WOMEN — VOLUME I

A PDI RESEARCH REFERENCE WORK

WOMEN — VOLUME I

A PDI RESEARCH REFERENCE WORK

FLORENCE L. DENMARK
Coordinating Editor

ROBERT W. WESNER
Editorial Director

FIRST EDITION — 1976

PSYCHOLOGICAL DIMENSIONS, INC.
500 FIFTH AVENUE, NEW YORK, N. Y. 10036

COPYRIGHT © 1976 PSYCHOLOGICAL DIMENSIONS, INC.

LIBRARY OF CONGRESS CATALOG CARD NUMBER LC76-5161

ISBN: 0-88437-001-1

0987654321

PRINTED IN THE UNITED STATES OF AMERICA

Contents

PART III: OCCUPATIONAL SCENE

PART IV: SEXUALITY AND GENDER

PART V: SEX ROLES

Contributors

Thelma G. Alper

Department of Psychology
Wellesley College

Sandra L. Bem

Department of Psychology
Stanford University

Nancy S. Cole

Educational and Social Research
*   Department*
The American College Testing Program
Iowa City, Iowa

Anne Constantinople

Department of Psychology
Vassar College

Nancy Datan

Department of Psychology
University of West Virginia

Kay Deaux

Department of Psychological Sciences
Purdue University

Florence L. Denmark

Doctoral Program in Psychology
Graduate School and University Center
City University of New York

Cynthia F. Epstein

Bureau of Applied Social Research
Columbia University

Dee Garrison

History Department
Livingston College
Rutgers University

Ruth Bader Ginsberg

School of Law
Columbia University

Nancy Goldman

Department of Sociology
University of Chicago

Walter R. Gove | *Department of Sociology*
Vanderbilt University

Helen Mayer Hacker | *Department of Sociology*
Adelphi University

Douglas T. Hall | *Department of Management*
Graduate School of Business
Michigan State University

Jack H. Hedblom | *Department of Sociology*
Wichita State University

Ravenna Helson | *Institute of Personality Assessment*
and Research
University of California, Berkeley

James A. Kenny | *Department of Psychology*
Saint Joseph's College

Birgitta Linner | *Municipal Family Guidance Clinic*
Stockholm, Sweden

John Money | *Department of Medical Psychology*
Johns Hopkins University and Hospital

Patrick H. Munley | *Psychological Service*
Veterans Administration Hospital
Lyons, New Jersey

Mary B. Parlee | *Department of Psychology*
Barnard College

Joseph H. Pleck | *Department of Psychology*
University of Michigan, Ann Arbor

Virginia Ellen Schein | *Personnel Research*
Metropolitan Life Insurance Company
New York, N.Y.

Catherine Bodard Silver | *Department of Sociology*
Brooklyn College
The City University of New York

Charles P. Smith | *Doctoral Program in Psychology*
Graduate School and University Center
City University of New York

Graham Staines | *Department of Psychology*
University of Michigan, Ann Arbor

Aletha H. Stein &
Margaret M. Bailey | *Department of Human Development*
Pennsylvania State University

Janet Taynor | *Clark County Comprehensive Mental*
Health Program
Springfield, Ohio

Sheila Tobias   *Associate Provost and Lecturer*
                                 in History
                                 Wesleyan Universtiy
                                 Middletown, Conn.

David Tresemer   *Private practice*
                                 Brattleboro, Vt.

J. Richard Udry   *Department of Maternal & Child Health*
                                 School of Public Health
                                 University of North Carolina

Rhoda K. Unger   *Department of Psychology*
                                 Montclair State College, New Jersey

Juanita H. Williams   *Women's Studies*
                                 University of South Florida

Thomas M. Wolf   *Child Development Clinic*
                                 St. Louis Universtiy

Acknowledgments

The publisher acknowledges with appreciation the following permissions to reprint from copyright holders and others for the articles appearing in this volume:

Chapter 1. Anne Constantinople, "Masculinity-Femininity: An Exception to A Famous Dictum." Psychological Bulletin, vol. 80, 5, 1973, pp. 389–407.

Chapter 2. Sandra L. Bem, "The Measurement of Psychological Androgyny." Journal of Consulting and Clinical Psychology, vol. 42, 2, 1974, pp. 155–162.

Chapter 3. Juanita H. Williams, "Sexual Role Identification and Personality Functioning in Girls." Journal of Personality, 1973, 41, pp. 1–8. © Duke University Press.

Chapter 4. Mary B. Parlee, "The Premenstrual Syndrome." Psychological Bulletin, 1973, vol. 80, No. 6, pp. 454–465.

Chapter 5. Ravenna Helson, "Heroic and Tender Modes in Women Authors of Fantasy." Journal of Personality, 1973, 41, pp. 493–512. © 1973 by Duke University Press, Box 6697, College Station, Durham, North Carolina 27708. vol. 41, No. 4 (December, 1973).

Chapter 6. Aletha H. Stein and Margaret M. Bailey, "The Socialization of Achievement Orientation in Females." Psychological Bulletin, November, 1973, vol. 80, pp. 345–366.

Chapter 7. Thelma G. Alper, "The Relationship between Role Orientation and Achievement Motivation in College Women." Journal of Personality, © by Duke University Press, Box 6697 College Station, Durham, North Carolina 27708, copyright 1973.

Chapter 8. Cynthia F. Epstein, "Bringing Women In: Rewards, Punishments, and the Structure of Achievement." Annals of the New York Academy of Sciences, 1973, pp. 62–70.

Chapter 9. Florence L. Denmark, Bernice K. Baxter and Ethel Jackson Shirk, "The Future Goals of College Women." Paper read at American Personnel and Guidance Association, Atlanta, Georgia, April 1974.

Chapter 10. Charles P. Smith, "Fear of Success: Qualms and Queries" Presented at American Psychological Association convention, New Orleans, Louisiana, September, 1974.

Chapter 11. Nancy S. Cole, "On Measuring the Vocational Interests of Women." Journal of Counseling Psychology, vol. 20, 1973, pp. 105–112.

Chapter 12. Patrick H. Munley, et al, "Female College Students' Scores On The Men's and Women's Strong Vocational Interest Blanks." Journal of Counseling Psychology, vol. 20, 1973, pp. 285–289.

Chapter 13. Douglas T. Hall and Francine E. Gordon, "Effects of Career Choices On Married Women." Journal of Applied Psychology, vol. 58, 1973, pp. 42–48.

Chapter 14. Cynthia P. Epstein, "Positive Effects Of The Multiple Negative: Explaining the Success of Black Professional Women." American Journal of Sociology, January 1973, vol. 78, No. 4.

Chapter 15. Sheila Tobias, "New Views of Rosie the Riveter." Original manuscript written for Panel on Women in World War II, October 1974. Author of "What Really Happened to Rosie the Riveter" MSS Modular Publications, MSS Information Corp., New York, New York.

Chapter 16. Dee Garrison, "The Tender Technicians: The Feminization Of Public Librarianship, 1876–1905." Journal of Social History, Rutgers University, Winter, 1972–73.

Chapter 17. Nancy Goldman, "The Changing Role of Women In The Armed Forces." American Journal of Sociology, vol. 78, pp. 892–911. © 1973 University of Chicago Press. All rights reserved. Also in "Changing Women in a Changing Society" ed. Joan Huber, University of Chicago Press, 1973, pp. 130–149.

Chapter 18. Ruth Bader Ginsberg, "Comment: Frontiero V. Richardson." Women's Rights Law Reporter, Summer, 1973, vol. 1, No. 5.

Chapter 19. Graham Staines, et al., "Alternative Methods For Measuring Sex Discrimination in Occupational Incomes." Reprinted from the 1969–70 Survey of Working Conditions: Chronicles of An Unfinished Enterprise. Published by the Survey Research Center—Institute for Social Research, University of Michigan, R. P. Quinn & T. W. Mangione, et al. 1973.

Chapter 20. John Money, "Phyletic and Idiosyncratic Determinants of Gender Identity." Danish Medical Bulletin, vol. 19, 1972, pp. 259–264. pp. 259–264.

Chapter 21. John Money, "Identification And Complementation In The Differentiation of Gender Identity." Danish Medical Bulletin, vol. 19, No. 8, 1972, pp. 265–268.

Chapter 22. J. Richard Udry, et al., "Effect of Contraceptive Pills on Sexual Activity In The Luteal Phase Of The Human Menstrual Cycle." Archives in Sexual Behavior, vol. 2, 1973, pp. 205–215.

Chapter 23. James A. Kenny, "Sexuality of Pregnant And Breast-feeding Women." Archives of Sexual Behavior, vol. 2, 1973, pp. 215–229.

Chapter 24. Jack H. Hedblom, "Dimensions of Lesbian Sexual Experience." Archives of Sexual Behavior, vol. 2, 1973, pp. 329–341.

Chapter 25. David Tresemer and Joseph Pleck, "Sex-Role Boundaries And Resistance To Sex-Role Change." Gordon and Breach Science Publishers Ltd. "Women's Studies," 1973, vol. 1, pp. 000–018.

Chapter 26. Thomas M. Wolf, "Effects of Live Modelled Sex-Appropriate Play Behavior In A Naturalistic Setting." Developmental Psychology, vol. 9, 1973, pp. 120–123.

Chapter 27. Virginia Ellen Schein, "The Relationship Between Sex Role Stereotypes And Requisite Management Characteristics." Journal of Applied Psychology, vol. 57, 1973, pp. 95–100.

Chapter 28. Walter R. Gove, "Adult Sex Roles and Mental Illness." Written with J. F. Tudor, American Journal of Sociology, 78, 1973, pp. 812–835.

Chapter 29. Janet Taynor and Kay Deaux, "When Women Are More Deserving Than Men: Equity, Attribution, and Perceived Sex Differences." Journal of Personality and Social Psychology, vol. 28, No. 3, 1973, pp. 360–367.

Chapter 30. Rhoda K. Unger, Beth J. Raymond and Stephen M. Levine, "Are Women A "Minority" Group? Sometimes!" International Journal of Group Tensions, vol. IV, No. 1, March 1974.

Chapter 31. Birgitta Linner, "Status Of Women-Population-Development." Paper delivered at the "Global Problems of Modern Civilization" Symposium in Prague, 1973.

Chapter 32. United Nations Economic and Social Council/Commission on the Status of Women, "Study on the Interrelationship of the Status of Women And Family Planning (Report of the Special Rapporteur-Addendum).

Chapter 33. Catherine B. Silver, "Salon, Foyer, Bureau: Women And The Professions in France." American Journal of Sociology, vol. 78, No. 4, January 1973. Reprint—The University of Chicago Press.

Chapter 34. Nancy Datan, "Your Daughters Shall Prophesy: Ancient And Contemporary Perspectives On The Women Of Israel." Paper read at convention of Academic Association for Peace in the Middle East, Chicago, 1972. Reprinted from Israel: Social Structure and Change—Michael Curtis, Mordecai Chertoff, eds. New Brunswick, New Jersey, Transaction Books, Inc. 1973.

Chapter 35. Helen Mayer Hacker, "The Socio-Economic Context of Sex and Power: A Study of Women, Work and Family Roles in Four Israeli Institutional Frameworks." A grant proposal submitted by Helen Mayer Hacker, 1973.

Chapter 36. The Economist, "The Life and Death of Ms. Solomon Grundy."

Introduction

In recent years, in the wake of the intense social change and intellectual questioning of the past decade, there has been a growing interest in studies of women by the social and behavioral sciences. Such interest, which both reflects and promotes this legitimate area of scientific investigation, has resulted in an ever-increasing number of scholarly papers, articles, and lectures. In fact, it becomes more and more difficult to "keep up" with the ever-burgeoning amount of knowledge generated. The serious scholar cannot read every journal, attend every scientific meeting, and be aware of the problems and the delineation of findings that is occurring.

For these reasons, the concept of a reference volume on women that is periodically updated is an invaluable tool to disseminate significant research findings.

These reference volumes are designed to supplement, not supplant existing sources. The panel of editors represents a wide variety of specialities and viewpoints in psychology, sociology, and other disciplines. From the material they read, prepublished, unpublished and published, as well as the talks they have heard, the editors submitted what they felt were among the most significant papers they had been exposed to in the last two years.

The readers of this annual thus have a preselected collection of material which would not otherwise be readily available to them. This volume includes both published and unpublished papers. Those which are published come from a wide variety of sources found both in the United States as well as abroad. Hardly any individual would have access to all these sources.

We are not claiming to have included *everything* that is important. In some cases, only one of several similar articles was selected. Due to space restrictions, the less familiar, less available material was sometimes selected over the more accessible in order to introduce the reader to materials she/he may have missed. However, what has been included in this volume presents to the reader an excellent cross-section of valuable papers highly representative of the type of material appearing in 1973–74. The selections represent different viewpoints and approaches, different theories and methodologies. The papers present a selective but broad overview of the field. There was no attempt to limit sources or to delimit the type of paper included other than by its scientific and/or informational merits. Some papers were included despite controversial features because they raise issues which should generate further research.

The contents have been divided into six major sections: Personality, Achievement, The Occupational Scene, Sexuality and Gender, Sex Roles, and Cross-Cultural Studies. Each section is preceded by a brief introduction. These areas reflect the included papers; thus, designation of the sections followed rather than preceded selection of the material. The period covered was heavy on achievement and occupations; other potential areas provided less in the way of significant studies. However, this will probably change in the next two years and our succeeding volume will reflect these changes.

The selections reflect the "state of the art" of research on women. Over a period of time, a collection of these volumes will represent a history of this discipline and what research was important to the discipline over varying periods of time.

Twenty-nine (29) papers are included in this volume from 17 different sources. Seven have not as yet been published. The sources and number of papers from each follow,

SOURCES	NUMBER OF PAPERS
Journals:	
American Journal of Sociology	4
Annals of the New York Academy of Sciences	1
Archives of Sexual Behavior	3
Danish Medical Bulletin	2
Developmental Psychology	1
International Journal of Group Tensions	1
Journal of Applied Psychology	2
Journal of Consulting and Clinical Psychology	1
Journal of Counseling Psychology	2
Journal of Personality	3
Journal of Personality and Social Psychology	1
Journal of Social History	1
Psychological Bulletin	3
The Economist	1
Women's Rights Law Reporter	1
Women's Studies	1
Book:	
Israel, Social Structure and Change	1
Unpublished:	7

This volume will keep the reader abreast of what is happening in the study of women, will be an essential reference work for the serious scholar, and will also serve to stimulate research and research ideas among experienced scientists and graduate students.

PART I

PERSONALITY

PERSONALITY

Personality is broadly defined in this section of the reference volume. Articles dealing with measurement of masculinity, femininity and androgeny have been grouped together with other articles dealing with female adolescent personality functioning, premenstrual symptoms, and creativity. Single selections on these topics resulted in their being grouped within a broad framework.

1

ANNE CONSTANTINOPLE [1]

Masculinity-Feminity:
An Exception to a Famous Dictum

The major tests of masculinity–femininity (M–F) in adults are reviewed with special attention to the ways in which their construction and use reflect three untested assumptions about the nature of the M–F construct: (*a*) that it is best defined in terms of sex differences in item responses; (*b*) that it is a single bipolar dimension ranging from extreme masculinity at one end to extreme femininity at the other; and (*c*) that it is undimensional in nature and can be adequately measured by a single score. Evidence which questions the validity of these assumptions and, therefore, of the tests of M–F is presented, with the conclusion that further theoretical and empirical work is necessary in all aspects of the problem.

Students in psychology often learn a famous dictum that expresses a fundamental axiom in psychological measurement: "Everything that exists, exists in some quantity, and if it exists in some quantity, it can be measured." When one reviews the history of attempts to measure masculinity-femininity (M–F) in adults, one is tempted to ask whether the reverse of the dictum is also true: That if something cannot be measured, it does not exist. Strong words when there is a 40-year history of inventories and scales designed to measure M–F. But a careful look at the definitions and assumptions inherent in the measurement process eventually leads one to ask what evidence there is for these instruments *as measures of M–F*. In order to answer this question, the most widely used verbal measures of M–F *in adults* are reviewed with particular reference to assumptions about the concept that are involved in the construction of the measures; occasional reference is made to research with children where it helps to elucidate the issues involved.

A definitive review of the concept of M–F itself is well beyond the scope of this paper; however, some of the biases of the author in dealing with the concept should be made explicit at this point. One recurring question

[1] The author wishes to thank Henrietta Smith and Vincent Nowlis for their thought-provoking and clarifying comments on earlier versions of this manuscript.

Requests for reprints should be sent to Anne Constantinople, Department of Psychology, Vassar College, Poughkeepsie, New York 12601.

that is reflected in varying terminology throughout the paper is whether M–F is a single bipolar dimension or whether there may not also exist two separable dimensions of masculinity (M) and femininity (F), either in addition to or instead of the M–F dimension. A further problem is raised by the use of the term "existence," as in the introductory paragraph, when referring to a hypothetical construct such as M–F. The very fact that the terms masculinity and femininity have a lengthy history in common discourse indicates that they are useful at least to the layman in organizing experience, enabling him to "construe reality" or "replications of events" more effectively (Kelly, 1963). The "existence" of M–F in the psychologist's conceptual and methodological world must be evaluated by more stringent criteria, however. With the logical positivists, one must ask whether this term and our methods of measuring it are useful in the prediction, control, and understanding of behavior. Although there is some clear convergence of data supporting the importance of sex differences in various aspects of physical, intellectual, and personality development (Garai & Scheinfeld, 1968), there is no similar body of data which indicates that M–F, or M or F alone, consistently is related to other variables in predictable ways (except whether or not the subject is male or female!). At this point in the history of the term M–F as a psychological construct, it is not clear whether our approach to its measurement is at fault or whether the term as such should be dropped from the psychologist's vocabulary because its referents vary so widely that it adds little to our understanding of behavior.

The last decade has seen a resurgence of concern with sex differences and sex-related aspects of development, both among professionals (e.g., Bardwick, 1971; Maccoby, 1966; Money, 1965) and in the general public. Masculinity and femininity, their hallmarks and salience in personal development, are widely discussed in relation to both individuals and groups, and it often seems that value judgments are implicit in both general and professional applications of these terms. The analogy with the use of the term "intelligence" seems apparent here. In both cases, we are dealing with an abstract concept that seems to summarize some dimension of reality important for many people, but we are hard pressed as scientists to come up with any clear definition of the concept or indeed any unexceptionable criteria for its measurement. In addition, M–F, like intelligence, is assumed to be in some way inherent in the individual and to be at least partially determined by biological factors. As such, both concepts are thought to be of limited potential for change through experience, and their measurement is assumed to reflect some characteristic of the organism that is fundamental to its nature. Because society attaches value statements, implicitly or explicitly, to the results of psychological testing in both of these areas, it becomes more important than usual to know what we are in fact measuring. An additional hazard in M–F measurement comes from the belief, often incorporated in test construction, that deviation from the norm of one's own sex in M or F may imply deviation in sexual orientation or homosexuality as well. Although the literature on this hypothesized relationship between M–F and homosexuality has been largely omitted from the present review, it should be understood that almost all of the available data contradict such an interpretation of deviant M–F scores.

DEFINITION OF MASCULINITY–FEMININITY

Criterion Groups and Item Selection

The terms, masculinity and femininity, have a long history in psychological dis-

course, but both theoretically and empirically they seem to be among the muddiest concepts in the psychologist's vocabulary. A search for definitions related to some theoretical position leads almost nowhere except to Freud (1965) and Jung (1956); it seems as if the terms were taken over whole from the public domain with no attempt to explicate them in the manner suggested by Mandler and Kessen (1959). The most generalized definitions of the terms as they are used by those developing tests of M–F would seem to be that they are relatively enduring traits which are more or less rooted in anatomy, physiology, and early experience, and which generally serve to distinguish males from females in appearance, attitudes, and behavior.

When one turns to empirical evidence as a source of concept definition, one finds that different investigators have chosen to emphasize different dimensions of the concepts in the measurement process, making generalizations across their measures difficult. The one factor common to most tests is reliance on an item's ability to discriminate the responses of males from those of females; therefore, M–F is defined at least partially in terms of sex differences in response. The content of such items varies enormously, however, both between and within tests. In some cases, item content would appear to be logically related to an intuitive definition of masculinity or femininity, but in many other cases the content seems to be irrelevant to any identifiable definition of the concept. The strictly empirical approach to test construction would seem to lead to an even muddier concept, since anything that discriminates men from women. usually at a particular point in time in a particular culture, is taken as an indicator of M–F with no assessment of the centrality of that trait or behavior to an abstract definition of M–F. In the absence of an accepted definition of the construct, it seems that the empirical approach alone will not suffice to generate a definition.

Relationship of Masculinity–Femininity to Other Concepts

The relationship between a theoretical definition and the measures of M–F is further complicated by the confusion of such related terms as sex role adoption, sex role preference, and sex role identity. These terms have been variously defined and implicated in both definitions and measures of M–F (e.g., Brown, 1958; Kohlberg, 1966; Lynn, 1969). In general, sex role preference can be distinguished from sex role adoption on the basis of activities or traits one would prefer to engage in or possess versus those that one actually manifests. It is not at all unusual to find a discrepancy between measures of these two constructs; for instance, in young girls a preference measure might indicate a relatively masculine personality while an adoption measure would reflect a preponderance of femininity. This extrapolation from either preference or adoption to M or F is made more often than not. Conceptually, however, neither measure alone would seem to be an adequate indicator of M–F; rather, there seems to be some notion of identity that should be included when making a statement about an individual's masculinity or femininity, unless one is thinking purely in terms of its social stimulus value. Sex role identity includes both cognitive and affective factors which reflect both self-evaluation and the evaluation of others as to one's adequacy as a male or female. Such an evaluation would probably include several components (e.g., appearance, reproductive capacity, social and/or occupational role), and one's definition of adequacy would probably vary with the kinds of standards of sex role appropriateness to which one had been exposed in the process of development.

The necessity for clarity in the use of these terms can be underscored by Hooker's (1965) data on nonpatient male homosexuals. These subjects showed no hesitation in designating themselves as males in their conscious gender identity, although there was considerable variation in the degree to which they preferred and/or adopted masculine or feminine attributes of behavior or personality. There were also variations in the degree to which they saw themselves as masculine or feminine, whether the basis for such definition was the so-called active versus passive role in homosexual relations or the more customary vocational and avocational interests or personality traits. There was no stable relationship across

subjects among the various factors that could be taken as indicators of M–F; on what basis, then, could one make an M–F classification of these subjects?

Sex role preference and sex role adoption are more easily measured than either sex role identity or M–F, as there are fewer steps between the observable characteristics of the individual and the construct inferred. In addition, when looking at sex role identity and M–F, the potential importance of unconscious factors increases, increasing the difficulties of the measurement process and the specification of appropriate external criteria for validation. Existing M–F tests tend to confound items that appear to be more directly related to sex role preference, adoption, or identity. While all three aspects may well underlie and be included in M–F, the clarification of the interrelationships among these constructs is essential to defining the M–F concept itself and to its measurement.

Dimensionality and Bipolarity of Masculinity-Femininity

The definition of M–F that has been implicitly used by most test developers has contained two assumptions, unidimensionality and bipolarity, neither of which has been tested for the validity of its application to the M–F construct. The dimensionality question can be raised in two ways: (*a*) Is M–F a single bipolar dimension ranging from extreme masculinity at one end to extreme femininity at the other, or is it possible that there are also two separable dimensions of masculinity and femininity which vary independently of each other. (*b*) Within the constructs of M, F, or M–F are we dealing with unitary or multidimensional traits? It seems quite clear from the available evidence that none of the existing tests is measuring a unitary trait and that one will derive different estimates of a person's relative M–F level depending on the kinds of behaviors sampled. If the M–F characteristic is multidimensional, a single summary score that ignores variations in what could be designated as subtraits would seem to be less appropriate than a profile of scores on the various subtraits measured.

The more basic issue of the bipolarity of one M–F dimension is unanswerable at present, since no measure of M–F has been devised that does not incorporate bipolarity from the start. English and English (1958), in their definition of bipolarity as it refers to dimensions of personality, not only stated that it implies a single continuum ranging from one extreme through a zero point to the other but that behaviors defining one end point are *opposite* to those at the other and thus should be negatively correlated. Carlson (1972), in discussing the pervasiveness of dualities in psychological theory and measurement, made particular reference to the problem of M–F and cautioned against the simplistic notion of a single bipolar continuum. She urged instead that many of the dualities inherent in human nature be viewed as interactive forces which may be working in some complex fashion toward integration. The problem of polarity in the domain of M–F is intensified by the fact that it is viewed as the psychological correlate of biological dimorphism, although the findings of Hampson (1965) and Money (1965) would cast doubt on the appropriateness of the monolithic either/or approach even in the biological substrate.

In M–F test construction, the assumption of bipolarity is evident in at least three ways: (*a*) The dependence on biological sex alone as the appropriate criterion for an item's M–F relevance, since item selection is usually based solely on its ability to discriminate the responses of the two sexes; (*b*) the implication that the opposite of a masculine response is necessarily indicative of femininity, especially in tests where only two options are provided; and (*c*) the use of a single M–F score which is based on the algebraic summation of M and F responses and places the individual somewhere on a single bipolar dimension.

REVIEW OF MAJOR TESTS OF MASCULINITY–FEMININITY

Terman and Miles: Attitude-Interest Analysis Test (M–F Test)

Terman and Miles (1936) believed that "mental masculinity and femininity" was a central trait of temperament, that it acted as a core around which the rest of the personality was formed. Terman and Miles offered no definitions of the trait which are grounded in theory and acknowledged that the measure-

ment process is crude and inexact, due both to the vagueness of the concept and the state of psychometric development. They cited three sources of confusion: (*a*) Our too ready acceptance of overt behavior as the appropriate criteria; (*b*) lack of sufficiently general sampling opportunities; and (*c*) the traditional biases which we all carry, some of which may vary with the age, sex, social class, or temperament of the individual judge.

Terman and Miles' purpose was to extend the generality of the measurement of M–F by increasing the range of demonstrable differences between the sexes which the test attempts to sample; they therefore relied heavily on known findings of sex differences in choosing the domains of behavior to be included in their test. The final form of the test includes seven exercises: Word Association, Ink-Blot Association, Information, Interests, Introversion, Emotional and Ethical Attitudes, and Opinions. These exercises vary considerably in their split-half reliabilities; after much work to improve test content, rs ranged from .32 to .90, with a median r of .64. The two exercises with very low reliabilities were included in the final form in the interest of keeping the range of behaviors sampled as wide as possible.

Items were selected for inclusion in the exercises on the basis of the extent to which they yielded significant differences in responses of the sexes in a number of different groups tested. Attempts were made to weight each item for the *degree* to which it discriminated the sexes, but the finding that neither reliability nor degree of overlap was significantly changed led to the use of unit scoring throughout the test. In addition, in a statement which implies some dissatisfaction with sex differences as the only criterion of M–F, Terman and Miles (1936) concluded,

One may reasonably argue that the only way to avoid making the test too much a measure of accidental differences in experience is to take account only of the *number* of M–F differences without regard to their size [p. 53].

In scoring the individual items, bipolarity is generally assumed and an item is scored plus for a masculine response and minus for a feminine one. The score for each exercise is the algebraic sum of the plus and minus scores, while the total score is the algebraic sum of the exercise scores with some weighting based on individual exercise reliability and overlap measures. Terman and Miles' data indicated that, in the general population sample of males, the mean score is +52.58 ($SD = 49.9$), while for the females the mean is −70.65 ($SD = 47.5$).

Although Terman and Miles (1936) chose to use the total score on the assumption that a "high *average* of masculinity or femininity in the fields covered by the test probably affects the total personality picture [p. 58]," the unidimensionality of the M–F trait was not demonstrated. In fact, the low intercorrelations among the exercises (.27 to .49) led Terman and Miles to believe that there was no use in searching for general factors through factor analysis. They also hoped to strengthen the individual exercises to permit profile scoring, as they thought it likely that specific behavior patterns might be more highly correlated with specific profile patterns than with total score.

The issue of the validity of the test is hard to settle in the absence of a clear definition of masculinity and femininity. Terman and Miles (1936) felt that the fact that test content tends to exaggerate true differences between the sexes is significant since the major purpose of the test is to highlight responses which "diverge from the mean of his sex on *just those items to which the sexes do tend to respond differently* [p. 65]." Yet Terman and Miles also asserted that "no one knows what amount of overlap would be found if the totality of M–F traits were adequately and reliably measured [p. 53]." Independent validation of the test is difficult to demonstrate, since Terman and Miles felt that ratings of M–F made by judges are notoriously unreliable, but they did feel that it is important to find behavioral correlates of the M–F score. An investigation of relationships of M–F score to physical measurements and secondary sex characteristics produced generally low and nonsignificant *r*s. There was a significant tendency for especially early puberty to be positively related to masculinity in boys and femininity in girls, but it was unclear how much this relationship was mediated by social role expectations. There were also some low-to-moderate relationships to such personality and achievement-related behaviors as introversion–extraversion, scholastic performance, and athletic prowess, as well as to occupational interests. A group of so-called passive male homosexuals did score significantly more feminine than any other group of men tested, but Terman and Miles warned against use of the test to identify overt or latent homosexuality.

In the Terman and Miles measure of M–F, then, we find evidence for the multidimensionality of the trait while unidimensionality is implicit in the scoring procedure. Bipolarity is assumed in the scoring of both individual items and the test as a whole. The construct is defined purely in terms of sex differences in response, although Terman and Miles expressed some reservations about the adequacy of this criterion alone. They repeatedly acknowledged the crudeness of their attempts to develop an M–F measure, but they also set the pattern which others have since followed in this field.

Strong: Masculinity–Femininity (MF) Scale of the Vocational Interest Blank

The MF scale of the Strong Vocational Interest Blank (SVIB) is based on the differential responses of men and women to 202 of the 400 items originally selected for the purpose of measuring vocational interests. Since the MF scale is subsidiary to the major interests of Strong, there is little discussion of the rationale for including an MF scale apart from the fact that men and women will seek somewhat different careers (Strong, 1936). Although the SVIB has gone through a number of revisions (Campbell, 1966, 1969), the present discussion is based almost exclusively on the work of Strong himself on the early versions of the MF scale, since scale construction is most relevant to the issues being considered here.

Like Terman and Miles, Strong used a variety of groups covering different age and education levels in deriving earlier versions of the scale. The final form is based on the combined responses of 1,200 men and women who had constituted the high school, college, and adult samples; the selection of items to be included in the MF scale and the individual item weights (from +4 to −4) were based on sex differences in response to each item. In general, the 400 items of the total test have "like," "indifferent," and "dislike" categories for response. For the MF scale, a plus weight was assigned when the responses of men predominated in that category and a minus weight when more women chose that option, while the numerical value was determined by the size of the difference in proportions responding.

Although different kinds of questions are included in the SVIB, only one total MF score is provided, which is the algebraic sum of all the keyed responses, taking into account both size and direction of the weight. On the SVIB for Men, the mean raw scores for men are 82.1 for the high school sample, 60.6 for the college sample, and 46.8 for adults, while for women they are −85.7 for high school, −111.8 for college, and −110.2 for adults (Strong, 1943). The SVIB for Women includes a Femininity–Masculinity scale, very similar in content and rationale to the MF scale but where a feminine response is scored plus and a masculine one minus. In comparing the mean scores of men and women in his various samples, Strong concluded that his MF scale adequately differentiates the sexes and that it is not significantly inferior to the Terman-Miles M–F scale in this regard. When all samples are combined, distribution overlap is 21.7%, which approximates that for the Terman-Miles when correction is made for the different methods of computation.

There are several points of comparison between the SVIB MF and the Terman-Miles M–F measures:

1. On the Terman-Miles, items were selected for inclusion in the test on the basis of significant differences in responses of men and women, while on the SVIB, all items that show any differentiation are included. It is not clear whether the SVIB items with a weight of + or −1 would meet Terman's criteria for inclusion.

2. The two tests are similar in the assumption of inherent bipolarity implicit in the plus and minus weighting of scores which are masculine or feminine; however, the SVIB includes many more instances in which a response may be scored as irrelevant to M–F.

3. Terman turned to unit scoring because he felt that it was important not to magnify the extent of differences between the sexes by differentially weighting those items which showed greater discriminant power. Strong chose the opposite approach, although he acknowledged that, on the test as a whole, similarities vastly overshadowed differences between the sexes.

Strong was very careful to point out the diagnostic limitations of the SVIB MF scale and to keep the focus on the fact that only items relevant to occupational interests are being measured, although their content is very heterogeneous. He found no diagnostic implications for a highly divergent MF score if the occupations in which the subject expresses interest are in the same direction as his MF score.

Minnesota Multiphasic Personality Inventory Masculinity–Femininity Scale (Mf)

According to the Minnesota Multiphasic Personality Inventory (MMPI) manual (Hathaway & McKinley, 1943), the *Mf* scale is designed to measure "the tendency toward masculinity or femininity of interest pattern [p. 5]," but the three major sources of the MMPI on item selection and validation procedures agree that its major aim is to identify sexual inversion in males. The progression of item selection procedures is somewhat unclear but would seem to be as follows: (*a*) Retention of all items from the original MMPI pool which discriminated men from women; (*b*) the discarding from this subpool all items which failed to discriminate the responses of 13 male homosexuals and an unspecified number of men with high inversion scores on the Terman Inversion scale from 54 "normal" male soldiers; and finally, (*c*) a check for male–female discrimination in both the original group of normals and the smaller groups of soldiers and airline employees (Dahlstrom & Welsh, 1960). The final scale consists of 60 items, 37 from the original MMPI pool and 23 from the work of Terman and Miles. This scale is considerably shorter than the two previously discussed and seems to be one of the most widely used in research; however, its derivation should produce some caution since homosexuality is explicitly included in the definition of the construct.

The response options are true, false, and cannot say (?) for each of the 60 items; responses are keyed so that a high T score is indicative of deviation from the norm of one's own sex when the appropriate form for each sex is used. Responses are keyed plus when they reflect femininity in men and masculinity in women. Although a high T score is thought to be related to homosexuality in men, there is no such diagnostic implication in a high T score for women, since efforts to establish a relationship to inversion in women have met with no success.

Dahlstrom and Welsh (1960, p. 64) noted that the item content of the Mf scale is very heterogeneous; they summarized an unpublished study which judgmentally identified five dimensions to characterize the item content. These categories were thought to be ego sensitivity, sexual identification, altruism, endorsement of culturally feminine occupations, and denial of culturally masculine occupations. Further evidence for the multidimensionality of the Mf scale can be found in the work of Dempsey (1963) using contextual analysis and in a factor-analytic study by Graham, Schroeder, and Lilly (1971) which resulted in seven factors for the 60-item scale. It should be noted that in both the judgmental categories and in this factor analysis, masculine and feminine interests were not found to be opposite ends of a single bipolar continuum but were separate categories or factors.

An indicator of the validity of the MMPI Mf scale can be found in the fact that mean scores consistently show large differences between the sexes. However, Goodstein (1954) has raised serious questions about the appropriateness of its use with college men, as his data indicate that such groups across the country score one-half to one standard deviation above the mean reported for Minnesota normals. Murray (1963) found that 20 of the 60 items did not discriminate between the sexes at the .05 level or better and that recomputation of the scores for men excluding these items brought them predominantly into the normal range.

In his assessment of the MMPI in general,

Cronbach (1960) noted that the Mf scale is especially weak. The nature and size of the criterion groups should certainly raise questions about its adequacy as a measure of M–F in the general population, even if one is not concerned with the problems of dimensionality and bipolarity.

Gough: The Femininity Scale

In devising the Femininity (Fe) scale, Gough's (1952) goals were to make it relatively brief, of fairly subtle content, and a reliable means of differentiating males from females and "sexual deviates from normals [p. 427]." The scale was largely empirically derived by comparing responses of high school and college men and women on some 500 items that had originally been written for a study of political behavior. Gough argued that these items are by definition not obvious in content, since they were written for another purpose besides the identification of M–F; however, an unspecified number of items was added to the original pool because their content was thought to be relevant to the psychological concept of femininity. The final version of the 1952 scale consisted of 58 items that significantly discriminated between males and females in both the high school and college samples. Percentage overlap was very small for the high school sample but rose to about 10% for the college sample; however, all samples tested revealed highly significant critical ratios between the two sex groups.

The Fe scale was reduced to 38 items ($r = .95$ with the 58-item version) when it was included in Gough's (1966) California Psychological Inventory with the purpose of defining a personological syndrome that can be called masculine at one pole and feminine at the other. Each item is keyed true or false for a "feminine" response, and the item is scored +1 if the subject answers in the feminine direction; the total score is a simple summation of all plus scores, and the mean standard score of 50 corresponds to a raw score of 16.3 for men and 23.0 for women (Gough, 1964).

Gough identified several clusters into which the content of the 58-item scale falls: (*a*) Emphasis on white-collar work; (*b*) sensitivity to social interaction; (*c*) social timidity and lack of confidence; (*d*) compassion and sympathy; (e) lack of interest in abstract, political issues; and (f) restraint and caution versus braggadoccio. Although Gough (1952, p. 427) stood by the relative subtlety of item content, it should be noted that his summary descriptions of the item clusters resemble those generally found in M–F tests and might well be identified as stereotypic aspects of M–F. In addition, their variety indicates probable multidimensionality in the scale; however, since no factor analyses of the Fe scale have been carried out, no more definitive statement is possible at this time.

Gough (1952) offered as evidence of the validity of the 58-item Fe scale data from a special study on the social stimulus value of 10 high- and 10 low-scoring men who were subjects in an ongoing intensive study by psychologists who rated them on an adjective checklist. Composite scores across nine judges revealed that high scorers were more often described by such adjectives as affectionate, courageous, dependent, gentle, honest, modest, sensitive, and tolerant, while low scorers were seen as ambitious, cool, dignified, hard-headed, humorless, self-centered, self-confident, tense, and wary. The adjective, feminine, did not discriminate the two groups. (One wonders whether these adjectives really are more appropriately seen as aspects of M–F or of social sensitivity or even flexibility.) Further evidence for the validity of the Fe scale is found in correlations of −.41 with SVIB MF and +.43 with MMPI *Mf* on samples of males only (Gough, 1964), and in point-biserial correlations with sex of respondent that range from .64 to .78. It should be noted that the California Psychological Inventory, unlike the other tests, is probably more appropriate for use with high school and college samples than with the general population because of the normative groups involved in its construction.

Guilford: The Masculinity Scale

The Masculinity (M) scale is one of many scales derived by Guilford and his colleagues in their continuing attempts to discover basic dimensions of personality through factor-analytic procedures. It first appeared as a factor in the analysis of 36 items thought to measure introversion–extraversion and was characterized by high loadings from such

items as "is a male," "not absent-minded," "likes to sell things," "has not kept a personal diary," and "more interested in athletics than intellectual things" (Guilford & Guilford, 1936). A new questionnaire containing 123 items thought to be relevant to the five factors found in the original analysis was administered to approximately 800 male and female college students. Criterion groups for the evaluation of the new items were formed on the basis of weighted scores on the original items for each of the factors, and top and bottom quartiles were compared. It is important to note that the criterion for the M scale was not sex but score on the first short scale; in fact, the top quartile contained 16 women and the bottom, 12 men. Item content and extensive overlapping caused Guilford to question whether the M factor represented a masculine ideal rather than a sex-difference factor; he also considered that it might even more appropriately be thought of as measure of dominance or ascendance–submission. He concluded that, of the five factors identified, M needed the most additional work on reliability and what it was actually measuring (Guilford & Guilford, 1936), but the scale was still included as a masculinity factor in the general activity, ascendance versus submission, masculinity versus femininity, confidence versus inferiority feelings, and calmness, composure versus nervous (GAMIN) inventory.

The M factor as it appears in Inventory GAMIN has 40 items of somewhat heterogeneous content; in a subsequent test of factor purity, these items were clustered into six tests on the basis of content and cluster scores as follows: fearfulness, inhibition of emotional expression, masculine vocational interests, masculine avocational interests, disgustfulness, and sympathy. Items from all the other factors were similarly clustered and were scored for the new factor analysis as +1 or 0 as keyed to the appropriate general factor. The new analysis yielded orthogonal factors similar to those produced earlier, which was regarded by Guilford and Zimmerman (1956) as effective refutation of the criticisms of factor purity. In particular, the M factor was defined by high loadings from the following tests: sex membership, .77; masculine vocational interests, .72; masculine avocational interests, .64; inhibition of emotional expression, .39; fearfulness, −.60; emotional excitability, −.52; sympathy, −.48; disgustfulness, −.45; and liking for limelight, −.30. In evaluating the M factor, Guilford and Zimmerman (1956) concluded that "Comparatively speaking, it is not a stable, unitary variable. . . . [and that it will be] defined in any particular analysis by the experimental variables in which there are substantial sex differences [p. 12]," making it highly subject to variation due to item content.

Factor M was incorporated into the Guilford-Zimmerman (1949) Temperament Survey, with a reduction from 40 to 30 items. Answer options are "yes," "?," and "no," but only "yes" or "no" is keyed +1 when scoring a factor, whereas "?" is always scored 0. The total score is the simple arithmetic summation of keyed responses; for Factor *M* the mean raw score is 19.9 for men and 10.8 for women, a highly significant difference. Although sex was never used as a criterion for item inclusion in the scale, Guilford offered as evidence of the internal validity of M its point-biserial correlation of .75 with sex of respondent, which is comparable to those reported by Gough for the Fe scale.

Other Measures of Masculinity-Femininity

There have been a number of attempts to develop verbal measures of M-F in adults that do not involve the standard inventory or questionnaire format, among them are adjective checklists (Berdie, 1959; Heilbrun, 1964), a word association test (Goodenough, 1946), and a semantic differential technique (Reece, 1964). In general, the basis for item selection has again been the differential response patterns of the two sex groups, with the hope that the items are less tainted by sex role stereotypes than those in questionnaires, thereby producing a "truer" measure of M-F. Goodenough is the only one who seems to be aware of the bipolarity problem and no one attempts to deal with the issue of dimensionality.

It should be noted here that some nonverbal projective tests of M-F have also been developed (Caligor, 1951; Franck & Rosen, 1949; May, 1971; Webster, 1953), but only

the Franck and Rosen Drawing Completion Test has been used in a substantial number of studies. The criterion for these measures as tests of M-F is their ability to discriminate the responses of men from those of women. Since they are thought to tap a relatively more unconscious assessment of oneself as masculine or feminine than is true of verbal measures, their low intercorrelations with the latter are not thought to reflect on their validity; indeed, the work of Lansky (1960) supported the notion that a discrepancy between conscious and unconscious components can be an important moderator of relationships to other variables.

DIMENSIONALITY OF MASCULINITY–FEMININITY

The research to be reviewed in this section deals primarily with the issue of dimensionality in terms of whether or not M-F is a unitary trait to be measured with one total score rather than a set of subtraits which may be more accurately represented and related to other variables through profile scoring. The other aspect of the dimensionality issue, the separability of M-F into independent M and F dimensions, is largely deferred to the next section on bipolarity.

The potential utility of the profile scoring procedure is evident in a report by Webster (1956) of developmental changes in M-F found in Vassar students. Items known to discriminate the sexes were divided into three subscales on the basis of item content: I, Conventionality, or preference for conventionally feminine roles and interests; II, passivity, or items reflecting docility, modesty, moral sensitivity, and lack of dominance, aggression, and manipulativeness; and III, feminine sensitivity, with items covering emotionality, fantasy, introspection, "neurotic trends," and aesthetic interests. Differences between freshmen and seniors were small, but seniors did score significantly lower than freshmen on Scales I and II; after lengthening Scale III by the addition of highly correlating non-M-F items, they scored significantly higher than the freshmen. Webster concluded that college women become more masculine in the sense of becoming less conventional and less passive but more feminine in greater awareness of their inner life. The customary use of one total score would have obscured these findings.

Webster's contention that multidimensionality is basic to both the M–F construct and inherent in most existing measures can be supported by both correlational and factor-analytic studies.

Correlational Studies

The reliability of the tests reviewed is generally high enough that one would expect moderately strong correlations between any two M–F measures if they are in fact measuring the same construct and that construct is of a unitary nature. In evaluating the size of a correlation, it is important to note whether the sample is of one or both sexes, as the reliability of all M–F measures is higher, sometimes substantially, in combined- than in single-sex groups because of the greater heterogeneity of scores. In reporting the following correlations, signs are ignored as confusing, since different scales run in different directions; however, the signs are almost always in the expected direction.

The highest correlations are to be found between the MMPI *Mf* scale and the SVIB MF scale, with *r*s approximating .70 in mixed-sex groups (Heston, 1948; Nance, 1949). Among males only, they range from .32 to .53, with a concentration around .50 (Barrows & Zuckerman, 1960; Himelstein & Stoup, 1967; Nance, 1949; Shepler, 1951; Wright & L'Abate, 1970), while for females only they range from .20 to .55 (Klopfer, 1966; Nance, 1949; Shepler, 1951). It is generally agreed that the "interest" aspect of both scales is the major contributor to these correlations; one would therefore expect that the MMPI would correlate even more highly with the Terman-Miles, since in both of these scales the major clusters of items reflect interests and emotional attitudes. In fact, few correlations between these two tests have been reported: de Cillis and Orbison (1950) found *r*s of .30 and .36 for 129 men and 50 women, respectively, while Shepler (1951) reported *r*s of .65 and .53 for 57 men and 67 women. Shepler found correlations of approximately the same magnitude between the Terman-Miles and the SVIB in the only reported relationship between these two measures.

As previously indicated, Gough (1964) offered *r*s of .43 and .41 in males only between the Fe scale and MMPI and the SVIB scales, respectively, as evidence for the validity of the Fe scale. Using separate groups of 31 men and 29 women, McCarthy, Anthony, and Domino (1970) reported correlations of .45 and .42 between the Fe and the MMPI *Mf* scales, while Lunneborg (1970) found a correlation of .80 when a mixed-sex group was used.

Guilford's M scale shows somewhat lower correlations with M–F measures, as might be expected since its derivation was somewhat different. In single-sex groups, the *r*s range from .08 with Fe (Gough, 1964) to .48 with the MMPI *Mf* (Murray & Galvin, 1963) for males; however, the majority of the correlations in both male and female groups fall between .20 and .30 (Barrows & Zuckerman, 1960; Himelstein & Stoup, 1967; Nance, 1949). Correlations are much stronger in the mixed-sex groups, with Nance reporting *r*s of .60 with the SVIB and .72 with the MMPI, while Lunneborg (1970) found a correlation of .62 between the Inventory GAMIN Factor M and the MMPI *Mf*.

In summarizing these data, it seems fair to say that although the tests have something in common, a considerable proportion of the variance associated with any two tests is not held in common. The universe of known sex differences is large indeed, and it is not unreasonable to expect that these differences reflect more than one underlying dimension. All of these data point to the greater power of M–F measures when combined-sex groups are used, but a cursory review of M–F-related research reveals a preponderance of single-sex studies. One should also note that the tests seem weaker when applied to women than they do when measuring M–F in men, which may suggest that femininity is not adequately conceptualized as simply a reversal of masculinity.

Factor-Analytic Studies

Although correlational studies between two supposed measures of the same construct can contribute some information concerning dimensionality, factor analysis remains one of the most effective methods for identifying the degree to which the total variance of a test or group of tests can be attributed to more than one underlying factor. Factor analysis of the items in an individual scale can give information about the dimensionality of that particular measure of M–F, while analysis of items from several measures can contribute to our knowledge of the dimensions of the construct in general.

Terman and Miles (1936) had concluded that it was unlikely that there was a *general* M–F factor underlying scores on their seven exercises, but their discussion of profile scoring leaves open the possibility that there may be several *common* factors which contribute to M–F scores in a predictable way. Ford and Tyler (1952), using over 300 ninth grade boys and girls, factor analyzed responses to the Terman-Miles, omitting the Ink-Blot Identification and Opinions exercises because of their low reliabilities. The items in the five remaining exercises were divided into 14 clusters on the basis of content, and scores on these clusters, not the individual items, were the basis for their analysis. Two factors were extracted from the matrix for males: (*a*) toughness or insensitivity, with high loadings from anger, disgust, pity, ethical attitudes, and interests; and (*b*) interests, with interests, books, and activity preference showing high loadings. The first two of the three factors extracted for females were very similar to those for the males, while the third was designated as a social role factor which reflects a girl's awareness of the part she is to play in society. Ford and Tyler concluded that the Emotional and Ethical Attitudes and Interests exercises of the Terman-Miles represent the two factors fairly well and that M–F is not a unitary trait. Marke and Gottfries,[2] in constructing a measure of M–F for use with a Swedish population, used the results of the Ford and Tyler analysis in selecting items, mostly from the original Terman-Miles, which would relate primarily to interests and emotionality as the principal components of M–F. On the basis of item content and preliminary statistical analyses, they devised several subscales to measure each of the two components

and subjected scores on these subscales to a series of within-sex factor analyses. Two factors appeared regularly: (*a*) interests, with high loadings from the subscales occupations, books, and hobbies; and (*b*) emotionality or sensitivity, with high loadings from the pity, disgust, and ethics subscales. Factor 3 is less clear, but Marke and Gottfries concluded that it is a stereotype toughness factor, since the subscales showing the highest loadings seem to "contain characteristics considered to typify pseudomasculinity or compensatory masculinity" (see Footnote 2, p. 38). Not surprisingly, this third factor is the only major difference from the results of Ford and Tyler, although it may be related to their Factor 1 for males.

Abbott (1969), using 199 male and 208 female high school students, developed a measure of 150 self-report items from previous tests which discriminated the sexes in her sample at the .05 level or better. She performed cluster analyses on the interitem correlations within the two sex groups and subjected the resulting 13 clusters from each group to factor analysis. For the males, three factors were extracted, each accounting for 16-25% of the variance: (*a*) tough, self-assertive; (*b*) impersonal, self-sufficient; and (*c*) enterprising, realistic. Four factors, accounting for 16-20% of the variance each, were extracted for the females: (*a*) self-concerned, timid; (*b*) insecure, dependent; (*c*) considerate of others; and (*d*) interests. These factors seem closer to the emotional or sensitivity dimension of Ford and Tyler, and to be subdivisions thereof; it is interesting to note that the interest factor did not appear in the matrix for males, although the age groups in both studies were similar as was the item content.

The question of multidimensionality in M–F scales and the nature of the construct lies at the heart of the work of Lunneborg (1972), who asserted that factor analysis of M–F items should produce one of three possible outcomes:

(1) A single dimension that underlies MF, (2) a small number of MF factors capable of psychological definition common to both sexes, or (3) a very large number of weak factors, which would suggest that sex differences have been tapped over a wide variety of personality traits [p. 313].

---

[2] S. Marke & I. Gottfries. Measurement of masculinity and femininity. Psychological Research Bulletin, Lund University, Sweden, 1967, VII, 4.

Both the second and third outcomes would point to multidimensionality; however, the second alternative would allow the construction of several homogeneous, orthogonal scales which could be used in combination as a profile measure of M–F, while the third outcome would cast doubt on any attempt to devise a measure reflecting a psychological dimension of M–F. In an earlier study (Lunneborg & Lunneborg, 1970), using 136 items from the MMPI, Inventory GAMIN, and Gough measures of M–F with 169 college sophomores as subjects, factor analysis of interitem correlations across scales had resulted in the extraction of 11 factors labeled as follows: (a), feminine interests; (b) emotional sensitivity; (c) Philistine versus artistic; (d) self-confidence; (e) masculine interests; (f) rejection of adventure; (g) neurotic symptoms; (h) indifference; (i) social adequacy; (j) extraversion; and (k) unsociable nonconformity. Factors a and b are defined by 22 and 10 items having loadings of .40 or higher, while all other factors have 6 or fewer items that meet this criterion. Factor scores were computed and tested for their ability to discriminate the sexes. Feminine interests and social adequacy were correlated with female sex status ($r = .82$ and $.34$), while Philistine versus artistic, masculine interests, and indifference were related to male sex status ($r = .32$, $.35$, and $.28$); however, the shortness of the scales and the modest size of the correlations are not particularly encouraging. The authors concluded that the 6 factors that were not related to sex of respondent should not be regarded as "true M–F" factors since ability to discriminate the sexes is a prime requirement for the definitions of such a factor.

Lunneborg (1972) computed interitem phi coefficients among 450 items taken from nine measures thought to be related to sex differences in response; the computations were done separately for each sex and the two resulting intercorrelation matrices were factor analyzed. All 450 items were included in this analysis although only 177 items discriminated the sexes at the .01 level in two separate administrations. Nine factors accounting for 20% of the variance were extracted for the females and 10 factors accounting for 28% were extracted for males. Lunneborg main-

tained that the lower reliabilities of true–false measures violate the usual assumptions about the reliability of items being factor analyzed and that the extracted factors actually account for 40% and 57% of the *reliable* variance associated with this pool. Four factors of those extracted were judged to be common to the two sexes: neuroticism, power, scientific interest, and less significantly, religiosity. Although the number of items defining these four factors in the separate analyses for men and women ranged from 7 to 40, the number of items in common for each factor were 19, 7, 7, and 5, respectively. The percent of variance accounted for by these four factors was not indicated but it cannot be greater than 20. The additional factors extracted for one sex but not the other bear more than a passing resemblance, which Lunneborg did not explore, to those found in the earlier analysis. She maintained that these factors reflect stereotyped notions of sex differences, but one could assert that single-sex factors could be indicative of dimensions of masculinity or femininity which differentiate levels of these traits within one sex but not necessarily across the sexes. Although Lunneborg (1972) concluded, on the basis of her results, that "MF is neither the unidimensional, mythical belief popularly held, nor is it nonexistent [p. 317]," one can hardly take her four factors as a final statement on the nature of the dimensions of M–F, as she seemed to imply. Instead, one can only endorse her plea for profile analysis and hope for further work that will be more definitive in identifying M–F traits.

BIPOLARITY IN MASCULINITY–FEMININITY MEASUREMENT

The question of the validity of the assumption of inherent bipolarity in M–F is harder to deal with than was that of multidimensionality. Although a number of people have commented on the issue, very little work has been done which bears directly on the problem; rather the impetus to its reassessment comes primarily from work in other areas. As examples, one can look at Beller's (1955) demonstration of the independence of two measures of dependency and independence in preschool children and Nowlis' (1970) repeated findings of orthogonality among 11 mood factors originally hypothesized to be bipolar.

At least three aspects of bipolarity as found in M–F measurement can be distinguished: (*a*) The implication that M–F is a single dimension ranging from extreme masculinity at one end through a zero point to extreme femininity at the other; (*b*) the use of a dichotomous variable, such as sex, to validate a continuous one like M–F, necessarily implying two poles, even if there is no distribution between them; and (*c*) the tendency to define *A* as not-*B* and not-*A* as *B*, or of logical reversal. Almost all the measures reviewed have used the power of an item to discriminate the sexes in defining M–F relevance and most rely primarily on a binary choice in response options; thus, the second and third aspects of the bipolarity issue are implicated in most measures. The first aspect is present whenever a single distribution of total scores reflecting both M and F is provided for; it is most apparent in the Terman-Miles and the SVIB, where scores are positive in the masculine end and negative in the feminine end, and the total score is based on an algebraic summation. However, the assumption is also present in the MMPI *Mf* and the Gough Fe scales; Gough (1964) indeed stated that a low score on Fe indicates masculinity. The construction of the M scale (Guilford & Zimmerman, 1949) comes closest to avoiding the problems of bipolarity, but many of its users ignore the fact that the authors do *not* indicate that a low score is indicative of femininity. However, it seems safest to look primarily to work done with other measures besides those reviewed in attempting to adduce evidence for or against the central issue of whether M–F is possibly divisible into separate M and F dimensions, either in addition to or instead of the single bipolar dimension of M–F.

Rosenberg and Sutton-Smith (1959), using a sample of 183 fourth to sixth graders, developed a games and activities preference measure, in which items were weighted on the basis of the extent to which they differentiated the responses of boys from girls, but were subsequently assigned only to a masculinity or a femininity scale. The authors were not particularly concerned with the nature of the

M–F dimension as bipolar and made no decision about whether one or both scales should be used with any single-sex group. In a subsequent study, however, Rosenberg, Sutton-Smith, and Morgan (1961) found that high scores on the *opposite*-sex scale were more clearly related to neuroticism, impulsiveness, and anxiety among fourth to sixth graders than were differences of any kind on the same-sex scale. This relationship would probably have been obscured by using the typical M minus F single score, since children scoring high on the opposite-sex scale had a wide distribution of scores on the same-sex scale.

Sannito, Walker, Foley, and Posavac (1972) have done considerable work with the Thorne Femininity Scale, which attempts to measure only one-half of the M–F dimension, in order to demonstrate the reliability and validity of a measure which is designed to elucidate only aspects of femininity with no reference to masculinity. However, the construction of this particular measure seems to suffer from so many other weaknesses that no real conclusions can be drawn as to the potential effectiveness of this kind of approach to the bipolarity issue.

Vroegh (1971) explicitly is less concerned with the ability of an item to discriminate between the sexes and more with its potential for discriminating appropriate gender identity within sex. She obtained teacher and peer ratings of masculinity and femininity and self-ratings on the Cattell Children's Personality form for over 400 upper-middle-class boys and girls in Grades 1 to 8. The purpose of the study was to establish the major interrelationships among teacher and peer ratings of masculinity and femininity and personality factor scores. Teacher/peer agreement was found to be only moderate, which may be due in part to different rating methods used by the two groups; the correlations were nonsignificant in Grade 1 but otherwise they ranged from .45 to .64 for masculinity in boys and from .38 to .76 for femininity in girls for the other seven grades. The essential findings for the purposes of this paper concern the fact that there is a *positive* relationship between the correlates of masculinity and of femininity in Grades 1–3 and 4–6 for the ratings by peers. The relationship does not hold for

Grades 7–8, nor is there any significant relationship among the correlates of teachers' ratings at any grade level. The overlap is seen most clearly in Grades 4–6 where both masculine boys and feminine girls are high on "competence" factors on the Cattell Children's Personality form.

Although the use of judges' ratings has many known hazards, it seems imperative that some way of establishing indicators of M and F independently of the sex discrimination criterion be developed, both to allow the use of a criterion that is not built on logical reversal and to permit an independent test of the adequacy of sex discrimination as a necessary characteristic of "true M–F," as Lunneborg has asserted. Goodenough (1946), using a word association test, originally attempted to use the Terman-Miles weighting procedure to develop a scoring key for M–F in both men and women. However, she concluded that a "feminine" woman is not the same as a "feminine" man, and subsequently developed separate scoring keys for the two sexes based on contrasting responses of the top and bottom quartiles (under the original scoring key) within each sex. Thus, with the new scoring key, the same response may be weighted +1 M on the key for males and +4 F on the key for females. The questions of definition and criteria of M–F become critical in evaluating results which indicate that the same factors may be highly related to both M and F, as Goodenough and Vroegh have asserted, since by one definition this is a logical impossibility.

Jenkin and Vroegh (1969) have assumed that M–F is not a single bipolar dimension but two separate dimensions, each applying only to one sex, and that appropriate criterion groups are not males or females but imaginary or "ideal" most and least masculine and feminine concepts. In a study using 189 adjectives and semantic differential scales with 50 adults, correlations between "most" and "least" were −.82 for masculinity and −.80 for femininity. However, the correlation between "most masculine person" and "most feminine person" was +.42, and of the 45 adjectives descriptive of "most masculine" and the 32 for "most feminine," 17 were in common. Further, correlations between "most masculine" and "least feminine" and between

"most feminine" and "least masculine" were *negative,* −.36 and −.47, respectively, which is contrary to the logical bipolarity assumption. Jenkin and Vroegh noted the possible contamination from social desirability factors. In addition, when the object of a rating is "ideal" man, woman, or self, higher ratings are given to valued characteristics that are usually associated with the opposite sex; thus ratings are less reflective of extreme masculine and feminine responses.

The most methodologically innovative study of bipolarity in M–F measurement is that of Gonen and Lansky (1968), who also present a clear review of the problem of bipolarity in M–F testing. Whereas Murray (1963) had concluded that the 20 MMPI *Mf* items which did not discriminate the sexes in his sample were M–F irrelevant, Gonen and Lansky hypothesized that they might be relevant to M or F but not to M–F, and therefore would reflect a unipolar dimension that did not discriminate the sexes. For each MMPI item, the subject was asked to indicate whether the content would be indicative of greater or lesser masculinity *and* greater or lesser femininity if answered "true" by a man *and* by a woman. Since the MMPI allows true and false responses, an alternate form was prepared in which the stimulus contained the opposite option from that used on the first form. On each of the 60 items, 8 responses were possible and the subject could check from 0 to 8 boxes. Bipolarity was indicated by any combination of 2 to 4 checks in which a change in masculinity was mirrored by a reverse change in femininity, while unipolarity was indicated by any combination of checks in which there was no clear implication about a change in masculinity from a response to femininity. When no boxes were checked, the response was designated M–F irrelevant. Gonen and Lansky found that, as they had predicted, more of the 40 discriminating items were rated in a bipolar way, but their prediction that more of the 20 nondiscriminating items would be seen as unipolar was not supported, although the tendency was in this direction. Many of these latter items were indeed rated as M–F irrelevant. Although Gonen and Lansky expressed dissatisfaction with the conclusiveness of their results, they did conclude that at least three complex dimensions should be considered in M–F research: masculinity, femininity, and masculinity–femininity.

It would seem that some variation of the Gonen and Lansky method could be used not only to examine the bipolarity of traits previously identified as M–F relevant, but also to answer the question of whether all three dimensions, if they exist, are relevant to both sexes. Although Jenkin and Vroegh (1969) explicitly stated that the separate dimensions of M and F are applicable to only one sex group, Webster (1953) concluded that "psychological femininity may also be considered a personality variable (which is present in both sexes) [p. 36]." Webster's position is consistent with both Jungian theory and Carlson's (1972) position that dualities be treated as complex interactive forces. Clearly this is another aspect of the M–F definition which needs further work.

OTHER PROBLEMS IN MASCULINITY–FEMININITY MEASUREMENT

Item Content and Stereotypy

Cultural lag is an important contributor to the dilemma of what we are measuring in most M–F tests; for example, answers given to Gough's Fe scale by his normative sample in the 1950s probably reflected in part actual sex differences in behavior at that time and in part the respondent's expectation of how she *should* respond to such a question as "I think I would like to drive a racing car." That "should" response is based on a stereotype for the female role derived from folk theory and data that is probably at least 20 years older than the college-age respondent.

That fairly clear-cut and persistent sex role stereotypes exist has been amply demonstrated (e.g., McKee & Sherriffs, 1957; Rosenkrantz, Vogel, Bee, Broverman, & Broverman, 1968), as has the fact that they contribute to the "fakability" of M–F measures (e.g., Bieliauskas, Miranda, & Lansky, 1968; Lunneborg, 1970). Just how serious this problem is when attempting to measure "true M–F" has been clearly demonstrated by Nichols (1962), who attempted to separate M–F items with "actual behavioral similarity to a given sex" from those which reflect self-at-tributed sex role. He administered 356 items from existing M–F measures to 100 men and 100 women under standard instructions and computed the ability of each item to discriminate the sexes, using the phi coefficient. The items were then given to a new group of 48 men and 64 women who were asked to indicate whether the item was more indicative of masculinity or femininity. Nichols constructed a scatterplot in which the coordinates represented the actual sex differences and the stereotypic differences. Items were placed on the plot according to the magnitude and direction of their two phi coefficients. "Obvious" items were high on both stereotype and actual discrimination, "subtle" items were high on actual discrimination but low on the stereotype, while "stereotype" items showed the reverse pattern. Three scales were derived and scores from the original sample plus those from a cross-validation sample were computed. The subtle scale contained only 30 items and was of low reliability, but did yield some discrimination of the sexes. The stereotype scale, containing 61 items, had high reliability and produced greater discrimination in the cross-validation sample than it had in the original. Its content reflects neuroticism, suspiciousness, and morality, plus some exaggeration of actual sex differences. The obvious scale had 58 items and, as might be expected, was high on both reliability and validity in terms of discrimination of the sexes. Nichols reported negative correlations between the subtle and stereotype scales, a finding which he interpreted as an indication of defensiveness, and positive correlations between the obvious scale and several existing measures of M–F. Using Nichols' method with a non-M–F measure, the Edwards Personality Inventory, Lunneborg (1970) obtained similar results and concluded that what is measured by the typical M–F scale is partly determined by stereotypes, although discriminant power between the sexes may be weak because of the influence of social desirability factors.

While it is clear from the above that item content, sex role stereotypy, and social desirability interact in measures of M–F making it difficult to obtain a relatively pure measure, it is not yet clear how (and how much) to control for their effects.

Demographic Factors

Social class, geographic location, and education have all been found to be associated with M–F scores, although the nature of the relationship is not always consistent across different studies. It is probable that the influence of all three is, at least in part, dependent on the rigidity and pervasiveness of the appropriate sex role stereotype, and that this factor may act as a mediator between M–F and these demographic variables. The usual finding that education contributes to a moderation of M–F scores in men and women (Gough, 1964; Strong, 1943; Terman & Miles, 1936; Webster, 1956) thus might be attributable to increasing flexibility in the stereotype which results from higher education. It is not clear whether the recurrent finding that many items no longer discriminate the sexes among college students is due to generation differences or to differences in education from the normative sample.

Geographical factors as well as education are apparent in the results of Goodstein (1954), who found that the mean score of college men on the MMPI was consistently one-half to one standard deviation higher than the norm, but that the size of the deviation varied with samples from different parts of the country. In an earlier study using the Terman-Miles, Disher (1942) found that both male and female high school and college students in Florida scored as more feminine that did the normative samples taken largely from the Pacific Northwest, with the most outstanding differences being in the areas of Emotional and Ethical Attitudes and Interests.

There has been little work on the effects of social class on M–F measurement in adults, but there is some indication that particular aspects of the stereotype become less important as one moves up the social ladder and that M–F scores become less extreme. Kaplan (1967) found that an index of cultural opportunity was a useful moderator variable which increased the ability of an unspecified M–F test to predict peer ratings of masculinity among 421 army recruits, although father's occupation and standard of living did not prove helpful. Vincent (1966) matched 50 high- and low-scoring females and 60 high- and low-scoring males on the California Psychological Inventory Fe scale for familial and social class factors and found that, contrary to his expectations, the low-Fe females and the high-Fe males showed a nonsignificant but consistent trend of having higher, or more healthy, scores on the other scales of the California Psychological Inventory. In an effort to clarify this result, Vincent examined item content and concluded that a number of items are time and/or culture bound. Males will score high if they have developed sensitivity, intuition, and responsiveness to others, while "successful" females will continue to score low as long as traditional items reflecting fear, excitement, and change are included. Vincent saw a definite social class bias in items which discriminate high- and low-Fe males, in that such behaviors as spitting on the sidewalk and fighting will not be endorsed by middle-class males.

Age

Both Terman and Miles (1936) and Strong (1943) presented evidence for increasing "femininity" with age among males, at least from the age of 18 or 19 on, but their data on changes among females are conflicting, with Terman finding more evidence for increasing femininity than did Strong. Gough (1964) indicated some trend toward increasing femininity among males and increasing masculinity among females in his samples of 15–25-year-olds, but these effects are compounded by educational differences. Similarly, Barrows and Zuckerman (1960) found some evidence of increasing femininity on the SVIB and MMPI in their study of 2,300 male white-collar workers. Evidence from research with children indicates that masculinity is more salient at an earlier age and is more persistent across age groups for boys than is femininity for girls, which has been interpreted as a result of greater cultural pressure toward sex role adoption in boys. Vroegh (1971), in interpreting the results of her study in which masculinity and femininity were positively related in the earlier grades but not in Grades 7–8, contended that this is a reflection of the pressure due to puberty to maximize sex differences which were less salient earlier and can be relaxed in later adolescence once gender identity has stabilized.

There are a number of indications that the relationships between age, "maturity" or "mental health," and M–F score need further investigation. It may be that a relatively extreme score on masculinity or femininity is positively related to maturity in early adolescence when this is an active area of conflict, but that it may be negatively related in adulthood. Such personality theories as those of Erikson (1963), Jung (1956), and Maslow (1962) certainly imply that the healthy adult of either sex will incorporate characteristics which are generally designated as opposite-sex appropriate by the stereotypes, such as sensitivity in men and self-confidence in women.

If further work on the interrelationships of these demographic factors, age, sex role stereotypes, and M–F substantiates the results of these preliminary studies, it may be necessary to provide detailed information or separate normative groups in order to facilitate the interpretation of individual scores. Given these data, however, one would also be forced to ask whether M–F is a true personality variable with some relationship to biological sex as is usually assumed.

SUMMARY AND CONCLUSIONS

The purpose of the present paper was to examine the adequacy of current approaches to M–F measurement in adults and to raise certain questions about the utility and validity of the concept of M–F as it is reflected in our measurement tools. The development and characteristics of the major tests of M–F in adults were reviewed with particular attention to those aspects of their construction that bear on the following issues: (*a*) Definition of M–F as a construct and the selection of appropriate criterion groups for item selection; (*b*) the dimensionality of the M–F construct, to be indicated by one summary score or by a profile of scores on subtraits; and (*c*) M–F as reflecting a single bipolar dimension as opposed to some combination of unipolar masculinity and femininity dimensions. In addition, the effects of demographic factors and sex role stereotypes on M–F measurement were considered briefly.

Current tests are judged to be largely inadequate for a variety of reasons: (*a*) Available data clearly point to multidimensionality, even if the concept of one bipolar M–F dimension is retained, and none of the tests is characterized by homogeneous subscales that can be scored separately; (*b*) all of the tests are built on an assumed bipolarity in the M–F dimension, but there is enough evidence for separate masculinity and femininity dimensions, possibly in addition to a bipolar M–F dimension, to warrant empirical tests of the bipolarity hypothesis before a final judgment can be reached; and (*c*) the use of sex differences in response as the sole criterion for an M–F indicator is open to question, but the hazards of other criteria are serious enough to indicate that this problem will probably be the least susceptible to experimental elucidation.

This article began with the question of whether or not something that cannot be measured does not exist. While it is clear that something is being measured by the tests of M–F, namely, sex differences in response, the theoretical explication that would tie sex differences, regardless of content, to masculinity and femininity is absent. In all probability, the length of the big toe would discriminate men and women, but does having a longer big toe than most women make a woman less "feminine," and can one have more confidence that she is less "feminine" because she scores deviantly on a number of items with similarly critical content?

Finally, one is left with the question of whether or not M–F is a useful dimension in studying a normal population. If M–F reflects a number of subtraits, such as aggressiveness, sensitivity, self-confidence, etc., is there anything to be gained by combining these measures in ways that are most characteristic of men and women? Multidimensional analysis may reveal that there are certain patterns of traits that appear more often in healthy males than healthy females, but the pattern may be different for most masculine versus least masculine men and most feminine versus least feminine women. Only further research will reveal whether or not there is some regular configuration of these traits that would justify their being handled under the summary term of M–F. Which is a specific instance of a general conclusion: Only a combination of further theoretical and experimental explication will permit a rational evaluation of the validity of the M–F concept per se and, by extension, the methods of its measurement.

REFERENCES

ABBOTT, M. M. *An analysis of the components of masculinity and femininity.* (Doctoral dissertation, Columbia University) Ann Arbor, Michigan: University Microfilms, 1969, No. 69-3048.

BARDWICK, J. M. *Psychology of women.* New York: Harper & Row, 1971.

BARROWS, G. A., & ZUCKERMAN, M. Construct validity of three masculinity–femininity tests. *Journal of Consulting Psychology,* 1960, 24, 441–445.

BELLER, E. K. Dependency and independence in young children. *Journal of Genetic Psychology,* 1955, 87, 25–35.

BERDIE, R. F. A femininity adjective check list. *Journal of Applied Psychology,* 1959, 43, 327–333.

BIELIAUSKAS, V. J., MIRANDA, S. B., & LANSKY, L. Obviousness of two masculinity–femininity tests. *Journal of Consulting and Clinical Psychology,* 1968, 32, 314–318.

BROWN, D. G. Sex-role development in a changing culture. *Psychological Bulletin,* 1958, 55, 232–242.

CALIGOR, L. The determination of the individual's unconscious conception of his own masculinity–femininity identification. *Journal of Projective Techniques and Personality Assessment,* 1951, 15, 494–509.

CAMPBELL, D. P. *Revised manual for Strong Vocational Interest Blanks.* Stanford: Stanford University Press, 1966.

CAMPBELL, D. P. *1969 supplement to revised manual for Strong Vocational Interest Blanks.* Stanford: Stanford University Press, 1969.

CARLSON, R. Understanding women: Implications for personality theory and research. *Journal of Social Issues,* 1972, 28(2), 17–32.

CRONBACH, L. J. *Essentials of psychological testing.* (2nd ed.) New York: Harper, 1960.

DAHLSTROM, W. G., & WELSH, G. S. *An MMPI handbook.* Minneapolis: University of Minnesota Press, 1960.

DE CILLIS, O. E., & ORBISON, W. D. A comparison of the Terman-Miles M–F Test and the Mf scale of the MMPI. *Journal of Applied Psychology,* 1950, 34, 338–342.

DEMPSEY, P. The dimensionality of the MMPI clinical scales among normal subjects. *Journal of Consulting Psychology,* 1963, 27, 492–497.

DISHER, D. R. Regional differences in masculinity–femininity responses. *Journal of Social Psychology,* 1942, 15, 53–61.

ENGLISH, H. O., & ENGLISH, A. B. *A comprehensive dictionary of psychological and psychoanalytical terms.* New York: Longmans, Green, 1958.

ERIKSON, E. H. *Childhood and society.* (2nd ed.) New York: Norton, 1963.

FORD, C. F., JR., & TYLER, L. E. A factor analysis of Terman and Miles' M–F Test. *Journal of Applied Psyhcology,* 1952, 36, 251–253.

FRANCK, K., & ROSEN, E. A projective test of masculinity–femininity. *Journal of Consulting Psychology,* 1949, 13, 247–256.

FREUD, S. *New introductory lectures on psychoanalysis.* (Trans. and ed. by J. Strachey) New York: Norton, 1965.

GARAI, J. E., & SCHEINFELD, A. Sex differences in mental and behavioral traits. *Genetic Psychology Monographs,* 1968, 77, 169–299.

GONEN, J. Y., & LANSKY, L. Masculinity, femininity, and masculinity–femininity: A phenomenological study of the Mf scale of the MMPI. *Psychological Reports,* 1968, 23, 183–194.

GOODENOUGH, F. L. Semantic choice and personality structure. *Science,* 1946, 104, 451–456.

GOODSTEIN, L. D. Regional differences in MMPI responses among male college students. *Journal of Consulting Psychology,* 1954, 18, 437–441.

GOUGH, H. G. Identifying psychological femininity. *Educational and Psychological Measurement,* 1952, 12, 427–439.

GOUGH, H. G. *California Psychological Inventory: Manual.* Palo Alto: Consulting Psychologists Press, 1964.

GOUGH, H. G. A cross-cultural analysis of the CPI Femininity scale. *Journal of Consulting Psychology,* 1966, 30, 136–141.

GRAHAM, J. R., SCHROEDER, H. E., & LILLY, R. S. Factor analysis of items on the Social Introversion and Masculinity–Femininity scales of the MMPI. *Journal of Clinical Psychology,* 1971, 27, 367–370.

GUILFORD, J. P., & GUILFORD, R. B. Personality factors S, E, and M and their measurement. *Journal of Psychology,* 1936, 2, 109–127.

GUILFORD, J. P., & ZIMMERMAN, W. S. *The Guilford-Zimmerman Temperament Survey: Manual of instructions and interpretations.* Beverly Hills, Calif.: Sheridan Supply, 1949.

GUILFORD, J. P., & ZIMMERMAN, W. S. Fourteen dimensions of temperament. *Psychological Monographs,* 1956, 70(10, Whole No. 417).

HAMPSON, J. L. Determinants of psychosexual orientation. In F. A. Beach (Ed.), *Sex and behavior.* New York: Wiley, 1965.

HATHAWAY, S. R., & MCKINLEY, J. C. *The Minnesota Multiphasic Personality Inventory.* New York: Psychological Corporation, 1943.

HEILBRUN, A. B. Conformity to masculinity–femininity stereotypes and ego identity in adolescents. *Psychological Reports,* 1964, 14, 351–357.

HESTON, J. C. A comparison of four masculinity–femininity scales. *Educational and Psychological Measurement,* 1948, 8, 375–387.

HIMELSTEIN, P., & STOUP, D. Correlation of three Mf measures for males. *Journal of Clinical Psychology,* 1967, 23, 189.

HOOKER, E. An empirical study of some relations between sexual patterns and gender identity in male homosexuals. In J. Money (Ed.), *Sex research: New developments.* New York: Holt, Rinehart & Winston, 1965.

JENKIN, N., & VROEGH, K. Contemporary concepts of masculinity and femininity. *Psychological Reports,* 1969, **25**, 679–697.

JUNG, C. G. *Two essays on analytical psychology.* New York: Meridian Books, 1956.

KAPLAN, H. *The use of moderator variables in the analysis of masculinity and femininity.* (Doctoral dissertation, George Washington University) Ann Arbor, Mich.: University Microfilms, 1967, No. 67-14,403.

KELLY, G. A. *A theory of personality.* New York: Norton, 1963.

KLOPFER, W. G. Correlation of women's MF scores on the MMPI and Strong VIB. *Journal of Clinical Psychology,* 1966, **22**, 216.

KOHLBERG, L. A cognitive-developmental analysis of children's sex-role concepts and attitudes. In E. E. Maccoby (Ed.), *The development of sex differences.* Stanford: Stanford University Press, 1966.

LANSKY, L. Mechanisms of defense: Sex identity and defenses against conflict. In D. R. Miller & G. E. Swanson (Eds.), *Inner conflict and defense.* New York: Holt, Rinehart & Winston, 1960.

LUNNEBORG, P. W. Stereotypic aspects in masculinity-femininity measurement. *Journal of Consulting and Clinical Psychology,* 1970, **34**, 113–118.

LUNNEBORG, P. W. Dimensionality of MF. *Journal of Clinical Psychology,* 1972, **28**, 313–317.

LUNNEBORG, P. W., & LUNNEBORG, C. E. Factor structure of Mf scales and items. *Journal of Clinical Psychology,* 1970, **26**, 360–366.

LYNN, D. B. *Parental and sex-role identification.* Berkeley, Calif.: McCutchan, 1969.

MACCOBY, E. E. (Ed.) *The development of sex differences.* Stanford: Stanford University Press, 1966.

MANDLER, G., & KESSEN, W. F. *The language of psychology.* New York: Wiley, 1959.

MASLOW, A. H. *Toward a psychology of being.* Princeton: Van Nostrand, 1962.

MAY, R. R. A method for studying the development of gender identity. *Developmental Psychology,* 1971, **5**, 484–487.

MCCARTHY, D., ANTHONY, R. J., & DOMINO, G. A comparison of the CPI, Franck, MMPI, and WAIS Masculinity–Femininity indexes. *Journal of Consulting and Clinical Psychology,* 1970, **35**, 414–416.

MCKEE, J. P., & SHERRIFFS, A. C. The differential evaluation of males and females. *Journal of Personality,* 1957, **25**, 356–371.

MONEY, J. Psychosexual differentiation. In J. Money (Ed.), *Sex research: New developments.* New York: Holt, Rinehart & Winston, 1965.

MURRAY, J. B. The Mf scale of the MMPI for college students. *Journal of Clinical Psychology,* 1963, **19**, 113–115.

MURRAY, J. B., & GALVIN, J. Correlational study of the MMPI and GZTS. *Journal of General Psychology,* 1963, **69**, 267–273.

NANCE, R. D. Masculinity–femininity in prospective teachers. *Journal of Educational Research,* 1949, **42**, 658–666.

NICHOLS, R. C. Subtle, obvious, and stereotype measures of masculinity–femininity. *Educational and Psychological Measurement,* 1962, **22**, 449–461.

NOWLIS, V. Mood: Behavior and experience. In M. Arnold (Ed.), *Feelings and emotions.* New York: Academic Press, 1970.

REECE, M. Masculinity and femininity: A factor analytic study. *Psychological Reports,* 1964, **14**, 123–139.

ROSENBERG, B. G., & SUTTON-SMITH, B. The measurement of masculinity and femininity in children. *Child Development,* 1959, **30**, 373–380.

ROSENBERG, B. G., SUTTON-SMITH, B., & MORGAN, E. The use of opposite-sex scales as a measure of psychosexual deviancy. *Journal of Consulting Psychology,* 1961, **25**, 221–225.

ROSENKRANTZ, P., VOGEL, S., BEE, H., BROVERMAN, I., & BROVERMAN, D. M. Sex-role stereotypes and self-concepts in college students. *Journal of Consulting and Clinical Psychology,* 1968, **32**, 287–295.

SANNITO, T., WALKER, R. E., FOLEY, J. M., & POSAVAC, E. J. A test of female sex identification: The Thorne Femininity Study. *Journal of Clinical Psychology,* 1972, **28**, 531–539.

SHEPLER, B. F. A comparison of masculinity–femininity measures. *Journal of Consulting Psychology,* 1951, **15**, 484–486.

STRONG, E. K. Interests of men and women. *Journal of Social Psychology,* 1936, **7**, 49–67.

STRONG, E. K. *Vocational interests of men and women.* Stanford: Stanford University Press, 1943.

TERMAN, L., & MILES, C. C. *Sex and personality.* New York: McGraw Hill, 1936.

VINCENT, C. E. Implications of changes in male–female role expectations for interpreting M–F scores. *Journal of Marriage and the Family,* 1966, **28**, 196–199.

VROEGH, K. Masculinity and femininity in the elementary and junior high school years. *Developmental Psychology,* 1971, **4**, 254–261.

WEBSTER, H. Derivation and use of the masculinity–femininity variable. *Journal of Clinical Psychology,* 1953, **9**, 33–36.

WEBSTER, H. Personality development during the college years: Some quantitative results. *Journal of Social Issues,* 1956, **12**(4), 29–43.

WRIGHT, F. H., & L'ABATE, L. On the meaning of the MMPI Mf and SVIB MF scales. *British Journal of Social and Clinical Psychology,* 1970, **9**, 171–174.

(Received January 3, 1973)

2

SANDRA L. BEM

The Measurement of Psychological Androgyny

This article describes the development of a new sex-role inventory that treats masculinity and femininity as two independent dimensions, thereby making it possible to characterize a person as masculine, feminine, or "androgynous" as a function of the difference between his or her endorsement of masculine and feminine personality characteristics. Normative data are presented, as well as the results of various psychometric analyses. The major findings of conceptual interest are: (*a*) the dimensions of masculinity and femininity are empirically as well as logically independent; (*b*) the concept of psychological androgyny is a reliable one; and (*c*) highly sex-typed scores do not reflect a general tendency to respond in a socially desirable direction, but rather a specific tendency to describe oneself in accordance with sex-typed standards of desirable behavior for men and women.

Both in psychology and in society at large, masculinity and femininity have long been conceptualized as bipolar ends of a single continuum; accordingly, a person has had to be either masculine or feminine, but not both. This sex-role dichotomy has served to obscure two very plausible hypotheses: first, that many individuals might be "androgynous"; that is, they might be *both* masculine and feminine, *both* assertive and yielding, *both* instrumental and expressive—depending on the situational appropriateness of these various behaviors; and conversely, that strongly sex-typed individuals might be seriously limited in the range of behaviors available to them as they move from situation to situation. According to both Kagan (1964) and Kohlberg (1966), the highly sex-typed individual is motivated to keep his behavior consistent with an internalized sex-role standard, a goal that he presumably accomplishes by suppressing any behavior that might be considered undesirable or inappropriate for his sex. Thus, whereas a narrowly masculine self-concept might inhibit behaviors that are stereotyped as feminine, and a narrowly feminine self-concept might inhibit behaviors that are stereotyped as masculine, a mixed, or

This research was supported by 1ROIMH 21735 from the National Institute of Mental Health. The author is grateful to Carol Korula, Karen Rook, Jenny Jacobs, and Odile van Embden for their help in analyzing the data.

Requests for reprints should be sent to Sandra L. Bem, Department of Psychology, Stanford University, Stanford, California 94305.

androgynous, self-concept might allow an individual to freely engage in both "masculine" and "feminine" behaviors.

The current research program is seeking to explore these various hypotheses, as well as to provide construct validation for the concept of androgyny (Bem, 1974). Before the research could be initiated, however, it was first necessary to develop a new type of sex-role inventory, one that would not automatically build in an inverse relationship between masculinity and femininity. This article describes that inventory.

The Bem Sex-Role Inventory (BSRI) contains a number of features that distinguish it from other, commonly used, masculinity-femininity scales, for example, the Masculinity–Femininity scale of the California Psychological Inventory (Gough, 1957). First, it includes both a Masculinity scale and a Femininity scale, each of which contains 20 personality characteristics. These characteristics are listed in the first and second columns of Table 1, respectively. Second, because the BSRI was founded on a conception of the sex-typed person as someone who has internalized society's sex-typed standards of desirable behavior for men and women, these personality characteristics were selected as masculine or feminine on the basis of sex-typed social desirability and not on the basis of differential endorsement by males and females as most other inventories have done. That is, a characteristic qualified as masculine if it was judged

TABLE 1

ITEMS ON THE MASCULINITY, FEMININITY, AND SOCIAL DESIRABILITY SCALES OF THE BSRI

Masculine items	Feminine items	Neutral items
49. Acts as a leader	11. Affectionate	51. Adaptable
46. Aggressive	5. Cheerful	36. Conceited
58. Ambitious	50. Childlike	9. Conscientious
22. Analytical	32. Compassionate	60. Conventional
13. Assertive	53. Does not use harsh language	45. Friendly
10. Athletic	35. Eager to soothe hurt feelings	15. Happy
55. Competitive	20. Feminine	3. Helpful
4. Defends own beliefs	14. Flatterable	48. Inefficient
37. Dominant	59. Gentle	24. Jealous
19. Forceful	47. Gullible	39. Likable
25. Has leadership abilities	56. Loves children	6. Moody
7. Independent	17. Loyal	21. Reliable
52. Individualistic	26. Sensitive to the needs of others	30. Secretive
31. Makes decisions easily	8. Shy	33. Sincere
40. Masculine	38. Soft spoken	42. Solemn
1. Self-reliant	23. Sympathetic	57. Tactful
34. Self-sufficient	44. Tender	12. Theatrical
16. Strong personality	29. Understanding	27. Truthful
43. Willing to take a stand	41. Warm	18. Unpredictable
28. Willing to take risks	2. Yielding	54. Unsystematic

Note. The number preceding each item reflects the position of each adjective as it actually appears on the Inventory.

to be more desirable in American society for a man than for a woman, and it qualified as feminine if it was judged to be more desirable for a woman than for a man. Third, the BSRI characterizes a person as masculine, feminine, or androgynous as a function of the difference between his or her endorsement of masculine and feminine personality characteristics. A person is thus sex typed, whether masculine or feminine, to the extent that this difference score is high, and androgynous, to the extent that this difference score is low. Finally, the BSRI also includes a Social Desirability scale that is completely neutral with respect to sex. This scale now serves primarily to provide a neutral context for the Masculinity and Femininity scales, but it was utilized during the development of the BSRI to insure that the inventory would not simply be tapping a general tendency to endorse socially desirable traits. The 20 characteristics that make up this scale are listed in the third column of Table 1.

ITEM SELECTION

Both historically and cross-culturally, masculinity and femininity seem to have represented two complementary domains of *posi-*

tive traits and behaviors (Barry, Bacon, & Child, 1957; Erikson, 1964; Parsons & Bales, 1955). In general, masculinity has been associated with an instrumental orientation, a cognitive focus on "getting the job done"; and femininity has been associated with an expressive orientation, an affective concern for the welfare of others.

Accordingly, as a preliminary to item selection for the Masculinity and Femininity scales, a list was compiled of approximately 200 personality characteristics that seemed to the author and several students to be both positive in value and either masculine or feminine in tone. This list served as the pool from which the masculine and feminine characteristics were ultimately chosen. As a preliminary to item selection for the Social Desirability scale, an additional list was compiled of 200 characteristics that seemed to be neither masculine nor feminine in tone. Of these "neutral" characteristics, half were positive in value and half were negative.

Because the BSRI was designed to measure the extent to which a person divorces himself from those characteristics that might be considered more "appropriate" for the opposite sex, the final items were selected

TABLE 2

MEAN SOCIAL DESIRABILITY RATINGS OF THE MASCULINE, FEMININE, AND NEUTRAL ITEMS

Item	Male judges			Female judges		
	Masculine item	Feminine item	Neutral item	Masculine item	Feminine item	Neutral item
For a man	5.59	3.63	4.00	5.83	3.74	3.94
For a woman	2.90	5.61	4.08	3.46	5.55	3.98
Difference	2.69	1.98	.08	2.37	1.81	.04
t	14.41*	12.13*	.17	10.22*	8.28*	.09

* $p < .001$.

for the Masculinity and Femininity scales if they were judged to be more desirable in American society for one sex than for the other. Specifically, judges were asked to utilize a 7-point scale, ranging from 1 ("Not at all desirable") to 7 ("Extremely desirable"), in order to rate the desirability in American society of each of the approximately 400 personality characteristics mentioned above. (E.g., "In American society, how desirable is it for a man to be truthful?" "In American society, how desirable is it for a woman to be sincere?") Each individual judge was asked to rate the desirability of all 400 personality characteristics either "for a man" or "for a woman." No judge was asked to rate both. The judges consisted of 40 Stanford undergraduates who filled out the questionnaire during the winter of 1972 and an additional 60 who did so the following summer. In both samples, half of the judges were male and half were female.

A personality characteristic qualified as masculine if it was independently judged by both males and females in both samples to be significantly more desirable for a man than for a woman ($p < .05$).[3] Similarly, a personality characteristic qualified as feminine if it was independently judged by both males and females in both samples to be significantly more desirable for a woman than for a man ($p < .05$). Of those characteristics that satisfied these criteria, 20 were selected for the Masculinity scale and 20 were selected for the Femininity scale (see the first and second columns of Table 1, respectively).

[3] All significance levels in this article are based on two-tailed *t* tests.

A personality characteristic qualified as neutral with respect to sex and hence eligible for the Social Desirability scale (*a*) if it was independently judged by both males and females to be no more desirable for one sex than for the other ($t < 1.2$, $p > .2$) and (*b*) if male and female judges did not differ significantly in their overall desirability judgments of that trait ($t < 1.2$, $p > .2$). Of those items that satisfied these several criteria, 10 positive and 10 negative personality characteristics were selected for the BSRI Social Desirability scale in accordance with Edwards' (1964) finding that an item must be quite positive or quite negative in tone if it is to evoke a social desirability response set. (The 20 neutral characteristics are shown in the third column of Table 1.)

After all of the individual items had been selected, mean desirability scores were computed for the masculine, feminine, and neutral items for each of the 100 judges. As shown in Table 2, for both males and females, the mean desirability of the masculine and feminine items was significantly higher for the "appropriate" sex than for the "inappropriate" sex, whereas the mean desirability of the neutral items was no higher for one sex than for the other. These results are, of course, a direct consequence of the criteria used for item selection.

Table 3 separates out the desirability ratings of the masculine and feminine items for male and female judges rating their *own* sex. These own-sex ratings seem to best represent the desirability of these various items as perceived by men and women when they are asked to describe *themselves* on the inven-

TABLE 3

MEAN SOCIAL DESIRABILITY RATINGS OF THE
MASCULINE AND FEMININE ITEMS
FOR ONE'S OWN SEX

Item	Male judges for a man	Female judges for a woman
Masculine	5.59	3.46
Feminine	3.63	5.55
Difference	1.96	2.09
t	11.94*	8.88*

* $p < .001$.

tory. That is, the left-hand column of Table 3 represents the phenomenology of male subjects taking the test and the right-hand column represents the phenomenology of female subjects taking the test. As can be seen in Table 3, not only are "sex-appropriate" characteristics more desirable for both males and females than "sex-inappropriate" characteristics, but the phenomenologies of male and female subjects are almost perfectly symmetric: that is, men and women are nearly equal in their perceptions of the desirability of sex-appropriate characteristics, sex-inappropriate characteristics, and the difference between them ($t < 1$ in all three comparisons).

SCORING

The BSRI asks a person to indicate on a 7-point scale how well each of the 60 masculine, feminine, and neutral personality characteristics describes himself. The scale ranges from 1 ("Never or almost never true") to 7 ("Always or almost always true") and is labeled at each point. On the basis of his responses, each person receives three major scores: a Masculinity score, a Femininity score and, most important, an Androgyny score. In addition, a Social Desirability score can also be computed.

The Masculinity and Femininity scores indicate the extent to which a person endorses masculine and feminine personality characteristics as self-descriptive. Masculinity equals the mean self-rating for all endorsed masculine items, and Femininity equals the mean self-rating for all endorsed feminine items. Both can range from 1 to 7. It will be recalled that these two scores are logically independent. That is, the structure of the test does not constrain them in any way, and they are free to vary independently.

The Androgyny score reflects the relative amounts of masculinity and femininity that the person includes in his or her self-description, and, as such, it best characterizes the nature of the person's total sex role. Specifically, the Androgyny score is defined as Student's t ratio for the difference between a person's masculine and feminine self-endorsement; that is, the Androgyny score is the difference between an individual's masculinity and femininity normalized with respect to the standard deviations of his or her masculinity and femininity scores. The use of a t ratio as the index of androgyny—rather than a simple difference score—has two conceptual advantages: first, it allows us to ask whether a person's endorsement of masculine attributes differs significantly from his or her endorsement of feminine attributes and, if it does ($|t| \geq 2.025$, $df = 38$, $p < .05$), to classify that person as significantly sex typed; and second, it allows us to compare different populations in terms of the percentage of significantly sex-typed individuals present within each.[4]

It should be noted that the greater the absolute value of the Androgyny score, the more the person is sex typed or sex reversed, with high positive scores indicating femininity and high negative scores indicating masculinity. A "masculine" sex role thus represents not only the endorsement of masculine attributes but the simultaneous rejection of feminine attributes. Similarly, a "feminine" sex role represents not only the endorsement of feminine attributes but the simultaneous rejection of masculine attributes. In contrast, the closer the Androgyny score is to zero, the more the person is androgynous. An "androg-

[4] A Statistical Package for the Social Sciences (SPSS) computer program for calculating individual t ratios is available on request from the author. In the absence of computer facilities, one can utilize the simple Androgyny difference score, Femininity − Masculinity, as the index of androgyny. Empirically, the two indices are virtually identical ($r = .98$), and one can approximate the t-ratio value by multiplying the Androgyny difference score by 2.322. This conversion factor was derived empirically from our combined normative sample of 917 students at two different colleges.

ynous" sex role thus represents the equal endorsement of both masculine and feminine attributes.

The Social Desirability score indicates the extent to which a person describes himself in a socially desirable direction on items that are neutral with respect to sex. It is scored by reversing the self-endorsement ratings for the 10 undesirable items and then calculating the subject's mean endorsement score across all 20 neutral personality characteristics. The Social Desirability score can thus range from 1 to 7, with 1 indicating a strong tendency to describe oneself in a socially undesirable direction and 7 indicating a strong tendency to describe oneself in a socially desirable direction.

PSYCHOMETRIC ANALYSES

Subjects

During the winter and spring of 1973, the BSRI was administered to 444 male and 279 female students in introductory psychology at Stanford University. It was also administered to an additional 117 male and 77 female paid volunteers at Foothill Junior College. The data that these students provided represent the normative data for the BSRI, and, unless explicitly noted, they serve as the basis for all of the analyses that follow.

Internal Consistency

In order to estimate the internal consistency of the BSRI, coefficient alpha was computed separately for the Masculinity, Femininity, and Social Desirability scores of the subjects in each of the two normative samples (Nunnally, 1967). The results showed all three scores to be highly reliable, both in the Stanford sample (Masculinity $\alpha = .86$; Femininity $\alpha = .80$; Social Desirability $\alpha = .75$) and in the Foothill sample (Masculinity $\alpha = .86$; Femininity $\alpha = .82$; Social Desirability $\alpha = .70$). Because the reliability of the Androgyny t ratio could not be calculated directly, coefficient alpha was computed for the highly correlated Androgyny difference score, Femininity − Masculinity, using the formula provided by Nunnally (1967) for linear combinations. The reliability of the Androgyny difference score was .85

for the Stanford sample and .86 for the Foothill sample.

Relationship between Masculinity and Femininity

As indicated earlier, the Masculinity and Femininity scores of the BSRI are logically independent. That is, the structure of the test does not constrain them in any way, and they are free to vary independently. The results from the two normative samples reveal them to be empirically independent as well (Stanford male $r = .11$, female $r = -.14$; Foothill male $r = -.02$, female $r = -.07$). This finding vindicates the decision to design an inventory that would not artifactually force a negative correlation between masculinity and femininity.

Social Desirability Response Set

It will be recalled that a person is sex typed on the BSRI to the extent that his or her Androgyny score reflects the greater endorsement of "sex-appropriate" characteristics than of "sex-inappropriate" characteristics. However, because of the fact that the masculine and feminine items are all relatively desirable, even for the "inappropriate" sex, it is important to verify that the Androgyny score is not simply tapping a social desirability response set.

Accordingly, product-moment correlations were computed between the Social Desirability score and the Masculinity, Femininity, and Androgyny scores for the Stanford and Foothill samples separately. They were also computed between the Social Desirability score and the absolute value of the Androgyny score. These correlations are displayed in Table 4. As expected, both Masculinity and Femininity were correlated with Social Desirability. In contrast, the near-zero correlations between Androgyny and Social Desirability confirm that the Androgyny score is not measuring a general tendency to respond in a socially desirable direction. Rather, it is measuring a very specific tendency to describe oneself in accordance with sex-typed standards of desirable behavior for men and women.

TABLE 4

CORRELATION OF MASCULINITY, FEMININITY, AND ANDROGYNY WITH SOCIAL DESIRABILITY

Sample	Masculinity with social desirability		Femininity with social desirability		Androgyny with social desirability		|Androgyny| with social desirability	
	Males	Females	Males	Females	Males	Females	Males	Females
Stanford	.42	.19	.28	.26	.12	.03	.08	−.10
Foothill	.23	.19	.15	.15	−.07	.06	−.12	−.09
Stanford and Foothill combined	.38	.19	.28	.22	.08	.04	.03	−.10

Test–Retest Reliability

The BSRI was administered for a second time to 28 males and 28 females from the Stanford normative sample. The second administration took place approximately four weeks after the first. During this second administration, subjects were told that we were interested in how their responses on the test might vary over time, and they were explicitly instructed not to try to remember how they had responded previously. Product-moment correlations were computed between the first and second administrations for the Masculinity, Femininity, Androgyny, and Social Desirability scores. All four scores proved to be highly reliable over the four-week interval (Masculinity $r = .90$; Femininity $r = .90$; Androgyny $r = .93$; Social Desirability $r = .89$).

TABLE 5

CORRELATION OF THE MASCULINITY–FEMININITY SCALES OF THE CALIFORNIA PSYCHOLOGICAL INVENTORY (CPI) AND GUILFORD-ZIMMERMAN SCALE WITH THE MASCULINITY, FEMININITY, AND ANDROGYNY SCALES OF THE BSRI

Scale	CPI		Guilford-Zimmerman	
	Males	Females	Males	Females
BSRI Masculinity	−.42	−.25	.11	.15
BSRI Femininity	.27	.25	.04	−.06
BSRI Androgyny	.50	.30	−.04	−.06

Note. The CPI scale is keyed in the feminine direction, whereas the Guilford-Zimmerman scale is keyed in the masculine direction.

Correlations with Other Measures of Masculinity-Femininity

During the second administration of the BSRI, subjects were also asked to fill out the Masculinity–Femininity scales of the California Psychological Inventory and the Guilford-Zimmerman Temperament Survey, both of which have been utilized rather frequently in previous research on sex roles. Table 5 presents the correlations between these two scales and the Masculinity, Femininity, and Androgyny scales of the BSRI. As can be seen in the table, the Guilford-Zimmerman scale is not at all correlated with any of the three scales of the BSRI, whereas the California Psychological Inventory is moderately correlated with all three. It is not clear why the BSRI should be more highly correlated with the CPI than with the Guilford-Zimmerman scale, but the fact that none of the correlations is particularly high indicates that the BSRI is measuring an aspect of sex roles which is not directly tapped by either of these two scales.

NORMS

Table 6 presents the mean Masculinity, Femininity, and Social Desirability scores separately by sex for both the Stanford and the Foothill normative samples. It also presents means for both the Androgyny t ratio and the Androgyny difference score. As can be seen in the table, males scored significantly higher than females on the Masculinity scale, and females scored significantly higher than males on the Femininity scale in both samples. On the two measures of androgyny, males scored on the masculine side of zero

TABLE 6

Sex Differences on the BSRI

Scale score	Stanford University			Foothill Junior College		
	Males (*n* = 444)	Females (*n* = 279)	*t*	Males (*n* = 117)	Females (*n* = 77)	*t*
Masculinity						
M	4.97	4.57		4.96	4.55	
SD	.67	.69	7.62*	.71	.75	3.86*
Femininity						
M	4.44	5.01		4.62	5.08	
SD	.55	.52	13.88*	.64	.58	5.02*
Social Desirability						
M	4.91	5.08		4.88	4.89	
SD	.50	.50	4.40*	.50	.53	*ns*
Androgyny *t* ratio						
M	−1.28	1.10		−.80	1.23	
SD	1.99	2.29	14.33*	2.23	2.42	5.98*
Androgyny Difference score						
M	−0.53	.43		−.34	.53	
SD	.82	.93	14.28*	.97	.97	6.08*

* $p < .001$.

and females scored on the feminine side of zero. This difference is significant in both samples and for both measures. On the Social Desirability scale, females scored significantly higher than males at Stanford but not at Foothill. It should be noted that the size of this sex difference is quite small, however, even in the Stanford sample.

Table 7 presents the percentage of subjects within each of the two normative samples who qualified as masculine, feminine, or androgynous as a function of the Androgyny *t* ratio. Subjects are classified as sex typed, whether masculine or feminine, if the Androgyny *t* ratio reaches statistical significance

($|t| \geq 2.025$, $df = 38$, $p < .05$), and they are classified as androgynous if the absolute value of the *t* ratio is less than or equal to one. Table 7 also indicates the percentage of subjects who fall between these various cutoff points. It should be noted that these cutoff points are somewhat arbitrary and that other investigators should feel free to adjust them in accordance with the characteristics of their particular subject populations.

CONCLUDING COMMENT

It is hoped that the development of the BSRI will encourage investigators in the areas of sex differences and sex roles to ques-

TABLE 7

Percentage of Subjects in the Normative Samples Classified as Masculine, Feminine, or Androgynous

Item	Stanford University		Foothill Junior College	
	Males (*n* = 444)	Females (*n* = 279)	Males (*n* = 117)	Females (*n* = 77)
% feminine ($t \geq 2.025$)	6	34	9	40
% near feminine ($1 < t < 2.025$)	5	20	9	8
% androgynous ($-1 \leq t \leq +1$)	34	27	44	38
% near-masculine ($-2.025 < t < -1$)	19	12	17	7
% masculine ($t \leq -2.025$)	36	8	22	8

tion the traditional assumption that it is the sex-typed individual who typifies mental health and to begin focusing on the behavioral and societal consequences of more flexible sex-role self-concepts. In a society where rigid sex-role differentiation has already outlived its utility, perhaps the androgynous person will come to define a more human standard of psychological health.

REFERENCES

BARRY, H., BACON, M. K., & CHILD, I. L. A cross-cultural survey of some sex differences in socialization. *Journal of Abnormal and Social Psychology,* 1957, **55,** 327–332.

BEM, S. L. Sex-role adaptability: One consequence of psychological androgyny. *Journal of Personality and Social Psychology,* 1974, in press.

EDWARDS, A. L. The measurement of human motives by means of personality scales. In D. Levine (Ed.), *Nebraska symposium on motivation: 1964.* Lincoln: University of Nebraska Press, 1964.

ERIKSON, E. H. Inner and outer space: Reflections on womanhood. In R. J. Lifton (Ed.), *The woman in America.* Boston: Houghton Mifflin, 1964.

GOUGH, H. G. *Manual for the California Psychological Inventory.* Palo Alto, Calif.: Consulting Psychologists Press, 1957.

KAGAN, J. Acquisition and significance of sex-typing and sex-role identity. In M. L. Hoffman & L. W. Hoffman (Eds.), *Review of child development research.* Vol. 1. New York: Russell Sage Foundation, 1964.

KOHLBERG, L. A cognitive-developmental analysis of children's sex-role concepts and attitudes. In E. E. Maccoby (Ed.), *The development of sex differences.* Stanford, Calif.: Stanford University Press, 1966.

NUNNALLY, J. C. *Psychometric theory.* New York: McGraw-Hill, 1967.

PARSONS, T., & BALES, R. F. *Family, socialization, and interaction process.* New York: Free Press of Glencoe, 1955.

(Received August 13, 1973)

3

JUANITA H. WILLIAMS

Sexual Role Identification and Personality Functioning in Girls: A Theory Revisited

Clinicians have traditionally ascribed different characteristics to masculine and feminine personalities in our culture (Broverman, I. K., Broverman, D. M., Clarkson, Rosenkrantz, & Vogel, 1970; Erikson, 1971; Freud, 1959). Furthermore, those characteristics describing the healthy male personality represent socially valued behaviors, while those describing the female do not. Contemporary clinicians believe that a healthy woman is, among other things, submissive, dependent, noncompetitive, and unaggressive (Broverman et al., 1970).

Recently, Rychlak & Legerski (1967) presented a sociocultural theory of sexual role identification which argues that, in the developmental process, the learning of the appropriate sexual role behaviors is more important for healthy adjustment than is the sex of the parent model. Males in our society, according to the theory, are expected to take an ascendant-dominant behavioral role, while females are expected to be retiring and passive. They state, "This is the most viable pattern. . . . Individuals who depart from these sexual role expectancies . . . will be more prone to personal maladjustments than will those who fulfill them" (p. 33). This theory predicts, then, that females who identify with a retiring-passive parent will show better personal adjustment than will those who identify with an ascendant-dominant parent, and that the opposite effect will hold for males.

The paper presents two studies which offer tentative support for his theory, especially for males. The data, however, do not support the theory when it is applied to delinquent girls, and offer very meager support indeed to such a generalization for normally functioning girls.

The present study tested the hypothesis that the four patterns of identification described by Rychlak & Legerski, ascendant-dominant father (A-D F), ascendant-dominant mother (A-D M), retiring-passive father (R-P F), and retiring-passive mother (R-P M), are differentially predictive of level of personality functioning in normal girls. Specifically, girls identifying with a retiring-passive mother should emerge as healthiest and best-adjusted, while girls identifying with an ascendant-dominant father should appear as least well-adjusted.

METHOD

Subjects

The entire senior class of 59 Caucasian girls attending a Roman Catholic high school were the subjects. The girls were predominantly from middle- and upper-middle-class families. The curriculum is college preparatory, and 90 percent of the students matriculate at a college or university. Ages ranged between 16 and 19.

A letter was sent to parents requesting permission for their daughters to participate in a study of personality functioning in normal girls. In no case was permission refused, and all members of the class elected to participate.

Sexual Role Identification Patterns

The identification measure consisted of 24 statements, printed on 3×5 inch index cards, which were categorized as follows:

Masculine ascendant-dominant: Is able to give orders, is firm but just, is practical, can get tough when necessary, has confidence in him- (her-) self, says exactly what he (she) thinks;

Masculine retiring-passive: Has very little courage, gets along with others, punishes him- (her-) self, is big-hearted and not selfish, is really bitter, is friendly;

Feminine ascendant-dominant: Enjoys taking care of other people, is always giving advice, always protects other people, likes everyone to admire her (him), is satisfied with her- (him-) self, is jealous;

Feminine retiring-passive: Is tender, lets others make the decisions, depends on other people, wants to be led, likes to be taken care of, is easily embarrassed.

Each subject was asked to sort these statements into envelopes marked "like self" and "unlike self," and, one week later, into envelopes marked "like father" and "like mother." If a subject had more A-D cards than R-P cards in the like-self envelope, she was scored as A-D. Following the second administration, she could be classified as, e.g., A-D M or A-D F identifier, depending upon the number of matches she made between her like-self sort and her like-mother or like-father sort. Similar categorizations were made for the R-P M and R-P F identifiers. If ties made it impossible to classify a subject she was called an Indefinite identifier. The rationale for and development of this scale and reliability studies are described in Rychlak (1967).

The Draw-a-Person (D-A-P) with inquiry was included for further data on identification, as it has been observed that 75–85 percent of subjects draw a figure of their own sex (Machover, 1951).

Level of Personality Functioning

During the second session, in addition to completing the identification procedure, subjects took the California Psychological Inventory (CPI). The CPI has demonstrated validity in determining antisocial tendencies (Adelson, 1969). It also yields data on interpersonal adequacy, socialization, achievement potential, intellectual efficiency, and other variables relevant to the study (Gough, 1969). Such characteristics are likely to be related to the favorable and positive aspects of personality, and are meaningfully applicable to normal subjects.

RESULTS

The breakdown of the sample into the sexual role identification categories (Table 1) reveals that almost half the girls in this normal sample were A-D F identifiers, while two-thirds ascribed to themselves mostly ascendant-dominant behavioral traits. Only 14 percent identified with a retiring-passive mother, and identifiers in both the retiring-passive categories accounted for only 24 percent of the total sample. This distribution is remarkably different from that obtained in the earlier study (Rychlak, 1967) for a sample of 26 nondelinquent girls. The most frequent category for that group was R-P M (31 percent), while A-D F and R-P F tied at 11 percent.

Fewer than half the subjects drew females for the D-A-P (Table 2); sexual role category membership made no difference in the sex of the figure drawn. There was a sidelight to these data which may be of interest to clinicians. In examining the drawings, it was necessary for the author to refer to the inquiry to determine the sex of 38 (64 percent) of the drawings. Most of the figures were wearing pants and had long hair, and sex differentiation was not possible without further information.

Table 1. Sample breakdown into sexual role identification groups.

Identification	N	%
A-D Father	28	47
A-D Mother	10	17
R-P Father	6	10
R-P Mother	8	14
Indefinite	7	12
Total	59	100

Table 2. Identification groups and sex of figure drawing.[a]

	Sex of drawing			
	Female		Male	
Identification	N	%	N	%
A-D Father	16	27	12	21
A-D Mother	5	8	5	8
R-P Father	3	5	3	5
R-P Mother	4	7	4	7
Indefinite	1	2	6	10
Total	29	49	30	51

[a]Chi square was not significant.

Table 3. Kruskall-Wallis analysis of variance for identification groups.

Scale	df	MSS	H[a]
Dominance	4	55560	9.50*
Capacity for status	4	55100	
Sociability	4	57499	14.92**
Social presence	4	56394	11.18**
Self-acceptance	4	55695	9.72*
Well-being	4	55641	9.63*
Responsibility	4	55427	
Socialization	4	54336	
Self-control	4	54466	
Tolerance	4	55696	9.72*
Good impression	4	56702	12.22**
Communality	4	53846	
Achievement/conformance	4	55900	9.90*
Achievement/independence	4	55631	
Intellectual efficiency	4	55911	9.90*
Psychological-mindedness	4	53607	
Flexibility	4	53338	
Femininity	4	54085	

[a]Corrected for ties.
*$p < .05$.
**$p < .01$.

To assess the levels of personal adjustment, analyses of variance were tried across the identification categories for each of the 18 variables of the CPI (Table 3). Differences among categories were significant for nine of these. On the CPI, high scores are associated with positive descriptions of behavior.

Examination of the mean profiles based on the scores of the four parental identification categories for the nine significant variables revealed that the A-D F identifiers scored higher than did the R-P Ms on all of them (Figure 1). In other words, A-D F identifiers had healthier profiles on the CPI than did their R-P M counterparts.

All scores of the A-D F group were within the range defined by the mean standard score (50) plus or minus 10. Only three of the R-P M scores were within this range, the others

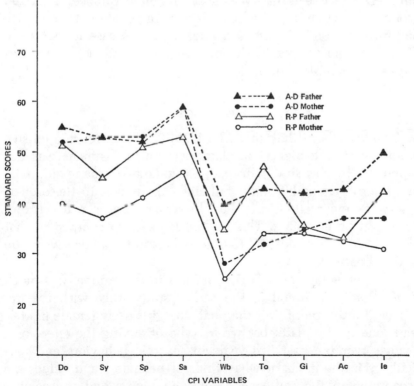

Figure 1. Mean profiles of identification groups on significant CPI variables. (See Table 2 for meaning of abbreviations.)

falling below 40. The remaining three groups, A-D M, R-P F, and Indefinite, had profiles which tended to be intermediate with respect to the high A-D F and the low R-P M groups.

Girls, then, who ascribed to themselves ascendant-dominant characteristics, and who perceived these also as descriptive of their fathers, were more confident, self-reliant, competitive, assertive, and self-accepting than were the girls who saw both themselves and their mothers as being retiring and passive. The A-D F girls were also more outgoing and adventurous, more direct in taking action, and more impatient with delay. They tended to be realistic, to be interested in achievement, and to use their skills effectively.

Looking again at the earlier study, in which adequacy of adjustment was measured by the HSPQ (Cattell, Beloff, & Coan, 1958), A-D F subjects were more guilt-prone and excitable; but A-D M subjects had the most favorable profiles of all the groups. Although it is difficult, often impossible, to compare performances on different instruments, in this case it seems obvious that the sample in the present study did not behave as the earlier sample did.

DISCUSSION

The hypothesis that girls who identify with a retiring-passive mother have the highest level of personal adjustment was not supported by this study. Instead, ascendant-dominant girls who saw themselves as like their fathers with respect to these characteristics emerged as the healthiest with respect to current personality functioning. This finding is in sharp contrast to that of Rychlak & Legerski, and therefore constitutes a negative claim to the theory under test.

The percentage of A-D F identifiers in this sample was much larger than that found in the earlier study; this, with the unexpected result that fewer than half the girls drew female figures, leads one to speculate that we may be observing the effect of a change over the past five years in sex role behaviors and particularly in the limits of what kinds of behaviors and values are acceptable in the self-concept of young girls and in society's capacity for tolerance of these changes.

Traditional conceptions of sex roles are not immutable and can vary as a function of individual experience (Vogel, 1970). Indeed, Rossi (1964) has proposed that traditional conceptions of masculinity and femininity are neither necessary nor appropriate, perpetuating, as they do, a differential status for the sexes. Behaviors such as assertiveness, constructive aggression, and striving for achievement have typically been highly valued in males. These same behaviors have also typically been negatively reinforced in girls and women. Even clinicians have employed a double standard to evaluate personality health in the two sexes (Broverman et al.). As society moves toward an androgynous conception of sex roles, these kinds of behaviors, as well as warmth, compassion, and empathic perception, heretofore considered feminine, will perhaps be equally valued as positive for both sexes. For the present, the notion that females need to identify with a retiring-passive parent in order to manifest viable patterns of personality functioning requires an attitude of scepticism.

SUMMARY

The study tested a recently published theory (Rychlak & Legerski, 1967) that females who identify with a retiring-passive mother will show better personal adjustment than will those who identify with an ascendant-dominant parent of either sex. Fifty-nine high school senior girls were classified into parental identification categories: ascendant-dominant father (A-D F), ascendant-dominant mother (A-D M), retiring-passive father (R-P F), and retiring-passive mother (R-P M). The California Personality Inventory (CPI) was used to measure level of personality functioning. Groups differed significantly on 9 of the 18 CPI variables, with A-D F identifiers scoring higher than R-P M identifiers on all of them. Other categories were intermediate. Identification with a retiring-passive mother for this group of girls was neither necessary nor desirable for optimum personality functioning.

REFERENCES

Adelson, J. Personality. *Annual Review of Psychology*, 1969, **20**, 217–245.
Broverman, I. K., Broverman, D. M., Clarkson, F. E., Rosenkrantz, P. S., & Vogel, S. R. Sex-role stereotypes and clinical judgments of mental health. *Journal of Consulting and Clinical Psychology*, 1970, **34**, 1–7.

Cattell, R. B., Beloff, H., & Coan, R. W., *Handbook for the IPAT high school personality questionnaire.* Champaign, Ill.: Institute for Personality and Ability Testing, 1958.

Erikson, E. H. Sex differences in the play configurations of preadolescents. In D. L. Schaeffer (Ed.), *Sex differences in personality.* Belmont, Cal.: Brooks/ Cole Publishing Co., 1971.

Freud, S. In E. Jones (Ed.), *The collected papers of . . .* New York: Basic Books, Inc., 1959.

Gough, H. G. *California psychological inventory manual.* Palo Alto: Consulting Psychologists Press, Inc., 1969.

Machover, K. Drawings of the human figure. In H. H. Anderson & G. L. Anderson (Eds.), *An introduction to projective techniques.* Englewood Cliffs, N.J.: Prentice-Hall, 1951.

Rossi, A. S. Equality between the sexes. In R. J. Lifton (Ed.), *The woman in America.* Boston, Mass.: Houghton Mifflin, 1964.

Rychlak, J. F., & Legerski, A. T. A sociocultural theory of appropriate sexual role identification and level of personal adjustment. *Journal of Personality,* 1967, **35**, 31–49.

Siegel, S. *Nonparametric statistics for the behavioral sciences.* New York: McGraw Hill, 1956.

Vogel, S. R., Broverman, I. K., Broverman, D. M., Clarkson, F. E., & Rosenkrantz, P. S. Maternal employment and perception of sex roles among college students. *Developmental Psychology,* 1970, **3**, 384–391.

Manuscript received August 30, 1971.

4

MARY BROWN PARLEE

The Premenstrual Syndrome[1]

Psychological studies of the premenstrual syndrome are discussed in four methodological categories: (a) studies reporting a positive correlation between specific behavioral acts and phase of the menstrual cycle; (b) those using retrospective questionnaires concerning symptom and mood changes; (c) studies involving day-to-day (self-) ratings of various behaviors, symptoms, and moods; and (d) thematic analyses of verbal material gathered in an unstructured situation throughout the cycle. The scientific status of the hypothesis of a premenstrual syndrome is considered, together with more general topics—in particular the question of control groups, the choice of a base line for describing changes in behavior, and the difficulties involved in physiological explanations of psychological phenomena. Brief consideration is given to publication practices of psychological journals as they affect the kind of scientific information available on behavioral changes associated with the menstrual cycle.

Considerable biological evidence is now available to support Seward's (1934) observation that "Rhythm is a universal characteristic of natural phenomena [p. 153]." In human beings, circadian rhythms have been reported to exist in a variety of processes including cell division, adrenal cortical activity, and glucose tolerance, as well as in sleeping and waking, pain tolerance, and susceptibility to asthmatic attacks (Luce, 1970). Cyclic changes with periods of greater than 24 hours are also well established (Richter, 1968). One rhythm that has been studied in detail is the menstrual cycle of the human female.

Southam and Gonzaga (1965) extensively reviewed studies of physiological changes occurring throughout the menstrual cycle. While a full specification of the neuroendocrine mechanisms controlling menstruation depends upon the development of appropriate techniques (e.g., Neill, Johansson, Datta, & Knobil, 1967), these mechanisms are understood in rough outline and will no doubt eventually provide explanations for the various bodily changes observed. Of more interest to the psychologist, however, are the numerous reports of behavioral changes associated with the menstrual cycle. Such studies would seem to be important for at least two reasons, the first being that psychological changes accompanying the menstrual cycle are phenomenologically significant to many women and are thus an appropriate topic for psychological research. The second reason, however, lies not in their contribution to the body of scientific knowledge, but in the fact that they raise methodological and theoretical issues which have implications for the study of other psychological phenomena as well. The purpose of the present article is to consider the literature on those psychological changes associated with the menstrual cycle which have been called the premenstrual syndrome(s) (Dalton, 1964; Moos, 1968) or premenstrual tension (Frank, 1931; Rees, 1953a). Another major topic in the study of behavioral changes accompanying the menstrual cycle—fluctuations in sexual behavior—will not be included here; this literature has been reviewed by Kane, Lipton, and Ewing (1969).

THE PREMENSTRUAL SYNDROME: FOUR TYPES OF STUDIES

Correlational Data

The syndrome first described by Frank (1931) as a premenstrual feeling of "indescribable tension," irritability, and "a desire to find relief by foolish and ill-considered actions [p. 1054]" has been studied in a variety of ways, one of which is simply to look for cor-

[1] This work was supported in part by Training Grant 5-T02-MH8533-08 from the National Institute of Mental Health to the Psychology Department, Wellesley College; the assistance of Ellen Zimmerman is thankfully acknowledged. The author is grateful to Laurel Furumoto of Wellesley College for many stimulating discussions.

[2] Requests for reprints should be sent to Mary Brown Parlee, Radcliffe Institute, 3 James Street, Cambridge, Massachusetts 02138.

relations between the phase of the menstrual cycle and statistical data on the occurrence of specific, well-defined behaviors. Correlations have been reported, for example, between the premenstrual or menstrual phase of the cycle and commission of violent crimes (Cooke, 1945; Dalton, 1961; Morton, Additon, Addison, Hunt, & Sullivan, 1953; Ribeiro, 1962), death from accident or suicide (MacKinnon & MacKinnon, 1956; Mandell & Mandell, 1967), accidents (Dalton, 1960b), admission to a hospital with acute psychiatric illness (Dalton, 1959; Janowsky, Gorney, Castelnuovo-Tedesco, & Stone, 1969), taking a child to a medical clinic (Dalton, 1966), and loss of control of aircraft (Whitehead, 1934). Such data were summarized by Dalton (1964) who has been a major contributor in this area of research.

In statistical studies, the behavioral act—when considered as one term of the correlation—is readily identifiable; it either occurs (and often becomes part of a public record) or it does not. It is usually the case that the other term of the correlation—the phase of the menstrual cycle—is also objectively determined by the investigators either by questioning the women shortly after the behavioral event (Dalton) or by basal body temperature (Altman, Knowles, & Bull, 1941; Ivey & Bardwick, 1968), vaginal smears (Benedek & Rubenstein, 1939a, 1939b), or data from autopsies (MacKinnon & MacKinnon, 1956; Ribeiro, 1962). Some frequently cited correlational studies, however, are methodologically less than sound. Morton et al. (1953), for example, reported that 62% of violent crimes committed by women took place during the premenstrual week, 19% during midcycle, and 17% during menstruation, but they did not define the length in days of these latter two phases. Nor did they say precisely how they determined the phase of the cycle at the time of the crime. "Review of the inmates' records . . . [Morton et al., 1953, p. 1191]" suggested that onset of menstruation may be part of a prisoner's record, but in a table presenting the data themselves (p. 1189), 8 of the 58 women are listed in a "cannot remember" category which does not support the notion that a record was kept for all prisoners.

In spite of possible weaknesses in method, however, the Morton et al. (1953) study does not have as many flaws as some others of this correlational type. Cooke (1945), for example, whose study is cited by Morton et al., Greene and Dalton (1953), MacKinnon and MacKinnon (1956), and Coppen and Kessel (1963) in support of a relationship between menstrual cycle phase and commission of violent crime, included exactly one sentence on the topic. It reads:

That this ["the hypersensitization of the nervous system which occurs during the premenstrual phase of the cycle"] is a very potent factor in the psychology of women is evidenced by the report of a Parisian prefect of police: that 84 per cent of all the crimes of violence committed by women are perpetrated during the premenstrual and early menstrual phases of the cycle [Cooke, 1945, p. 459].

Although several relatively recent papers refer to an association between the menstrual cycle and crashes by women airplane pilots (Dalton, 1960b; Moos, 1968, 1969b; Pierson & Lockhart, 1963), the only reference offered is to Whitehead (1934) or to Dalton (1964) who cited only Whitehead. Whitehead's article consisted of reports of three airplane crashes over a period of eight months in which the women pilots were said to be menstruating at the time of the crash.

While methodologically sound in terms of specifying both the behavioral event and the phase of the menstrual cycle, even Dalton's much-cited work does not always establish the correlations between menstrual cycle and behavior as clearly as might be desirable. As Sherman (1971) and Sommer (1972) pointed out, Dalton (1960a) reported a decrease in 27% of her schoolgirl subjects' test performance during the premenstrual phase of the cycle but did not provide a statistical test of the significance of this decrease, and references to her work fail to note that a premenstrual increase in 17% of the schoolgirls' performance was also found, while 56% of the girls showed no change.

Reynolds (1966) has documented the persistence of at least one "myth" in psychology (that there are sex differences in color discrimination) and suggests that such myths tend to be perpetuated when authors cite studies from other reviews or repeat the original author's conclusions without checking the data as they appeared in the original report. Given the variable quality of the basic data in correlational studies of the menstrual cycle, it would seem necessary for contemporary authors to be familiar with the methodological adequacy of the original studies before citing them as factual evidence—a caution which does not, of course, apply alone to studies of the premenstrual syndrome.

Putting aside questions of method, however, and assuming that many of the correlations between phase of the cycle and behavior are true as reported, how should the studies be interpreted and to whom can the results be generalized? Most of the investigators in this area do not explicitly point to a causal relationship between hormonal changes and the occurrence of various behaviors, but they do use phrases which tend strongly to imply that the hormones are the cause of the behaviors. Rarely is it suggested that it is the behavioral events that affect the menstrual cycle, a-though gynecology texts state that psychological stress may delay menstruation (Lloyd, 1962, p. 473) or precipitate its onset (Benson, 1964, p. 573); Balint (1937) offered an elaborate psychodynamic interpretation of how this might occur.[3] It is also important to note in interpreting correlational studies that data from particular groups cannot provide a basis for a generalization about all women or about any woman selected at random unless it is assumed that women are equally likely to be or become a member of the groups in which the data were collected. From knowing, for example, that crimes are likely to *have been committed* during certain phases of the cycle, it is not possible to assume the truth of the inverse—that women in these phases of the

cycle are more likely to commit crimes; this latter is true only for women who will at some time commit crimes. It is possible that studies of different populations of women might reveal correlations between the premenstrual and menstrual phases of the cycle and more positively valued acts such as, for example, bursts of creative energy. Without further correlational studies of more diverse populations, and in the absence of additional information as to which subgroup a woman belongs (e.g., potential criminal, potential artist), it is difficult to predict anything about an individual's behavior from the fact that she is in the premenstrual or menstrual phase of the cycle.

Retrospective Questionnaires

A second type of data which is available to support the hypothesis of a premenstrual syndrome is based upon questionnaires asking women to report (their memory of) their experience of various "symptoms" and moods at different phases of the cycle. The symptoms and moods listed on the questionnaires are usually negative ones, and the subjects are questioned primarily about their experiences just before and during menstruation. Moos (1968, 1969b) has described the development of a comprehensive questionnaire of this sort; Coppen and Kessel (1963) and Sutherland and Stewart (1965) provided earlier examples. None of these questionnaires can be considered well-developed psychometric instruments, since no reliability data or external validity data (with the exception of Coppen & Kessel) are offered to support their usefulness. The Moos Menstrual Distress Questionnaire, which is relatively recent and frequently used (Moos, Kopell, Melges, Yalom, Lunde, Clayton, & Hamburg, 1969; Silbergeld, Brast, & Nobel, 1971), suffers from additional methodological inadequacies. In his articles describing the development of the questionnaire, Moos failed to report the fact that of the 839 subjects in the normative sample, 420 were taking oral contraceptives, 81 were pregnant, and 40 did not answer the questions about their use of oral contraceptives. These data are presented elsewhere (Moos, 1969a) along with the fact that significant differences in responses on the questionnaire were found between those women who were taking the pill and those who were

---

[3] The suggestion that behavior can indeed influence levels of reproductive hormones is supported by the recent finding that testosterone levels in primates are affected by manipulations of the social setting (Rose, Gordon, & Bernstein, 1972). McClintock's (1971) study demonstrated in another context the effects of social factors on the timing of menstruation in human beings: Menstrual cycles of females living together in a college dormitory were found to become more closely synchronized over the course of an academic year. While it is clear that many of the correlational data mentioned above cannot be interpreted in this way, a consideration of possible psychological effects on the menstrual cycle as well as the reverse would be useful in assessing the extent and limitations of the statistical evidence cited in support of a hormone-"related" (with connotations of "caused") premenstrual syndrome of "neurotic and antisocial reactions [Janowsky et al., 1969, p. 189]."

not. In light of the suggestion that clinical studies and retrospective questionnaires have been the primary source of evidence that there are behavioral changes associated with the menstrual cycle (Moos et al., 1969, p. 37), the methodological soundness of individual questionnaires must be carefully considered in evaluating the relevance of such data to the hypothesis of a premenstrual syndrome.

Daily Self-Reports or Observations

Another approach to the study of the premenstrual syndrome also involves women's self-ratings of various symptoms and moods, but is different from the simple questionnaire in that the ratings are made regularly throughout the cycle and do not depend upon a retrospective account. McCance, Luff, and Widdowson (1937) collected self-reports from 167 women (over 4–6 menstrual cycles) of their experience of 10 carefully defined symptoms and moods. The data, consisting of records kept over 780 cycles, showed discrepancies between the daily-record technique and the results of a preliminary questionnaire on menstrual cycle symptoms given before the study was made, discrepancies "so frequent that they throw considerable doubt upon the value of any work on this subject based upon history or a questionnaire [pp. 579–580]." McCance et al. reported that the majority of individual records showed no evidence of rhythm during the period of the study. When records were combined, however, cyclic changes were observed, related to the menstrual cycle, in fatigue, abdominal and—to a lesser extent—back pain, headache, breast changes, sexual feelings and intercourse, tendency to cry, irritability, and effort required for intellectual work. Rees (1953a) also collected day-to-day records of reports of symptoms from 30 women (over a period of "some months") and found overall patterns of premenstrual increases in tension, irritability, depression, emotional lability, anxiety, swelling of extremities and breasts, fatigue, and headaches. In a similar study with more subjects, Rees (1953b) noted that 56% of the women did not report any significant "premenstrual tension symptoms"; the method section is not sufficiently detailed, however, to determine precisely what data were collected to support this conclusion. The

Nowlis (1965) Mood Adjective Check List has been used to study daily changes in self-ratings over the course of the menstrual cycle, with inconsistent results (Moos et al., 1969; Silbergeld et al., 1971).

Altman et al. (1941) followed 10 subjects over a total of 55 menstrual cycles, recording variations in physiological events associated with ovulation (basal body temperature, "bioelectric ovulatory potentials," skin temperature) and psychological changes (sleep, physical and mental activity, mood, worry, tension, irritability, and fatigue). The psychological changes were assessed by the experimenter during daily interviews which apparently were conducted after the physiological measures had been taken (see pp. 200–201). Their psychological data showed the presence at ovulation of elation and activity, and the presence during the premenstrual phase of depression, tension, and activity. Individual women showed considerable variability in patterns of behavior. Abramson and Torghele (1961) reported changes in daily recordings of weight, temperature, and "psychosomatic symptomatology" (ratings of abdominal pain, irritability, bloating, depression, etc.). As was the case in Rees' reports, information which might have been gained in a longitudinal study is lost since the authors did not report the ratings for individual symptoms at different points throughout the cycle; instead, they presented bar graphs of the total number of times individual signs and symptoms were reported. The most frequently indicated symptom was headache, which was mentioned 90 times (the study involved 34 subjects who reported in all approximately 3,000 times on the presence or absence of headache). In the absence of a fuller presentation of the data and of control groups of nonmenstruating individuals, it is unclear whether such "psychosomatic symptomatology" can be taken as evidence of a premenstrual syndrome. Dalton's (1964) use of control groups, unusual in studies of this kind, raises an interesting question about the interpretation of any fluctuations in day-to-day records of activities; she reported that punishment records in prisons and schools failed to show 28-day cycles for males but did show them for female prisoners and schoolgirls, both those who were menstruating *and those who had not yet begun to menstruate* (pp. 81–82).

Thematic Analysis of Unstructured Verbal Material

A final approach to the study of the premenstrual syndrome is one which also records data on a day-to-day basis, but this technique, first put in quantitative form by Gottschalk, Kaplan, Gleser, and Winget (1962), differs from those above in that the subjects are not rated or asked to rate themselves on specific symptoms, but rather are requested to talk into a tape recorder for five minutes "about any life experience they cared to [p. 301].' Gottschalk and his co-workers developed a standardized method of scoring which allowed them to analyze the verbal material gathered in this way in terms of the levels of "hostility directed inwards," "hostility directed outwards," and "anxiety" manifested by the subject. Studying five women over a period of 30–60 days, they found that "four of the 5 women showed statistically significant rhythmical changes in the magnitude of at least one of the affects . . . during the sexual cycle [test and significance level not specified]. The changes in these affects were not similar among the women [Gottschalk et al., 1962, pp. 307–308]." It should be noted that they did not say that these rhythmic changes are linked to the phase of the menstrual cycle.

Using the Gottschalk technique with a larger sample of subjects (26 women, data collected four times over the course of two cycles), Ivey and Bardwick (1968) confirmed the Gottschalk et al. (1962) report of transient "decreases in levels of anxiety and hostility [p. 307]," finding that the ovulatory anxiety level was significantly lower than that during the premenstrual phase. Paige (1971) also gathered unstructured verbal material from an even larger sample at four different times throughout the cycle, and used Gottschalk's scoring procedure to assess anxiety, hostility, and negative affect (the latter being the sum of the anxiety and hostility scales). In the 38 subjects not taking oral contraceptives, she found that all three scores varied significantly throughout the cycle. These cyclic variations were not present in the group of 52 subjects who were taking oral contraceptives containing both estrogens and progestin.

While not relying upon a standardized scoring technique such as Gottschalk, Benedek, and Rubenstein's (1939a, 1939b) classic study also involved day-by-day analysis of women's speech in a relatively unstructured setting. In their case, the data consisted of "verbal material" (not verbatim records) collected over the course of psychoanalysis of women diagnosed as neurotic. Studying nine patients over a total of 75 cycles, Benedek found that she could predict, solely on the basis of a patient's reports of dreams, the day on which ovulation occurred, a prediction which was corroborated independently by Rubenstein's analysis of vaginal smears. Benedek (1963) noted the difficulty she experienced in formalizing what it was in the records which allowed her to make such precise predictions; the fact that her data are described in terms which are inseparable from her theoretical orientation makes it difficult to specify operationally the procedures by which she was able to infer the phase of the menstrual cycle from the women's reports of their dreams.

SCIENTIFIC STATUS OF THE PREMENSTRUAL SYNDROME

The four kinds of studies discussed above—correlations between behavioral acts and phase of the menstrual cycle, retrospective questionnaires, daily self-ratings or observations, and thematic analyses of verbal material—represent the sorts of evidence that are cited in support of the hypothesis of the existence of a premenstrual syndrome. Given the variety of types of supporting data, it is not surprising that the terms "premenstrual syndrome" and ts associated "symptoms" seem to have been used somewhat broadly. Premenstrual syndrome, for example, has been taken to include the "recurrence of [any] symptoms always at the same time in each menstrual cycle [Dalton, 1954, p. 339]" or even "any combination of emotional or *physical* features which occur cyclically in a female before menstruation [Sutherland & Stewart, 1965, p. 1182; italics added]." Moos (1969b) found from a review of the literature that over 150 different symptoms have been associated with the menstrual cycle, including such various ones as elation, depression, back pain, sexual desire, and a great many other more or less specific behaviors and inferred psychological states. Sutherland and Stewart suggested .that "the only common denominator to all the symptoms described is that, when they occur, they do so at regular [28-day?] intervals [p. 1183]." Given the broad and not always consistent use of "premenstrual syndrome" and its constituent "symptoms," estimates of the prevalence of "menstrual symptoms" or of the premenstrual syndrome are useless for most purposes (Ferguson & Vermillion, 1957; see Moos, 1968, p. 854, for other references).

In spite of the lack of agreement on the precise nature of the premenstrual syndrome or even its relationship to the phases of the menstrual cycle, a wide variety of physiological factors have been proposed in the past to account for it. Among them are "female sex hormones" (Frank, 1931), estrogen-progesterone imbalance (Morten et al., 1953), altered suprarenal cortex activity (MacKinnon & MacKinnon, 1956), water retention caused by high estrogen-progesterone ratio (Greene & Dalton, 1953); see Southam and Gonzaga (1965) for others. This physiologic explanatory bias dictated some of the early attempts to "cure" the syndrome: Sterilization by X-ray was reported to have been successful for some of Frank's (1931) patients; Greene (1954) reported, however, that "not only does hysterectomy fail to cure the premenstrual syndrome, but it may actually initiate it, a fact which we have so far failed to explain [p. 338]." Less drastic measures such as diuretics (Eichner & Waltner, 1955) and hormone therapy (Rees, 1953a) were also reported.

Recently, several investigators have suggested that monoamine oxidase activity might be the means through which estrogens and progesterone affect neural firing and behavior (Grant & Pryse-Davies, 1968; Klaiber, Broverman, Vogel, Kobayashi, & Moriarty, 1972; Paige, 1971). As in the case of earlier proposals, evidence supporting a hypothetical mechanism involving monoamine oxidase is indirect, and a number of currently untested assumptions about physiological processes are required.[4] On the basis of available data, such

[4] The argument is that estrogens and progesterones affect levels of monoamine oxidase which in turn affect catecholamine-mediated neural activity in the brain;

an hypothesis seems premature since physiological knowledge is not yet sufficiently detailed to put serious limits on the kinds of physiological processes which might mediate this central nervous system activity is, according to the hypothesis, related to psychological states of depression and irritability. Supporting evidence is indirect: (a) endometrial monoamine oxidase fluctuates throughout the human menstrual cycle (Cohen, Belensky, & Chaym, 1965; Southgate, Grant, Pollard, Pryse-Davies, & Sandler, 1968), (b) drugs which inhibit monoamine oxidase activity—and possibly affect other physiologically significant substances as well—transiently relieve psychological depression (Crane, 1970), (c) oral contraceptives affect both endometrial monoamine oxidase levels and psychological depression (method for assessing "depression" not stated; Grant & Pryse-Davies, 1968). Several assumptions are obviously required if these data and others like them are to be interpreted as supporting the hypothesis that naturally occurring fluctuations in estrogen and progesterone levels during the menstrual cycle are responsible—by means of a mechanism involving monoamine oxidase—for clearly established cycles in depression and irritability. Some of these assumptions are (a) that the pharmacologic doses of estrogen and progesterone present in oral contraceptives have similar psychological effects on the physiologic levels of these hormones; (b) that peripheral, systemic measures of monoamine oxidase activity (blood plasma, endometrial monoamine oxidase) reflect central levels; (c) that monoamine oxidase regulates the functional levels of catecholamines in the brain; and (d) that central nervous system activity involving catecholamines as transmitter substances is directly related to psychological states of depression and irritability. Relevant to these assumptions, respectively, are the following considerations: (a) behavioral effects of drug substances are not always a monotonic function of dosage; (b) one of the basic functions of the blood-brain barrier is to maintain constant levels of some substances in the brain in the presence of fluctuating systemic levels; (c) even if there were direct evidence that monoamine oxidase influences absolute levels of brain catecholamines, it would still be necessary to establish that monoamine oxidase affects direct measures of neural transmission in the same way; and (d) no evidence is available showing the existence of a one-to-one relationship between brain activity of a specified kind and psychological states. As an example of the relationship between the sort of physiological knowledge now available and the psychophysiological assumptions required by the monoamine oxidase–catecholamine hypothesis, compare Assumptions b and c above with the Southgate et al. (1968) report in which they were able to show a correlation between two methods for assessing human endometrial monoamine oxidase activity. In this article they noted that "at present there is insufficient information to decide whether the observed changes are localized to the endometrium or are part of a more generalized cyclical variation in MAO [monoamine oxidase] activity [p. 724]" and that "in recent years it has become increasingly obvious that there are hormone–behavior relationships, and more importantly, psychological studies have not yet clarified the nature and extent of the behavioral changes which are to be explained by the proposed mechanism.

There is clearly a need for a more precise definition of the premenstrual syndrome and for a specification, in terms of the methods used to identify them, of the symptoms of which it is thought to be composed. This definition should be accompanied by a conceptual scheme for relating to each other the data collected by different methods. Is a premenstrual increase in irritability (e.g., found in daily self-ratings) causally related to a premenstrual increase in commission of violent crimes? Is the anxiety found through thematic analysis related to the increased likelihood of a mother's taking her child to a clinic? Questions such as these illustrate the need for an explicit statement of the hypothetical psychological mechanisms relating one kind of data to another. Before such theories can be elaborated and tested, however, it must be shown that data collected by different methods are in fact correlated, since one would expect that any psychological state that is included in a description of the premenstrual syndrome would be measurable by more than one method. There is some evidence that this is not always the case. The premenstrual syndrome as assessed by the Moos (1968, 1969b) Menstrual Distress Questionnaire, for example, includes symptom scales labeled Autonomic Reactions and Concentration (which includes as one item "lowered motor coordination"), but in his own work with Kopell, Lunde, Clayton, and Moos (1969), Moos reported failure to find fluctuations throughout the menstrual cycle in galvanic skin potential and in reaction time. Pierson and Lockhart (1963) and Zimmerman and Parlee (1973) also reported failure to find

changes in reaction time and in galvanic skin potential. McCance et al. (1937) found cyclic variations in subjects' self-ratings of "effort required for intellectual work," but Sommer (1972) could not demonstrate changes in intellectual performance when subjects were tested repeatedly over the course of the menstrual cycle. Using three different measures within a single study—the Moos Menstrual Distress Questionnaire (retrospective questionnaire), the Nowlis Mood Adjective Check List (daily self-report), and the Gottschalk technique of thematic analysis—Silbergeld et al. (1971) concluded that "the three methods of behavioral assessment produced scores which were, at best, only weakly correlated [p. 411]."

Coppen and Kessel (1963) have attempted to make the generalized use of premenstrual syndrome more precise by distinguishing between dysmenorrhea—pain specifically associated with and occurring during menstruation—and the premenstrual syndrome which they define in a more limited way as irritability, depression, nervousness or tension, and anxiety. While it is not clear that all of the symptoms which have previously been studied in conjunction with the menstrual cycle can be placed reliably into one of these two categories (e.g., how would "headache" be classified?), the distinction does have some empirical justification. On the basis of a retrospective questionnaire administered to 500 women, Coppen and Kessel reported that the premenstrual syndrome as they defined it is correlated with neuroticism (Maudsley Personality Inventory), while dysmenorrhea is negatively correlated with age and with parity, and is uncorrelated with neuroticism. Although the authors offered no speculation concerning the causes of either dysmenorrhea or the premenstrual syndrome, their discussion implied that dysmenorrhea has a more direct physiological basis (it occurs during menstruation and is not "a psychosomatic condition or one that calls for psychological treatment, [p. 720]") while "the subjects with premenstrual symptoms had abnormal personality traits [p. 718]." Lennane and Lennane (1973) have also noted that, contrary to a considerable body of medical opinion, evidence strongly suggests that dysmenorrhea is primarily of physiological rather than psychogenic origin.

---

not one but a series of MAOs, each differing in its action towards substrates and inhibitors [p. 725]."

While none of the assumptions required by the monoamine oxidase hypothesis is itself inherently implausible, considerable physiological and psychophysiological research would be needed to establish each of them, research which is not cited by supporters of the monoamine oxidase–catecholamine hypothesis. In view of the considerations bearing on the correctness of each assumption, furthermore, any hypothesis which depends upon the validity of all of them must be regarded as far from established.

Thompson (1950), Shainess (1961), Paige (1971), and others have suggested, on the other hand, that a woman's psychological response to the physiological changes associated with her menstrual cycle may also be shaped or modified by cultural practices which attach values to menstruation and to femininity. In this view, what Coppen and Kessel (1963) call the premenstrual syndrome would be the result of complex psychological processes arising from an interaction between physiological changes and environmental factors specifically related to femininity and sexuality. As such, it would be associated with other aspects of the personality to the extent that these also are related to sexuality, and considerable individual differences might be expected.

Whether a distinction between dysmenorrhea and a more limited and precise definition of the premenstrual syndrome will prove useful for psychological theory construction remains to be seen, but in its present form it represents one attempt to deal with at least some of the various and complex factors which must be considered in dealing with phenomena involving both physiological and psychological processes. Statements which simply assume a direct causal relationship between physiological processes and complex psychological experiences and behaviors are abundant in the literature,[5] but they are inadequate as contributions

to psychology since they neither specify in at least outline form the nature of the hypothetical mechanism supposed to link physiological and psychological events nor make explicit the underlying beliefs about the conceptually difficult relationship between mind and body (Borst, 1970; Fodor, 1968).

GENERAL ISSUES

Many of the studies of the premenstrual syndrome discussed above involve certain assumptions which, when made explicit, raise some interesting general questions about the description and explanation of behavior. One of these assumptions is that the syndrome (however it may be defined in a particular study) can best be described as a premenstrual or menstrual "increase" in certain symptoms, moods, or behaviors. With some exceptions, the data seem equally consistent with an hypothesis of a midcycle syndrome of lowered incidence of crime (Dalton, 1961) and epileptic seizures (Hamburg, 1966), increased self-esteem and elation (Ivey & Bardwick, 1968), and increased sexual desire and sexual activity (Benedek & Rubenstein, 1939a, 1939b; McCance et al., 1937). What is the base line compared with which *changes* in behavior are described as an increase or decrease? If control groups of males are used in studies of cyclic behavior, the question of what to use as a base line for description of behaviors also arises. To take a hypothetical example, if female performance on a digit-symbol substitution task should be found to fluctuate with the menstrual cycle, it would seem incomplete and therefore misleading to say only that females' performance is worse at certain times in the cycle than at others, since it may at all times be better than the average performance of males on this task. One can say, of course, that male performance is by definition irrelevant to the study of behavioral changes associated with the menstrual cycle, but it is not irrelevant—

---

[5] "The personality changes associated with the menstrual cycle occur in spite of individual personality differences and may even be extreme; they are consequences of endocrine and related physical changes . . . [Bardwick, 1971, p. 27]." "We felt assured that the phases of ovarian function were reflected in psychic processes [Benedek, 1963, p. 315]." "There was a tendency for the levels of tension measured—specifically, anxiety and hostility inward—to decrease transiently around the time of ovulation. The presumed cause is some hormonal change . . . [Gottschalk et al., 1962, p. 308]." "The menstrual cycle imposes on the human female a rhythmic variability encompassing all aspects of her being, from the biochemical to the psychosocial [Silbergeld et al., 1971, p. 411]." "The theory that the pathological emotional findings are hormonally influenced is widely accepted [Janowsky Gorney, & Kelley, 1966, p. 243]." Janowsky et al., regard these hormonal influences as having considerable scope, listing the following as

some [sic] of the cyclically recurring phenomena of the premenstrual and menstrual phases . . . depression, irritability, sleep disturbances, lethargy, alcoholic excesses, nymphomania, feelings of un-

reality, sleep disturbances, epilepsy, vertigo, syncope, paresthesias, nausea, vomiting, constipation, bloating, edema, colicky pain, enuresis, urinary retention, increased capillary fragility, glaucoma, migraine headaches, relapses of meningiomas, schizophrenic reactions and relapses, increased susceptibility to infection, suicide attempts, admission to surgical and medical wards, crime rates, work morbidity, manic reactions, and dermatological diseases [p. 242].

though it is not often investigated—to studies of rhythmic changes in human behavior, which may be a more useful concept in a general psychological theory.

The question of control groups, then, points to a second assumption which seems to underlie studies of the premenstrual syndrome—that is, the assumption that the menstrual cycle is relevant to the interpretation of a great many cyclic changes in behavior in human females. In view of the evidence of the pervasiveness of cyclic phenomena in human beings (Luce, 1970), control groups would appear to be essential for proper interpretation of data on adult female subjects. Hersey (1931), for example, has reported finding cycles of emotionality in males (determined on the basis of daily observations of behavior and self-reports. These cycles varied from three and one-half to nine weeks in length, but were constant, within ± one week, and predictable for a given individual. Lieber and Sherin (1972) have reported finding lunar cycles in the occurrence of violent crimes—whether committed by males or females. As noted above, Dalton (1964) described 28-day cycles in the behavior of prepubertal schoolgirls, cycles comparable to those found in menstruating females of various ages (though not found in men and boys). Whatever the cause of such rhythmic behaviors in nonmenstruating individuals, their existence points to the necessity of control groups for interpretation of cyclic phenomena as well as for determining a base line for describing any changes which may be found only in one sex.

A final issue which is raised by the literature on the premenstrual syndrome has to do with some of the conventions governing the publication of psychological research. One of these is the generally accepted practice of not publishing "negative" results. In the menstrual cycle literature, for example, numerous investigators have tested reaction time at various phases of the menstrual cycle and have found no changes (the data were included as part of a report of a larger study in which some other change was found; e.g., Kopell et al., 1969). There is, on the other hand, at least one report of positive findings (Voitsechovsky, 1909) which presumably could be cited in support of a claim that reaction time varies throughout the menstrual cycle. Given the conventions governing the availability of "facts" in psychology, it is difficult to document a claim of "no change" or "no difference." The issue of negative results is, of course, a complex one, involving questions about the sensitivity of the tests used, random sampling errors and the like. Nevertheless, in a problem area where there may be a general expectation of finding a "result," there would seem to be a danger that the literature will be encumbered with more Type II errors than is desirable simply because a result frequently sought may occur by chance at least a few times and make its way into print.

Also related to publication practices is another difficulty illustrated by the menstrual cycle literature, one which arises when investigators have data on which a large number of correlations can be computed. What should be the editorial policy regarding publication of such data when only a few of the correlations are significant? In studies of the menstrual cycle, this generally occurs when correlations are computed between each item on a lengthy questionnaire and individual items on other questionnaires or tests. Kopell et al. (1969), for example, found 12 of at least 72 correlations (the exact number cannot be determined from their report) to be statistically significant, Levitt and Lubin (1967) found 14 of 75, and Silbergeld et al. (1971) found 13 of 129 variables to vary significantly during the cycle. In interpreting such data, it seems that either the authors do not attempt to make even ad hoc sense out of the data in terms of a coherent psychological theory (Silbergeld et al., 1971), or else they draw a conclusion which seems more elaborate than is justified by the data. Kopell et al., for example, found that time estimation varied significantly during the menstrual cycle; time estimation and two-flash threshold were found to be positively correlated on three out of four tests; and self-ratings of "concentration" and "social affection" were negatively correlated with time estimation at each of the four phases of the cycle tested. From these data they posed the "intriguing question" of whether the "subjective changes experienced during the premenstrual period" are "an expression of a distortion of the basic time sense which, in turn, might be part of a very mild, transient, confusional state [p. 186]."

In light of these various methodological and theoretical considerations, then, it seems fair to conclude:

1. Psychological studies of the premenstrual syndrome have not as yet established the existence of a class of behaviors and moods, *measurable in more than one way*, which can be shown in a longitudinal study to fluctuate throughout the course of the menstrual cycle, or even a class of such behaviors which is regularly correlated with any particular phase of the cycle for groups of women. This is not to say that such a set of behaviors does not exist—many women spontaneously attest that they do—but that as a scientific hypothesis the existence of a premenstrual syndrome has little other than face validity.

2. Psychological studies of the premenstrual syndrome are difficult to interpret without control groups to establish a base line for describing changes in behavior in one sex and to determine the presence or absence of cyclic changes in the behaviors of nonmenstruating individuals. The use of control groups—automatic in most psychological studies—might yield new data on rhythmic behaviors of hitherto unsuspected generality and, if so, would broaden the interpretation of those previously studied only in adult females.

3. Given the paucity of data showing actual changes in nonverbal behavior throughout the menstrual cycle, careful consideration should be given to the nature of the data in a particular study: Do they show what the subject *says* about menstruation or what she does—nonverbally—throughout the cycle? In view of the prevalence of culturally transmitted beliefs and attitudes about menstruation, this distinction is important in considering the relative influence of social and physiological factors both in interpreting the data and in formulating new hypotheses.

4. Given the variety of methods and the variable quality of data on the premenstrual syndrome, investigators proposing a physiological mechanism to explain hormone–behavior relationships should make clear both what behaviors they propose to account for and also the nature of the empirical and conceptual assumptions upon which their psychophysiological hypotheses rest.

REFERENCES

ABRAMSON, M., & TORGHELE, J. R. Weight, temperature changes, and psychosomatic symptomatology in relation to the menstrual cycle. *American Journal of Obstetrics and Gynecology*, 1961, 81, 223–232.

ALTMAN, M., KNOWLES, E., & BULL, H. D. A psychosomatic study of the sex cycle in women. *Psychosomatic Medicine*, 1941, 3, 199–224.

BALINT, M. A contribution to the psychology of menstruation. *Psychoanalytic Quarterly*, 1937, 6, 346–352.

BARDWICK, J. M. *Psychology of women: A study of biocultural conflicts*. New York: Harper & Row, 1971.

BENEDEK, T. An investigation of the sexual cycle in women: Methodologic considerations. *Archives of General Psychiatry*, 1963, 8, 311–322.

BENEDEK, T., & RUBENSTEIN, B. B. The correlations between ovarian activity and psychodynamic processes: I. The ovulative phase. *Psychosomatic Medicine*, 1939, 1, 245–270. (a)

BENEDEK, T., & RUBENSTEIN, B. B. The correlations between ovarian activity and psychodynamic processes: II. The menstrual phase. *Psychosomatic Medicine*, 1939, 1, 461–485. (b)

BENSON, R. C. *Handbook of obstetrics and gynecology*. Los Angeles: Lange Medical Publications, 1964.

BORST, C. V. (Ed.) *The mind/brain identity theory*. New York: Macmillan, 1970.

COHEN, S. BELENSKY, L., & CHAYM, J. The study of monoamine oxidase activity by histochemical procedures. *Biochemical Pharmacology*, 1965, 14, 223–228.

COOKE, W. R. The differential psychology of the American woman. *American Journal of Obstetrics and Gynecology*, 1945, 49, 457–472.

COPPEN, W. R., & KESSEL, N. Menstruation and personality. *British Journal of Psychiatry*, 1963, 109, 711–721.

CRANE, G. E. Use of monoamine oxidase inhibiting antidepressants. In W. G. Clark & J. del Giudice (Eds.), *Principles of psychopharmacology: A textbook for physicians, medical students, and behavioral scientists*. New York: Academic Press, 1970.

DALTON, K. Discussion on the premenstrual syndrome. *Proceedings of the Royal Society of Medicine*, 1954, 48, 339–346.

DALTON, K. Menstruation and acute psychiatric illness. *British Medical Journal*, 1959, 1, 148–149.

DALTON, K. Effect of menstruation on schoolgirls' weekly work. *British Medical Journal*, 1960, 1, 326–328. (a)

DALTON, K. Menstruation and accidents. *British Medical Journal*, 1960, 2, 1425–1426. (b)

DALTON, K. Menstruation and crime. *British Medical Journal*, 1961, 2, 1752–1753.

DALTON, K. *The premenstrual syndrome*. Springfield, Ill.: Charles C Thomas, 1964.

DALTON, K. The influence of mother's menstruation on her child. *Proceedings of the Royal Society of Medicine*, 1966, 59, 1014.

EICHNER, E., & WALTNER, C. Premenstrual tension. *Medical Times*, 1955, 83, 771–779.

FERGUSON, J. H., & VERMILLION, M. B. Premenstrual tension: Two surveys of its prevalence and a description of the syndrome. *Obstetrics and Gynecology*, 1957, 9, 615–619.

FODOR, J. A. Functional explanation in psychology. In M. Brodbeck (Ed.), *Readings in the philosophy of the social sciences*. New York: Macmillan, 1968.

FRANK, R. T. The hormonal causes of premenstrual tension. *Archives of Neurology and Psychiatry*, 1931, 26, 1053–1057.

GOTTSCHALK, L. A., KAPLAN, S. M., GLESER, G. C., & WINGET, C. M. Variations in magnitude of emotions: A method applied to anxiety and hostility during phases of the menstrual cycle. *Psychosomatic Medicine*, 1962, 24, 300–311.

GRANT, C., & PRYSE-DAVIES, J. Effects of oral contraceptives on depressive mood changes and on endometrial monoamine oxidase and phosphates. *British Medical Journal*, 1968, 1, 777–780.

GREENE, R. Discussion on the premenstrual syndrome. *Proceedings of the Royal Society of Medicine*, 1954, 48, 337–338.

GREENE, R., & DALTON, K. The premenstrual syndrome. *British Medical Journal*, 1953, 1, 1007–1013.

HAMBURG, D. A. Effects of progesterone on behavior. *Research Publications. Association for Research in Nervous and Mental Diseases*, 1966, 43, 251–265.

HERSEY, R. B. Emotional cycles in man. *Journal of Mental Science*, 1931, 77, 151–169.

IVEY, M., & BARDWICK, J. M. Patterns of affective fluctuation in the menstrual cycle. *Psychosomatic Medicine*, 1968, 30, 336–345.

JANOWSKY, D. S., GORNEY, R., CASTELNUOVO-TEDESCO, P., & STONE, C. B. Premenstrual-menstrual increase in psychiatric hospital admission rates. *American Journal of Obstetrics and Gynecology*, 1969, 103, 189–191.

JANOWSKY, D., GORNEY, R., & KELLEY, B. "The curse" —Vicissitudes and variations of the female fertility cycle: Part I. Psychiatric aspects. *Psychosomatics*, 1966, 7, 242–247.

KANE, F. J., LIPTON, M. A., & EWING, J. A. Hormonal influences in female sexual response. *Archives of General Psychiatry*, 1969, 20, 202–209.

KLAIBER, E. L., BROVERMAN, D. M., VOGEL, W., KOBAYASHI, Y., & MORIARTY, D. Effects of estrogen therapy on plasma MAO activity and EEG driving responses of depressed women. *American Journal of Psychiatry*, 1972, 128, 1492–1498.

KOPELL, B. S., LUNDE, D. T., CLAYTON, R. B., & MOOS, R. H. Variations in some measures of arousal during the menstrual cycle. *Journal of Nervous and Mental Diseases*, 1969, 148, 180–187.

LENNANE, M. B., & LENNANE, R. J. Alleged psychogenic disorders in women—a possible manifestation of sexual prejudice. *New England Journal of Medicine*, 1973, 288, 288–292.

LEVITT, E. E., & LUBIN, B. Some personality factors associated with menstrual complaints and menstrual attitude. *Journal of Psychosomatic Research*, 1967, 11, 267–270.

LIEBER, A., & SHERIN, C. The case of the full moon. *Human Behavior*, 1972, 1, 29.

LLOYD, C. W. The ovaries. In R. H. Williams (Ed.), *Textbook of endocrinology*. (3rd ed.) Philadelphia: W. B. Saunders, 1962.

LUCE, G. G. *Biological rhythms in psychiatry and medicine*. (USPHS Pub. No. 2088) Washington, D. C.:

U. S. Department of Health, Education and Welfare, 1970.

MACKINNON, P. C. B., & MACKINNON, I. L. Hazards of the menstrual cycle. *British Medical Journal*, 1956, 1, 555.

MANDELL, A., & MANDELL, M. Suicide and the menstrual cycle. *Journal of the American Medical Association*, 1967, 200, 792–793.

MCCANCE, R. A., LUFF, M. C., & WIDDOWSON, E. E. Physical and emotional periodicity in women. *Journal of Hygiene*, 1937, 37, 571–605.

MCCLINTOCK, M. K. Menstrual synchrony and suppression. *Nature*, 1971, 229, 244–245.

MOOS, R. H. The development of a menstrual distress questionnaire. *Psychosomatic Medicine*, 1968, 30, 853–867.

MOOS, R. H. Assessment of psychological concomitants of oral contraceptives. In H. A. Salhanick et al. (Eds.), *Metabolic effects of gonadal hormones and contraceptive steroids*. New York: Plenum Press, 1969. (a)

MOOS, R. H. Typology of menstrual cycle symptoms. *American Journal of Obstetrics and Gynecology*, 1969, 103, 390–402. (b)

MOOS, R. H., KOPELL, B. S., MELGES, F. T., YALOM, I. D., LUNDE, D. T., CLAYTON, R. B., & HAMBURG, D. A. Fluctuations in symptoms and moods during the menstrual cycle. *Journal of Psychosomatic Research*, 1969, 13, 37–44.

MORTON, J. H., ADDITON, H., ADDISON, R. G., HUNT, L., & SULLIVAN, J. J. A clinical study of premenstrual tension. *American Journal of Obstetrics and Gynecology*, 1953, 65, 1182–1191.

NEILL, J. D., JOHANSSON, E. D. B., DATTS, J. K., & KNOBIL, E. Relationship between the plasma levels of leutinizing hormone and progesterone during the normal menstrual cycle. *Journal of Clinical Endocrinology*, 1967, 27, 1167–1173.

NOWLIS, V. Research with the Mood Adjective Check List. In S. S. Tomkins & C. E. Izard (Eds.), *Affect, cognition, and personality*. New York: Springer, 1965.

PAIGE, K. E. Effects of oral contraceptives on affective fluctuations associated with the menstrual cycle. *Psychosomatic Medicine*, 1971, 33, 515–537.

PIERSON, W. R., & LOCKHART, A. Effect of menstruation on simple reaction and movement time. *British Medical Journal*, 1963, 1, 796–797.

REES, L. The premenstrual tension syndrome and its treatment. *British Medical Journal*, 1953, 1, 1014–1016. (a)

REES, L. Psychosomatic aspects of the premenstrual tension syndrome. *Journal of Mental Science*, 1953, 99, 62–73. (b)

REYNOLDS, L. T. A note on the perpetuation of a "scientific fiction." *Sociometry*, 1966, 29, 85–88.

RIBEIRO, A. L. Menstruation and crime. *British Medical Journal*, 1962, 1, 640.

RICHTER, C. P. Periodic phenomena in man and animals: Their relation to neuroendocrine mechanisms (a monthly or near monthly cycle). In R. P. Michael (Ed.), *Endocrinology and human behavior*. London: Oxford University Press, 1968.

ROSE, R. M., GORDON, T. P., & BERNSTEIN, I. S. Plasma testosterone levels in the male rhesus:

Influences of sexual and social stimuli. *Science,* 1972, 178, 643–645.

SEWARD, G. H. The female sex rhythm. *Psychological Bulletin,* 1934, 31, 153–192.

SHAINESS, N. A re-evaluation of some aspects of femininity through a study of menstruation: A preliminary report. *Comparative Psychiatry,* 1961, 2, 20–26.

SHERMAN, J. A. *On the psychology of women: A survey of empirical studies.* Springfield, Ill.: Charles C Thomas, 1971.

SILBERGELD, S., BRAST, N., & NOBEL, E. P. The menstrual cycle: A double-blind study of symptoms, mood and behavior, and biochemical variables using Enovid and placebo. *Psychosomatic Medicine,* 1971, 33, 411–428.

SOMMER, B. Menstrual cycle changes and intellectual performance. *Psychosomatic Medicine,* 1972, 34, 263–269.

SOUTHAM, A. L., & GONZAGA, F. P. Systemic changes during the menstrual cycle. *American Journal of Obstetrics and Gynecology,* 1965, 91, 142–165.

SOUTHGATE, J., GRANT, E. C. G., POLLARD, W., PRYSE-DAVIES, J., & SANDLER, M. Cyclical varia-

tions in endometrial monoamine oxidase: Correlation of histochemical and quantitative biochemical assays. *Biochemical Pharmacology,* 1968, 17, 721–726.

SUTHERLAND, H., & STEWART, I. A critical analysis of the premenstrual syndrome. *Lancet,* 1965, 1, 1180–1193.

THOMPSON, C. Some effects of the derogatory attitude toward female sexuality. *Psychiatry,* 1950, 13, 349–354.

VOITSECHOVSKY, N. V. [The influence of menstruation upon the nervous and psychic apparatus of women.] Thesis from the Imperial Military Academy, St. Petersburg, Russia, 1909, No. 6. Cited by G. H. Seward, The female sex rhythm. *Psychological Bulletin,* 1934, 31, 153–192.

WHITEHEAD, R. E. Women pilots. *Journal of Aviation Medicine,* 1934, 5, 47–49.

ZIMMERMAN, E., & PARLEE, M. B. Behavioral changes associated with the menstrual cycle: An experimental investigation. *Journal of Applied Social Psychology,* 1973, in press.

(Received March 13, 1973)

5

RAVENNA HELSON

Heroic and Tender Modes in Women Authors of Fantasy[1]

In a previous study, a sample of 27 male authors of literary fantasy was subdivided into five groups on the basis of the creativity and motive-pattern of their books (Helson, 1973). These groups of men were found to differ in personality, work style, and personal history according to hypotheses taken from Rank (1945) and Neumann (1954 a, b). The present study will show how a similar analysis applies in a sample of women authors.

The first hypothesis is, briefly, that creativity is related to a *non*conventional *integration* of personality, where less creative individuals tend either to a conventional adjustment or to rebellious conflict (Rank, 1945; MacKinnon, 1965). It is further hypothesized that major dimensions of variation in the literary product express these personality patterns.

Although the study of male authors did not go into the general question of the socialization process in adjusted, conflicted, and creative subjects, this topic seems important in understanding the data from women. Rank believed that creative integration had its origins in the "counterwill" manifested by the child against the restraints and demands of the parents. The "adusted" type of person minimized his counterwill, patterned it with the grain of the culture, and thus came to identify his own will with that of his parents and later with the dictates of wider society. The "conflicted" type of individual reacted with guilt and vacillation over the assertion of counterwill against his parents, whom he loved and upon whom he was dependent. The creative individual was either so fortunate as to have had parents who accepted him as a separate individual and thus encouraged him to develop autonomy with a minimum of guilt, or he was able to find a resolution to the conflict between will and counterwill (MacKinnon, 1965).

1. This research was supported by a grant from the Frances G. Wickes Foundation.

It is in the spirit of Rank's point of view to suggest that, in the normal course of reconciling will and counterwill, there are two main strategies, one counteractive to fear that the ego will be trapped or dependent, and another counteractive to the fear that the ego will be isolated (see also Bakan, 1966; Carlson, 1971). The first, which will be referred to here as the heroic strategy, is regarded as particularly appropriate for boys. It consists in overcoming one's dependent involvement in early relationships and striving toward new relationships in which one has a more equalitarian, independent, or dominant role. Heroic development is thus chronological, ego-assertive, achievement-oriented, outward-looking. The other strategy, which will be called the tender, is to a greater extent contemporaneous, ahistorical (past merging with present), a field-force phenomenon. It seeks to find a natural rhythm or patterning of will and counterwill, a good gestalt for whatever are the prevailing conditions. As the heroic strategy tends to use discipline, practice, abstraction, analysis—techniques which *minimize* feeling and *sever* relationship, the tender strategy tends to use techniques which *employ* feeling and emotion—identification, empathy, emotional climates, suggestion, charm, etc. Girls use this strategy more than boys, but its amorphous nature and perhaps our cultural prejudice in favor of the heroic make it hard to see and describe. As the last statement implies, societies may incline to one strategy or the other, and there has been a long-term trend from the "matriarchal" to the "patriarchal" (Neumann, 1954a; Lomax, 1972). Individual families also differ in their encouragement of one style or the other.

Let us assume with Jung (1966) that the relation between the individual and society has a counterpart in the relation between the ego and the unconscious. The ego of the individual who *adjusts* to society is *resistant* to the unconscious, because rebellious and maladaptive impulses aggregate there. The conflicted individual is hyperreceptive in some ways and overdefended in others, in a pattern that reverses the conscious attitude. The creative individual, who tends to *detachment* in relation to society, shows emotional *involvement* in a clearly structured relationship between the ego and unconscious. In the heroic type of relationship, the ego confronts the unconscious and uses the instruments of the ego and a sense of high purpose in the interests of an expansion of personality. In the tender relationship the ego broods and is concerned with the realization of organic cognitiv,e-emotional patterns. These two types of thought-process have been described by Neumann (1954b) as patriarchal and matriarchal consciousness, and they have been demonstrated in several studies of sex differences in creative style (Helson, 1967) and in studies of differences among creative men (Helson & Crutchfield, 1970; Helson, 1973). Neumann believed that there was a close relationship between the matriarchal and the creative, and this too has found support (Helson, 1970).

This schema organizes and anticipates the material to follow. After presentation of the findings, some parts of it will receive further elaboration.

Method

Sample

Books. A sample of 72 books was originally drawn for use in a study of sex differences in creative products (Helson, 1970). The books were works of fantasy written since 1930 for 8–12 year-old children. They were mentioned in at least two of six British and American compilations published during the 1950's and 1960's, or they were nominated for inclusion by one of the 15 persons who served the study as consultants or judges of creative excellence.

Authors. Invitations to participate in a study of children's literature were extended to all still-living authors of the books included in the previous study, and to authors of some 20 additional books. Eighty percent of the women who were asked to participate accepted the invitation. Of 28 subjects, 17 are American, 9 are British, 1 is Canadian and 1 is Scandinavian. Data were obtained by mail.

Assessment of Works of Fantasy

Two rater-analysts filled out a questionnaire about each book (see Helson, 1970). In particular, they ranked the relative importance of five formal dimensions: setting or mood; personality or relationships between characters; plot; verbal play or humor; and analysis of parts. They also rated ten "needs" on a 5-point scale. The needs were taken from the Murray system (1938) but were adapted to make them more clearly applicable to the sample, and to the special concerns of the study with relations between the ego and the unconscious. A Tryon-type cluster analysis (Tryon & Bailey, 1970) of these 15 variables had been carried out for the original 72 books, but was now repeated for the new sample of 91 books.

In the earlier study, eight West Coast judges in the field of children's literature had rated the books on overall creative excellence. Five judges were added, two from the U.S. and three from England. Ratings of the new group of five judges show a correlation of .92 with the ratings of the original group of eight.

Assessment of Authors

The authors sorted 56 statements about work style according to how well the items described their own way of working. These items constituted the Writers Q Sort, modeled after the Research Scientists Q Sort (Gough & Woodworth, 1960) and the Mathematicians Q Sort (Helson, 1967). Data from the Writers Q Sort were subjected to a cluster analysis.[2]

Personality characteristics of authors were assessed by the California Psychological Inventory (CPI) (Gough, 1964), the Male Form of the Strong Vocational Interest Blank (SVIB) (Strong, 1959), and the Adjective Check List (ACL) (Gough & Heilbrun, 1965). The subjects also filled out a questionnaire in which they answered questions about their family background and life history. Descriptions of parents were rendered anonymous and rated on several variables, with adequate reliability, by psychologists unconnected with the study.[3]

RESULTS

Cluster Analysis of Books

The cluster analysis of the formal dimensions and "needs" of the 91 books yielded three clusters (Table 1). The clusters will be labeled heroic, tender, and comic, respectively. The first cluster consists of variables having to do with purposiveness, achievement, and overcoming opposition, and would thus seem to evidence a high level of the ego-assertiveness hypothesized to be counteractive to fear of dependence. The second cluster consists of variables which describe a nonanalytical "field-dependent" orientation emphasizing the tender feeling and relationship hypothesized to be compensatory to fear of isolation. The third cluster describes a "Walter Mitty" syndrome—wish-fulfillment, achievement, and humor. Cluster scores were obtained for all books on these three motive-stylistic patterns. Of the books which received a score of 60 or above on any one of the clusters, the great majority were rated in the upper half of the sample on

2. I am grateful to Lloyd Alexander for his collaboration in developing the Writers Q Sort, and to Susan Hopkin for her statistical advice and aid.
3. I am grateful to Alfred Bloch and Lillian Cartwright for their ratings.

Table 1. Cluster analysis of needs and stylistic dimensions in 91 fantasies written for children.

Defining variables	Oblique factor coefficient
Cluster I. Heroic (reliability: .78)	
Aggression	.85
Order (overcoming dissident elements)	.73
Achievement (individual exploit)	.66
Accomplishment (group effort)	.46
Cluster II. Tender (reliability: .86)	
Analysis of parts	−.77
Tender emotion	.76
Setting or mood	.70
Personality or relations between characters	.61
Plot	−.54
Order (bringing things into the right relationship)	.54
Cluster III. Comic (reliability: .57)	
Verbal play, humor	.58
Achievement (individual exploit)	.46
Wish-fulfillment	.41

creativity ($p < .001$). The fact that these patterns describe the more creative books better than the less creative, and the additional fact that books by men and women were combined probably accounts for the somewhat low reliability of some of the clusters. In particular, few books by women scored high on the comic cluster.

Cluster Analysis of the Writers Q Sort

The cluster analysis of the Writers Q Sort for all authors, male and female, yielded six clusters. The defining variables of three of these clusters of importance for the present study are shown in Table 2. The first cluster has to do with receptivity to mood and emotional involvement in creative work, as contrasted with businesslike attitudes and responsiveness to external rewards. The second cluster describes productive, assertive ego activity as contrasted with sensitivity and submission to emotional Gestalten. This cluster seems to approximate what Neumann referred to as patriarchal vs. matriarchal style. The third cluster contrasts interest in the concrete, practical, and pecuniary with a somewhat hyper-intuitive receptivity, particularly to inner life.

Correlates of Creativity of the Literary Product

The first hypothesis to be evaluated is that the correlates of creativity describe a personality that is integrated and directed but not in the conventional mold.

Table 2. Cluster analysis of the Writers Q Sort for 54 authors of fantasy.

Defining variables	Oblique factor coefficient
Cluster 1. Emotional involvement in work (reliability: .76)	
Experiences fluctuating moods without apparent cause	.74
Feels depressed after work is finished	.60
Would welcome having work adapted to mass media	−.53
Has an active, efficient, well-organized mind	−.45
Generates many ideas for plots and characters	−.44
Cluster 2. Assertive ego (reliability: .76)	
Writing stints are accompanied by marked fluctuations in sexual interest	−.71
Is productive; turns out a large amount of work	.65
Productivity runs in cycles	−.53
Is flexible in thinking; able rapidly to consider many alternatives in plotting and to foresee consequences	.47
Is aware of personality changes which seem related to developments in writing	−.45
Enjoys power of manipulating characters and plot	.39
Easily distracted; tries to secure optimum conditions for concentration	−.38
Fears someone else is writing something similar	−.35
Cluster 3. Practical reality vs. receptive intuition (reliability: .70)	
Insights often come in dreams, upon waking, just before sleeping, or at some time other than during a period of concentration	−.71
Interested in production processes (typesetting, printing, etc.)	.60
Solution to a problem comes from an unexpected direction	−.48
Feels emotionally tense when a solution to a problem seems imminent	−.47
Finds it difficult to read the work of other writers in his field and prefers to spend time on own work	.38
Publications are of uneven quality	−.34
Desire for money is an important motivating factor	.32

On the Writers Q Sort, creativity ratings are correlated with Cluster 1, Emotional involvement in work, and with several individual items connoting depth of personal involvement or commitment, as contrasted with external concerns or "ego-spinning" (Table 3).

Two correlations with CPI scales, positive with Psychological Mindedness and negative with Dominance, suggest a somewhat introverted integration of tough and tender thinking undisrupted by an impulsive power drive. Three negative correlations with ACL scales, Self-confidence, Affiliation, and Personal adjustment, would seem to indicate reserve and some deviation from conventional social attitudes.

On the SVIB there is a considerable body of correlations

Table 3. Correlates of creativity of literary product for 28 women authors of fantasy for children.

Variable	r
Writers Q Sort	
Cluster 1. Emotional involvement in work	.39*
Places literary goals above all others	.64**
Writes for reader rather than for self	—.43*
Generates many ideas for plots and characters	—.40*
California Psychological Inventory	
Dominance	—.46*
Psychological mindedness	.44*
Femininity	—.35
Adjective Check List	
Self-confidence	—.55**
Affiliation	—.44*
Personal adjustment	—.40*
Strong Vocational Interest Blank[a]	
Group I (Artist, Architect, Dentist)	.55**
Group II (Physicist, Chemist, Engineer)	.56**
Group V (Personnel manager, Vocational counselor, School Superintendent, Music teacher, $p < .01$, and others, $p < .05$)	—.42*
Group IX (Real estate salesman, Life insurance salesman)	—.48*
Mortician (Group VIII)	—.53**
Masculinity-femininity	.60**
Personal History Questionnaire	
Respect for mother	.42*
Respect for father	.38*
Difference in respect for the two parents	—.46*
Present age	.02

[a]Individual scales in each group which show significant correlations are listed in parentheses.

*$p < .05$.
**$p < .01$.

showing a pattern of strong symbolic interests, both artistic and scientific, in marked contrast to social and practical interests. Among the male authors, there were virtually no significant correlations on the SVIB. This fact would seem to emphasize the importance, for creativity in women, of an integration of the masculine at a high level of interest and intellect, as opposed to its simpler expression at the level of extraverted assertiveness or practical or stereotyped categorization.

Finally, there are several correlations with respect for parents and similarity in respect for the two parents. These findings were not obtained in the male sample. The discrepancy may be related to the fact that writing fantasy for children is a more sex-appropriate field for women than for men.

In sum, the correlations of creativity describe an integration of personality around directed symbolic activity, and one that diverges from conventional feminine adjustment. The findings would thus seem consistent with Rank's conceptualization of creativity as associated with a non-conventional integration of personality.

Creative and Comparison Subgroups

The next hypotheses to consider are whether the authors of creative fantasy separate, on the basis of their work, into groups which approximate the patriarchal and matriarchal types described by Neumann, and whether the comparison groups, on the basis of their work, separate into the adjusted and conflicted types as described by Rank.

Groups of authors were constituted on the basis of the creativity and motive-pattern of their books. Books rated above the mean of the sample were designated as "creative," and those rated at the mean or below as "comparison." Books with a standard score over 50 on the heroic cluster were classified as heroic. Half of the books fell into this category, and for all of them the score on the heroic cluster was their highest, or, in one case, tied for highest. Of the other 14 books, three stood apart as having low scores on both the heroic and tender clusters and high scores on the comic cluster. One of these books was creative and two were comparison. Since the comic cluster shows a correlation of .39 with the heroic cluster and —.59 with the tender cluster, these books were combined with the works of heroic fantasy. The remaining 11 books will be designated as tender, although several of them have scores below 50 on all three clusters. Personality data from an author of one of these "tender" books are incomplete.

There are thus four groups of books and authors: the creative heroic and tender and the comparison heroic and tender. Table 4 shows mean scores for the four groups on the criterion ratings of creativity, the motive-patterns, three clusters of the Writers Q Sort, and those scales of the CPI and SVIB which showed differences significant at the .05 level in any of the comparisons now to be discussed.

Creative groups. Let us consider each group as compared with all other subjects, paying particular attention to the relative positions of, first, the two creative groups, later the two com-

Table 4. Comparisons of subgroups of authors on measures of personality and work style.

| | Mean Scores | | | | t Heroic groups | t Tender groups |
| | Creative | | Comparison | | | |
	Heroic N = 6	Tender N = 5	Heroic N = 11	Tender N = 5		
Creativity criterion	26.3*	25.6ᵃ	20.3*	17.0**	5.55**	4.90**
Motive-stylistic patterns						
Heroic	59.0*	39.1**	55.7ᵃ	44.7	—	—
Tender	50.3	62.1**	49.4	50.8	—	
Comic	58.7**	40.6ᵃ	46.8	44.3	2.48*	—
Writers Q Sort						
1. Emotional involvement in work	50.0	54.5	50.8	40.2*	—	2.74*
2. Assertive ego	53.0	40.2**	53.6	53.1	—	−2.78*
3. Practical reality vs. receptive intuition	46.2	47.7	40.7*	54.4*	—	—
California Psychological Inventory						
Dominance	25.0	24.2ᵃ	29.7	32.0ᵃ	—	−4.33**
Sociability	22.8	20.2	22.1	26.4*	—	−2.15ᵃ
Socialization	39.8	36.8	33.7*	40.4	2.30*	—
Self-control	33.0	31.2	26.4*	34.0	2.23ᴬ	—
Communality	24.8	23.2*	24.6	25.4	—	−2.84*
Achv. via conformance	28.2	25.0ᵃ	27.0	33.0**	—	−4.54**
Achv. via independence	26.8ᵃ	25.2	23.4*	26.0	2.18*	—
Intellectual efficiency	43.2	39.8	39.9	42.6	—	−2.67*
Strong Vocational Interest Blank						
Group I (Artists, etc.)	67.2**	62.6	59.4	55.4*	2.51*	3.35*
Group II (Mathematicians, etc.)	45.2**	38.4	34.8	28.4*	2.22*	4.11**
Group IX (Sales Manager, etc.)	26.4	30.0	32.0	37.2*	—	2.03ᵃ
Masculinity of interests	29.0*	25.6	23.6	2.03ᵃ	—	20.0ᵃ

Note.—Superscripts by mean scores indicate that the group differs significantly from all other women by two-tailed *t* test.
ᵃDifference between means is significant at the .10 level of confidence.
*p < .05.
**p < .01.

parison groups. Of all four groups, the authors of creative heroic fantasy are the least distinctive. As one would expect, they have high scores on creativity and on the heroic cluster, and one may note in Table 4 that they also score high on the comic cluster. Otherwise, they differ significantly ($p < .05$) from the rest of the sample only on scales of the SVIB. On this test they have higher scores on Group I and Group II scales and on masculinity of interests, and they differ also on many individual scales not shown in Table 4. What stands out about them most, then, is their humor and their strong symbolic interests, involving intuitiveness, objectivity, sustained effort, and autonomous integration.

The authors of creative tender fantasy score high on the tender cluster, of course, and also distinctively low on the heroic cluster. On the Writers Q Sort they score lower than other women on the Assertive Ego cluster ($p < .01$), indicating that they work in a "matriarchal style" in close touch with mood and feeling. On the CPI they score lower than other women on the Communality scale ($p < .05$). The negative end of the Communality scale might be described as "narcissistic expression." They also score somewhat lower ($p < .10$) on Dominance and Achievement via Conformance. To the casual observer, these women might appear as narcissistically preoccupied, as somewhat unpredictable, or perhaps as a bit distant, awkward or stubborn. However, what is important is going on inside; the strong tender motive-pattern and the Assertive Ego cluster of the Q Sort, turned "upside down," suggest what this inner process is like.

Compared with each other, the authors of creative heroic and tender fantasy differ significantly on the Assertive Ego cluster ($p < .05$). The items of the Writers Q Sort which these two groups place highest in their self-descriptions (Table 5) show only one common item: Enjoys using language accurately and expressively. In Table 5 note the emphasis on intuition, originality, and drive in the items placed highest by the authors of heroic fantasy; the emphasis on feeling and passive concentration in the items placed highest by the authors of tender fantasy.

Comparison groups. The authors of comparison tender fantasy have the lowest ratings of the sample on creativity, as Rank would have predicted for persons of the "adjusted" personality type (Table 4). On the Writers Q Sort, their extreme low scores on cluster 1 show them to be the most concerned with external rewards and expectations. They also score at the extreme end of cluster 3 in the direction of Practical Reality, where the comparison heroic authors score at the extreme in the direction of Receptive Intuition. The CPI findings add strong support for the hypothesis that the authors of comparison tender fantasy may be considered "adjusted" and the authors of comparison heroic fantasy "conflicted": The former group scores *higher* than other

Table 5. Items of the Writers Q Sort placed highest in self-description by authors of creative heroic and tender fantasy.

	Creative Heroic ($N = 6$) mean	Creative Tender ($N = 5$) mean
Items placed highest by authors of heroic fantasy:		
Enjoys using language accurately and expressively	5.0[a]	4.6
Insights come in dreams, upon waking, etc.	4.3	3.8
Is a person with marked intuitive power	4.3[a]	2.8*
Work is characterized by inventiveness and ingenuity	4.2[a]	2.4**
Grasps ideas of others quickly	4.0[a]	3.0
Uncomfortable when not creating	4.0	3.0
Has strong powers of visualizing scenes	4.0	3.6
Items placed highest by authors of tender fantasy:		
Enjoys using language accurately and expressively	5.0	4.6
Easily distracted; tries to secure optimum conditions for concentration	3.3	4.2*
Solution comes from an unexpected direction	3.3	4.0
Major gratification is the clarification and sharing of feelings	3.5	4.0
Patient; does not get upset when progress is slow	3.3	4.0[a]

Note.—Q-sort items were sorted on a five-point scale.
[a]Difference between means for group indicated and all other women is significant at the .10 level of confidence by two-tailed t test
*$p < .05$.
**$p < .01$.

women on Sociability and on Achievement via Conformance; the latter group scores *lower* than other women on Socialization, Self-control and Achievement via Independence. Finally, the comparison authors of tender fantasy have lower scores than the rest of the sample on several SVIB scales indicative of strong symbolic interests, and higher scores on scales reflecting manipulative extraversion.

Tender Groups and Heroic Groups

According to the schema offered in the introduction, the heroic and tender motive-patterns can be considered as reflecting distinctive strategies for reconciling will and counterwill. However, the previous findings suggest that personality characteristics associated with motive-pattern vary with level of creativity. The following comparisons of the two tender groups with each other and the two heroic groups with each other clarify the nature of these differences.

Tender groups. The last column of Table 4 shows that the

authors of creative and comparison tender fantasy differ significantly on ten measures, most of which have to do with extraversion and conventionality. On the ACL (not shown in Table 4) the comparison women have a peak standard score of 58 on *Favorableness* of self-description, the creative subjects a peak of 64 on *Unfavorableness* of self-description. The creative group has a very sharp profile on the motive-pattern clusters; the comparison group has low scores and a flatter profile.

Heroic groups. Here again, the creative group has the sharper motive-pattern. Its humor is particularly conspicuous. The two groups differ on the CPI scales Socialization, Self-control, and Achievement via Independence. On the ACL the creative group has a peak score of 54 on Self-control; the comparison group a peak of 55 on Abasement, a scale assessing feelings of unworthiness and self-punishing tendencies.

Table 6 compares the two tender and the two heroic groups on features of life-history, and also on several variables describing their books. No difference between the two tender groups reaches the .05 level of significance, but there are several significant

Table 6. Comparisons of the different groups of authors on life history variables and themes in fantasy.

	Heroic			Tender		
	Creative N = 6 Mean	Com- parison N = 11 Mean	t	Creative N = 5 Mean	Com- parison N = 5 Mean	t
Life History						
Size of community	1.5	2.5	−2.49*	2.0	1.4	—
Number of siblings	3.3	1.4	2.61*	2.0	1.4	—
Neurotic tie to parent	1.0	2.6	−5.85**	1.5	2.4	—
Respect for mother	8.3	6.9	2.30*	8.3	7.4	—
Respect for father	8.3	5.0	3.78**	7.0	7.4	—
Works of fantasy						
Characters (6-point scale)						
Alliance with a wise or powerful male	2.7	5.0	−3.54**	3.0	2.8	—
Relationship among peers	5.8	5.0	—	4.3	4.4	—
Themes (10-point scale)						
Struggle with the demonic	5.7	7.8	a	2.5	3.8	a
Opposition to convention	7.0	4.4	b	8.0	4.4	b

aHeroic fantasy rated higher, $p < .01$.
bCreative books rated higher, $p < .01$.
*$p < .05$.
**$p < .01$.

differences between the two groups of authors of heroic fantasy. Although there were no significant differences in education or occupation of parents, the comparison subjects grew up in larger communities, had fewer siblings, particularly fewer brothers, described their parents with less respect, particularly the father, and more frequently reported a neurotic or difficult relationship with a parent. Only four of the 11 were married, as compared with five of six creative subjects. Where the books written by the comparison authors usually involve a struggle with demonic forces and an alliance with a wise or powerful male, the books by the creative group more frequently concern a group of peers in opposition to conventional society and its law-enforcing representatives.

DISCUSSION

This study has shown that the major types of fantasy for children which are written by women are the work of authors whose personalities fit the Rankian schema of adjusted, conflicted, and creative. The pattern of relationships duplicates that obtained in the study of male authors, except that where adjusted women write dilute tender fantasy and conflicted authors write in the heroic mode, among men the adjusted subjects write mock-heroic (comic) fantasy and conflicted men write in the tender mode.

A second major finding is that women authors of creative heroic and tender fantasy differ in personality and work style. The former group are conspicuous for their strong and versatile symbolic interests, the latter group for their introverted "narcissism," or submission of the ego to emotional Gestalten. Results in the male sample were similar. There is thus additional support for the concepts of patriarchal and matriarchal styles as advanced by Neumann in his contributions to Jungian theory.

The study of male authors developed the idea that motive-pattern in literary fantasy expresses quite directly the relationship between the ego and unconscious, at least in creative individuals. The fact that comparison men did not seem to show these relationships so clearly was attributed somewhat vaguely to their greater conventionality and defensiveness. The present study has inquired more carefully into the psychology of both creative and comparison subjects. As a consequence of this wider view, several new questions have presented themselves.

The first has to do with a possible integration of Rankian and Jungian concept-systems. One's task in making a track of Jung's explorations, relating his concepts of the inner world and its outer roots to the Rankian outer constructs and their inner roots, and then making inferences about where the terrain revealed in the present study would fit on these conjoined maps—this task clearly involves free, rather than precise and detailed cartography. Nevertheless, there are broad areas where the fit seems compelling. Let us consider whether the Rankian categories of adjusted, conflicted, and creative, when regarded from the point of view of inner adjustment, may not correspond to the Jungian stages in the relation between the ego and unconscious, those defined by the dominance of the persona, then by awareness of the shadow, then the animus, and after that, stages in which appear the archetypes of integration, meaning, and selfhood (Jung, 1959, 1966).

The adjusted woman would be, in Jung's terminology, one who was strongly identified with her persona or social role. Just as such a person is susceptible to social influence, says Jung, so is she susceptible to influence from the unconscious. Such individuals tend to employ defenses such as repression, suppression, and reaction-formation which maintain the proper persona and keep shadow impulses white or out of awareness. But reliance on these defenses stands in the way of a genuine relationship between the ego and unconscious (Fordham, 1966).

The adjusted writers show, in their self-descriptions, the most favorable self-presentations, and in their works the weakest motive-patterns. One might say, then, that they are the most dominated by the persona and have the shallowest relationship to the unconscious.

Jung says that knowledge of the shadow is necessary before experience of the animus begins to become conscious. Thus an author who shows concern with the animus would be expected to have a closer relationship to the unconscious than an author concerned to maintain the persona and suppress the shadow. In this study, the authors who have been designated as "conflicted" on the basis of Rankian conceptions present themselves much less favorably than the "adjusted" women, and their books show stronger motive-patterns. Furthermore, in their books the struggle with the demonic is one important theme, and the other main element is the alliance with a wise or powerful male.

The Jungian literature does not discuss, I believe, how the animus might be expected to differ in women who show different degrees of awareness of the shadow. A number of findings reported in this study suggest that both adjusted and conflicted authors have characteristics that have been attributed to "animus women" (Emma Jung, 1957). Their high Femininity, high Dominance, and low Psychological-Mindedness can be interpreted to mean that the hyperfemininity reported by the comparison subjects—their sensitivity, preference for feminine occupations, etc.— is mixed with "inferior masculinity"—a tendency to bossiness, harsh criticism of self or others, pedantic ways, slightly excessive efficiency, slightly grandiose philosophizing. However, the high scores of the conflicted women on Abasement, among other similar findings, suggest that in their case a significant portion of the aggression of the animus is directed against themselves. This intropunitive criticism would have the effect of increasing their awareness of the inferior aspects of the personality. If one assumes that the dominance and stereotypy of the adjusted women are organized into their persona of self-confident conventionality, where the expressions of the animus in the conflicted women lack this protective cover, one gains another view of why the animus is said to emerge after the individual becomes separated from her persona.

It is perhaps to be expected that the creative authors, who show the best integration of masculine intellectual interests and attitudes, seldom have conspicuous animus figures in their books. They are presumably further along in the realization of the self. Perhaps their search is expressed in themes such as the attempt to create an order in which "the parts are brought into the right relationship." This theme also recurs in books by creative men (Helson, 1970).

Among men, adjusted and conflicted subjects as a group showed more stringent self-control than creative subjects; this self-control could be interpreted as a defense against the anima, that is, against the primitive moods and emotions of undifferentiated and unassimilated femininity. The adjusted subjects scored higher than other men on various indices of conventionality, where the conflicted subjects were less conventional and placed higher than all other men the Writers Q-Sort item, "Experiences fluctuating moods without apparent cause." Thus, the concepts of persona, shadow and animus or anima seem to be applicable in both samples.

As a consequence of attempting to conceptualize what the heroic and tender dispositions have in common at different levels of creativity, the relevance of the Jungian theory of types became apparent (Jung, 1971; von Franz & Hillman, 1971; Detloff, 1972). This well-known typology involves the attitudes of extraversion and introversion, in combination with the perceptive functions of sensing and intuiting and the evaluative functions of thinking and feeling. All three pairs are seen as consisting of polar opposites. Of the four functions, one is "dominant," and whichever it is, the other in the pair is assumed to be the "inferior" function, since it is presumed to be difficult to use two ways of perceiving or of evaluating at the same time. If the dominant function is introverted, the auxiliary or second-best function tends to be extraverted, though not necessarily. Women are usually more highly developed in feeling than thinking, and it is the opposite with men. Individuals whose dominant function is a perceptive one are said to be less orderly and more open, spontaneous and restless than those whose dominant function is evaluative.

There have been many empirical studies of these personality dimensions, especially extraversion-introversion, but rarely is one able to investigate the patterning of the functions that is essential to the concept of typology (Carlson & Levy, 1973). In the following attempt to explore this patterning within a Jungian framework, I shall omit reminders that ambiguities abound and that there are alternative ways of interpreting the data.

Let us assume that women authors of fantasy will tend to introversion, intuition and feeling. The SVIB data support this inference. A main source of variation in the sample, then, would consist in whether individuals have intuition or feeling as the dominant function. The nature of the two main motive-patterns is consistent with this analysis: the "heroic" cluster consists of items having to do with assertive action toward future goals, and the "tender" cluster contrasts feeling and analytical thinking. The contrast to be expected from intuitive and feeling types is also evident in Table 5, where the creative authors of heroic fantasy describe themselves as having intuitive power and as inventive, perceptive and restless; and the creative authors of tender fantasy describe themselves as patient, concerned with the clarification and sharing of feelings, surprised by solutions (because not actively searching) and as *not* inventive or markedly intuitive. They are also distractible, a trait that might reflect the low level of control by thinking, which would be the feeling type's inferior function. Can we also assume that "conflicted" comparison authors of heroic fantasy are intuitive types and the "adjusted" comparison authors of tender fantasy feeling types? The only difficulty is presented by the latter group, who have no clear motive-pattern and score high on cluster 3 in the direction of Practical Reality.

This difficulty brings up the role of the persona and the animus in the typological organization. That the authors of comparison tender fantasy tend to introversion, intuition and feeling, like their fellow authors, is suggested by the fact that their highest SVIB scores are on the Group I scales (Artist, Architect, Psychiatrist, etc.). This fact, together with their high scores on Practical Reality on the Writers Q Sort and Achievement via Conformance on the CPI, leads to the conjecture that these comparison authors have developed extraverted sensation as their auxiliary function, as indeed would be most likely for introverted women of the feeling type. The extraverted sensation function is well-suited to maintain the persona. Since a feminine image is an important part of the persona, the development of masculine potential, the animus, is restricted and remains primitive.

The creative authors of tender fantasy, on the other hand, might be said to have a bland, negative or poorly differentiated persona, because they describe themselves unfavorably and have low scores on Sociability, Communality and Achievement via Conformance. According to Jung (1966) a woman with a poorly developed persona tends to have a well-developed animus. Perhaps the auxiliary function of the creatives, whether intuition or sensation, remains predominantly introverted, and serves to explore or mediate the inner world, and thus fulfills important functions which have been assigned in Jungian theory to the animus.

The comparison and creative authors of tender fantasy differ strikingly in conventionality, however one chooses to conceptualize this difference. The authors of heroic fantasy on the other hand, differ chiefly in socialization, capacity for sustained independent effort, and in masculinity of interests. In Jungian terms one would say that the creatives show better control of the thinking function and have integrated the animus or masculine potential more harmoniously.

Let us assume that both the creative and comparison authors of heroic fantasy used the heroic strategy to separate from one relationship and go on to another, but because their histories were different, different complexes press for expression in their fantasy. The conflicted subjects return to the problem of changing allegiance from the mother to the father, a separation made difficult for them by the close attachment to the mother, the small family, the lack of respect for the father, etc. (Table 6). They became "mothers' daughters," carriers of the mother's ambitions, but lacking male figures to support them in achieving emotional independence. In their fantasy they are trying to separate from the mother's influence, which has become restrictive, and make contact with the archetypal father (Perry, 1962). The creative subjects on the other hand, go to a point further on, using the heroic strategy to try to achieve a separation from the father and move on to an equalitarian relationship between the sexes. Their greater socialization, self-control, autonomy, and masculine interests reflect their further progress along the developmental continuum.

In sum, the heroic and tender modes may be regarded as the "voice" of the functions of intuition and feeling, respectively. Our simplifying assumptions then help to show this pattern: the similarity that would be expected between the creative and comparison authors of tender fantasy is masked by the difference between them in the importance of persona, and the similarity between the creative and comparison authors of heroic fantasy is masked by their different experience of the father with its consequences for the development of the animus. Presumably these are the sorts of factors, perhaps the main factors, which make types difficult to recognize and conceptualize.

The character of the heroic and tender modes in this study seems to fit Rank's conceptualization of a basic dichotomy between fear of death (loss of autonomy) and fear of life (exposure, isolation). But in terms of the Jungian types, this dichotomy between intuitive and feeling types would seem to be merely one of a number of possible contrasts. A comparison of artists and scientists might contrast intuitive and thinking types, and so forth for other possible pairs throughout a three-dimensional sphere,

If the Rankian dichotomy is more basic than the others, one reason is perhaps that the contrast between intuition-thinking and sensing-feeling is more closely related to sex differences and socialization processes.

SUMMARY

Criterion ratings of creativity and measures of stylistic-motive patterns were obtained for a sample of works of literary fantasy. Data describing personality and work habits are presented for 27 women authors of these works. Creativity of the books was correlated with emotional involvement in work, integration of masculine interests and attitudes, and freedom from one-sided or neurotic relationships with parents. The authors were subdivided into four groups on the basis of high or low creativity and whether their work was heroic-comic or tender. The creative and comparison tender groups differed on the dimension of conventionality; the two heroic-comic groups on the dimension of social maturity and integration of the masculine. The various groups had distinctive characteristics which paralleled, in main features, previous findings for male authors of fantasy. Considered from the point of view of the relation between the individual's will and that of society, the results fit Rank's conceptualization of adjusted, conflicted, and creative types. Considered from the point of view of inner adjustment, they also approximate Jung's conception of stages in the relationship between the ego and the unconscious. There is discussion of the significance of the heroic and tender modes and the characteristics of the four groups in terms of the Jungian theory of types.

REFERENCES

Bakan, D. *The duality of human existence.* Chicago: Rand McNally, 1966.

Carlson, R. Sex differences in ego functioning: Exploratory studies of agency and communion. *Journal of Consulting and Clinical Psychology,* 1971, 37, 267–277.

Carlson, R., & Levy, N. Studies of Jungian typology: I. Memory, social perception, and social action. *Journal of Personality,* 1973, 41, 559–576.

Detloff, W. K. Psychological Types: Fifty years after. *Psychological Perspectives,* 1972, 3, 62–73.

Fordham, F. *An introduction to Jung's psychology.* Middlesex, England: Penguin, 1966.

Gough, H. G. *Manual for the California Psychological Inventory.* (Rev. ed.) Palo Alto, Calif.: Consulting Psychologists Press, 1964.

Gough, H. G., & Heilbrun, A. B., Jr. *Manual for the Adjective Check List.* Palo Alto, Calif.: Consulting Psychologists Press, 1965.

Gough, H. G., & Woodworth, D. G. Stylistic variations among professional research scientists. *Journal of Psychology,* 1960, 49, 87–98.

Helson, R. Sex differences in creative style. *Journal of Personality,* 1967, 35, 214–233.

Helson, R. Sex-specific patterns in creative literary fantasy. *Journal of Personality,* 1970, 38, 344–363.

Helson, R. The heroic, the comic, and the tender: Patterns in literary fantasy and their authors. *Journal of Personality,* 1973, 41, 163–184.

Helson, R., & Crutchfield, R. S. Creative types in mathematics. *Journal of Personality,* 1970, 38, 177–197.

Jung, C. G. *Psychological types: Or the psychology of individuation. Collected works,* Vol. 6. Princeton: Princeton University Press, 1971.

Jung, C. G. *Two essays on analytical psychology. Collected works,* Vol. 7. Princeton: Princeton University Press, 1966.

Jung, C. G. *Aion: Researches into the phenomenology of the self. Collected works,* Vol. 9, Part II. Princeton: Princeton University Press, 1959.

Jung, E. *Animus and anima.* New York: Spring Publications, 1957.

Lomax, A. The evolution of culture and expressive style: A comparative approach to social change. In G. V. Coelho & E. A. Rubinstein (Eds.), *Social change and human behavior: Mental health challenges of the seventies.* Rockville, Maryland: NIMH, 1972.

MacKinnon, D. W. Personality and the realization of creative potential. *American Psychologist,* 1965, 20, 273–281.

Murray, H. A. et al. *Explorations in personality.* New York: Oxford University Press, 1938.

Neumann, E. On the moon and matriarchal consciousness. *Spring,* 1954, 83–100 (Analytical Psychology Club of New York). (a)

Neumann, E. *The origins and history of consciousness.* New York: Bollingen Foundation, 1954. (b)

Perry, J. W. Reconstitutive process in the psychopathology of the self. *Annals New York Academy of Sciences,* 1962, 96, 853–876.

Rank, O. *Will therapy and truth and reality.* New York: Knopf, 1945.

Strong, E. K., Jr. *Manual for Strong Vocational Interest Blanks for men and women, revised blanks (Forms M and W).* Palo Alto, Calif.: Consulting Psychologists Press, 1959.

Tryon, R. C., & Bailey, D. W. *Cluster analysis.* New York: McGraw-Hill, 1970.

von Franz, M., & Hillman, J. *Jung's typology.* Zurich: Spring Publications, 1971.

Manuscript received September 5, 1972.

PART II

ACHIEVEMENT

ACHIEVEMENT

The importance of child-rearing practices and sex role orientation to achievement motivation in women are included in this section in addition to an analysis of several fear of success studies and the questions they raise. Another article notes that women have not been encouraged to achieve and that change which admits women to achieve at all levels will occur gradually. A final article deals with a specific technique enabling young women to set goals and achieve at higher levels.

If women are encouraged and permitted to achieve without restrictions then measures of achievement motivation may be useful in predicting achievement behavior.

6

ALETHA H. STEIN[2] AND MARGARET M. BAILEY[1]

The Socialization of Achievement Orientation in Females

The literature on achievement motivation and achievement-related behavior in females is reviewed in an attempt to identify theoretical relationships and child-rearing antecedents of these variables. The impact of sex role definitions on achievement striving is examined with particular attention to the hypothesis that females' primary goal is affiliation. Individual differences in integrating achievement striving with sex role definitions are discussed, and the patterns of variables such as level of aspiration, expectancy of success, and fear of failure are examined. Finally, the literature on parental socialization of achievement orientation is reviewed.

The purpose of this article is to review the literature on achievement motivation and achievement-related behavior in females from a developmental perspective. Although females achieve at relatively high levels in childhood, their ultimate levels of achievement are considerably lower than those of males. There has been intense concern about the high rates of academic and emotional problems that males experience during the elementary school years with particular attention to the alleged "feminine" nature of school during this period (e.g., Kagan, 1964). Little concern has been expressed, however, about low rates of achievement shown by females in adulthood, though this phenomenon also seems tied to sex role definitions. The ratio of female to male underachievers increases with age until the college years when the proportion of female underachievers exceeds the proportion of male underachievers (Raph, Goldberg, & Passow, 1966). Our purposes are to explore some factors that may affect females' achievement strivings, to determine the effects of sex role expectations on achievement orientation, and

[1] The authors are grateful to Virginia Crandall, Carolyn Sherif, and Dale Harris for their careful reading of earlier drafts of the manuscript and for many helpful suggestions.
[2] Requests for reprints should be sent to Aletha Huston Stein, who is now at the Department of Psychology, Box 265, Temple University, Philadelphia, Pennsylvania 19122.

to identify child-rearing practices that may enhance achievement behavior in females.

The article is focused on achievement motivation and achievement related behavior rather than academic performance. Although the two are related, our concern is with a general pattern of independent striving for excellence in self-selected areas. Even within the intellectual achievement area, striving for excellence can be discriminated from simple "grade getting." For instance, Crandall and Battle (1970) separated subjects with high intellectual achievement striving from those with high academic achievement striving. The former group exhibited effort in intellectual activities not required by their vocations or academic status; the latter group exhibited effort specifically directed toward receipt of academic or vocational rewards.

The focus on females' achievement striving in self-selected activities is particularly needed because of the relative neglect of females in much theory and research on achievement motivation. There appears to be a need for females to develop achievement orientations and to express them in a variety of areas including, but not restricted to, academic and occupational attainment. Nevertheless, the male pattern of achievement is not necessarily an ideal model for females to emulate. More development of achievement orientations by females might lead to new patterns that do not conform to current definitions of either the male or female roles. The emphasis on female patterns has led us to exclude most studies dealing only with male subjects, and to be sensitive to previous interpretations of data that smack of sex stereotypes instead of research-based accounts of females' attitudes and behavior.

The literature reviewed falls primarily in the period from 1958 to 1972. Studies measuring achievement behavior are given more weight than those restricted to projective or psychometric measures of achievement motivation because behavioral indexes appear to have greater validity, particularly for females and young children of both sexes. The term "achievement motivation" comes from a particular theoretical context (McClelland, Atkinson, Clark, & Lowell, 1953). Other theories focus on achievement striving and achievement behaviors. We use the term "achievement orientation" as a general rubric to encompass both types of research.

Coverage is restricted to middle-class whites because most of the research has been conducted with this group. The few studies of working-class or black groups suggest that different patterns exist (e.g., Solomon, 1969). Conclusions from middle-class whites cannot be safely generalized to other demographic groups.

THEORIES OF ACHIEVEMENT MOTIVATION AND BEHAVIOR

The most widely known theory of achievement motivation was initially proposed by McClelland et al. (1953). They conceptualized achievement motivation as a relatively stable disposition to strive for success in *any* situation where standards of excellence are applicable, that is, as a motive that generalized across achievement areas. This conceptualization has received reasonably good support in studies of males but not with females. The projective measures of achievement motivation typically used are not correlated with achievement effort or with academic and intellectual performance for females (Entwisle, 1972). Arousal conditions in which intelligence and leadership are stressed do not lead to increases in females' scores (Alper & Greenberger, 1967; Veroff, Wilcox, & Atkinson,

1953). In the Veroff et al. studies, females' scores in both neutral and aroused conditions were equivalent to those obtained from males following arousal.

In one of the more recent formulations (Atkinson & Feather, 1966), two motives have been proposed: hope of success and fear of failure. Hope of success corresponds to the original achievement motive. Fear of failure is operationally defined as test anxiety. In a particular situation, the aroused motivation is thought to be a function of *expectancy* of success and the *incentive value* of success or failure as well as the relative strength of hope of success and fear of failure. The principal behavioral indicators of aroused motivation are achievement effort (e.g., persistence) and level of aspiration.

Adult males for whom hope of success is greater than fear of failure set moderate levels of aspiration and show their greatest achievement effort on moderately difficult tasks. Those for whom fear of failure predominates set very low or very high levels of aspiration and show the greatest achievement effort on easy or difficult tasks (Atkinson & Feather, 1966). Virtually no research has been conducted with females using this expanded theoretical formulation.

The Crandalls (Crandall & Battle, 1970; Crandall, Katkovsky, & Preston, 1960) have proposed a model that applies to children and adults of both sexes in which there are three determinants of motivation in a given situation: *expectancy of success, attainment value* (the value attached to a particular type of achievement), and *standards of performance*. The minimum standard of performance is defined as the lowest level that an individual considers satisfactory. The principal index of motivation is *achievement behavior* such as task persistence, attempts at mastery, and working alone. It is assumed that motivation is specific to particular achievement areas rather than being generalized. This assumption of specificity is useful in explaining the absence of confirmation of the McClelland-Atkinson theory with females. In studies testing that theory, motivation usually has been measured in situations stressing intellectual and leadership skill. It is likely that cultural sex role definitions lead many females to show motivation in other areas that are more sex appropriate.

SEX ROLE EFFECTS ON FEMALE ACHIEVEMENT STRIVING

Sex Role Definitions of Achievement Areas

Children learn cultural sex role definitions of achievement areas by early elementary school, and these are well ingrained by adolescence. In two studies, children from the second through twelfth grades considered social, verbal, and artistic skills feminine and considered mechanical, spatial, and athletic skills masculine. Math was also considered masculine by adolescents but not by younger children (Stein, 1971; Stein & Smithells, 1969).

Attainment Values and Standards of Performance

Attainment value refers to the value an individual attaches to performing well in a given achievement area. Minimum standard of performance is the lowest level of competence that satisfies the individual. Females exhibit higher attainment values and standards of performance in sex-appropriate achievement areas, particularly social skill, than in sex-inappropriate skills. In three studies, including students from the sixth to twelfth grades, females had higher attainment values and standards for English, verbal skills, social skills, and artistic accomplishments than for natural sciences, athletic, and mechanical skills. Lowered value for math occurred only for the twelfth graders (Battle, 1965, 1966; Stein, 1971). In one study of elementary school children (Crandall, Katkovsky, & Preston, 1962), females had higher attainment values than males for intellectual skills when they rank ordered the importance of intellectual, artistic, athletic, and mechanical skills. The higher rank assigned to intellectual skills by females is probably a result of the sex-typed character of the other achievement areas. In an experimental study (Stein, Pohly, & Mueller, 1971), sixth-grade females exhibited higher attainment values and expectancies of success on tasks labeled "feminine" and "neutral" than on "masculine" tasks.

Attainment value for a given area of achievement is a good predictor of females' achievement effort and performance in that area. Studies of various age groups have shown substantial correlations between attainment value for an area of achievement and persistence at tasks in that area (Battle, 1965; Crandall et al., 1962; Stein et al., 1971). Attainment values are also correlated with competence in a given area (Battle, 1966; Crandall et al., 1962). Minimum standards were positively related to competence in one study of junior high school students (Battle, 1966), but not in a study of elementary-school-age children (Crandall et al., 1962).

Effects of Social Arousal

Arousal treatments that stress one important feminine area, social acceptability and skill rather than intelligence and leadership, do sometimes lead to increased achievement motivation for adult females. When college females were told they were socially acceptable *or* that they were not, their achievement motivation scores were higher than in a neutral condition; no effects of this arousal treatment appeared for males (Field, 1953). In two more recent studies of college women, arousal stressing social skill was given to part of the sample. Subjects had previously taken a "value orientation" scale designed to tap intellectual values and traditional women's role values (primarily social skills). In the first study (French & Lesser, 1964), women who attended colleges in which most students valued women's role activities showed increased achievement motivation after social skills arousal. Friedrich and Harding[3] attempted to replicate this finding by comparing individuals within the same college who varied in women's role values, but found no differences in their response to social skills arousal. This suggests that the French and Lesser findings may have been due to the

[3] L. K. Friedrich & J. Harding. Achievement motivation and academic performance in women. Final report to the National Institute of Mental Health, 1968. (The report may be obtained from Lynette Friedrich, S-105 Human Development Building, Pennsylvania State University, University Park, Pennsylvania 16802.)

impact of social norms rather than to internalized value systems of individuals.

It appears from these findings that many females (though not all) are likely to express their achievement motivation in areas that are defined as part of the traditional women's role, particularly social skill. One important finding from the Friedrich and Harding (see Footnote 3) study lends further support to this view. In addition to scoring achievement motivation in the standard way (intellectual need for achievement), they scored imagery concerning women's role activities such as marriage, heterosexual popularity, and social leadership in which the goal was attainment of excellence rather than affiliation (women's role need for achievement). There were low positive correlations of women's role achievement motivation with grade average and with achievement *effort* (i.e., amount produced) on a "social skills" test.

Performance

The sex appropriateness of a task can also affect performance. Milton [4] performed a series of studies in which mathematical and logical problems were administered to males and females in two versions. One had masculine content, the other had feminine content. The operations involved were otherwise identical, for example, dividing a circle or dividing a cake. Two samples of college females performed better on the feminine version than on the masculine version; males showed the reverse pattern. This finding was not replicated with high school students or with another group of college students when mathematical ability was controlled (Hoffman & Maier, 1966). A more indirect piece of evidence comes from a study by Carey (1958) in which a discussion aimed at improving attitudes toward problem solving was effective in improving females' performance on mathematical problems but had no effect on males' performance.

---

[4] G. A. Milton. *Five studies of the relation between sex-role identification and achievement in problem solving.* (Tech. Rep. 3) New Haven: Yale University, Department of Industrial Administration and Department of Psychology, December 1958.

Summary

The findings reviewed support the hypothesis that females' achievement orientations are likely to be manifested in areas which represent culturally defined sex-appropriate activities. Perhaps the most important area, especially for adult females, is social skill. Females set high attainment values and standards of performance in sex-appropriate areas, and these values and standards predict their effort and performance. Arousal treatments stressing social skill often result in increased achievement imagery; furthermore, imagery involving achievement in female-role-related activities is correlated with effort and performance. Finally, feminine content in a task results in better performance than when the content is masculine.

AFFILIATION AS A GOAL OF ACHIEVEMENT BEHAVIOR

The importance of social skill to females' achievement orientations has frequently been interpreted in a different framework than that used in the previous section. Many writers have hypothesized that female achievement behavior is instigated by affiliation motivation or need for social approval rather than by achievement motivation. The evidence is discussed in some detail because we do not believe it provides adequate support for the hypothesis. Instead, it suggests that social skill and interpersonal relations are often important areas of achievement (i.e., attainment of excellence) for females.

Crandall's Hypothesis

Crandall (1963) proposed that achievement behavior of both boys and girls is initially directed toward obtaining social approval. With development, he suggested that boys internalize standards of excellence and come to rely on their own satisfaction in meeting these standards rather than on reinforcement from others. Girls' achievement efforts were thought to remain more dependent on external social rewards, though the reasons for this sex difference were not specified. As one piece of evidence for his hypothesis, Crandall cited a study in which young girls' achievement efforts in free play were correlated with approval seeking, while those of boys were not (Crandall, Dewey, Katkovsky, & Preston, 1964). Females also score higher than males on a questionnaire measure of concern with social desirability or with receiving social approval, but this measure does not relate consistently to females' achievement efforts (Crandall, 1966). That is, in some fashion, females may be more concerned with social approval than males, but this concern does not determine their achievement behavior.

Social Approval and Disapproval

If Crandall's hypothesis were correct, one would expect relatively low achievement effort by females in experimental situations where no social rewards are given and relatively high effort when praise is received. In the large literature on social reinforcement, there are not consistent sex differences of this kind even when conditions involving social praise are compared with conditions where the child works alone (Cotler & Palmer, 1971; Stein, 1969; Stevenson, 1965).

Similarly, females respond to social disapproval or criticism in an achievement situation with at least as much achievement effort and learning as males. Elementary school boys and girls showed similar reactions to criticism of their performance in studies measuring rate of response (Hill, 1967; Stein, 1969), expectancies of success (Montanelli & Hill, 1969), reading performance (Cotler & Palmer, 1971), and persistence and accuracy on a pursuit-rotor task (McManis, 1965). In two studies of college students, females manifested greater effort and better performance than males when their performance was criticized (Hetherington & Ross, 1963; Yonge, 1964).

Correlations of Social and Achievement Behaviors

Another source cited by Crandall was a study of fifth- and sixth-grade children[5] in which a projective measure of affiliation mo-

[5] P. S. Sears. *The effects of classroom conditions on the strength of achievement motive and work output of elementary school children.* (Cooperative Research Project No. 873), Washington, D. C.: U. S. Office of Education, 1963.

tivation predicted achievement test scores of females slightly better than achievement motivation scores. Affiliation motivation did not predict task-oriented classroom behavior, however, nor did it predict "social work," defined as "any social remark, interchange, or action which is work-oriented." Furthermore, the high-IQ females in the sample maintained stable levels of task orientation during the school year despite the fact that the teachers switched from positive ratings of task-oriented girls in the fall to negative ratings in the spring on such dimensions as how much they liked the student. Apparently such behavior by girls resulted in a withdrawal of reinforcement by the teachers. Social work among bright girls, by contrast, was associated with positive ratings by the teacher suggesting that teachers reinforced achievement orientations if they were evidenced in a social context, but reacted negatively to female task orientation which did not have the social component. This pattern did not occur for boys.

Veroff's Hypothesis

Veroff (1969) also proposed that females' achievement motivation is more dependent on external social cues and rewards than that of boys, but his developmental formulation contradicts that of Crandall (1963). His initial stage for both sexes is autonomous achievement motivation, a period in which the child learns to evaluate his performance against his own standards. The second step is social comparison achievement motivation during which the child learns to compare his or her performance with others. Finally, these two types of motivation are thought to be integrated. He proposed that females pass through this developmental sequence more slowly than males and less often reach the final stage of integration, though again the reasons are unclear.

Although this formulation is concerned with the sources of the child's standards, it is assumed that autonomous motivation is associated with internalized rewards and social comparison motivation with dependence on social rewards. This assumption is questionable, but even if one accepts it, the data provide skimpy support for the theory. High motivation is indicated by the selection of *moderate* levels of aspiration when the subject has information about his own past performance (autonomous) or about other children's performance (social comparison). Among samples from 5 to 11 years old, females' autonomous motivation scores were higher than males' after first grade, but the sexes did not differ on social comparison scores. Integrated motivation was measured with a projective device. Males' scores were higher, but all of the stimulus pictures contained male figures!

Veroff (1969, p. 77) also cited as evidence a study of second graders by Lahtinen in which both males and females responded to a threat of social rejection with increased task persistence. Only the males also responded to mastery arousal, but this difference may be due to differential appropriateness of the tasks for females and males (lifting weights and untying knots). The author dismissed this differential appropriateness rather lightly. One wonders whether he would be so willing to draw conclusions about males if they were asked to dress and undress dolls. In any case, as both sexes responded to social arousal, this study does not support the hypothesis that females are more concerned about social approval than males.

Achievement in Social Skills

We propose that the evidence discussed supports the hypothesis that social skills are a central area of *achievement* concern for many females, not that female achievement efforts are instigated primarily by affiliation motives or desire for social approval per se. The goal is attainment of a standard of excellence, but the areas in which such attainment is most important are somewhat different from males. The argument that achievement rather than affiliation is the important motivational system is supported by the fact that social arousal led to achievement imagery, not affiliation imagery, in the studies cited earlier. This revised hypothesis also explains the absence of sex differences in experimental studies of social reinforcement. In those studies, the task or area of achievement is nonsocial; the reinforcement serves as information about performance. Finally, the Crandall et al. (1964) and Sears (see Footnote 5)

findings may be interpreted as indicating that females combine social activity with achievement strivings more often than males, partly because adults reinforce them for doing so. That is, females are not necessarily more sensitive to social approval; they may receive social approval for a more social pattern of achievement behavior than males do.

IMPACT OF SEX-TYPED PERSONALITY ATTRIBUTES

The argument thus far has been focused on the differential prescriptions of sex role definitions for activities or tasks in which achievement is appropriate. Many of the personality attributes that are generally defined as feminine such as nonassertiveness, avoidance of competition, and dependency are in conflict with achievement motivation as it is usually manifested in intellectual and occupational contexts. For example, females in our culture are taught that competition, particularly with a male, is unfeminine and may result in social rejection ("Don't ever let a boy know you're smarter than he is, dear, or he won't want to date you."). Horner (1972) demonstrated that college females often manifested a "fear of success" in competitive situations with males. In response to a story about a woman who was at the top of her medical school class, many females produced story completions indicating a fear that such success would lead to social rejection, loss of attractiveness to males, or a lack of femininity. Females who expressed this fear performed more poorly on a test administered in a group situation with "competitive" cues than they did when they were alone. Males, and the smaller group of females who showed little fear of success, performed better in the group situation than alone.

College women also showed reduced effort on a dynamometer when they attained higher scores than a male partner (Weiss, 1962). At the same time, the women manifested increased social–emotional interaction toward their male partners, evidently using their social skills to make the man feel better. In the posttest inquiry, many of the women expressed discomfort about reducing their effort. In this study, the partners were working for a combined score, so there was no official sanction for competition between partners.

Weiner (1966) studied same-sex and cross-sex pairs of college students in a situation where the two people were instructed to compete against each other. He found greater recall of incompleted tasks for individuals paired with females than for those paired with males, but this trend was stronger for male subjects than for female subjects. The recall measure was correlated with achievement motivation only for men, so its meaning is unclear for women. It may be that for males, comparing unfavorably to a female is more "arousing" or threatening than comparing unfavorably to a male because females are perceived as less competent.

INDIVIDUAL DIFFERENCES IN PATTERNS OF INTEGRATING ACHIEVEMENT STRIVING AND FEMININITY

Ambiguity of Societal Expectations

While many women appear to channel their achievement orientations into activities that are consistent with traditional feminine role definitions, there are many individual and group departures from this pattern. Some groups of women appear to adjust their concepts of femininity or their identifications with that role to include more "masculine" patterns of achievement striving. One important reason is probably the low status of most activities and spheres of work, such as child care and domestic responsibilities, defined as feminine in American society (see Sherman, 1971). The apologetic, "I'm just a housewife" or "I don't do anything" that one frequently hears reflects the low status of the traditional domestic role. Thus, although there are pressures to engage in feminine role-related activities, there are relatively few rewards for doing so. On the other hand, there are rewards as well as negative feedback for the woman who chooses to pursue occupational achievement in her own right. In a sense, there is no path that a woman can choose that is as highly rewarded and relatively conflict free as high occupational achievement is for a man. It is not surprising then that women have evolved a variety of patterns and techniques for engaging in achieve-

ment striving and integrating that activity with their roles as females.

Variations in Sex Role Definitions

Cultural sex role stereotypes are widely known and understood, but some females appear to define achievement-related behavior as more feminine than others. When they define achievement as feminine, they are more likely to manifest achievement-related behavior (Stein, 1971). A study by Lesser, Krawitz, and Packard (1963) also suggested that high school females who performed well in school considered achievement more sex appropriate than underachievers did. Achievers produced increased achievement imagery in stories about females following an arousal treatment; underachievers showed such increases only in stories about men. Among college students, Sundheim (1963) found no differences in sex role concepts among majors in science, liberal arts, and education, but Lipman-Blumen (1972) found that young women with nontraditional sex role concepts had higher educational aspirations and were more likely to consider their own achievement (as opposed to their husband's) important than women with more traditional sex role standards.

Variations in Sex Role Identification

Knowledge of sex role definitions does not necessarily lead to adoption of or identification with that role. If achievement striving is a masculine characteristic, it might be related to identification with the masculine role by females. Some evidence suggests that this is the case, at least when striving is measured in achievement areas that are generally considered masculine. Sixth-grade females who expressed high preferences for the masculine sex role were more persistent on a masculine task than girls with low masculine preferences (Stein et al., 1971). An independent measure of feminine preferences in this study was unrelated to persistence. Ferguson and Maccoby (1966) also found that fifth-grade females with high spatial ability had low sex role acceptance. Oetzel [6] found that masculin-

[6] R. Oetzel. The relationships between sex role acceptance and cognitive abilities. Unpublished master's thesis, Stanford University, 1961.

ity was positively related to spatial ability and negatively related to verbal ability. Again, girls with spatial and verbal ability did not differ in femininity. In four studies of high school and college students, Milton (see Footnote 4) found positive correlations between masculine identification and performance on problems with masculine content. There were no correlations when the problems had feminine content. Crandall and Battle (1970) found that play with opposite-sex toys was a significant antecedent of females' intellectual achievement striving and academic performance in adulthood. However, Stein (1971) found no relation between sex role preferences and attainment value, expectancy, or standards in several sex-typed areas of achievement.

High achievement motivation is characteristic of women who manifest "masculine" interests by choosing a field of endeavor that departs from traditional feminine pursuits. In one study of college women, science majors had higher achievement motivation than language majors who were in turn higher than elementary education majors (Sundheim, 1963). Both Shelton (1968) and Baruch (1967) found that middle-aged professional women had higher achievement motivation than housewives of comparable ability and social status.

Lest these findings be interpreted as confirming a stereotype of the achieving woman as aggressive, pushy, and unfeminine, it is important to note that identification with the masculine role does not necessarily imply low femininity. Studies that have measured masculinity and femininity as two dimensions rather than opposite poles of one dimension have found zero-order correlations between the two (Stein et al., 1971; see also Footnote 6). Furthermore, Oetzel (cited in Maccoby, 1966) found that both characteristics were correlated with IQ for fifth-grade girls. This finding is consistent with reports that creativity is associated with characteristics of the opposite sex for both boys and girls (Maccoby, 1966). Perhaps children who are most effective in intellectual and creative endeavor have expanded their behavioral repertoires and self-perceptions to include

attributes associated with both sex roles rather than being restricted to one.

Vicarious Satisfaction

If a woman pursues a traditional feminine role, some satisfaction of achievement needs may be obtained vicariously through the accomplishments of a husband or children. Lipman-Blumen (1972) asked approximately 1,000 young college-educated married women whether they derived their primary satisfaction from their own accomplishments, their husband's accomplishments, or both equally. The majority of the sample considered their husband's accomplishments more gratifying. This pattern of vicarious gratification was more prevalent for women who espoused traditional views of the feminine role than for those with more "liberated" views.

Vicarious satisfaction of achievement needs may also be indicated by the finding that women produce more achievement imagery when given pictures or stories containing men than they do when the stimuli contain women (French & Lesser, 1964; Lesser et al., 1963; Veroff et al., 1953). This pattern is particularly marked for underachieving females (Lesser et al., 1963) or when intellectual achievement is emphasized (French & Lesser, 1964).

Feminine Career Choice

A woman may satisfy achievement needs while reducing some of the conflict with cultural sex role demands by choosing a feminine occupation or by remaining in a low status position in her occupation. Females fall disproportionately into careers that involve traditional feminine activities such as working with children, caring for the sick, and helping people. These career choices do not result entirely from internalized personality attributes. Strong negative sanctions are often applied to a woman who attempts to enter a "male" career such as medicine or engineering. Choice of a feminine career probably reduces both internally generated conflict and externally imposed negative feedback.

Concealing Accomplishments and Lowering Effort

In an earlier section, evidence was presented that public accomplishment, particularly in competitive situations, is sometimes threatening to females. One reaction to such conflict is reduced effort (Weiss, 1962). Another way of coping is concealing accomplishments, particularly from male peers. For instance, women report that they tell males that they received a lower grade than they actually attained (Horner, 1972).

Superwoman

Finally, a woman may "compensate" for her achievement striving by being super-feminine in appearance and personality. A woman who is physically attractive and who exhibits feminine qualities such as nonassertiveness, social–emotional forms of interaction in groups, and submissiveness can avoid many of the negative sanctions often associated with achievement striving. People may even comment that she is not like a "career woman" (i.e., she does not fit their stereotype of the loud, aggressive, domineering woman).

A related means of compensation involves performing all the functions of the traditional domestic role in addition to a career. Such a woman attempts to provide her husband and her children with all the "benefits" that they would have if she were fully devoted to a traditional feminine role. She may entertain lavishly, keep her house immaculate, assume full responsibility for child care, and cook gourmet meals. Such a pattern may, of course, reflect generalized achievement motivation that is expressed in women's role activities as well as intellectual activities. To these authors, it appears to be a physically and emotionally exhausting way of living that may have considerable psychological costs.

Summary

Both achievement striving and adherence to the traditional feminine role result in mixed rewards and punishments for women. Women have evolved a variety of means of combining the two and reducing, if not eliminating, the conflict between them. Females

with high achievement motivation define achievement as being more feminine than those with low motivation. Those who manifest achievement effort in areas that are usually considered masculine have relatively high masculine role identification, but not necessarily low identification with the feminine role.

Within the traditional feminine role, achievement needs may be partially satisfied vicariously through the accomplishments of a husband. Choice of a feminine career area is a more direct means of expressing achievement motivation while avoiding some sex role conflicts. Concealing achievement or temporarily reducing effort is another way of coping with the conflict generated by public accomplishment in competitive situations. Finally, conflicts may be reduced by manifesting feminine personality attributes and by performing traditional feminine role functions well while engaging in achievement striving.

DEVELOPMENTAL CHANGES

Many of the patterns discussed appear to develop gradually from the preschool years on, but some authors have suggested that adolescence is a particularly important time because of a sudden increase in pressures to be feminine and attractive to males. One study demonstrated that high school female underachievers had normal levels of achievement until junior high, whereas male underachievers had been chronically poor in school from third grade on (Shaw & McCuen, 1960). At the same time that social pressure for sex role conformity increases sharply, females are becoming more aware that academic achievement is not directly relevant to the future goals dictated by the feminine role. Adolescent females studied by Douvan and Adelson (1966) had much less realistic and clear goals for their adult lives than males. Their ambivalence was manifested in the fact that when they were asked what they expected to do in adulthood most of these females named a career rather than saying housewife. The careers, however, were more often on a fantasy level (e.g., movie star) than on a level permitting realistic planning.

Recent data (reported by Horner, 1972) suggest that the college years may be also a time of changing social pressures for females. As a woman nears the end of her college career, her parents and peers often become intensely concerned with her marrying; earlier value on academic accomplishment appears to drop considerably. Females often begin to major in "masculine" subjects such as science, but switch to majors in the humanities and education later in the college years; they also lower their career aspirations. The small proportion of females who do not manifest "fear of success" are exceptions to these trends.

Adolescence (including college) probably is an important period, but longitudinal data indicate that motivation in early adolescence and adulthood is correlated with motivation during the elementary years for females (Crandall & Battle, 1970; Kagan & Moss, 1962). Adolescence does not create entirely new patterns. Rather, it is likely that a female's response to the changes in social expectations in adolescence depends partly on her earlier patterns of achievement-related behavior.

During adulthood, data from one study (Baruch, 1967) indicate that intellectual achievement motivation declines during the period usually devoted intensively to child rearing, then increases for well-educated women. The increase appears to precede slightly the time when family responsibilities are reduced and active professional activity can readily be undertaken. These conclusions are, however, based on cross-sectional comparisons, so some of the differences may be due to generation rather than developmental period. The women with the lowest achievement motivation graduated from college in the early 1950s, an era that has been characterized as the height of the "feminine mystique" of domesticity and motherhood (Friedan, 1963).

FEMALE PATTERNS OF ACHIEVEMENT-RELATED CHARACTERISTICS

In the theories that form the basis for most of the achievement motivation research, several variables in addition to those already discussed are postulated as determinants of achievement behavior. These include expectancies of success, level of aspiration, anxiety about failure, and belief in personal responsibility for success and failure. In this section, these variables are examined to determine the extent to which they form an integrated pattern of determinants for females. This analysis includes comparisons of females with males, examination of the correlations of these variables with indices of achievement effort and performance for females, and discussion of developmental changes.

Expectancy of Success

Crandall (1969) reported a series of studies on various age groups showing that females had lower expectancies of success than males even when their performance was superior. For example, during a two-year period, the expected course grades of women students at Antioch were lower than grades men expected despite the fact that the female's actual grades were slightly higher. Similar sex differences are reported by Battle (1966), Deaux and Emswiller,[7] Montanelli and Hill (1969), Stein (1971), and Strickland (1971). These sex differences occur across many achievement areas. Crandall (1969) tested and found no evidence for the following as possible reasons for expectancy differences: differences in past success or reinforcement history, parental differences in expectations and standards, differences in the sex appropriateness of making high verbal estimates of one's ability, and differences in immediate assimilation of positive and aversive consequences in achievement situations. There was some indication of long-term differences in assimilation when feedback had been neutral or contradictory.

One reason for lower female expectancies may be the generalized sex role stereotype in the culture that females are less competent than males. The professional and artistic work of females is often perceived as less competent than that of males even when the products being rated are identical. In one study (Goldberg, 1968), college women rated professional articles less favorably when the alleged author was female than when it was male. This finding was not replicated in a later study (Baruch, 1972) perhaps because the sample

[7] K. Deaux & T. Emswiller. Explanations of successful performance on sex-linked tasks: What's skill for the male is luck for the female. Unpublished manuscript, Purdue University, 1972.

was more sophisticated or more aware of issues raised by the women's movement during the years intervening between the two studies. Students also rated identical artistic works labeled with female names less favorably than those with male names, but this difference was eliminated when the paintings were presented as contest winners, that is, when there was some external evidence of the artist's success (Pheterson, Kiesler, & Goldberg, 1971). Chairmen of 147 psychology departments rated credentials of potential faculty members with male and female names randomly assigned (Fidell, 1970). The mean academic rank that would be offered to females was significantly lower than that offered males with identical credentials, and there was some tendency to less favorable ratings of the females. The kindest interpretation that can be made is that these department chairmen are influenced by a sex role stereotype of which they are largely unaware. Even when females are perceived as performing competently, their performance is more likely to be attributed to luck as opposed to skill than that of males. This difference is particularly apparent when performance on a masculine task is rated (see Footnote 7). Finally, an anecdote. One of the authors recently asked a gas station attendant for directions and was told he would explain the easy way "so the lady can find it."

Despite the mean sex difference, expectancy of success predicts achievement behavior and performance for adolescent and college females about as well as for males. In four studies of this age group, Crandall and her associates (Crandall, 1969) found low to moderate correlations between females' expectancies and academic performance. Expectancies in math were also related to persistence on a math problem (Battle, 1965). There is some indication, however, that elementary school females' expectancies are not positively related to achievement behavior (Crandall et al., 1962; Stein et al., 1971) or to performance on intelligence and achievement tests (Crandall et al., 1962). Positive relations did occur for males in these studies. More data are needed to draw firm conclusions, but these findings suggest that expectancies are not good predictors before adolescence. Another developmental

pattern was suggested in a study of sixth and ninth graders (Stein, 1971). The expectancies of the older females were lower than those of the younger girls; the reverse pattern occurred for males (middle-class subjects). This trend is congruent with the fact that females' superiority in school achievement decreases with age.

Level of Aspiration

Level of aspiration and expectancy are sometimes used interchangeably in the literature, but there is an important distinction between the two. Expectancies measure what the individual believes she will be able to do, while level of aspiration measures what level of difficulty the individual chooses to *attempt*. The goals chosen probably reflect not only expectancy of success but the level of risk the person is willing to tolerate.

Females typically set lower levels of aspiration than males. In one study (Crandall & Rabson, 1960), elementary school girls were more likely than boys to repeat a task on which they had previously succeeded than one on which they had failed, but this finding was not replicated on a slightly older sample (Butterfield, 1965). Using a variety of tasks, Veroff (1969) found that female children chose a very easy task more often than males. Males chose a very difficult task more often than females. The proportion of females who chose tasks of intermediate difficulty was either equal to or slightly higher than the proportion of males making such choices. By Veroff's definition, selection of the intermediate difficulty level is indicative of high achievement motivation. It is usually the most adaptive choice for attainment of long-range success. The fact that the sexes are about equally likely to set this adaptive level of aspiration is important because boys' higher levels of aspiration have sometimes been interpreted as indicators of greater motivation. That interpretation is not consistent with achievement motivation theory. Instead, the sex difference occurs in the direction taken by those children who set less adaptive goals. Girls err in the direction of overcautiousness by choosing easy tasks; boys err in the direction of undercautiousness by choosing difficult tasks. These trends occur across achievement areas.

The age trends in these studies initially appear contradictory. On Veroff's tasks, choice of intermediate and difficult tasks increased with age in samples from 5 to 11 years old. On the other hand, in the Crandall and Rabson (1960) and Butterfield (1965) studies, there was either no increase or a slight decrease with age in the number of girls who chose to repeat previously failed tasks. In both studies, boys showed an increase with age. The critical difference between these studies and those reported by Veroff (1969) appears to be the experience of failure. We tentatively conclude that females' levels of aspiration increase during the elementary years (as do males'), but there is also a developmental increase in their tendency to avoid situations involving failure when they are given a choice.

Anxiety about Failure

It appears that females are more anxious about failure in academic situations than males and that their anxiety levels increase during the elementary years more than males. Females score higher than males on questionnaire measures of test anxiety (Feld & Lewis, 1969; Hill & Sarason, 1966; Sarason, Lighthall, Davidson, Waite, & Ruebush, 1960; Wallach & Kogan, 1965). In a five-year longitudinal study, Hill and Sarason (1966) found that sex differences were absent in the first grade but had appeared by the third grade. Though both sexes showed some increase with age, the gap between males and females was larger the older the children were. As all of these studies are concerned with academic tasks, it is not possible to tell whether these differences generalize to other achievement areas.

The validity of these findings is sometimes questioned on the grounds that females are more willing than males to admit anxiety on a questionnaire. It is true that males score higher on scales designed to detect defensiveness and false reporting (Hill & Sarason, 1966). Nevertheless, the same cultural norm that permits females to express anxiety more easily may also lead them to experience it more readily and to defend against it less effectively. The differences in expectancies, levels of aspiration, and response to failure

discussed above support the hypothesis of a real difference in anxiety. The pattern described for females is very similar to that obtained from highly anxious males in other research (Atkinson & Feather, 1966).

In an earlier review, Maccoby (1966) concluded that anxiety was negatively related to achievement for females but not for males. The literature at this date does not support that sex difference. Anxiety is usually correlated negatively with achievement for both sexes, although the data are not entirely in agreement. Sarason et al. (1960) and Lunneberg (1964) found negative correlations of anxiety with achievement test performance. In experimental situations, Cotler and Palmer (1971) and Lekarczyk and Hill (1969) reported negative correlations between anxiety and learning; Hill and Dusek (1969) found a negative correlation between anxiety and expectancies. Other studies have found no correlation between anxiety and school achievement (Crandall et al., 1962; Lekarczyk & Hill, 1969; Stanford, Dember, & Stanford, 1963). Finally, one discrepant result if IQ is interpreted as achievement: Increases in IQ from age 6 to 10 were positively related to anxiety for female children in the Fels sample (Sontag & Baker, 1958).

Belief in Personal Responsibility

Crandall, Katkovsky, and Crandall (1965) devised a measure of internal control specific to achievement situations called intellectual achievement responsibility. It is designed to determine the extent to which the person perceives that consequences in achievement situations are due to his own behavior (internal) or due to factors outside his control (external). There are two subscales that are not highly correlated with each other: I+ indicating the degree of responsibility assumed for success and I−, assumed responsibility for failure. Females score higher than males throughout the school years on I−, and the gap increases in adolescence. Females generally score higher on the total score as well. This tendency to assume increasing responsibility for academic achievement, especially failure, is congruent with the hypothesis that females become more anxious and concerned about failure as they progress through the school years. Again, these studies are concerned only with academic achievement, not other areas.

Generally, intellectual achievement responsibility is not as good a predictor of achievement-related behavior for females as for males. Crandall et al. (1962) reported that females' internal responsibility scores were not related to achievement behavior in free play or to intelligence and achievement test scores. Females' scores also did not predict task efficiency or frustration–anxiety behaviors during a problem-solving task involving assembling a "Chinese puzzle." [8] Adult females' achievement effort was not predicted by internal responsibility during childhood and adolescence (Crandall & Battle, 1970). In each instance the parallel correlations were positive for males.

There is some evidence that internal responsibility is related to academic and problem-solving performance for females. On a large sample of third through fifth graders, internal responsibility was positively related to grades and achievement test scores for females. This finding was not replicated, however, on a smaller sample including older children (McGhee & Crandall, 1968). The relation was positive for males in both samples. Performance on an embedded figures task was related to internal responsibility for both sexes (see Footnote 8).

Achievement Behavior in Response to Failure

When females are exposed to failure on a task, they exhibit as much achievement effort and learning as males do. Among preschool children, Wyer (1968) found no sex differences in persistence on a difficult task with no social approval. Zunich (1964) found that girls were more likely than boys to attempt to solve a difficult task alone, to seek information, and to seek contact from an adult and were less likely to seek help, be destructive, or rationalize. In a recent series of three studies, Crandall [9] found that fourth- and

---

[8] V. C. Crandall. *Parents' influences on children's achievement behavior.* (Progress report to National Institute of Mental Health) Yellow Springs, Ohio: Fels Research Institute, December 1965.

[9] V. C. Crandall. *Progress report on the achievement development project.* (Progress report to the National

eighth-grade females responded with greater effort when they were failing to meet a previously established standard than when they were succeeding. Males showed the same pattern in two studies, but not in the third. The studies cited earlier on response to social disapproval also support the absence of sex differences in response to failure. Thus, despite the fact that females are more anxious about failure and are less likely to select tasks that threaten failure when given a choice, they apparently can function at least as efficiently and with at least as much persistence as males when they must cope with failure.

Summary

These studies form a picture suggesting that females are more anxious about failure, more cautious in risking failure, and more likely to assume responsibility for failure when it occurs than is the case for males. Some of these differences apply across achievement areas; others have been demonstrated only in relation to academic achievement. All of these characteristics appear to increase during middle childhood and adolescence. Females also have lower expectancies of success and in turn are perceived as less competent than males even when their work is identical. During the elementary school years, levels of aspiration increase, but there is some evidence that expectancies of success decrease in adolescence. Females are as likely as males to set moderate levels of aspiration, but those who do not are more likely to set low levels rather than high ones. In addition, when confronted with a task involving failure rather than a situation involving a choice of tasks, females show as much effort and learning as males do.

Some of these characteristics are less consistently related to achievement behavior and academic performance for females than for males. Internal responsibility is less often related to achievement effort for females than for males, but is generally related to academic performance. Expectancies are correlated with performance in adolescence, but not necessarily for younger children. Some studies

Institute of Mental Health) Yellow Springs, Ohio: Fels Research Institute, 1972.

show negative correlations of anxiety with performance; others find no relation.

SOCIALIZATION BY PARENTS

Now that the various patterns of achievement orientation and behavior that appear to characterize the development of females have been described, we turn to the socialization literature to gain some insight into the ways in which children learn these patterns. As the focus of the article is on understanding how females may become more motivated to independent achievement, the literature on child rearing is examined with that end in mind. Correlations within groups of females are discussed; sex differences in child rearing are not our concern here. Some females have developed strong achievement orientations that have been congruent with their roles as women; information about their child-rearing experiences may help to understand how that pattern is acquired.

Stable patterns of achievement-oriented behavior and related dispositions such as independence are acquired by females in childhood, and parental socialization during that period appears to have long-term effects. In longitudinal studies (Crandall & Battle, 1970; Kagan & Moss, 1962), achievement behavior and independence from middle childhood through early adolescence are predictive of adult achievement behavior and independence for females. Similarly early child-rearing practices are associated with adolescent and adult behavior with surprising frequency. In the following section, socialization practices from early childhood through adolescence are examined in relation to achievement-oriented behavior and accompanying characteristics such as independence and activity (as opposed to passivity).

Two dimensions emerge most frequently in factor analyses of child-rearing practices (Becker, 1964). The first is warmth–hostility, the second is permissiveness–restrictiveness.

Warmth–Hostility

The weight of the evidence indicates that a moderate, but not high, level of warmth or nurturance is most conducive to achieve-ment behavior in females. Both very high levels of nurturance and high levels of punishment or rejection are associated with relatively low achievement behavior. For three separate samples from the Fels longitudinal study, early babying, protectiveness, and warmth were negatively associated with later achievement behavior. Crandall and Battle (1970) found a negative correlation between adult intellectual achievement effort and earlier maternal babying and protectiveness. Kagan and Moss (1962) found that early protection was related to adult passivity and feminine interests while adult achievement behavior of females was positively related to early maternal hostility. Adolescent females who tended to withdraw from achievement tasks had mothers who had been highly accepting and affectionate during the early years (Kagan & Freeman, 1963). Achievement motivation was also positively related to adolescent females' tendency to be critical and aggressive toward their mothers (Lansky, Crandall, Kagan, & Baker, 1961). As adults, females who were high on intellectual achievement effort recalled their fathers as being hostile and rejecting (Crandall & Battle, 1970).

Among preschool children, maternal nurturance was not related to achievement behavior in free play, but the amount of reinforcement that the mother gave specifically for achievement effort and for approval seeking was related to achievement behavior. Nevertheless, the mothers who rewarded achievement efforts were less affectionate and less positive in their responses to dependency than those who did not reward achievement efforts (Crandall, Preston, & Rabson, 1960).

Relatively low levels of nurturance are also conducive to acquisition of achievement-related behavior in experimental studies. Preschool children were more persistent on a task when the experimenter was nonnurturant than when she was nurturant (Mandel, 1968). When a model exhibited high standards of performance to elementary school children, they imitated more when the model was non-nurturant than when he or she was nurturant (Bandura, Grusec, & Menlove, 1967). This find is striking because nurturance facilitates imitation of many other kinds of behavior (Bandura, 1969).

The studies reported thus far suggest a negative linear relation between achievement behavior and maternal nurturance rather than a curvilinear one. It is likely, however, that the range of nurturance and hostility sampled in many of the studies cited is not sufficient to show negative effects of extreme hostility and rejection. A curvilinear relation did appear in a longitudinal assessment in which child-rearing practices at age 5 were studied in relation to level of aspiration at age 18 (Crowne, Conn, Marlowe, & Edwards, 1969). Low levels of aspiration were related to early protectiveness, warmth, and low punishment; high levels, to early punishment and low warmth. Thus, the moderate levels of aspiration usually associated with high achievement motivation occurred for children whose mothers were moderate on the warmth–hostility dimension.

Studies of independence, responsibility, and leadership also support a curvilinear relation. In an extensive analysis of competence in preschool children (Baumrind, 1971; Baumrind & Black, 1967), children whose parents used coercive punishment extensively and were authoritarian had very low autonomy and achievement-oriented behavior. Independence and achievement-oriented behavior were associated with a pattern, described as authoritative, that included moderate warmth and some punishment. Among adolescent females, Bronfenbrenner (1961) found that high levels of either parental nurturance or parental rejection and hostility were associated with low responsibility and leadership for females. Douvan and Adelson (1966) also found that achievement-oriented female adolescents had pleasant, but not close, relations with their families. Heilbrun and his colleagues (Heilbrun, Harrell, & Gillard, 1967; Heilbrun & Orr, 1965) have found few consistent relations of nurturance to achievement-related behavior for college women, perhaps because they split the subjects into high- and low-nurturance groups that obscured possible curvilinear trends.

One exception to the pattern described was the finding by Katkovsky, Crandall, and Good (1967) that high personal responsibility for achievement was positively associated with babying and protectiveness and negatively

related to rejection. These findings were only partly replicated on a second sample, possibly because of the use of a questionnaire rather than observation. The pattern of parental socialization that leads to high personal responsibility may be more typical of female children than males. This may be why females score higher than males, but personal responsibility does not predict females' achievement behavior as well as it does that of males.

The findings concerning nurturance make sense when one examines the relation between achievement orientation, dependence–independence, and the feminine sex role. High levels of maternal nurturance typically generate femininity for little girls (Mischel, 1970) with the accompanying patterns of dependency, passivity, and nonassertiveness. This appears particularly true when nurturance involves babying, protectiveness, and other forms of holding the child close to the mother. Achievement orientation, on the other hand, is associated with emotional independence, assertiveness, and competitiveness, all of which are traditionally unfeminine characteristics. The development of these attributes apparently requires sufficient affection and support to provide confidence and security, but not so much that the child does not move away from the mother. In addition, Baumrind (1971) suggested that moderate amounts of punishment and hostility may have a "toughening" or desensitizing effect that enables the child to handle challenge, competition, and risk of failure.

Restrictiveness–Permissiveness

Permissiveness in a context of moderate to high warmth is associated with independence in children while restrictiveness in such a context is associated with dependency and conformity (Becker, 1964). It is important to differentiate restrictions from demands for mature behavior or for high performance. Restrictiveness–permissiveness refers to the number of rules imposed that prohibit behaviors such as aggression, sexual expression, damage of property, and so on. Parents at either end of the continuum may or may not make demands for mature behavior.

In general, permissiveness is positively associated with achievement orientation for females, though it appears that other variables such as high demands on the child may be important additional factors. Baumrind (1971) found that permissiveness by both parents was associated with achievement-oriented behavior for female preschoolers. Independence and achievement behavior also occurred for children with authoritative parents—a pattern of firm control, moderate warmth, and use of reason associated with some punishment, but one in which the parents were not highly restrictive or coercive. Highly restrictive families had children who were low in achievement-oriented behavior. Among adolescent females, parental restrictiveness is associated with low achievement aspirations (Douvan & Adelson, 1966), low responsibility and leadership (Bronfenbrenner, 1961), and low levels of aspiration (Crowne et al., 1969).

By contrast, restrictiveness is positively related to femininity and passivity for young children and for adolescents (Douvan & Adelson, 1966; Hetherington, 1967; Kagan & Moss, 1962; Sears, Rau, & Alpert, 1965). Again, the child-rearing practices that lead to femininity are antagonistic to those associated with achievement behavior and related characteristics.

Independence Training

Early theorizing about the development of achievement motivation stressed independence training as an important variable (McClelland et al., 1953). Independence appears to be an important correlate of achievement striving for females, but the studies of independence training have generated mixed results (see Crandall, 1963).

One reason for the discrepancy in results appears to be that many studies have been focused on the training of instrumental independence, that is, on the mother's expectations that the child learn to do things for herself at an early age. The more critical variable appears to be emotional independence, or the ability of the child to move away from the parent emotionally and function on her own.

Emotional independence is apparently facilitated by differential reinforcement for independent behavior (Crandall, Preston, & Rabson, 1960) and by expectations for self-

care and autonomy (Nakamura & Rogers, 1969). The relation of independence training to achievement behavior is less clear. Baumrind (1971) found positive relations between encouragement of independence and achievement-oriented behavior. Hatfield, Ferguson, and Alpert (1967) found that preschool girls' achievement standards were negatively related to *both* pressure for independence and restrictions on independence, suggesting one reason for the conflict in findings. Independence training may involve permissiveness and supportive encouragement to venture out or it may involve rejection. The former should facilitate achievement motivation while the latter should inhibit it.

On a more molecular level, Hermans, ter Laak, and Maes (1972) examined the helpgiving reactions of parents when their children were performing achievement tasks. Parents of children with high achievement motivation gave more nonspecific help and less specific help than those whose children had low motivation. By contrast, those whose children had high anxiety were more likely to give specific help, especially to female children. It appears that high achievement motivation and low anxiety are most likely when the parent provides some general direction and interest but expects the child to perform on her own.

Encouragement of Achievement

Achievement orientation and behavior are positively related to various forms of parental encouragement of achievement effort including positive reinforcement, attempts at acceleration, and criticism for lack of effort. In one study of preschool children, achievement behavior in free play was positively related to maternal reinforcement for achievement effort (Crandall, Preston, & Rabson, 1960). Early attempts at achievement induction by the mother were associated with moderate and high levels of aspiration for middle-class preschool girls in another (Callard, 1968). For elementary school children, achievement efforts were positively related to the mother's instigation to high achievement activity and to the father's instigation, encouragement, and participation in such activity with the child (Crandall, 1963, p. 429). When parents were observed, positive task-oriented reinforcement was associated with high achievement motivation, whereas withholding reinforcement after success was related to test anxiety (Hermans et al., 1972). One exception to this pattern was the finding that preschool girls' achievement standards were negatively associated with observed maternal involvement in the child's task performance (Hatfield et al., 1967), but the measures of achievement-related behavior in this study were more limited than in the others cited.

Achievement efforts in adolescence and adulthood are also related to early maternal acceleration. Maternal acceleration reflects the degree to which the mother shows excessive concern for her child's development and places excessive expectations on the child's level of achievement (Kagan & Moss, 1962, p. 206). Acceleration during early years was positively related to females' achievement behaviors in both childhood and adulthood, to adult concern with intellectual mastery (Kagan & Moss, 1962), and to intellectual achievement efforts in adulthood (Crandall & Battle, 1970). Attainment value for intellectual mastery in adolescence was unrelated to early maternal acceleration in Kagan and Freemans' (1963) study, but daughters whose mothers had made little attempt to accelerate their development were more likely to withdraw from achievement situations than those with highly accelerating mothers.

These data indicate that achievement-oriented behavior results from explicit reinforcement and attempts to accelerate the child's development. In some sense, the pushy mother appears to produce the effects that she probably wants. The role of the father is less clear, though it appears that reinforcement and instigation to achievement by the father are also important. If the father approves of achievement, this male encouragement may enable a female to integrate high achievement into her concept of femininity more readily than she would without such encouragement, but more data on the father's role in females' achievement development are needed to evaluate this suggestion.

An additional pattern of restrictiveness, encouraging dependence, and reinforcing achievement concurrently appears to lead to a feminine pattern of achievement. Bing (1963) compared mothers of children with two patterns of discrepant abilities: high verbal (low math or spatial) and low verbal (high math or spatial). The mothers of high verbal females were quite demanding and intrusive during an observation in which the child performed a task. These mothers also reported more restrictions on activities such as object experimentation and more training for cautiousness than mothers of low verbal girls.

Modeling

Although achievement standards and behavior can be learned through imitation (Bandura et al., 1967; Mischel & Liebert, 1966), identification with the mother by female children appears to be antagonistic to achievement orientation unless the mother is an atypical model, that is, unless she does not conform to traditional feminine role definitions. In the Douvan and Adelson (1966) study, adolescent females with high traditional feminine interests and low achievement aspirations named their mothers and other female relatives when asked who their models were. Those with high achievement aspirations, regardless of whether or not they also had feminine interests, more often named nonfamily models. In another study (Lansky et al., 1961), adolescent females who were highly critical of their mothers had high motivation but low levels of maternal identification.

While identification with the mother is usually associated with low motivation, the presence of an achieving maternal model appears to facilitate achievement-oriented behavior for females. Maternal employment in middle-class families is associated with high educational and occupational aspirations for young females (Banducci, 1967; Nye & Hoffman, 1963; Stein, in press) and with professional activity for middle-aged offspring (Shelton, 1968). In one study (Baruch, 1972), daughters of working mothers also assessed the professional competence of females more highly than those of nonworking mothers. In that study, the women's attitudes about careers and achievement for females were not related to maternal employment (an exception to the other findings) but were related to the mother's perceived attitudes on the same subject.

Daughters of working mothers also adopt traditional feminine characteristics less often than those of nonworking mothers. In one study of college women, maternal employment was associated with high achievement motivation, dominance and endurance (independently assessed as masculine characteristics), and low succorance and abasement (passive feminine characteristics; Stein, in press). These effects were not due to the educational level of the mothers. In Douvan and Adelson's (1966) study, daughters of working mothers also expressed less traditional feminine interests than those of nonworking mothers. However, Lipman-Blumen (1972) found no relation of maternal employment to young women's sex role ideologies, perhaps because the ideology question was a fairly gross measure.

Summary

Perhaps the major theme that emerges from the socialization data is that the child-rearing practices that are conducive to feminine sex typing are often antagonistic to those that lead to achievement-oriented behavior. A female child is most likely to develop achievement behavior and independence when her parents are moderately warm, moderately to highly permissive, and when they reinforce and encourage achievement efforts. Encouragement of independence apparently leads to independence but is not clearly related to achievement behavior. Some concomitant features of the practices in families of highly achievement-oriented females are moderate punitiveness, high demands on the child, and acceleration attempts by the mother. Achievement orientation can also be stimulated by a mother who engages in a career (i.e., is an achieving female model). These child-rearing practices are in many instances the reverse of those that typically lead to high femininity.

A brief contrast with the findings for males indicates a possible sex difference in the effect of the warmth–hostility dimension on achievement orientation. Warmth is more often correlated with males' than with females' achievement orientations (Crandall, 1963). There is also some indication that males fare better

with slightly less permissiveness than females (Baumrind, 1971; Bronfenbrenner, 1961). It may be assumed that the mother's model of achievement differently affects females and males. A less traditionally feminine mother may be especially important to her daughter by providing a model of alternatives to the stereotyped sex role.

CONCLUSIONS

There are some general themes and some directions for future research that emerge from the literature. First, like much psychological theory, achievement-motivation theory was developed to explain the behavior of males. Then attempts were made to use that theory for females. Not surprisingly, it does not work as well for females. The expected correlations between achievement motivation, achievement behaviors, and performance of various kinds are often absent for females, and the situations that arouse achievement motivation fairly reliably for males do not do so consistently for females. It appears that better theory will result from a direct examination of females rather than from attempts to apply concepts derived from studies of males that may be inappropriate.

This article does not pretend to present new theoretical concepts, but we have attempted to describe the patterns of achievement-related behavior that characterize females and to explore some of the variables that influence those patterns. During the early school years, females achieve well, particularly in school, by applying a pattern of careful, cautious work habits bolstered by a high sense of responsibility for any failure. They value achievement and set high standards for themselves, though they appear more anxious about failure and less confident of their abilities than males. Many of these behaviors that help in school achievement are less adaptive for continued achievement striving outside the school setting or even within the school setting at advanced educational levels.

Reduced achievement efforts occur for many young women as they reach adolescence and adulthood partly because there is pressure to adhere to feminine role definitions and because females internalize the low expectations of the culture for their continued achievement. Attainment in the occupational world not only produces some negative sanctions but often requires the self-esteem and assertiveness that are contrary to traditional feminine personality attributes. Although achievement striving may simply drop out of some females' repertoires, it appears that it is often manifested in various channels that are at least partially congruent with the feminine sex role. Some of these patterns have been described.

One of the most important areas for female achievement is social skill. Achievement striving and social activity are more closely linked for females than for males. This link has frequently been interpreted as indicating that females' achievement striving is motivated by need for affiliation or external social approval rather than by an internalized desire to meet a standard of excellence. The examination of the literature presented here led to a rejection of that interpretation. Instead, it appears that attainment of excellence is often a goal of females' achievement efforts, but the areas in which such attainment is sought are frequently social skills and other areas perceived as feminine.

While achievement orientations and feminine role performance can be combined in a variety of ways, there is some inherent conflict between them. Some of the personality characteristics associated with achievement behavior such as independence, assertiveness, competitiveness, and belief in one's own competence are antagonistic to cultural demands on females for sex-role-appropriate behavior. Further, the child-rearing practices that are associated with achievement orientation for females are, in many instances, the reverse of those that lead to high femininity.

Some female children are trained to be achievement oriented, and the literature is remarkably clear in indicating what parental characteristics are involved. The pattern that fosters achievement striving for females is not entirely consistent with the stereotypical notions of the best child rearing for happy, mentally healthy children. It involves some pressures on the child, some withholding of nurturance, and some punitiveness, although none of these characteristics appears in extremes. Nevertheless, the ideal child rearing depends on one's goals for the child. Bronfenbrenner (1961) suggested that there is a danger of oversocializing girls by too much warmth and/or too much restrictiveness so that they become obedient, conforming, and feminine, but do not develop more independent qualities such as responsibility and leadership. The review presented here is consistent with that view in suggesting that moderate levels of warmth, a fair amount of permissiveness combined with high standards and reinforcement for achievement efforts are likely to facilitate achievement behavior in female children, whereas their opposites are likely to lead to conforming, dependent, and feminine patterns of behavior.

Possible directions for future research are almost limitless, but a few areas are mentioned here that show especially obvious gaps in the literature. There is relatively little information on achievement-related behavior in classes and ethnic groups other than the white middle class. The studies that do exist suggest that the concepts and generalizations developed on middle-class males do not apply well to other groups. All other research suggestions implicitly include these populations.

There is a need for more developmental studies, probably longitudinal. A possible "flight into femininity" at adolescence with a concomitant reduction in achievement motivation has been widely assumed, but there is little if any documentation for it. The information that does exist indicates a high level of consistency of achievement strivings from middle childhood to adulthood among females, suggesting that changes in adolescence may be less striking than has been assumed. More data are needed to understand the developmental patterns involved.

The effect of fathers is relatively neglected in this area as in other parts of the socialization literature. There is some indication that fathers may be particularly important for encouraging achievement behavior and independence in females, especially if their mothers are rather traditional women. In other areas of achievement-related behavior, such as anxiety about failure, there is little information about the impact of either fathers or mothers.

The patterns of achievement behavior that are reinforced by teachers and other adults need to be studied for females. The finding that teachers reacted negatively to task-oriented behavior in bright girls but positively to socially oriented achievement behavior, suggests a possible basis for the link between social and achievement orientations among females. Generally, there is almost no research on the impact of socializing agents other than parents.

A related problem concerns the compromises and attempts at integration that females make to reconcile achievement orientations and femininity. Women do sometimes reduce their efforts in order to avoid successful competition with men, but there is some suggestion in the literature that they feel uncomfortable about it. It appears that women are also sometimes reluctant to make their accomplishments public. Other sex-role-related characteristics such as perceptions of incompetence and anxiety about failure need exploring to determine their impact on achievement effort.

Finally, achievement motivation needs to be conceptually and operationally defined in a way that is appropriate to females. It will be useful only if it predicts achievement efforts and other forms of achievement behavior. The "women's role achievement motivation" developed by Friedrich and Harding (see Footnote 3) is one promising effort in this direction. At the same time, the constellation of variables and predictors related to achievement motivation needs to be better identified.

REFERENCES

ALPER, T. G., & GREENBERGER, E. Relationship of picture structure to achievement motivation in college women. *Journal of Personality and Social Psychology*, 1967, 7, 362–371.

ATKINSON, J. W., & FEATHER, N. T. (Eds.) *A theory of achievement motivation.* New York: Wiley, 1966.

BANDUCCI, R. The effect of mother's employment on the achievement, aspirations, and expectations of the child. *Personnel and Guidance Journal*, 1967, 46, 263–267.

BANDURA, A. Social-learning theory of identificatory processes. In D. A. Goslin (Ed.), *Handbook of socialization theory and research.* Chicago: Rand McNally, 1969.

BANDURA, A., GRUSEC, J. E., & MENLOVE, F. L. Some social determinants of self-monitoring rein-forcement systems. *Journal of Personality and Social Psychology*, 1967, 5, 449–455.

BARUCH, G. K. Maternal influences upon college women's attitudes toward women and work. *Developmental Psychology*, 1972, 6, 32–37.

BARUCH, R. The achievement motive in women: Implications for career development. *Journal of Personality and Social Psychology*, 1967, 5, 260–267.

BATTLE, E. S. Motivational determinants of academic task persistence. *Journal of Personality and Social Psychology*, 1965, 2, 209–218.

BATTLE, E. S. Motivational determinants of academic competence. *Journal of Personality and Social Psychology*, 1966, 4, 634–642.

BAUMRIND, D. Current patterns of parental authority. *Developmental Psychology*, 1971, 4(1, Pt. 2).

BAUMRIND, D., & BLACK, A. E. Socialization practices associated with dimensions of competence in pre-school boys and girls. *Child Development*, 1967, 38, 291–328.

BECKER, W. C. Consequences of different kinds of parental discipline. In M. L. Hoffman & L. W. Hoffman (Eds.), *Review of child development research.* Vol. 1. New York: Russell Sage, 1964.

BING, E. Effect of childrearing practices on development of differential cognitive abilities. *Child Development*, 1963, 34, 631–648.

BRONFENBRENNER, U. Some familial antecedents of responsibility and leadership in adolescents. In L. Petrullo & B. M. Bass (Eds.), *Leadership and interpersonal behavior.* New York: Holt, 1961.

BUTTERFIELD, E. C. The role of competence motivation in interrupted task recall and repetition choice. *Journal of Experimental Child Psychology*, 1965, 2, 354–370.

CALLARD, E. D. Achievement motive of four-year-olds and maternal achievement expectancies. *Journal of Experimental Education*, 1968, 36, 14–23.

CAREY, G. L. Sex differences in problem-solving performance as a function of attitude differences. *Journal of Abnormal and Social Psychology*, 1958, 56, 256–260.

COTLER, S., & PALMER, R. J. Social reinforcement, individual difference factors, and the reading performance of elementary school children. *Journal of Personality and Social Psychology*, 1971, 18, 97–104.

CRANDALL, V. C. Personality characteristics and social and achievement behaviors associated with children's social desirability response tendencies. *Journal of Personality and Social Psychology*, 1966, 4, 477–486.

CRANDALL, V. C. Sex differences in expectancy of intellectual and academic reinforcement. In C. P. Smith (Ed.), *Achievement-related motives in children.* New York: Russell Sage, 1969.

CRANDALL, V. C., & BATTLE, E. S. The antecedents and adult correlates of academic and intellectual achievement effort. In J. P. Hill (Ed.), *Minnesota Symposia on Child Psychology.* Vol. 4. Minneapolis: University of Minnesota Press, 1970.

CRANDALL, V. C., KATKOVSKY, W., & CRANDALL, V. J. Children's beliefs in their own control of reinforcements in intellectual-academic achievement situations. *Child Development*, 1965, 36, 91–109.

CRANDALL, V. J. Achievement. In H. W. Stevenson (Ed.), *Child psychology: Sixty-second yearbook of the National Society for the Study of Education.* Chicago: University of Chicago Press, 1963.

CRANDALL, V. J., DEWEY, R., KATKOVSKY, W., & PRESTON, A. Parents' attitudes and behaviors and grade-school children's academic achievements. *Journal of Genetic Psychology,* 1964, 104, 53–66.

CRANDALL, V. J., KATKOVSKY, W., & PRESTON, A. A conceptual formulation for some research on children's achievement development. *Child Development,* 1960, 31, 787–797.

CRANDALL, V. J., KATKOVSKY, W., & PRESTON, A. Motivational and ability determinants of children's intellectual achievement behaviors. *Child Development,* 1962, 33, 643–661.

CRANDALL, V. J., PRESTON, A., & RABSON, A. Maternal reactions and the development of independence and achievement behavior in young children. *Child Development,* 1960, 31, 243–251.

CRANDALL, V. J., & RABSON, A. Children's repetition choices in an intellectual achievement situation following success and failure. *Journal of Genetic Psychology,* 1960, 97, 161–168.

CROWNE, D. P., CONN, L. K., MARLOWE, D., & EDWARDS, C. N. Some developmental antecedents of level of aspiration. *Journal of Personality,* 1969, 37, 73–92.

DOUVAN, E., & ADELSON, J. *The adolescent experience.* New York: Wiley, 1966.

ENTWISLE, D. R. To dispel fantasies about fantasy-based measures of achievement motivation. *Psychological Bulletin,* 1972, 77, 377–391.

FELD, S. C., & LEWIS, J. The assessment of achievement anxieties in children. In C. P. Smith (Ed.), *Achievement-related motives in children.* New York: Russell Sage, 1969.

FERGUSON, L. R., & MACCOBY, E. E. Interpersonal correlates of differential abilities. *Child Development,* 1966, 37, 549–571.

FIDELL, L. S. Empirical verification of sex discrimination in hiring practices in psychology. *American Psychologist,* 1970, 25, 1094–1097.

FIELD, W. F. The effects on thematic apperception of certain experimentally aroused needs. Cited by D. C. McClelland, J. W. Atkinson, R. A. Clark, & E. L. Lowell, *The achievement motive.* New York: Appleton-Century-Crofts, 1953.

FRENCH, E., & LESSER, G. S. Some characteristics of the achievement motive in women. *Journal of Abnormal and Social Psychology,* 1964, 68, 119–128.

FRIEDAN, B. *The feminine mystique.* New York: Norton, 1963.

GOLDBERG, P. A. Are women prejudiced against women? *Trans-Action,* 1968, 28–30.

HATFIELD, J. S., FERGUSON, L. R., & ALPERT, R. Mother-child interaction and the socialization process. *Child Development,* 1967, 38, 365–414.

HEILBRUN, A. B., HARRELL, S. N., & GILLARD, B. J. Perceived maternal childrearing patterns and the effects of social nonreaction upon achievement motivation. *Child Development,* 1967, 38, 267–281.

HEILBRUN, A. B., & ORR, H. K. Maternal childrearing control history and subsequent cognitive and personality functioning of the offspring. *Psychological Reports,* 1965, 17, 259–272.

HERMANS, H. J. M., TER LAAK, J. J. F., & MAES, P. C. J. M. Achievement motivation and fear of failure in family and school. *Developmental Psychology,* 1972, 6, 520–528.

HETHERINGTON, E. M. The effects of familial variables on sex typing, on parent-child similarity, and on imitation in children. In J. P. Hill (Ed.), *Minnesota Symposia on Child Psychology.* Vol. 1. Minneapolis: University of Minnesota Press, 1967.

HETHERINGTON, M., & ROSS, L. E. Effect of sex of subject, sex of experimenter, and reinforcement condition on serial verbal learning. *Journal of Experimental Psychology,* 1963, 65, 572–575.

HILL, K. T. Social reinforcement as a function of test anxiety and success-failure experiences. *Child Development,* 1967, 38, 723–738.

HILL, K. T., & DUSEK, J. B. Children's achievement expectations as a function of social reinforcement, sex of subject and test anxiety. *Child Development,* 1969, 40, 547–558.

HILL, K. T., & SARASON, S. B. The relation of test anxiety and defensiveness to test and school performance over the elementary-school years: A further longitudinal study. *Monographs of the Society for Research in Child Development,* 1966, 31(2, Serial No. 104).

HOFFMAN, L. R., & MAIER, N. R. F. Social factors influencing problem solving in women. *Journal of Personality and Social Psychology,* 1966, 4, 382–390.

HORNER, M. S. Toward an understanding of achievement-related conflicts in women. *Journal of Social Issues,* 1972, 28, 157–176.

KAGAN, J. Acquisition and significance of sex typing and sex role identity. In M. L. Hoffman & L. W. Hoffman (Eds.), *Review of child development research.* Vol. 1. New York: Russell Sage, 1964.

KAGAN, J., & FREEMAN, M. Relation of childhood intelligence, maternal behaviors, and social class to behavior during adolescence. *Child Development,* 1963, 34, 899–911.

KAGAN, J., & MOSS, H. A. *Birth to maturity.* New York: Wiley, 1962.

KATKOVSKY, W., CRANDALL, V., & GOOD, S. Parental antecedents of children's beliefs in internal-external control of reinforcements in intellectual achievement situations. *Child Development,* 1967, 38, 765–776.

LANSKY, L. M., CRANDALL, V. J., KAGAN, J., & BAKER, C. T. Sex differences in aggression and its correlates in middle class adolescents. *Child Development,* 1961, 32, 45–58.

LEKARCZYK, D. T., & HILL, K. T. Self-esteem, test anxiety, stress, and verbal learning. *Developmental Psychology,* 1969, 1, 147–154.

LESSER, G. S., KRAWITZ, R. N., & PACKARD, R. Experimental arousal of achievement motivation in adolescent girls. *Journal of Abnormal and Social Psychology,* 1963, 66, 59–66.

LIPMAN-BLUMEN, J. How ideology shapes women's lives. *Scientific American,* 1972, 226, 34–42.

LUNNEBERG, P. W. Relations among social desirability, achievement, and anxiety measures in children. *Child Development,* 1964, 35, 169–182.

MACCOBY, E. E. Sex differences in intellectual functioning. In E. E. Maccoby (Ed.), *The development of sex differences.* Stanford: Stanford University Press, 1966.

MANDEL, S. L. Nurturance, persistence and distraction in preschool children. *Dissertation Abstracts,* 1968, 29(5-B), 1845.

MCCLELLAND, D. C., ATKINSON, J. R., CLARK, R. A., & LOWELL, E. L. *The achievement motive.* New York: Appleton-Century-Crofts, 1953.

MCGHEE, P. E., & CRANDALL, V. C. Beliefs in internal-external control of reinforcements and academic performance. *Child Development,* 1968, 39, 91–102.

MCMANIS, D. L. Pursuit-rotor performance of normal and retarded children in four verbal-incentive conditions. *Child Development,* 1965, 36, 667–683.

MISCHEL, W. Sex typing and socialization. In P. H. Mussen (Ed.), *Carmichael's manual of Child Psychology.* Vol. 2. (3rd ed.) New York: Wiley, 1970.

MISCHEL., W., & LIEBERT, R. M. Effects of discrepancies between observed and imposed reward criteria on their acquisition and transmission. *Journal of Personality and Social Psychology,* 1966, 3, 45–53.

MONTANELLI, D. S., & HILL, K. T. Children's achievement expectations and performance as a function of two consecutive reinforcement experiences, sex of subject, and sex of experimenter. *Journal of Personality and Social Psychology,* 1969, 13, 115–128.

NAKAMURA, C. Y., & ROGERS, M. M. Parents' expectations of autonomous behavior and children's autonomy. *Developmental Psychology,* 1969, 1, 613–617.

NYE, F. I., & HOFFMAN, L. W. *The employed mother in America.* Chicago: Rand McNally, 1963.

PHETERSON, G. I., KIESLER, S. B., & GOLDBERG, P. A. Evaluation of the performance of women as a function of their sex, achievement, and personal history. *Journal of Personality and Social Psychology,* 1971, 19, 114–118.

RAPH, J. B., GOLDBERG, M. L., & PASSOW, A. H. *Bright underachievers.* New York: Teacher's College Press, 1966.

SARASON, S. B., LIGHTHALL, F. F., DAVIDSON, K. S., WAITE, R. R., & RUEBUSH, B. K. *Anxiety in elementary school children.* New York: Wiley, 1960.

SEARS, R. R., RAU, L. R., & ALPERT, R. *Identification and child rearing.* Stanford: Stanford University Press, 1965.

SHAW, M. C., & MCCUEN, J. R. The onset of academic underachievement in bright children. *Journal of Educational Psychology,* 1960, 51, 103–108.

SHELTON, P. B. Achievement motivation in professional women. *Dissertation Abstracts,* 1968, 28(10-A), 4274.

SHERMAN, J. A. *On the psychology of women.* Springfield, Ill.: Charles C Thomas, 1971.

SOLOMON, D. The generality of children's achievement-related behavior. *Journal of Genetic Psychology,* 1969, 114, 109–125.

SONTAG, L. W., & BAKER, C. T. Personality, familial and physical correlates of change in mental ability. *Monographs of the Society for Research in Child Development,* 1958, 23(2, Serial No. 68).

STANFORD, D., DEMBER, W. N., & STANFORD, L. B. A children's form of the Alpert-Haber Achievement Anxiety Scale. *Child Development,* 1963, 34, 1027–1032.

STEIN, A. H. The influence of social reinforcement on the achievement behavior of fourth-grade boys and girls. *Child Development,* 1969, 40, 727–736.

STEIN, A. H. The effects of sex-role standards for achievement and sex-role preference on three determinants of achievement motivation. *Developmental Psychology,* 1971, 4, 219–231.

STEIN, A. H. The effects of maternal employment and educational attainment on the sex-typed attributes of college females. *Social Behavior and Personality,* in press.

STEIN, A. H., POHLY, S. R., & MUELLER, E. The influence of masculine, feminine, and neutral tasks on children's achievement behavior, expectancies of success, and attainment values. *Child Development,* 1971, 42, 195–207.

STEIN, A. H., & SMITHELLS, J. Age and sex differences in children's sex role standards about achievement. *Developmental Psychology,* 1969, 1, 252–259.

STEVENSON, H. W. Social reinforcement of children's behavior. In L. P. Lipsitt and C. C. Spiker (Eds.), *Advances in child development and behavior.* Vol. 2. New York: Academic Press, 1965.

STRICKLAND, F. R. Aspiration responses among Negro and white adolescents. *Journal of Personality and Social Psychology,* 1971, 19, 315–320.

SUNDHEIM, B. J. M. The relationships among "n" achievement, "n" affiliation, sex-role concepts, academic grades, and curricular choice. *Dissertation Abstracts,* 1963, 23, 3471.

VEROFF, J. Social comparison and the development of achievement motivation. In C. P. Smith (Ed.), *Achievement-related motives in children.* New York: Russell Sage, 1969.

VEROFF, J., WILCOX, S., & ATKINSON, J. W. The achievement motive in high school and college age women. *Journal of Abnormal and Social Psychology,* 1953, 48, 108–119.

WALLACH, M. A., & KOGAN, N. *Modes of thinking in young children.* New York: Holt, Rinehart & Winston, 1965.

WEINER, B. Achievement motivation and task recall in competitive situations. *Journal of Personality and Social Psychology,* 1966, 3, 693–696.

WEISS, P. Some aspects of femininity. *Dissertation Abstracts,* 1962, 23, 1083.

WYER, R. S., JR. Effects of task reinforcement, social reinforcement, and task difficulty on perseverance in achievement-related activity. *Journal of Personality and Social Psychology,* 1968, 8, 269–276.

YONGE, G. D. Sex differences in cognitive functioning as a result of experimentally induced frustration. *Journal of Experimental Education,* 1964, 32, 275–280.

ZUNICH, M. Children's reactions to failure. *Journal of Genetic Psychology,* 1964, 104, 19–24.

(Received March 2, 1973)

7

THELMA G. ALPER

The Relationship Between Role Orientation and Achievement Motivation in College Women[1]

Achievement motivation within the McClelland, Atkinson, Clark, and Lowell (1953) framework has, from the beginning, attracted a large number of investigators. Moreover, for the most part, the original theoretical formulations continue to be supported, especially when the subjects are males. By comparison, the literature on females is both sparse and inconsistent.[2] Why the lesser interest in females, and why the inconsistencies? Horner's (1970) study seems to provide some basic clues. Taken literally, Horner's data indicate that, unlike men, most women in our society do not really want to be achievers, at least not in a field traditionally regarded as more appropriate for men than for women. Given the verbal cue "After first term finals, Anne finds herself at the top of her medical school class," over 65 percent of Horner's coeds told *avoidance-of-success* stories, whereas, in response to the "John" form, over 90 percent of the males told *success* stories. The typical avoidance themes in the female stories were fear that no one would like Anne now and questioning her femininity. Assuming that Horner's subjects are representative, the shortcomings of much of the past research and the directions for the future become clearer. If women do not want to achieve and men do, then both the theory and the techniques for testing the theory are male-specific and, as such, are not likely to yield comparable results for females. In other words, unless either the male or the female sample is atypical, the re-

1. Based in part on a paper presented at a symposium on women on April 16, 1971 during the EPA meetings in New York City. The two studies reported here were completed under a research grant from the Radcliffe Institute during the years 1968–1970.
2. For reviews of the relevant literature, see, e.g., Alper and Greenberger (1967); Bardwick (1971); French and Lesser (1964); Kenny (1964); Lesser, Krawitz, and Packard (1963); McClelland, Atkinson, Clark, and Lowell (1953); Murstein (1961, 1965); Smith (1969); and Veroff (1961).

sults for the two sexes should be different. Angelini's (1955) study is a case in point. Commenting on this study, Lesser, Krawitz, and Packard (1963) note that, as a group, the female subjects here were likely to have been both highly competitive and achieving. Otherwise, they could not have survived the Latin American prejudice against higher education for women. If so, unlike Horner's subjects, in Angelini's sample the coeds would have wanted to be achievers and the results of the two studies should be different: high need Achievement scores in Angelini's study, fear of achievement in Horner's.

Instead of abandoning the area of achievement motivation in women, then, what seems to be needed is a shift in focus, away from insistence on extrinsic parsimony across the sexes to a search for intrinsic lawfulness. To do this requires more knowledge of the achievement values of women and the conditions under which these values emerge. At this point, the relevant data are slim, but what there is is relatively consistent: highly competitive women (Angelini, 1955), bright, academically achieving high school girls (Lesser et al., 1963), and intellectually-oriented coeds (French & Lesser, 1964) show achievement-motivation patterns similar to those found in males, while under-achieving high school girls (Lesser et al., 1963), woman's role-oriented coeds (French & Lesser, 1964) and unselected samples of coeds (Horner, 1970) do not. In short, some women may accept achievement as female-appropriate while others do not. In the present paper, the role-orientation variable is given primary consideration. The construction of a new role-orientation measure, The Wellesley Role-Orientation Scale, or WROS, is described, and differences in the thematic content of the fantasies of subjects who score at opposite ends of the scale are reported. The results of two experiments are included here, the initial one in which the role-orientation measure was first used, and a subsequent partial replication study. In both, the sex of the stimulus-figure variable and methods of scoring for achievement imagery are evaluated.

Assumptions and Specific Hypotheses

Starting with the basic assumption that achievement fantasies in women are positively related to personal role preferences, it was anticipated that strongly achievement-cued stimuli would evoke significantly different achievement fantasies in subjects who accept the traditional sex role imperatives, as compared with subjects who reject them. In an oversimplified form, these imperatives are: woman's place is in the home, man's place in the professions, business, industry or politics (cf., for example, Mead, 1949; and Levinson & Huffman, 1955). If this assumption is valid, using stimuli typical of most of the past research, namely, pictures, we should be able to predict which subjects will tell success stories and which will not and to relate the results to previous research in this area. To this end, two sets of hypotheses were formulated: Hypotheses I A through II B focus on strength of achievement motivation as a function of the sex of the stimulus-figures; Hypotheses III A through III C on the thematic content of the fantasies. The first set is consistent with the theory formulated by Lesser et al. (1963) to account for their unexpected sex of stimulus-figure effects, a theory partially supported in the subsequent study of French and Lesser (1964). The second applies projective test theory to the sex-role framework of the present studies.

Hypothesis I A. The mean need Achievement score of high feminine subjects (those whose role-preference scores fall in the upper third of the distribution of scores on the WROS) will be significantly higher when the stimulus involves male, rather than female, figures.

Hypothesis I B. The mean need Achievement score of low feminine subjects (those whose role-preference scores fall in the lower third of the distribution of scores on the WROS) will be significantly higher when the stimulus involves female rather than male figures.

Hypothesis II A. The male picture cue will evoke significantly higher need Achievement scores in high- than in low-scoring subjects.

Hypothesis II B. The female picture cue will evoke significantly higher need Achievement scores in low- than in high-scoring subjects.

Hypothesis III A. In response to the female picture-stimulus, low-scoring subjects more often than high-scoring subjects will tell unambivalent success stories, success itself being the valued goal.

Hypothesis III B. Success stories in which the success is instrumental to the gratification of love-oriented needs rather than personal accomplishment will be more characteristic of high- than of low-scoring subjects.

Hypothesis III C. In response to the female picture stimulus, high-scoring subjects more often than low will tell avoidance of success stories.

Given the assumption that it is the high scorers who regard achievement as more appropriate for men than for women, one might expect a strongly achievement-cued male picture to evoke unambivalent success stories more often in high scorers than in low. But such an expectation omits an important factor: to view achievement as appropriate only for men, as high scorers do, prepares us logically for success themas from high scorers in response to the male picture. But to view achievement as appropriate for women, as low scorers do, does not logically preclude the possibility of their giving success themas in response to the male picture. Since the same logic applies to the other hypotheses here, thema predictions in Set III have been limited to the female stimulus cue.

THE ROLE-ORIENTATION MEASURE

Construction of the WROS

The WROS, a 24-item paper and pencil scale, was designed to measure the sex-role preferences of college women.[3] Three aspects of role-preference are tapped.

1. Traits college girls generally regard as "feminine" rather than as "masculine";

2. Role activities college girls find acceptable for themselves as women;

3. Career, or career-oriented, activities college girls consider appropriate only for men.

3. Of the various scales already available, the Fe subscale of the CPI (Gough, 1957) had originally seemed most promising. Pilot work with this scale led us to abandon it as our major instrument since most subjects quickly identified what the test was measuring. (See Bieliauskos, Miranda, & Lansky, 1968 for a report on the "obviousness" of this scale).

In constructing the scale, students in an introductory psychology course were each asked to submit a number of sex-role relevant statements. These were to include traits as well as the roles appropriate for each sex. Analysis of the statements yielded the above categories. Final selection of 21 items, 7 for each of the categories, plus three "filler" items was arrived at on the basis of two successive Q sorts performed by members of the class.[4] The first sort, into clearly feminine, clearly masculine, and ambiguous, or unrelated to sex roles, was used to eliminate items in the latter category. A second sort was then performed, and only items for which there were consensus sorts were retained. These items, along with several "filler" items, were then pilot-tested under conditions of group administration, using other undergraduates as subjects. Items which were either uniformly accepted or uniformly rejected by the pilot group were dropped. This step left a 24-item scale. Two examples from each of the subscales, and a "filler" item, are shown below. In each case, the "feminine" score is indicated in the parenthesis following the statement.

Feminine trait subscale:

Aggressiveness and drive are valuable personality attributes. (Disagree)
Most girls would prefer something frivolous rather than something practical for a present. (Agree)

Feminine role activities subscale:

A married woman with children should not work. (Agree)
Just because a woman has chosen a career rather than marriage does not mean that she is less feminine. (Disagree)

Male-oriented careers subscale:

It is more difficult to have confidence in a female doctor than in a male one. (Agree)
I see no reason why a woman should not be elected President of the United States. (Disagree)

A "filler" item:

All colleges should adopt the honor system. (Not scored)

4. The contributions to and assistance of the following students in the initial stages of the test construction are gratefully acknowledged: • Lynn M. Anderson, Patricia A. Challender, Carole J. Goldstein, Betsy A. MacGregor and Elizabeth F. Robbins.

Validity of the WROS

A brief questionnaire appended to the WROS asked the subject to indicate (1) what she expected to be doing one year after graduation from college and 10 years after, and (2) what she would like to be doing one year after and 10 years after. The answers to these questions, obtained from the subjects in the first experiment, support the basic assumptions of the study and provide, therefore, an initial validation of the scale.

As shown in Table 1, the answers to the questionnaire fell into two main categories: (1) graduate school, with or without a job, and (2) marriage, with or without a job. Answers limited to "working" were included in the second. To validate the test, more low- than high-scoring subjects should be planning on a career. The expectation data for a year after graduation tend to support this ($p < .10$), the preference data clearly do so ($p < .01$). The data for 10 years after graduation yield no differences. In accord with Rostow's (1964) data for middle-class

Table 1. Expectations and preferences of high- and of low-feminine role-oriented college women in the initial study reported in terms of frequency of occurrence within a category.

	One year after graduation			Ten years after graduation		
	Highs (n=13)	Lows (n=11)	P[a]	Highs (n=13)	Lows (n=11)	P
Expectation						
Graduate school, with or without a job	3	7	<.10	0	0	—
Marriage, with or without a job, or job only	10	3		12	9	
Miscellaneous	0	1	—	1	2	—
Preference						
Graduate school, with or without a job	1	4	<.01	0	0	—
Marriage, with or without a job, or job only	12	6		13	11	
Miscellaneous	0	1	—	0	0	—

[a]All P values based on Fisher's Exact Probability Test.

samples, our subjects, both high and low scorers, want eventually to marry. Few foresee for themselves a combination of career and marriage.

Repeated attempts to correlate the WROS with two seemingly relevant personality measures, e.g., the Fe subscale of the CPI (Gough, 1957) and the Crowne-Marlowe (1964) Social Desirability Scale, have failed to yield significant relationships. However, correlations with the Traditional Family Ideology Scale (Levinson & Huffman, 1955) have consistently been positive and highly significant. Significant correlations in the expected direction, negative, between the WROS and the sex-stereotype measure devised by Rosenkrantz and his associates (1968) have been obtained with only one sample, a group of lower-middle-class junior college females.

Reliability of the WROS

Reliability, tested by means of the split-half method, was well within the limits of statistical significance in both the initial and the replication study. In the former, the value of Spearman's Rho was .58, the $p < .01$; in the latter, Rho $= .60$, $p < .01$.

No test-retest measure of reliability was available for either sample. Retest data for a small group of 25 upperclassmen, retested after a semester, however, were well within the limits of acceptability (Rho $= .70$, $p < .01$).

Instructions to the Subject

The instructions for the WROS indicated that the scale was part of a questionnaire designed to sample opinions and attitudes toward problems facing college girls; that there were no right or wrong answers; that some people agreed with some of the statements and others disagreed. The subject's task was merely to check "agree" if she agreed with a given statement, "disagree" if she disagreed with it.

Scoring Procedure

As noted in the examples above, "agree" for some items is scored as "feminine," "disagree" for others as "masculine." Where the wording is reversed, "agree" is scored as "masculine," "disagree," as "feminine." The subject's WROS score was computed merely by totaling the number of "feminine" responses. The possible range of scores here is 0 to 21, with 0 at the low feminine end and 21 at the high feminine end.

THE MOTIVATION MEASURE

To assure strongly achievement-cued stimuli, two pictures from the Veroff et al. (1960) set were initially selected, the Chem Lab, and the Machine Shop, since in the Veroff et al., (1960) national survey study these two had emerged as most effective for arousing achievement imagery in female and male subjects, respectively.[5] The former shows two women in a laboratory setting, the latter two men in a machine shop.

Instructions to the Subjects

All subjects were given the McClelland et al. (1953, p. 166) "creative imagination" instructions.

Scoring Procedures

Two types of scoring procedures were used, the McClelland et al. (1953, pp. 110–138), for measuring strength of achievement motivation, and a thema analysis for measuring content of the fantasy. For the latter, the categories originally included two success themas (Unambivalent and Instrumental) and three nonsuccess themas (Failure, Task Involvement, and Unrelated to Achievement). The failure thema was subsequently relabeled "Achievement can be dangerous," since this turned out to be the major thrust in such stories, and Task and Unrelated stories were combined into a single category, "Themas unrelated to achievement."

THE INITIAL STUDY

Subjects. Thirty five Wellesley College undergraduate women, 20 freshmen and 15 juniors, served as subjects. All were volunteers.

Materials. The WROS, the expectation and preference question-

5. Two other pictures, the Boy and Violin (Murray, 1943, TAT Card 1) and Girl in Classroom (Michigan Picture Test, 1953, Card 11G), were also used in the initial study. The data derived from them are not included here since they relate to a different set of hypotheses.

naire, instructions for the motivation measure, and sheets for writing each story were compiled into the test booklet handed to each subject at the beginning of the testing hour.

Procedure. Half of the freshmen and half of the juniors were given the WROS first and the motivation measure second. For the other half, the order was reversed. Group administration was used for both groups with the writer serving as the experimenter.

Since previous research has shown that order of presentation of pictures has little or no effect on need Achievement scores (Veroff et al., 1960; Lesser et al., 1963; Alper & Greenberger, 1967), picture order was kept constant for all subjects.

RESULTS[6]

The subjects in this study differed with respect to two variables, order of presentation of instruments and class status. Analyses by means of the Mann-Whitney U Test revealed no differences for either variable. The 35 subjects could therefore be treated as a single sample for all subsequent analyses.

The WROS Scale

The scores on the WROS ranged from a low of 5 to a high of 17. The median was 8.5, the mean, 9.14. Dividing the sample into thirds, the range for the lower third was 5 through 7; for the middle third, 8 through 9; for the upper third, 10 through 17.

The Picture Stimuli as Evokers of Achievement Imagery

Analysis of the number of achievement imagery stories aroused by each of the pictures clearly supports the Veroff et al. (1960) finding that these pictures are indeed strongly achievement-cued. As shown in Table 2, both pictures arouse achievement imagery significantly beyond chance. The *P* value for the Chem Lab picture is beyond .02, that for the Machine Shop, beyond .01. There are no differences between high and low scorers within either picture.

Strength of Achievement Imagery and Role-Orientation

Of the four hypotheses relating strength of need Achievement and role-orientation, one is clearly supported, one approaches

6. Unless otherwise noted, the *P* values presented in the tables below are based on one-tailed tests, if specific hypotheses are supported.

Table 2. Number of achievement imagery stories told by high- and by low-feminine role-oriented college women to each of the picture stimuli in the initial study.

	Chem Lab Picture			Machine Shop Picture		
	Yes	No	p^a	Yes	No	p^a
Highs	11	2	—	12	1	—
Lows	10	1		10	1	
χ^b	6.03			7.52		
p^b	<.02			<.01		

[a]Tested by means of Fisher's Exact Probability Test.
[b]Based on a two-tailed test, corrected for continuity.

Table 3. Mean strength of achievement imagery in high- and in low-feminine role-oriented college women in the initial study, using the McClelland et al. (1953) scoring categories.

	Highs	Lows	p^a
Chem Lab Picture	3.25	4.36	.06
Machine Shop Picture	2.77	1.82	—
p^b	—	<.025	

[a]Tested by means of the Mann-Whitney U Test.
[b]Tested by means of the Wilcoxin Matched-Pairs Signed-Ranks Test.

significance and two receive no support at all. Specifically, the male picture does evoke stronger achievement imagery in high-than in low-scoring subjects (IIA, $p < .025$), and within the high scorers it tends to be more effective than the female picture (IA, $p < .06$). But contrary to IIB and IB, respectively, the female picture neither pulls more achievement imagery in low scorers than in high, nor is it more effective than the male picture for doing so with low scorers. In short, when scored in terms of the McClelland et al. (1953) procedures, sex of the stimulus-cue appears to be a more differentiating determinant of strength of achievement motivation for high WROS scorers than for low.

Thema Analysis

The Thema analysis results are summarized in Table 4. As anticipated, though the two pictures do evoke the same themas,

Table 4. Relationship between role-orientation and themes in the initial study.

Chem Lab picture stimulus				Machine Shop picture stimulus			
Achievement is unambivalently valued				Achievement is unambivalently valued			
	Yes	No	Pa		Yes	No	P
Highs	2	11		Highs	4	9	
			.05				—
Lows	8	3		Lows	4	7	
Achievement is instrumental to the satisfaction of another need				Achievement is instrumental to the satisfaction of another need			
	Yes	No	P		Yes	No	P
Highs	4	9		Highs	1	12	
			.07				—
Lows	0	11		Lows	0	11	
Achievement can be dangerous				Achievement can be dangerous			
	Yes	No	P		Yes	No	P
Highs	5	8		Highs	7	6	
Lows	2	9	—	Lows	6	5	—
Themas unrelated to achievement				Themas unrelated to achievement			
	Yes	No	P		Yes	No	P
Highs	2	11		Highs	1	12	
Lows	1	10	—	Lows	1	10	—

aAll P values based on Fisher's Exact Probability Test.

significant differences occur only for the female picture. For this cue, Hypothesis IIIA is clearly supported (more low than high scorers do tell unambivalent success stories, $p = .05$), and Hypothesis IIIB tends to be supported (more high scorers tend to tell instrumental achievement stories, $p = .07$). But contrary to Hypothesis IIIC, avoidance-of success stories are not more characteristic of high scorers than of low. This holds both when the dangers-of-achievement and unrelated-to-achievement themas are separately analyzed, and when the two are combined into a single avoidance of success category.

The comparable results for middle WROS scorers, as a group, were: 54.5 percent, avoidance of success; 45.5 percent, Unambivalent Success. No middle scorer told an instrumental-achievement story. Adding the middle scorers, the percentages for the total sample are 53.2 percent avoidance, 45.7 percent unambivalent success, and 1.1 percent instrumental success. As in Horner's (1970) data, then, in absolute terms more subjects do tell avoidance than success stories. But unlike Horner's data, in the present study, the difference is not statistically significant.

Differences in the content of the achievement fantasies of high and low scorers can best be demonstrated by quoting from stories told to the Chem Lab picture. As the examples make clear, low scorers do expect women to be able to achieve personal fame through their own efforts, while high scorers do not. What high scorers want to achieve is marriage now. When their stories are future-oriented, they focus on women serving as assistants to men, with the women doing the chore work men have no time for. The major themes and subthemes under each are illustrated below. The WROS scoring category, high or low, is indicated in each case.

The *Unambivalent Success* theme includes five subthemes, the various conditions under which women can be achievers: hard work pays off, support by an achieving female model, cooperation between women, rivalry between women, and if women are to achieve they must work harder than men.[7] The first is more characteristic of low scorers than of high, the next three occur only in low scorers, the last, only in high.
Hard work pays off:

> This lady scientist, like Madame Curie, is about to make an amazing discovery. She has been trying for months to find a cure for cancer and in spite of almost giving up because of repeated failures, she and her assistant know that this is the moment. If she drops the right amount of solution into the tube, it will neutralize and that will be the answer to her years of effort. She will do it. [Told by a Low.]

Support by an achieving model:

> The instructor is showing her student how to do a step in a complicated experimental procedure. The student has been working on the experiment for some time, and is nearly at the end of her work. She is observing carefully what the other woman does, and, when she returns to her

7. The fact that the assisting person, model, rival, etc., is referred to as a woman in these stories, is, of course, overdetermined. Both figures in the stimulus cue *are* women.

own work, will repeat the procedure with care and pre-
cision and will be able to finish her project and achieve
significant results. The instructor would like the student to
become an able scientist, and is pleased with her work.
[Told by a Low.]

Cooperative effort:

These are two sisters, working on a new live virus serum.
Their interest in it is understandable since most of their
family has died of the disease.—The serum is finally per-
fected and saves innumerable lives. [Told by a Low.]

Achievement despite initial underlying rivalry:

These two very great scientists are working together to
try to come up with a cure for cancer. Though they are
natural enemies—they are persuaded to work together by
a career foundation with lots of money.—They come up
with a cure and share the fame. [Told by a Low.]

To achieve, women have to work harder than men:

It is a time when women scientists are not common. They
are in the minority and are often looked down upon by
men. Therefore they have to work extra hard to prove
themselves. These two female technologists are working
on a biochemistry experiment. The one standing is trying
to train the younger woman whom she feels has much
potential. Through their hard work and dedication to their
project they will succeed. They will not only make a name
for themselves—. [Told by a High.]

Note that the project is successful. But whether the achievement
finally wins them acceptance by men, is less certain. The story
remains unfinished. Moreover, a downgrading of the status of
women (here to technologists), occurs only in stories told by
Highs.

The *Achievement is Instrumental to the Gratification of Another Need* theme involves a different type of success. Found
only in high-scoring subjects, it is made up of two subcategories.
One, achievement in the service of winning affection or love,

is present-oriented; the other, helping men to be the real achievers, is future-oriented. An example of each follows.

What women really want is marriage, not personal achievement:

> Two unmarried Wellesley College chemistry professors are titrating a solution. They expect to find a new theory of nuclear activity involved in the solution process that will be crucial to the instant coffee concerns. They hope to make a lot of money so they can go to the Bahamas on a cruise and meet some eligible bachelors. They both fall in love with MIT professors and live satisfiedly ever after. [Told by a High.]

Woman as man's helper, not as an independent achiever:

> These two ladies are Ph.D. holders in chemistry who are working for the hospital in a surgeon's research laboratory. They are married but wanted to do something for a career with research work filling the bill. They don't want fame but rather to help mankind in their small way to find a cure for hepatitis. They will be of great assistance to the doctor and will perform a valuable function in doing the tasks that the doctor doesn't have time to do. [Told by a High.]

The *Avoidance of Success* theme includes two types of stories, one focuses on the dangers of achievement-striving, the other avoids the whole issue either by unrelated imagery or by mere task-involvement (the McClelland et al., 1953, UI and TI categories, respectively). While such stories tend to be more characteristic of high scorers than of low, the danger projected by the two groups is different: for low scorers, it is the project which fails; for high scorers, it is the achiever who is endangered since her achievement arouses the envy and dislike of others. Thus, the avoidance of success pattern, which Horner (1970) also describes, is a better fit for high than for low scorers. The examples below illustrate this difference.
Achievement can be dangerous:

> Two women are working in a science laboratory—trying to grow a particular culture of bacteria. Something un-

expected has happened to the culture, and they are preparing for tests—. They are hoping this new occurrence
will bring some important discovery. However, it will
only be a freak and on further testing will prove to be due
to their mistakes. They will entirely give up on this
project. [Told by a Low.]

The woman with the test tube is a famous Latin American
scientist; the other an American scientist.—Both want the
experiment to prove successful, though the American is
somewhat skeptical. —The experiment is a success. The
American congratulates, somewhat enviously, the other
scientist. [Told by a High.]

Other high scorers see even more serious dangers ahead
for the woman who aspires to be an achiever. Here is an example:

The lady with the test tube is a movie star who has sunk
to doing TV commercials. The other is an admiring no-
body (who) pities her.—They both fade into oblivion.
No one will hire them or pay any attention to them.—
The star commits suicide and the other marries a florist
and gets fat. [Told by a High.]

The moral here seems to be that a career, even a glamorous one,
can lead only to "oblivion"; better to settle for the more conventional, if somewhat unshapely, role of the married woman.

Unrelated imagery and stories involving only task imagery
occur less frequently than the danger subthema within the
avoidance of success category. When they do appear there are
no striking differences between high scorers and low. In these
stories, the women are either engaged in a routine laboratory
exercise (TI), or the fantasy is completely unrelated to achievement (UI).

THE PARTIAL REPLICATION STUDY

This study, undertaken two years after the initial study, was
designed as part of a series of studies on role ambivalence. It
included, among other pictures, the Chem Lab, but not the

Machine Shop picture. The results serve, therefore, only as a partial replication of the original experiment.

With two exceptions, the design was basically the same as that of the initial study. The exceptions were: (1) the source of the subjects and (2) control for the sex of the experimenter. Twenty-eight of the 50 subjects were fulfilling a course requirement that they serve as a subject in a given number of psychological experiments while the other 22 were tested during a regular meeting of the psychology course in which they were enrolled. In other words, none of these subjects was really a volunteer. The writer served as the experimenter for the first group and Mr. Bartlett Stoodley, a male faculty member of comparable academic status and age, was the experimenter for the second group. Since analysis of the WROS data revealed no differences, the two groups have been combined into a single sample.

RESULTS

The WROS scale

The WROS scores here ranged from a low of 4 to a high of 13, with a median of 8, and a mean of 7.84. Dividing the sample into thirds, scores for low-scoring subjects fell between 4 and 6, for middle-scoring subjects, between 7 and 8, for high-scoring subjects between 9 and 13. Comparing this distribution with that obtained in the initial study reveals that the scores for this group tended to be lower ($p < .06$, two-tailed test). Tested two years later, this difference could be a reflection of the growing interest of this age group in the women's liberation movement.

The Chem Lab picture as an evoker of achievement imagery

As in the initial study, this stimulus continues to be a strong evoker of need Achievement. Of the 50 subjects, 38 tell achievement stories ($\chi^2 = 11.52$, $p < .001$).

Thema Analysis

These data, summarized in Table 5, in essence corroborate the findings of the initial study: Low scorers significantly more often

Table 5. Relationship between role-orientation and themas in the replication study, *Chem Lab picture stimulus.*

Achievement is unambivalently valued				Achievement can be dangerous			
	Yes	No	P[a]		Yes	No	P
Highs	4	15		Highs	8	11	
			<.025				<.10
Lows	11	6		Lows	2	15	
Achievement is instrumental to the satisfaction of another need				Themas unrelated to achievement			
	Yes	No	P		Yes	No	P
Highs	0	19		Highs	7	12	
			—				—
Lows	0	17		Lows	4	13	

[a]All P values based on Fisher's Exact Probability Test.

than high tell success stories ($p < .025$), and high scorers more often than low tell avoidance stories. In the latter, either the dangers of achieving are stressed, or achievement imagery, as defined by McClelland et al. (1953), is completely absent. Combining the two types yields a P value beyond .025 in favor of high scorers. Contrary to the initial study, however, now the Instrumental Achievement thema occurs only in high middle-scoring subjects, not in the high.

For the sample as a whole, 48 percent tell avoidance of success stories, 46 percent unambivalent success stories, and 6 percent, instrumental success stories. As in the initial experiments, the percentage differences between success and avoidance are not significant. Thus, despite the more constricted WROS range, thematic differences between extreme scorers, as well as for the sample as a whole, remain relatively constant. In fact, had the original cutting-points for the initial study also been used for the replication, the relationships shown in Table 5 would still pertain.

DISCUSSION AND CONCLUSIONS

The results of the present studies support the prediction that achievement motivation in women is significantly related to sex role-orientation. In testing this relationship, strongly achievement-cued picture stimuli were used as well as a scoring procedure which focuses on the thematic content of the subjects' achievement fantasies. The McClelland et al. (1953) scoring procedures commonly used in research in this area, both presence and absence of achievement imagery, and strength of the achievement imagery, failed to reveal differences between subjects who scored at opposite ends of The Wellesley Role-Orientation Scale, a newly constructed self-rating instrument. A thema analysis approach applied to stories told to the Veroff et al. (1960) Chem Lab picture, however, does get at the differences. Subjects who score as low feminine on the WROS usually tell stories in which the women are engaged in critical tasks, such as seeking cures for dread diseases, and their efforts are typically highly successful. A few high feminine scorers also tell success stories, but the achievement goal is likely to be very different: present-oriented stories focus on unmarried women attaining marriage mates; future-oriented stories, on married women who take jobs, presumably after their children are grown. In the former, the task on which the women are working is likely to be female-oriented, for example, manufacturing a perfume which will make women irresistable to men, or perfecting a household gadget. The product, if successfully marketed, enables the women to find husbands, and in the words of one high scorer, to "live satisfiedly ever after." In future-oriented success stories, high scorers write about women doing the chore work for men. In other words, women serve as assistants to the real achievers, men, but women are not themselves the achievers. Some subjects in both groups speak of the dangers of achievement striving. This thema corresponds to Horner's (1970) fear of success. But here again, there is a difference between low scorers and high. In low scorers' stories, the project fails; in high scorers' stories, interpersonal relationships are threatened, jealousy arises, jobs are lost, the fruits of the achievement do not endure.

The Veroff et al. (1960) male Machine Shop picture evokes similar themes but now there are no between group differences and, on logical grounds, none had been anticipated: both high and low scoring subjects may regard achievement as male-appropriate, high scorers because the culture so dictates, low because female achievement would not necessarily preclude male achievement. On the other hand, since the male stimulus evokes a high percentage of "danger" themes in both groups, this explanation is not too convincing. Perhaps what needs to be explored next is the effects of a stimulus-cue showing males in a situation with which middle-class coeds could more readily identify, for example, a picture showing men in a chem lab rather than in a machine shop.

A replication study, limited to the Chem Lab stimulus, indicates that the relationships reported here are relatively stable. How, then, do these findings fit in with the results of other studies in this area and to what extent can they account for the equivocal nature of much of the earlier literature involving female subjects? Space limitations permit only a few examples.

To begin with, contrary to Horner's (1970) findings, our subjects did not tell significantly more avoidance of success than success stories. Even when middle scorers are included, avoidance of success characterizes only 53.2 percent of the subjects in the initial, and 48.0 percent in the replication study. Assuming a random distribution of sex-role preference in Horner's female sample, a justifiable assumption unless some unspecified, selective factor was operating, should not the percentage of avoidance of success stories in the two studies be more nearly the same? On the other hand, does it matter that Horner's subjects were in a coeducational setting and, therefore, perhaps less willing than our subjects to be competitive (French & Lesser, 1964; Horner, 1970)? There is also the difference in stimulus cues, a picture in the present study, a verbal cue in Horner's. But probably more important than this structural difference is the content difference. Horner's stimulus presents a subject with an accomplished fact—Anne *has* achieved, she *is* at the top of her class. In the present study, success (failure) is wholly a product of a subject's own projective processes. Moreover, in Horner's cue, the success is in medicine, a field long regarded as more appropriate for males than for females. Had the setting been more neutral, say a liberal arts college for women, or at least one more culturally defined as female-appropriate, for example, a school of nursing, our data would lead us to expect a significant drop in avoidance of success stories. To be sure, in a random sample, some high scorers might still feel threatened even by such success, but middle and low scorers probably would not. Two additional Wellesley studies are relevant here. Dropping the medical school reference and leaving only "After first term finals, Anne finds herself at the top of her class," yielded 50 percent avoidance and 50 percent success stories (Grainger, Kostick & Staley, 1970). The subjects were undergraduates in two noncoeducational, nonintegrated women's colleges in the South, one for black students, the other for white. On the other hand, a consciousness-raising, women's lib group at Wellesley, given the medical school form (Calkins & Dingman, 1971), yielded significantly fewer than 50 percent avoidance stories, as well as a very narrow range of WROS scores, 1 through 8! Thus, differences from study to study in explicitness and area of achievement (cf. also French & Lesser, 1964; Veroff, Feld & Gurin, 1966), sex of the stimulus figures (Alper, 1957; Lesser et al., 1963; French & Lesser, 1964), strength of the stimulus cues (Vogel, 1954), as well as in the nature of the instructional set (Field, 1951), all could have been contributing to the seemingly inconsistent and/or equivocal findings in the female need Achievement literature.

Still another difference between studies is the scoring method. Horner (1970) and the present writer independently have used a thema analysis. Most other investigators have used the McClelland et al. (1953) methods successfully with male subjects, but less successfully with female subjects. The Veroff et al., (1966) study is especially noteworthy here. Using postcollege-age mothers, some of whom were working, others not, and scoring only for presence or absence of achievement imagery, Veroff et al. (1966) were not able to reproduce the results obtained with postcollege-age males. To be sure, factors such as the age range of the mothers (Baruch, 1967) and how the mother feels about working or not working (Yarrow, Scott, de Leeuw, & Heinig, 1962) might also have beclouded the Veroff et al. (1966) results. A measure of "feelings of inadequacy" had been included here, but it failed to show a relationship to need Achievement, as scored. Perhaps a thema analysis would have been more successful.

But what of the other side of the coin? Can our results account for significant findings, where these *have* occurred? Of particular interest here are the studies of Angelini (1955), Lesser et al. (1963) and French & Lesser (1964). In all of these, the increase in achievement-motivation scores under achievement-oriented conditions, so typical of male subjects, did occur. Angelini's highly competitive and presumably highly achieving university women, the Lesser et al., bright, high achievers and the French and Lesser intellectually value-oriented subjects all show the pattern characteristic of our low feminine role-oriented subjects, a seeming acceptance of the sex-appropriateness of female achievement by females who have themselves, in fact, achieved. On the other hand, the achievement-motivation pattern of the Lesser et al. bright underachievers, and the French and Lesser woman's role-oriented subjects parallels that of our high scorers, a seeming acceptance of the cultural stereotype that achievement is appropriate for men, but not for women. The absence of ability differences between our high and low scorers, as measured by their weighted S.A.T. scores,[8] yet a tendency for low scorers to achieve a higher grade average at the end of the year in which they served as subjects ($p = .10$, two-tailed test) makes these across sample comparisons all the more meaningful. As in the Lesser et al. (1963) study, then, the fantasy measure would turn out to be a better predictor of academic achievement than the ability measure. Results reported by Hout and Entwisle (1968) point in this same direction: matched for verbal ability, high school girls who accepted competition for grades as appropriate to the female role achieved higher grades than those who did not.

Clearly, many factors influence the achievement motivation and achievement behavior of women, not the least of which, apparently, are the differences in the roles assigned to men and women by the culture. That these values may even override personal role-preferences is evident in the unpredicted finding reported by French & Lesser (1964) that motivation scores of female subjects were always higher under intellectual arousal when male figures were used in the stimuli and under woman's role arousal when female figures were used. Whether the "most girls here" format for the value-orientation measure in the French & Lesser (1964) study would tend to maximize cultural stereotyping for the sample as a whole, and a more personal focus,

8. The weighted S.A.T. score takes into account a predictive measure of academic success.

such as the one used in the present study, to minimize it, remains to be tested.

Further testing of The Wellesley Role-Orientation Scale is, of course, needed. It was constructed as a measure of sex-role acceptance and it appears to have validity as such. On the other hand, the fact that it fails to correlate with some of the other seemingly relevant measures is puzzling. Is this scale so much less obvious as to what it is measuring than the Fe subscale of the CPI (Gough, 1957; see also Bieliauskos et al., 1968), the Rosenkrantz et al. (1968) sex-stereotype measure, or the Crowne-Marlowe (1968) Social Desirability Scale? Or is some other factor, such as the format differences mentioned above, affecting the results? We hope studies now underway will provide the answers.

REFERENCES

Alper, T. G. Predicting the direction of selective recall: Its relation to ego strength and *n* Achievement. *Journal of Abnormal and Social Psychology,* 1957, **55,** 149–165.

Alper, T. G., & Greenberger, E. Relationship of picture structure to achievement motivation in college women. *Journal of Personality and Social Psychology,* 1967, **7,** 362–371.

Angelini, A. L. Um novo método para avaliar a motivação humano. [A new method of evaluating human motivation]. *Boletin Faculdade de Filosofia Ciencias San Paulo,* 1955, No. 207.

Atkinson, J. W. (Ed.). *Motives in fantasy, action and society.* Princeton, N.J.: Van Nostrand, 1958.

Bardwick, J. M. *Psychology of women.* New York: Harper and Row, 1971.

Baruch, R. The achievement motive in women: Implications for career development. *Journal of Personality and Social Psychology,* vol. 15, 1967, 260–267.

Bieliauskos, V., Miranda, S., & Lansky, L. M. Obviousness of two masculinity-femininity tests. *Journal of Consulting Psychology,* 1968, 314–319.

Calkins, K. V., & Dingman, A. F. A Woman's liberation group serves as the Ss in a study of the motive to avoid success. Unpublished paper, 1971.

Crowne, D. P., & Marlowe, D. A new scale of social desirability independent of psychopathology. *Journal of Consulting Psychology,* 1960, **24,** 349–354.

Field, W. F. The effects of thematic apperception of certain experimentally aroused needs. Unpublished doctoral dissertation, University of Maryland, 1951.

French, E., & Lesser, G. S. Some characteristics of the achievement motive in women. *Journal of Abnormal and Social Psychology,* 1964, **68,** 119–128.

Gough, H. G. *California psychological inventory.* Palo Alto, Calif.: Consulting Psychologists Press, 1956–57.

Grainger, B., Kostick, B., and Staley, Y. The role of the stimulus-cue in Horner's motive to avoid success. Unpublished paper.

Horner, M. S. Femininity and Successful Achievement. A Basic Inconsistency. In Bardwick, Douvan, Horner and Gutman, *Feminine personality and conflict.* Belmont, Calif.: Brooks/Cole, 1970, pp. 45–74.

Houts, P. S., & Entwisle, D. R. Academic achievement effort among females. Achievement attitudes and sex-role orientation. *Journal of Consulting Psychology*, 1968, 15, 284–286.

Kenny, D. T. Stimulus functions in projective techniques. In B. Maher (Ed.), *Progress in experimental personality research.* Vol. 1. New York: Academic Press, 1964, pp. 285–354.

Lesser, G. S., Krawitz, R. N., & Packard, R. Experimental arousal of achievement motivation in adolescent girls. *Journal of Abnormal and Social Psychology*, 1963, 66, 59–66.

Levinson, D., & Huffman, P. Traditional family ideology and its relation to personality. *Journal of Personality*, 1955, 23, 251–273.

McClelland, D. C., Atkinson, J. W., Clark, R. A., & Lowell, E. I. *The achievement motive.* New York: Appleton-Century-Crofts, 1953.

Mead, M. *Male and female.* New York: Morrow, 1949.

Michigan picture test. Chicago: Science Research Associates, 1953.

Morrison, H. W. Validity and behavioral correlates of female need for achievement. Unpublished master's thesis, Wesleyan University, 1954. Cited in D. C. McClelland (Ed.), *Studies in motivation.* New York: Appleton-Century-Crofts, 1955.

Murray, H. A. *Thematic apperception test.* Cambridge, Mass.: Harvard University Press, 1943.

Murstein, B. I. (Ed.). *Handbook of Projective Techniques.* New York: Basic Books, 1965.

Murstein, B. I. The Role of the Stimulus in the Manifestation of Fantasy. In J. Kagan & G. S. Lesser (Eds.), *Contemporary issues in thematic apperceptive methods.* Springfield, Ill.: Charles C. Thomas, 1961, pp. 229–273.

Rosenkrantz, P., Vogel, S., Bee, H., Broverman, I., & Broverman, D. M. Sex-role stereotypes and self-concepts in college students. *Journal of Consulting and Clinical Psychology*, 1968, 32, 287–295.

Rostow, E. G. Conflict and accommodation. *Daedalus*, 1964, 736–760.

Smith, C. P. (Ed.). *Achievement-related motives in children.* New York: Russell Sage, 1969.

Veroff, J. Thematic apperception in a nationwide survey. In J. Kagan & G. S. Lesser (Eds.), *Contemporary issues in thematic apperceptive methods.* Springfield, Ill.: Charles C. Thomas, 1961, pp. 83–111.

Veroff, J., Atkinson, J. W., Feld, S. C., & Gurin, G. The use of thematic apperception to assess motivation in a nationwide interview study. *Psychological Monographs*, 1960, 74 (12, Whole No. 499).

Veroff, J., Feld, S. C., & Crockett, H. J. Explorations into the effects of picture-cues on thematic apperceptive expression of achievement motivation. *Journal of Personality and Social Psychology*, 1966, 3, 171–181.

Vogel, M. D. An investigation of the affiliation motive in college age women using low cue strength pictures. Unpublished honors thesis, University of Michigan, 1954. Cited in J. W. Atkinson (Ed.), *Motives in fantasy, action and society*, Princeton, N.J.: Van Nostrand, 1958.

Yarrow, M. R., Scott, P., deLeeuw, L., & Heinig, C. Child-rearing in families of working and non-working mothers. *Sociometry*, 1962, 25, 122–140.

Manuscript received September 13, 1971.

CYNTHIA F. EPSTEIN

Bringing Women In; Rewards, Punishments, and the Structure of Achievement*

I have found it curious that merely pondering the issue of "women and success" has seemed to raise personal anxiety among my female colleagues as well as in myself. Only recently it occurred to me that this distress was probably a variation of the process that Matina Horner has identified as the motive to avoid success,[1] a syndrome to which women especially fall prey, in this case from simply *thinking* about women and success.

This analysis will not, however, deal with the psychological dimension of success. It will be restricted to a set of sociological explanations of the processes that I believe lead to success, or rather, the processes in the society—and thus in the minds of women—that place severe limits on their attainment of success.

It is my conviction that anxiety about success is not the major problem. Although the dynamics of the achievement motivation process remain unclear, we see that while at some levels anxiety destroys motivation, at other levels it drives individuals toward achievement. The far greater problem, I believe, is the general statistical reality that women do not have much success. Perhaps the anxiety that Dr. Horner has so ingeniously identified arises because women's success is in such short supply, and, as with all scarce commodities that we value, we worry about wanting it, feel guilty about having it, and don't quite know how to cope with it when we get it.

From one analytic perspective, the low incidence of success among women is a pathological state in the society, a state of structural imbalance. Considering the vast participation of women in the occupational sphere and their infinitesimal degree of success, it is apparent that a large investment must be made on their behalf to create even a modest ratio of input to payoff. Until some reasonable ratio is developed, the tiny number of women who have been successful are destined to be regarded as pathological and gender anomalies. In addition, because women are not generally counted among the successful, *all* women are regarded as deficient. Thus, women outside as well as inside the professions and occupations are regarded as second-class citizens, as incompetents dependent on males to make the important decisions; as giggling magpies who will contaminate the decorum of the male luncheon clubs and bars; as persons who can't be trusted to be colleagues.

I do not think that these last observations are antiquated. Contrary to the beliefs of many, the world has not changed much in the last five years or two years or two months—in spite of the recent legislation aimed at guaranteeing women and other success-deficient groups a larger share of the places at the top. Informants who wish to remain anonymous report that the male gatekeepers of the channels and the structures of success commonly voice strong objections to bringing women in, suggesting that standards of performance will surely be diminished by their presence. Somewhat contradictorily, these same gatekeepers

* This paper was prepared with the support of a grant by the Research Foundation of the City University of New York.

believe that bringing women in poses *unfair* competition to the special needs of men: economically, as dutiful providers for the family; and psychologically, because their fragile egos would be impaired. The mixed bag of accusations against women and assertions about their incapacities or special strengths; the images, models of human nature, and the nature of man—all seem to have the consequence of assigning women (and resigning them) to supporting roles in the human drama. They are almost never heroes.

The topic around which the papers in this volume is organized—successful women—is not a simple one; it calls into question the entire set of standards used in assessing women's accomplishments in this society. The underlying assumption in this assessment is the use of occupational criteria of success, the dominant standard in the culture. But in American Society there is actually a double standard of success: one for males, another for females.

Although this forum is directed at examining determinants of success of women in the sciences, it is probably reasonable to assume that similar processes affect women's success in almost any domain.

One thing is clear about those women regarded as successful in the United States. Women at the top are at the *bottom* of the top, just as they are at the bottom of any stratum in which they happen to be represented. The occupational spread of women is bottom-heavy. As service workers, women cluster in the lowest paying domestic jobs, ranking lower even than porters and janitors (male jobs); as clerical workers, they hold the lowest ranking jobs as file clerks and typists; in the school system, the women teach and the men administrate. Women lawyers still seem to be found primarily in the specialties considered low ranking, such as matrimonial and real estate work; women doctors cluster in the lower-ranking areas of public health and psychiatry (see Ref. 2, p. 163). In the university, women are most often found in the ranks of lecturer and assistant professor, and fade into statistical obscurity as one goes to the top. The best-situated women, those who hold top ranks as professors or lawyers in Wall Street firms, are not really in and of their elites. Even the most talented and productive are balanced at the outer edge or hold ancillary posts as special assistants to the presidents of prestigious institutions, as adjunct or visiting professors. A striking example is the Noble Laureate Maria Mayer, who held auxiliary and adjunct posts for many years of her career, not becoming a full professor of physics (at the University of Chicago) until 1959, when she was 53 years old. Even today, bringing women into elite structures means creating special posts for them, not in the mainstream of a field but often in the newly created women's specialties—women's studies in English and sociology; the first law professors appointed in the law schools tend to teach courses on women in the law.

Of course, in the natural sciences women are so few and far between that it is hard to assemble statistics about their specialties. Chance seems to play a big role. I understand, for example, that there are women crystallographers in England who have achieved some distinction and whose careers were developed partly through the sponsorship of Dame Kathleen Lonsdale. Lonsdale herself would have settled down to become a "good wife and mother" after her marriage (as she reports in an article of "reminiscences",[3] except that her husband pushed her to return to science and Sir William Bragg persuaded the managers of the Royal Institution to provide her with £50 to pay for the services of a daily domestic helper.† This was in 1929, and one may assume that not many such fellowship

† I am indebted to Professor Harriet Zuckerman for passing on this reference, as well as for the note on Maria Mayer, from her substantial knowledge of Nobel Laureate lore.

awards for the services of a domestic helper have been granted since or are being considered.‡

The chance award, the especially sensitive husband, the protected work situation,[4] a high degree of accident (see Ref. 5, p. 403), the crisis of war—all these idiosyncratic elements have resulted in the success patterns of the few women whom we rate as successes. But there are some more general patterns, as well. Successful women tend more than men to come from higher-income families and to have mothers who have been professional workers. Yet this is not so surprising. The women who come closest to belonging to elites could never have surmounted all the obstacles in their way had they not had some special benefits, had not some of the barriers been lowered. Yet "drift" characterizes even successful women, and their lack of long-range career strategy processes is documented by the studies by Fogarty and the Rapoports of women in top jobs in England[6] and in all the available American literature.

The pressures on American women *not* to achieve (in the *normative,* not the psychological dimension) are strong and more complex than has been realized. Although we have become very sophisticated about early socialization and its clear and present danger to women's careers, there is less cognizance of the *later* dangers to girls' self-images. The fact that girls do not aspire is not just linked to early socialization and the fact that the mothers in children's primers are never seen reading a book or a newspaper, much less scouting adventure. Long after their earliest influences, girls and women are constantly encountering pressures directing them toward the home as a compelling and socially legitimated activity. No balancing pull exists to keep them in the occupations. My studies on women's careers in law indicated that women were as likely to drop out at the peak of their careers as at the start. The late dropouts were clearly engaged in rather successful and rewarding activities and usually no longer had young children demanding constant attention. These women had surmounted the obstacles of the early professional years to drop out at a time when they were supposed to have increased career commitment.

Why?

I think that it comes from the general orientation of girls, young women, and even older women, toward "others" (in David Reisman's sense of being "other directed"). Women are constantly urged to consider "Am I doing the right thing?" and "What shall I be or do that will please my husband, children and parents?" Occupational success never comes out as the positive answer to these questions. Pleasing others and doing the "right thing" always means holding back, and retreating from a position of strong ambition and career commitment.

Black women, ironically, are getting subjected to a strong dose of this orientation today as an outgrowth of the black political movement. They are asked to weigh their life choices from the perspective of how their actions will be viewed by black men, rather than from the perspective of how their choices will give them a richer life or a wider set of options.

Men also face the problems of making important life decisions and experience anxiety about competition and the drive to success, but they have the firm approval of a society that says, "Yes, you are a person, a potential contributor to society; you are on the right course, aim high, be something!" That's quite different from

‡ There is a further footnote to this apocryphal tale. Dame Lonsdale's housekeeper was a woman named Mrs. Snowball, and through her efforts, certainly a kind of "snowball effect" was produced that created careers for a number of women crystallographers in Great Britain.

the message given women: "Explain why you want to be something or somebody and make sure your reason is a good one."

Women do not hear insistent voices saying they *must* do, as do men.

Both men and women are probably afraid of the heights of ambition, achievement, and accomplishment; all these have their costs. But men are forced to face their fears. For those who are successful in conquering them, the lives they chart may be rich and meaningful. Women are not challenged to face their fears and thus never lose them, and remain self-doubting. Without the support to do their best, to be their best, and to enjoy doing well, most of those who could "make it," don't.

It was curious to find in my research on black professional women that in spite of enormous obstacles, they could often be their own person, depending on their own resources and not on the coattails of a husband or a mentor, as do so many women of the white middle class, not because black men don't wish to supply the coattails (it is probably gratifying and power-affirming for the male to know he can carry himself and also his wife and family), but because white society makes it impossible for them to do so.

Why could black women be their own persons? Not because there is anything unique about their sense of competence. In fact, they were behaving much like women lawyers I interviewed earlier who came from white immigrant families, who also went to work with enthusiasm and a sense of commitment and purpose. The thread that connected them was the fact that they *had* to work. That is, the *economic* rationale—the most legitimate in American Society—gave them the answer to the question that all women face: "Why aren't you at home, and aren't you denying your family something by not being there?"

As a footnote to the question still asked in America about women's capacities for distinction in work, some further data on the black women is instructive. Considering the tiny total pool of black women in the prestigious professions (less than 1,000),§ of the eleven doctors I interviewed, two had performed ground-breaking research: one in kidney disorders and the other in pediatric blood disorders. Clearly, this indicates that once women get a foot in the door, quality is not a problem.

A further deterrent to women's success stems from the fact that they are asked to demonstrate competence in a *range* of roles, their female roles as well as their occupational roles, in order to be deemed successes. Occupational excellence is not sufficient for them to be considered really successful. In exchange for this multirole achievement, women are permitted to perform somewhat less than men in their occupational roles and still be considered a success ("for a woman"). Men, on the other hand, must succeed or fail primarily on the basis of occupational achievement. They get few extra credits for being good husbands and fathers.

Does society grant women permission to perform less well than men occupationally because of the awareness of the other crucial societal functions women perform? Or is lower performance structured and guaranteed for women, making it idiosyncratic for them to aim for the top and become professional stars?

Consider some of the dimensions of the problem:

There is probably far more compatibility and structure to the performance of women in the institutions of the family and work than appears on the surface.

Each institution supports the other. The demands by the family on the woman keep her out of real competition in the occupations; reciprocally, the lack of

§ According to the 1960 Census, there were 222 black women lawyers, 487 black women physicians.

positive reinforcement she faces in the occupations sends her back to the home to seek rewards there. This may not be the manifest intent of decision-makers in these institutions, but the consequences are the same.

Part of this is a phenomenon of simple definition. Although 40% of the work force is composed of women, the cultural view is that women do *not* work and are in the home. It is an ideal view and not a real one; but it serves the purpose of forming images and placating discontents. Even the women who are working are convinced that they are not really "workers" and do not think in terms of ambitions, goals, demands, and rights. They may be pleased that they are permitted to work at all, particularly at interesting work. Consider the professors' wives who have been teaching and research assistants on college campuses through the years. Many or most of these held low ranks but were uncomplaining, aware that many others in their position couldn't get jobs at all.

Women's success also is directly affected by the general system of social control in the occupations. The social control system typically operates to undercut the sense of commitment and ambition of those persons not considered potential members of the elite; it acts to make the route to the top clear only to those deemed the preferred candidates.¶

Further, it is characteristic of the world of work that the rewards and punishments are supposed to be clear. A man is supposed to feel that if he is clever enough and hard-working enough, he can "make it." True, there are obstacles, and not everyone possesses talent. But there does seem to be some rationality and coherence about the whole process: reward for performance; punishment for failure.

The messages are shaped to be direct, instructive, and motivating for the person who will be brought inside, and to be confusing and exclusionary for women, blacks, and others regarded as outsiders.

The problem of *demonstration* of competence is in itself a problem, which, once recognized, can be justly rewarded and lead to success.

It is often impossible for the aspiring elite recruit who is unwanted to acquire competence, especially the competence learned after formal training, in an informal professional setting. This later training is necessary if the professional is to operate at the highest levels.

There are a number of dimensions to the creation of competence. One was long ago identified by the sociologist Max Weber as "charismatic education," the education of persons selected to assume leadership roles. Weber included in his description not only the technical knowledge necessary to become warrior, medicine man, priest or legal sage, but the *secret* know-how, and the creation of a sense of distinction by passing through often torturous initiation ceremonies.[8] But who gets this elite education? What are the selection criteria? Who is permitted to learn the secret chants, the etiquette, the names of the gods, to become able to perform miracles, make discoveries, or heal the sick?

The standard selection criteria for graduate education and professional education are fairly well known. But less information is available about the ways in which senior scientists pick members of their research teams, the ways in which authors select collaborators, or how chiefs of staff are chosen. There are no civil

¶ This section is drawn largely from my analysis of social control in the professions reported in two papers: Ambiguity as social control: consequences for the integration of women in professional elites. *In* Varieties of Work Experience. Stewart & Cantor, Eds. Schenkman Publishing Co. Cambridge, Mass. In Press. Women lawyers and their profession: inconsistency of social controls and their consequences for professional performance. *In* The Professional Woman. Athena Theodore, Ed. Schenkman Publishing Co. Cambridge, Mass. 1971.

service exams for any of these elite statuses; entry to structures from which success emanates is problematic.

A degree from a good school will not guarantee that the doctor who graduates high in his class is a brilliant diagnostician, nor can a recently graduated lawyer become a persuasive courtroom advocate through courses in litigation. There are no objective tests for competence at high levels. Here the status-judges of the profession and, to some extent, one's clients bestow the crown of competence. The lawyer doesn't really learn law until he has had the experience of handling actual cases and courtroom situations. He learns partly by trial and error, but better, he learns from the tutoring of an older partner who sees it his duty to guide the neophyte through the maze.

In science, medicine, law, and the academic world (and this is true for business as well), competence is created by exposing the new professional to the tasks, giving him the opportunity to learn the techniques and avoid the pitfalls. He must be given access to persons who can help him, and to information about the important people in the system. The accepted newcomer learns by observing and performing because he is put in a position where he can observe and *must* perform. His important colleagues will watch how he does and give him feedback vital for his improvement as a professional.

Those who teach the young professional and those who lead the profession usually agrees that the "appropriate" candidates are competent and will later become more competent in important ways beyond their talents and formal training. They agree, too, that the "inappropriate" candidates cannot become competent. It is believed that those with the "wrong" statuses cannot be part of the subtle, informal collegial system, will be unable to catch the messages, will be ill-prepared in the necessary etiquette of professional behavior and rules of reciprocity, and will be incapable of proper behavior toward a hierarchy that may not be clearly labeled—for them.[2] Cleverness is not sufficient, nor is a professional degree. Because failure is presumed, few act as sponsor for the *unwanted* professional. "The creation of competence" is a result of on-the-job training given only when important gatekeepers decide that a person has talent that will develop and that he or she will continue to perform well. Residents in hospitals are picked partly because of their past records as medical students and interns, but mainly on the judgment of potential by senior staff members. The new assistant professor is hired because it is believed that the person will later produce competent works and be a colleague of worth.

In short, gatekeepers can structure success for those whom they judge will become competent. Because they are usually men, no one at the gate asks about their hormones, whether they have lovers, children, or spouses. The man of erratic flashes of insight and emotion often will be said to have an interesting mind or a creative nature. He will be told that great things are expected from him and he will be protected from the mundane routines. The woman who is erratic may be labeled muddleheaded. Consider the disesteem suffered by Rosalind Franklin, even though her contributions to current genetic theory were of prime importance. She was considered more odd than a usually "eccentric" scientist.[9]

Women do not fit the *image* of competence held in the society. The woman's commands are heard as shrill. The study by Fogarty and the Rapoports of English women managers[5] reports that women's managerial styles are not thought to be successful. Women are said to be more liable than men to nag, to whine, to "flap like wet hens" when something goes wrong, to be unaware of how to handle colleagues, or to react to extremes: "dragons in an older generation, ineffectual nice mice" in the present one; in any case, ineffective as managers, whatever their style (see Ref. 5, p. 403). There is a self-fulfilling prophecy in this. *Any* female command style is interpreted as inept.

Are men constrained to be so perfectly balanced?

But what of the women who do manage to pass the gatekeepers and are judged to be among the potentially competent? For them the key question is whether they are truly brought into the inner core of professional elites.

As we know from early childhood studies, belonging is as much geared to the discipline structure as to the reward structure. It is my hypothesis that women are often not subjected to the disciplines of their professions as are the men, and thus do not learn how to improve or refine their behavior. Often they are rewarded for merely adequate performance (*any* performance by a woman is considered unique), or their deficiencies are attributed to women as a class of persons, rather than to the individual. What I am pointing to here is a structure of ambiguity. Women don't know where they stand and may not find out until they realize they are out of the picture entirely. As a *class of persons* they are subject to the subtle cooling-out process that men also experience, but the latter undergo it as individuals. Women are rewarded for irrelevant performances or ignored entirely.

Furthermore, I believe that knowledge that they stand in peripheral places undermines women's motivation. Again, we can draw on numerous studies indicating that persons who feel they do not have a stake in an organization have less commitment to it and are more likely to leave.[10,**] Women are often seduced into a type of high commitment by rewards directed at their sex status (such as affection and attention) rather than their occupational status,[11] money, rank, and coauthorship. It is doubtful that the resulting commitment will lead to the major contributions that result in success. The inappropriate rewards women get generate commitment directed to a person, a set of persons, or an institution, rather than more diffusely, to the profession or the discipline.

The secondary rewards women typically receive also pull them off course. They do not compete, nor do they ever put their capacities and talents on the line. Women do not expect or believe that there are *tests* for them as there are for men, and that, like men, they can succeed or fail in the society on the basis of their occupational contributions.

Were this to happen, they would expect that if they did contribute, they would rise in rank and be paid accordingly; they would expect deference and respect. On the other hand, if they did not do well, they could expect the same loss of face that men suffer.

Equality for women means that they should no longer be judged by a different set of standards, because this has typically meant *no* standards at all or debilitating ones.

Equality means the right to the same sanctions, fears, and punishments: the same set of forces that drive men within the reward structure. Where merit is at issue, there must be one standard for all.

I am suggesting that until now there has been virtually no success for women; not that women have not performed well, but because of the multiple standards, the acceptance of a different set of measures that have cheated them of their due. The work of great women painters is often assessed in comparison with other women painters, and not with *all* painters. Women writers suffer the same fate.

** See also the testimony of Judith Long Laws before the Federal Communications Commission, Washington, D.C. 1971 Docket No. 19143. Causes and Effects of Sex Discrimination in the Bell System.

I don't think women have ever had much of a chance to demonstrate greatness in architecture, or as jurists. Uniquely in science, the work of women that has surfaced has been given the same assessment as the work of men, because contributions in science defy sexualizing.

More typically, however, women are encouraged to fail. The "new" woman is a perfectly balanced person who does a little of everything—a little writing and research; a little gourmet cooking; a little loving; a little mothering. But nowhere is she expected to rise to the top of her profession or field of work.

Occupational success probably is a developing phenomenon for women. We will probably witness less fear of success and more movement toward success.

A hypothesis has grown out of my research, which can easily be summed up by the old homily that "nothing succeeds like success!"

Women who have had any success find that in fact it is more pleasant than failing. Women who fear taking jobs with authority find that people will listen to them, and that they *can* be effective task leaders and administrators.

Too often we explain phenomena in terms of the charisma of the leader and not the charisma of the office. The person who is given a role with high ranking attached finds that he (or she) is more successful in effecting changes than the person who has a low-ranking position. Success breeds success. Once we cast the mantle of success on a person, the wheels are set in motion for greater authority. (How much more noble is the judge in his robes than in his golf jacket; how much more sage he is on the bench than at the breakfast table.) Women have always been denied this charisma of office, the halo effect of *place*. (Male colleagues may not hear the wise comments of the female member of the department, but if she is made chairman, their hearing will become more acute.)

I do not anticipate rapid change toward admission of women to the true in-groups of elite structures and stimulation of competence for women at the top. Opening the doors to some women somehow seems to create more apprehension in the hearts of men than opening the doors to members of minority groups. Some of these fears are real, of course. It is certainly true that women, who constitute a substantial pool of the educated and professionally acculturated, could take over a good proportion of men's jobs tomorrow, if they were so inclined and were given the opportunity.

I think that given the taste and experience of success, women will not only not fear it any longer, they will actively seek it and enjoy it. Certainly the women in the sciences have proved that as a class of persons, women can do work that meets the criteria for success in this society. Furthermore, the inclusion of more women in the elite sphere will probably do much to raise the general level of talent and discovery in the society.

The stimulation of the intellectual arena comes from the challenge and confrontation of good minds. Bringing women in is likely to make it more productive for the entire society.

References

1. HORNER, M.   1969.   Psychology Today 3(6): 36. November.
2. EPSTEIN, C. F.   1970.   Woman's Place. The University of California Press. Berkeley, Calif.
3. LONSDALE, K.   1962.   Reminiscences. *In* Fifty Years of X-Ray Diffraction. : 598. P. P. Ewald, Ed. International Union of Crystallography.
4. EPSTEIN, C. F.   The Woman Lawyer. University of Chicago Press. Chicago, Ill. To be published.
5. FOGARTY, M. P., R. RAPOPORT & R. N. RAPOPORT.   1971.   Sex, Career and Family. Sage Publications. Beverly Hills, Calif.

6. FOGARTY, M., A. J. ALLEN, I. ALLEN & P. WALTERS. 1971. Women in Top Jobs. George Allen & Unwin Ltd. London, England.
7. EPSTEIN, C. F. 1973. Positive effects of the multiple negative: explaining the success of black professional women. Am. J. Sociol. Jan. In press.
8. WEBER, M. 1968. Economy and Society. : 1143. Bedminster Press. New York, N. Y.
9. WATSON, J. D. 1968. The Double Helix. Atheneum Press. New York, N. Y.
10. BLAUNER, R. 1964. Alienation and Freedom: the Factory Worker and his Industry. The University of Chicago Press. Chicago, Ill.
11. EPSTEIN, C. F. 1972. Sex Role Stereotyping, Occupations and Social Exchange. Paper presented at the Radcliffe Institute Conference. Radcliffe College, Cambridge, Mass. April 18.

FLORENCE L. DENMARK, BERNICE K. BAXTER AND ETHEL JACKSON SHIRK

The Future Goals of College Women

It is now well known and almost universally recognized, that one of the most formidable barriers to women's full participation in the professions and management fields is their own lack of confidence in themselves regardless of their professional qualifications and skills. Horner (1969, 1972) concludes that "fear of success" is a major obstacle which prevents women from achieving their full potential. Her findings viewed in the context of the rapidly expanding market for professional women have made the need for career information and a new approach to counseling vital for college women.

In the past investigators have dealt exclusively with the tradition-al methods of individual and leader-directed group counseling. Studies of student counseling in small groups have been concerned with therapeut-ic problem solving and the utilization of role playing techniques (Ohlson, 1970). Other studies investigated the occupational and career interests of employed male adults (Miller, et. al., 1970).

This growing market for professional women in various educa-tional, social, industrial, and government agencies, in business and the traditional professions means that the shortage in counseling services will handicap scientific and technical development of manpower and womanpower resources as reported by Torpey (1966) a specialist in the President's Office of Emergency Planning. The need for new and different counseling programs for college women who are career goal oriented is obvious.

This study is concerned with the development and clarification

of school and career goals of women through the use of self-directed group
techniques which is one of the most expedient and productive means of extending and enhancing available counseling services. The approach is
self-instructional, thereby eliminating the need for trained group leaders.
This technique is aimed at improving self-understanding of values and life
goals through the sharing of similar experiential situations, since it enables
women, who experience dilemmas of role identification, to articulate their
problems among peers in a non-inhibited supportive setting (Cook, 1970).
This experience enables the female student to probe her inner feelings
regarding her role as wife, mother and careerist as well as to share and
establish rewarding and productive interpersonal relationships with her peers.

When subjected to the "give and take" and the cooperative interaction of an unstructured group setting, individual doubts and seemingly
insurmountable problems tend to lose some of their intensity, aspiration
levels rise, and goals appear more attainable. Evidence of the importance
of moral support and social sanction cultivated in informal sessions among
women were reported by Farmer and Bohn (1970) who found that home-career
conflicts were often reduced experimentally by verbally providing social
sanction for professionally demanding career roles. Subjects were told to
pretend that men liked intelligent women and that women could be good
homemakers as well as successful careerists. The investigators found that
irrespective of married or single status the level of vocational aspiration
in subjects in the experimental group increased significantly. It is hypothesized that women who participate in self-directed group counseling will
show a greater degree of satisfaction with career goals as well as increased
clarity in pursuit of their goals than will non-participants.

METHOD

Subjects: The subjects used in the present study included 48 nursing
majors enrolled in a four-year nursing program at Hunter College, CUNY,

prior to open enrollment. All of the Ss were female entering freshmen who
lived in the dormitory and took the major portion of their courses at the
Bellevue Hospital complex.

Procedure: Half of the subjects, whose high school grades did not differ
from the other 24 students, participated in a preliminary version of PROBE,
a self-directed group exercise, and half were assigned to a control group.
This exercise, in which the experimental group participated, consisted of
a self-evaluation questionnaire and discussion guidelines, which formed the
basis of discussions carried out by the three-member group. The exercise
consisted of 61 specific items, of which 47 were personal concerns related
to S's future educational and career goals such as academic skills, motivation, personal and social adjustment, and family commitments. 14 items were
addressed to college concerns dealing with the relevance of certain administrative features toward the attainment of S's educational goals. In order
to tap concerns which the participants themselves felt were relevant, and
which might not have already been covered, four blank items were included.
After answering these questions, Ss stated the realistically attainable
specific goals which they expected to reach within two years. They prepared actions plans for attaining these goals and then met with the other
two members of their group to further clarify their goals and action plans.
These discussions ranged well beyond the items suggested by the questionnaire
and included topics such as dating, marriage, the world situation, etc. Following that discussion, each participant had the opportunity to review and
revise their action plans. The total exercise took approximately three hours
to complete.

    Six weeks following the small group discussions, all Ss
were adminstered a post-session questionnaire. This questionnaire contained personal interest items dealing with college life, career goals
and other relevant issues, which were some of the topics covered in the
group discussion. The 15 items are shown in Table 1.

Table 1

15 Item Questionnaire Dealing with College Life and Future Goals

Administered to All Subjects

1. Have you ever given systematic attention to your own career plans by formally writing out personal goals, programs, schedules, etc.? (check <u>one</u>)

   ___I have a formal career plan which I think about and update regularly.

   ___I have made a formal career plan in the past, but I don't think much about it now.

   ___I have never made a formal career plan.

2. Do you think about your long-term career plans (what you would like to be doing in 10 or 20 years) (check one)

   __very often __ rather often __sometimes __seldom ___never

3. Do you discuss your long-term career plans with friends your age or with classmates? (check <u>one</u>)

4. Do you discuss your long-term career plans with your parents or teachers? (check <u>one</u>)

   ___very often ___rather often ___sometimes ___seldom __never

5. Have you ever discussed your long-term career plans with career or guidance counselors or other professional advisors? (check <u>one</u>)

   ___very often __ rather often ___sometimes ___seldom ___never

6. Check the box below which best describes how clear your career objectives are:

   ___I have a very clear picture of what my future career will be; I am deeply committed to it; I will almost certainly devote my efforts to preparing for this career.

   __I have a pretty good idea of a likely future career, but a few related areas are also possible.

   ___I have a number of specific career areas in mind which are rather different from each other.

   __I have several general career areas in mind, but no particular objectives I'm now working toward.

   ___I have no idea at all about the kind of career I'll be in ten or twenty years from now.

7. Have you discussed your career plans with <u>anyone</u> in the last four weeks? (check <u>one</u>)

___not at all ___rather little ___ some ___rather much ___very much

8. All things considered, how satisfied are you with the academic program at your school? (check <u>one</u>)

____Very   ____Somewhat   ____Neutral   ____Fairly   ____Very
    Dissatisfied   Dissatisfied   Satisfied   Satisfied

9. All things considered, how satisfied are you with your own academic performance in school? (check <u>one</u>)

____Very   ____Somewhat   ____Neutral   ____Fairly   ____Very
    Dissatisfied   Dissatisfied   Satisfied   Satisfied

10. All things considered, how satisfied are you with the physical environment in which you work and study (buildings, laboratories, living quarters, etc.)? (check <u>one</u>)

____Very   ____Somewhat   ____Neutral   ____Fairly   ____Very
    Dissatisfied   Dissatisfied   Satisfied   Satisfied

11. All things considered, how satisfied are you with the career you have chosen?

____Very   ____Somewhat   ____Neutral   ____Fairly   ____Very
    Dissatisfied   Dissatisfied   Satisfied   Satisfied

12. In general how friendly and easy to talk with are your classmates? (check <u>one</u>)

____Very   ____Rather   ____Somewhat   ____Rather   ____Very
    Friendly   Friendly   Friendly   Unfriendly   Unfriendly

13. Do you and your classmates exchange ideas and opinions about schoolwork? (check <u>one</u>)

____Very   ____Rather   ____Sometimes   ____Rather   ____Practically
    Often   Often   Seldom   Never

14. Do you feel that you and your classmates belong to a team that works well together? (check <u>one</u>)

____Very   ____Rather   ____Sometimes   ____Rather   ____Very
    Much   Much   Little   Little

15. All things considered do you feel you have much influence and control over your own career plans? (check <u>one</u>)

____Very   ____Rather   ____Some   ____Rather   ____Very
    Little   Little   Much   Much

Grade point averages were obtained after one college year.

Results: Surprisingly, average grades differed between the two groups. The experimental group had a grade point average of 2.8; the control group's average was 2.4 (p $<$ .01).

A multivariate test of equality of mean vectors yielded a significant F at the .01 level between the nursing experimental and control groups on the 15 item scale. As shown in Table 2, significant differences emerged between the twp groups on the following four specific variables:

Friendly classmates - easy to talk with (p $<$ .01)

Influence and control over career plans (p $<$ .01)

Clarity of career objectives (p $<$ .03)

Satisfaction with physical environment of school (p $<$ .03)

Table 2

Multivariate and Univariate F Ratios for the 15 Variables Administered to Nursing Experiment and Control Groups

F Ratio for Multivariate Test of Equality of Mean Vectors Over All 15 Variables = 2.96, p $<$ .01.

Variable*	Univariate F	P Value
1	.03	N.S.
2	2.29	N.S.
3	1.00	N.S.
4	1.94	N.S.
5	.03	N.S.
6	5.82	$<$.02
7	.09	N.S.
8	1.58	N.S.
9	.00	N.S.
10	5.31	$<$.03
11	.69	N.S.
12	8.12	$<$.01
13	1.10	N.S.
14	.41	N.S.
15	6.12	$<$.01

* For description of variable see Table 1

As expected, the Experimental group reported that classmates were more friendly and easy to talk with, they felt they had more influence and control over their career plans, and had greater clarity with regard to their career objectives, thus supporting the hypothesis. However, the Experimental group expressed more physical dissatisfaction with the physical environment in which they worked and studied.

Students complained about the length of the questionnaire in the original version and felt that there were too many items to keep in mind for the single discussion period scheduled at the completion of the questionnaire. They also complained because the exercise took three hours. However, many of the students reported to the investigators that they continued their discussions long after they returned to the dormitory following the official end of the exercise.

Discussion: As hypothesized, the nursing students who participated in PROBE, the self-directed group counseling session, showed increased clarity over their career plans, than did non-participants. The fact that the experimental group found it easier to talk with their classmates indicated that this type of exercise could be a valuable aid in developing friendships among students. Promoting early adjustment to the college scene is an important goal of college administration and seems to have also had an impact on grades.

The counseling participants expressed greater dissatisfaction with the school and hospital buildings, laboratories and living quarters in the follow-up study than did the controls. It is possible that their emergent greater commitment made them more demanding and thus more aware of the deficiencies that existed in their work, study and living environ-ments. This was not too surprising a finding since criticism of the facilities available to them emerged in the small group discussion, and awareness of this increased through the verbal sharing of common experiences.

This study indicates that the use of small informal group

experiences can be a worthwhile means for meeting the counseling needs of
career-oriented college women. Although the Ss were in a career oriented
program directed toward a specific goal, the results cannot be attributed
solely to this fact. Similar results were found with a group of women
uncommitted to any specific major enrolled in a special program at City
University and with a group of Liberal Arts women at the University of
Rochester, as well as with a group of high school seniors. Since the
students in this study were freshmen, they were not at all firmly
committed toward a particular goal. In addition, the exercise was concerned
with those desired goals which could be attained within the next two years,
such as improved study habits, improved reading and writing skills, skill
in taking examinations, ability to work out their own problems, maturity
and independence in thinking, etc., rather than goals attainable at the
end of four years of college.

As a consequence of the study, the criticisms voiced by the
participants were taken into account and the exercise was redesigned
(Denmark, Baxter, Shirk, 1972) to provide a shorter questionnaire which
is divided into two parts. The first part is concerned with career and
educational objectives and the second part with personal objectives,
each part being followed by a separate discussion period. It consists
of 12 basic steps which allow participants to first examine their goals
individually, then to further clarify and develop them through small group
interaction. This new exercise (PROBE)[1] ends with a restatement of goals
and actions. Test administrations indicate this redesign effectively
deals with the criticisms voiced by the students of the present experiment
and provides a more effective and shorter (under two hours) instrument for
delineating and clarifying the future goals of college women.

[1] published by Transnational Programs Corporation, Scottsville, New York

10

CHARLES P. SMITH

Fear of Success: Qualms and Queries

> Where were the women who were <u>really</u> free, who
> didn't spend their lives bouncing from man to
> man....Almost all the women we admired most were
> spinsters or suicides. Was <u>that</u> where it all led?
>
> I scrapped two [books of poems] and the third was
> published. Then a whole new set of problems began.
> I had to learn to cope with my own fear of success
> for one thing, and that was almost harder to live
> with than the fear of failure.
>
> Erica Jong <u>Fear of Flying</u>

Since Horner's (1968) original study of fear of success,
there has been a spate of research on women's achievement problems. Surely it is no coincidence that this scholarly activity
coincides with a period of heightened concern about women's
rights. But perhaps for that very reason we should be wary
of its merit and ask if this flare-up of interest is a flash
in the pan. Does it simply document the fact that because
society has proscribed certain avenues of accomplishment for
women, they have learned to fear competition and attainment?
If so, is the outpouring of research on fear of success only
a descriptive statement about a particular society at a particular time, but of little scientific merit? Does it merely
exemplify the operation of an already-understood scientific
principle (e.g., that fears can be learned) or does it tell
us something more fundamental and universal about human motivation, gender differences, social interaction, or the mechanisms by which culture influences personality? I shall return to this question at the conclusion of these comments.

The purpose of these remarks is to raise some general
questions about fear of success research and to discuss some
issues growing out of a set of papers on this topic that deal
with how fear of success affects behavior, how pervasive it

is, how realistic it is for a person to fear success, and
with other achievement problems that accompany fear of success.
The findings of these studies, taken together, form a complementary body of information and add substantially to our knowledge of fear of success.[1]

Matina Horner's (1968) initial study of fear of success
is so well known by now that only a few summary statements
are needed to set the stage for the discussion of subsequent
studies. Horner's college subjects wrote stories to a verbal
lead. For females the lead was, "After first term finals Anne
finds herself at the top of her med school class." For males
the lead was the same except that "John" was substituted for
"Anne". Horner found evidence of fear of success in the stories
of more than 62 percent of the females and less than 10 percent
of the males. She also found a tendency (p < .10) for more Honors
women to express fear of success than non-Honors women, a finding consistent with her assumption that "fear of success should
be more strongly aroused in women who are highly motivated to
achieve and/or highly able" (Horner, 1974, p. 99). Two possible
negative consequences of success for women are suggested: (1) loss
of a sense of femininity and self-esteem, and (2) social rejection. Horner views fear of success as indicative of a motive
to avoid success. In the present discussion, the term "fear
of success" will be used throughout for the sake of consistency
even though some authors use the term "motive to avoid success."

In a study of "The Motive to Avoid Success and Instructional
Set" Rosemarie Patty (1974) theorized that women who do not fear
success "will excel in situations which are difficult, important,
and/or reflections of their individual ability, i.e., those
which are personally significant." Conversely, women who do

---

[1] The present paper is a revision of comments made by the author
as a discussant at a session on Fear of Success and Achievement
at the meetings of the American Psychological Association in
New Orleans, Louisiana, September, 1974.

fear success "will perform well on tasks where the negative
consequences of success are minimal, e.g., easy tasks or tasks
which say little about their individual ability." Women without
fear of success were expected to perform more effectively
following instructions to the effect that the task is difficult
or instructions stressing internal locus of control, while the
opposite was expected for women with fear of success.

Patty obtained stories from undergraduate women in response
to two verbal cues: "After first term finals, Anne finds herself at the top of her med school class," and "Joan while still
in high school wins national awards for her science projects."
The stories were scored for presence or absence of fear of success using Horner's (1968) coding system except that subjects
who wrote bizarre stories were dropped. Digit span (backwards)
was used as the performance task.

In the first experiment approximately half the subjects
were told that the task was easy while the rest were told the
task was difficult. In a second experiment approximately half
the subjects were instructed that "success is a matter of effort
and ability--there is little room for chance or luck" while the
rest were told that "success is sometimes a matter of luck or
chance rather than effort or ability."

The results were clear-cut (see Table 1). In both experiments there was a significant interaction between presence or
absence of fear of success versus instructions. As predicted,
women without fear of success performed best following instructions that the task was difficult, or those emphasizing internal
control. On the other hand, women with fear of success performed less well when the task was presented as difficult than
when it was presented as easy, and when it was presented as a
task on which one's score was due to effort and ability rather
than to good or bad luck. As Patty observed, for the women
with fear of success, "it may simply have been less threatening
to be successful on a task which was easy or affected by chance,
making them both less personally significant."

Table 1

Digit Span (Backwards) Performance of College Women

following Two Different Instructional Sets

(Adapted from Patty, 1974)

Motive to Avoid Success		Instructional Set			
		Difficult (Experiment I)	Easy	Internal (Experiment II)	External
Present	$\overline{X}$	8.19	10.00	7.67	9.30
	SD	2.69	2.68	2.75	2.50
	N	16	13	13	10
Absent	$\overline{X}$	9.86	7.07	10.00	8.44
	SD	1.46	2.09	1.78	2.13
	N	14	15	18	16

On the basis of these results one might speculate that
following success on an ambiguous task, the two types of women
would make different kinds of attributions. Women with fear
of success might be expected to attribute success to external
factors such as good luck or the easiness of the task, while
women without fear of success might be expected to attribute
success to internal factors such as effort and ability. Unfortunately these speculations are essentially the opposite of
the findings reported in a study of attribution and fear of
success by Feather and Simon (1973). The discrepancy may be
due to methodological factors, or it may be that the Australian
college women in the Feather and Simon study who indicated
fear of success also had strong achievement motivation, and
their attribution patterns may have reflected their achievement
motivation rather than their fear of success. The apparent
discrepancy between the two studies remains an unsolved puzzle
at this time.

It is important to note that there were no main effects
in Patty's study due to fear of success or to instructions.
That is, women who do not fear success are not superior in
performance under all conditions. For example, women with fear
of success performed just as well following "task easy" instructions as women without fear of success following "task difficult"
instructions. (See Table 1.) These findings may be seen as
consistent with those of Feather and Simon (1973) who found no
difference in performance between subjects with and without
fear of success. We will have occasion to return to this point,
and to Patty's main finding that fear of success is most likely
to impair a woman's performance on difficult tasks and on tasks
where one is personally responsible for the outcome.

A study that extends research on fear of success beyond
the college population was conducted by Kristin Moore (1974)
based on a survey of a representative sample of 576 male and
female adults in Detroit, Michigan. An interviewer recorded
stories told by each respondent in response to a single verbal
cue: "Anne (or John) has just graduated at the top of her (his)

college class." ("Medical school," as in Horner's cue, was
changed to "college" to make the topic more realistic for a
non-academic sample.) Two-thirds of the respondents received
the Anne cue and one-third the John cue. The stories were
coded for presence or absence of fear of success imagery using
Horner's scoring system.

Two clear overall trends emerge from the data: (1) Black
respondents produced significantly fewer fear of success stories
than White respondents, regardless of gender of respondent or
cue character, and (2) among White males and females, the highest percentage of fear of success stories (from 53 to 71 percent)
occurs in the youngest age group (18 to 24 yrs.) in response to
both the Anne and John cues. A similar age trend in the percentage of fear of success stories occurs among Black respondents, except for the lack of a clear age difference among
Black females in response to the Anne cue. Thus, as Moore
points out, the prevalence of fear of success in our society
may have been exaggerated in previous studies that have assessed
fear of success primarily in persons of this age group, namely,
college students.

Moore opens up an important new area of research by relating
fear of success to fertility rates. She hypothesizes that women who fear success will have more children than women who do
not as a socially-acceptable means of avoiding competitive occupational achievement. The results support her hypothesis
for White women, and the finding holds up when income and
religion are controlled. The opposite relationship between fear
of success and number of children is obtained for Black women,
however, possibly because they can less easily afford to leave
employment in response to pregnancy.

Moore also found that males and females more often wrote
fear of success stories about Anne the higher their education
level, and the higher their occupation level. (Examples of
high-level occupations were: professional, managerial, technical.) However, the frequency of fear of success stories
about John in relation to education and occupation level tended

to go in the opposite direction. This pattern of responses
suggests that men and women may share a stereotype of the
consequences of success for Anne, and that these differ from
those expected for John. However, the existence of a shared
stereotype about the unfavorable consequences of success for
women does not preclude the possibility that the stereotype
may be true and/or that the existence of such a stereotype may
contribute to the development of such fears in women.

It is possible, therefore, that women who write fear of
success stories about Anne are reflecting their own motivation
as well as a socially-shared stereotype. If we assume that
women in high-level occupations have a relatively high degree
of fear of success, then we may ask whether women high in
fear of success enter such jobs, or whether such jobs arouse
normal levels of fear of success to their highest pitch after
women enter them. There is some suggestive evidence that
both alternatives may be true. Horner assumed that fear of
success would be highest in persons with high achievement motivation and/or high ability, and found some evidence consistent
with that assumption. Moreover, in a subsequent analysis of
the data from her original study, Horner (1972) found that 78
percent of her females with fear of success came from upper-
middle or middle class homes, while only 33 percent of the
women without fear of success came from such backgrounds.

Since women who attain high-level occupations are likely to come from higher social classes and to have relatively
high ability, it seems likely that the women who make it to
the high-level jobs are those who had the highest fear of
success even during their college years. But what a price
they pay, if Patty's analysis is correct! The very conditions most debilitating to a person with strong fear of success, namely, a difficult task and a high degree of personal
responsibility, are the conditions that accompany professional,
managerial, and technical positions. Thus, while all women
in high-level jobs need not have strong fear of success, some

women who do have strong fear of success may indeed attain
such jobs, and the realistic possibility of success in such positions may then arouse their fears to the maximum strength.

Moore's results suggest that there are two types of women
who fear success--those who opt out of competitive achievement
activities (e.g., those who have babies instead of careers) and
those who engage in such activities despite their fear of success (e.g., those who attain high-level occupations). One
way to account for this difference is to assume that women in
the first group have relatively less achievement motivation
than fear of success, so that their overall reaction to
achievement situations is avoidance and withdrawal. Women
in the second group, on the other hand, may be assumed to
have achievement motivation predominate over fear of success
and to react to achievement situations with approach tendencies. Both groups should experience an approach-avoidance conflict, but avoidance wins out in one group and approach in
the other.

It seems likely that the woman with fear of success who
attains a high-level occupation also has relatively high ability and a record of past successes. Thus, she should have a
realistic chance of success, even in a demanding job, and this
should arouse her fears of success more strongly than such
fears would be aroused in persons whose chances of success are
remote. This line of thought describes a person who achieves
at great cost because of the anxieties that accompany goal
striving.

Intensive life history information about particular individuals could provide a much richer picture of such conflicts
than experimental data, and fortunately Karen Horney (1942) has
provided us with an excellent example of such a case. Clare,
who has become a magazine editor, has come for therapy at the
age of thirty because of paralyzing fatigue that interferes
with her work and her social life. In spite of being relatively
successful in her career, she lacks self-confidence. She has
a number of problems that might be regarded as symptomatic of

fear of success including compulsive modesty, low aspirations, inability to give orders or to take a critical stand toward anyone or anything, except in editing, and finally she performs poorly if she is about to win in games in order not to come out on top. Secretly Clare wishes to triumph over others, but she is afraid that if she does she will alienate them, and since she is a very dependent person, she dare not risk rejection. The analysis brings out the fact that Clare was an unwanted child who won acceptance by subjugating her own wishes and acceding to the demands of others. In spite of the manifestation of high ability and ambition in high school and college, Clare was seriously blocked in her efforts to achieve by her fears and resentments. As the therapy progressed, Clare's compulsive modesty was reduced. This, in turn, reduced her dependency and her need to triumph over others, liberated her energies, and made it possible for her to express her ambition effectively in her work.

The case of Clare provides a concrete illustration of a person with high ability and a strong desire to achieve who has actually attained a high-level job, yet whose functioning is impaired because of her fear of the consequences of asserting her ambition and expressing her abilities.

There is yet another factor that should be added to the picture. Women, as a rule, have stronger fear of failure than men (cf. Smith, 1969); and fear of failure, like fear of success, is aroused when there is a realistic chance of actually failing. Thus, the woman with high fear of success, who is successful in a career, may possess the following qualities:

Approach Tendencies	Conflict	Avoidance Tendencies
achievement motivation	→ ←	fear of failure
high ability		fear of success

All of these qualities are exemplified by the heroine, Isadora, of the (possibly autobiographical?) novel <u>Fear of Flying</u> by Erica

Jong. Isadora's mother failed to fulfill her own ambitions:

> Of course my mother had a rationalization for
> it all...the age-old rationalization of women
> seething with talent and ambition who keep
> getting knocked up.
> "Women cannot possibly do both," she said,
> "you've got to choose. Either be an artist or
> have children."

The mother (who is reminiscent of the type of woman who opts
out) expects Isadora to attain the success that she herself had
not enjoyed, and Isadora, bursting with talent and ambition,
finds herself crippled by fear of failure. Then, after extensive
psychotherapy helps to reduce it sufficiently to permit her a
limited taste of success, she experiences fear of success.

To sum up this argument, I suspect that intensive studies
of successful women in high-level jobs who express fear of
success would demonstrate even higher levels of achievement
motivation, together with high ability and probably a considerable amount of fear of failure. Such a woman, while not performing at her best, should perform well, but at the cost of tension, fatigue, uncertainty, and a vague discomfort with her
achievements.

Now let us turn to some additional studies. In a paper
on "Female Role Perception and Attitudes toward Competence as
Related to Activism in Housewives" Rhoda Unger and Diane Krooth
(1974) investigate fear of success outside the college population.
The 53 housewives (out of 132) who responded to their mailed
questionnaire were married adult women between the ages of 25
and 50 who were white, middle-class, and college educated. They
responded to two verbal leads, one describing a person whose
novel becomes a best seller, and another describing a professor
who is named department chairman. The stories were scored for
presence or absence of fear of success according to criteria
listed by Scott (1958).

Contrary to their expectations, the authors found a
non-significant tendency for activist women (members of groups
that promote social change) to more often express fear of success

than non-activist women. Unger and Krooth raise the interesting question of whether, if a woman achieves the traditional female goal of marriage and a family, she will manifest less fear of success. Since fear of success was not assessed in their subjects prior to marriage, their design does not permit an answer to that question. However, their data suggest that being married and not being in competition with men in jobs probably does not reduce the expression of fear of success, since 85 percent of the women wrote stories containing fear of success imagery. The authors speculate that Americans today may value achievement less than before, and that the term "hostility toward success" rather than "fear of success" may be more appropriate as a description of negative attitudes toward success.

In dealing with the question of whether or not it is realistic for women to fear success, Linda Davis and Michael Spiegler (1974) present evidence that men may not, in fact, discriminate against bright and ambitious women when choosing social partners. The authors hypothesized that both sexes would prefer a bright, ambitious person as a partner for an intellectual task, but would not discriminate between bright and average individuals for a social task.

Their subjects were 87 single college males and 84 single college females who were asked to choose partners for a social situation and for a competitive task. Subjects witnessed a video tape interview of two members of the opposite sex who were confederates of the experiementer. This procedure permitted control of attractiveness and other physical characteristics. One potential partner was made to appear bright and ambitious, the other "average." In the social condition the subjects were asked to choose a partner for a situation that was intended to resemble a first date--spending half an hour at a campus coffeehouse. In the intellectual situation, subjects were asked to select a partner with whom to work in competition against another team in solving puzzles.

The results concerning male choice of female partners are

most pertinent here. The hypothesized distinction between the
two types of situation did not occur. Instead, there was a
non-significant tendency for men to select bright women as
partners more often for both kinds of tasks. (The males did,
however, discriminate against bright women when making a hypothetical choice among female partners for a date.)

The authors conclude that it is not realistic for women
to fear social rejection by males if the women are bright and
ambitious. Instead, they suggest that it may be the responses
of other women that cause women to fear social rejection following success. This idea is supported by some results obtained
by Karabenick and Marshall (1974) whose female subjects believed that following a competitive success they were less
well liked by female opponents than by male opponents.

The provocative results of this study leave several questions
in the mind of the reader. First, is spending half and hour
at a coffeehouse with a girl as part of an experiment the equivalent of a first date? Did some men, in choosing the "average"
partner discriminate against the bright woman, even though
many, by selecting the bright woman, clearly did not? Might
some males have chosen the bright partner in that situation
because they felt it was socially desirable to do so? And
finally, the fact that the hypothetical choices of the males
discriminated against bright women suggests that some men may
at least talk as if they make such distinctions, and thereby
foster the view that "men don't make plays for girls who make
A's."

Patricia Campbell and Ann McKain (1974) investigated the
question of why females are more likely to decline in I.Q.
during adolescence than males. Their subjects were 290 girls
and 181 boys from two public and two parochial schools. I.Q.s
obtained at the end of the twelfth grade were compared with
those obtained with the same type of test at the beginning of
the seventh grade.

As expected on the basis of previous findings, more males

than females increased in I.Q. during adolescence, while
more females than males decreased in I.Q. (p < .005).

The subjects were also given the FIRO-B test, a semantic
differential scale on "myself," and an inventory of jobs to
categorize as jobs for males, females or both. Results from
these measures provided suggestive evidence that "young women
who declined saw themselves as being closer to the passive
non-assertive ideal of a woman than did young women who did not
decline. Since part of that ideal is not to be smarter than
the men, it would appear that young women who decline are again
fitting themselves to the feminine ideal by ignoring or not
using their abilities" (Campbell and McKain, 1974).

Campbell and McKain do not mention the finding of Sontag,
Baker and Nelson (1958) that during the elementary school
years girls' I.Q.s less often increase and more often decrease
than boys'. Since girls' test anxiety also appears to increase
more than that of boys during these years, and since children
whose test anxiety increases tend to decrease in intelligence,
anxiety may be responsible for the decline (cf. Smith, 1969,
Chapter 9). As Horner has pointed out, test anxiety scores
may reflect fear of success as well as fear of failure. An increase in either of these types of anxiety throughout either
the elementary or high school years might be expected to have
a detrimental effect on intelligence test performance.

In a study of "Sex Differences in Academic Expectations and
Achievement," Vaughter, Gubernick, Matossian, and Haslett (1974)
compared the estimated and obtained course grades of 69 female
and 79 male college psychology students. As anticipated more
men than women expected to make As, but there were no clear
differences between males and females in grades obtained. The
authors suggest that women's expectations are influenced by
two aspects of sex-role prescriptions: the assumption that
women are less competent to excel, and a response set of verbal
modesty on the part of females regarding achievement as contrasted with a norm of confidence on the part of males.

To pursue this line of reasoning, we might postulate that attributions and expectancies are mediating processes intervening between sex-role stereotypes and impaired performance on tests of intelligence or achievement. For example, the stereotype of lesser female competence in some areas of endeavor might lead to the attribution on the part of females that success, when it occurs, must be due to good luck, whereas failure must be due to lack of ability. The attribution of success to good luck would produce no feeling of pride, and no increase in expectancy of success, but an attribution of failure to low ability would produce humiliation and lower expectancies of future success. These factors, should, in turn, weaken motivation to engage in achievement activities at a later date.

Concluding Comments

The studies reviewed here greatly extend the scope of research on fear of success. They suggest that it is a relatively pervasive problem for both men and women, manifested more under some conditions than others, and responded to in more or less maladaptive ways.

On the negative side, some of the studies described employ relatively small and/or possibly atypical samples from which conclusions must be drawn with care. Of particular methodological importance is the fact that interscorer agreement between two independent scorers is not always reported--a must for research concerning the amount of imagery obtained in different social groups. Little attention is given to the adequacy of the original Horner measure of fear of success, and modifications of the Horner cue make it difficult to compare the results of different studies.

Most serious, however, is the lack of concern with theory. Most of the papers seem to accept the theoretical framework provided by Horner and give little explicit attention to theoretical issues. It would seem that if research on this topic is to be of lasting value, attention must be paid to such theoretical issues as whether fear of success is a unitary construct. For example, is it fear, or hostility toward success, or both? And if it is

fear, is it fear of rejection, fear of retaliation, fear of
conscience (guilt), fear of independence, or what? And if it
is primarily fear of rejection, why not call it that rather than
fear of success? Are there differences between the fears of males
and females, and if so, does it make sense to call them both fear
of success?

Theory and research are needed on the attributional implications of fear of success. Further work on the prevalence of fear
of success in different social groups will be of limited value
so long as the meaning of such imagery is in doubt. For example,
does fear of success imagery reflect a motive or a sex-role
stereotype, or, in some instances, both? If future studies of
fear of success are to be of genuine scientific interest and not
simply of topical or practical interest, they must make a contribution to the theory of human motivation and/or to a general theory
of sex differences in behavior.

References

Campbell, P. B. & McKain, A. E. Intellectual decline and the adolescent
woman. Unpublished paper. American Psychological Association
Convention. Fall, 1974.

Davis, L. S. & Spiegler, M. D. Bright and ambitious: Kiss of death for
women? Unpublished paper. American Psychological Association
Convention. Fall, 1974.

Feather, N.T. & Simon, J. G. Fear of success and causal attribution
for outcome. Journal of Personality. 1973, 41, 525-542.

Horner, M. Sex differences in achievement motivation and performance in
competitive and non-competitive situations. Unpublished doctoral
dissertation. University of Michigan, 1968.

Horner, M. Toward an understanding of achievement-related conflicts in
women. Journal of Social Issues, 1972, 28, 157-176.

Horner, M. The measurement and behavioral implications of fear of success
     in women. In J. W. Atkinson & J. O. Raynor (Eds.) Motivation and
     achievement. Washington, D. C.: Winston, 1974. Pp.91-117.

Horney, K. Self-analysis. New York: Norton, 1942.

Karabenick, S. A. & Marshall, J. M. Performance of females as a function
     of fear of success, fear of failure, type of opponent, and performance-
     contingent feedback. Journal of Personality, 1974, 42, 220-237.

Jong, E. Fear of flying. New York: Signet, 1974.

Moore, K. Fear of success: The distribution, correlates, reliability and
     consequences for fertility of fear of success among respondents in a
     metropolitan survey population. Working Paper #111. Center for Research
     on Social Organization. University of Michigan. Ann Arbor, Michigan,1974.

Patty, R. A. The motive to avoid success and instructional set. Unpublished
     paper. American Psychological Association Convention. Fall, 1974.

Scott, W. A. The avoidance of threatening material in imaginative behavior.
     In J. W. Atkinson (Ed.) Motives in fantasy, action, and society.
     Princeton, N.J.: Van Nostrand, 1958. Chapter 40.

Smith, C. P. (Ed.) Achievement-related motives in children. New York:
     Russell-Sage Foundation, 1969.

Sontag, L. W., Baker, C. T., and Nelson, V. L. Mental growth and personality
     development: A longitudinal study. Monographs of the Society for Research
     in Child Development, 1958, 23, Serial No. 68.

Unger, R. K. & Krooth, D. M. Female role perception and attitudes toward
     competence as related to activism in housewives. Unpublished paper.
     American Psychological Association Convention. Fall, 1974.

Vaughter, R.,Gubernick, D., Matossian, J. & Haslett, B. Sex differences in
     academic expectations and achievement. Unpublished paper. American
     Psychological Association Convention. Fall, 1974.

PART III

OCCUPATIONAL SCENE

OCCUPATIONAL SCENE

Several articles are concerned with interest inventories and their usefulness in vocational counseling for women. Moving from occupational interests to those engaging in occupations, other studies consider the career choices of married women and their effects on satisfaction and conflict, the success of black professional women, the feminization of librarianship and its concurrent inhibiting effect on professionalism in this field, and the role of women in the armed forces. Finally one paper points out that women encounter significant sex discrimination in occupational incomes, while another is concerned with a Supreme Court decision which significantly advanced equal rights for fringe benefits for working women.

The occupational scene shows advances for women, albeit that the change is slow, the discrimination and problems confronting some women, as well as lessons to be learned from what has occurred.

11

NANCY S. COLE[1]

On Measuring the Vocational Interests of Women

Analyses of the interrelationships of scales on common interest inventories and of the interest patterns of women selecting various occupations support the similarity of the structure of women's interests to the structure previously found for men. This information should be used to provide women with information about more and more diverse career options than are now commonly available.

The application of civil rights laws to discrimination against women in hiring practices and in salary levels, the public attention gained by the women's liberation movement, and the increasing number of women who enter the work force each year seem to be combining to produce a large number of women with access to a greatly increasing variety of careers. Vocational interest inventories that often have been constructed primarily for use with men are used commonly to assist women in making career decisions. However, the investigation of such use necessarily has been limited to the occupations that women have entered in great numbers, traditional women's occupations. The appropriateness of present inventories for use with women who have access to the whole range of occupations should be examined carefully.

Research has suggested that present inventories yield much meaningful information about women's vocational interests. A number of studies have reported similar differences between career-oriented and home-oriented women (Astin, 1968; Gysbers, Johnston, & Gust, 1968; Harmon, 1970; Hoyt & Kennedy, 1958; Rand, 1968; Schissel, 1968; Surette, 1967; Wagman, 1966). Astin (1968) and Harmon (1970) have studied the development of vocational interests in women using standard inventories, and Harmon (1969) examined the long-term stability of interest measures for

[1] Requests for reprints should be sent to Nancy S. Cole, The American College Testing Program, P.O. Box 168, Iowa City, Iowa 52240.

women. Many occupational scales for women have been validated (e.g., Campbell & Soliman, 1968; Darley & Hagenah, 1955; Harmon & Campbell, 1968; Strong, 1943). Much useful information about women's vocational interests is provided by present inventories.

However, a number of questions remain about the use of present inventories with women considering vocations not traditionally associated with women. When the results of inventories center around women's occupational scales that have been limited to traditional women's occupations, students and counselors may limit consideration to the occupations presented, although, in fact, the options may be much broader. If the patterns and interrelationships of women's interests are similar to those for men, inferences may be possible from data for women to the entire range of men's occupations, thus eliminating the limiting effect of using only the traditional women's vocations. The purpose of this paper is to consider this possibility by examining the structure of women's interests in terms of inventory scales and occupational groups, to compare this structure with that for men, and finally, to suggest what inferences can be made from women's interests to the entire career spectrum.

STUDY 1: STRUCTURE OF WOMEN'S INTEREST

In a recent article, Cole and Hanson (1971) examined the structure of vocational interests of men in several interest inventories. Their results indicated a common structure (or pattern of interrelationships) of interests across all the inventories considered. The common structure followed the two-dimensional circular arrangement of scales proposed by Roe (1956) and Holland, Whitney, Cole, and Richards (1969). In Holland's terms, the circular arrangement is from Realistic to Intellectual to Artistic to Social to Enterprising to Conventional and back to Realistic.

Cole and Hanson (1971) suggested that knowledge of such a circular arrangement could assist in the interpretation of the inventories, particularly with occupations for which no specific scales exist. In the case of women, useful interpretation in the absence of particular occupational scales could be useful in this time of vocational transition. Therefore, the purpose of the first study was to examine the structure of women's interests in the Strong Vocational Interest Blank, the Kuder Occupational Interest Survey, Holland's Vocational Preference Inventory, and the American College Testing (ACT) Vocational Interest Profile to discover if a common structure existed and, if so, to explore how it compared with that for men.

Method

The analysis of spatial configuration. Following Cole and Hanson (1971), an analysis of spatial configuration (Cole & Cole, 1970) was used to examine the relationship of scales for women in the four inventories, the Strong, the Kuder, Holland's inventory, and the ACT instrument. The analysis gave (a) the degree to which the variation on the scales can be accounted for by a two-dimensional configuration of the scales and (b) the particular configuration of the interest scales when plotted on a two-dimensional surface.

Data. Separate correlation matrices of the scales in each of the interest inventories were

submitted to the analysis described. The intercorrelations of 27 Strong Occupational scales for 300 women were given in Strong (1959), and those for 19 Strong Basic scales for women were taken from Campbell (1971, p. 168). The *Kuder Occupational Interest Survey Manual* (Kuder, 1966, pp. 56–57) gave intercorrelations of 21 core scales for 280 women. The intercorrelations of the six Holland scales for 2,433 women were reported in the *ACT Guidance Profile Manual* (American College Testing Program, 1968) and those for the 8 scales of the ACT inventory for 655 women were given in the *Handbook for the ACT Career Planning Program* (American College Testing Program, 1972).

The Kuder inventory posed a special problem as the 21 core scales on which data were reported for women included 14 scales constructed on men but scored for women along with 7 scales constructed on women. In addition, of the 14 men's scales, there were 9 occupational groups and 5 groups of educational majors, while 2 of the 7 women's scales also were educational majors. The seven women's scales were traditional women's occupational areas, primarily of the social type that would be expected to give only a small segment of the Holland circle. Because of this unusual mix of scales and because comparisons across scales derived on different sex groups is not recommended on the Kuder, only the nine male-constructed Occupational scales were analyzed. These scales seemed most likely to show any whole circle configuration that might exist.

Results

Goodness of fit of the two dimensions. The goodness of fit of a planar surface to the points representing scales of an inventory was measured by the percentage of the trace given by the first two dimensions in the analysis of spatial configuration. The percentage of the trace may be interpreted as the proportion of the variance of the scale points accounted for by two dimensions.

Table 1 presents the results for the fit of the plane for each of the five analyses. The results were comparable to those found with men by Cole and Hanson (1971) in each case. Four of the five analyses indicated a good fit of the scale configuration to the plane with percentages of the trace near 60%. The Strong Basic scales give a much poorer fit (as occurred with men) as was expected since the scales were constructed to be as independent as possible.

Planar configurations. The scale points were projected onto the best-fitting planar

TABLE 1

GOODNESS OF FIT OF THE PLANES

Number of scales	Inventory	Percentage trace
27	Strong Occupational scales	59.0
19	Strong Basic scales	34.3
9	Kuder Occupational scales	61.7
6	Holland's VPI scales	59.7
8	·ACT VIP scales	59.5

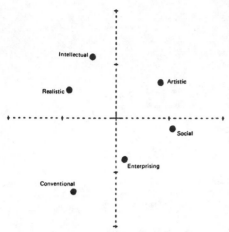

Fig. 1. Spatial configuration for women of Holland's six Vocational Preference Inventory scales.

that reported by Holland et al. (1969) and Edwards and Whitney (1971) and showed the circular ordering from Realistic to Intellectual to Artistic to Social to Enterprising to Conventional.

The configurations of the 27 Strong Occupational scales, the 19 Strong Basic scales, the 9 Kuder scales, and the 8 ACT scales are given in Figures 2, 3, 4, and 5, respectively. In each case the configurations tended to follow the Holland ordering and were, in addition, similar to the comparable configurations for men reported in Cole and Hanson (1971). For example, of the Strong Occupational scales in Figure 2, math-science teacher, dentist, physician, psychologist, author, life insurance salesman, and office worker were located in positions similar to the corresponding scales for men (Cole & Hanson, 1971, p. 481); and in both cases, the scales conformed to the Holland circular ordering. For each inventory examined, the Realistic and Intellectual scales tended to be found in the upper left quadrant, the Artistic scales to the upper right, and the Social, Enterprising, and

surface for each of the inventories, and the configurations were oriented in the same general way for visual comparisons. Figure 1 gives the configuration of Holland's six scales. The configuration corresponded to

Fig. 2. Spatial configuration for women of 27 Strong Vocational Interest Blank Occupational scales.

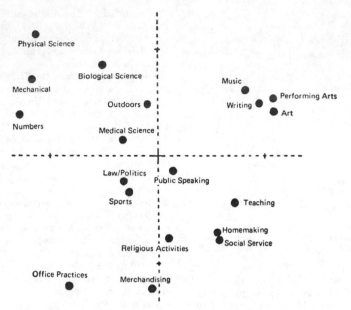

Fig. 3. Spatial configuration for women of 19 SVIB Basic scales.

Conventional scales from right to left in the lower half of the configuration.

Discussion

In this study we found that women's interests can be represented in a two-dimensional configuration and that the configurations generally conform to those reported by Cole and Hanson (1971) for men. The existence of a structure in the interests of women similar to that found for men could be valuable in interpreting women's inter-

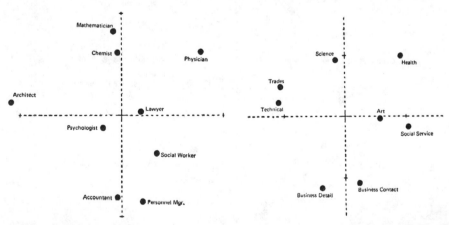

Fig. 4. Spatial configuration for women of nine Kuder Occupational Interest Survey scales.

Fig. 5. Spatial configuration for women of eight American College Testing Vocational Interest Profile scales.

ests, especially in cases where specific scales for women in careers dominated by men are unavailable.

In Study 2, we examined interest inventory scores of women selecting particular vocations to get further information about the pervasiveness of the Holland configuration in the vocational interests of women.

STUDY 2: OCCUPATIONAL CONFIGURATIONS

Additional information about the interest patterns of women in a variety of occupations can be obtained by constructing occupational configurations. Cole, Whitney, and Holland (1971) used the analysis of spatial configuration to construct a configuration of occupations for men based on Holland's VPI. The results both confirmed and supplemented the analyses of Cole and Hanson (1971). In this study, we constructed two occupational configurations for women— one based on Holland's VPI and one based on the ACT VIP—in order to compare the occupational configurations with the inventory scale configurations and to gain additional information about occupational groups for which no scales are available.

Method

Data. The data for one of the occupational configurations were scores on the six scales of Holland's VPI and expressed vocational choice of 6,143 female college freshmen in a sample described by Abe, Holland, Lutz, and Richards (1965). Expressed vocational choice was obtained by asking the students to select from a list of over 70 occupations "the occupation you plan to enter." Mean VPI scores were computed for all students selecting each of 22 occupations with adequate frequency of selection and expected diversity in the configuration.

For the second occupational configuration, the data were scores on the eight scales of the ACT VIP and expressed vocational choice for women entering 2-year colleges. The students selected their vocational choices from a list of over 150 occupations. Mean ACT VIP scores were computed for students selecting each of 13 occupations.

Analysis. Cole and Cole (1970) described a procedure for projecting group means onto the space of the variables produced from the analysis of spatial configuration described in Study 1. The analysis yields a projection matrix with which the occupational group means can be plotted on the same surface as the scale configuration. The result is then a configuration of occupational groups. This

procedure was used by Cole et al. (1971) to obtain an occupational configuration for men based on scores on Holland's VPI. In this study the analysis was applied to data for women from Holland's inventory and from the ACT VIP to obtain two occupational configurations for women.

Results

Figure 6 gives the occupational map for 22 women's vocational choice groups based on Holland's VPI. The map in Figure 6 can be superimposed on that of the Holland scales in Figure 1 to relate the inventory scales and the occupational groups. The configuration in Figure 6 was compatible with the scale configuration in Figure 1; that is, social-type occupations such as social worker, elementary school teacher, history teacher, and counselor fell in the same area as the Social scale. In addition, the configuration of occupations was similar to that found for men by Cole et al. (1971).

In Figure 7, the configuration is given for 13 occupational choice groups based on the ACT VIP scores of a sample of women entering 2-year colleges. No scientific occupations were available on this group and therefore the upper left quadrant is vacant. However, even on this different sample of women, the occupations again conformed to the scale configuration in Figure 4 and to the general Holland circular ordering.

Discussion

The similarities of the occupational configurations based on two samples of women (one sample of 4-year college students and another of 2-year college students) and two different inventories lend further support for the pervasiveness of the Holland circular ordering in the vocational interests of women.

IMPLICATIONS AND CONCLUSIONS

The primary concern of this article has been to determine how interest inventories can be used with women in order to provide useful information about the full range of careers currently being opened to them. As was noted earlier, the use of traditional women's occupational scales may have a severely limiting effect on the careers women consider. Yet at this time of transition, the

Fig. 6. Spatial configuration of occupations based on women's responses to Holland's Vocational Preference Inventory. (The number in each occupational group is given below.)

Accountant–174	Lawyer–32
Art Teacher–93	Mathematician–54
Business Teacher–89	Math Teacher–114
Buyer–55	Medical Technician–111
Clinical Psychologist–48	Musician–43
Counselor–76	Music Teacher–74
Elementary School Teacher–1497	Nurse–301
English Teacher–306	Physician–79
History Teacher–154	Science Teacher–45
Housewife–122	Secretary–267
Journalist–57	Social Worker–140

only data available are those on traditional women's occupations. In this section we examine the implications of the studies presented here for a different kind of use of present interest inventories with women with newly increased career options.

The two studies in this article indicated that when women's interests were compared with those of other women, the resulting structure of interests was essentially the same as that found for men. In addition, when there were occupations that both, men and women pursue, these occupations tended to fit in similar positions within the

structure for both men and women. These results suggested that by locating a woman's interests within the observed circular structure, one could indicate similarities not only with the locations of women's occupations but also with men's occupations at a corresponding location in the structure for men.

The Holland VPI and the ACT VIP are well suited to this approach since they contain scales that refer to areas of the circular structure and are identical for men and women. Thus, on these two inventories one need only identify the scales on which a

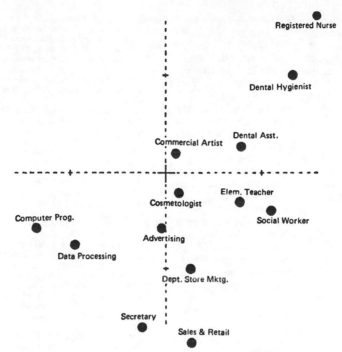

Fɪɢ. 7. Spatial configuration of occupations based on women's responses to the ACT Vocational Interest Profile. (The number in each occupational group is given below.)

Advertising–20	Department Store Marketing–22
Commercial Artist–38	Elementary School Teacher–89
Computer Programmer–178	Registered Nurse–843
Cosmetologist–158	Sales & Retail–79
Data Processing–231	Secretary–988
Dental Assistant 313	Social Worker–58
Dental Hygienist–129	

woman's scores are relatively high when compared with scores of other women, and refer the woman to both the men's and women's occupations that relate to those scales.

The same type of information also is available in the Strong and in the Kuder, although in a less direct way. For these two inventories, the present scales should be used *only* to locate a woman's interests on the circular structure or in the primary categories of the structure. Then lists of both men's and women's occupations that relate to that location should be provided. On the Strong, either the women's Occupational scales, the women's Basic scales, or the new Strong–Holland scales could be used at the

initial step. The women's Occupational scales on the Kuder are so limited that the male-derived scales are probably better suited for the purpose of locating women's interests on the circular structure.

Two additional implications should be mentioned. First, the procedures suggested here are different from the tradition of empirical group comparison common to both the Strong and the Kuder (although not inconsistent with the more recent work on the more general Strong Basic scales). We do not necessarily argue against the empirical approach but the lack of available data should not be used to limit women's career options, especially when a viable alternative exists. A second point deserving notice is that the results of the studies presented here do not imply that women's and men's interests do not differ. In fact, there is abundant evidence that distinct differences do exist in present society. The results implied instead that the interrelationships of interests do not differ and, for example, that a woman whose interests are relatively more scientific than those of other women may look more like a scientist in her interest pattern even though she may still have the high social interests of most women.

In summary, while present interest inventories sometimes include traditional women's occupational scales that could limit women's career options, the present inventories show a common structure of women's interests that parallels that found for men. By using this structure, women may be given information about how their interests relate to the full spectrum of occupations, including those associated traditionally with either men or women.

REFERENCES

ABE, C., HOLLAND, J. L., LUTZ, S. W., & RICHARDS, J. M., JR. A description of American college freshmen. *ACT Research Report No. 1.* Iowa City, Iowa: American College Testing Program, 1965.

AMERICAN COLLEGE TESTING PROGRAM. *ACT Guidance Profile Manual.* Iowa City, Iowa: Author, 1968.

AMERICAN COLLEGE TESTING PROGRAM. *Handbook for the ACT Career Planning Program.* Iowa City, Iowa: Author, 1972.

ASTIN, H. S. Career development of girls during the high school years. *Journal of Counseling Psychology,* 1968, **15,** 536–540.

CAMPBELL, D. P. *Manual for the Strong Vocational Interest Blank.* Stanford: Stanford University Press, 1966.

CAMPBELL, D. P. *Handbook for the Strong Vocational Interest Blank.* Stanford: Stanford University Press, 1971.

CAMPBELL, D. P., & SOLIMAN, A. M. The vocational interests of women in psychology: 1942–66. *American Psychologist,* 1968, **23,** 158–163.

COLE, N. S., & COLE, J. W. L. An analysis of spatial configuration and its application to research in higher education. *ACT Research Report No. 35.* Iowa City, Iowa: American College Testing Program, 1970.

COLE, N. S., & HANSON, G. R. An analysis of the structure of vocational interests. *Journal of Counseling Psychology,* 1971, **18,** 478–486.

COLE, N. S., WHITNEY, D. R., & HOLLAND, J. L. A spatial configuration of occupations. *Journal of Vocational Behavior,* 1971, **1,** 1–9.

DARLEY, J. G., & HAGENAH, T. *Vocational interest measurement: Theory and practice.* Minneapolis: University of Minnesota Press, 1955.

EDWARDS, K. J., & WHITNEY, D. R. *A structural analysis of Holland's personality types using factor and configural analysis.* (Center for Social Organization of Schools Resch. Rep. No. 103) Baltimore: Johns Hopkins University, 1971.

GYSBERS, N. C., JOHNSTON, J. A., & GUST, T. Characteristics of homemaker- and career-oriented women. *Journal of Counseling Psychology,* 1968, **15,** 541–546.

HARMON, L. W. Predictive power over 10 years of measured social service and scientific interests among college women. *Journal of Applied Psychology,* 1969, **53,** 193–198.

HARMON, L. W. Anatomy of career commitment in women. *Journal of Counseling Psychology,* 1970, **17,** 77–80.

HARMON, L. W., & CAMPBELL, D. P. Use of interest inventories with nonprofessional women: Stewardesses versus dental assistants. *Journal of Counseling Psychology,* 1968, **15,** 17–22.

HOLLAND, J. L. *Manual for the Vocational Preference Inventory.* (6th rev.) Palo Alto: Consulting Psychologists Press, 1965.

HOLLAND, J. L., WHITNEY, D. R., COLE, N. S., & RICHARDS, J. M., JR. An empirical occupational classification derived from a theory of personality and intended for practice and research. *ACT Research Report No. 29.* Iowa City, Iowa: American College Testing Program, 1969.

HOYT, D. P., & KENNEDY, C. E. Interest and personality correlates of career-motivated and homemaking-motivated college women. *Journal of Counseling Psychology,* 1958, **5,** 44–48.

KUDER, G. F. *Kuder Occupational Interest Survey general manual.* Chicago: Science Research Associates, 1966.

RAND, L. Masculinity or femininity? Differentiating career-oriented and homemaking-oriented college freshman women. *Journal of Counseling Psychology,* 1968, **15,** 444–450.

ROE, A. *The psychology of occupations.* New York: Wiley, 1956.

SCHISSEL, R. F. Development of a career-orientation scale for women. *Journal of Counseling Psychology,* 1968, **15,** 257–262.

STRONG, E. K., JR. *Vocational interests of men and women.* Stanford: Stanford University Press, 1943.

STRONG, E. K., JR. *Strong Vocational Interest Blank manual.* Palo Alto: Consulting Psychologists Press, 1959.

SURETTE, R. F. Career versus homemaking: Perspectives and proposals. *Vocational Guidance Quarterly,* 1967, **16,** 82–86.

WAGMAN, M. Interests and values of career and homemaking oriented women. *Personnel and Guidance Journal,* 1966, **44,** 794–801.

(Received March 25, 1972)

12

PATRICK H. MUNLEY, ET. AL.[1]

Female College Students' Scores on the Men's and Women's Strong Vocational Interest Blanks

Men's and women's forms of the Strong Vocational Interest Blank (SVIB) were administered to a sample of 90 undergraduate women. Significant differences were found between mean scores on Occupational scales common to both forms and on mean number of B+ and A ratings on the men's and women's forms. Occupational scale scores and number of B+ and A interest ratings were examined in relationship to career versus homemaker orientation. Students differentiated on the basis of career orientation obtained significantly different mean numbers of B+ and A interest ratings on the Women's SVIB. Results are discussed in terms of implications for vocational counseling, and use of both forms of the SVIB is recommended in vocational counseling with college women.

The vocational interests of women have received considerably less attention than those of men. While certain consistent differences between the interests of men and women have been described (Carter & Strong, 1934; Strong, 1943; Terman & Miles, 1936; Traxler & McCall, 1941; Yum, 1942), the question of whether or not men and women engaged in the same occupations have the same interest patterns still remains unanswered. In spite of some evidence that men and women have similar interests within certain occupations (Hornaday & Kuder, 1961; Seder, 1940), interest inventories such as the Strong Vocational Interest Blank (SVIB) still appear with separate scales for men and women.

From the point of view of the counselor who uses the SVIB, separate forms have been a drawback in counseling females. Due to the slow development of research on women's interests and difficulties in obtaining criterion groups, the women's blank has had a history of being more limited in scope than the men's blank. Even with the 1969 revision of the women's blank and the appearance of a number of new Occupational scales for occupations entered primarily by

women, many Occupational scales on the men's blank which might be considered relevant for women, for example, veterinarian, psychiatrist, biologist, architect, personnel director, and pharmacist, were not scaled for women. This discrepancy in scope and type of occupational coverage offered by the two forms has influenced counselors to use the men's blank with women (Darley & Hagenah, 1955). However, such practice has been disputed by Strong (1955, 1966).

While, ideally, the issue should be decided by research, prior research relevant to the use of the men's blank with female clients has not yielded a conclusive answer (Laime & Zytowski, 1963; Stanfiel, 1970). This inconclusiveness stems, in part, from the small number of studies relevant to the topic, incompatible results among existing studies, and the obsolescence of some research due to the publication of the new Women's Form, TW 398. In brief, the professional situation that exists is one with conflicting recommendations and few empirical guidelines. As such, counselors still must rely largely on their own intuitive judgments about the usefulness of the men's blank in vocational counseling with women.

The present investigation provides research relevant to a vocational counselor's

[1] Requests for reprints should be sent to Bruce R. Fretz, Department of Psychology, University of Maryland, College Park, Maryland 20742.

decision on this issue by comparing female college students' interest scores on the men's and women's forms of the SVIB. Occupational interest scores and number of B+ and A interest ratings are examined on both blanks, testing two hypotheses derived from the research of Laime and Zytowski (1963) and Stanfiel (1970).

● Hypothesis 1: For the Occupational scales appearing on both forms of the SVIB, female college students' scores on the men's blank are significantly higher than their scores on the corresponding Occupational scales on the women's blank.

● Hypothesis 2: Considering *all* scales on both forms, female college students obtain a significantly greater proportion of B+ and A interest ratings on the men's blank in comparison with their proportion of B+ and A interest ratings on the women's blank.

Interest ratings also are examined in relationship to career orientation, a potential moderator variable suggested by the authors just cited as well as by Darley and Hagenah (1955). Career orientation here is defined as rating oneself more favorably as a career woman than as a homemaker. Subjects who scored high on career orientation and low on career orientation (homemaker oriented) were compared with respect to the mean number of B+ and A ratings obtained on three sets of scales: (*a*) Occupational scales common to both the men's and women's blank (common scales); (*b*) Occupational scales appearing only on the men's blank (men's unique scales); and (*c*) Occupational scales appearing only on the women's blank (women's unique scales).

METHOD

Subjects

The subjects for the study were 90 female undergraduate students enrolled in introductory psychology who received research credit for participating. They were informed that the research dealt with women's occupational interests and that they would be taking and receiving the results of two vocational interest inventories.

Instruments

Three measures were completed by each subject, the men's and women's forms of the SVIB (Forms

T 399 and TW 398) and a career orientation questionnaire. The career orientation questionnaire was constructed by the present authors to differentiate between career-oriented and homemaker-oriented women. The questionnaire consisted of a semantic differential with two concepts, "Myself as a Homemaker" and "Myself as a Career Woman," each with the same 11 evaluative bipolar adjectives, for example, successful–unsuccessful, wise–foolish. The rationale for using these concepts was that women do differ in their evaluations and perceptions of themselves as homemakers and career women and that, while some women may find being a homemaker and a career woman equally attractive, women who rate themselves more favorably as a career woman should be more career oriented than those who rate themselves more favorably as a homemaker. A pilot investigation compared scores of two groups of female college students on the career orientation questionnaire. One group (*n* = 10), composed of students who planned on attending graduate school, scored significantly higher (*p* < .05) than a second group of students (*n* = 10) who did not plan on attending graduate school.

Procedure

Testing was conducted in the Counseling Center Testing Room under standard testing conditions. Administration of the men's and women's forms of the SVIB was counterbalanced to control for order effects. After completion of both forms of the SVIB, subjects completed the career orientation questionnaire; most subjects completed all forms in from 1½ to 2 hours. All SVIBs were scored by National Computer Systems. Subjects were contacted a second time, approximately 3 weeks after testing, and given the results of the SVIBs. Following test interpretations of both forms, all subjects responded to the question, If you could take only one form of the SVIB, which one would you choose, men's or women's form?

RESULTS

Table 1 presents the comparative data for the scales that appear on both men's and women's blanks of the SVIB. Dependent *t* tests on the means of corresponding scales yielded the following results: (*a*) Significantly higher means were obtained on the men's blank scales for 13 of the 21 pairs of scales. These were the Dentist, Physician, Psychologist, Mathematician, Chemist, Social Worker, Social Science Teacher, Librarian, Artist, Musician, Performer, Music Teacher, Lawyer, and Business Education Teacher scales. (*b*) Significantly higher means were obtained on four of the women's blank scales: Army Officer,

TABLE 1

WOMEN'S SCORES ON CORRESPONDING SCALES OF THE MEN'S AND WOMEN'S
FORMS OF THE STRONG VOCATIONAL INTEREST BLANK

Scale	Men's blank		Women's blank		Pearson r	t
	M	SD	M	SD		
Dentist	30.95	10.86	21.46	11.38	.504	8.07*
Physician	35.40	13.93	25.60	14.08	.679	8.23*
Psychologist	29.85	9.99	18.07	14.95	.820	12.55*
Mathematician	22.73	9.92	10.90	14.82	.701	10.55*
Chemist	23.78	12.54	5.61	16.66	.706	14.51*
Engineer	18.37	10.64	18.26	12.85	.574	.09
Army Officer	12.81	11.12	27.45	10.06	.396	−11.83*
Math-Science Teacher	25.31	9.61	29.61	11.58	.729	−5.06*
YMCA-YWCA Staff Member	34.00	12.86	33.00	12.38	.792	1.15
Social Worker	34.85	12.94	19.96	13.26	.742	14.90*
Social Science Teacher	36.44	10.02	29.67	10.75	.526	6.20*
Librarian	43.21	8.46	23.08	13.45	.678	19.15*
Artist	35.77	10.89	25.00	12.45	.752	12.17*
Musician–Performer	48.50	10.65	30.94	11.76	.579	16.03*
Music Teacher	41.23	10.66	16.75	13.36	.687	23.51*
Accountant	18.75	12.26	16.98	13.53	.618	1.47
Banker–Bankwoman	23.27	10.40	23.80	12.11	.754	−.61
Lawyer	32.41	7.28	19.50	11.61	.398	11.09*
Physical Therapist	35.41	12.19	39.02	13.10	.718	−3.57*
Computer Programmer	25.77	10.82	30.84	10.07	.651	−5.45*
Business Education Teacher	30.93	11.83	19.58	11.93	.759	12.97*

Note. $N = 90$.
* $p < .001$.

Math-Science Teacher, Physical Therapist, and Computer Programmer. (c) No Significant differences were found for the four remaining pairs of scales. A total of 17 of 21 differences were in the hypothesized direction; a sign test (Siegel, 1956) was significant at the .004 level.

Table 2 presents the comparative data on the mean number of B+ and A interest ratings obtained on both forms. A t test comparing the total mean number of B+ and A ratings obtained on both forms yielded no

TABLE 2

MEAN NUMBER OF B+ AND A INTEREST RATINGS
OBTAINED ON THE COMMON AND UNIQUE SCALES

Scale	Men's blank		Women's blank		t
	M	SD	M	SD	
Common	5.64	1.86	2.96	2.43	9.73*
Unique	5.14	2.63	8.27	4.15	−5.52*
Total	10.78	3.60	11.24	5.38	−.86

* $p < .001$.

significant difference and consequently fails to support Hypothesis 2. However, t tests of mean number of B+ and A ratings obtained on the common scales (the Occupational scales that appear on both forms of the SVIB) indicated a significantly ($p < .001$) greater number of B+ and A ratings on the men's forms.

Table 2 also indicates that all subjects attained a significantly greater number of B+ and A ratings on women's unique scales than on the men's unique scales. This result of course mitigated against finding a significantly larger total number of B+ and A ratings on the men's form.

Tables 3 and 4 present the results of empirical tests regarding the influence of career orientation on interest patterns. High and low career orientation subjects were defined as those whose scores on the questionnaire were in the top and bottom 27% of the sample. High and low career orientation subjects did not differ significantly on the number of B+ and A ratings on the men's

TABLE 3.

MEAN NUMBER OF B+ AND A INTEREST RATINGS
OBTAINED BY HIGH AND LOW CAREER
ORIENTATION STUDENTS ON THE
WOMEN'S SVIB

Scale	High career orientation		Low career orientation		t
	M	SD	M	SD	
Common	4.12	2.98	2.24	2.28	2.45*
Unique	7.24	3.19	9.56	4.29	−2.12*
Total	11.36	5.43	11.80	5.55	−.27

* $p < .05$.

blank. However, high career orientation students obtained a significantly greater mean number of B+ and A ratings on the women's common scales and low career orientation students obtained a significantly greater mean on the women's unique scales.

DISCUSSION

The results obtained support the recommendation that a counselor consider the men's form of the SVIB a useful instrument with female clients. Although the high scores the women obtained on the men's form cannot be considered an index of occupational similarity with *women* in those occupations, the scores do indicate that the clients have interests in common with members of those occupations who happen to be men. If such information is useful to a female client in terms of exploring career choices, then the administration of the men's form is clearly appropriate.

The above recommendation suggests the administration of the men's form *in addition* to the women's form, not in place of it. Administering both forms of the SVIB to female clients has some advantages. The higher mean scores and the significantly greater number of B+ and A ratings obtained by females on the scales common to both forms as well as a mean of over five B+ and A ratings on scales only on the men's form indicate that if a counselor chooses only the women's form, occupational areas in which the client has interests significantly similar to men may be overlooked. A client may be led inappropriately to believe that she lacks interests in common

with people in a certain occupation when a more accurate assessment would be that the client lacks interests in common with women in that occupation. When given a forced-choice question after receiving their interest results on both forms, 48% of all subjects stated they would prefer, if they could take only one form, to take the men's form.

The present results confirm an earlier hypothesis proposed by Laime and Zytowski (1963). In attempting to explain why the significant score differences occurred for women completing both the men's and women's common scales, they noted Strong's observation that women in various occupations tended to be more heterogeneous in interests. They assumed that it might be harder for women to obtain high occupational similarity ratings and went on to conclude that when a woman takes the male form, she will show greater interest similarity when compared to men. Such results were obtained in the present study.

Of further importance are the results of the empirical tests of the relationship between career orientation and SVIB interest scores. Comparing the results shown in Tables 3 and 4 reveals that low career orientation subjects are the ones who have the greatest increase in number of B+ and A ratings on the men's form as compared to the women's form ($\bar{X}s$ of 5.76 and 2.24, respectively). Paradoxically, non-career-oriented women are most logically the clients given only the women's form.

The remaining results in Tables 3 and 4 are all in accord with logical deductions from the construct of career orientation. On the women's form where the unique scales

TABLE 4

MEAN NUMBER OF B+ AND A INTEREST RATINGS
OBTAINED BY HIGH AND LOW CAREER
ORIENTATION STUDENTS ON THE
MEN'S SVIB

Scale	High career orientation		Low career orientation		t
	M	SD	M	SD	
Common	5.92	1.69	5.76	1.72	.32
Unique	5.24	2.38	4.88	2.77	.48
Total	11.16	3.50	10.64	3.52	.51

reflect homemaker, non-career-oriented vocations, low career orientation obtained significantly more B+ and A ratings. On the scales common with the men's form (the more career oriented vocations) high career orientation subjects obtained the greater number of B+ and A ratings. Finally, on the men's form the absence of significant group differences could be explained by the greater similarity concerning career orientation of men in all occupations as compared to women in all occupations.

In summary, not to administer both forms of the SVIB to female clients may be an actual disservice to them. The fact that men and women in a given occupation may have different interests does not preclude using the men's scale with women. Such a procedure precludes only using the men's form as an index of occupational similarity with women. The writers believe that it is most appropriate to allow women, at least college women, to compare their interests with those of men as well as women and consequently recommend the administration of both forms of the SVIB to college women requesting vocational counseling. Only if such a practice is adopted will college female clients be assured a complete picture of their interests.

REFERENCES

CARTER, H. D., & STRONG, E. K. Sex differences in occupational interests of high school students. *Personnel Journal,* 1934, **12,** 166–175.

DARLEY, J. G., & HAGENAH, T. *Vocational interest measurement: Theory and practice.* Minneapolis: University of Minnesota Press, 1955.

HORNADAY, J. A., & KUDER, G. F. A study of male occupational scales applied to women. *Educational and Psychological Measurement,* 1961, **11,** 859–863.

LAIME, B. F., & ZYTOWSKI, D. G. Women's scores on the M and F Forms of the SVIB. *Vocational Guidance Quarterly,* 1963, **12,** 116–118.

SEDER, M. A. The vocational interests of professional women. *Journal of Applied Psychology,* 1940, **24,** 130–143.

SIEGEL, S. *Nonparametric statistics for the behavioral sciences.* New York: McGraw-Hill, 1956.

STANFIEL, J. D. Administration of the SVIB Men's Form to women counselees. *Vocational Guidance Quarterly,* 1970, **19,** 22–27.

STRONG, E. K., JR. *Vocational interests of men and women.* Stanford: Stanford University Press, 1943.

STRONG, E. K. JR. *Vocational interests 18 years after college.* Minneapolis: University of Minnesota Press, 1955.

STRONG, E. K. JR. *Manual for the Strong Vocational Interest Blanks.* (Rev. ed.) Stanford: Stanford University Press, 1966.

TERMAN, L. M., & MILES, C. C. *Sex and personality.* New York: McGraw-Hill, 1936.

THAXLER, A. F., & McCALL, W. C. Some data on the Kuder Preference Record. *Educational and Psychological Measurement,* 1941, **1,** 253–268.

YUM, K. S. Student preferences in divisional studies and their preferential activities. *Journal of Psychology,* 1942, **13,** 193–200.

(Received August 25, 1972)

13

DOUGLAS T. HALL[2] AND FRANCINE E. GORDON[3]

Effects of Career Choices on Married Women[1]

Conflicts, pressures, and satisfactions associated with three career options available to married women were studied. The options are full-time employment, part-time employment, and being a full-time housewife. The main hypothesis, that satisfaction would be related to the extent to which women actually did what they ideally prefer to do, was supported in the case of housekeeping and volunteer activities but not for full-time or part-time employment. Role involvements and conflicts were generally greater for workers than housewives, although full-time workers differed greatly from part-timers and were the most satisfied of the three groups.

A key issue in the concern with equal opportunities for women is the range of choices of possible careers and life styles available to women. This paper considers the outcomes of conflict, coping, and satisfaction resulting from three different career choices made by married women: full-time homemaking (with perhaps some volunteer or community responsibilities), part-time employment, and full-time employment.

The main hypothesis predicts that those women who are performing activities they choose to perform will be more satisfied than women whose roles do not match their preferences. This hypothesis is consistent with studies showing that a woman's role performance and attitudes are less positive if she works out of economic necessity rather than by choice (Kligler, 1954; Orden & Bradburn, 1969).

The differences in conflicts, related coping, and satisfaction for women in the different career groups were also explored. More evidence of role conflict and related coping was expected among employed women than among the full-time housewives, since care of the home and family is generally the responsibility of the wife in our culture, whether she is employed or not.

METHOD

The initial sample was a group of women on the mailing lists of several women's organizations and college alumnae clubs in the New Haven, Connecticut, area. Most of these women were college educated, a factor related to greater adjustment and satisfaction in working (Nye, 1963; Orden & Bradburn, 1969; Sobol, 1963). Questionnaires were sent to 250 women who had previously been invited to a 1-day symposium on women's roles in which one author participated. A total of 109 usable questionnaires were received out of the approximately 250 mailed out.

The questionnaire covered the following issues to be examined here: marital status, present work activities, preferred work activities, present roles, role conflicts, and satisfaction. Present work activities were measured with the following:

Please check below the category (or categories) which describe your work activities.

___Full-time housewife
___Full-time volunteer work
___Part-time volunteer work
___Full-time employment
___Part-time employment
___Other (Please specify) _____.

Preferred activities were measured as follows:

___Full-time housewife
___Full-time volunteer work
___Part-time volunteer work
___Full-time employment
___Part-time employment
___Other (Please specify) _____.

[1] This research was supported in part by a Ford Foundation grant to the Department of Administrative Sciences, Yale University, with which the authors were previously affiliated, and in part by a Ford Foundation grant to the Faculty of Administrative Studies, York University.

[2] Requests for reprints should be sent to Douglas T. Hall, who is now at the Department of Management, Graduate School of Business, Michigan State University, East Lansing, Michigan 48823.

[3] The cooperation of the alumnae and the Alumnae Office of the University of Connecticut is gratefully acknowledged. The authors are also indebted to Donald D. Bowen, Ronald J. Burke, Leona Burns, and Lois Lehman for comments on an earlier draft.

Roles were measured by asking the person to list the roles "which seem most salient or prominent to you." Then the person was asked to "list any conflicts or strains you experience or have experienced" between roles. Satisfaction was measured as follows:

Overall, how *satisfied* do you feel with your career?

    a. Dissatisfied
    b. Neutral: neither dissatisfied nor satisfied
    c. Mildly satisfied
    d. Very satisfied
    e. Extremely satisfied.

A second sample was also drawn in order to provide a more clearly identifiable population than the first and to replicate and extend the now-versus-preferred activity analysis of the first sample. Since the first sample was found to have very few full-time workers, a more representative sample was needed.

The second sample consisted of women from the University of Connecticut's graduating classes of 1948, 1953, 1958, 1963, and 1968. Questionnaires were mailed to 450 women, 90 from each class. With one follow-up, usable responses were received from 261. The response rate was roughly the same for each class. For nonrespondents, data were not available on marital status, work status, or other background variables against which we could test for sample bias. Of the 261 respondents, 229 were married or were widowed or divorced mothers. The remaining women (single women with no children) were not included in the present analysis.[4]

For the present analysis, the questions used in the second questionnaire were similar to those in the first, with one exception—happiness—which was measured following Gurin, Veroff, and Feld (1960):

In general, how happy would you say you are? (Circle one)

| Very Happy | Happy | Not Very Happy | Unhappy | Very Unhappy |

The correlation between satisfaction and happiness was .73.

RESULTS

Conflicts Reported

Conflict is viewed here as resulting from two or more competing pressures (after Hall & Lawler, 1971). The conflicts experienced by the women in the sample were coded in terms of the sources of pressure which produced them.

---

[4] Data reported elsewhere (Gordon, 1971) indicate that single women are less satisfied and happy than married women who work full time. Single women do not differ significantly from married women who are part-time employees or full-time housewives.

The following sources of pressure were identified from the questionnaire responses: *home* (e.g., wife, mother, and housekeeper roles), *nonhome* (e.g., employment, volunteer work), and *self* (e.g., personal desire for free time to develop interests, take courses). Another factor, *time*, did not involve any particular role, but it was mentioned so frequently with no further qualification that it was also coded. On a sample of 20 questionnaires, intercoder reliability was .74. The equation used to compute reliability was:

$$r = \frac{2 \times (\text{number of agreements})}{(\text{number of units coded by coder 1}) + (\text{number of units coded by coder 2})}.$$

Also, each questionnaire was coded in terms of the presence or nonpresence of conflict.

Role Activities and Satisfaction

It was predicted that women performing activities they prefer to do will be more satisfied than women who are either (*a*) performing activities that they would not prefer to do, given the choice, or (*b*) not performing activities that they would prefer to do, given the choice. Mean satisfaction scores from both samples for women in these various conditions are shown in Table 1.

The hypothesis received support for some, but not all, types of role activities. The results were similar in both samples. Full-time housewives who indicated they preferred this role were significantly more satisfied than those who indicated they would prefer not to be full-time housewives ($p < .01$, both samples). A similar significant difference also existed in both samples between part-time volunteers who did, and those who did not, express a preference for this role ($p < .01$). Furthermore, in the initial sample, those who preferred and were doing part-time volunteer work were significantly more satisfied than those who would prefer such work but were not currently engaged in it ($p < .01$). In fact, the women preferring and doing part-time volunteer work seemed to be the most satisfied group in both samples.

In both samples the hypothesis was not supported in the case of part- or full-time em-

TABLE 1

SATISFACTION RELATIVE TO WORK ACTIVITIES: PRESENT AND PREFERRED

Sample	Now only		Prefer only		Now and prefer	
	No. responses	Mean satis-faction	No. responses	Mean satis-faction	No. responses	Mean satis-faction
Initial						
Full-time housewife[a]	25	3.28	0	—	37	3.86
Part-time volunteer[a,c]	24	3.20	9	2.77	38	4.00
Full-time employment	9	3.55	5	2.60	2	—
Part-time employment	9	3.00	37	3.35	24	3.54
Connecticut						
Full-time housewife[a]	68	3.45	5	3.60	53	4.03
Part-time volunteer[b]	18	3.44	22	3.63	19	4.05
Full-time worker[d]	28	4.00	6	3.16	44	3.93
Part-time worker	5	3.20	84	3.63	36	3.63

[a] Now and prefer > now only, $p < .01$, one-tailed.
[b] Now and prefer > now only, $p < .025$, one-tailed.
[c] Now and prefer > prefer only, $p < .01$, one-tailed.
[d] Now only > prefer only, $p < .01$, two-tailed.

ployment. For women who preferred working, those who were presently working part time were not significantly more satisfied than those who were not working. Also, women who were working and preferring to work were not significantly more satisfied than those who were working but would prefer not to. Furthermore, for part-time work activity in both samples, women in the "now only" category were less satisfied than those in the "prefer only" and "now and prefer" categories; in the case of full-time employment, however, women in the "now only" category were more satisfied than those in the other two categories.

In each sample, women preferring and doing part-time work reported lower satisfaction than women doing and preferring the other three work activities. Despite this low satisfaction for women preferring and doing part-time work, in both samples more women expressed a preference for part-time work than for any other career activity. Also, let us consider the percentage of women for each work activity who would prefer *not* to be doing what they are presently doing, defined as

$$\frac{\text{No. in "now only" column}}{\text{No. in "now only" and no. in "now and prefer."}}$$

Summing across both samples, the percent-

ages who would prefer a different role are:

Full-time housewife, 93/183 = 51%
Part-time volunteer, 42/99 = 42%
Full-time employment, 37/83 = 45%
Part-time employment, 14/74 = 19%.

Despite their low satisfaction scores, the percentage of women who would change roles is far lower for part-time workers than for any other group.[5]

Obviously the role dynamics of working women are different from those of nonworking women. Further, there seem to be important differences between women who work full-time and those who work part-time. The remaining data were collected in the Connecticut sample to help understand more about these differences.

Profiles of the Three Career Groups

Respondents in the Connecticut sample were divided into three groups: full-time employees, part-time employees, and full-time housewives. Descriptive data for each of the three groups are reported in Table 2. Scores for college class were coded as follows:

[5] The authors are grateful to Donald D. Bowen for pointing out these data.

TABLE 2

PROFILES OF THE THREE CAREER GROUPS

Item	Part-time workers (PTW) (n = 42)	Full-time workers (FTW) (n = 73)	House-wives (H) (n = 114)	t test		
				PTW vs. H	PTW vs. FTW	FTW vs. H
Class[a]	2.19 (1.04)	3.23 (1.47)	2.72 (1.30)	−2.36**	−4.00***	2.47**
Number of roles	3.21 (1.09)	2.95 (1.29)	2.76 (1.07)	2.30*		
Proportion reporting conflict	.834 (.377)	.768 (.425)	.729 (.446)			
Proportion reporting *time* conflicts	.166 (.377)	.232 (.425)	.087 (.284)			2.68***
Proportion reporting *home* conflict	.761 (.431)	.561 (.499)	.640 (.482)		2.15*	
Proportion reporting *nonhome* conflicts	.452 (.503)	.438 (.499)	.236 (.427)	2.57***		2.89***
Proportion reporting *self* conflict	.190 (.397)	.178 (.385)	.245 (.432)			
Satisfaction	3.58 (.999)	3.95 (.862)	3.66 (.998)		−2.07*	2.03*
Happiness	4.09 (.655)	4.30 (.684)	4.22 (.746)			

Note. Numbers in parentheses are standard deviations, t = tests are two-tailed.
[a] Scores for college class were coded as follows: 1948 = 1, 1953 = 2, 1958 = 3, 1963 = 4, and 1968 = 5.
* $p < .05$.
** $p < .02$.
*** $p < .01$.

1948 = 1, 1953 = 2, 1958 = 3, 1964 = 4, and 1968 = 5.

Full-time workers tended to be significantly younger than both part-time workers or housewives as determined by college class, and part-time workers were the oldest. The relative youth of the full-time workers is in contrast with the common belief that women generally wait until their children are grown before they enter the labor force full time.

Generally, the two groups of working women experienced more conflict than the housewives.[6] Both working groups reported significantly more conflicts from nonhome pressures than housewives. Part-time workers reported more home-related conflicts than the

[6] Naturally the type or quality of the woman's job would moderate these and other correlates of employment, just as the quality of her family relationships moderates the effects of being a full-time housewife. However, the present focus is on the *degree* of employment—full time, part time, or nonemployed (i.e., housewife)—rather than the nature of the work itself.

other groups (significantly more than full-time employees). Part-timers also reported the greatest number of salient roles (significantly more than housewives). The full-time workers experienced more time conflict than the other two career groups (significantly more than housewives). Despite these conflicts, however, full-time employees reported significantly greater satisfaction than part-time workers or housewives. The housewives reported the fewest salient roles, and they are distinguished by very low occurrences of time and nonhome pressures and relatively high incidences of self-related conflicts.

Sources of Conflict

The relationships among the sources of conflict were examined next within each career group. The correlations are presented in Table 3.

For all three groups, home pressures were the most important contributor to women's role conflicts, with nonhome sources next in

TABLE 3

RELATIONSHIPS AMONG DIFFERENT TYPES OF PRESSURE
FOR DIFFERENT WORK STATUSES

Pressure	Presence of conflict	Time	Home	Nonhome
Full-time housewives				
Time	.18			
Home	.81**	−.15		
Nonhome	.34**	.11	.41**	
Self	.34**	−.10	.38**	.31**
Part-time workers				
Time	.20			
Home	.80**	−.20		
Nonhome	.40**	−.02	.39**	
Self	.21	.10	.12	−.19
Full-time workers				
Time	.30**			
Home	.62**	−.16		
Nonhome	.48**	−.16	.61**	
Self	.25*	−.17	.19	−.05

Note. $n = 114$, 42, and 73 for full-time housewives, part-time workers, and full-time workers, respectively.
* $p < .05$, two-tailed.
** $p < .01$, two-tailed.

importance. The main differences between groups lay in the other pressures that also related to conflict. Full-time workers showed the greatest range of pressures, with time, home, nonhome, and self pressures contribu-

ting to experienced conflict. Part-time workers were again at the opposite extreme from full-time employees, with only home and nonhome pressures related significantly to conflict. For housewives, home, nonhome, and self pressures led to conflict. Furthermore, the conflicts of the housewives involved self-pressures to a greater extent than did either of the other groups. Time pressures tended to be the least frequent contributor to overall conflict.

Sources of Satisfaction and Happiness

Table 4 shows correlations between satisfaction and happiness and the conflict and role variables. As one might expect, the incidence of conflict and pressure tended to relate negatively to happiness and satisfaction. For part-time workers, however, there were no significant relationships between conflict and happiness. The only clue about causes of positive outcomes for this group is a positive correlation ($r = .28$) between satisfaction and the number of roles the person has. For full-time workers, this relationship was negative ($r = −.21$). The difference between these two correlations is significant ($p < .02$).

Self-pressures were again important for only the housewives, since these pressures were negatively related to satisfaction and happiness. Time pressures were again important only to the full-time workers, since these pressures were negatively correlated with satisfaction. The incidence of nonhome pressure

TABLE 4

SATISFACTION AND HAPPINESS RELATIVE TO CONFLICT

Conflict	Total sample		Full-time housewives		Part-time workers		Full-time workers	
	Satisfaction	Happiness	Satisfaction	Happiness	Satisfaction	Happiness	Satisfaction	Happiness
Presence of	−.28**	−.31**	−.34**	−.40**	.07	−.03	−.40**	−.27*
Time	−.07	−.07	.00	−.05	−.07	−.06	−.24*	−.14
Home	−.26**	−.30**	−.30**	−.32**	.10	.00	−.36**	−.37**
Nonhome	−.01	−.03	.01	−.03	.07	.08	−.18	−.10
Self	−.17*	−.15*	−.29**	−.25**	−.04	−.07	−.01	.00
No. roles	.06	.04	.03	−.01	.28	.14	−.21	−.16

Note. $n = 229$, 114, 42, and 73 for the total sample, full-time housewives, part-time workers, and full-time workers, respectively.
* $p < .05$, two-tailed.
** $p < .01$, two-tailed.

was not related to these outcomes for any group or for the total sample.

DISCUSSION

Work and the Primacy of the Home

The hypothesized relationship between a woman's satisfaction and the fit between what she prefers to do and what she actually does was found to exist for nonemployment activities (volunteer and housewife work), but not for part-time or full-time employment. This result is especially noteworthy in the case of part-time work, since more women in the sample state a preference for this than for any other activity.

These results suggest first that the career choices of the work-oriented married woman are more difficult to implement successfully than are the choices of home-oriented women. Home-related tasks and volunteer activities are part of the traditionally accepted roles of wife and mother. The woman who by her own choice prefers to do these activities will find external role support, acceptance, admiration, and intrinsic satisfaction for doing them. Since employment is outside the traditional home roles, the woman preferring to work may encounter increased role conflicts, time pressure, prejudice, and discrimination when she seeks employment. These problems may offset the satisfaction which a work-oriented woman would otherwise receive by doing what she prefers to do.

This reasoning is supported by the data on role conflicts. For all groups, employed or not, home pressures were the most important contributors to experienced conflict, low satisfaction, and low happiness. The most consistent combination of pressures was the classic home versus nonhome clash. These data support the primacy of home-related activities for married women, whether they happen to be personally oriented toward full-time home activities or not.

Part-Time versus Full-Time Work

A second conclusion to be drawn from the results is that the difference between part-time and full-time work is as distinct as that between working and not working.

Full-time workers experienced greater satisfaction than women who worked part time. Part-time workers had a higher proportion of conflicts (particularly of home-related conflicts) and more roles to manage than either of the other two groups (significantly more than housewives). Indeed, part-time workers reported the lowest satisfaction of any women doing what they preferred, even though more women preferred part-time work than any other activity. Examination of the comments written in on the questionnaires suggested four possible explanations for this.

First, part-time jobs are often not especially challenging and rewarding. A second reason why part-time work is not more satisfying is that for some women it represents an incomplete resolution of the internal conflict about a career, a compromise between working full time and not being employed at all.

A closely related factor is the role overload resulting from such a compromise. The questionnaires of part-time workers indicated that they also performed several other activities such as volunteer work and being full-time housewives.

It has also been shown earlier that part-time workers have more roles and experience more conflicts and home pressures than women in the other groups. The part-time worker, because of the less demanding nature of part-time work, may have made fewer role reductions than one might expect and is therefore spread very thin.

A fourth possible explanation for the low satisfaction of part-time work is that in addition to the role overload of part-time workers, they may have also developed less effective resources and strategies for coping with role conflicts. This hypothesis was tested by comparing the frequency of different types of coping techniques for part-time versus full-time workers, using a system developed by Hall (1972). No significant differences were found. Therefore, insufficient coping does not appear to be an important factor in the relatively low satisfaction experienced by part-time workers.

There is some indication that the part-time worker is simply a different type of person from the full-time worker and that she may not mind role overload. First, in contrast to full-time workers and housewives, her satisfaction and happiness are not affected by pressure or conflict. Even though she is less satisfied than women in the other groups, she strongly prefers to remain a part-time employee. Finally, even though she is already suffering from role overload, she reports significantly greater satisfaction from multiple roles than does the full-time employee. The part-timer's satisfaction may come from multiple involvements—activity qua activity—whereas full-time employees and housewives seek deeper involvements and achievements in a more limited number of activities.

Unique Features of Each Group

Each career group showed distinctive patterns of role pressures and outcomes. The unique characteristic of part-time workers was role overload and apparent satisfaction resulting from overload. Full-time employees were the most satisfied group, experienced the greatest time pressures, and stood midway between part-time employees and housewives in many respects. Housewives were unique in the salience of self-pressures as a factor in conflicts and satisfaction.

REFERENCES

GORDON, F. E. Where happiness lies: Self-image, stereotypes, work status, and happiness. Working paper, Department of Administrative Sciences, Yale University, 1971.

GURIN, G., VEROFF, J., & FELD, S. *Americans view their mental health.* New York: Basic Books, 1960.

HALL, D. T. A model of coping with role conflicts: The role behavior of college-educated women. *Administrative Science Quarterly,* 1972, **17,** 471–486.

HALL, D. T., & LAWLER, E. E. Job pressures and research performance. *American Scientist,* 1971, 59, 64–73.

KLIGLER, D. H. The effects of the employment of married women on husband and wife roles. Unpublished doctoral dissertation, Yale University, 1954.

NYE, F. I. Personal satisfaction. In F. I. Nye & L. W. Hoffman (Eds.), *The employed mother in America.* Chicago: Rand McNally, 1963.

ORDEN, S. R., & BRADBURN, N. M. Working wives and marriage happiness. *The American Journal of Sociology,* 1969, **74,** 392–407.

SOBOL, M. G. Commitment to work. In F. I. Nye & L. W. Hoffman (Eds.), *The employed mother in America.* Chicago: Rand McNally, 1963.

(Received March 20, 1972)

CYNTHIA F. EPSTEIN

14

Positive Effects of the Multiple Negative: Explaining the Success of Black Professional Women[1]

Despite American society's myth and credo of equality and open mobility, the decision-making elites and elite professions have long remained clublike sanctuaries for those of like kind (Goode 1957; Merton, Reader, and Kendall 1957; Hughes 1962; Hall 1948; Epstein 1970*b*, p. 968).

To be Jewish, black, foreign born, or a woman have all been bases for exclusion from law, medicine, engineering, science, the supergrades of the civil service, architecture, banking, and even journalism. Only a few in the professions find that good can come from being born of the wrong sex, race, religion, or ethnic group. This is a report on a set of these deviants who possess at least two—and often more—statuses deemed to be "wrong." It attempts to analyze why they nevertheless were successful in the occupational world.

In the exchange system of American society, women's sex status and blacks' racial status have typically cost them prestigious and remunerative jobs because society did not evaluate them as being high in either capacity or potential. Those who did succeed had to be brighter, more talented, and more specialized than white males in a comparable labor pool, whom the society ranked higher. Thus, they paid more for the same benefits (or "goods"), if they were permitted to acquire them at all.

Where categories of persons have more than one of these negative statuses, there often tends to be a cumulative negative effect. The costs of having several negatively evaluated statuses are very high and lead to social bankruptcy when people simply cannot muster the resources to pay them. This effect has been elsewhere conceptualized as "cumulative disadvantage" and has explained the poor representation of blacks (among others) in skilled occupations. Black women, for example, because of their

[1] This is publication A-662 of the Bureau of Applied Social Research, Columbia University. It is a revision of a paper presented at the Annual Meeting of the American Sociological Association, 1971, in Denver, Colorado, and was prepared with the support of grants from the Research Foundation of the City University of New York, no. 1079 and grant no. 91-34-68-26 from the Manpower Administration, U.S. Department of Labor. The author is indebted to Diana Polise for help in its preparation and to Florence Levinsohn and Howard Epstein for editorial suggestions. Critical issues were raised by William J. Goode, Gladys G. Handy, Jacqueline J. Jackson, Robert K. Merton, and Lauren Seiler (some resolved, others not).

two negatively evaluated statuses, are situated at the very bottom of the occupational pyramid.

Indeed, the status set which includes being black and being a woman has been one of the most cumulatively limiting.

These ascribed sex (female) and race (black) statuses are dominant;[2] they are visible and immutable and impose severe limits on individuals' capacities to alter the dimensions of their world and the attitudes of others toward them. In the elite professions, blacks and women have been considered inappropriate and undervalued, and as a result they have constituted only a tiny proportion of the prestigious professionals.[3] Not only have they been prevented from working in the elite professions, but the few who do manage to become professionals tend to work in the less remunerative and prestigious subfields (Epstein 1970c, p. 163).

Women typically have jobs which rank lower than men at every class level, and, contrary to some current misconceptions about the existence of a black matriarchy, black women are most typically at the very bottom of the occupational pyramid. They earn less than white women who, in turn, make less than men, white or black.[4] This economic distribution is constant for every category of worker, including professionals, with the sole exception of domestic workers. Although black women earn less, they are also much more apt to work than white women of the same age and education (Bureau of the Census, *Current Population Reports,* P-60, no. 75 [1970], table 50, p. 113).[5]

Yet there are black women who have achieved success in the popular definition of the term, becoming professionals of high prestige and acquiring high incomes as well. For them the effect of status sets with two immutable negatively evaluated statuses—the sex status of female and the race status of black—did not result in negative consequences but formed a positive matrix for a meaningful career.

[2] According to Robert K. Merton, statuses are dominant when they determine the other statuses one is likely to acquire (see Epstein 1970c, p. 92). Part of this analysis (as that in my earlier work [1970b, 1970c]) draws on Robert K. Merton's conceptualization of the dynamics of status sets, part of which is found in *Social Theory and Social Structure* (1957, pp. 368–84), and much of which has been presented in lectures at Columbia University and is as yet unpublished (see footnotes in Epstein 1970b, p. 966).

[3] In 1960, blacks constituted 1.3% of all lawyers, and the proportion of women in law was 3.4%.

[4] Median earnings of full-time, year-round workers were reported as follows for 1967: Negro women—$3,194; white women—$4,279; Negro men—$4,777; white men —$7,396 (U.S. Bureau of Census, *Current Population Reports,* ser. P-60, no. 60, table 7, p. 39). Although figures went up in 1970 the relationship remained the same (U.S. Bureau of Census, *Current Population Reports,* ser. P-60, no. 75, table 45, pp. 97–98).

[5] In 1968, 49% of Negro women were in the work force compared with 40% of white women (Brimmer 1971, p. 550).

This paper is based on interviews with a sample of 31 such women who achieved occupational success in the prestigious male-dominated professions and occupations of law, medicine, dentistry, university teaching, journalism, and public relations.[6]

Studying these successful black professional women we located three major patterns resulting from the interaction between statuses which accounted for their success. They may be outlined as follows:

1. Focusing on one of the negatively valued statuses canceled the negative effect of the other. (That is, raised its "worth." For example, in a white professional milieu, a black woman is viewed as lacking the "womanly" occupational deficiencies of white women—for example, seeking a husband—and the black woman's sex status is given a higher evaluation.)

2. Two statuses in combination create a new status (for example, the hyphenated status of black-woman-lawyer) which may have no established "price" because it is unique. In this situation, the person has a better bargaining position in setting his or her own worth. This pattern may also place the person in the role of a "stranger," outside the normal exchange system and able to exact a higher than usual price.

3. Because the "stranger" is outside the normal opportunity structure, he or she can choose (or may be forced to choose) an alternate life-style. This choice was made by many black women forced to enter the occupational world because of economic need, and, in turn, it created selective barriers which insulated the women from diversions from occupational success and from ghetto culture, thus strengthening ambition and motivation.

In the sections which follow, we will locate black professional women among other professionals to demonstrate their very special position in the social structure and further illustrate the process by which they were able to "make it" in American society.

BLACK WOMEN IN THE PROFESSIONS

Like the pattern for whites over 25, black women currently in the labor force have had more median years of schooling than black men, and more of them have been high school graduates. Furthermore, although black men in college now exceed black women, more black women over 25 are college graduates than are men in this age group (U.S. Department of Commerce,

---

[6] Because no lists exist of black women in any of these professions, there was no way to systematically sample the universe of black women professionals. Instead, respondents were obtained by referral from friends and colleagues. Because of the extremely small absolute number of black women in these fields, and because the study was limited to the New York area, a great deal of time was spent simply trying to find subjects.

Statistical Abstract 1968 [1968], table 156, p. 110; *Statistical Abstract 1970* [1970], table 157, p. 109; data derived from the *U.S. Census of the Population: 1960,* vol. 1, and *Current Population Reports,* ser. P-20, nos. 169, 194). Their educational advantage accounts partly for their greater access to professional jobs, and a significantly higher proportion of black women than men hold professional jobs—60% of the total numbers of blacks holding such jobs—as reported by the 1960 census (Bureau of the Census, *1960 Subject Reports. Occupational Characteristics,* PC(2) and 7A, table 3, p. 21). Of all employed black women, 7% were professionals, in contrast to 3% of all employed black men (Ginzberg and Hiestand 1966, p. 210).

Like all American college women, black women are often steered into teaching and nursing careers. Black college women generally have taken B.A. degrees in education[7] and found employment in the segregated school systems of the South (Ginzberg and Hiestand 1966, p. 216). Although the census has always counted teachers as professionals, teaching has always ranked low in occupational prestige,[8] and black men, like white men, did not enter teaching in any numbers.[9]

There are no census figures on the total number of graduate and professional degrees earned by black men and women,[10] and seemingly contra-

---

[7] In predominantly Negro colleges and universities, for the years 1963–64, the proportion of women students majoring in elementary education was 24.4% as compared with 6.4% of the men (McGrath 1965, p. 80). The field of education alone accounted for 38% of all bachelor's degrees earned by women in 1967. Education also accounted for 51% of the master's and 29% of the doctor's degrees earned by women in 1967 (*Handbook of Women Workers 1969,* pp. 192–93); 53.5% of black women in the "Professional, Technical & Kindred Workers" category in the U.S. census were elementary (43.1%) and secondary (10.4%) school teachers (Ginsberg and Hiestand 1966, p. 215).

[8] Teaching ranked thirty-sixth in the NORC study of occupational prestige in 1947 and rose to twenty-sixth place in 1963, still placing it far below medicine, law, banking, college teaching, etc.

[9] Black men have gone into teaching to a somewhat greater degree than white men but not nearly to the extent of the women. Of professional men, 11.9% were elementary school teachers and 13.1% were secondary school teachers; the absolute numbers being considerably smaller as well, as the table below indicates:

PERCENTAGE OF NEGRO PROFESSIONAL, TECHNICAL AND KINDRED CENSUS
CATEGORY WHO WERE TEACHERS, BY SEX, 1960

TEACHERS	MEN		WOMEN	
	Number	%	Number	%
Elementary	13,451	11.9	75,695	43.1
Secondary	14,823	13.1	18,194	10.4

SOURCE.—Ginsberg and Hiestand 1966, pp. 210, 215.

[10] Statistics on doctorate production of blacks can only be based on the number of graduate degrees produced by the predominantly black colleges and by estimates of

dictory figures appear in the sources available. A study of Negro colleges—where the majority of blacks have earned their graduate degrees (Blake 1971, p. 746)—shows that black women earned 60% of the graduate and professional degrees awarded in 1964–65 (United Negro College Fund 1964–65, appendix I). However, a Ford Foundation study (1970) of all black Ph.D. holders in 1967–68 (p. 3) indicated that of a 50% sample of the total, only 21% were women. Another source covering black colleges for the same period as the UNCF report (1964) lists more women than men earning M.A.'s (799 as compared with 651; probably a majority were education degrees) but more men than women earning Ph.D.'s (five men and two women) (Ploski 1967, p. 527).[11]

If one compares the proportion of black women with black men in those professions higher in prestige than teaching, we find a more traditional picture. More black men than women are editors, doctors, lawyers, scientists, and college teachers (Bureau of the Census, *1960 Subject Reports. Occupational Characteristics*, PC (2)-7A, table 3, p. 21). Furthermore, they consistently have higher median incomes than do the women in these professions (Bureau of the Census, *1960 Subject Reports. Occupational Characteristics*, PC (2)-7A, table 25, p. 296; table 26, p. 316).[12]

But relative to their male colleagues, black career women have done better than their white sisters; they constitute a larger proportion of the black professional community than women in the white professional world. Only 7% of white physicians are women, but 9.6% of black doctors are women; black women make up 8% of black lawyers but white women constitute only 3% of all white lawyers. Black women approach real equality with black men in the social sciences—they are 34% of all blacks in the profession—although the absolute numbers are small (data derived from same Bureau of the Census 1960 as indicated above).

In most professional groups, black women constitute a larger proportion of women than black men do among males in these groups (U.S. Bureau of the Census, *1960 Subject Reports. Occupational Characteristics*, PC (2)-

---

the number of blacks in the integrated colleges. Statistics are unavailable because of fair educational practices laws. The absolute number of black doctorates ever held is small, estimated by Horace Mann Bond (1966) at 2,485 (comprising those awarded 1866–1962) (Ginsberg and Hiestand 1966, p. 564). The Ford Foundation study cited herein found 2,280 current holders of Ph.D. degrees in 1967–68.

[11] Although the Ford study included education doctorates, we suppose that the high figure for women graduates in black institutions is probably due to the high proportion of education doctorates awarded by Negro institutions when compared with the range of doctorates awarded by white institutions. This is probably due to perennial fiscal problems and inability to fund programs in the hard sciences until quite recently.

[12] If one uses nonwhite categories (which, for the general population, is 92% black) to get figures for blacks in the professions, a misleading impression will result. Certain professions (see n. 15) have almost equal numbers of blacks and other nonwhites, such as Chinese, Japanese, etc.

7A, table 3, p. 21). In terms of earnings they are also far more equal to white women than black men are to white men. In fact, black women accountants, musicians, professional nurses, and social workers exceeded their white female colleagues in earnings, according to the 1960 census (U.S. Bureau of the Census, *1960 Subject Reports. Occupational Characteristics,* PC (2)-7A, table 25, p. 296; table 26, p. 316).

However, one cannot ignore the fact that for all professions the absolute numbers of blacks are small, and the numbers of black women are so tiny that they may go unreported and unanalyzed. In the 1960 census, only 220 black women lawyers and about 370 black women social scientists were counted. No doubt there have been increases in all fields, but this remains conjectural in view of the fact that the proportion of all women in the professions has remained fairly static over the past 40 years (Epstein 1970*b*).

BLACK WOMEN HAVE GREATER ACCESS

It is believed that in some sectors, probably as professionals in white firms, hospitals, and communities, black women have done better than black men. Historically, black women have had more access to white society than black men and have had opportunities to learn the "ropes" of the white world. Because they were desired as house servants, nurse-maids, and sexual partners, black women often became intimates of whites, learnings their values and habits. They could be intimates because as women they were not only powerless but were never regarded as potentially powerful, an attribute which has its analogue in their admission to the male-dominated professions.

Although it is difficult, if not impossible, to document the sense of threat with which white male professionals react to the thought of black men as colleagues, it is clear that black men and women perceive this reaction as a barrier to them. It was a common feeling among the black women in this study that this perceived threat was not as great for them. Being a woman reduced the effect of the racial taboo.

On the other hand, black women are found in professions and occupations known to be difficult for white women to penetrate. Because these women are black they are perhaps not perceived as women; they may be regarded as more "serious" professionals than white women; they may not be viewed as sexual objects nor be seen as out to get a husband. The stereotypes attached to the so-called feminine mind, emotions, or physiology may not seem easily transferable to black women, for whom there seem to be fewer stereotypes in the context of the professionally trained.

We have concentrated on several themes: (1) the special conditions which created for these women an image of self and an achievement value structure, (2) the problems attached to playing out traditional, idealized female dependency roles; and (3) the reinforcing components of the work situation.

WOMAN AS DOER

Although the situation of the black woman is in many ways unique, many of the problems she faces are also experienced by other groups of women with negatively evaluated statuses. The mechanisms she uses to cope with strain are mirrored in their experiences as well. But perhaps more than the others, the black woman has been the subject of myths and misinterpretations often applied to behavior of minority group members (see Hyman 1969; Mack 1971).

The most pernicious of the popular stereotypes about the black woman holds that a black matriarchy exists and is a key factor in the social disorganization of the Negro family and the "irresponsibility" of the male as provider and authority. It is a perfect example of the "damned if you do, damned if you don't" syndrome (Merton 1957, p. 480).

Although a greater proportion of black women than white women work, and a greater proportion are the heads of families, the assumption that these factors have an independent negative effect has been challenged. The great majority of black families are intact families and, although a higher proportion of black wives work than do white wives, the typical pattern of black family life is an equalitarian one rather than one of wife-mother dominance. The strong mother figure is prevalent in the black family, but as Ladner (1971) has recently pointed out, strength is not the same as dominance. There have been many instances of strong mother figures in American history (immigrant mothers and pioneer mothers) who have been idealized as women who made it possible for their families to endure in punishing situations. Somehow, these other women were subjected to a different set of norms in contexts in which work was considered appropriate, in which running the shop, sitting at the cash register, or administering the farm was not viewed as masculine or, worse "castrating" behavior. Sometimes the work was done side by side with the husband, sometimes alone because of his incapacity or unavailability. Only the rich could afford to keep their women unoccupied and unhelpful.[13]

The analogue of the immigrant woman probably fits the black woman's situation best, for she also was aware that the men in her family might

---

[13] The managerial ability of women throughout history has been understated. Although women have always worked in agrarian societies and at the lower strata in all societies, upper-class women have assumed economic roles in a variety of circumstances. Women of rank managed estates in France and England in the absence of male heirs or when men went off to war.

not be able to provide for it entirely. Sharing or assuming work obligations were real expectations, and enough women did so to become models for generations to come. Both this study of black women professionals and my earlier study of women lawyers, many of whom came from immigrant families, showed that these women had in their lives models of mother-provider figures[14]—a mother or grandmother who, as a domestic worker or proprietor of a small store, or as a seamstress and, later, teacher and suffragette, generated a positive image of woman as doer, not as a passive and dependent person. The mother-provider figure appeared not in the absence of a father but often as the figure who worked with a father in a family business or who shared the economic burden by working at another enterprise. In fact, the mother-provider as heroine is a common image in many of these case studies because the activity of these women was so positively experienced and cherished.

The following description of a mother, offered by a woman physician in the study, is typical: "My mother was not the stronger of my parents but she was the more aggressive, always planning and suggesting ideas to improve the family's situation. A dressmaker by trade, she would slip out to do domestic work by the day when times got hard, often not telling my father about it. He was a bricklayer and carpenter but had trouble finding work because he was unable to get union membership."

Most of this sample of black women came from intact families. What was important was that their mothers, forced to work, canceled the "female effect" of motivation and offered an alternative model of adult women to that of the larger white culture. The black women interviewed showed a strong maternal influence; of the 30 interviewed, only four said their mothers had never worked (and one of these "nonworking" mothers had 13 children). Even more unusual was the fact that many of the mothers had been professionals or semiprofessionals. Seven had been teachers, one a college professor, two were nurses, and one a physician. This heritage is unique for any population of women, including professional women, whose mothers are more likely to have worked.

MIDDLE-CLASS VALUES

Most women interviewed in this study came from families which stressed middle-class values, whether or not their incomes permitted middle-class amenities. I have already noted the high proportion of mothers who held

[14] In my sample of women lawyers, nearly all of whom were white, 20% had mothers who were or had been engaged in professional occupations, nine of whom were teachers. Thirty percent never worked (Epstein 1968, p. 96). In Rita Stafford's larger study of women in *Who's Who,* 11.5% of the mothers of lawyers were in a profession and close to 70% were housewives (Epstein 1968, p. 236).

professional jobs, and although far fewer of the fathers' jobs ranked high (five of the 30), the fathers all had occupational talents and skills. Generally the fathers held a variety of jobs which defy ordinary classification because, though not middle-class jobs by white standards (e.g., as truckers and post office employees), they were at the time good opportunities for blacks.

THE SPECIAL CASE OF THE WEST INDIANS

Considering the size of its population in the United States, an unusually large proportion of my sample (one-third) is West Indian, and this helps account for the high level of aspiration found in the sample. It is generally believed that black professionals are of West Indian extraction in far greater proportion than could be expected by chance.[15] The situation of the black women of this group is illustrative of the "positive" effect of holding two or more negative statuses.

The experience of West Indians in the United States is different from that of other blacks because they face double discrimination—from the larger society for being black and from the black community for being

[15] West Indians have contributed disproportionately to the current Negro leadership, including Stokely Carmichael, Lincoln Linch, Roy Inniss, and other accomplished people. Glazer and Moynihan (1963) assert that in the 1930s foreign-born persons were to make up as much as one-third of the Negro professional population, especially physicians, dentists, and lawyers. We can assume these foreign born were predominantly West Indian. This seems to hold true today if one examines the proportion of foreign-born nonwhites in the professions. Almost one-half of the nonwhite male college instructors, presidents, etc., were listed as foreign born in the 1960 census, about 20% of the natural scientists, about 40% of the doctors, but only a tiny percentage, 0.8, of the lawyers. This also holds true for black women with almost 11% of the nonwhite female college faculty being foreign born, 26% of the natural scientists, 60% of the doctors, and no lawyers listed (U.S. Bureau of Census 1963, vol. 2, PC [2]-7A, table 8, pp. 114–15). And the census figures do not include the large numbers of professionals who were born here of West Indian parentage. Although the nonwhite population is 92% black, and the category in the census data is often taken to mean "mostly black," one must be wary of the percentages for certain professions because tiny numbers of blacks are often matched in number by other nonwhites, such as Chinese. This can be seen in the following table:

NUMBER OF NEGRO AND OTHER NONWHITES IN SELECTED OCCUPATIONS, UNITED STATES, 1960

	Negroes	Other Nonwhites
College pres., prof., instruct.	5,910	2,794
Chemists 1,799		1,115
Physicians, surgeons	5,038	5,007
Lawyers, judges	2,440	530

SOURCE.—*U.S. Census of the Population*, vol. 2, *1960 Subject Reports, Occupational Characteristics*, PC (2)-7A, table 3, pp. 21–22.

foreign.[16] West Indian children are often persecuted and taunted as "monkey chasers." Their way of speech identifies them to other blacks as foreigners, and they experience the same kind of ostracism as white immigrants who bear visible negatively valued statuses. But, as a group, West Indians are known to have a sense of pride, to value education, and be characterized by Protestant Ethic strivings. Although the assimilation of second-generation immigrants into the main culture is common, and they may have difficulty maintaining their values in the context of competing views of work and study in the ghetto, being a West Indian black does create a circumscribed set of possibilities and insulation from the larger society, black and white. Marginality to black society (as immigrants) and to white society (as blacks) means an absence of diversion from the group's goals and competing values. Because they are isolated and the young women are segregated by their parents even more than the men,[17] the threat of the street and the illegitimate opportunity structure is cut off. At the same time, West Indian youth receive a heavy dose of achievement input from parents and their extended-kinlike community.[18] Many prominent West Indians referred repeatedly to their British training in thrift and self-esteem, to the importance given by their elders to education, to respect for adults, and at the same time, to the importance of being "spunky."

SELF-CONFIDENCE

Black women seem to have acquired a sense of confidence in their competence and ability. Interviews with these black professional women revealed a strong feeling of self-assurance. Further support comes from Fichter's study of graduates from predominantly black colleges, which indicates that college-educated black women have more confidence in their abilities than

---

[16] Cruse (1967, p. 121) suggests that native (New York) Negroes frowned on West Indians mainly because the islanders presented a threat of competition for jobs available to blacks. The West Indian influx into New York in the 1920s coincided with the great migration of Negroes from the South. However, he does note the severe antipathy of native blacks to West Indians because of their alleged "uppity" manner.

[17] One women commented: "I was not only protected; I was overprotected. West Indians are real Victorians regarding the behavior of their girls."

[18] The isolation and special character of the black West Indian have probably emphasized a sense of community bolstered by mutual benevolent associations (also known as "meetings" and "hands") which are often church associated. Members have pooled resources to meet mortgage payments on homes, appraised property, and in other ways have acted as pseudokin groups in assisting talented youngsters with college scholarships. Often these groups had a geographic base and were Jamaican, or Trinidadian, etc. Paule Marshall's *Brown Girl, Brownstones* (1959) is a vivid portrait of a Barbadian community in Brooklyn, focusing on a young girl growing up, her hard-working mother, and the influence of a Barbadian community organization in reinforcing work, ownership, and scholarship norms.

a comparable group of white women graduates (1964, p. 12; table 5.17, p. 92).

Asked by Fichter if they thought they had personalities suitable to a career as business executives, 49% of the white women interviewed but 74% of the black women thought they did (1964, table 5.18, p. 93).

This high degree of self-confidence may result from their special condition of having gone to college, a very special event in the black community. Their self-confidence is probably reinforced as they overcome each obstacle on the way to the top.

EDUCATION AND ITS STRUCTURE

It is commonly believed that a greater premium is placed on the higher education of girls than boys in the black community.[19] Until recently the greater numbers of black women college graduates have supported this assumption. This view and the statistics supporting it have their origins in the structure of discrimination; even with college degrees, black men could not penetrate the high-ranking occupations, while black women graduates could always go into schoolteaching. Thus it has been suggested that contrary to the pattern believed to be true of underprivileged white families, in which male children got preference if not all could be sent to college, in the black family the female child would get preference.

However, the number of black men in college has grown steadily in the past decade and by 1963 surpassed the number of black women students. Further, if one measures the proportion of women among blacks in professions other than teaching, it is not true that more girls get professional training than men. Only 9.6% of black doctors are women (again a higher percentage than in the white community, where only 7% of doctors are women). Certainly black families, like many white immigrant families in the past, could not afford sex discrimination when they needed the contribution of any family member who showed promise. As one dentist of West Indian extraction put it: "Girls or boys—whoever had the brains to get education was the one pushed to do it and encouraged."

Although white families support the notion of college education for girls, they are somewhat ambivalent about encouraging them to go beyond the B.A., viewing professional training as a waste, detrimental to marriage chances, or simply inappropriate for a woman (Epstein 1970c, p. 62). Not a single black woman in the study reported opposition from her family

---

[19] See, for example, Silberman's assertion about the black woman: "Her hatred of men reflects itself in the way she brings up her own children; the sons can fend for themselves but the daughters must be prepared so that they will not have to go through what she has gone through" (1964, p. 119). And Cogan's statement: "In the Negro family the oldest girl is most protected and most often encouraged to go on with her education" (1968, p. 11).

on the matter of professional training; many referred to their parents' attitudes in the same terms as the dentist quoted above, and with the intensity characterized by a physician: "From the time you could speak you were given to understand that your primary interest in life was to get the best education you could, the best job you could. There was no other way!"

Where the parents could, they paid for the education of their daughters, often at the cost of years of savings and great personal sacrifice. Most of the women interviewed received at least a small amount of financial help from their parents and supplemented the costs of education by working while in school or through scholarship aid.

The black woman's education is considered a real investment in her future. She could not expect, like a white woman, to put her husband through college in order to enjoy a life of leisure on her husband's achievement and income. She knows, too, that a stable marriage is much more problematical as she moves up in educational status.

Of the black women college graduates studied by Noble, 90% said that "preparing for a vocation" was first in a list of reasons for going to college (1956, p. 46, table 16). These responses followed a pattern reported in two earlier studies (Johnson 1938; Cuthbert 1942). And it should be noted that, far more than for the black man, a college education radically improves the income potential of the black woman; her median income is even higher than that of white women with college degrees (*The Social and Economic Status of Negroes in the United States, 1970*, table 102, p. 125, and table 25, p. 34).

In general, black women are more concerned with the economic rewards of work than are white women (Shea, Spitz, and Zeller 1970, p. 215).

Furthermore, the economic necessity expected by black women indicates a canceling of female occupational role stereotypes. The black women interviewed were not bound by conventional stereotypes of the professions deemed suitable "for a woman"; instead, they weighed the real advantages and disadvantages of the occupation. Although my earlier study of white women lawyers found that some of their parents had tried to deter them from that male-dominated occupation, the black women interviewed for this project reported their parents not only encouraged them but a number had suggested they try law or medicine. One woman who wanted to be a nurse was persuaded by her mother to become a physician.

PROFESSIONAL SCHOOLS

Most of the women interviewed were educated at white schools, a number of them having gone to private white elementary schools, to white colleges (79%), and to white professional schools (70%). A little more than half of the physicians went to white medical schools (and most of these attended the very top schools—Yale and Columbia, for example), and the rest went to predominantly Negro schools.[20] This is extremely unusual because the great majority of black doctors have always been educated in black medical schools.

No figures exist on the proportion of male and female black students admitted to white medical schools, and one can only suppose that black women had as hard a time getting admitted as any women or any blacks. A few of the doctors interviewed, however, felt that they had a slight edge over both groups—again the interaction effect of their two negative statuses; their uniqueness made their admission more likely. None, however, could say exactly why they thought this was true. One commented: "I think that being both black and female may have been an asset, in a peculiar sense, both in getting into medical school and subsequently."

Being black attenuated the effect of feminine roles in the university setting. Dating was difficult because there were so few black men; furthermore, being a specially selected female meant a high commitment to scholarship. The girls who went to all-white schools were good students, and most reported they had virtually no social life.

MARRIAGE

For most women, getting married and becoming a mother are still the most salient decisions in the setting of a life course. These decisions usually follow a fairly certain pattern and serve as limits on the acquisition of other statuses, especially occupational ones. But marriage is not by any means a certainty for black women, and for those who do marry being a wife may not offer the security to replace a career.

The factors which result in the educated black woman's contingent marital status derive from the marginal position of blacks in American society and from their inability to conform to a number of norms in the family setting which are rooted in patriarchal-focused values. The black male's marginality makes it doubtful he will acquire a professional career; whatever the level of occupation he attains, he will have difficulty in providing a middle-class life-style on his income alone. The educated black woman thus is unlikely to find a mate of similar social rank and education, and it is doubtful she can expect to play the traditional middle-class housewife role played by educated white women.

Lacking the usual guarantee that Prince Charming will come equipped with a good profession and a suburban home, or will come at all, the

[20] Seventy percent of Negro medical students in 1955–56 attended black medical schools as opposed to only 30% who attended white medical schools (Reitzes 1958, p. 28).

educated black girl is prepared in both subtle and direct ways to adapt if the dream should fail. The women in our sample reported that their parents did not push them toward marriage, and though they generally married late if they married at all (one-third had not), they did not feel anxious about being unmarried.[21] Although there is some change today, most white girls have internalized enormous pressures to marry and marry early. Not only do black women probably invest less in the good-life-through-marriage dream, there is evidence that a great proportion feel they can do without it.

Bell (1971, p. 254) suggests that "marriage has limited importance to black women at all educational levels" and that it is also possible that "if education were held constant at all levels, black women would show a greater rejection of marriage than would white women." At lower-class levels it is clear that the rejection of marriage comes because it is perceived as unreliable, and at upper-class levels because of the small pool of eligible men and the competition for husbands.

Although the white college-educated woman is strongly deterred from focus on a career when she marries (though she may work), the black woman who marries a black college-educated man cannot consider withdrawing from the marketplace. She knows that her husband's education is no guarantee of his financial success. It has been clearly established that the discrepancy in income between white and black male college graduates is wider than the gap between incomes of those who are less well educated (Sheppard and Striner 1966, p. 24). Educated black women, like other black women who seem able to trim their expectations to the realities of their lives, know they will have to share the financial responsibilities for a middle-class standard of living. One-half of the college-educated black women studied by Fichter (1964, p. 81) said they preferred to combine their family role with an occupational role. This made them twice as likely as Southern white women or the comparable group of other white women in a national NORC sample to select a combination of marriage, child rearing, and employment.

It seems probable, too, that black women view careers differently than white women who expect to combine marriage and career. White women like to view their work as supplemental to the husband's. They tend not to think of their work as a career growing out of their own life aims. Black women tend less to view their work as a "hanger-on" activity. One gets the feeling in interviews with them that the quality of their lives is determined by their own endeavor and is less a response to their husband's occupation situation. Perhaps this is a function of their relatively high

---

[21] But generally women in the male-dominated professions marry late and a substantial proportion are unmarried (see Epstein 1970*a*, p. 905).

self-confidence. White women lawyers I studied who practiced with their husbands typically referred to their work as "helping their husbands" and not in terms of a real career (Epstein 1971). Of course, black women have less opportunity to reason so circuitously. They are not in any structure where they could work for a husband. None of the lawyers had lawyer husbands, and only one of the doctors had a husband who was a physician. All of the doctors made more money than their husbands. There was almost no occupational homogamy and very little occupational-rank homogamy between husbands and wives, contrary to the marriage pattern for white women professionals, in which occupational homogamy is exceptionally strong.[22]

Our respondents, following a pattern common to other educated black women,[23] often married down occupationally. Although some white women in my study of lawyers had husbands who earned less than they did, they appeared more threatened by this situation than the black women studied. Some of the white women, faced with developing careers, checked them to assure they would have lower-ranking, lower-paying jobs than their husbands.[24] Black women also consider checking their career progress for this reason, but feel the costs are too great. Although the white woman usually can withdraw from her profession and continue to live at the same economic standard, the black woman who does so pulls the family to a lower standard of living. If the black woman acts like a woman occupationally, she is failing as a mother in helping her family.

The negative rank differential present in most marriages of black professional women has an important effect on their commitment to career. Although black women are probably as hopeful as white women for a long and happy life with their husbands, they face the reality of a higher probability of marital breakup. Divorce and separation rates for blacks

---

[22] Compared by race, marriages tend to be homogamous—husbands and wives coming from similar social, religious, ethnic, and educational background. Within this general similarity, there is some tendency for men to marry a little below their own level, so that they are slightly hypogamous while their wives tend to be slightly hypergamous. The reverse tends to be true for blacks; women tend to marry below their own level (Bernard 1966, p. 90).

[23] Noble reported that more than 50% of the husbands of college-educated black women in her study were employed in occupations of lower socioeconomic level than those of the wives. In more than 60% of this study's cases in which wives reported on their husband's education, the man had a lower level of education than his wife. Noble reports low levels of response for both these items in her questionnaire (1956, p. 51).

[24] Perhaps this is a manifestation of the ambivalence women feel toward success. Matina Horner's work suggests that most women will explore their intellectual potential only when they do not need to compete—least of all with men. They feel success is unladylike and that men will be put off by it (1969, p. 62).

are higher than for whites,[25] and their remarriage rates are lower. Although rates of dissolution for black women professionals are the lowest of any category of black women workers, they are still higher than those for white women in similar jobs (Udry 1968, p. 577). Eight of the 24 women we studied who had ever been married had been divorced.

Caroline Bird suggests that black professional women's deviant place in the structure of marriage expectations "frees" them: "Negro career women are 'freer than white career women not to marry, to marry outside their race or class. . . . They are . . . much less bound than white women by the role duties most frequently cited as universal and inescapable limitations on the career aspirations of all women forever" (1969, p. 38). Whether or not they are free, it is certainly true that their lack of a safe haven in marriage gives them independence, motivation, and perhaps more reinforcement of self-confidence than the white woman who may retreat to full-time marriage at the first feeling of fear or insecurity as a professional.

MOTHERHOOD

Although getting married may determine whether or not a woman takes her career seriously, it is the demands on her as a mother and how she deals with those demands which become most important in her ability to focus on career.

Having children is costly for a family not only because of what it takes to feed, clothe, and educate them, but because typically the wife leaves the labor force—and her income—for long periods to care for them. And for black families it has been imperative that both wife and husband work to maintain their hold on a middle-class life-style.

Although blacks generally exceed the fertility pattern of whites, the fertility rates of upper-class Negro families are the lowest of any group (Moynihan 1965, p. 758).[26] Noble's study of Negro women college graduates found that although the majority of her sample married, more than 40% were childless and 38% had only one child (1957, p. 17). Of the 24 ever-married women in my study, 17 had children and seven did not. Of those who had children, more than half had two or more. Strikingly, all of those with two or more children were upper-income professionals—an editor, a lawyer, a dentist, and a half-dozen physicians. The sample's only mother of five is a practicing M.D.

[25] Black women appear more likely to encounter marital discord than whites. In 1970, 19% of all black women who at some time had been married were either divorced or separated as contrasted with 6% of white women who had been married (*New York Times,* July 26, 1971, p. 1).

[26] Although there are no data for fertility of women by their own occupation, the

Though black women who have careers can be assumed to reduce demands made on them by having fewer children than their white counterparts, it is more interesting to see the ways in which they handle their role demands as mothers and the unique aspects of the black social structure which help them do so.

The black mothers interviewed seemed far less anxious about their children than whites. They did not insist that it was their sole responsibility to care for their children, nor did they fear that their absence from home during the children's early years would be harmful to their psychic and physical growth. They seemed freer to accept help from relatives (particularly grandparents, who often volunteered it), to leave the children for long periods, and even to let the children accompany them to work if that became necessary. Hill (1971) suggests that black families are generally more adaptable to absorbing new members—other relatives' children, grandchildren, or grandparents—and that often the "new" older members play important roles in caring for young children while the mother works (p. 5).

Black women, whether of Southern or of West Indian origin, share an extended family tradition in which "others" can routinely perform tasks which middle-class white society would see as exclusively the responsibility of the husband and wife. This aspect of the black social structure meshes neatly with the needs of the black professional woman; it makes it possible for her to continue studies or career after having children, and makes combined motherhood and career a rational decision to be made on its merits.

CAREERS

The occupational spread of the 31 women interviewed ranged from physicians (12, including four psychiatrists), to lawyers (eight), dentists (two), a university professor, three journalists, and several in public relations work, business management, and top administrative posts in social services. (One was in library science, a "woman's field" except in administration; this woman was in charge of a noted collection.) We excluded nursing, social work, and teaching, which are not only women's fields but are low in prestige and considered professions almost solely by the United States census.

An early decision to go into professional work was characteristic of most of the women in the sample. They share this history with male professionals of both sexes (Rogoff 1957, p. 111) and with other black women

---

percentage of nonwhite wives of professional men who were childless in 1950 was 33% (Whelpton, Campbell, and Patterson 1966, p. 153).

professionals (Ostlund 1957; Brazziel 1960). Considering the years of preparation, both in terms of anticipatory socialization and formal educational requirements, early deciders have an advantage over those who choose late.

Blacks, however, suffer from having fewer real role models in their decision matrix, although doctors (in particular) and lawyers have always been held in high esteem in the black community. Until recently, physician was the highest status occupation a black person could hold, but the absolute number has been, and remains, small. In 1956 New York City had only 305 black physicians, the largest number of any city in the country, and in 1960 the total census figure for the United States was 5,038, of whom 487 were women.[27]

In contrast to the strong family encouragement of professional careers already noted, most black women recall, as do white women, being urged by primary and high school teachers and guidance counselors to go into schoolteaching or social work. This advice was based on their racial and sex statuses, although black men, too, are sometimes directed into these occupations because of the barriers they face in the more prestigious professions. But the significant messages for them were from their parents, who were encouraging them to be whatever they wanted and who did not raise objections to their trying a white, male profession.

Eight of the physicians went to "white" medical schools (NYU, New York Medical College, Boston University, Philadelphia Women's) or to elite white schools (Columbia's Physicians and Surgeons and Yale).

Despite their educational credentials, most of the doctors work in the black community. Elite medical careers require not only degrees from good schools but a status sequence of internships at elite training hospitals which are hard for any black to get, and which most of the women did not get, or which they did not seek because they felt their chances were nonexistent. None of the women who went to a black medical school was able to work within the medical "establishment," although a few had some contact with it under new programs pairing private teaching hospitals with municipal hospitals.

The lawyers interviewed went exclusively to white law schools; four to Columbia, one to the University of Michigan, two to NYU, and one to Brooklyn Law School, a lower-ranking school with an evening program.

---

[27] Michel Richard figured that by interviewing 98 black physicians in New York in 1965 he had a sample of about 28% of all black doctors in New York City, using an estimate of 355 for 1965 (1969, p. 21). By doing a little creative statistical calculation, we figured that using the national percentage of black women doctors (9.6% of black doctors) would mean that there are about 28 black women doctors in New York. We interviewed 12, which would be about 40% if one allowed for a general increase in the total number of black doctors by 1968–69, when most of these interviews were done.

Two of the lawyers who achieved elite establishment careers did so after a top-rank legal education during which they had performed at the top of their class. Following another typical route for the ethnic minorities, the Brooklyn Law School graduate achieved a high-ranking position within the city government. Nearly all of the women interviewed found, regardless of educational attainment, that some professional gates were simply locked. It was one thing to get admitted to school, another to find a job.

Like blacks and women, following the negative effect of holding "inappropriate statuses," they tended to go into protected work settings. Most of the doctors and lawyers started in salaried jobs—government work and clinics—where getting clients was not an immediate problem. Many of the doctors took residencies in municipal hospitals and went directly onto the staffs of these same hospitals or into clinics in the black community. Some of the psychiatrists later mixed private practice with their institutional jobs, but only one could be said to have a truly full-time private practice. It was not only the closed opportunity structure which led these women into clinics and municipal hospitals, but also their sense of service and duty to the black community. Later, some with research interests were able to work in private hospitals within the structure of new programs.

Six of the doctors interviewed were on the staff of Harlem Hospital (the hospital has 15 women physicians, a few of whom are white). This was partially the result of sampling by referral and partially because Harlem Hospital is one of the few U.S. hospitals that has any number of black physicians. It is unique in that women doctors are heads of three departments. All of the women interviewed were specialists. In 1952, out of 33,000 medical specialists, only 190 were Negroes (*Negroes in Medicine* [1952], p. 6, cited in Lopate [1968]). With the exception of three (one of whom had done breakthrough research on the "kidney machine") all were in specialties which historically have been relatively open to women and blacks: four were psychiatrists, two were pediatricians, one was in community medicine, and one in dermatology. A few now in psychiatry had been practicing pediatricians. One can see that their specialization and superior training placed them high on the eligibility list. Most black physicians have not had top-rank educations; more than four-fifths of black physicians were graduated from Meharry Medical College and Howard University (Altman 1969, p. 38). The fact that they claimed to work very hard and the somewhat greater tolerance of black men to women's participation in the professions made it possible for black women to get better posts than most white women can aspire to.

The lawyers followed the pattern of protected salaried positions to a lesser degree than the doctors. Three had their own practices, and two had become public figures. One was salaried but had attained the super-elite position of partnership in a Wall Street firm. One was the first woman assistant district attorney in New York, and another was moving from a poverty program into private practice. All had been affected by the social changes in attitudes toward racial discrimination in New York; all were exceptionally attractive or outstanding in some way, all were highly articulate; all had solid educational credentials. With one exception, all worked in the white world. All felt that being black and women gave them additional possibilities than they might not have had as only women or as only black. The lawyers' extremely unique status combination made them highly visible, and in the law, where performance is quite open to the scrutiny of peers, news of one's excellence spreads quickly.

Women lawyers interviewed in my previous study emphasized their need to be better than others so that no one could use incompetence or lack of devotion to work against them. Black women professionals also stressed this motivating factor and were even more passionate about it. Their need to prove themselves and be the best was often tied in with self-consciousness about their visibility and their sense of responsibility for others of their race and sex. These remarks were typical:

> Being a black woman . . . . It's made me fight harder. . . . I think probably one of the strengths of being black or being a black woman is that if you have the native material you really do learn to fight and try to accomplish and all the rest. If I had been white, with the same abilities, I'm not sure the drive would have been the same.

> Women have some advantages as trial lawyers, for one thing they are well remembered, or remembered, well or not, depends on how they perform. The judge is not as likely to forget them if he has ever seen them before, because we women are in the minority. And, of course, for a Negro woman, she is very likely to be remembered. It is always a help, not to be forgotten.

Some of the younger women were well aware of today's emphasis on having women and blacks in hospitals, firms, corporations, and schools. Most spoke of it with irony, but with an air of confidence and a sense that they deserved whatever benefits came out of the new social awareness. Some recognized they were useful because an employer could kill two birds with one stone by hiring a black woman; one said pithily: "I'm a show woman and a show nigger, all for one salary." Some older women felt they had been accepted in their professional work because being a Negro woman was not as bad as being a Negro man. About a third said they believed Negro men were "a threat" to white men or alluded to that belief as if it were well known to all, and that a black woman constituted less of a threat.

Whether or not this is true (and certainly, no data are available on it), the belief may act to discourage black men from seeking entry into white domains and encourage the black woman because she thinks she has more of a chance. Black women doctors and dentists who worked with white patients (one had almost a totally white practice) felt that because most of their patients were children, and therefore brought in by mothers, no "male threat" was operative in their relationship.[28]

Black women probably get "straighter" treatment in white professional setting than do white women. For one thing, white men do not as often see black professional women as romantic partners, or feel the black woman is out "to catch" one of them as a husband, and therefore respect their serious intent. In black settings, the black professional women report suspicious views of their competence and career involvement similar to those encountered by white women in white male settings, but the fact that the working woman is a more familiar image to the black man, and the "woman as doer" is more familiar to him (as it is for the woman), means that attitudes are more tempered.

Black women professionals also seem to have higher regard for each other than white women professionals. I encountered far less self-hatred among them than among the white women lawyers interviewed earlier. The latter shared the (male) negative stereotypes of women lawyers as excessively aggressive and masculine. The black women interviewed seemed to have a more matter-of-fact attitude toward their sister professionals; they never indicated doubts about the competence of other women, and some said they favored women as colleagues because they were more reliable and more willing to work than the men they knew. Few white women professionals favored other women professionals.

These phenomena in the professional world, which grow out of black women's unique position, probably reinforce their self-confidence and act to motivate them toward a career line similar to that of the white male. However, given the limits imposed by the current social structure, only the most extraordinary black women, those who are intellectually gifted and personally attractive, can make it. The fact that some do indicates that an enormous amount of energy in the social system must be directed to keeping others out.

The chance to become professionals developed out of a structure which narrowed their choices, made them visible and unique. For these few, the

---

28 William J. Goode suggests (personal communication) a general psychodynamic interpretation—that perhaps there is such a cultural emphasis on the fragility of the male ego that the typical traditional male professional may, indeed, play it safe in choosing his colleagues (certainly in choosing someone to act in an authority position over him, as a patient does when he chooses a doctor). The black woman professional may not only face less resistance from a white women client (she might prefer a male doctor but certainly would choose a black woman over a black male doctor) but she herself might be willing to challenge the professional setting to a greater extent in attempting to enter the white establishment than the black man because, being a woman, she is not so sensitive to the fear of "losing face" (the woman in American society not being socialized to think she has much face to lose, anyway).

effects of living in a world otherwise beset with limits fed their determination and made them feel the only road to survival lay in occupational success. For those without the special support of family and personal networks of these women, and without their extraordinary ability to drive ahead, the limits of the occupational structure could only be defeating, even to those with ability. The self-maintaining mechanisms of the present stratification system within the professions clearly operate to keep the participation of certain persons low in spite of their possible intellectual contributions. Ironically for this small sample of black women, the effect of mechanisms within the larger stratification system (which operate to keep blacks and women down) served to reinforce their commitment to careers which would be normally closed to them, and by defining them as superunique, made it possible for some to rise within the professional structures. It has become clear that the elaborate filtering system which keeps elite spheres clear of alien groups is costly and self-defeating. It is rare that those who do push through emerge unscathed by the passage. Those who fall on the way are lost to the greater society. But the mechanisms which contribute to the status quo are often not consciously known even by those who participate in their exercise, and only by analyzing the various structural nexus in which they occur can they be isolated and evaluated for what they are.

REFERENCES

Altman, Lawrence K. 1969. "Funds Urged to Attract Negro Doctors." *New York Times,* October 5, 1969.
Bailyn, Lotte. 1964. "Notes on the Role of Choice in the Psychology of Professional Women." *Daedalus* 93 (Spring): 700–710.
Bell, Robert R. 1971. "The Related Importance of Mother-Wife Roles among Black Lower-Class Women." In *The Black Family: Essays and Studies,* edited by Robert Staples. Belmont, Calif.: Wadsworth.
Bernard, Jessie. 1966. *Marriage and Family among Negroes.* Englewood Cliffs, N.J.: Prentice-Hall.
Bird, Caroline. 1969. "Black Womanpower." *New York Magazine* 2 (March): 35–42.
Blake, Elias, Jr. 1971. "Future Leadership Roles for Predominantly Black Colleges and Universities in American Higher Education." *Daedalus* 100 (Summer): 745–71.
Bond, Horace Mann. 1966. "The Negro Scholar and Professional in America." In *American Negro Reference Book,* edited by John P. Davis. Englewood Cliffs, N.J.: Prentice-Hall.
Brazziel, William F., Jr. 1960. "Occupational Choice in the Negro College." *Personnel and Guidance* 39:739–42.
Brimmer, Andrew. 1971. "Economic Outlook and the Future of the Negro College." *Daedalus* 100 (Summer): 539–72.
Cogan, Lee. 1968. *Negroes for Medicine.* Baltimore: Johns Hopkins Press.
Cruse, Harold. 1967. *The Crisis of the Negro Intellectual.* New York: Apollo Editions.
Cuthbert, Marion. 1942. "Education and Marginality." Ph.D. dissertation, Teachers College, Columbia University.
Epstein, Cynthia F. 1968. "Women and Professional Careers: The Case of the Woman Lawyer." Ph.D. dissertation, Columbia University.

————. 1970*a*. "Current and Emerging Occupation-centered Feminine Life-Career Patterns and Trends." *Annals of the New York Academy of Science* 175:898–909.
————. 1970*b*. "Encountering the Male Establishment." *American Journal of Sociology* 75:965–82.
————. 1970*c*. *Woman's Place: Options and Limits of Professional Careers.* Berkeley: University of California Press.
————. 1971. "Law Partners and Marital Partners: Strains and Solutions in the Dual-Career Family Enterprise." *Human Relations* 24 (December 1971): 549–64.
————. Forthcoming. *The Woman Lawyer.* Chicago: University of Chicago Press.
Fichter, Joseph H. 1964. *Graduates of Predominantly Negro Colleges—Class of 1964.* Public Health Services Publication, no. 1571. Washington, D.C.: Government Printing Office.
Ford Foundation. 1970. *The Black American Doctorate.* New York: Office of Reports, 320 E. 42 St.
Ginzberg, Eli, and Dale L. Hiestand. 1966. "Employment Patterns of Negro Men and Women." In *American Negro Reference Book,* edited by John P. Davis. Englewood Cliffs, N.J.: Prentice-Hall.
Glazer, Nathan, and Daniel Patrick Moynihan. 1963. *Beyond the Melting Pot.* Cambridge, Mass.: Harvard University Press and M.I.T. Press.
Goode, William J. 1957. "Community within a Community: The Professions." *American Sociological Review* 22:195–200.
Hall, Oswald. 1948. "The Stages of a Medical Career." *American Journal of Sociology* 53:327–36.
Hill, Robert. 1971. "Strengths of the Black Family." Mimeographed. Washington, D.C.: National Urban League.
Horner, Matina. 1969. "A Bright Woman Is Caught in a Double Bind." *Psychology Today* 3 (November): 36, 62 ff.
Hughes, Everett C. 1962. "What Other." In *Human Behavior and Social Processes,* edited by Arnold Rose. Boston: Houghton Mifflin.
Hyman, Herbert. 1969. "Black Matriarchy, Reconsidered." *Public Opinion Quarterly* 33 (Fall): 346–47.
Johnson, Charles S. 1938. *The Negro College Graduate.* Chapel Hill: University of North Carolina Press.
Ladner, Joyce. 1971. *Tomorrow's Tomorrow.* New York: Doubleday.
Lopate, Carol. 1968. *Women in Medicine.* Baltimore: Johns Hopkins Press.
McGrath, Earl. 1965. *The Predominantly Negro Colleges and Universities in Transition.* New York: Teachers College, Columbia University.
Mack, Delores E. 1971. "Where the Black Matriarchy Theorists Went Wrong." *Psychology Today* 4 (January): 24, 87 ff.
Marshall, Paule. 1959. *Brown Girl, Brownstones.* New York: Random House.
Merton, Robert K. 1957. *Social Theory and Social Structure.* Glencoe, Ill.: Free Press.
Merton, Robert K., George Reader, and Patricia Kendall. 1957. *The Student Physician.* Cambridge, Mass.: Harvard University Press.
Moynihan, Daniel Patrick. 1965. "Employment, Income and the Ordeal of the Negro Family." *Daedalus* 94 (Fall): 745–70.
Noble, Jeanne L. 1956. *The Negro Women's College Education.* New York: Stratford.
————. 1957. "Negro Women Today and Their Education." *Journal of Negro Education* 26 (Winter): 15–21.
Ostlund, Leonard A. 1957. "Occupational Choice Patterns of Negro College Women." *Journal of Negro Education* 26 (Winter): 86–91.
Ploski, H. 1967. *The Negro Almanac.* New York: Bellwether.
Reitzes, Dietrich C. 1958. *Negroes and Medicine.* Cambridge, Mass.: Harvard University Press.
Richard, Michel. 1969. "Ideology of Negro Physicians: A Test of Mobility and Status Crystallization Theory." *Social Problems* 17:20–29.
Rogoff, Natalie. 1957. "Decision to Study Medicine." In *The Student Physician,*

edited by Robert K. Merton, George Reader, and Patricia Kendall. Cambridge, Mass.: Harvard University Press.

Shea, John, Ruth S. Spitz, and Frederick A. Zeller. 1970. *Dual Careers: A Longitudinal Study of Labor Market Experience of Women.* Vol. 1. Columbus: Center for Human Resources Research, Ohio State University.

Sheppard, Harold L., and Herbert E. Striner. 1966. *Civil Rights, Employment, and the Social Status of American Negroes.* Report of the U.S. Commission on Civil Rights. Washington, D.C.: Government Printing Office.

Silberman, Charles. 1964. *Crisis in Black and White.* New York: Random House.

Udry, J. Richard. 1968. "Marital Instability by Race, Sex, Education, Occupation, and Income, Using 1960 Census Data." In *Selected Studies in Marriage and the Family,* edited by Robert F. Winch and Louis W. Goodman. New York: Holt, Rinehart & Winston.

United Negro College Fund. 1964–65. "Statistical Information, UNCF Office of Development and Educational Services." Report of member institutions of UNCF. New York: United Negro College Fund.

U.S., Bureau of the Census. 1963. *1960 Subject Reports. Occupational Characteristics.* Final Report PC (2)–7A. Washington, D.C.: Government Printing Office.

———. 1967. *Current Population Reports.* Series P-60, No. 60. Washington, D.C.: Government Printing Office.

———. 1970. *Current Population Reports.* Series P-60, No. 75. Washington, D.C.: Government Printing Office.

U.S., Department of Commerce. 1968. *Statistical Abstract, 1968.* Washington, D.C.: Government Printing Office.

———. 1969. *Changing Characteristics of the Negro Population.* Washington, D.C.: Government Printing Office.

———. 1970. *Statistical Abstract, 1970.* Washington, D.C.: Government Printing Office.

U.S., Department of Commerce and Department of Labor. 1970. *The Social and Economic Status of Negroes in the United States, 1970.* BLS Report No. 394, and Current Population Reports, Series P-23, No. 38. Washington, D.C.: Government Printing Office.

U.S., Department of Labor. 1967. *Negro Women in the Population and the Labor Force.* Washington, D.C.: Government Printing Office.

———. 1970. *Handbook of Women Workers 1969.* Women's Bureau Bulletin No. 294. Washington, D.C.: Government Printing Office.

Whelpton, Pascal K., Arthur A. Campbell, and John E. Patterson. 1966. *Fertility and Family Planning in the United States.* Princeton, N.J.: Princeton University Press.

15

SHEILA TOBIAS AND LISA ANDERSON

New Views of Rosie
The Riveter

Two questions of importance to women's history and to the history of the labor movement in the United States find their formulation if not their answers in the person and the mythology surrounding Rosie the Riveter: Who was the American working woman during World War II and what was her level of consciousness?

Rosie the Riveter was World War II's second favorite pin-up (after Betty Grable). A pompadoured fresh-faced female welder appeared on countless posters in the period, responding vacuously to a message like, "Longing will not bring him back sooner...Get a War Job." More realistic but no less propagandistic views of women abound in old copies of LIFE magazine and in archives, their long hair tied in bandanas, their eyes behind dark glasses, cutting metal plates with acetylene flames in one picture, working on the wings of a bomber in another, operating, this time wearing hard-hats, on a bolt-cutting machine in a shipyard in a third.

In a recent article describing governmental sources relating to women war workers during the forties, in which the posters described above are reproduced, Eleanor F. Straub seems to accept at face value the posters and the view that "...potential Rosie the Riveters were courted, cajoled and flattered in an attempt to induce women to accept war jobs."[1] The War Information Office, she reports, encouraged the media to convince women that just as men must fight, women must work. Her article suggests that the women's sense of patriotism had to be aroused before they would take on full-time positions as factory workers.

Although the Straub article is to be welcomed as one of the few serious commentaries on Rosie the Riveter to appear in the decades since Rosie disappeared from public consciousness, the interpretation rests, as does much that was written about Rosie during the war, on what is in our opinion a fundamental fallacy concerning the definition of women war workers and one that fails to appreciate their place in American labor history. Behind the "induction" metaphor lies an assumption that prior to World War II Rosie the Riveter was a non-working woman. This is undoubtably true of some number of female war workers who were either in school or at home when the war broke out and the posters issued by the government agencies were doubtless directed at these women. But missing from

[1] Eleanor F. Straub, "United States Government Policy Toward Civilian Women during World War II," *Prologue* (Winter 1973), National Archives, p. 240ff.

the numerous commentaries about Rosie the Riveter is a recognition
that there were a substantial number of "other" Rosies, women who
were employed prior to Pearl Harbor. How and why did they migrate
to war work? And how were they to cope with unemployment after the
war?

Our own research, entitled "What Really Happened to Rosie
the Riveter" (1973) began by challenging what appeared to us to be
a middle-class model of Rosie the Riveter associated with the notion
of "induction." For if, as we hypothesized, most Rosie the Riveters
were not middle-class housewives, but instead underpaid domestic,
retail and service workers, employed before the war at low wages in
insecure industries, then merely opening up jobs for women in war-
related plants would have sufficed to "induce" them to apply for
these new positions. And if, in turn, these women saw themselves as
continuing to work after the war, functioning as a main source of
income for self, family, parents or dependents, they would have been
seriously dislocated first by the laying-off that began in war-
related work as early as the summer of 1944, and then by industrys'
unwillingness to hire them back at the same job or at comparable
wages after the war.

Indeed, if Rosie were as we hypothesized a working woman and
not a glamourous housewife-on-leave as depicted in the posters, she
might have identified with issues that were not among the National
Women's Bureau's more traditional priority, protective legislation.[2]
She might have been more concerned about equal pay, equal access to
men's only jobs and equal seniority rights and union participation.
She might have been or might have become for all we know a working-
class feminist. Though this last may be far-fetched, we have some
evidence that for whatever combination of reasons she did not
voluntarily give up her job at war's end.

Our data indicates that women workers were disproportionately
"bumped" in the last year of the war and not rehired in terms of their
seniority. Where they landed in the economy thereafter is purely
speculative. It is possible that a good many women factory workers
slid back down into service-related, restaurant, laundry and retail
work, where wages were lower and workers unorganized. Since the
twelve million women who had been working full-time and full-season
before the war were not recognized as war workers in popular mythology,
there was never any suggestion that there should be a post-war national
policy along the lines of the GI Bill to protect, retrain and re-equip
women war workers for the post-war world.

[2]The Women's Bureau of the United States Department of Labor was
established after the first World War to protect women workers.
This agency was given no regulatory laws to administer, and
therefore relied upon "fact-finding and fact furnishing" to achieve
its ends. Numerous studies conducted by the Bureau during the 1940's
chart changes in female employment patterns.

The detailed story of their post-war dislocation is yet to be researched but certain patterns emerge. Given the enormous amount of physical movement during the war toward better paying jobs, it is probable that a large proportion of the suddenly unemployed women did not return home. Their story, then, may be a significant section in the history of other post-war labor migrations, a partial explanation for central city overcrowding and for the increase in welfare needs. While racism has now been accepted as a tangible cause of poverty and underemployment, sexism has not yet been perceived or studied in that same way. If thoroughgoing analysis of the fate of women war workers reveals a decline since the war in female earning power and a corresponding increase in numbers among the female working poor, then the rise and fall of industrial employment opportunities for women is surely to blame.

The second question, as to Rosie's consciousness of herself as woman and as worker, is even harder to explore, for the public Rosie showed little aggressiveness or self-righteousness in the face of war-time discrimination and post-war neglect. One possibility is that she took the message of the posters to be true and since neither the media nor the government depicted her as a bona fide member of the working class, her own class identity might have become confused. To the Woman's Bureau in Washington, the participation of women in defense production, as Straub's review and our research points out again and again, was not a permanent phenomenon to be adjusted to, but a "situation", temporary in nature, owing to war, absent husband, special circumstances or color of skin. Therefore it was considered more appropriate for the Woman's Bureau to worry about protecting women workers from dangers on the job than to battling inequities in separate seniority listings for example. Who then saw Rosie as worker? The Unions? Management? Herself?

We do not have answers to these questions, but we continue to be intrigued by the resiliance of the mythology. The propaganda may have been designed as much to disguise Rosie the Riveter as to glamourize her and women's history and labor history are the worse for this sleight of hand.

The Macro Picture

In the little that has been written about women war workers, the emphasis has been on two aspects of their labor-market participation: the increase in the numbers of women working from 13.8 million just before the war, or 27.5 percent of the total work force to a high of 19.4 million, or 36.7 percent of the total work force in 1944,[3] and the increase in the proportion of married women working. In 1940, single women had constituted 48.5 percent of the female work force, married women 36.4 percent and widows and divorcees, 15.1 percent. During the war, however, these figures changed to 40.9

---

[3]U.S. Department of Commerce, Bureau of the Census, Current Population Report, 1950.

percent single, 45.7 percent married and 13.4 percent widowed or [4]
divorced (of the married women 11 percent had husbands in service.)
These figures must be appreciated in terms of the changing size of
the total labor force: 46 million in 1940, 53.5 million in 1944,
plus 12 million in the armed services. After 1947, when the conversion to a peace-time economy was more or less complete, the work
force numbered 56.7 million, well above the 40 million 1940 figure,
and the female work force numbered 15.8 million, substantially above
the 13.8 figure in 1940 though well below the high of 19.6 million
registered in 1944.

Information about occupational shifts in employment of men
and women during this period is even more interesting than these
gains in numbers and in percent married, given our hypothesis that
Rosie had migrated up to factory work. We wanted to understand the
internal dynamics of both the demand side of the labor picture and
the supply side as well, so that eventually we would be able to
chart where women who went into manufacturing had come from. We
did not entirely succeed in this task but we did discover the
following: male and female employment in the munitions manufacturing
industries and in the federal war agencies increased by seven million
between 1940 and 1945.[5] In general, these increases were at the
expense of agriculture, construction and trade, all of which lost
ground. Craftsmen (and women) and operatives gained five million
new workers. Industrial workers who had previously, in 1940,
accounted for fewer than 30 percent of total civilian employment,
accounted for 35 percent by 1945. White collar work also expanded,
rising by two million, though professional workers, many of whom were
inducted into the armed forces, dropped by 200,000 over the five-year
period.

Most important, about 15 percent of women employed both before
Pearl Harbor and in 1945--or about 2 million women workers--changed
their jobs and occupational groups. In most cases, according to
Pool and Pearlman, the change was from farm, service and sales
occupations to manufacturing. Details follow: one-sixth of the
women previously employed in service occupations and one-tenth of
the sales women were in industrial jobs by March 1944. An even more
dramatic way of presenting this data is in percent of total employed:
In 1940 women workers constituted eight percent of all workers in
durable goods; at the war-time peak, they constituted 25 percent of
all durable goods workers and in 1947, but 13 percent.

The entry of women into industries and occupations previously
reserved almost exclusively for men was the most striking labor market
development of the war period although women's employment also shifted
into clerical and sales, replacing men. Domestic industries,

[4]U.S. Bureau of the Census, "Marital Status of Women in the Population and Labor Force, 1940, 44, 47, 42."

[5]Harold Pool and Lester M. Pearlman, "Recent Occupational Trends in
   the United States," Monthly Labor Review, Dept. of Labor, Bureau of
   Labor Statistics, August 1947, Vol. 65, No. 2, p. 139ff.

laundries and even schools found themselves bereft of women workers, as females moved into better-paying jobs in industry, but the shift to manufacturing was the most salient and most significant for change in female earning-power.

One further research project would be to go back to the raw data on which Pool and Pearlman rest their all too brief report, written just after the war, and to try to disaggregate the figures. For what we need to know with some accuracy are answers to questions like the following:

1. From what other industries were women recruited most likely to be recruited for war-time work?

2. How far geographically did they migrate for work in industry?

3. Did the industrial employer show any preference for previously working women over housewives-on-leave?

4. What were the relations between these two groups of women on and off the job?

5. Where did women from each of, say, 20 of the largest munitions manufacturing plants in the country go to work after the war?

Another measure of the shift in women's employment from non-manufacturing to manufacturing can be inferred from the total number of women in labor unions. In 1919, there had been but 250,000 unionized women; in 1937, 500,000 and in 1944, 3.5 million. Industrial unions, then as now, were quicker to open their doors to women. Craft unions remained closed or gave a form of temporary membership which would be rescinded with the end of the war-time emergency.

Possibly the most dramatic shift in type of employment was registered by Negro women during the war. In 1940 two out of every five Negro women worked compared with two out of every eight white women. Of the total 1.5 million working in 1940, more than half were in service occupations, agriculture, domestic help, cooking, waiting or were seeking work (unemployed). But by 1945 two million Negro women were working as craftsmen, foremen, factory workers and in the armed services, not only in munitions but in food, clothing textiles, leathers and other manufacturing.[6]

Geographic shifts were also measured by the Women's Bureau. The numbers of women working in 1940 and in 1944 increased as follows in the cities named:[7] Detroit, 182,000 to 387,000; San Francisco

[6]"Negro Women War Workers", The Women's Bureau, Bulletin 205, Washington, D.C. 1945

[7]F.M. Brewer "Women Workers after the War", Editorial Research Report 16, Washington, D.C. 1944, p. 291

137,000 to 275,000 and Mobile, Alabama, 7,800 to 27,000. It remains again to disaggregate the data and try to ascertain whether these women came from outlying rural areas or from other manufacturing cities and whether they remained in their temporary homes after the war.

Motivation to Work

There was an enormous amount of nonsense written before, during and after the war about women's commitment to work. The posters only emphasized the patriotic dimension of war work, as we have seen, and even newspapers as realistic as the Wall St. Journal saw women as "choosy" when it came to selecting jobs, easily bored and always ready to "fade" away. If one were to depend on popular descriptions of women at war work, one might conclude that the wearing of pants was more interesting to them than the paycheck, but this, too, was part of the continuing mythology that women do not work for money.

There is no question that factory work was better paying, in general, and in particular during the war and that working women cared about that paycheck and were willing to protest unequal pay for equal work throughout the period. Some standard pay ranges easily document this: In the best paying defense industry, namely aircraft (the industry on which most of our longer study focused in the area in and around Detroit), the low hourly wage in this period was about $1.02 and the high $1.15. In other defense manufacturing, the range was from 89¢ to 93¢ per hour, and in non-defense manufacturing 60¢ to 85¢ per hour. This made possible a nation-wide average for females (for forty-eight hours worked) of $44.21 during this period, a wage at least equivalent to highly skilled and professional work before the war.[8]

As for continuing to work after the war, more than 80 percent of the women who had been employed before Pearl Harbor, according to a survey done by the Women's Bureau in 1944, intended to keep on working. Among women who had been in school before Pearl Harbor, 75 percent expected to continue working and more than half the former housewives had similar plans.[9] United Auto Worker surveys show even higher rates: 85 percent of the women interviewed wanted to continue to work after the war. Of the married women 68.7 percent responded yes, 98.5 percent of the single women and 100 percent of the widows.[10] Elsewhere, in other surveys, women specified that what they wanted above all was to continue in factory work. Much of the reason was financial: in a survey done by the United Electrical Radio and Machine Workers of America, one-fifth of the women working indicated they were the only wage earners in their family and one-half were the main source of income for relatives living elsewhere. More than 80 percent of this group planned to continue working, 93

[8]National War Labor Board, Memorandum on Equal Pay, 1944.

[9]Women's Bureau, "Women Workers in Ten War Production Areas and Their Post-War Plans," Bulletin No. 209, Washington, D.C. 1946

[10]Statement of R.J. Thomas, UAW "On Employment of Women after the War," March 10, 1944 archives.

percent of these for financial reasons.[11]

We cannot document all the reasons for female labor participation during the war. As the work of Mirra Komarovsky[12] and Lee Rainwater[13] have amply shown, the blue-collar woman has many and mixed motivations for work, some of which she cannot admit even to herself. Our conclusion so far is, rather, a negative one: that the public view of female labor participation during World War II does not bear up under any kind of analysis, largely because the women who worked at these jobs were not indifferent to money or to job security. They were, in large part, working women who had always worked, would go on working, and for as long as it lasted, would benefit from the opportunity to do men's jobs at men's wages.

The Micro Picture

The aircraft industry in and around Detroit was chosen by us for detailed study, largely because it was among the industries most affected by war production needs. Automobile production was cut as the factories were re-tooled for war-related work. The establishment of a Women's Department within the United Auto Workers in 1944, a relatively unusual move, also stimulated our interest in this particular industry. This department was responsible for conducting surveys, collecting statistics, and in general, representing women's interests within the automobile-aircraft industry. Further studies might possibly focus on the steel and the electrical industries, though the story in the last-named field would be unduly complicated by the internal political dynamics of the electrical workers union. Another approach might be to concentrate on a single geographic area, or to select a number of still-living Rosie the Riveters and survey their remembered attitudes and experiences.

Our primary goal was to investigate what we had felt to have been a disproportionate laying-off of women who wanted to continue working at their jobs at war's end. Here, too, the popular press was misleading, for the implication was that women were restless at work, anxious to get home and back to the business of raising their families. Within the UAW files, we found ample evidence to support our suspicion that women were rather brutally laid off, their seniority notwithstanding and, indeed, unwelcome even two to three years later at the old jobs or at comparable jobs in the same location, despite their training and experience.

Our conclusion after reading UAW grievances on file at the Labor and Urban Affairs Archives at Wayne State is that for the most part women war workers expected and did not especially resent being laid off as cutbacks marked the end of the war. What they did

[11]"Why Women Work," Department of Labor, N.Y., March 1946 archives.

[12]Mirra Komarovsky, Blue-Collar Marriage (N.Y. Random House, 1964)

[13]Lee Rainwater, Richard Coleman and Gerald Handel, Workingman's Wife (N.Y., Oceana Publications, 1959)

resent and what caused them to file grievances was that they were not rehired in accordance with their perceived seniority when the plant was reconverted to postwar production. They did not want "special treatment" as a December 1944 UAW conference on women said explicitly; but they wanted equal access to jobs. The issue of seniority, then, is a central one, made complicated by the fact that one cannot make generalizations about seniority arrangements, since they vary by union contract and by industry.

In aircraft parts plants where women had amounted to 42.2 percent of the total working population, they were 60.2 percent of the workers laid off in 1944. In aircraft engine plants, where women had been 39.2 percent of the workers employed, they were 86 percent of the layoffs. In the truck and agriculture implements industry, women had been 13.1 percent of the work force, and were 51.6 percent of the layoffs. In ordinance, at 25.6 percent of the work force, they were 61 percent of the total layoffs.[14]

Other plants reported 98 percent of the layoffs to have been female, and in some cases 100 percent. Sometimes the cutbacks were rationalized as having to do with a conversion back to "heavy assembling" where "light assembling" had been done before. Even more ambiguously, jobs were described as "not suitable" for female workers. Often an entire plant closed down and when it reopened, women were not rehired. Whether or not this was legal in terms of union contracts and seniority was hotly debated in the years just after the war. One issue, that of the desirability of a "successor clause" which would have obligated any newly converted plant to rehire all workers who had worked in its war facility, was voted down by the International United Auto Workers in 1945.[15] The successor clause that the union preferred was one that permitted the Corporation to rehire only those it found "suitable," "experienced" and "qualified", restrictions that the unions had been trying to prevent management from making in regard to male workers for years. Clearly, where white women (and Negro males and females) were concerned, the old protections were not going to be defended.

During the war there had been substantial debate about separate seniority listings, which we followed in some detail in our longer study. The interesting point is, however, that much of this went by the board in the post-war allocation of jobs within individual plants. The following public statement by a union official describing the situation in a Springfield Ohio company, gave the union pause, but did not lead to anything like a protest:

[14]Folders entitled "layoffs" in the "Preliminary Inventory", Archives of Labor History and Urban Affairs, Wayne State Univ. Reports for individual locals were filed for the years 1943-45.

[15]Much material on this is in folders marked "Fair Labor Committee" in the Wayne State UAW archives.

> There are jobs in this plant at the present time,
> but they are not suitable for female workers.
> The work is too heavy. The girls may find work
> in this area, but naturally it will have to be at
> lower wages as most plants seem to be asking for
> male workers.[16]

Protests

Insofar as women protested discrimination during the war and differential laying-off after the war, the majority did so as individuals in the form of grievances. The only collective response to inequalities that we could uncover in our study was in the form of conferences. Toward the end of World War II, in anticipation of a recurrence of the problems of converting from a war to a peacetime economy, a number of conferences were held around the country. Organizations ranging in type from the YWCA and ad-hoc committees to union and government agencies focused on possible discrimination confronting women workers after the war. There was, however, no woman's movement in the political arena, no separate organizations representing working women, no caucuses within the unions, and no opportunities for women to move into leadership positions there. There do not seem to have been any strikes by women or on behalf of women that we could uncover.

During the war the issues affecting women were many: seniority, coequal status of women doing men's jobs with the men on those jobs; equal pay for equal work; unemployment compensation; implementation (or suspension) of protective legislation; union representation and child care. After the war, the issues centered on equal rights to re-employment.

Throughout the war, of course, formal striking had been prohibited. Yet among the many wildcat (unofficial) strikes, particularly in the year of greatest labor disturbance, 1943, women were conspicuously absent from the ranks of participants, and issues of interest to women were never at stake. We have done, to be sure, only a superficial survey of wildcatting largely through reports in the N.Y. Times, but it was disturbing not to discover among these any references to women or to women's issues. It may be of course that the women's presence was ignored by their male co-workers and by the news media. But even where there was a reference to the equal pay for equal work issue, the concern was rather with differential payments to male workers.[17]

Strikers are always referred to as "men," but again this does not tell us whether women were present, because women workers may have been subsumed under the word "men." Still it is noteworthy that in 1943, when as we know from other sources about 50% of the workers at any one aircraft plant must have been women, R.J. Thomas,

[16]Letter from president of local union at Oliver Co. Springfield, Ohio
to UAW International, May 17, 1945

[17]N.Y. Times, May 21, 1943, p. 11

President of the UAW, told the N.Y. Times, "The men involved in the strikes...have legitimate and serious grievances..."[18] We can only assume that women's participation in unauthorized work stoppages to pursue their own or their co-workers' grievances did not take place to any great extent. Further research is required to ascertain whether, indeed, this judgment based on a review of thirty-three wildcat strikes holds out, but it is even more important to understand why women were not involved. After the war, by contrast, we find some evidence of female participation in a dispute involving the Ford Highland Motor Plant (December 1945). The women picketed over alleged discrimination practices.

If evidence of collective action is unavailable, individual grievances, on the other hand, abound in the files of the UAW, some of them not filed until as late as 1949-51. Of the many instances we looked at, the typical pattern involved as re-classification of jobs after the war such that a woman could not qualify for a job she had held during the war. For a time, judging by the dearth of grievances filed immediately after the war, the women workers seemed content to allow the companies to reconvert, but they complained as the months stretched into years and they were barred from jobs they knew were available to men.

The role of unions (in this case the UAW) both on a local and on a national level is worth a study of its own. If historical judgments were to rest exclusively on documentary sources, the UAW leadership--R.J. Thomas, Walter and Victor Reuther, Brendon Sexton, Emil Mazey--would have to be praised for its even-handed and sensitive approach to women workers during World War II. Certainly, the union wanted women workers to join. The purpose of the Women's Department and of Sister Sue's columns in the official UAW newspaper Ammunition, was precisely to argue for the benefits to women workers of union membership. But when it came to the gut issues, the union either retreated behind global goals (e.g. full employment for everyone) in order to avoid taking sides between men and women, or took great pains to guarantee the rights and benefits of male workers, in the process of supporting women.

Two issues will illustrate this strategy. The struggle for equal pay for equal work, (after women found themselves doing men's work at women's wages), was complicated by the fact that though the War Labor Board came out unequivocally on the side of equal pay for women, it was mandated to curb inflation by not allowing wage and price increases.[19] Thus, the union feared men's and women's hourly rates on similar jobs would be equalized by cutting men's wages and not by increasing women's. This of course would not have satisfied anyone, but it is interesting to note the care with which the union leadership protected the higher rates from change.

[18]N.Y. Times, ibid.

[19]War Labor Board's policy promulgated 9/26/42

William Chafe, author of The American Woman (Oxford University Press) has suggested to us in a personal communication that the union was also mindful of post-war wage rate-setting and anxious to undermine in advance any attempt by management after the war to lower rates on those jobs that had been held by women during the war. This would suggest that the leadership all along anticipated that men would replace women where women had replaced men, and was interested in a longer-run strategy. Still, the very idea of equal pay for equal work between women and men was progressive. It was not until 1963 that this standard was made into law.

Another example of union strategy was in the response given to women leaders about post-war work opportunities for women war-workers. When pressed for a statement or a position on the subject of female employment after the war, Thomas would speak only of a national full-employment policy of 60 million post-war jobs. The women leaders inside and outside the UAW also ducked the issue of potential male-female competition. At a 1944 conference to discuss the needs of women workers, the final resolution proposed by the women called for "no special consideration for women in post-war planning."[20]

On the local level, for all the female grievances that were taken up by the union, there were at least as many that died at the door of the local shop steward or by vote of the local membership.

Conclusion

The generation of women war workers, symbolized by Rosie the Riveter, has not been seriously analyzed by historians. Perhaps it is because the women disappeared as a recognizable group after the war, in pursuit, according to popular mythology of the "best years of their lives" (the title of a popular postwar film) that the war had postponed; or, as Betty Friedan suggested fifteen years later in her book, The Feminine Mystique,[21] they were hoodwinked by returning magazine editors selling a new product called "suburbia." In either case, the conventional view of Rosie's generation is that they were temporary workers; they had entered the work force for patriotic reasons only, donning unfamiliar working-class aprons and riveter masks; and they departed from factory work altogether as soon after the war as they could manage.

Although there was at least one "Back to Mamma" club founded in the late years of the war with the express purpose of persuading women to quit,[22] most experts, among them Frances Perkins, Roosevelt's female Secretary of Labor, predicted that American women would go on

[20] Detroit News, November 18, 1944, report on the conference.

[21] Betty Friedan, The Feminine Mystique (New York, 1963).

[22] "Are Wives People?" Independent Woman XXIV (November 1946): 332.

preferring domesticity to factory work.[23] Others, and among these
were union leaders, some of whom were anxious to avoid competition
between war workers and returning veterans, hoped that women would
retire voluntarily.[24] But what the contemporaries failed to notice
and what history has not yet set right is the degree to which the
women were forceably laid off their jobs in the postwar period.

Three million fewer women were employed in 1946 than at the
peak of the war. The critical questions are whether women were
unjustly laid-off against their will or merely accommodated in their
wish to go home; and, if they were laid-off, where they landed in the
economy. Our hunch is that Rosie did not run to the suburbs so much
as fall into a lower-paying, more traditional female job after the
war. Since we know that by 1950 the number of employed women was
almost back to the wartime peak, our suspicion is that Rosie stopped
riveting, but she did not stop working. Further research will be
needed to substantiate this view.

Mythology dies hard. Although it is beyond the scope of this
paper to speculate on Friedan's allegation that the feminine mystique
was revived to keep women from maintaining the economic gains they
had won during the war, the issues of equal pay, desegregation of
job categories, and government-supported child care, which were much
discussed during the war, did not surface again until the 1960s.
The quiescence of women in the fifties may well be the result not
of Rosie's choice but of Rosie's frustration, which is another good
reason for laying the myths surrounding Rosie the Riveter to rest.

[23]Brief, issued April 22, 1944, of F.M. Brewer, "Women Workers After
    the War," Editorial Research Report 1, no. 16 (Washington, D.C.,
    1944).

In this brief the prediction made by Secretary of Labor Perkins as
to the number of women who would voluntarily withdraw from the
labor force following the war is contrasted with the predictions
made by the Women's Advisory Committee of the War Manpower
Commission. Perkins is quoted as saying "many women now at work
will leave their jobs to retire, to go back to school, or to
return to the homes they left for patriotic reasons." The Women's
Advisory Committee predicted that "a relatively small portion"
of women would voluntarily withdraw from paid employment. See also
the New York Times article dated February 13, 1945, p. 26 in which
Secretary Perkins outlines her reconversion program. She advocates
a strengthening of protective legislation, and moves that women
"who took jobs only because of the war" be encouraged to leave the
labor market.

[24]Statement of R.J. Thomas, President, UAW-CIO. "On Employment of
    Women After the War," March 10, 1944.

The foregoing was based on a lengthy study of women war workers in auto-aircraft industry, published under the title "What Really Happened to Rosie the Riveter" by MSS Modular Publications, 655 Madison Avenue, New York, New York 10021 (1974). In the longer study can be found a detailed bibliography. The work relied heavily on manuscript collections in the United Auto Workers Archive and the Archives of Labor History and Urban Affairs. Pertinent government documents were found in the Women's Bureau Archives, Department of Labor, Wayne State University, Detroit, Michigan. In addition, the following books and articles were made use of:

Books

Chafe, William, The American Woman: Her Changing Social, Economic and Political Role, 1920-1970 (New York: Oxford University Press, 1972)

Friedan, Betty, The Feminine Mystique (New York: Dell, 1963)

O'Neill, William, Everyone Was Brave (Chicago: Quadrangle Press, 1969)

Thomas, R.J., Automobile Unionism, volumes 1940, 1942, 1943, · 1944, 1946

Government Sources

Frieda Miller, "Employment Opportunities in Characteristic Industrial Occupations of Women," Women's Bureau Bulletin, January, 1945.

"Women Workers in Ten War Production Areas and Their Post-war Employment Plans," Women's Bureau Bulletin no. 209, 1946.

"Negro Women War Workers," Women's Bureau Bulletin no. 205, 1945.

"The Woman Worker a Year After VJ Day," by Frieda Miller, n.d.

Other Government Agencies

Pool, Harold and Pearlman, Lester M. "Recent Occupational Trends in the United States," Monthly Labor Review, U.D. Department of Labor, Bureau of Labor Statistics, August 1947, volume 65, no. 2, pp. 139ff.

"Straight-time Average Hourly Earnings in Selected Occupations, Miscellaneous Metalworking Establishments (excluding foundries), Benton Harbor and St. Joseph, Michigan, Wage Area," U.S. Department of Labor, Bureau of Labor Statistics, Serial no. 8-5, August 1943.

Newspaper and Magazine Articles and Research Reports

Brewer, F.M., "Women Workers After the War," Editorial Research Reports, Washington, D.C., volume I, no. 16.

Greenbaum, Lucy, "Women Who Need to Work," New York Times Magazine, April 29, 1945, p. 16.

Greenbaum, Lucy, "Industries in U.S. Replacing Women," New York Times, January 1946.

Miller, Frieda, "What's Become of Rosie the Riveter?" New York Times Magazine, May 5, 1946.

Trey, Joan, "Women in the War Economy," The Review of Radical Political Economics, (New York, July 1972) IV, no. 3.

"Women in the Post-war Labor Market: Does Full Employment Include Jobs for 18 Million Women?" Forum; October 1945.

16

DEE GARRISON

The Tender Technicians: The Feminization of Public Librarianship, 1876–1905

T he law of nature destines and qualifies the female sex for the bearing and nurture of the children of our race and for the custody
of the homes of the world," stated the Wisconsin Supreme Court in
1875 when ruling that women could not be admitted to their bar.
The judges conceded that the "cruel chances of life" might leave
some women free of the sacred female duties. "These may need
employment, and should be welcome to any not derogatory to their
sex and its proprieties."[1] Most Americans of the time would have
agreed with the Court that only financial need justified a woman's
going to work and that only limited jobs should be opened to her.
But in the decades before and after 1900 Americans became the
unobservant participants in a social revolution, as profound changes
took place in the attitudes toward women and their work. The
American public libraries played an important role in the revolution, for the feminization of librarianship proceeded rapidly. In
1852 the first woman clerk was hired at the Boston Public
Library;[2] by 1878 fully two thirds of the library workers there were
female.[3] In 1910 78½ percent of library workers in the United
States were women; only teaching surpassed librarianship as the
most feminized "profession."[4]

Educated women, while meeting resistance in other more established professions, flooded into library work during the last quarter
of the nineteenth century for a variety of reasons. Librarianship
was a new and fast-growing field in need of low-paid but educated
recruits. With a plentiful number of library jobs available, male
librarians offered no opposition to the proliferation of women
library workers, partly because women agreed that library work

Professor Garrison is a member of the history department of Livingston College, Rutgers
University.

matched presumed feminine limitations. Librarianship was quickly adjusted to fit the narrowly circumscribed sphere of women's activities, for it appeared similar to the work of the home, functioned as cultural activity, required no great skill or physical strength and brought little contact with the rougher portions of society. For all these reasons, Melvil Dewey could predict, when writing at the turn of the century of the ideal librarian, that "most of the men who achieve this greatness will be women."[5] The feminization of librarianship, however, had unexpected long-range results. The prevalence of women would profoundly affect the process of professionalization and the type of service the library would provide. The nature of library work itself, one of the few sources of economic opportunity open to educated women in the late nineteenth century, would serve to perpetuate the low status of women in American society. Above all, female dominance of librarianship did much to shape the inferior and precarious status of the public library as an important cultural resource and to cause it to evolve into a marginal kind of public amusement service.[6]

The rapid growth of libraries in size, number and complexity between 1876 and 1905 was an important cause of the feminization of librarianship. The monumental 1876 "Report on Public Libraries" listed 3,682 libraries containing a little over twelve million volumes.[7] Total yearly additions of library books in the nation passed the one million mark in 1876.[8] A conservative estimate raised the total to forty million volumes held in 8,000 libraries in 1900.[9] Because a heavy demand for trained librarians coincided with other national developments, particularly the advance of women's education and the increase of women workers, many women found employment in library service. Very probably, women would have flocked into any new field into which their entry was not opposed. Because male librarians heartily welcomed women into library service, the eventual feminization of the library staff was assured.

The low cost of hiring women was perhaps the most important reason that male library leaders welcomed women assistants. The public library, supported by taxes and voluntary donations, was by necessity obliged to practice thrifty housekeeping. Trustees and taxpayers expected that the major portion of the yearly income would be invested in books. Because women were notoriously low-paid, the annual cost of library administration could be appreciably lowered by the introduction of women workers. Frederick Perkins, in an 1876 article entitled "How to Make Town Libraries Successful," recommended that "women should be employed as librarians and assistants as far as possible." Perkins was no crusader for women's equality; he only pointed out that the hiring of women, along with the use of "mechanical appliances...better arrangements of book rooms and other sufficient contrivances of that American ingenuity," would lessen the excessive cost of library administration.[10] Justin Winsor, speaking at .the 1877 conference of British and American librarians in London, emphasized the importance of women workers in American libraries.

In American libraries we set a high value on women's work. They soften our atmosphere, they lighten our labor, they are equal to our work, and for the money they cost—if we must gauge such labor by such rules—they are infinitely better than equivalent salaries will produce of the other sex....We can command our pick of the educated young women whom our Colleges for Women are launching forth upon our country—women with a fair knowledge of Latin and Greek, a good knowledge of French and German, a deducible knowledge of Spanish and Italian, and who do not stagger at the acquisition of even Russian, if the requirements of the catalogue service make that demand. It is to these Colleges for Women, like Vassar and Wellesley, that the American library-system looks confidently for the future.[11]

The limited opportunities open to educated women for paid employment served to bring larger numbers of competent women than competent men into low-paid library jobs during this period. Of the eight leading women librarians of the time, four had some college and the rest at least a high school education.[12] In view of the constant references made in library literature to the necessity of finding workers with an educated knowledge of books, a high intelligence and preferably a familiarity with a few languages, it is safe to assume that most women entering library service at this time were either self- or formally-educated to at least the extent expected of an urban schoolteacher.[13] The same economic factors were at work in librarianship and teaching, for educated women, with few other job opportunities flocked into both fields, with a depressing effect on wages. Library work required similar qualifications to teaching and was little worse in pay. In librarianship women could exercise their presumed special feminine talents and could, besides, remain isolated, in a way teachers could not, from the rough workaday world.[14]

The feminine movement into new occupations like nursing and teaching or clerical and industrial employment began in the middle of the nineteenth century when both the right to individuality and the myth of women's sphere held extremely important places in American popular thought. Two such conflicting ideas could not exist together unless individualism was reserved for man alone. Thus man took the world and all its activities as his "sphere," while confining women to domesticity and the guardianship of culture. Women were just as guilty of inconsistency. The gradual expansion of women's claim to the right of individual choice was on the whole unaccompanied by any feminine calls for radical social change. Instead, as each new job became filled by women, charming theories were developed by both sexes to explain why the feminine mind and nature were innately suited to the new occupation. Thus it was decided that teaching was much like mothering; women, it was said, were uniquely able to guide children into piety, purity and knowledge. Women were cleared to work as writers, musicians and artists because of their inherent sensitivity, elevated moralism and love of beauty. Women doctors and nurses were intuitively kind, sympathetic and delicate of touch. The woman social worker expressed inborn feminine qualities of love, charity and idealism. Factory, business and clerical work fit the feminine nature, for women were naturally industrious, sober and nimble-fingered, as well as better able than men to endure the boredom of detailed or repetitive tasks. These various expansions of the work of women served to modify the concept of woman's proper sphere but the process was gradual and involved no radical threat to traditional social ideals.[15] Yet each expansion led to others, with a snowballing effect, so that within a hundred years the limits of woman's claim to individual freedom of choice had undergone considerable and drastic change.

This redefinition of woman's sphere, always in accord with the characteristics presumed to be innately feminine, also came to encompass librarianship as one of the proper fields open to women. The course to library work had already been cleared for women because libraries held books and books denoted Culture with a capital "C". By the late nineteenth century, woman's sphere decidedly included the guardianship and enjoyment of culture. It was believed that through their refining and spiritualizing influence women could exalt all human society. It would be almost impossible to overemphasize the Victorian conviction that men were physically tamed and morally elevated by the sway of the gentle female. Moreover, by the 1870s American popular literature was consciously designed to please feminine readers. Therefore the advent of women to library work required little stretching of the popular ideal regarding the female, for "books...should be treated by reverent hands... should be given out as a priest dispenses the sacrament, and the next step to this ideal ministry is to have them issued by women."[16]

The librarian...is becoming...the guardian of the thought-life of the people....The library, in its influence, is whatever the librarian makes it; it seems destined to become an all-pervading force...moulding [sic] public opinion, educating to all of the higher possibilities of human thought and action; to become a means for enriching, beautifying, and making fruitful the barren places in human life....Librarians have an important part to play in the history of civilization and in the conservation of the race.[17]

Women in librarianship were merely making more visible the female position as the guardian of cultural ideals.

Just as the concept of "culture" had been generally accorded to the care of women, so the functions of providing education and of overseeing charity to the poor had been deemed suitable fields for female concern. The provision of education and moral uplift to the masses was a prominent mission of the early library; thus, women library workers, with their presumed inborn talents and temperaments, seemed uniquely suited to the new field of librarianship. The popular library brought the librarian "in hourly contact with her constituency of readers, advising, helping and elevating their lives and exerting a far-reaching influence for good not to be exceeded in any profession open to women...."[18] The great mass of men in all fields worked to secure prestige or a higher income but the librarian worked "with as distinct a consecration as a minister or missionary....The selfish considerations of reputation or personal comfort, or emolument are all secondary."[19] For Melvil Dewey, library work offered more opportunity to the altruistic than did the work of the clergyman or teacher. The library would reach those who never entered a church or who did not go to school.

Is it not true that the ideal librarian fills a pulpit where there is service every day during all the waking hours, with a large proportion of the community frequently in the congregation?...[The library is] a school in which the classes graduate only at death?[20]

Dewey encouraged educated women who might ordinarily have become teachers to consider a library career. Physically the library was less exacting than the school. The librarian avoided the "nervous strain and the wear and tear of the classroom" and escaped the bad air of crowded rooms. Dewey could think of no other profession "that is so free from annoying surroundings or that has so much in the character of the work and of the people which is grateful to a refined and educated woman."[21] The genteel nature of library work would compensate, he believed, for the regretable fact that women librarians normally received half the pay of men librarians and often received even less than urban teachers did.

As women became dominant in library work, library literature began to reflect the concept that the ideal library would offer the warmth and hospitality of the home to its patrons. To nineteenth-century man, of course, woman's sphere was, above all, the home, for which she was originally intended and which she was so exactly fitted to adorn and bless. Not surprisingly, it was anticipated that the feminine influence of the librarian would soften the library atmosphere. Like a visitor to a home, the reader must be welcomed; he must be given kind and individual attention; he must be treated with tact and gentle manners. Not the cold impersonality of the business world should pervade but rather the warmth of the well-ordered home, presided over by a gracious and helpful librarian. Counsel like the following is pervasive in the library literature of the 1870s and 1880s:

Something may be said of the desirableness of making the library wear a pleasant and inviting look. The reading-room offers perhaps the best opportunity for this. A reading-room lately seen has a bright carpet on the floor, low tables, and a few rocking-chairs scattered about; a cheerful, open fire on dull days, attractive pictures on the walls, and one can imagine a lady librarian filling the windows with plants. Such a room is a welcome in itself, and bids one come again.[22]

It was this ideal of the librarian as the accommodating and heartily receptive hostess which Miss Theresa West had in mind when she said that "the personal equation of the librarian may easily become the exponent of the power of the library."[23] On the surface the likening of the library to the home was but one of several devices which library leaders used to entice the reluctant patron and to make the library into a more "popular" institution. Operating more subtly, underground, were the effects of the prevalence of women in library work. Just as the school had been likened to the home, in order to make more acceptable the dominance of women teachers, so did the library readjust to reflect the widening of woman's sphere. The position of librarian required a certain "gracious hospitality" and here "women as a class far surpass men." Women would not feel humiliated by serving, by playing in the library the part they played in the home: "Here it is said her 'broad sympathies, her quick wits, her intuitions and her delight in self-sacrifice' give her an undoubted advantage."[24]

Women workers were also preferred, it was generally conceded, for the tedious job of cataloging. Again, it was the unique nature of woman which qualified her for this work because of her "greater conscientiousness, patience and accuracy in details."[25] Because women had greater ability than men to bear pain with fortitude, women had stored great reserves of patience and thus could perform the most monotonous tasks without boredom. All the routine, repetitive work of the library was quite generally agreed to fall within the scope of women's special talents.[26]

It is evident that the role of domesticity imposed upon women also worked to create the emphasis which was early given to library service for children.[27] By 1900 the children's library had "passed its first stage—all enthusiasm and effervescence—"[28] and had moved into its current position as a major department of the public library. From the beginning, the supervision of children's reading was given over to the woman librarian.

The work for children in our libraries, like many other of our best things, is woman's work. To them it owes its inception, its progress and present measure of success, and its future is in their hands.[29]

Here in the children's sections was woman's undisputed domain. And here the librarians waxed eloquent over the attributes and accomplishments of the reigning queen. Work with children is "the most important, and in its results, the most satisfactory of all library work," reported Minerva Sanders. "As our personal influence is exerted, in just such a proportion will our communities be uplifted."[30] Another librarian commented that woman, alone, has "that kind of sympathetic second-sight that shall enable her to read what is often obscure in the mind of the child."[31] Edwin M. Fairchild summed up the prevailing attitude toward woman's natural role in library work—not as a bluestocking, but as a traditionally defined female with intrinsic traits.

The chief source of enthusiasm for the children's library is the librarian....[She] needs to be...a woman grown, herself the realization of the educational ideal, which by the way is not the smart, but the intelligent, great souled woman....[32]

Originally conceived and theoretically maintained as an educational institution, the children's department was, in fact, even by the turn of the century, becoming mainly a provider of recreational reading for pre-adolescents.[33] Misgivings over the nature of library service to children were rarely expressed, however. Most often, sentimentality over-ruled any attempt at a realistic assessment of the work being accomplished in the children's department. The romantic air of enthusiastic tenderness so prominent in any discussion of children in the library is in sharp contrast to the more normal tendency of librarians to indulge in searching self-criticism in every other phase of library work. This incongruity becomes more understandable when it is remembered that the children's section of the library was created and shaped by women librarians. Here, as in no other area, library women were free to express, unchallenged, their self-image. Because their activities did not exceed the Victorian stereotype of the female, their endeavors remained substantially unquestioned and unexamined by male library leaders.

Despite the respect paid them, however, women soon learned that they were seldom paid the same as men who were doing the same work; and that even though women easily dominated the library field in numbers, male librarians headed the largest and most prestigious libraries. In the library literature of this period there is hardly a hint that the hundreds of women librarians across the country were seriously disturbed at the inequality which was freely admitted to be their lot.[34] Rather, one finds feminine pride repeatedly expressed over the prevalence of women in the library, at the increased participation of women in the national association and of America's flattering contrast with England where women were meeting resistance in library work. A situation which really amounted to the exploitation of women in the American library was publicly touted as a liberal concession to women in America and was contrasted with women's supposedly less favorable position in the Old World to indicate the superiority of American freedoms and the liberal attitudes of the male leaders of the American library movement.[35]

The twelve women present at the 1876 American Library Association meeting set the submissive tone which few women librarians were to challenge. They were "the best of listeners, and occasionally would modestly take advantage of gallant voices, like Mr. Smith's, to ask a question or offer a suggestion."[36] The next year Miss Caroline Hewins had the distinction of being the first woman to speak up at the national convention; she asked if the dog tax were used to support a library outside Massachusetts. Perhaps this small temerity earned her the reputation of fearless spokesman for it was Miss Hewins who presented in 1891 the first general discussion of the "woman question" in the *Library Journal*.

Library work was difficult for women, Miss Hewins said. For a salary varying from three to nine hundred dollars annually, a library assistant must write steadily six or seven hours a day, know half a dozen languages, be absolutely accurate in copying, "understand the relation of all arts and sciences to each other and must have...a minute acquaintance with geography, history, art and literature." A successful woman librarian would work eight to ten hours a day and "those who are paid the highest salaries give up all their evenings." Miss Hewins added that "librarians and library attendants sometimes break down from overwork." With unconscious humor, the intrepid Miss Hewins had a remedy for impending exhaustion—"plenty of sleep and nourishing food, with a walk of two or three miles every day."[37] Presumably this stroll was to be taken in the hours of early dawn or late evening.

The year after Miss Hewin's article appeared there was an abortive attempt to establish a Woman's Section in the national organization. The sole meeting of women in 1892 was a tame affair, with only the barest expression of stifled rage at women's low wages and subordinate position. An official statement secured from 25 of the nation's most prominent libraries revealed that "women rarely receive the same pay for the same work as men."[38] But no matter. "The palm of honor and of opportunity waits for her who shall join a genius for organization...to the power of a broad, rich, catholic and sympathetic womanhood." In "the long run" the woman librarian "will win appreciation."[39]

The Woman's Section of the American Library Association did not meet again, although the 1892 session appointed a committee to report at the next conference in Chicago. There was no formal explanation of the failure of this committee to report but it may be that a protest movement, sparked by Miss Telsie Kelso of the Los Angeles Public Library, would explain the demise of the Woman's Section. Miss Kelso stoutly disapproved of any deference paid to women as a group.[40]

In the...14th American Library Association Conference I note that there is a movement toward establishing a woman's section....For years woman has worked, talked, and accepted all sorts of compromises to prove her fitness to hold the position of librarian, and to demonstrate that sex should have no weight where ability is equal. In all these years the accomplishment is seen in the table of wages paid women librarians in comparison with those paid men....For women to now come forward with the argument that a woman librarian has a point of view and such limitation that they must be discussed apart from the open court of library affairs is a serious mistake....The use of the name of the association should not be permitted in such a direction....[41]

Such a truculent defense of women's equality, however, was not in accord with the expressed attitude of most women librarians. They accepted with little protest the traditional view of women as inherently limited in the working world. Certainly women library leaders had no utopian plans for woman's sexual and social emancipation. Of course they wanted to do things not customary for women in the past, such as managing a library with pay equal to men's, but this they considered as no more than a slight modification of the traditional ideal, and certainly not as a basic change in the male-structured view of women. As late as 1896 the influential Mary Ahern, editor of *Public Libraries,* warbled that "no woman can hope to reach any standing...in the library profession...who does not bring to it that love which suffereth long and is kind, is not puffed up, does not behave itself unseemly, vaunteth not itself, thinketh no evil...." Every woman owes it to herself to live up to the ideals expected of womanhood; "no woman striving ever so hard to play the part of a man has ever succeeded in doing more than to give just cause for a blush to the rest of her kind." Every woman in library work should seek not "to detract from the reputation so hardly earned of being faithful conscientious workers."[42]

In 1904 one hundred representative libraries were asked by the American Library Association to comment on the limitations of women library workers.[43] Economic reasons were most often cited to explain women's low pay scale; women who did not demand as much salary as men were in abundant supply. Women were generally acknowledged to be hampered by their "delicate physique" and "inability to endure continued mental strain." Mary Cutler (now Mrs. Fairchild), an important woman library leader, commented that she could not see how women's physical disability could ever be eliminated. Whether women would ever hold high positions in the library "may remain perhaps an open question." While having decided advantage wherever "the human element predominates," Mrs. Fairchild went on, women too frequently lacked the will to discharge executive power and most trustees "assume that a woman would not have business capacity." Reviewing all the facts she concluded that "on account of natural sex limitations, and also actual weakness in the work of many women as well as because of conservatism and prejudice, many gates are at present closed to women."[44]

Recognition of women's limited potential was probably justified when applied to women library workers in general. The average woman accepted the current ideal which taught that her success in life would be judged by her marriage and not by her work. With this concept central in her mind, she was being wholly practical if she spent much of her time in conforming to the popular ideal of "femininity" rather than in thinking about business achievement. Women librarians who had given up hope for marriage were also less apt to strain for advancement since they realized that society would discourage them from a display of "male" aggressiveness. Of course, some talented and energetic women librarians did realize their ambitions to a considerable degree, primarily because these ambitions were exceedingly modest and did not threaten the prevailing notion of woman's place.

Perhaps the most striking point to be made about women's adaptation to library work is the extent to which they supported the traditional feminine concern for altruism and high-mindedness. They invoked the Victorian definition of proper female endeavors at the same time as they were widening it. Librarianship, when defined as self-denying and spiritual, offered women the opportunity not to change their status but to affirm it, not to fulfill their self but their self-image. When women's advance became justified in terms of the good they could do, rather than of their human right to equality, it became conditional in nature.

Even if some librarians did not subscribe to the concept of woman's sphere, with all its connotations, they had to appear to do so in order not to offend the many who did. Not to surrender to the Victorian mystique was to run the terrible risk of being judged deviants in their society, of being judged abnormal because of a challenge to well-established norms. Perhaps, too, both men and women librarians wished to avoid any real discussion of the injustice which library women suffered because of the eagerness of all library leaders to establish librarianship as a profession. To publicize the prevalence of women in the library or to increase their influence could only harm the drive toward professionalization. A woman-dominated profession was obviously a contradiction in terms.

Librarians have been absorbed to a marked degree, from 1876 to the present, with the question of professionalization. Melvil Dewey and other early library leaders made repeated claims to professional status.[45] Not until the Williamson report of 1923 was there open and general admission among librarians that significant elements common to professional work were lacking in librarianship.[46] In the effort to win professional standing, librarians have concentrated upon improvements in their system of library schools. The education of librarians, it has been commonly lamented, includes too much detail and attention to method, only producing good craftsmen and technicians. True professional education, on the other hand, should present a systematic body of theory and a scientifically-based abstract knowledge upon which the profession rests.

Throughout the debate among librarians as to how best to receive recognition as professionals, the dominant influence of women on librarianship has been strangely shunted, buried under a multitude of words concerning recruitment, accreditation, curriculums and other factors thought to be inhibiting professionalization. There has been no systematic consideration given to the way in which feminization has shaped, in a most significant way, the development of library education and the entire range of activities associated with the field of library work. Carl White, who has written the best study of library education as it developed before 1923, gives thoughtful and scholarly attention to the social and educational setting in which library education began and relates it brilliantly to the traditions which remain today from that early inheritance.[47]

Yet White curiously refrains from considering the effect of the prevalence of women workers upon the shaping of those traditions. Only sociologist Peter Rossi, in a symposium of 1961, has tackled the existence of feminization head-on and applied it to library development. Rossi commented upon the puzzling absence of any real consideration being given to the influence of women upon library history.

I kept expecting...some comment on *the major reason* [italics mine] why librarians find it difficult to achieve a substantial spot in the array of professions. Any occupation in which there is a high proportion of women suffers a special disability.... Women depress the status of an occupation because theirs is a depressed status in the society as a whole, and those occupations in which women are found in large numbers are not seen as seriously competing with other professions for personnel and resources. It is for this reason that professions such as education, social work, and librarianship develop within themselves a division of labor and accompanying status along sex lines.[48]

Rossi added that the status of librarianship could be raised by a radical division of labor such as that accomplished in medicine where nursing was done by females and doctoring by males. This sharp differentiation between male and female librarians, however, runs counter to the central development of library history. Once formed, the solutions—both planned and accidental—found workable by nineteenth-century librarians closed the possibility of starting over with a clean slate. For this reason it is important that librarians assess the basic meaning of feminization and give precise attention to their early history, for the dominance of women is surely the prevailing factor in library education, the image of librarianship and the professionalization of the field. Women's role in the library was established in the last 25 years of the nineteenth century. An examination of the principal factors in this period of library history should include an emphasis upon the underrated effect of women students in library schools and its relationship to the constant search of librarians for professional standing.

The process of professionalization has received increasing attention by sociologists and historians in recent years.[49] Although it is generally agreed that professions have certain characteristics differentiating them from other occupations, there is no agreement on the precise nature of those characteristics. The conceptual model for this study will be devised so as to examine the professionalization of librarianship under three headings: service orientation, knowledge base and degree of autonomy. These components of professionalization will be examined, first as they apply to nineteenth-century librarianship in general and then as they relate to the feminization of the field.

The service orientation of librarianship exhibits most of the qualities expected in the ethical code of a profession. The professional, in contrast to the non-professional, is primarily concerned with his client's needs or with the needs of society, rather than with his own material interests. A profession also has direct relevance to basic social values on which there is widespread consensus. In law and medicine, for example, the services provided by the professional are justice and health. In librarianship the basic social value served is education. Early library leaders were firm in their commitment of the library to educational purposes; they definitely relegated the recreational function of the library to a secondary place. William Poole's comment typifies this view.

Our public libraries and our public schools are supported by the same constituencies, by the same methods of taxation, and for the same purpose; and that purpose is the education of the people....If public libraries shall, in my day, cease to be educational institutions; and serve only to amuse the people and help them to while away an idle hour, I shall favor their abolition.[50]

The librarian also showed a professional acceptance of the ideal of sacrificial service to the community. Librarianship was deemed to be second only to the ministry in its aims and standards.[51] Additionally, librarians had the sense of community which is common to professionals. They felt an affinity with other librarians in a way which the plumber, for example, does not feel for all other plumbers. Librarians, like the ministers with whom they liked to compare themselves, sensed an identity as a group, sharing a common destiny, values and norms.

The service and collectivity orientation of librarianship, then, conform to certain important characteristics of a profession. The characteristics used in the definition of the term "profession" are variables, forming a continuum along which an occupation's rise to professionalism can be measured. Although librarianship certainly showed a number of professional traits, significant elements of a truly professional code of service were missing. Specifically lacking in the librarian's professional service code are a sense of commitment, a drive to lead rather than to serve and a clear-cut conception of professional rights and responsibilities. The feminization of library work is a major cause of these deficiencies.

The concentration of women served to lower a professional work-commitment within librarianship. The culture defined woman's responsibility to the home as her primary one and this definition was all-pervasive before 1900. It was perfectly understandable, for example, that Theresa West would in 1896 leave her job as the leading woman librarian heading an important library when she married Henry Elmendorf. Indeed, it would have been shocking if she had chosen otherwise. Nineteenth-century complaints of high employee turnover and of low commitment to excellence among library workers are directly related to the place which women accepted in society. For the library assistant of the nineteenth century to become highly work-committed would require from her an atypical value orientation.[52] The majority of librarians were no doubt eager to marry and to leave library work. Of the eight women leaders selected for this study, five were unmarried and one was a widow. Of the two who married, late in life, both continued to work in the library field, although not as head librarians. All eight of these women were highly educated by the standards of their time. In each case, professional success, high status, extensive training and spinsterhood served to increase their vocational commitment. Despite the positive work commitments demonstrated by these women leaders, it remains generally true that within the field of librarianship, from 1876 to the present, the dominance of women significantly lessened a trend toward professional, life-long commitment to the field of library service.[53]

In established professions the practitioner assumes the responsibility for deciding what is best for his client. Whether or not the client agrees with him is theoretically not a factor in the professional's decision. Thus in the medical field, the doctor does not give the patient whatever treatment he requests, but instead prescribes the treatment which, for professional reasons, the doctor thinks is correct. In contrast to this professional attitude, librarians tended to "serve" the reader, rather than to help him. They felt a strong obligation to meet the needs of the public and were self-consciously sensitive to requests and complaints of the client.[54] This is partly a result of the tax-supported nature of the library and of its early efforts to attract a large public following. But this passive, inoffensive and non-assertive "service" provided by the librarian is also a natural acting-out of the docile behavioral role which females assumed in the culture.[55]

Theoretically the nineteenth-century library could have developed a less demand-oriented code of service. John Dana, Melvil Dewey, William Fletcher and William Poole often urged the librarian to lead his community, to educate the reader and the public. These men strongly felt that the librarian's role was to teach the standards that the public *should* want, not merely to provide access to what the public *did* want. Dewey argued that it was unwise "to give sharp tools or powerful weapons to the masses without some assurance of how they are to be used."[56] The public library, said William Fletcher,

...has too often been regarded somewhat as a public club; a purely democratic association of the people for mutual mental improvement or recreation....The public library is an educational and moral power to be wielded with a full sense of its mighty possibilities and the corresponding danger of their perversion.[57]

The assumption of a definitive intellectual leadership, however, did not come to characterize the public librarian. Modern librarians have laid the blame for their general passivity and inferior status upon various factors: the lack of a scientifically-based abstract body of knowledge; the public's lack of differentiation between the "professional" librarian and the library clerk and the inherently weak position of the librarian as implementor rather than creator of intellectual and cultural advance. Rarely given its due as a determinant is the overwhelming presence of women in librarianship. The negative traits for which librarians indict themselves—excessive cautiousness, avoidance of controversy, timidity, a weak orientation toward autonomy, little business sence, tractability, over compliance, service to the point of self-sacrifice and willingness to submit to subordination by trustees and public—are predominantly "feminine" traits.[58] Dana and others who sought to give librarianship a position of community leadership and intellectual authority were vastly outnumbered by the thousands of women who were shaping library development across the country. There is no evidence to indicate that these women opposed society's views of woman's nature and function. The traditional ideals of feminine behavior held by women librarians and the reading public had a profound impact upon the development of the public librarian's non-assertive, non-professional code of service.

The second component of library professionalization—the body of knowledge—does not contain as many professional attributes as does the service ideal of librarians. Professional knowledge is generally defined as that knowledge which (1) is organized in abstract principles, (2) is continually revised or created by the professionals, (3) places strong emphasis upon the ability to manipulate ideas and symbols rather than physical objects and (4) requires a long enough term of specialized training so that the society views the professional as possessing skills which are beyond the reach of the untrained layman. William Goode has commented,

Librarians themselves have found it extremely difficult to define their professional role and the knowledge on which it rests. To use a phrase like 'specialization in generalism' is insufficient....The repeated calls which librarians have made for a 'philosophy of librarianship' essentially expresses the need to define what *is* the intellectual problem of the occupation.[59]

In short, the librarian does not know who he is. Is he a library mechanic, having to do with such clerical, technical work as cataloguing, shelf arrangement and signing-in-and-out management? Or is he an expert guide, with considerable training in knowledge retrieval and organization?

One point, at least, seems clear. Despite the expressed desire of librarians to become admired professionals whose expertise would make available the world of knowledge, the system of library education which developed in the nineteenth century was a form of schooling, in origin and by design, which merely produced good craftsmen, trained to perform jobs which were chiefly mechanical in nature. This relatively low level of training, which made a small intellectual demand on the student, did not evolve entirely because of the feminine majority in library schools. The rate of expansion in both size and numbers of libraries was the first influence. The demand for a rapid production of library workers encouraged library schools to grind out graduates after only a brief course of instruction in the fundamental skills of library economy. The older system of in-service training could not produce enough self-made librarians to satisfy the manpower needs of the country. Carl White has outlined the second great influence on library education—the nineteenth-century development of technical education to fill the vacuum created by the breakdown of the classical curriculum and the medieval system of apprenticeship.[60] Library leaders were aware that a concentrated practical training has been demonstrated in other fields to produce the same results as learning by doing, but in less time and more systematically. Thus, detailed instruction in technical routines became the solid core of library training. Library education was in no sense designed to cultivate intellectual leadership, to produce trained high-level administrators or to develop an abstract knowledge base for library science.

The predominance of women in library schools, on library-school faculties and in library work functioned as an unmentioned but inflexible framework into which "professional" education would have to be fitted. An emphasis upon the influence of women is not meant to downgrade the other elements which shaped library education or to deemphasize the other inherent weaknesses in the librarian's claim to professional status, nor is it meant to impose chauvinistic attitudes upon male library leaders. Nineteenth-century librarians, however, were men and women of their time, governed by traditional views of woman's role in society. They were faced with an unorthodox problem—how to devise "professional" training for young women. Their answer was caught between the upper and the nether millstones. The upper millstone was their hope that librarians would become indispensable educational leaders, with professional scope and value. The nether millstone was the reality of the library school student—a woman who most likely lacked scholarly ambitions or preparation, had no life-long vocational commitment and whose attitudes toward feminine sex roles led her to accept, and expect, administrative controls, low autonomy and subordination to clerical, routine tasks.[61]

No study of why library training developed as it did would be complete without a consideration of how it was influenced by the thought of Melvil Dewey. Dewey so molded library education that the whole period before 1923 is called the "Dewey period." Librarians, too, have their folk heroes; Dewey's whirlwind passage through library history is the source of much of librarianship's most colorful annals. The narrators who have given accounts of intimate contact with Dewey share a common characteristic—they are breathless, either with admiration or with rage.

Tall, powerfully built, astonishingly handsome, Melvil Dewey was priggishly devoted to the truth as he saw it. He had no use for the trivial frolics of life; wasted time was to him a moral issue. He even developed in his wife the habit of writing precise compilations of how each minute of the day had been spent. He was, above all, pragmatic, looking only for what was workable, then and there, to produce the desired results. Dewey has been called a "man-child," for his idealism, enthusiasm and impatience with any obstacle. Childish too was his simplistic assessment of the world and his mission in it. There is something maddeningly pretentious about a man who can decide, at 17, "to inaugurate a higher eduction for the masses,"[62] and who can write, at age 76, in the same shallow prose,

As I look back over the long years, I can recall no one I ever intentionally wronged, or of whom I should, now, ask forgiveness....I have tried to do right, and so, if my race is run, I can go down into the last river serene, clear-eyed and unafraid.[63]

Yet burning zeal can carry one very far. Dewey's contributions to library development are unequaled by any one man and his personal courage and unflinching faith in his mission will long be admired. It was Dewey who initiated library school education and aggressively promoted his standards of technical training in library mechanics.

A predominant characteristic of Dewey's, and important for its relationship to library education development, is his inordinate fondness for women. His men friends were few; his women friends appear to have been numerous. All through his life he preferred the company of women to men. He worked with them, played with them and repeatedly got into trouble over them.

The trouble began as early as 1883 when Dewey hired six young women graduates of Wellesley to assist him in the organization of the Columbia University Library. At that time Columbia College was closed to women. Four years later Dewey again scandalized the campus by his insistence that women students be admitted to the first library school ever established. When the Trustees refused to allow Dewey classroom space because of the presence of women in the school, he furnished an unused storeroom on the campus and opened on schedule in defiance of the Trustees' orders. Shakily supported by President Frederick A. P. Barnard, the library school survived until 1889 when Dewey submitted his resignation to the Trustees shortly before his impending dismissal. During the time at Columbia, Dewey was sharply criticized for his open recruitment of women students and for his startling application form which included in it a request for height, weight, color of eyes, color of hair and a photograph.[64] Little tempered by time, Dewey's congenial intimacy with women set wagging in 1905 the "tongue of slander in sex matters," which even his eulogistic biographer concedes to have sent "stories sweeping like storms among the library leaders of the nation."[65] Dewey apparently had been guilty of some vaguely defined, but unorthodox, familiarities. The scandal prompted his wife to write scorching letters to the tale-bearers.

Women who have keen intuitions know by instinct that they can trust Mr. Dewey implicitly. He has so many proofs of this and is so sure of his own self-control, that unconsciously his manner has grown more and more unconventional and familiar....It is most unwise for any man to pass the bounds of convention, and he has been frequently warned of the danger. Knowing that I was absolutely free from jealousy and understood him perfectly, he has doubtless gone farther than with a wife who felt it necessary to watch her husband....A wife who has lived more than a quarter of a century with her husband is surely the best judge as to whether he is pure minded....[66]

Dewey's compatibility with women gave him insight which was unusual among men of his time. This remarkable statement was delivered before the Association of Collegiate Alumnae in 1886:

Would a father say to his son, 'My boy, your mother and I are lonely without you; you must stay at home, go out to afternoon teas with us, and keep us company in the big, empty house. I have enough for us all, so there is no need of your bothering your head about supporting yourself.' Would he expect his son to be happy under such circumstances? Why, then, his daughter?[67]

Dewey had sincere respect for the intellect of women and successfully contended that Mary Salome Cutler should be chairman of the library exhibit committee for the World's Columbian Exposition of 1893 because she was the most highly qualified candidate. He has often been praised because his defense of women's capabilities led him at times to suffer real personal sacrifice, as at Columbia. Any admiration for his support of women's rights, however, must be tempered by a recognition that Dewey had an unusually strong personal desire for feminine company and an equally strong indifference to the presence of men. Indeed, his role as champion of women is a complex and intriguing one, for beneath it lies a grating note of paternalism. He did not call on women to assert themselves but instead set himself up as their valiant spokesman.

Dewey, with a progressive (as well as erotic) affinity for women, was obviously deflected by his sexist attitudes from his progressive design for a strong, highly intellectual new profession. The library school curriculum which Dewey devised at Columbia and later continued at the New York State Library School ruled out any "attempt to give general culture or to make up deficiencies of earlier education." Dewey, in a characteristically pragmatic decision, would reconcile the library needs of the country with the status of women in society by concentrating upon schooling which would teach the technical skills necessary to perform work on the lower rungs of the library ladder. The American Library Association's committee on the proposed library school at Columbia remarked that those who came to the school would probably wish to become administrators. Dewey quickly corrected them; the committee was told that "the plans all contemplate special facilities and inducements for cataloguers and assistants who do not expect or desire the first place."[68]

By 1905 library education had crystallized around Dewey's core of practical instruction of routine detail to a predominantly female force. Yet even though librarians had established library education as a system of non-professional training for library mechanics, they continued to wonder at the "appalling misconception" in the public mind of their "professional" qualifications and to bemoan the fact that the public had made them "the poorest paid professionals in the world."[69] In that year the American Library Association found an answer of sorts to the dilemma—the great librarians, it was agreed, were born, not made.

Pooles and Winsors are not and never will be wholly produced by library schools.... Such eminent examples are born librarians. The born librarian will not need a school to teach him principles of classification...he will evolve systems of classifications and cataloging, and methods of administration without ever going near a school....But there will never be many of him, and there will be thousands of library employees.[70]

It was for the low-level employee "that our schools are at present intended."[71] In the discussion that followed a consensus was reached by important library spokesmen like E. C. Richardson, Frederick M. Crunden, S. S. Green, Melvil Dewey and Herbert Putnam.[72] It was agreed that librarians of genius had no need of formal training. Unconsciously the national association had focused upon a central library truth. While females from the library schools became clerks and assistants and heads of small libraries, the most honored and well-paid librarians were men. The "best" librarians of the time were indeed not made, but born—born male.

The prevalence of women librarians also served to strengthen a non-professional bureaucratic system of control and low autonomy base for the library worker. In librarianship, as in teaching and social work, the dominance of women made more likely the development of an authoritative administrative structure with a stress on rules and generally established principles to control the activities of employees. In these feminized fields the highest success was secured through promotion to the administrative levels of the organization. This is in contrast to the pattern within established professions. In university teaching, for example, the productive practitioner is usually more honored within his profession than is the high level administrator of the university. Within librarianship and other feminized occupations, compliance to sex roles caused women to assume low levels of autonomy. Because sexist attitudes still prevail in the society, this basic situation has undergone little change since the nineteenth century.[73]

The changing image of librarianship graphically illustrates the many alterations which feminization brought to library work in the late nineteenth century. To call the public image of librarianship a stereotype does not make it an entirely erroneous concept for the popular image of librarians is a by-product of deeper social realities. In the 1870s the popular concept of the librarian was that of a pre-occupied man in black—a collector and preserver who was never so happy as when all the volumes were safely on the shelf. He was thought to be ineffectual, grim and "bookish." Library literature of this period reflects the attempt of librarians to replace the image of the "old" librarian with a picture of the "new" librarian.

The mechanical librarian is no more a finality than the acquisitive and conservative librarian. He is succeeded by...a type who is not content with removing the obstacles to circulation that his predecessors have built up, but tries actually to foster it; who leans more to the missionary and pastoral side of librarianship; who relies more on personal intercourse; who goes in for reference lists and annotated and interesting bulletins; who does not so much try to make it easy for an interested public to help itself among the books as to create an interested public.[74]

The popular image had shifted by 1905 to portray the librarian as a woman. The public's mental image of the librarian was consistently deprecatory. Meek, mousy and colorless had been added to the original "old" male librarian's traits of eccentricity, frustration, grouchiness and introversion. The public librarian came to be stereotyped as an inhibited, single middle-aged woman.[75] Librarian Harold Lancour quipped that he had heard so much about this lady that he was "growing rather fond of the old girl."[76] Howard Mumford Jones, musing on the caricature of the librarian, suggested that the image was "partly the product of limited budgets, and in part the product of genteel tradition....This is not to say that all librarians are maiden ladies, but enough of them are to rank librarians with school teachers, Y. W. C. A. secretaries and social workers as persons less likely to go to night clubs than are receptionists or department-store buyers."[77] Unlike the librarians who had shaped public library standards, Jones understood well the chief reason why professionalization continued to elude library workers: the training of librarians should include more about the insides of books and "less technical lore about what to do with the book as an object in space."

The feminization of public librarianship did much to shape and stunt the development of an important American cultural institution. The socially designated sexual roles which women elected to act out had a major influence upon the development of the library's "homey" atmosphere and its staff of "helpful" non-assertive hostesses. Increasingly librarians are seeking to change the traditional role of the public librarian. The hope is to establish librarianship on a scientifically-oriented, abstract-knowledge base and to train the librarian as the indispensable expert in knowledge retrieval. The communication explosion has decidedly created a need for such a person; as the printed material grows to an unmanageable mass certainly someone, if not the public librarian, will move in to perform this vital function. However, until the librarian deals with the implications of feminization—with its varied inhibitory effects on intellectual excellence and leadership— progress toward professionalization will be limited. So long as sexist attitudes essentially govern the society, the basic situation which supported the service ideal and knowledge base of the nineteenth-century librarian seems unlikely to change.

FOOTNOTES

1. Cited in Robert W. Smuts, *Women and Work in America* (New York: Columbia University Press, 1959), 110.

2. [Charles Evans] (ed.), *The Athenaeum Centenary* (Boston: The Boston Athenaeum, 1907), 42. William Poole is generally credited with the hiring of the first woman librarian at the Boston Athenaeum in 1857. Poole's predecessor had barred women from the staff on the grounds that part of the library should be closed to impressionable female minds.

3. "The English Conference: Official Report of Proceedings," *Library Journal*, II (January-February, 1878), 280. The *Library Journal*, organ of the American Library Association, is hereafter cited as *LJ*.

4. Joseph Adna Hill, *Women in Gainful Occupations, 1870-1920*, Census Monograph, No. 9 (Washington: Government Printing Office, 1929), 42. Librarianship has been termed a "profession" by the U. S. Census and is used in that sense here. Hill cites 43 women library workers in 1870, 3,122 in 1900 and 8,621 in 1910. See Sharon B. Wells, "The Feminization of the American Library Profession, 1876-1923" (unpublished Master's thesis, Library School, University of Chicago, 1967) for statistics on the number of women employed in all American libraries, including public libraries, and the number of women enrolled in library schools. Miss Wells counts 191 men and 18 women managing collections of over ten thousand volumes in 1875.

5. Melvil Dewey, "The Ideal Librarian," *LJ*, XIX (January, 1899), 14.

6. This analysis of the feminization of public librarianship rests upon a larger study of the socio-economic backgrounds and social and literary ideals of 36 library leaders in the period from 1876 to 1900. The selected librarians represent the profession's most influential spokesmen and are primarily the heads of urban libraries in the east, although important western library leaders are also included in the group.

7. U. S. Bureau of Education, *Public Libraries in the United States of America: Their History, Condition and Management*, Special Report, Part I (Washington: Government Printing Office, 1876), iii. Hereafter cited as "1876 Report."

8. Carl M. White, *The Origins of the American Library School* (New York: The Scarecrow Press, Inc., 1961), 14.

9. R. R. Bowker, "Libraries and the Century in America: Retrospect and Prospect," *LJ*, XXVI (January, 1901), 5.

10. "1876 Report," 430. It is interesting to note that Perkins, who deserted his family to go West and to become the surly librarian at the San Francisco Public Library, left behind his young daughter, Charlotte Perkins Stetson Gilman, who later became a noted spokesman for women's rights.

11. "The English Conference...," *loc. cit.*

12. The eight women among the selected 36 library leaders are: Mary Bean, Eliza G. Browning, Mary Cutler, Theresa Elmendorf, Caroline Hewins, Hannah James, Mary Plummer and Minerva Sanders.

13. Because librarians, at least until about 1885, were so vocal in their contempt for the low intellectual-abilities of teachers in general, I deduce that most women librarians were better educated or of higher social standing than were most women teachers.

14. Mabel Newcomer, *A Century of Higher Education for American Women* (New York: Harper and Brothers, 1959) offers a good overview of the employment opportunities open to educated women in the late nineteenth century. The economic causes which she cites of the predominance of women teachers can also be applied to the feminization of librarianship. In 1870 three fifths of all teachers were women. Also see, Robert E. Riegel, *American Women: A Story of Social Change* (Cranbury, New Jersey: Associated University Presses, Inc., 1970), 132-200.

15. Aileen S. Kraditor (ed.), *Up from the Pedestal* (Chicago: Quadrangle Books, 1968) and William L. O'Neill, *Everyone Was Brave* (Chicago: Quadrangle Books, 1969).

16. Richard le Gallienne, quoted in M. S. R. James, "Women Librarians," *LJ*, XVIII (May, 1893), 148.

17. Linda A. Eastman, "Aims and Personal Attitude in Library Work," *LJ*, XXII (October, 1897), 80.

18. "Library Employment vs. the Library Profession," *Library Notes*, I (June, 1886), 50.

19. *Ibid.*, 51.

20. Melvil Dewey, "Libraries as Related to the Educational Work of the State," *Library Notes*, III (June, 1888), 346.

21. Melvil Dewey, "The Attractions and Opportunities of Librarianship," *Library Notes*, I (June, 1886), 52. See also, Melvil Dewey, Address before the Association of Collegiate Alumnae, March 13, 1886, *Librarianship as a Profession for College-Bred Women* (Boston: Library Bureau, 1886).

22. Lilian Denio, "How to Make the Most of a Small Library," *Library Notes*, III (March, 1889), 470.

23. Theresa H. West, "The Usefulness of Libraries in Small Towns," *LJ*, VIII (September-October, 1883), 229. .

24. Mary Salome Cutler Fairchild, "Women in American Libraries," *LJ*, XXIX (December, 1904), 162.

25. *Ibid.*

26. Celia A. Hayward, "Woman as Cataloger," *Public Libraries*, III (April, 1898), 121-23; "Female Library Assistants," *LJ*, XIV (April, 1889), 128-29; John Dana, "Women in Library Work," *Independent*, LXXI (August 3, 1911), 244.

27. Robert Weibe, *The Search for Order: 1877-1920* (New York: Hill and Wang, 1967), 122-23, discusses how sexual roles were expressed in this period by women social workers, lawyers and doctors in their service to children.

28. *LJ*, XXV (August, 1900), 123.

29. *Ibid.*

30. Minerva Sanders, "Report on Reading for the Young," *LJ*, XV (December, 1890), 59.

31. Annie Carroll Moore, "Special Training for Children's Librarians," *LJ*, XXIII (August, 1898), 80.

32. E. M. Fairchild, "Methods of Children's Library Work as Determined by the Needs of the Children," *LJ*, XXII (October, 1897), 26.

33. Sophy H. Powell, *The Children's Library: A Dynamic Factor in Education* (New York: H. W. Wilson Co., 1917), 1-7, 191-96, 255-71, is a careful study of the limited educational function of the children's section of the library. For a history of the development of library service to children see Harriet G. Long, *Public Library Service to Children: Foundation and Development* (Metuchen, New Jersey: The Scarecrow Press, Inc., 1969) and Effie L. Power, *Work With Children in Public Libraries* (Chicago: American Library Association, 1943).

34. For examples of women's mild tone see, Mary S. Cutler, "What a Woman Librarian Earns," *LJ*, XVII (August, 1892), 90; Mary E. Ahern, "The Business Side of a Woman's Career as a Librarian," *LJ*, XXIV (July, 1899), 62; Martha B. Earle, "Women Librarians," *Independent*, XLIX (February 18, 1897), 30.

35. "Woman's Meeting," *LJ*, XVII (August, 1892), 89-94.

36. "Proceedings," *LJ*, I (November 30, 1876), 90.

37. Caroline M. Hewins, "Library Work for Women," *LJ*, XVI (September, 1891), 273-74.

38. Cutler, 90.

39. *Ibid.*, 91.

40. "Library Association of Central California," *LJ*, XXII (June, 1897), 308. Miss Kelso later became a successful businesswoman in the field of publishing and remained an outspoken feminist.

41. Tessa L. Kelso, "Woman's Section of the A.L.A.," *LJ*, XVII (November, 1892), 444.

42. Ahern, 60-62.

43. Fairchild, 153-62.

44. *Ibid.*, 162.

45. Melvil Dewey, "The Profession," *LJ*, I (September, 1876), 5-6; Ernest C. Richardson, "Being a Librarian," *LJ*, XV (July, 1890), 201-02.

46. The first library school opened in 1887 at Columbia College. As a result of Williamson's critical survey of library schools in 1923, the curriculum standards in library education were revised and a national system of accreditation was established. Charles C. Williamson, *Training for Library Service: A Report Prepared for the Carnegie Corporation of New York* (Boston: The Merrymount Press, 1923); Sarah K. Vann, *The Williamson Reports: A Study* (Metuchen, New Jersey: The Scarecrow Press, Inc., 1971); C. Edward Carroll, *The Profes-*

sionalization of Education for Librarianship (Metuchen, New Jersey: The Scarecrow Press, Inc., 1970). For discussions of library professionalization see: Phillip H. Ennis (ed.), *Seven Questions About the Profession of Librarianship* (Chicago: University of Chicago Press, 1961); Pierce Butler, "Librarianship as a Profession," *Library Quarterly*, XXI (October, 1951), 235-47; Robert D. Leigh, *The Public Library in the United States* (New York: Columbia University Press, 1969); Robert B. Downs (ed.), *The Status of American College and University Librarians* (ACRL Monograph, No. 22 [Chicago: American Library Association, 1958]); William J. Goode, "The Theoretical Limits of Professionalization," *The Semi-Professions and their Organization: Teachers, Nurses, Social Workers,* ed. Amitai Etzioni (New York: The Free Press, 1969), 266-313.

47. White, *passim.*

48. Ennis, 83.

49. A. M. Carr-Saunders, *The Professions* (Oxford: Clarendon, 1933); T. A. Caplow, *The Sociology of Work* (Minneapolis: University of Minnesota, 1954); Ernest Greenwood, "The Attributes of a Profession," *Social Work,* II (June, 1957), 139-40; Howard M. Vollmer and Donald Mills (eds.), *Professionalization* (Englewood Cliffs, New Jersey: Prentice-Hall, 1966); Ronald M. Pavalko, *Sociology of Occupations and Professions* (Itasca, Illinois: F. E. Peacock Publishers, Inc., 1971); Raymond M. Merritt, *Engineering in American Society* (Lexington, Kentucky: University Press of Kentucky, 1969); Daniel H. Calhoun, *Professional Lives in America* (Cambridge, Massachusetts: Harvard University Press, 1965); Kenneth S. Lynn (ed.), *The Professions in America* (Boston: Houghton Mifflin Company, 1965).

50. William F. Poole, "Buffalo Conference Proceedings," *LJ,* VIII (September-October, 1883), 281. See also, William H. Brett, "The Present Problem," *LJ,* XVIX (December, 1894), 5-9; S. S. Green, *Libraries and Schools* (New York: F. Leypoldt, 1883), 56-74; Max Cohen, "The Librarian as an Educator and Not a Cheap-John," *LJ,* XIII (November, 1888), 366-67; Melvil Dewey, "Public Libraries as Public Educators," *LJ,* XI (June, 1886), 165.

51. Charles Knowles Bolton, "The Librarian's Duty as a Citizen," *LJ,* XXI (May, 1896), 219-22; S. S. Green, "Personal Relations Between Librarians and Readers," *LJ,* I (November 30, 1876), 74-81.

52. Smuts, 36.

53. For a thorough documentation of characteristic behavior of women workers see Richard L. and Ida Harper Simpson, "Women and Bureaucracy in the Semi-Professions," in Etzioni, 196-265. The nineteenth-century woman would demonstrate even more strongly the traits which the Simpsons outline.

54. Ennis, 7, 9; Marjorie Fiske, *Book Selection and Censorship* (Los Angeles: University of California Press, 1959), 100-12.

55. Sociologist Talcott Parsons has also noted the "tendency for women to gravitate into 'supportive' types of occupational role, where functions of 'helpfulness' to the incumbent of more assertive and ultimately, in the social function sense, more responsible roles, is a major keynote." Parsons points to sex composition as "both a symptom and a partial determinant" of the pattern of "the 'quietness,' the rather passive character of the attributes of librar-

ians as a group, wishing as it were to be unobtrusively 'helpful' but avoiding assertiveness." Talcott Parsons, "Implications of the Study," *The Climate of Book Selection*, ed. J. Periam Danton (Berkeley: University of California, 1959), 94-95.

56. U. S. Bureau of Education, *Report of Commissioner of Education, 1887-1888* (Washington: Government Printing Office), 1033.

57. William Fletcher, *Public Libraries in America* (Boston: Roberts Brothers, 1894), 32-33.

58. My interviews with a leading university librarian and with several public librarians indicate a recent twentieth-century trend toward male homosexuals in library work. Their presence may be connected to the role-playing assumed by librarians in general. That is, to the extent that the homosexual male takes on the characteristics of femininity, he proves quite adaptable to playing a female service role. It may be, too, that male homosexuals, having been driven from most of the high status professions by prejudice, find women less hostile to their presence and thus feel more comfortable in a feminized working environment. On this point, note the formation of the Task Force on Gay Liberation during the 1970 American Library Association annual meeting.

59. William E. Goode "The Librarian: From Occupation to Profession?" Ennis, 13.

60. White, 32-33.

61. Normal schools were faced with similar problems during this period. A predominantly bureaucratic control is evident in school-teaching and librarianship. See Simpson and Simpson, 196-221.

62. Fremont Rider, *Melvil Dewey* (Chicago: American Library Association, 1944), 8.

63. Grosvenor Dawe, *Melvil Dewey: Seer, Inspirer, Doer* (Albany, New York: J. B. Lyon Company, 1923), 76.

64. Ray Trautman, *A History of the School of Library Service: Columbia University* (New York: Columbia University Press, 1954), 3-23.

65. Dawe, 70.

66. Letter from Annie Godfrey Dewey, June 15, 1906, cited in Dawe, 70.

67. Dawe, 91-92.

68. "Report of the Committee on the Proposed School of Library Economy," *LJ*, X (September-October, 1885), 293.

69. Lutie E. Stearns, "The Question of Library Training," *LJ*, XXX (September, 1905), 68, 70.

70. "Fifth Session," *LJ*, XXX (September, 1905), 167-68.

71. *Ibid.*

72. *Ibid.*, 164-76.

73. Simpson and Simpson, 260-65. For current feminist protest see, Anita R. Schiller, "The Widening Sex Gap," *LJ*, LXXXXIV (March 15, 1969), 1098-100; Janet Freedman, "The Liberated Librarian," *LJ*, LXXXXV (May 1, 1970), 1709-711; Anita R. Schiller, "The Disadvantaged Majority: Women Employed in Libraries," *American Libraries*, IV (April, 1970), 345-49.

74. "Editorial," *LJ*, XVII (September, 1892), 371. For discussions of the old and new librarian see, "The New Librarians," *LJ*, XV (November, 1890), 338; R. R. Bowker, "The Work of the Nineteenth Century Librarian for the Librarian of the Twentieth," *LJ*, VIII (September-October, 1883), 247-50.

75. William H. Form, "Popular Images of Librarians," *LJ*, LXXI (June 15, 1946), 851-55; Robert Leigh and Kathryn W. Sewny, "The Popular Image of the Library and of Librarians," *LJ*, LXXXV (June 1, 1960), 2089-091.

76. Ennis, 74.

77. Howard Mumford Jones, "Reflections in a Library," *Saturday Review*, XXXXIII (April 9, 1960), 34.

17

NANCY GOLDMAN

The Changing Role of Women in the Armed Forces[1]

The position of women in the armed forces—the epitome of a male-dominated establishment—offers a striking and limiting case of the changing role of women in occupational and bureaucratic structures. In his analysis of the American military, Charles Moskos has spoken of "the military as a vestige of male sanctity" (1970, p. 64). Traditionally, in the United States military, women are excluded from direct combat roles and from significant assignments in administration. In fact, since the end of World War II, the armed forces have not even filled the 2% authorized quota for women. In the U.S. forces they are entirely volunteers, although the basic military structure for manpower has rested on a draft system.

However, during the second half of the 1960s the number of uniformed women in the armed forces increased, and there is evidence of a trend toward a very gradual expansion of their roles. While the concentration of these women will remain limited, the armed forces anticipate, in the decade of the 1970s, an increase in their number and percentage from less than 2% to approximately 4%.

The encountered and projected increase of women in the armed forces reflects, first, external social change in the United States and the conscious effort of the military to recognize and incorporate such· change. Second, because of the relatively low status of the profession, the traditional anti-military attitudes in the society, and the negative impact generated by the war in Vietnam, the movement to an all-volunteer force requires the military to intensify its search for sufficient personnel. The armed forces have traditionally recruited some from the margins of American society; they have recruited heavily from the rural areas, particularly the South; and more recently, personnel have been sought in the black community (Janowitz 1971, pp. 79–101; Moskos 1970, pp. 108–18). Women are also a potential source of labor, especially since they are already recruited on a volunteer basis. Third, the changing character of the military establishment, together with its great emphasis on administration, logistics, and the like, plus its increasing emphasis on deterrence (Kissinger 1965), alter the organizational milieu of the armed forces and potentially broaden sex roles in a direction favorable to women.

This paper will examine the profound organizational resistances and role strains associated with increasing the concentration of women in

[1] I wish to acknowledge the helpful comments of Beth Coye, Otis Bryan, Morris Janowitz, Charles Moskos, William Zierdt, and the support of the Inter-University Seminar on Armed Forces and Society.

the armed forces. However, it is necessary to examine more specifically the symbolism and ideology found in an institution which manages violence, since changes in the position of women tend to be limited in such organizations. (Similar problems exist in the role definition of women in the police force.) Two basic issues are offered as points of departure. First, the movement toward. "occupational and professional equality" for women in the military establishment occurs without their involvement in jobs similar to those held by men, that is, without systematic incorporation into "operations" and other key military assignments. What form and degree of strain will result from such a process of organizational adaptation? One hypothesis is based on the notion of relative deprivation. If there is no possibility of effective equality for women in the military, increasing the number and roles of women in the armed forces will produce greater women's militancy. An alternative hypothesis, which seems to be supported by the limited available evidence, is that selective recruitment will limit the strain.[2] This hypothesis assumes that those women who voluntarily select the military profession would be likely to accept its existing authority structure and its internal values.

The recruitment pattern of women into the military is not expected to produce cadres who are committed to militant demands for "complete equality," but groups who are, instead, mainly concerned with extending the roles of women into a wide range of assignments, including those associated with the deterrence functions. Therefore, the analysis of the roles of women in the military offers a locus for the analysis of the trend toward equality without similarity of task—or "functional equality" versus "functional similarity."

Second, with the introduction of an all-volunteer force, new mechanisms of integration of the armed forces into civilian society will be required to maintain civilian supremacy and to prevent the social isolation of the military profession. At the end of the draft in 1973, even with a marked reduction in the overall size of the armed forces to 2 million or less, the military establishment will be a large-scale organization capable of developing and maintaining its own internal subculture. Thus, in the years ahead it will be necessary to ascertain the impact—if any—of more women on the organizational climate of the military as it becomes less of an all-male organization.

.A wide range of official documentary sources, reports, and statistical data on manpower were reviewed in the preparation of this paper. In conjunction with the trend toward an all-volunteer force, the armed forces have conducted personnel studies such as *The American Soldier in the 70's*

---

[2] Although black women in the military have already demonstrated the strongest degree of militant demands and behavior, their response should be seen more as a reflection of the black community in the military than of the women's group.

(1971) in which data have been assembled on women. A study project by Lt. Comdr. Beth F. Coye (1971) based on survey interviews with 34 women naval line officers produced relevant data on their attitudes and conceptions of professionalism. In addition, I interviewed 30 military officials and personnel officers, both active duty and retired, both on and off military bases, in each case the subject being aware that the material was being collected for university-based research. In addition, strikingly candid contents and reports contained in newspapers published commercially for military personnel provided useful material.

TRENDS IN THE UTILIZATION OF WOMEN

Until World War II, women in the United States who served as military personnel did so as nurses. The only exception was the "Yeomanettes" who, during World War I, were organized as a woman's naval auxiliary to free men for sea duty. However, this service was dissolved in 1919 after the Armistice. Civilian women first served as military nurses in 1854, when Florence Nightingale was asked to organize a group of nurses to care for the wounded in the Crimea (Woodham Smith 1950). In the United States, women served similarly during the Civil War. However, the history of women as uniformed personnel in the armed forces began in 1902 during the Spanish-American War, when the Army Nurse Corps was formed. In 1908 the Navy Nurse Corps was established. It was not, however, until after World War I that nurses were granted military rank. During World War II one-fourth of all American professional nurses volunteered for service. Following the format of the nursing profession in civilian life, the military nurse became rapidly institutionalized and distinct from the women's military corps (Jamieson, Sewall, and Suhrie 1966).

At this time, each of the armed services also established a women's auxiliary unit which has gradually become more and more a permanent and integral part of the service. The navy spelled out its initial, temporary intentions when in 1942 it labeled its women personnel WAVES, namely, Women Accepted for Volunteer Emergency Service. The army established the Women's Army Auxiliary Corps (WAAC) in 1942, and a year later redesignated it the Women's Army Corps (WAC), indicating the trend from an auxiliary service to a regularized component. With the establishment of an independent air force in 1947, Women in the Air Force (WAF) automatically came into being (from 1943 to 1947 they were called Air WACS). Both the marines and the Coast Guard (SPARS) created women's auxiliaries in 1942, although the SPAR corps was dissolved after World War II, except for a small group of reserves. These wartime measures were designed to mobilize effective manpower and to be a symbolic device representing the inclusion of women in the national war effort.

Although the introduction of women into the military during World War II was seen as a short-term wartime measure, even the most male-oriented officers were satisfied with the ability of the forces to use female personnel. However, after the Korean conflict in the late 1950s the position of women in the armed forces remained doubtful, with the prospect that they might become a vestigial element. In the late 1960s, changes in the civilian social structure and the advent of the all-volunteer force made reevaluations by the military necessary and resulted in a limited trend toward the revitalization of the women's element.

Historically, the increase in number and the expansion of women's assignments in the United States armed forces created resistances comparable with those found in other professions such as law, medicine, and university teaching. The oft-quoted assertion by General Lewis Hershey perhaps overstated the issue but reflected, in more picturesque language, the organizational realities. "There is no question but that women could do a lot of the things in the military services. So could men in wheelchairs. But you couldn't except the services to want a whole company of people in wheelchairs." In his study of *The Professional Soldier,* completed in 1960, Morris Janowitz did not find it necessary to deal in any depth with women personnel because of their derivative role and lack of impact on the organizational climate of the profession (Janowitz 1971, pp. 417–30). While Janowitz foresaw the end of the mass army and the movement toward a more contractual system, he did not anticipate an increased emphasis on the recruitment of women into the military. Charles Moskos, a decade later, still had to point out that the position of women in military organizations is almost completely unresearched (Moskos 1971*b,* p. 286).

The trend in the use of women in the armed forces has been examined in this study for the period from 1945 to spring 1972. In 1945, the military reached a high point of over 12 million active officers and enlisted persons, with 265,006 women. As part of a process of "total" mobilization, the percentage of 2.18 women in the armed forces was the high point in their utilization. By 1950, the total number of women in service had declined to 22,069 or 1.51% of the forces. During the Korean War, the number of uniformed women rose to 35,191 in 1955 (1.27%). From 1960 to 1966, the number of women in the forces remained fairly constant, approximately 30,000, and the percentage decreased slightly (from 1.27 to 1.05) because of a limited increase in total personnel.

In 1967, under the impact of Vietnam hostilities, recruitment was intensified and the number of women increased slowly from 35,173 to 42,814 in 1971, with the percentage moving steadily up toward the 2% level. On November 8, 1967, Public Law 90-130, in anticipation of a

TABLE 1

MILITARY PERSONNEL ON ACTIVE DUTY, 1960–SPRING 1972, BY SERVICE AND BY SEX

	Army	%	Navy	%	Air Force	%	Marines	%	Total	%
1960:										
Men	860,536	98.6	609,913	98.7	805,426	98.9	169,010	99.1	2,444,885	98.7
Women	12,542	1.4	8,071	1.3	9,326	1.1	1,611	0.9	31,540	1.3
Total	873,078	100.0	617,984	100.0	814,752	100.0	170,621	100.0	2,476,425	100.0
1965:										
Men	955,987	98.7	663,156	98.8	814,792	98.9	188,606	99.2	2,622,546	98.8
Women	12,326	1.3	7,862	1.2	3,841	1.1	1,581	0.8	30,610	1.2
Total	968,313	100.0	671,018	100.0	823,633	100.0	190,187	100.0	2,653,156	100.0
1970:										
Men	1,305,135	98.7	684,199	98.7	778,346	98.3	257,893	99.2	3,025,573	98.7
Women	16,724	1.3	8,683	1.3	13,654	1.7	2,418	0.8	41,479	1.3
Total	1,321,859	100.0	692,882	100.0	792,000	100.0	260,311	100.0	3,067,052	100.0
1971:										
Men	1,200,513	98.6	635,442	98.6	738,469	98.1	222,927	98.9	2,797,351	98.5
Women	16,865	1.4	8,801	1.4	14,850	1.9	2,298	1.1	42,814	1.5
Total	1,217,378	100.0	644,243	100.0	753,319	100.0	225,225	100.0	2,840,165	100.0
1972 (Spring):										
Men	868,965	98.1	586,200	98.5	731,774	97.8	193,807	98.8	2,380,746	98.2
Women	16,814	1.9	8,993	1.5	16,225	2.2	2,273	1.2	44,305	1.8
Total	885,779	100.0	595,193	100.0	747,999	100.0	196,080	100.0	2,425,051	100.0

SOURCE.—*Statistical Abstract of the United States.* Table published by Department of Defense, Comptroller: "Women Military Personnel on Active Duty, May 31, 1945 to Date."

demand for more female personnel, removed the 2% quota, but the expansion in the numbers of women has been very gradual.

Table 1 shows that for the past decade the army has employed the largest number of women. However, on a percentage basis the air force had the highest concentration. An indication of continued trends can be seen in a comparison of 1970, 1971, and 1972. Although the number of men was markedly reduced through demobilization, the total number of women was not. In fact, in 1970 there were 41,479 women on active duty and the number rose to 44,305 in 1972; thus, as of 1972, the overall percentage of women on active duty was 1.8, with corresponding increases over 1970 in all four services.

Despite the very low ratio of women to men in the military it is interesting to note that the ratio of officers to enlisted personnel is about twice as high for women as for men. Among male active-duty personnel in 1970, 13% were officers compared with 36% of the women. Of course, these women officers had a strong concentration of specialists, particularly nurses. Nevertheless, within the military, with its manifest rank system, the high proportion of female officers has the effect of giving greater visibility to women than they would have were the concentration of officers the same as among male personnel.

A comparison of the percentage of women officers in the armed forces, regardless of specialists, with women in other professions reveals that the practices of the military do not vary widely from those of the major professional groups. (Officers are the appropriate group for comparison with other professions.) As of 1970, 3.8% of the army's officers were women, while the air force had 3.6% and the navy, 4.0%. The most recent available data for civilian professions are for 1960, and they do not reflect changes over the last five years. In 1960, the percentage for engineers was 0.8, dentists, 2.1, lawyers, 3.5, while for doctors it was 6.8, and scientists, 9.9. These percentages are rising, as they are in the military, although women officers are not found in these particular specialties.

Because Great Britain has had an all-volunteer force for the past 10 years it is relevant to compare the percentage of women on active duty in the United States with that in Great Britain. Since service became fully volunteer, Great Britain has expanded the concentration of women to meet its personnel requirements. In 1970, it had 14,000 women out of 372,500 in the services (3.8%) (see table 2), or twice as many as in the United States. This difference cannot·be accounted for by any difference in age structure.

With the advent of the all-volunteer force scheduled for the summer of 1973, the concentration of women is likely to increase at a modest but steady rate. As already mentioned, the armed forces are more capable of

TABLE 2

PERSONNEL ON ACTIVE DUTY, UNITED STATES AND GREAT BRITAIN, 1970

	United States	%	Great Britain	%
Women	41,000	1.3	14,000	3.8
Men	3,025,000	98.7	358,500	96.2
Total	3,066,000	100.0	372,500	100.0

SOURCE.—*Britain 1971: An Official Handbook.*

meeting volunteer quotas of women than of men since women have always been recruited on a volunteer basis. The air force alone has, for example, a goal of 15,000 women by 1975. To meet these labor needs, the forces have instituted study groups on required organizational and professional changes and have instituted new recruiting programs. The air force has moved toward including women in its ROTC units. Both symbolically and in terms of professional roles, the incorporation of women into the military establishment will result in pressure for women graduates from the military academies. In the fall of 1971, Senator Jacob Javits and Congressman Jack McDonald each sought to have a young woman appointed to the United States Naval Academy from their states.

In September of 1971, the army undertook a staff study, in connection with the advent of the volunteer armed forces, that called for the permanent elimination of the ceiling of 2% on female personnel, a ceiling which was labeled "unrealistic and debilitating" (U.S. Army Combat Developments Command 1971, p. 93). The study showed that between 20% and 35% of army positions could be filled by women, and it also emphasized the necessity of training women in army ROTC units. An advisory commission of 50 civilian women first established in 1951 to investigate the position of women in the military (called the Defense Advisory Commission on Women in the Armed Forces, and during most of its existence relatively inactive) has in recent years been more involved in the debate on the role of women in the armed services.

Interview data with both male and female officers, especially with officers responsible for personnel planning, as well as the findings of the naval survey (Coye 1971, p. 33) indicated that the further increase of women and the expansion of their roles are resisted by some top women officers. One reason is that they see a change in opportunities for women in the military as a threat to their well-being and to their elite positions. Further, their age places them at some distance from the younger women.

Some male officers, because of traditional beliefs, oppose the increase of women and their greater roles; however, since the numerical goals are limited, there is actually very little ideological opposition. In fact, many traditional male officers are more likely to change their opinion about this issue than about many other issues associated with a volunteer force, such as modifications in military justice. There are, indeed, considerable diffuse and positive sentiments toward women. Many traditionalists feel that women entering the service will fit in, since they will make the military more like civilian organizations and will be an asset in the recruitment of young men, and many traditionalists are not adverse to having more "attractive young women" around military headquarters.

Concern about high personnel turnover because of marriage and pregnancy was expressed by military personnel officers. However, a period of three to five years of active duty service is more and more seen as meeting the cost of training and assignment. Also, special arrangements are being slowly developed for married women personnel. Since court cases on issues of pregnant military personnel are underway it is likely that maternity leaves will be instituted. Military women who have children may request to remain in the service once arrangements are made for the child's care (AR 635-200 and AR 635-120 [enlisted personnel separations and officer personnel separations]). Unwanted pregnancies are not a major problem and are infrequent; the effective dissemination of birth control information is probably more extensive in the military than in comparable civilian groups because of the high quality of medical services available. In fact, in 1970 the military medical services took steps to offer expanded abortion service to their personnel and dependents. However, President Richard Nixon issued a presidential order on April 1, 1971 requiring the services to follow local state law, but field observations indicate that military doctors tend to give a "liberal" interpretation to existing law and administration regulations.

Organizational living quarters constitute the greatest area of opposition to an increase in the number of women, since the idea of mixed barracks is strongly resisted by top-ranking female officers. In the air force, bachelor barracks were made coeducational but enlisted personnel still have sex-segregated living quarters.

ROLES OF WOMEN IN THE MILITARY

At the root of the changing roles of women in the armed forces are the special problems of "arming" women. The historical record during the last century in industrial societies indicates only a few cases of institutionalized arming of women, even in nations under the gravest national security threat. Russia, under Kerensky in 1917 during the "Great War," did form a women's battalion which went to the front to fight. This was a desperate attempt to stimulate patriotism and increase manpower. The results, however, were hardly successful. In addition to many losses, the women as a battalion were resented and ridiculed by the men (Beard 1946).

During World War I, England, with a shortage of personnel, organized women's auxiliary groups to a much greater extent than other nations— the Women's Army Auxiliary Corps (WAAC), Women's Royal Air Force (WRAF), and Women's Royal Naval Service (WRNS). Previously, as in the United States, women had served only as nurses (Haldane 1923). Although these auxiliary groups constituted a uniformed women's corps they were not given full military status: that is, they did not "enlist," they "enrolled," and were regarded as civilians.

During World War II, the democratic nations mobilized women both in uniform and in civilian war production far more than did the Axis powers, particularly Nazi Germany. About the possibility of employing German women to reduce the labor shortage during World War II, Speer reports, "Sauckel laid great weight on the danger that factory work might inflict moral harm upon German womanhood; not only might their 'psychic and emotional life' be affected but also their ability to bear" (1970, pp. 220–21). In Great Britain, in addition to inducting women into uniformed auxiliary services, the army employed females in the Auxiliary Territorial Army in air control and as radar operators, and they manned antiaircraft weapons—roles which involved defensive combat (Essame 1970). The Soviet Union trained and gave extensive publicity to a very limited number of women pilots in order to dramatize the need for wartime mobilization and commitment. The Soviet approach can be called "tokenism" rather than an institutionalized use of women in the armed forces. Women have also been used as parachutists behind enemy lines. In Communist China, throughout the whole guerrilla war of national liberation, women were not armed but were used as auxiliaries. Occasionally women have been armed as a result of accident or happenstance and they have been found in small detached guerrilla forces, but there is little evidence that they have been deployed as a significant part of mainline guerrilla forces. Che Guevara in his diary gives his view on the masculinity of the guerrilla status: "This type of fight gives us the opportunity of becoming revolutionaries, the highest level of human species, and it also permits us to graduate as men" (1968, p. xiii).

The case of Israel is particularly noteworthy. In Israel, the large and highly respected women's corps is given training in arms, namely with rifles and submachine guns. However, they are not regularly deployed with arms or mobilized as an armed formation during war (Rolbant 1970, p. 136). They are attached to combat units in training and in the reserves as educational officers (Bar-On 1964).

In the United States during World War II, women in uniform generally filled nursing, administrative, and clerical jobs, although a small minority held more varied posts, especially in naval intelligence and communications. After that conflict their assignments narrowed, and in all of the services women were employed mainly as clerks, secretaries, and in routine types of communications. Continuously since 1945, the U.S. military operated on the notion that women would be excluded from "armed combat," and this concept is applied to military planning for the future. Even the most innovative proposals and staff plans maintain this formal assertion (U.S. Army Combat Development Command 1971, p. 95). However, the changing nature of the military organization weakens the sharp distinction between male and female type of assignments. The military establishment has seen a long-term growth in the proportion and importance of both men and women assigned to logistics and communications and thereby a decline in the segregation of men and women. In fact, the range of functions which women perform has widened. The linkages of women with military missions can be seen in their recent or renewed entrance into intelligence, essential communications functions, and more complex aspects of logistics and maintenance administration.[3] It is also striking to note that selected occupations which are typed as "female" in civilian life have a higher concentration of males in the military, for instance, nurses and social workers, blurring sexual differentiation.

However, the root of the issue of sex-typed positions rests in the changing definitions of military roles. With the development of nuclear weapons and the emergence of deterrence as the central goal of the military, the significance of traditional combat roles is also altered. Women penetrate into the support and administration of deterrence tasks, decreasing the differences in the importance of tasks assigned to men and women (Moskos 1971*a*, p. 24). In other words, because of the importance of deterrence, many of the tasks of logistics, intelligence, communications and control, and command mean that while the distinction between combat and roles concerned with the mechanics and administration of deterrence is still operative, it becomes attenuated. The effect of deterrence is to expand the number and variety of sedentary noncombat tasks in which the "fighter spirit" is irrelevant. Potentially, women could perform many deterrence tasks such as surveillance by radar equipment, but they are still restricted. In this connection it is important to note that as of Spring 1972, the air force, which has the smallest number of traditional combat roles, had the highest concentration of women personnel. New definitions of sex-

[3] The wider range of assignments for females in the armed forces has very slowly increased the situations in which they supervise males. For a long period, female nurses had responsibilities which required them to be in charge of male personnel. Women officers are supervisors of enlisted personnel, both male and female, in selected administrative and logistics settings, but these are rare cases because of the limitations in the number of women military officers and the procedures for assigning personnel.

based roles and assignments nevertheless remain to be established and formalized. In Great Britain, naval experiments with women aboard ship were terminated, partly because the added manpower advantages seemed trivial and outweighed the personal inconveniences. In 1970 the U.S. navy, aside from their use of nurses, assigned one woman to an operational ship, and it was not a successful experiment.

CHANGING ATTITUDES OF WOMEN

The changing assignments of women in the military must be examined in the light of the demands by women both in civilian society and in the military. The movement for women's equality has a long tradition in the United States, but the current phase encompasses not only traditional goals of equality in economic, occupational, and public life, but also, in the name of women's liberation, includes a psychological and cultural dimension as well as a critique of the moral values of contemporary society. In particular, the militant dimension of women's liberation is linked to the opposition to the war in Vietnam and indifference, at least, about the position of women in the armed forces. However, it is my impression from conversations with militant advocates of the women's liberation movement that when they consider the issues of women in the armed forces, they hold the ideological belief that women should be armed just like men.

In contrast, women recruited into the military, or who are planning to enter, reveal that they are not attached to the militant women's liberation movement. Special effort was made to observe the attitudes of recently recruited women in order to infer any impact of the women's rights movement. The new and younger females entering the military are more self-assertive than the older and earlier recruited personnel. However, the pattern of self-recruitment is such that "militancy" is very low or effectively absent. Selecting the military as a place of employment goes hand in hand with a rejection or indifference to the militant women's liberation movement.

The new recruits—both officers and enlisted personnel—think of themselves as entering a service which has a strong emphasis on equal opportunities, made more emphatic by the fixed and uniform pay rates. Likewise, realistically or unrealistically, they assume that women in the military have better job security than in civilian employment. Sources of dissatisfaction are mainly with living quarters, irritation over administrative detail, and the quality of specific supervisors. "Relative deprivation," always difficult to assess, seems to be limited, not only by selective recruitment but also because resignation rather than opposition is the typical response to frustration and dissatisfaction. Thus, for example, of the 34 naval women officers interviewed, only three expressed dissatisfaction when questioned (Coye 1971, p. 32).

As a result, most of these women accept the existing rate of organization change. But there is an equivalent of a "subdued" women's movement whose manifestations and tactics are very restrained. As a response to the changing context of the military service, there have been continual rounds of official staff discussions, preparation of special internal staff papers plus pressure to change administrative regulations, and even individual court suits, as in the cases of women who have become pregnant and are faced with dismissal.

Outwardly, the demands of the women in the military are pragmatic, specific, and generally negotiable. Occupationally and professionally, the goal is to press for a broader range of assignments, often under the category of line- or unrestricted line-officers' duties. The formulation is that—potentially—women should be able to serve in the broadest range of assignments, depending on the requirements of the service and of the task to be performed. Married women personnel concerned with change are interested in administrative arrangements which would facilitate the utilization, retention, and careers of married women. In this regard, the key demands center around the issues of pregnancy and the right of female military personnel to have children and pursue their careers. The change in procedures desired by women officers and enlisted personnel are documented in considerable detail in the specialized "trade" publications, such as the *Army Times* and the *Air Force Times*, which circulate among military personnel. All these demands are tempered by the general belief—of those who wish to pursue a military career—that such a career imposes some limitations on personal freedom. With respect to child rearing, the demands of new arrangements are grounded in a highly matter-of-fact assertion, offered by both males and females and incorporated into planning documents, that effective birth control is available and, therefore, there is a real alternative to the disruptions associated with childbearing.

Underlying these specific issues and orientations, especially for women officers, is a set of diffuse attitudes which agree with concepts of military affairs and with changes in the structure and outlook of the male military professionals. In Coye's study, on the basis of informal interviews and a partial survey of the attitudes of 34 women naval officers, the range of opinions can be preliminarily identified (Coye 1971, pp. 27–32).

One essential source of data is the response elicited by the probe, "What do you think are the navy's reasons for maintaining women officers today?" The traditionalist's viewpoint rested on the "nucleus" notion—that active duty women (officers and enlisted) provide a trained nucleus in the event of mobilization. According to this view, the role of the women line officers is essentially the administration of women personnel. This concept of women's role in the military is based on a concept of military organization which antedates the introduction of nuclear weapons and the threat of mass destruction.

Second, closely related but less traditionalist, is the outlook that women, as a significant part of the labor force, are a resource base and should therefore be used. Moreover, they have proved their worth and competence and are available elements of the naval organization as it currently operates. Those with this point of view believe that women officers can be just as competent as men, but believe that before this is accepted (by the male officers) the image of women in the country must be changed. These less traditional women have a strong element of equalitarianism in their thinking, but they are resigned to accepting the system, and they anticipate that changes will come from the outside; they are in effect the gradualists.

The third group appears to be not only the most change oriented, with respect both to the status of women and to the naval organization, but they also appear to be the most aware that mobilization concepts are only partially valid, or in a "state of limbo," since the relevance of the naval force is mainly as a force in being. These women are thinking about greater equality through functional equivalences. This point of view was expressed in interviews by the following attitudes: "The navy wants women for their general and special talents, and at the same time, offers young women the opportunity to serve their country." "The quality of women officers has been steadily improving; women have proven themselves useful and have become an integral part of the navy." By inference, for these women, administration and being a generalist in administration are a partial equivalent to sea duty.

A scattered few held a "tough minded" point of view, namely that women were in the military because the armed forces were "stuck with them by law." All of these groups, as witnessed by their continued naval service, accepted the system in varying degrees. However, three out of a sample of 34 were outspokenly negative. For them, women in the navy did essentially secretarial and paperwork duties. Their responses included opinions such as "We are high-paid office managers doing the navy's paperwork. . . . We still get scruffy billets that the men don't want. . . . We are performing well, but are kept down in how we perform. . . . We are restricted."

INSTITUTIONAL MECHANISMS FOR CONTROLLING SEX ROLES

As in any organization, personal attitudes and role relations in the military are contained and controlled by a series of institutional mechanisms; but the military has special features which impinge directly on these attitudes and relations. The overall number of women in the armed forces is set by formal allocations or quotas. Once a decision has been made to increase the number or percentage, the institutional mechanisms of control reveal many of the requisites for integrating women into the formal structure. In fact, there are institutional mechanisms of control which facilitate the integration of women into the civilian professional and occupational structure found in the armed forces. To identify these mechanisms is not to overlook the crucial issue of sex typing of professional and occupational roles, especially as they are linked to the ideology and reality of combat. The military is exclusively in the public sector and under a civil service format. Women in occupations and professions generally fare better in the public sectors, as has been demonstrated in a variety of studies. The civil service concept, with all of its limitations, at least requires equal pay for equal work and emphasizes more explicit criteria for promotion.

Moreover, while the protégé system and collegial relations are dominated by men in the military, they operate mostly at the very top. Throughout the military there are powerful pressures for the development of elaborated and explicit standards of promotion, which serve to penalize the most gifted and creative of both sexes. Likewise, women in the uniformed services have never developed sex-segregated occupational associations believed by some sociologists to be devices for deflecting the integration of women in the larger organizational settings. Moreover, women officers have had access to officers' clubs although their role in these clubs has been marginal.

However, at the higher levels, despite the trend toward managerial authority, the military is a crisis-prone organization in which innovation is in the hands of charismatic leaders or under centralized control, devices which serve to hamper the extension of women into positions of authority.

Defined standards of performance assist in the integration of women. The military constantly emphasizes a skill structure of specialists. However, the idea of the generalist—the operations officer—is very powerful, and it is noteworthy that, while there is a strong concentration of women in specialist assignments, the woman contingent has developed a functional equivalent of the generalist in operations, namely, the generalist in administration.

Career length and professional relations, or, more specifically, a system of ranking, are another positive factor (Epstein 1970, pp. 979–81). In the military this variable is operative to a considerable extent because of the system of formal grades. The rank system in the armed forces serves to separate, to some extent, the office from the person, with special relevance for the position of women. Nevertheless, there is some evidence that the rate of promotion for women officers is at least in some cases different from that of men. Until recently there were no authorizations for female general rank officers, and women officers in the navy are at times assigned to "billets" which are rated below their military rank. In April 1971, 22% of the captains, 27% of the commanders, and 17% of the lieutenant commanders had such assignments (Coye 1971, p. 10). However, comparable data on the underutilization of men are not available.

Finally, the ability to perform formal professional roles and to shift rapidly into the informal role requirements of a woman is a positive factor in integrating women into an occupational structure. In the military environment, especially at the officer level, there is considerable emphasis on appropriate manners and protocol. However, for the military, which is a communal institution—a setting in which work and residential roles strongly overlap and where the elements of sexual symbols are linked to the imagery of the fighting man—it is necessary to examine the sex symbolism of professional roles in somewhat deeper categories.

SEX AND SEXUAL SYMBOLISM

The literature on military institutions reveals a relative neglect of the study of sexual relations and of sexual symbolism in the military community. One sociological issue is that of family relations in the military community; another is the imagery and life circumstances of female military personnel. Charles Moskos's study of the American enlisted man focuses on the sexual behavior of military personnel while they are stationed abroad during the period 1945–70, when over one-third were on overseas assignments (Moskos 1970, pp. 78–107). He presents the conclusion that "indeed, from the viewpoint of many bachelor soldiers, it is the widespread opportunity for sexual promiscuity that most distinguishes overseas from stateside assignments" (1970, p. 91). In Vietnam, under the impact of actual hostilities and in the setting of extensive local corruption, catering to the sexual desires of American servicemen becomes a major and openly tolerated enterprise. An article with the headline "U.S. Viet Bases Welcome Shady Ladies" states that "the army is permitting ladies of the evening to be signed onto central Vietnam bases officially to meet U.S. troops in their barracks. . . . [Officers] maintain that the risks are worthwhile in the interest of keeping the peace in an increasingly disgruntled and demoralized army" (Chicago *Sun-Times,* January 24, 1972, p. 4).

The issue at hand is that of sexual values as an aspect of the social personality of the military, if that construct has relevance and validity. The social personality of the military profession—officer or enlisted man— is a matter more of impressionistic observation and literary reference than of systematic research. Nevertheless, for career personnel, and especially for those in highly specialized volunteer units, selection and self-selection in terms of social personality do operate (Janowitz 1965, pp. 50–76).

Even in the absence of extensive documentation and without probing underlying personality dynamics, two themes characterize, in ideal typical terms, the conventional military establishment. On the one hand, it has been noted by Little (1971, p. 249) that the military establishment has a strong familistic culture. The cult of manliness which emphasizes sexual virility and sexual exploits is the alternate theme which, although contradictory in one sense, may not necessarily be antithetical to the maintenance of family ties, if these relationships are adequately institutionalized.

Both ideologically and in reality family life and the importance of family ties are dominant in the military (Janowitz 1971; Little 1971, pp. 247–71). Careful research by Williams on the air force notes the lower divorce rate as a reflection of the culture of the military family (Williams 1971). One is struck by the relative absence of unmarried male officers, the few divorced personnel, and the very few childless families.

The family is a device for accommodation to the strains of military life, and family instability is linked to the exodus of those who do not fit in. Traditionally, in the peacetime armed force an officer, or—increasingly —a top noncommissioned officer, does not move easily into the overlap between occupational and social obligations without a family (Little 1971, p. 253); the officer's wife is seen as an active ingredient of the military community and antedated the corporation wife. There is, as well, a widespread assumption (not necessarily based on fact) that promotions into the higher ranks and responsible assignments go to the family man. For example, in the air force, particularly in the Strategic Air Command with its responsibility for nuclear weapons, married men are thought of as being more safe and sane and having a sense of responsibility. In air force imagery, fighter pilots can well be single men but they are considered to be less appropriate members of a strategic deterrence bomber crew (Williams 1971).

Before World War II the social position of the military wife was relatively fixed. In addition to her family role, she participated in the elaborate social protocol of the military base and had definite although limited obligations in voluntary associations and in the military's system of mutual self-help. However, with the vast expansion of the military establishment, the extensive rotations of assignments, and the weakening of military protocol, the old system has been drastically undermined (Lang 1964, pp. 77–80). Therefore, the military has organized itself to assist family life, and elaborate programs involving professionals and volunteers have become necessary (Little 1971, p. 248).

Despite its strains, military life is a form of communal living; most military activities are carried out on the base, which is as well the locus of much of military family life (although housing shortages require that an important percentage of the military live elsewhere). Consequently, the unmarried female military personnel occupy an ambiguous position in the social life of the base. Women officers are, to some degree, incorporated into its formal social life and thereby come into contact with the wives of officers; but the gulf between enlisted women and the wives of noncommissioned officers is much wider.

The theme of the cult of masculinity, on the other hand, implies that the good fighter is the man of sexual power and exploits. In imagery, as much as in reality, this aggressive sexual symbolism is based on the assumption that an effective officer cannot be a sissy or a virgin. The more combat oriented the locus or setting, the more pronounced the sexual symbolism and mythology. The heroic officer is an active type of man; in the past, he engaged in horseback riding and even polo, while in the contemporary scene his activities are survival training, parachuting, and the like, plus a range of hard-driving sports. Drinking is standard, but drunkenness is considered in bad taste. Before World War II, many military bases in the United States assumed that nearby local communities would openly tolerate brothels frequented mainly by their enlisted men and young and unmarried officers. Within the confines of the military community, codes of conduct were well developed, since scandal, if revealed, was highly disruptive of the small, closely knit, and compact military establishment. Mass mobilization during World War II and the continued tensions of the Cold War strained the ability of the military to control and deal with these two themes of the family man and the cult of masculinity. As the number of women increased, both as civilian and as military personnel, the emphasis on appropriate and proper relations continued—but the cult of masculinity found more and more opportunities for expression within the military establishment. In the 1960s the changing mores of the outside world and the disruption of the military community caused by Vietnam only served to sharpen the dilemmas. In addition, the issues of homosexuality—including homosexuality among women—had to be faced in new and more explicit terms.

In the military community as in the civilian society, the role relations and protocol between the sexes are being redefined. The consequences of new trends in socialization cannot be anticipated and may produce strong reactions. However, the hypothesis can be offered that there will be a reduction in overt sexual competition, since the new generation appears to be more prepared for "coeducational" existence in most segments of their daily life. The military will not be able to differentiate itself sharply from civilian society in this respect, except in highly specialized units.

The coeducational format has already been introduced in important aspects of military training, with notable implications. The impact, even if limited to the specific training situation, has been to reduce or at least contain the cult of masculinity and render the organizational climate more pragmatic and less ritualistic. For example, during the period 1966–70, which included expansion of Vietnam hostilities, the officer training school of the air force contained a small but regular percentage of WAFs. In 1968, there were 7% in the class, a percentage large enough to make a direct impact (Wamsley 1972). Wamsley's analysis of this training institution concluded that the presence of women added a "measure of decorum and realism," and generally dampened the zeal and ferocity with which particular activities such as drill, discipline, and even room arrangements were approached. He quotes a training officer: "Some of the Mickey Mouse crap the cadets used to pull is beneath these guys and especially with the girls around. They feel just plain foolish pulling some of those stunts around the WAFs" (unpublished). The impact of the presence of women should not be exaggerated, but, in this case, some coeducational training was compatible with military requirements, as it would appear to be for a force committed to a deterrence philosophy. Likewise, leading educational officers in the Israeli defense forces emphasize that the presence of girls in the army is responsible for a polite atmosphere and the maintenance of more appropriate language and behavior among soldiers. It seems not to affect battle performance and probably contributes to the sense of civility found in the Israeli forces.

Data on the patterns of contacts of women military personnel with civilians in the local communities would be useful; these patterns will change both as the number of women in the military increase and as the military moves more toward a volunteer force. Although it is possible that these contacts may not serve to integrate the military into the civilian social structure, there is reason to believe that they may well work to prevent the social isolation of the military, since women are more likely to maintain their previous civilian contacts and many serve limited tours of duty.

Problems of personal and social adjustment rest more heavily on the unmarried enisted women than on officer personnel. Not only are women officers more readily accepted into the social life of the military base, but they enter with a stronger sense of personal competence and are afforded a more individualized life-style. They have generally been given separate quarters, which contributes to a feeling of esteem. As mentioned earlier, enlisted women are less likely to engage in social contacts with the families of the enlisted ranks and are less interested in doing so. Their social life is oriented to other unmarried personnel—male and female. The services are conscious of their problems of social adjustment. Nevertheless, their housing is most limited and generally in some form of barracks. The new female recruit finds herself in a situation in which there is a strong emphasis on appropriate form and protocol. The services, in fact, conduct seminars on "social maturity" and personal style in the military. But basically social adjustment is based on self-selection since those who find the life confining or unsatisfactory leave.

CONCLUSION

There is no reason to believe that the proportion of women in the armed forces will increase or that the range of their employment and responsibility will expand rapidly or dramatically with the advent of the all-volunteer armed force. However, I believe there is ample reason to expect a gradual increase in numbers and a slow but steady expansion of assignment. Conceptually, the position of women in the armed forces offers a special case for analyzing both the women's liberation movement and the search for occupational equality. The armed forces operate under the federal sanction of equal pay for equal work and in an ethos of institutional change oriented toward equality. However, the context of the armed forces and the nature of the military is such that women in the military present a clear-cut case of the search for equality on the basis of autonomy and functional equivalence without the opportunity for similarity of specialization or task. The greater emphasis on deterrence increases the opportunity for women to become more directly involved in new types of "military" assignments. But women are not likely to be trained and armed for assault or direct combat operations. The institutional need for such deployment is slight; and the larger society has not yet been receptive to the idea that such equality is an essential demonstration of women's equality. The need for the military to adjust to more women who have broader assignments will increase the strains in the establishment, especially in connection with child-rearing requirements and the symbolism connected with sexual relations. However, under an all-volunteer system, the armed forces have an organizational structure to accommodate such strains, especially since, from a social and ideological point of view, they will not be recruiting the most "militant" younger women.

REFERENCES

Bar-On, Moshe. 1964. *Education Process in the Israel Defense Forces.* Jerusalem: Israel Digest.
Beard, Mary R. 1946. *Woman as a Force in History: A Study in Traditions and Realities.* New York: Macmillan.
Coye, Beth F. 1971. "The Woman Line Officer in the U.S. Navy: An Exploratory Study." Paper presented to the September 1971 Inter-University Seminar on Armed Forces and Society, University of Chicago.
Epstein, Cynthia. 1970. "Encountering the Male Establishment: Sex-Status Limits on Women's Careers in the Professions." *American Journal of Sociology* 75 (May): 965–82.
Essame, Hubert. 1970. "The Second World War: The Years of Retreat, 1939–49." In

History of the British Army, edited by Peter Young and J. P. Lawford. London: Barker.

Guevara, Ernesto. 1968. *The Diary of Che in Bolivia, November 7, 1966–October 7, 1967.* Calcutta: National Book Agency.

Haldane, Elizabeth Sanderson. 1923. *The British Nurse in Peace and War.* London: Murray.

Jamieson, Elizabeth Marion, Mary F. Sewall, and Eleanor B. Suhrie. 1966. *Trends in Nursing History: Their Social, International and Ethical Relationships.* Philadelphia: Saunders.

Janowitz, Morris, in collaboration with Roger W. Little. 1965. *Sociology and the Military Establishment.* New York: Russell Sage Foundation.

Janowitz, Morris. 1971. *The Professional Soldier.* New York: Free Press.

Kissinger, Henry. 1965. *Problems of National Strategy: A Book of Readings.* New York: Praeger.

Lang, Kurt. 1964. "The Effects of Succession: A Comparative Study of Military and Business Organization." In *The New Military,* edited by Morris Janowitz. New York: Wiley.

Little, Roger W. 1971. "The Military Family." In *Handbook of Military Institutions,* edited by Roger W. Little. Beverly Hills, Calif.: Sage Publications.

Moskos, Charles C., Jr. 1970. *The American Enlisted Man: The Rank and File in Today's Military.* New York: Russell Sage Foundation.

————. 1971a. "The Emergent Military: Civilianized, Traditional or Pluralistic?" In *Public Opinion and the Military Establishment,* edited by Charles Moskos. Beverly Hills, Calif.: Sage Publications.

————. 1971b. "Minority Groups in Military Organization." In *Handbook of Military Institutions,* edited by Roger Little. Beverly Hills, Calif.: Sage Publications.

Rolbant, Samuel. 1970. *The Israeli Soldier: Profile of an Army.* South Brunswick, N.J.: Barnes.

Speer, Albert. 1970. *Inside the Third Reich.* New York: Macmillan.

United States Army Combat Developments Command. Personnel and Administrative Services Agency, Deputy Chief of Staff for Personnel, U.S. Army. 1971. *The American Soldier in the 70's.* Vol. 1, *The Personnel Offensive (Phase I).*

Wamsley, Gary. 1972. "Contrasting Institutions of Air Force Socialization: Happenstance or Bellwether?" *American Journal of Sociology* 78 (September): 399–417.

Williams, John. 1971. "Divorce and Family Dissolution." Paper presented at American Sociological Association Annual Meeting in Denver, September.

Woodham Smith, Cecil Blanche. 1950. *Florence Nightingale.* London: Constable.

Young, Peter, and J. P. Lawford, eds. 1970. *History of the British Army.* London, Barker.

18

RUTH BADER GINSBERG*

Comment: Frontiero v. Richardson

On May 14, 1973, the Supreme Court rendered a decision that significantly advances opportunities to achieve equal rights for women and men before the law. In FRONTIERO v. RICHARDSON,[1] in an 8-1 judgment, the Court declared unconstitutional a fringe benefit scheme that awarded male members of the military housing allowance and medical care for their wives, regardless of dependency, but authorized benefits for female members of the military only if they in fact supported their husbands. In effect, the FRONTIERO judgment notifies legislatures and lower courts that sex discrimination by law will no longer escape rigorous constitutional review in our nation's highest tribunal.

A resume of the Supreme Court's prior decisions in the area of sex discrimination indicates the importance of the FRONTIERO judgment. Until the current decade, the review standard for fifth and fourteenth amendment challenges to legislation according different treatment to women and men was deferential in the extreme. Legislative lines drawn between the sexes, however sharp, proved invulnerable to constitutional assult. Supreme Court decisions that span the years from 1873 to 1971 tell us this. Until the nineteenth amendment, women could be denied the right to vote. Of course they are "persons" within the meaning of the fourteenth amendment, but so are children, the Court observed in

1874.[2] The right to serve on juries could be reserved to men, a proposition the Court declined to reexamine in 1971, although Justice Douglas urged his brethren to do so.[3] Women, regardless of individual talent, could be excluded from occupations thought more suitable to men — lawyering and bartending, for example.[4]

Typical of the attitude that prevailed well into the twentieth century is the response of one of our nation's greatest jurists, Harlan Fiske Stone, author of the celebrated Carolene Products footnote[5] that supplied the rationale for the suspect classification doctrine. In 1922, when Chief Justice Stone was Dean of Columbia Law School, he was asked by a Barnard Graduate who wanted to study law: "Why doesn't Columbia admit women?" The venerable scholar replied in a manner most uncharacteristic of him: "We don't because we don't."[6]

In 1971, two legal scholars — both of them male — examined the record of the judiciary in sex discrimination cases. They concluded that the performance of American judges in this area "can be succinctly described as ranging from poor to abominable. With some notable exceptions they [judges] have failed to bring to sex discrimination cases those judicial virtues of detachment, reflection and critical analysis which have served them so well with respect to other sensitive social is-

---

* 1. 93 S.Ct. 1764 (1973). *Professor of Law, Columbia University School of Law.*

2. Minor v. Happersett, 88 U.S. 162, 167 (1874).

3. Alexander v. Louisiana, 405 U.S. 625 (1971); See also Hoyt v. Florida, 368 U.S. 57 (1961).

4. Bradwell v. Illinois, 83 U.S. 130 (1873); Goesaert v. Cleary, 335 U.S. 464 (1948).

5. United States v. Carolene Products Co., 304 U.S. 144, 152-3 n. 4 (1938).

6. C. F. Epstein, Women and Professional Careers: The Case of the Woman Lawyer, 140 (1968) (thesis on file at the Faculty of Political Science, Columbia University) (reporting interview with Frances Marlatt, Attorney, Mount Vernon, New York).

sues. . . . Judges have largely freed themselves from patterns of thought that can be stigmatized as 'racist' . . . . [But] '[s]exism' — the making of unjustified (or at least unsupported) assumptions about individual capabilities, interests, goals and social roles solely on the basis of sex differences — is as easily discernible in contemporary judicial opinions as racism ever was."[7]

In 1971, a new direction was signalled by the Supreme Court. In REED v. REED,[8] the Court invalidated an Idaho statute that gave preference to men over women for appointment as estate administrators. Repudiating one-eyed sex role thinking as a predicate for legislative distinctions, the REED opinion declared[9]

[the statute] provides that different treatment be accorded to the applicants on the basis of their sex; it thus establishes a classification subject to scrutiny under the Equal Protection Clause.

Recognizing that the governmental interest urged to support the Idaho statute was "not without some legitimacy,"[10] the Court nonetheless found the legislation constitutionally infirm because it provided "dissimilar treatment for men and women who are similarly situated."[11]

REED was assessed by discerning courts and commentators as a harbinger of fundamental change in the Supreme Court's perspective with regard to sex-based classifications.[12] Although the REED opinion was laconic, it was apparent that the Court had departed from the "traditional" equal protection standard familiar in review of social and economic legislation.[13] Sex-based distinctions were to be subject to "scrutiny," a word until REED typically reserved for race discrimination cases. "Traditional" equal protection rulings, by contrast, upheld a statutory classification if the Court "conceived" any state of facts to justify it.[14]

In FRONTIERO, the Court moved on beyond REED more swiftly than many had anticipated. While REED involved an obsolete statute repealed, although

not with retroactive effect, even before the Supreme Court heard the case, the differential involved in FRONTIERO reflects a common statutory pattern. For example, the same differential is made for Social Security purposes, in workmen's compensation and disability laws, and in benefit programs for federal, state and municipal employees.[15] Despite the obviously broad ramifications of rejection of a pervasive legislative pattern, the Court was unwilling to perpetuate lump treatment of men and women.

Four of the Justices joined in a plurality opinion by Justice Brennan that declares "classifications based upon sex, like classifications based on race, alienage, or national origin . . . inherently suspect,"[16] and therefore subject to "close judicial scrutiny." Adopting a position long urged by advocates of equal rights and responsibilities for women and men, the plurality opinion states:[17]

since sex, like race and national origin, is an immutable characteristic determined solely by the accident of birth, the imposition of special disabilities upon the members of a particular sex because of their sex would seem to violate "the basic concept of our system that legal burdens should bear some relationship to individual responsibility. . . ." [citation omitted] And what differentiates sex from such nonsuspect statuses as intelligence or physical disability, and aligns it with the recognized suspect criteria, is that the sex characteristic frequently bears no relation to ability to perform or to contribute to society. As a result, statutory distinctions between the sexes often have the effect of invidiously relegating the entire class of females to inferior legal status without regard to the actual capabilities of its individual members.

Justice Stewart offered a one sentence concurrence tersely acknowledging that the statutes in question "work an invidious discrimination in violation of the Constitution."[18] Further enlightenment on the review standard by which he measures sex differentials in the law has been left for another day. In the meantime, lower courts may well assume that Justice Stewart

---

7. Johnston & Knapp, *Sex Discrimination by Law: A Study in Judicial Perspective*, 46 N.Y.U.L. REV. 675, 676 (1971).

8. 404 U.S. 71.

9. 404 U.S. at 75.

10. 404 U.S. at 76.

11. 404 U.S. at 77.

12. See Gunther, *Foreword: In Search of Evolving Doctrine on a Changing Court: A Model for a Newer Equal Protection*, 86 HARV. L. REV. 1, 34 (1972); Note, 86 HARV. L. REV. 568, 583-88 (1973).

13. *E.g.* Dandridge v. Williams, 397 U.S. 471, 485 (1970).

14. McGowan v. Maryland, 306 U.S. 420, 426 (1961). *See also* Jefferson v. Hackney, 406 U.S. 535, 546 (1972).

---

15. For social security provisions that automatically qualify wives as dependent, whether or not they are in fact, but require proof of actual dependency of husbands, see BIXBY. WOMAN AND SOCIAL SECURITY IN THE UNITED STATES. DEPARTMENT OF HEALTH. EDUCATION AND WELFARE PUB. NO. (SSA) 73-11700 (1972). Other examples at the federal level are catalogued in Petition for Certiorari, Appendix E, Moritz v. Commissioner, No. 72-1298, filed March 1973.

16. 93 S.Ct. at 1768.

17. 93 S.Ct. at 1770.

18. 93 S.Ct. at 1772-73.

knows sex discrimination when he sees it, just as he "knows [hard-core pornography] when he sees it,"[19] and accordingly conclude that at least five Justices can be relied upon to closely scrutinize sex classifications.

Also concurring in the judgment, Justices Powell, Burger and Blackmun found it "unnecessary for the Court in this case to characterize sex as a suspect classification, with all of the far-reaching implications of such a holding." In their view[20]

by acting prematurely . . . the Court has assumed a decisional responsibility at the very time when state legislatures, functioning within the traditional democratic process, are debating the proposed [Equal Rights] Amendment.

Justice Rehnquist was the lone dissenter. He wrote no opinion but simply referred to the reasons for upholding the legislation announced by Judge Rives in the court below. Judge Rives had indicated that a sex classification is constitutionally permissible "if any state of facts rationally justifying it is demonstrated to or perceived by the courts."[21]

Justice Rehnquist apart, the Court regarded "administrative convenience" as insufficient justification for dissimilar treatment of men and women who are similarly situated. Moreover, the Court's remedy for the constitutional infirmity is of critical importance. Equality was not achieved by eliminating benefits previously granted to men but not to women. Rather, the Court struck the offending exclusion of women, in effect declaring the benefits available to both sexes.[22]

The 4-1-3-1 division in FRONTIERO should provide stimulating material for dissection in next year's law reviews. Justice Stewart's enigmatic concurrence may occasion speculation. Some may wonder why Justice Powell, speaking for three of the Justices, referred to the plurality opinion as action of "the Court."[23] The counsel of restraint against judicial preemption of political decisions, sternly offered by Justices Powell, Burger and Blackmun, may be contrasted with the less

deferential attitude displayed by these Justices in the abortion decisions rendered during the same term.[24]

Does FRONTIERO indicate that the Equal Rights Amendment is no longer urgently needed? Emphatically no. FRONTIERO is certain to encourage increased litigation attacking on the basis of the fifth or fourteenth amendment sex-based differentials in federal and state statutes and regulations. Legislative response to FRONTIERO is more problematic. Past behavior suggests that Justice Powell's counsel resembles the position of the most political branch: If the Equal Rights Amendment is adopted, the hard task of revision will be undertaken in earnest; absent ratification, comprehensive revision may continue to be regarded as "premature and unnecessary."[25]

Some persons have expressed fear of a "flood of litigation" in the wake of the Equal Rights Amendment. But the dramatic increase in sex discrimination litigation under the fifth and fourteenth amendments in the 1970's is indicative that, if anything, ratification of the Amendment will stem the tide. The Amendment will impel the comprehensive legislative revision that neither Congress nor the states have undertaken to date. The absence of long overdue statutory revision is generating cases by the hundreds across the country.[26] Legislatures remain quiescent despite the mounting judicial challenges, challenges given impetus by the Supreme Court's decision in FRONTIERO. Ratification of the amendment, however, would plainly mark as irresponsible any legislature that did not undertake the necessary repairs during the two-year period between ratification and effective date.

Although the proposed Amendment should not excuse the judiciary from its responsibility to interpret the present equal protection requirement in the light of reason and contemporary social conditions, our elected representatives surely have an obligation to the long silenced majority.[27] That obligation is most appropriately recognized by an explicit constitutional provision dedicating the nation to a system in which women and men stand as full and equal individuals before the law.

---

19. Jacobellis v. Ohio, 378 U.S. 184, 197 (1964) (Stewart, J., concurring).

20. 93 S.Ct. 1773.

21. Frontiero v. Laird, 341 F. Supp. 201, 206 (1972), citing United States v. Maryland Savings-Share Insurance Corp., 400 U.S. 4, 6 (1970).

22. The extension cure for legislation that benefits one sex only is apparently overlooked by unions that assail the Equal Rights Amendment on the grounds that it would deprive women of protections currently enjoyed. Since the technique is hardly obscure, failure to press for it renders these unions vulnerable to the charge that, in fact, what they seek to protect is men's jobs.

23. Cf. Comment, 24 U. CHI. L. REV. 99 (1956).

24. Roe v. Wade, 93 S.Ct. 705 (1973); Doe v. Bolton, 93 S.Ct. 739 (1973).

25. According to the Solicitor General, a recent government computer search revealed that 896 sections of the U.S. Code contain sex-based references. Brief for the Appellees at 20, n. 17, Frontiero v. Richardson, No. 71-1694, filed December, 1972. Despite overwhelming congressional approval of the Equal Rights Amendment, Congress has not yet turned its attention to legislative revision.

26. See, e.g., Women's Rights Project Legal Docket, issued periodically by the American Civil Liberties Union.

27. AMUNDSEN. THE SILENCED MAJORITY: WOMEN AND AMERICAN DEMOCRACY (1971).

19

GRAHAM STAINES, ET. AL.

Alternative Methods for Measuring Sex Discrimination in Occupational Incomes *

*This research was supported by a contract with the Employment Standards Administration of the U.S. Department of Labor. Interpretations or viewpoints stated in this report do not necessarily represent the official position or policy of the Department of Labor.

We would like to express our appreciation to Laura Klem for her generous assistance in planning the analysis. Thanks are also due to James Morgan and Robert Quinn for their helpful criticism of the manuscript.

The recent surge in the literature on sex discrimination has suggested that in the 1970s sex discrimination may receive the same rigorous attention that was devoted to racial descrimination in the 1960s. Five years ago, little research existed on sex discrimination. The last few years, however, have witnessed a determined effort on the part of social scientists and others to study sex discrimination -- at particular institutions (e.g., Fox et al, 1972), in particular occupations (e.g., La Sorte, 1971; Martin, 1972) and in the work force at large (e.g., Cohen, 1971; Martin and Poston, 1972).

Although the recent studies of sex discrimination in occupations span a wide range of approaches and varying levels of methodological sophistication, most of them attempt to document sex differences in job incomes and to interpret such income differentials, at least partially, in terms of sex discrimination. Discrepancies between the incomes of working men and women, however, are not solely attributable to discrimination. Cautious investigators must assess the extent to which other, non-discriminatory factors -- considered legitimate determinants of a worker's worth -- make a significant contribution to the income differential.

This paper compares and evaluates four alternative methods for detecting and measuring income differentials between comparably qualified men and women in the labor force. For brevity of reference, these are called analyses of occupational sex discrimination. The paper takes as

its point of departure a broadly based study of sex discrimination by Levitin, Quinn, and Staines (1971), which used data from the 1969 National
Survey of Working Conditions conducted by the Institute for Social Research.

The approach of Levitin et al., referred to as Method 1 in the present
context, began with the selection of six variables as legitimate predictors
of a worker's income on the basis of the prevailing achievement ideology which
justifies the allocation of rewards in terms of a person's merit or performance. The six variables chosen were a worker's education, amount of supervisory responsibility, tenure with present employer, tenure on present
job with employer, number of hours worked per week and occupational prestige as measured by the Duncan scale (Reiss, et al., 1961). Conventional
multiple regression was used to develop, on a random half of the male subsample, an equation for predicting incomes from scores on the six legitimate predictors. The weights for the predictors in the regression equation were assumed to be the best estimates of how occupational rewards
are distributed according to the achievement ideology among a population --
namely men -- who experience no sex discrimination. On the basis of this
same regression equation, the incomes of women were predicted in accordance
with their scores on the legitimate predictors. The discrepancies between
the predicted incomes for women (that is, the incomes they "merited" in
terms of their qualifications thus measured) and the actual incomes that
these working women were paid indicated the magnitude of the income discrimination they encountered on their jobs.

The study by Levitin et al., however, failed to cope adequately with
at least three major issues that concern the documentation and interpretation

of sex differentials in occupational incomes:

(1) Can the predictive power of legitimate determinants of job income
be exhausted by a simple regression equation which captures only linear
and additive relationships between the predictors and the criterion variable of income? Possible curvilinear and interactive relationships between the legitimate variables and income, that is, are necessarily ignored
in conventional regression analysis.

(2) Can the income differential between comparably qualified men and women
be attributed to sex alone? Potentially confounding variables such as
race and age should be controlled in reaching estimates of occupational
sex discrimination.

(3) While the Levitin et al. study indicates a strong relationship
between workers' sex and annual income, it does not determine the importance
for predicting income of a worker's sex when compared to occupational qualifications and other demographic factors.

Methods 2, 3 and 4 represent attempts, using the same 1969 national
survey data, to deal with the three deficiencies attributed to the original
methodology. Method 2, for example, departs in one important way from
Method 1. Since conventional multiple regression imposes upon the relationships between predictors and criterion the restrictive assumptions of lin-
earity and additivity, it remains possible that the resulting multiple
R^2 represents an underestimation of the amount of variance in income
scores that could be accounted for by legitimate predictors. An effective
way to avoid these two assumptions is provided by the combination of two
statistical techniques (Sonquist, 1970): Automatic Interaction Detector
(AID) and Multiple Classification Analysis (MCA). AID facilitates the

detection of interactions among independent variables and the construction
of pattern variables that represent these interactions. MCA, in turn, can
incorporate these pattern or 'interaction variables and, in addition, has
the capacity to detect curvilinear relationships. Thus the combined AID-
MCA strategy handles both non-additive and non-linear relationships and,
when substituted for the conventional multiple regression used in the
first method of Levitin et al., should provide a more powerful prediction
equation (represented by a higher R^2) for predicting incomes on the basis
of scores on the legitimate variables.

The third method, while similar to the second, provides a more precise
estimate of occupational discrimination attributable to sex. It was devised to explore the second major issue raised earlier, namely, that although Method 2 indicates how much of the sex differential in annual incomes cannot be attributed to legitimate achievement factors, it fails to
determine whether the residual differences are attributable to sex or to other
illegitimate factors which may be confounded with sex, such as race, age,
union membership, or living in a particular region of the country, which
have often been suggested as bases of income inequalities. The third
method adds these four additional, illegitimate variables to the list
of six legitimate ones used in the first two methods, repeats the AID-MCA
strategy of the second method and generates an estimate of income discrimination wholly attributable to sex.

The fourth method focuses upon the relative importance of sex as but
one among the many predictors of income, legitimate or otherwise. It thus
represents a sharp departure from the previous three approaches and provides a statistical model for predicting the annual income of men and women

in the labor force. The set of predictors includes most of the major
ones: the legitimate predictors, sex, and a variety of major occupational and demographic variables. The AID-MCA package once again
determines how the predictors may be combined to provide the best
predictions of annual income. According to the basic idea behind this
fourth method, sex discrimination on the job is present to the extent
that sex is a relatively powerful predictor of income, especially
when the other predictor variables are held constant.

Methodology

Sample

The sample for the 1969 Survey of Working Conditions was a
national probability sample of persons who were living in households,
were sixteen years old or older, and were working for pay twenty
hours a week or more. Data were obtained through personal interviews with all eligible workers in a household. Since each worker
therefore had an equal probability of being selected, the data were
self-weighting. The full sample included 539 women and 993 men. A
comparison between the demographic and occupational characteristics
of the sample and those of larger scale government surveys is
presented in Quinn et al. (1971, 25-28).

The analyses reported below excluded three groups of workers:
self-employed workers; part-time workers, defined as those working
35 hours a week or less; and workers who were seasonally or otherwise irregularly employed during the year. School teachers were not
regarded as seasonally employed. After these exclusions, the remaining sample consisted of 351 women and 695 men. For some analyses

with the first method, the sample of men was further randomly divided into two half samples.

Measures

   Predictors. The predictor variables, listed in Table 1, included

both demographic variables such as race, sex, and age, and variables that

define a worker's position on the job, such as supervisory status and job

tenure.

   Annual income. This was total annual income from the worker's pri-

mary job before taxes or other deductions. Where a worker held more than

one job all questions in the interview were asked with reference to the

job on which the worker spent the greatest number of hours.

Analytic Techniques

   Of the two major analytic techniques reported here, multiple regression and AID-

MCA, only AID-MCA warrants detailed explanation. Taken together, the two

computer programs -- AID and MCA -- enable the identification of useful

predictors and the measurement of individual and collective relationships of

these predictors to a criterion variable.

   Used first, the AID program examines the associations between pre-

dictors and a criterion variable in an attempt to determine the dichoto-

mous split, on any predictor, which will yield the greatest reduction of

variance in the criterion scores. Once AID has made this initial dichoto-

my, it examines each of the two new groups to determine the group, the

predictor, and the split point which account for the largest variation in

the criterion scores. AID makes the best split and then examines each of

the existing groups to find the best dichotomization at still a third

level, and a fourth, and a fifth, and so on. With this breakdown of the sample through such successive AID dichotomizations, the analysis comes to resemble a tree with one trunk, two major limbs, and increasing numbers of branches as one nears the tips of the tree. The tree configuration makes it possible to detect interaction effects by noting whether the relationship between predictors and criterion is of the same magnitude and direction in groups on different forks of the same branch (i.e., groups of workers dichotomized only one or two steps earlier in the AID analysis). If interactions are identified through AID, new pattern variables can be constructed which incorporate both the main effects and the interactions of the original variables. The AID algorithm, moreover, can handle non-linear as well as non-additive relationships in the data.

The MCA analysis program is able to take advantage of the findings from AID. MCA resembles a multiple regression using dummy variables, in which a criterion score consists of the sum of a series of main effects. These main effects are coefficients associated with membership in a particular response category of each predictor. The program thus handles curvilinear relationships since the distribution of coefficients may be curvilinear for any particular predictor. MCA is limited, however, by the assumption that the effects of the predictor variables on the criterion are strictly additive. That is, it assumes that there are no interactions among the predictors. Yet the AID findings concerning interaction may be applied to the MCA procedure. The interaction terms, or pattern variables, developed with AID may be included in the roster of additive components that are used in the final MCA analysis, in which case the original predictors on which the interaction terms were based must be excluded from the analysis. If, on the other hand, no substantial

interactions are identified, no interaction terms are constructed for
the MCA analysis and the MCA may proceed under the assumption that the
relationships in the data between the predictors and the criterion are
strictly additive. Clearly, the joint use of AID and MCA obtains the
advantages of both while compensating for weaknesses in the other.

Procedure

Method 1. As described in the report of Levitin et al., the first
method used conventional multiple regression upon half the male subsample
to build an equation for predicting income. This regression equation was
later validated upon the remaining half-sample of the male workers. The
legitimate predictors used were education, occupational prestige, number
of hours worked per week, supervisory status, employer tenure and job
tenure. The incomes for women were then predicted from this equation
and a discrepancy score for each woman was created by subtracting her
predicted income from her actual income.

Method 2. In the second method, the combined AID-MCA procedure
was substituted for multiple regression in the building, on the whole
male subsample, of an equation to predict incomes and in the generation
of income discrepancy scores for the women. The set of predictor variables was identical to the one used in Method 1.

Method 3. This method also used the AID-MCA procedure employed in Method
2 but differed by the addition of four illegitimate variables -- race, age,
union membership, and geographic region -- to the six legitimate

variables used previously.

Method 4. The fourth method for studying occupational sex discrimination bore little resemblance to the previous three. Its main purpose
was simply to determine the power of sex as a predictor of income in comparison to both legitimate predictors and other illegitimate predictors.
The sample used contained both men and women, and the predictors, listed
in Table 1, included major demographic and occupational variables. The
AID-MCA strategy was again employed to build the statistical model for
predicting incomes.

Results

Method 1. Table 2 presents the multiple R and beta weights of the
multiple regression equation generated by Levitin et al.'s study, that
is, by Method 1. For the first random half-sample of men, multiple
R = 0.53 when adjusted to correct for capitalization on chance in fitting
the model. Education (beta = 0.28) and occupational prestige (beta = 0.20)
were the strongest predictors of income.

The mean of the discrepancies for women between actual annual income and income predicted from the male-derived multiple regression equation was -$3,459 (standard deviation = $2,200; N = 323). The distribution of these discrepancies appears graphically in the shaded histogram
in Figure 1, which indicates that 50.3 percent of the women in the sample
had total annual income discrepancies ranging from -$3,000 through
-$5,999, and the mean annual income of 94.9 percent of the women was less
than the amount they should have received on the basis of the selected
achievement criteria.

Table 1

List of Predictors Used in Method 4

Predictor	Number of coding categories used in AID & MCA analyses
Education	6
Occupational prestige, estimated by Duncan decile scores	3
Working week hours -- total number of hours worked per week on primary job	7
Supervisory status -- whether or not the worker supervised anyone	2
Employer tenure -- how long worker had been with the present employer	7
Job tenure -- how long worker had been on his or her present job with his or her present employer	7
Race, excluding all races not codeable as Black or White	2
Age	4
Union membership -- whether or not worker belonged to a union or employee's association	2
Geographical region -- whether worker lived in West, North Central, Northeast, or, South	4
Collar color -- whether worker was a white-collar or a blue-collar worker (Farm workers were excluded)	2
Occupation -- major occupational group according to 1960 Census codes	7
Industry -- major industrial groups according to 1960 Census codes	7
Marital status	5
Number of children for whom worker was the major source of support	5
Sex	2

Table 2

Beta Weights of Predictors Obtained
by Four Different Methods

Predictor	Method 1 (men)	Method 2 (men)	Method 3 (men)	Method 4
Education	.28	.40	.39	.38
Occupational prestige	.20	.11	.09	.11
Working week hours	.18	.20	.19	.20
Supervisory status	.11	.11	.10	.07
Employer tenure	.09	.22	.17	.15
Job tenure	.01	.11	.10	.09
Race	-	-	.03	.01
Age	-	-	.12	.06
Union membership	-	-	.03	.00
Geographical region	-	-	.14	.11
Collar color	-	-	-	.22
Occupation	-	-	-	.27
Industry	-	-	-	.10
Marital Status	-	-	-	.06
Number of children	-	-	-	.11
Sex	-	-	-	.26
R	.53[a]	.57[b]	.59[b]	.69[c]
R^2	.28[a]	.32[b]	.35[b]	.47[c]
N	326[a]	645[b]	639[b]	923[c]

[a] The N is based on the first random half-sample of men. The R and R^2 values for Method 1 were adjusted to anticipated shrinkage according to a formula presented by Guilford (1956).

[b] Data are based on full sample of men. The computation of R and R^2 involves an internal adjustment that anticipates shrinkage and reduces the values accordingly.

[c] Data are based on full sample of men and women. The computation of R and R^2 involves an internal adjustment that anticipates shrinkage and reduces the value accordingly.

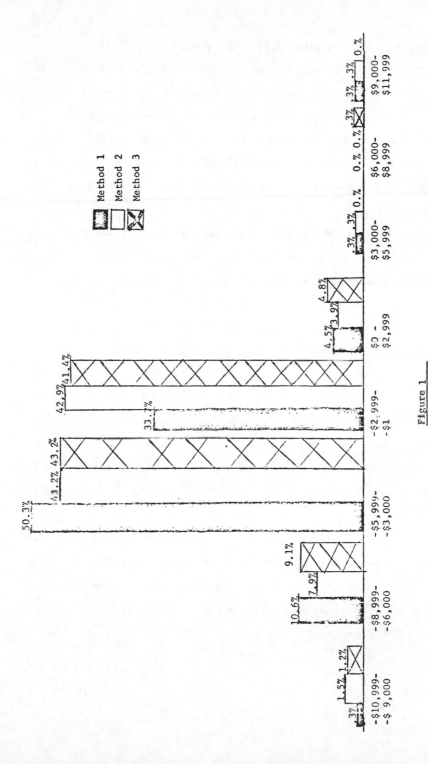

Figure 1

Percentage Distribution of Total Annual Income Discrepancies for Women by Methods 1, 2, and 3

Method 2. The results for Methods 1 and 2 were quite similar, so
only the slight differences in their findings need be emphasized. Table
2 presents the results of the AID-MCA procedure when it was applied to
the whole male sample with income as the criterion variable. Multiple
R for the MCA was 0.57, compared to 0.53 for the regression multiple R.
Both equations computed beta weights for each of the six legitimate predictors. Although the overall pattern was similar, the AID-MCA betas were
generally larger.

The mean for women of the actual minus predicted income discrepancies
generated by Method 2 was -$3,242 (Standard deviation = $2,289; N = 331),
a decrease of $217 from the estimate provided by Method 1. The distribu-
tion of the discrepancies computed by Method 2 is presented in Figure 1
and closely parallels that of the discrepancies computed by Method 1.

Method 3. The results of Method 3 were similar to those of the
first two methods. Table 2 contains the details of the AID-MCA procedure. Multiple R was 0.59, slightly higher than for Methods 1 and 2, and
the beta weights were similar to, though lower than, those for Method 2.
Because of the four extra predictors included in Method 3, four additional
beta weights were generated which had no counterparts in the first two
methods. Table 2 presents the beta weights for all ten predictors used
in Method 3.

The mean for women of the actual minus predicted income discrepancies
generated by Method 3 was -$3,280 (Standard deviation = $2,278; N = 331).
This mean was $179 lower than the comparable estimate provided by Method 1
but $38 higher than that provided by Method 2. The distribution of the
discrepancies from Method 3 is also shown in Figure 1.

Method 4. The final method employed all the predictors listed in Table 1 -- both legitimate and illegitimate -- to predict annual incomes for the full sample of men and women. The multiple R produced by this AID-MCA analysis was 0.69. The corresponding R^2 was 0.47, indicating that almost half the variance of annual income was explained by the 16 predictors. Since AID failed to uncover any interaction among predictors, the MCA-based R and R^2 values captured only additive predictor effects.

The beta weights generated by the MCA analysis are shown in Table 2. Sex, according to Method 4, was an important predictor of annual income. Its beta weight was third in magnitude among the 16 legitimate and illegitimate predictors, exceeded only by education and occupation.

MCA also estimates for every category of every predictor a value to be added or subtracted from the full-sample criterion mean to "adjust" for a worker's being in that category. The data indicated that by virtue of being a man, a worker's annual income was increased by $916 over the mean income earned by the sample; if the worker was a woman, she "lost" $1,830 per year. These adjustments were calculated with the effects of the remaining 15 predictors held constant.

Discussion

Methods 1, 2, and 3

Whereas Method 4 represents a wholly different approach to measuring sex discrimination in occupational incomes, the findings of Methods 1, 2, and 3 bear direct comparison. Method 1, however, did differ from Methods 2 and 3 in one minor way: the regression equation generated in Method 1 was based on a random half-sample of the men. The remaining half-sample was thereby made available for cross-validation. For Methods 2 and 3, this

additional step was not taken because the cross-validation in Method 1
had established that the mean of the income differentials for the second
half-sample of men was, as expected, close to zero (viz. -$27). The
equations generated by AID-MCA in methods 2 and 3 were therefore based
on the full subsample of men.

The major difference between Methods 1 and 2 lay in the power of
the analytic techniques used. Method 1 used conventional multiple
regression to build an equation for predicting income. Method 2 used
the AID-MCA technique. To the extent that the legitimate predictors
were related to the incomes of men by curvilinear and interactive (or
non-additive) relationships, AID-MCA was in principle able to create
a more powerful predictive equation. In this instance, however, the
search strategy provided by AID failed to uncover any interactions and
hence the assumption of additivity required for conventional multiple
regression proved to be unobjectionable. Using Method 2, however, MCA
did detect curvilinear relationships (e.g., between job tenure and
income) and the multiple R for AID-MCA (0.57) therefore exceeded the
multiple R for multiple regression (0.53). Since MCA was more
powerful in detecting a relationship between the legitimate predictors
and income, it attributed more of the gap between male and female
incomes to legitimate factors, thus lowering the dollar estimate of
sex discrimination obtained by Method 1. But perhaps what is most
striking about the comparison between multiple regression and AID-MCA
was how little the latter, more sophisticated strategy modified the
original findings. The assumption of additivity entailed no loss in
predictive power; and the assumption of curvilinearity altered the

estimate of average annual discrimination against working women by only $217.

Method 2 clearly provided a more accurate estimate of job discrimination than Method 1, but how accurate was the method in absolute terms?
In all likelihood, Method 2 somewhat exaggerated the amount of discrimination experienced by working women. Because of the unavailability -- for use
as legitimate predictors -- of variables not included in the survey's interview, the method probably failed to detect all the variance of income that
legitimate achievement factors could explain. Ideally, the prevailing
achievement ideology would be represented by direct measures of employee
performance -- the quantity and quality of work completed, absenteeism,
lateness, etc. But it has not yet proven feasible in surveys to use
either direct measures of performance or efficient measures of an individual's abilities and skills. In the absence of complete and direct measures
of predictors legitimated by an achievement ideology, less direct measures,
such as education and tenure, were substituted. Since the associations between legitimate predictors and income were possibly underestimated, the
estimate of objective sex discrimination based on the reported income differentials probably leaned, if in any direction, in the direction of inflating these differentials.

Method 3 corrected an additional limitation of Method 2. Although
Method 2 measured discrimination faced by women, it did not necessarily
measure discrimination solely attributable to sex. Women may have
faced discrimination because of their race, age, lack of union membership,
or residence in certain areas of the country. To arrive at an accurate
measure of discrimination attributable only to sex, these other illegitimate variables were controlled statistically. Method 3 thus added four

major illegitimate predictors -- race, age, union membership, and geographical
region -- to the six legitimate predictors. The income differentials from the
MCA analysis in Method 3 provided the best estimate of discrimination in annual
income that was directly attributable to sex -- namely, -$3,280. By adding con-
trols for other illegitimate predictors, Method 3 therefore raised Method 2's
estimate of income discrimination by $38. Far from explaining away some of the
observed income differentials between men and women, consideration of illegitimate
factors other than sex slightly increased the estimate of occupational sex
discrimination.

Age and race are the variables most likely to have raised Method 3's estimate
of discrimination above that of Method 2. Compared to men, women workers are
disproportionately black and, among blacks, the income for women workers is
closer to male incomes than it is among whites. Likewise, women workers tend
to be young (16 - 29 years), and in this age category women are paid more, relative to men, than in other age categories. When age and race are controlled,
it becomes irrelevant that women are found in better-paying categories on these
two variables and the estimate of sex discrimination is accordingly increased.
Union membership, in contrast, does not contribute to Method 3's higher estimate
of discrimination since women tend not to belong to unions and female non-union
members are paid relatively poorly. Geographical region is also irrelevant since
women workers do not cluster in regions that pay women well, relative to men.

Method 4

Two general properties of the analytic procedure developed in Method 4 are
critical to understanding its implications for sex discrimination. First, the sixteen predictors used in Method 4, including both legitimate and illegitimate predictors, accounted for roughly half the variance of income -- 47.4%. The remaining
variance may be attributable to measurement errors in predictors and criterion, or to
factors outside the predictors used, including performance on the job and dwelling

area (urban versus suburban versus rural). Second, the statistical power of Method
4, like that of Methods 2 and 3, was enhanced by its capacity to incorporate both
non-additive and non-linear relationships between the predictors and income. The
AID analysis program again uncovered no interactions, which was surprising in view
of the nature and number of variables used, and the non-additive feature of the
MCA procedure was therefore not required. The MCA procedure did, however, detect
non-linear relationships between income, the criterion variable, and various predictors -- both ordinal variables, such as age, and nominal ones, such as occupation and industry.

Method 4's identification of a worker's sex in and of itself as an important
predictor of income suggests the widespread presence of occupational sex discrimination. Sex was the third most important predictor of income, surpassed only by
occupation and education. Of the 47.4% of the income variance accounted for, sex
explained seven percent when the other 15 predictors were held constant.

Conclusion

Although they measure somewhat different things, the four methods described
may be compared and evaluated as measures of occupational discrimination attributable
to sex. Method 1, used by Levitin et al., assumed that the relationships between
six achievement factors and annual income were linear and additive, therefore under-
estimating the extent to which the sex differential in incomes could be explained in
terms of legitimate considerations. This first method estimated that, on an annual
basis, the average American working woman received $3,459 less than a comparably
qualified man.

Method 2 permitted non-linear and non-additive relationships between the achievement predictors and annual income and thus extracted greater predictive power from the
six legitimate predictors. With Method 2, the estimate of discrimination dropped
$217 to -$3,242.

Method 3 controlled for the possibly confounding effects of alternative forms of discrimination based on race, age, union membership and geographical area. Because it isolated sex discrimination from other types of discrimination, Method 3 provided the best dollar estimate of occupational sex discrimination, namely, -$3,280. The additional controls thus increased the estimate of discrimination by $38 over the figure provided by Method 2.

Method 4 demonstrated that, after education and occupation, sex was the most powerful of sixteen predictors of annual income. The results of all four methods suggested that American working women encounter significant sex discrimination in incomes from their jobs.

References

Andrews, F. M., Morgan, J. N., and Sonquist, J. A. The Multiple Classification Analysis Program. Ann Arbor, Mich.: Institute for Social Research, 1967.

Cohen, M. S. Sex differences in compensation. Journal of Human Resources, 1971, 6, 434-447.

Fox, G. L., Blanchard, C. B., Eckman, M., Foy, R., and Merriam, K. H. The Status of Women Faculty at Bowling Green State University: Report of the Faculty Senate Ad Hoc Committee on the Status of Women; May, 1972, Bowling Green State University, Bowling Green, Ohio.

Guilford, J. P., Fundamental Statistics in Psychology and Education. New York, N.Y.: McGraw-Hill Book Company, 1965.

La Sorte, M. A. Sex differences in salary among academic sociology teachers. American Sociologist, 1971, 6, 304-307.

Levitin, T., Quinn, R. P., and Staines, G. L. Sex discrimination against the American Working Woman. American Behavioral Scientist, 1971, 15, 237-354.

Martin, C. R. Support for Women's Lib: Management performance. Southern Journal of Business, 1972, 7, 17-28.

Martin, W. T. and Poston, D. L. The occupational composition of white females: Sexism, racism and occupational differentiation. Social Forces, 1972, 50, 349-355.

Quinn, R. P., Seashore, S., Mangione, T., Campbell, D., Staines, G. L., and McCullough, M. Survey of Working Conditions. Washington, D.C.: Government Printing Office, 1971.

Reiss, A. J., Jr., Duncan, O. D., Hatt, P. K., and North, C. C. Occupations and Social Status. New York: Free Press, 1961.

Sonquist, J. A. Multivariate Model Building: The validation of a search strategy. Ann Arbor, Mich.: Institute for Social Research, 1970.

Sonquist, J. A., Baker, E. L., and Morgan, J. M. Searching for structure. Ann Arbor, Mich.: Institute for Social Research, 1971.

References

Cook, B. Women search for a way of becoming, Journal of National Association of Women Deans and Counselors, 1970, 34.

Denmark, F. L., Baxter, B. K., Shirk, E. J. PROBE - A Program for Planning Ahead Educationally. Scottsville, New York: Transnational Programs, Inc. 1972.

Farmer, H. and Bohn, Jr., M. J. Home-career conflict reduction and the level of career interest in women. Journal of Counseling Psychology, 1970, 17, 222-223.

Horner, M. Toward an Understanding of Achievement Related Conflicts in Women. Journal of Social Issues. 1972, 28, 157-176.

Horner, M. Why bright women fail. Psychology Today, 1969, 3, 36-41.

Miller, J. A., Hoas, J. A., Bass, B. M., Ryterbauel, E. C. Exercise Future: A Program of Exercises for Management and Organizational Development, 1970, Juntod. Ltd., Second Edition.

Ohlson, Merle, M. Group Counseling, New York: Hart, Rhinehart and Winston, Inc. 1970.

Tarpey, W. G., Shortages of counseling personnel handicap scientific and technological development, Personnel Journal, 1966, 45, 489-493.

PART IV

SEXUALITY AND GENDER

SEXUALITY AND GENDER

The articles included in this section range from gender identity to adult female sexuality. There is no absolute dichotomy of male and female. Determinants of gender identity as well as the role of parents in terms of both identifications and complementation of gender identity are considered. Other articles deal with the effect of contraceptive pills, of pregnancy and breastfeeding on sexuality and the lesbian sexual experience.

Many of these topics are "underinvestigated" and deserve further study.

20

JOHN MONEY

Phyletic and Idiosyncratic Determinants of Gender Identity

If you have ever taken for granted that your own personal gender-identity was, after the fashion of a Platonic ideal, immanent in your genes at the moment of conception, needing only time for its inexorable unfolding, then you were wrong. Not only time was needed, but also an appropriately programed environment, because the program transmitted in the genes — the genetic code — does not express itself in a vacuum. The genetic code requires a permissive environment in which to express itself. Otherwise the code-carrying genes, and the chromosomes on which they cling, die and express nothing at all. The limits of permissiveness are phyletically prescribed and need to be empirically defined, species by species, for any given entity or variable. One such variable is gender identity of which the mirror image is gender role.

The environment in which the genes live and on which they are dependent for their survival is initially the cytoplasmic environment that surrounds the nucleus in which the genes themselves are located. In experiments on the frog, the genes in the nucleus of a cell have been shown to behave quite differently when they are located in a cell in

From the Department of Psychiatry and Behavioral Sciences and the Department of Pediatrics, The Johns Hopkins University School of Medicine and Hospital, Baltimore, Maryland 21205, USA.

the intestine as compared with when that same nucleus is implanted into an enucleated egg of the same species. The nucleus surrounded no longer by its intestinal cytoplasm, but by ovarian cytoplasm instead, can respond as the nucleus of an ovum and produce a tadpole, a replica of its one parent (G u r d o n 1968; G u r d o n & W o o d l a n d 1968)

Not only the cytoplasmic, but also the extra cellular environment will influence the way in which the genetic code expresses itself. The critical or sensitive developmental period, especially in embryonic life, is of key importance in this respect. Thus, by changing the hormonal environment of the embryonic anlagen of the genital anatomy, one can experimentally dictate that a genetic male will differentiate the reproductive organs of a female[1]. In the mammal, the experimental formula is this: remove the testes before they become embryonically active. The converse of this experiment is the masculinization of the genetic female. Experimentally it is more difficult to masculinize the internal than the external organs. The latter is easy. All that is needed is to inject the pregnant mother with sufficient dosages of testosterone during the critical days of fetal external genital differentiation.

In fish and amphibians, the influence of the extracellular hormonal environment on the genetic code of the fertilized egg is even more spectacular. With the sex-appropriate hormone dissolved in the water of the larvae of the killifish, Orizeas latipes (Y a m a m o t o 1962), genetic males will differentiate as phenotypic females, and genetic females as phenotypic males. Estrogen reverses the genetic males and androgen the females. In each of these

---

[1] Documenation for the statements made in this and succeeding paragraphs, together with a complete bibliography, will be found in J. Money and A. A. Ehrhardt. *Man and Woman, Boy and Girl: The Differentiation and Dimorphism of Gender Identity from Conception to Maturity.* Johns Hopkins University Press, 1972.

reversals, the individuals will be able to breed as members of their phenotypic sex. A genotypic-XX-phenotypic-male, if bred with a normal XX female will produce only XX females. A genotypic-XY-phenotypic-female, if bred with a normal XY male will produce 25 % YY males. Thus, by experimental environmental manipulation, it is actually possible even to change the male genotype, from XY to YY, in the killifish.

In human beings the external genital phenotype is sometimes hormonally reversed not experimentally, but as a result of spontaneous changes of the hormonal environment of the fetus in utero — or, more rarely, as a result of iatrogenic hormonal changes coinciding with the critical period of external genital differentiation. In such a case, a genotypic female may, indeed, be born with a penis and empty scrotum and, conversely, a genotypic male with a vulva and abdominal testes. When such a baby is born, the appearance of the external genitalia — the external phenotypic sex — determines the sex of assignment and the sex of rearing, provided there are no associated tell-tale diagnostic signs that lead to a contrary decision. Thereafter, if the sex of rearing is unambiguous, psychosexual differentiation, that is to say the differentiation of gender identity, takes places concordantly with the phenotype of the external genitals and the sex of assignment, irrespective of genetic sex.

Figure 1 represents schematically the sequence of determinants or events that lead to the differentiation of gender identity in childhood and adulthood. The figure can be interpreted metaphorically as a relay race, each entity being the equivalent of a runner that carries the program for gender identity differentiation and passes it on to a successor. Each runner must translate the program into instructions comprehensible to his successor. In some instances there may be paired successors, as happens when fetal sex hormone passes on instructions partly to sex-organ morphology and partly to pathways in the central nervous system.

One recipient of such a distribution may be time-delayed in carrying out its part of the program, as when the gonads delay the secretion of sex hormone postfetally until the age of pubertal onset.

With each change in the transmission of the program of gender-identity differentiation, there exists the possibility that an error may be introduced and subsequently transmitted. It is an empirical task to ascertain and catalogue potential errors and their consequences — a task which is

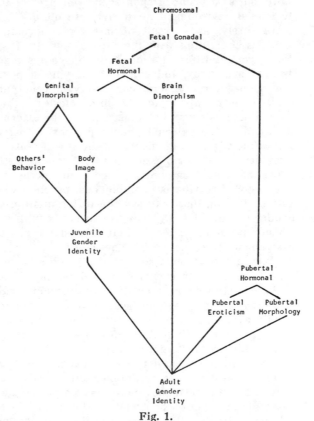

Fig. 1.

Schematic representation of the sequential nature of the determinants of gender-identity differentiation.

by no means complete at the present stage of the history of sexual science. Errors before birth do not, it would appear, have an automatic, direct-line, causal effect on the differentiation of gender identity, but only by way of changing the risk or probability of what may happen in the later stages of differentiation. To illustrate, consider the case of one of the cytogenetic anomalies, the inclusion of an extra X chromosome into the XY chromosomal constitution of a genetic male (Klinefelter's, or the 47, XXY syndrome)[2].

The supernumerary X chromosome does not preordain any unique feature of subsequent gender identity, but it does put the individual into a population at risk for impairment of central nervous system functioning and psychological development. Included among the psychopathologies likely, though not predestined, to appear in members of this population at risk are errors or anomalies of gender-identity differentiation. This increased risk may well be secondary to a deficiency of testicular androgen at the critical phase of fetal development when the hormone is known to have an effect on the central nervous system. Alternatively, or additionally, fetal cells carrying an extra X chromosome, as do all cells of the body in XXY individuals, may be weakly responsive to androgen.

In adulthood XXY men typically have low levels of plasma androgens, and their pubertal virilization is weak. Given exogenous androgens, their bodies do not utilize them with a good response, as does the body of a simple castrate. One consequence is that an XXY adult typically has the subjective experience and behavioral manifestation of a low level of sexual drive, regardless of how the gender identity has differentiated postnatally as masculine, feminine or bisexual, and regardless of whether unusual or paraphiliac tendencies in sexual behavior are present or not.

---

[2]) Parallel illustrations may be drawn from the 47,XYY and 45,X (Turner's) syndromes.

The bulk of today's evidence, particularly from the study of hermaphroditic biographies, points to the early postnatal years as constituting a very important developmental epoch in gender-identity differentiation. There is a parallel here with native language. According to the criterion of his ability to use language, a child by the age of five, at the latest, has an effective grasp of the principles of linguistics embedded in his native tongue. At that age there is, however, still enough flexibility for a second language to be acquired as if native, and spoken idiomatically and without an accent, which will seldom be possible later. Nonetheless, the second language will not eradicate the first, which will always remain subject to rapid reacquisition, even years later, should it have fallen into disuse.

By the age of five, a child's gender identity is imbedded firmly, like the native language. As a system in the brain, gender-identity programs a developing boy's own masculinely appropriate behavior and imagery while simultaneously programming the feminine counterpart as the complement of the boy's own reactions in relationship with the other sex. The reverse applies to the developing girl.

The years before age five are critical ones for the establishment of concordance versus discordance of the gender identity with the sex of assignment and with the prenatal components of gender. It is probable also that these are the years in which are established the behavior and imagistic anlagen of what will later be manifest as paraphilias, that is to say the behavioral disorders or errors of sexual functioning. The factors and experiences that lead to such errors are not yet systemically understood — only sporadically and anecdotally in terms of individual biographies. Thus, it is not clear whether experiences in later childhood and at the onset of puberty may leave an indelible mark.

It appears reasonably clear, however, that paraphilias do not become established in adolescence, but that they appear at that age on the basis of what was programed earlier in the biography. The function of the hormones of puberty is to lower the threshold of responsiveness to the erotic image and to increase the frequency of erotic expression. This principle applies irrespective of the erotic contents of both the image and the behavior, and irrespective of whether it is socially defined as normal or abnormal.

My purpose at this point is not to elaborate further on the postnatal components of gender identity differentiation, normal or otherwise, but to give special attention to the prenatal hormonal effect, specifically the behavioral sequelae of prenatal androgenization of the genetic female. There is a certain parallelism here between the observations made by Goy and his associates on the rhesus monkey and those made by myself and co-workers on human beings. In both cases, genetic females became androgenized in utero, so that the external sexual organs took on a masculine appearance. The human beings were surgically feminized at birth or soon thereafter, when the diagnosis (adrenogenital syndrome or progestin-induced hermaphroditism) was correctly recognized, and were assigned and reared as girls, with appropriate hormonal regulation as needed. A few, however, were not correctly recognized and were assigned and reared as boys, with appropriate surgical and hormonal intervention, as needed. The monkey hermaphrodites were not surgically corrected and not given postnatal hormonal treatment.

Tersely stated, the androgenized genetic females, monkey and human, developed behaviorally as tomboys. The monkeys gained scores more like those of normal male than female controls for rough-and-tumble play, for the initiation of play, for threatening and chasing play, and for mounting play.

Among the human beings, those raised as girls thought of themselves as tomboys and were so considered by others more than were their matched controls. They evinced a strong interest in vigorous outdoor energy expenditure at the expense of doll play and the rehearsal of maternal caretaking. They were not aggressive — an important point with reference to current hypotheses attempting to correlate aggression with androgen level — but they were capable of self-assertion, fighting if need be, for a position in the dominance hierarchy of childhood. Usually they underplayed the role of dominance assertion, in deference to the boys they liked to play with and who might otherwise not have accepted them. (Those reared as boys did not need to make this concession.) In keeping with their tomboyish play interests and activities, they preferred utility clothing styles and hair styles to decorative frills and curls, but did not repudiate feminine dressing-up for special occassions. They had little use for jewelry, but had no objection to perfume. From childhood onward, they envisaged themselves as giving preference to a nondomestic career as compared with a career as housewife and mother. They did not exempt themselves from marriage but rather projected marriage to a distant horizon. Those already in teenage were late in developing a romantic interest in boys, though not because of a lesbian preference instead. As a group, they tended to be high in IQ and academic achievement, quite possibly on the basis of an enhancing effect of excess prenatal steroidal hormones on ultimate postnatal intelligence. A point requiring further observation is that they may prove to be more easily aroused erotically by the visual image than are most women. In childhood, prenatally androgenized girls, unlike their monkey counterparts, did not manifest either more or less sexual play than their matched controls, presumably responding to the typical taboos of our culture in this respect.

Prenatally androgenized genetic females who are assigned and reared as girls, with appropriate and timely surgical correction and hormonal regulation, if needed, differentiate a feminine gender identity. Nonetheless, it is a feminine identity with a difference, the difference being the flavor, so to speak, of tomboyism contributed by the prenatal androgenic effect. This effect, if one may interpolate from experiments on lower mammals, is mediated by way of androgen-sensitive pathways in the fetal hypothalamus and, probably, the nearby structures of the limbic system. The effect of androgen is probably not sexually dimorphic in the sense of either/or, but rather in the sense of changing thresholds. Thus, a woman with the adrenogenital syndrome, late in getting married and apprehensive as to her mothering ability should she get pregnant, does eventually succeed in the parental caretaking function — in a fashion not unlike that of the child's father, if he is adept at infant care.

Fortunately for the fetally androgenized female reared as a girl, there is no cultural stigma attached to tomboyism in a girl in our society. The reverse is true for the fetally deandrogenized male reared as a boy. There is not even an acceptable name for him, like tomboy, unless it be that he is sensitive and artistic. Usually he is stigmatized as a sissy.

The change of threshold for sexually dimorphic behavior induced by fetal androgenization works in favor of the genetic female assigned and reared as a boy because of morphologic masculinization to the extent of having a penis and empty scrotum. Such a boy has no difficulty at all in differentiating a masculine gender identity in conformity with society's stereotype of what a boy and a man should be.

There is a theoretical principle to be drawn from the foregoing, the principle of phyletic and idiosyncratic interaction. It is incorrect to conceive of gender identity as the effect produced by a genetic ideal, in the Platonic sense of an ideal as an immanent cause awaiting its time. It is equally incorrect to juxtapose the genetic versus the environmental, for they are interactive. Likewise it is incorrect to juxtapose the biological versus the social, the innate versus the learned, or the constitutional versus the acquired, for they also are, respectively, interactive. More correctly, one might juxtapose the phyletic versus the idiosyncratically biographic.

The phyletic represents that which is shared by other members of one's species, or by other members of the same sex. Phyletic is not synonymous with genetic, but includes that which is the product of interaction between the genetic code, and its developmental environment, on the assumption that the developmental environment has been similar from individual to individual, with respect to those facets of the genetic code that they carry in common.

The idiosyncratic represents that which is not shared by the majority of the members of one's species of the same sex but is individual. This individuality may reside in the genetic code, or in some more or less unique factor in its developmental environment. A good example of the latter, already mentioned, is that of genetic females morphologically masculinized by androgen present in the fetal environment during the critical developmental period. The appearance of androgen in atypical amounts for a genetically female fetus so alters the subsequent stages of the program for gender-identity differentiation that the baby may be born with a penis, reared as a boy, and differentiated with a masculine gender identity that, apart from sterility, allows him to be behaviorally and psychologically indistinguishable from other husbands and fathers.

SUMMARY

Sexual science is now sufficiently advanced as to show that it is anachronistic to dichotomize heredity and environment, biological and social, or innate and acquired with respect to psychosexual phenomena, including the differentiation of gender identity. One gains extra theoretical freedom and flexibility by juxtaposing instead the phyletically determined versus the biographically idiosyncratic.

Both may be the product of interaction between the genetic code and its developmental environment.

SUMMARIO

John Money: DETERMINANTES PHYLETIC E IDIO-SYNCRATIC DEL IDENTITATE DE GENERE

Le scientia sexual es nunc sufficientemente avantiate quanto a monstrar que il es anachronistic dichotomisar hereditate e ambiente, biologic e social, o innate e acquirite, con reguardo a phenomenos psychosexual, incluse le differentiation del identitate de genere. On gania extra libertate e flexibilitate theoretic per, in loco de isto, juxtaponer le phyleticamente determinate contra le biographicamente idiosyncratic. Ambes pote esser le producto de interaction inter le codice genetic e su ambiente developpamental.

Acknowledgement: Supported by USPHS grants, HD00325 and HD18635.

References:

Gurdon, J. B.: Transplanted nuclei and cell differentiation. Scientific American 1968:*219*:24-35.

Gurdon, J. R. & Woodland, H. R.: Cytoplasmic control of nuclear activity in animal development. Biological Reviews 1968:*43*:233-267.

Yamamoto, T.: Hormonic factors affecting gonadal differentiation in fish. General and Comparative Endocrinology 1962, Supplement 1: 011-040.

Michael Pers: I want to thank Dr. Money for his vivid description of the tomboyism syndrome which was new to me. The only thing that I am not quite aware of is how it is defined from the somatic point of view. Did all these girls have influence of androgen during their fetal life or were they adrenogenital syndromes or were any of them in cortisone treatment, or did they not have any androgen stimulation at all at any time, I did not quite get this?

John Money: Well, all of the girls had a history of prenatal androgenization. There were ten of them whose androgen effect came from progestin given to the mothers to prevent a miscarriage. They had different varieties of synthetic progestin, but all of the variety that happen to be androgenic in chemical structure. The only strange thing, not fully explained, is that many other children whose mothers were similarly treated did not get an enlarged clitoris. There is not enough knowledge that can be retrieved to know whether it was simply a dose-response effect, or timing effect, or otherwise mysterious effect. These ten girls were studied with matched controls as were fifteen other girls whose history was one of the spontaneously occurring adrenogenital syndrome. They were fetally masculinized by their own adrenocortical androgen. Several other girls, not among these fifteen, were also adrenogenital girls. All of the girls with the andrenogenital syndrome have been kept regulated on cortisone since birth, so that their androgenic effect is a prenatal one only, as it is also for the girls with progestin-induced hermaphroditism, because as soon as they are born they are away from the masculinizing environment.

Michael Pers: May I add another question. Was clitorectomy done in all cases or in a few of them?

John Money: The only cases that don't get a clitorectomy (ideally in the neonatal period) are those in which the clitoris is sufficiently small and sufficiently in its "hiding place" where it does not appear as an embarrassment to either the parents or the doctor or, later on, to the child.

Herman Musaph: I would like to know, is there any planned psychotherapy for your patients and for the family problems, especially aroused by these disorders?

John Money: Yes, there is. Now I immediately have to make some modifications. All the parents are given quite a bit of my time, and the time of my assistants, at the crisis period when the baby is born, or when they first come to our hospital, to help them to understand the nature of hermaphroditism. If they are not given the right kind of help, they have only the imagery of the circus to draw on, and think of the baby as being a freak, a half boy and half girl. One of the most important little phrases that I have learned to tell parents is that their baby was born with its sex organs infinished. They can tell the brothers and sisters that — and the grandparents, and the aunts and uncles, and the neighbours.

I make a special plan also of helping the people who have to go home and reannounce the sex of the baby, if it was announced wrongly at the time of birth — which reminds me of the extraordinary capacity that many people have (people with a, shall I call it a strong ego Dr. Stoller?) to deal with adversity, when they are given the required amount of help. To my amazement it may be a rather small amount of help, in terms of total number of hours. I am also amazed how the community can accept a reannouncement of sex, and then keep its mouth closed, if the parents go home with a strong sense of conviction of the correctness of what they are doing, having been instructed in a program of how to deal with the community. I have helped myself in economizing on time for psychological counseling with these parents, and with the older children, by writing a book called: "Sex Errors of the Body", which is also available in German translation as a paperback. In this book are, among other things, the two diagrams which you saw on the screen of embryonic differentiation of the sex organs. Those diagrams have proven remarkably therapeutic for many people, especially when they can take them home to explain the intersexual condition in medical talk to their relatives. I have found that, if parents give their relatives an answer they could not have given themselves (and sound very learned, like those parents who go home with a few medical terms like hypospadias and hyperadrenocorticism), and if they obviously know what they are talking about, then, if at the conclusion they say, "I would now like you please to not talk about this, because it is for the child's own benefit in the future not to have this story running around", then parents really can form the behavior of the whole community of people. One of the clearest examples I have known is that of an isolated island in the Chesapeake Bay that has a total population of 600 people, all related to one another. They have been able to keep their mouths closed about a family that has three intersexual children in it. There are some parents for whom I have to try, to the best of my ability, to find regular and long term follow-up psychotherapy, but as it turns out that is not because of the problem of dealing with hermaphroditism in the family, but because of a problem they had in their love relationship together before they got married. They are the sick people that one would be seeing mostly in a psychotherapeutic practice, the people who come in with a "fractured ego", and who have great difficulty in dealing with adversity. I am really tremendously impressed, by reason of the opportunity that I have to work primarily in a endocrine clinic, to see people who can really cope with adversity. It is so different than when one draws a population only from a child guidance clinic or a psychiatric clinic, where one sees the people who can't manage. It gives me a renewed faith in the human race, that I need every now and again. I recommend all psychiatrists to get one patient a month from a pediatric endocrine clinic!

Isaac Marks: I wonder if you have any observations to offer on capacity for multiple orgasm along the female model of the different kinds of hermaphrodites?

John Money: I have one observation on that. Earlier today in the discussion group, I was talking about the problem of solipsism — of trying to get inside of the "egg shell" of another's mind to find out what is going on in there, in their own imagery and thoughts and feelings. Well, the best that I have been able to do, with regard to getting inside the egg-shell, is to recognize when I and the person I am talking to are tuned in on the same wave band. I first learned about this problem in trying to talk to colour-blind people — especially when I was being very nasty to one of them about the bad colour matching of clothes. Then it dawned on me, this was many years ago, that I was being brutally cruel. I got the colour-blind test out, and sure enough the person was colour-blind.

Well, with regard to talking about sexual response feelings and orgasm, I have had a chance to talk to men who have the partial androgen insensitivity syndrome. These men should really indeed have been assigned as girls, but alas for them a urologist found two "orange pips" in their groins, when they were little, and recognizing or assuming them to be testicles, required that the individuals be raised up as boys. When I talk to these men, I find that we are absolutely not talking on the same wave band. I try to orient myself to the fact that I perhaps would be talking to a woman who, erotically speaking, is posing as a man. Then I can begin to understand what they are telling me. One of the things they may report is that they have multiple orgasm. They don't have ejaculation, so it is a so-called dry run orgasm. By contrast, when I talk to a genetic female — these were genetic males with partial androgen insensitivity and a very small penis — when I talk to a genetic female who has been raised up as a man, with a repaired penis (even though it is a small one and being maintained on a sufficient dose of testosterone enanthate) I get more the feeling that I am tuned in to a man talking. But they do also have a capacity for more than one orgasm per session of sexual experience.

Actually, the best application I know of this particular "eggshell principle", if I may call it that, is in trying to find out whether a woman knows what a sexual climax is or not. I have found out that the way she gives her answer when one asks about orgasm, perhaps with a big smile from ear to ear, tells you very well that she knows what she is talking about. And if there is any if, or subjunctive quality to it, you can almost be sure that she has not really experienced orgasm properly.

21

JOHN MONEY

Identification and Complementation in the Differentiation of Gender Identity

The untutored mind of modern man knows of gray, of the land of the midnight sun, and of intersexuality, yet it retains its atavistic logic of dichotomies and thinks of black and white, day and night, male and female. Only with difficulty does it accommodate itself to the logic of gradations.

Chromosomal and Gonadal Dimorphism

Conceptual dichotomism in man's thinking undoubtedly has an ancient phyletic foundation, nowhere more anciently founded than with respect to sexual dimorphism which in its very origins is genetic, namely in the chromosomal dimorphism of sex. Yet even chromosomal dimorphism is not an absolute. Some individuals are born neither with the normally expected XX nor XY sex-chromosomal complement, witness the syndromes characterized as 45, X; 47, XXX; 47, XXY, 47, XYY and divers sex chromosomal mosaics.

The same absence of absolutism in sexual dimorphism may be observed also independently of chromosomal sex, in the fetal phases of sexual differentiation that follow the earliest beginnings when chromosomal sex is established. Thus, the gonads may differentiate not as ovaries or testes, but as various combinations of both, either separately, or as a histological mixture, ovotestes.

From the Department of Psychiatry and Behavioral Sciences and Department of Pediatrics, Johns Hopkins University School of Medicine and Hospital, Baltimore, Maryland, 21205, USA.

Fetal Androgenization and Hypoandrogenization

After gonadal sex has been developmentally established, lack of dimorphic absolutism may again
manifest itself in fetal hormonal functioning. An
excess of male sex hormone, whether produced by
the fetus itself (most commonly from malfunction
of the adrenal cortices) or of exogenous origin, will
allow the external genitalia of the chromosomal
female to masculinize. Thus the genetic female
with two ovaries and internal female differentiation may be born with a grossly enlarged clitoris
and partial fusion of the labia. In the extreme case,
the clitoris becomes a penis and the labia majora
fuse to become an empty scrotum.

The counterpart of such masculinization of the
genetic female occurs not as an influence of female
sex hormone on the genetic male fetus, but as a
failure of its male hormonal function. There are
two types of failure. One is the failure of the embryonic testes to release their mullerian inhibiting
substance, with the consequence that the uterus and
fallopian tubes differentiate and persist in an individual otherwise differentiated as male. The second
type of failure is that which occurs when the embryonic and fetal testes fail to release male sex hormone, or when the target cells prove incapable of
utilizing the male sex hormone that is released
(androgen intensitivity syndrome). In the extreme
case, the genetic and gonadal male then differentiates the external genitalia of a female. In the less
extreme case, the male organs are incompletely differentiated, with the penis small, its urinary canal
unfused, and its urinary orifice in approximately
the female position.

The hormonal exceptions to the rule of dimorphic absolutism that manifest themselves, as
above, in ambiguity or hermaphroditism of the
external genitalia influence also the differentiation
of pathways in the brain. More accurately, one
makes an inference to this effect on the basis of
experimental animal studies and human clinical
observations. In brief, it appears that the prenatally
androgenized genetic female has no difficulty postnatally in differentiating gender-dimorphic behavior culturally ascribed to the male, provided
the sex of assignment and rearing has been consistently as a boy, with concordant surgical and
hormonal treatments. The same individual assigned
as a girl, with appropriate surgical treatment and
hormonal regulation, differentiates a female gender
identity but with a tomboyish temperament. This

tomboyism means, in brief, hypertrophy of interest in athletic energy expenditure, exploratory curiosity, and capacity for competitive rivalry and dominance assertion in boys' play groups, together with hypotrophy of interest in the childhood rehearsals of maternalism as manifested in dollplay.

The counterpart of tomboyism in the androgenized girl is a kind of behavior in the hypoandrogenized boy for which there is no term in English. It is not sissiness, for sissiness implies effeminacy and homosexuality, but rather a quietism against which much effort is needed in order to match the behavioral demands that boys put on one another. Such quietism facilitates feminine behavioral development and feminine gender identity differentiation in a hypoandrogenized genetic male assigned and reared as a girl, with appropriate surgical correction as needed. In cases of total androgen failure, no feminizing surgery is needed, nor is hormonal therapy at puberty, since the body responds only to its own testicular estrogens, being insensitive to androgen. Pubertal insensitivity to androgen creates an insoluble problem when the child has been reared as a boy, for no amount of hormonal treatment will produce a masculine body build, masculine secondary sexual characteristics, and masculine aging and maturity of appearance.

Pairs Concordant for Diagnosis, Discordant for Rearing
Androgenization of the genetic female, and hypoandrogenization of the genetic male demonstrate, in their respective ways, the lack of dimorphic absolutism with respect to those aspects of gender-dimorphic behavior subject to prenatal hormonal influence: babies of either genetic sex can be assigned are reared as boy or girl. Then, typically, they differentiate a gender identity concordant with the sex of assignment and rearing, albeit flavored or tinted, so to speak, by the particular prenatal hormonal brain influence. Despite their value for science, however, matched pairs of hermaphrodites concordant for the prenatal variables of sex, and discordant for assigned sex, rearing, and gender-identity differentiation, do not have quite the same dramatic impact, heuristically, as does another type of case.

This other type is that of a normally born boy who in early life underwent traumatic ablation of the entire penis as a result of an accident of circumcision by cautery. The total number of such cases has not been recorded. Some few are known to have been reared as boys, but are lost to follow-up. Within the last ten years, two cases are known in which the posttraumatic dilemma was resolved in a decision to reassign the baby as a girl, following appropriate first-stage feminizing surgery of the genitalia — with the second stage, namely construction of a vaginal cavity, to follow in adolescence after a feminizing puberty has been induced by estrogen replacement therapy. The oldest of these two children is now in middle-childhood. Her gender specific behavior as a girl is quite remarkably evident by reason of its contrast with that of her identical twin brother. Her appearance and behavior as a girl elicit sex-appropriate behavior toward her from other people. At school her medical history is not known or suspected. The mother is explicitly aware of reinforcing and encouraging feminine behavior in the girl, and masculine behavior in the boy. The father simply takes for granted that one behaves as a girl, the other as a boy, and he responds accordingly. The end of the story, scientifically, will be written with the development of romance and falling in love in adolescence. One predicts then that the girl will continue the feminine gender identity already differentiated, basing the prediction on adult cases of male hermaphroditism with feminine sex assignment, rearing, and gender identity differentiation.

Hermaphroditic Sex Reassignment

Cases of sex reassignment, like the foregoing, occur also in some cases of hermaphroditism when the initial decision later proves to have been unwise. Usually it is not feasible to decide on a sex reassignment after an infant has begun to grasp sex differences imbedded in linguistic and other conventions and to apply them to the self. Thus, between eighteen months and two years of age is usually the limit for an imposed reassignment, unless it is later evident that differentiation of the gender identity has been equivocal. The age of eighteen months, however, is sufficiently advanced for it to become quite evident to parents and other adults that they do, indeed, have different programs and expectancies in their own behavior toward a boy as compared with a girl. Moreover, these programs and expectancies exist independently of the child's own sex-specific appearance and behavior, and can be changed if the child's sex is reassigned. There is no doubt, nonetheless, that a parent's behavior is reinforced by the sex-appropriate appearance and behavior of the child. Thus, the change of clothing style and haircut is of major importance in facilitating the change in parental behavior when their child's sex is reannounced — to say nothing of the appropriate surgical change of the genitalia. Visible changes also influence other people's responses to the child and as the child's behavior reciprocates a feedback effect is established.

Complementation and Identification Models

Sex reassignment demands that father and mother both reorient themselves and their behavior toward the child. Thus, the father whose erstwhile son comes from the hospital reassigned as a daughter no longer can act as a male identification model for a son, but must become a male complementation model for a daughter. Simultaneously, the mother changes from a complementation to a identification model. The principle is nicely illustrated in an anecdote given by the father of a son-become-daughter. Back from the hospital, the little girl showed an enthusiasm for copying her four-year-old brother's rough-house dancing, to be a big shot, like him. The father's impulse was to hold his daugther close to him in partner-to-partner dancing. Rebellious at first, she soon recognized her favored position, whereupon her brother wanted to share it. The father's reaction was negative. He taught his son to dance with his mother, instead, all four being together each evening for the children's play time with their parents.

Ideally, there will exist reciprocal concordance between parents regarding their respective roles as identification and complementation models, so that each reinforces the role of the other in interaction with the child. Disordance between the parents in this connection introduces ambiguity and conflict into the child's gender-identity differentiation. The roles of complementation and identification may both then become impaired in the child, and to a greater or lesser degree transposed or translocated, part of one being affixed to the other, and vice versa. Ideally, both parents — and other people too — agree on both roles, so that a child can establish each with clearly demarcated boundaries.

Clarity of the boundaries is more important than the content of the two roles themselves. In fact, there is no absolute dichotomy of male and female identification roles and their complements. The invariates or imperatives may be condensed to four: males impregnate, and females menstruate, gestate and lactate. Other criteria of sexual dimorphism of behavior are either derivatives of these irreducible four, or are optional according to time and place — as is obvious in studies of historical and cultural anthropology. In today's world, there is plenty of scope for reciprocal change with respect to the optional content and definition of male and female roles, in keeping with the new feminism of the Women's Liberation Movement. Ideally, for each child, both parents will agree on the change, even though reciprocal change is not predictably easy to achieve. Ideally, also, the child's own family will not be socially isolated in its definition of the two roles, since such social isolation easily stigmatizes a child among his age mates, and may force him to choose between parents and peers.

Gender Schemata in the Brain

Differentiation in the postnatal phase of gender identity by means of identification and complementation (manifestations of both types of behavior being reinforced by both parents) required, by implication, that the two patterns of gender-dimorphic behavior be encoded in the brain. In normal development, the one gender schema is encoded as positive, so to speak, which means identification, which means "this is how I do it". By contrast, the other, negatively coded, means complementation, which means "this is how it will be done by the other sex, and I shall respond in a complementary way".

Here again, to continue the thematic principle of this paper, there is no dichotomous absolutism. Part or all of the dimorphic gender schemata may become reciprocally translocated or transposed. Phenomenologically, the result is what is commonly considered to be a gender identity disorder, either minor or severe. As well as being either partial or complete, transposition may be also either chronic or episodic in its manifestations.

Transpositions in Gender Schemata

A partial chronic form of transposition is exemplified in the ordinary type of homosexuality in which there is a degree of discordance or dissociation between cognition of one's morphologic sex, on the one hand, and cognition of one's same-sex erotic partnership on the other, but not between morphologic sex and vocational or business partnerships.

A partial episodic form of transposition is exemplified in genuine bisexuality, in which dissociation between cognition of morphologic sex and of erotic partnership alternates with episodes in which there is no dissociation. In other words, the partner is sometimes of the same sex, and sometimes of the other sex.

A complete chronic form of transposition is exemplified in transexualism, in which there is a more or less complete dissociation between cognition of one's morphologic sex and cognition of one's gender identity plus its expression as gender role. The transexual person has an intense conviction, or idée fixe, that the only way to resolve the paradox is by way of hormonal and surgical change of sexual morphology.

A complete episodic form of transposition is exemplified in transvestism, in which dissociation between cognition of morphologic sex and gender identity/role alternates with episodes in which there is no dissociation. The dissociative episode has some kinship with a fugue state and is intimately associated with putting on the clothing of the opposite sex. A homosexual partnership, that is with a person of the same morphologic sex, is optional while the transvestite is cross dressed. Also, the clothing may have a fetishistic stimulus value, heightening the possibility of performance in a heterosexual partnership.

The above four examples are ideal types, so to speak, with various gradations and subtypes found in actual clinical manifestation. One special subtype is that in which transposition between the two gender schemas is, in addition to being partial, unstable — subject to chaotic shifts and fragmentation. The resultant dissociation between cognition of morphologic sex and of gender identity/role is unstable and disorderly, sometimes present, sometimes gone. It is likely to manifest itself primarily in the solipsistic privacy of thought and imagery, as in fantasy, dream or hallucination. Its public expression is likely to occur only in elliptical signs and symbols of either body language or verbal language. In its classic form, this type of dissociation is schizophrenic.

Brain Dysfunction

It is exceptionally rare to be able to trace a transposition of the gender schemata from its manifestation in behavior to its manifestation in demonstrable brain dysfunction. However, there are recorded cases in clinical neurosurgery which show that behavioral symptoms of such a transposition, in one case transvestism, may occur in connection with a brain lesion and the onset of temporal lobe epilepsy. Additionally, following successful temporal lobectomy for relief of seizures, the psychosexual symptom may disappear. One may then infer that the epileptogenic lesion opened a gating mechanism that permitted negatively coded behavior to escape, and that surgery, being successful, allowed the gate to close again. The escape of sexually dimorphic behavior that once was negatively coded is also symptomatic in some cases of brain deterioration in senility. The principle of escape is an example of the well known Jacksonian Law of Release which has hitherto been applied to the functioning of other brain systems, but not to sexual dimorphism as a brain system.

CONCLUSION

Clearly, the brain holds the secrets of the etiology of gender identity differentiation and its transposition disorders — secrets that pertain to fetal hormones, childhood developmental learning, and the impairments of maturity. When the brain will yield up all of these secrets — who know what the story will be?

SUMMARY

There is no absolute dichotomy of male and female, even with respect to chromosomal and gonadal sex. Hyperandrogenism in utero masculinizes the genetic and gonadal female. Hypoandrogenism demasculinizes, that is feminizes the genetic and gonadal male. Hyperandrogenized females differentiate a gender identity concordant with assigned sex and rearing, though as boys or girls they share those behavioral traits which in girls constitute tomboyism. Hypoandrogenized males also differentiate a gender identity concordant with assignment and rearing; and they lack tomboyish traits. Cases of sex reassignment in childhood hermaphroditism demonstrate that the same-sexed parent is an identification model, and the other parent a complementation model. Ideally they both agree on the boundaries of what constitutes sexual dimorphism of behavior. The irreducible imperatives of such dimorphis are that women menstruate, gestate and lactate, and that men impregnate. Complementation and identification are the basis of two gender schemata in the brain, which may possibly become reciprocally transposed, either partly or wholly, and either chronically or episodically. Transposition may be either stable and organized, or shifting and chaotic. Different types and degrees of transposition are manifested clinically as homosexuality, bisexuality, transexualism, transvestism and the schizophrenic type of gender-identity ambiguity. In very rare instances the behavioral manifestations of transposition can be correlated with demonstrable brain dysfunction.

Acknowledgement: Supported by USPHS Grants 5K03-HD18635 and 2R01-HD00325.

SUMMARIO

John Money: IDENTIFICATION E COMPLEMENTATION IN LE DIFFERENTIATION DEL IDENTITATE DE GENERE

Il ha nulle absolute dichotomia de mascule e feminin, mesmo quanto al sexo chromosomal e gonadal. Hyperandrogonismo in le utero masculinisa le genetic e gonadal feminin. Hypoandrogenismo demasculinisa, i. e. feminisa, le genetic e gonadal mascule. Feminas hyperandrogenisate differentia un identitate de genere in concordantia con le assignate sexo e education, benque como pueros o pueras illes ha in commun ille characteristicas que in pueras constitue "puero-ismo". Masculos hypoandrogenisate etiam differentia un identitate de genere in concordantia con le assignation e education; e illes care le characteristicas "puero-ista". Casos de reassignation sexual in hermaphroditismo del infantia demonstra que le parente del mesme sexo es un modello de identification, e le altere parente un modello de complementation. Idealmente illes ambes es de accordo concernente le limites de lo que constitue le dimorphismo sexual de conducta. Le imperativos irreducibile de tal dimorphismo es que feminas menstrua, gesta e lacta, e que masculos impregna. Complementation e identification es le base de duo schemas de genere in le cerebro, que pote possibilemente devenir reciprocamente transponite, sia partialmente sia integremente, e sia chronicamente sia episodicamente. Transposition pote esser sia stabile e organisate, sia variabile e chaotic. Differente typos e grados de transposition es manifestate clinicamente como homosexualitate, bisexualitate, transsexualismo, transvestismo, e le typo schizophrenic de ambiguitate del identitate de genere. In exemplos multo rar le manifestationes comportamental de transposition pote esser correlatate con demonstrabile dysfunction cerebral.

22

J. RICHARD UDRY, NAOMI M. MORRIS AND LYNN WALLER

Effect of Contraceptive Pills on Human Sexual Activity in the Luteal Phase of the Human Menstrual Cycle[1]

The results of a double-blind placebo study reveal changes of sexual behavior of 51 women followed over three menstrual cycles. Differences in sexual activity during the luteal phase of the cycle (days 18 to 25) were noted. Sexual activity increased for women on contraceptive pills but not on placebo. After examination of the data, hypotheses were rejected that the difference was due to contraceptive pills directly affecting the woman's feeling state or overall activity level. The data are consistent, however, with the following: The presence of endogenous progesterone during natural cycles affects the male so that he does not desire coitus as frequently during the luteal phase. The absence of endogenous progesterone during pill cycles removes whatever restraint progesterone has on coitus. No other interpretation is consistent with the data derived from this study. The influence on the human male may operate via a pheromone as is the case with male rhesus monkeys.

INTRODUCTION

The purpose of this paper is to discuss the effect of contraceptive pills in changing sexual activity during the luteal phase of the menstrual cycle. We have previously reported our finding from this study that the frequency of intercourse and orgasm of women on contraceptive pills peaks during the normally low luteal phase of menstrual cycle (Udry and Morris, 1970). The present paper is an attempt to explain this finding.

BACKGROUND

In previous research, we had reported the periodicity of intercourse and orgasm in two groups of women (Udry and Morris, 1968). This research showed

[1] This research was supported by funds from the Carolina Population Center and the University Research Council.

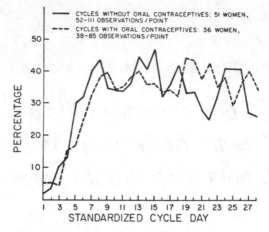

Fig. 1. Percentage of women reporting intercourse by standardized menstrual cycle day.

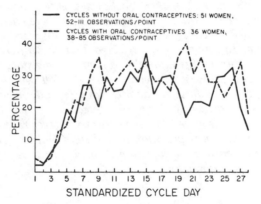

Fig. 2. Percentage of women reporting orgasm by standardized menstrual cycle day.

a definite decrease in sexual activity during the luteal phase of the menstrual cycle. In a double-blind placebo study (Udry and Morris, 1970), we found the luteal decline in sexual activity present in women during non-pill cycles, while women on contraceptive pills did not show the luteal decline.[3] Figures 1 and 2 present these data for comparison with data to be presented in this paper.

[3] For pill cycles, we have observed a *rise* in frequency of intercourse during the luteal phase. The peaks observed on days 19, 20, and 22 in Figs. 1 and 2 will not stand up under a test of significance as higher than other high points in the cycle. Therefore, until the pattern is replicated in further research we will state only that there is an "absence of a depression" in pill cycles.

In the previous paper, we suggested that the change presented by women on active pills during this period was due to the absence of endogenous progesterone normally present at this time in the cycle after ovulation. The *means* by which this absence actually affected sexual activity was not at that time considered. It is through a more detailed examination of these data that we can shed light on that question. In order to do so, we have redefined the period of interest to be the luteal phase, the period in which we have shown the pill to have affected sexual frequency. We have used the term *luteal phase* only for convenience in identification. During the menstrual cycle of women on contraceptive pills, technically there is no luteal phase We use the term in order to present comparable data for women, both with and without contraceptive suppression of the corpus luteum, during days 18 through 25 of their standardized 28-day menstrual cycle

METHODS

A complete discussion of the method of study is presented in the previously mentioned paper. In brief the final study group consisted of 51 women, all married, ranging in age from 18 to 35, none using oral contraceptives. Participants were assigned randomly to three groups and instructed to continue their regular methods of contraception because neither they nor the investigators would know whether they were receiving a contraceptive pill. The women were asked to wear pedometers and to mail in daily data slips which recorded whether or not they were menstruating that day, whether or not they had had intercourse and/or orgasm in the previous 24 hr, mileage clocked on their pedometers for the previous day, and their answers to questions concerning how they were feeling and whether their husbands had wanted intercourse. All participants sent in these data slips daily for their first cycles Each woman was given a strand of 60 numbered but unmarked capsules. After the first cycle group 1 was given lactose as a placebo, group 2 was given 0.1 mg mestranol combined with 2.0 mg norethindrone (Ortho-Novum-2), and group 3 was given 0.08 mg mestranol for the first 14 days and then 0.08 mg mestranol combined with 2.0 mg norethindrone (Ortho-Novum SQ). All capsules looked identical and not like commercial contraceptive pills. Since this study was double-blind, we were able to control the so-called psychological effects of contraceptive pills as an influence on behavior.

ALTERNATE HYPOTHESES

We pose the following possible hypotheses to explain how the absence of endogenous progesterone in the luteal phase of menstrual cycles during the use of oral contraceptives produces a level of sexual behavior which is above that occurring in natural cycles when natural progesterone is present.[4]

1. The natural progesterone acts as a general activity depressant. If this is so, then sexual behavior may be depressed as simply a single type of behavior among many. Our pedometer readings allow us to examine this possibility.

2. The natural progesterone makes women feel less well than usual, while its absence makes fewer feel less well than usual, or more feel better than usual than during its presence. This causes them to desire intercourse more frequently in the absence of endogenous progesterone and less frequently in the presence of progesterone. Our daily reports of the women's general feelings allow us to examine this possibility.

3. The natural progesterone causes the women to be less attractive to their sex partners, independent of any actual behavioral change in the females. A nonbehavioral cue such as a pheromone (chemical messenger), operating through olfaction is postulated, such as the recently demonstrated estrogen-dependent positive sex pheromone in the rhesus monkey (Michael *et al.,* 1971). This causes the men to seek coitus more frequently when the natural progesterone is absent than when it is present. A deleterious effect on sexual behavior has been convincingly demonstrated to occur in rhesus monkeys when estrogenized, ovariectomized female monkeys were given exogenous progesterone. Our daily reports from the women concerning whether or not their husbands wanted intercourse allow us to examine this possibility.

4. The natural progesterone does not in fact affect the sexual behavior, during either natural or pill cycles. Rather, the sex drive in females, like the male sex drive, is affected by androgenic hormones. If this is so, then the production of these androgens would be altered by the use of oral contraceptives, in a pattern similar to changes in sexual behavior. Comparison of our data with other reports on androgen production in females allows us to test this hypothesis.

Once we can explain how the absence of a luteal trough in sexual activity is produced in pill cycles, we may be in a position to understand through what mechanism the luteal trough comes about in natural cycles.

RESULTS

Sequential and combined cycles were first examined separately to determine whether we had different effects from the two kinds of pills. For neither intercourse, orgasm, nor "he wanted intercourse" rates were the graphs for the two types of pills different from one another. We conclude from this that the

---

[4] There is over ten times as much circulating progesterone present during the normal luteal phase as the amount present during cycles controlled by contraceptive pills (Thorneycroft and Stone, 1972). We refer to this normal luteal phase elevated level as *endogenous* or *natural progesterone,* as opposed to the low level provided by pills.

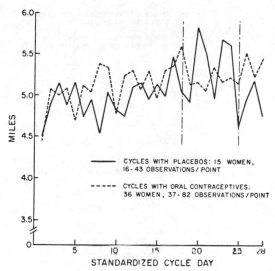

Fig. 3. Average pedometer readings in miles by standardized menstrual cycle day.

two types of pills, in spite of the different ingredients at different times, have the same effects on sexual interaction. We therefore proceeded to test the hypotheses, combining the groups on different active pills, in most cases.

1. According to the first hypothesis, the differences in sexual behavior between pill cycles and natural cycles are a manifestation of a decrease in general activity in the presence of endogenous progesterone and an absence of this decrease in the absence of endogenous progesterone. Figure 3 compares the pedometer readings during pill cycles with pedometer readings during placebo cycles. In looking at the critical luteal phase days 18 to 25, it is clear that there is no difference in pedometer readings associated with pill status. Accordingly, we reject this hypothesis as inconsistent with the data.

2. According to the second hypothesis, during pill cycles women should report feeling worse than usual less frequently during days 18 to 25 and should report feeling better than usual more frequently during this period. Figure 4 shows the proportion of women reporting that they felt better than usual by cycle day, and Fig. 5 shows the proportion reporting that they felt worse than usual. No difference of note appears between pill cycles and placebo cycles in Figs. 4 or 5. Thus we reject the hypothesis that the woman's overall sense of well-being directs the change of intercourse level during the luteal phase. This does not exclude the possibility that specifically *sexual* feelings of the woman, uncorrelated with general feelings, are responsible for the observed changes in sexual frequency. If so, the changes in sexual feelings could be related to androgen changes, discussed under hypothesis 4.

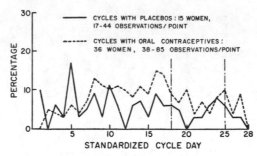

Fig. 4. Percentage of women reporting that they felt better than usual, by standardized cycle day.

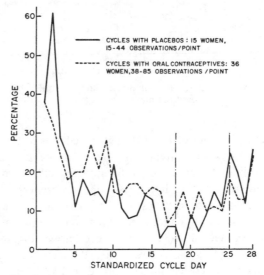

Fig. 5. Percentage of women reporting that they felt worse than usual, by standardized cycle day.

3. The third hypothesis says that independent of the woman's feelings, intercourse rates will be depressed during the luteal phase of natural cycles and will not be depressed during the same phase of pill cycles because of a nonbehavioral cue communicated to the man. This cue makes him desire coitus during the luteal phase of natural cycles less than during the same phase of pill cycles. During all reporting days, the woman indicated whether her sex partner wanted intercourse. These responses are compared for pill and natural cycles in Fig. 6. The critical period shows a greater difference between pill and natural cycles than is shown in Fig. 1, where sexual activity is recorded.

To get a more detailed picture of what is happening. we next examined individual group cycles within the three-group design. This drastically reduces

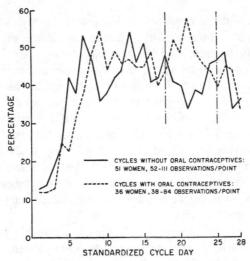

Fig. 6. Percentage of daily reports of women indicating that husband wanted intercourse, by standardized cycle day.

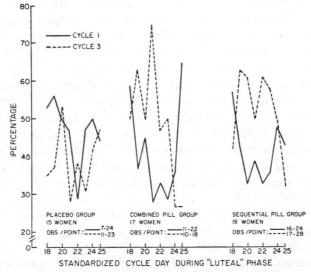

Fig. 7. Percentage of women reporting that husband wanted intercourse, by standardized cycle days 18 to 25 (luteal phase).

the number of observations on which each figure is based and therefore subjects the resulting figures to far greater random fluctuations. Under these circumstances, only the most clear-cut patterns remain. Figure 7 shows days 18 to 25 for the first and third cycle of each group. During cycle 1, no pills were taken by any group. During the third cycle, the placebo group was in the second month of taking placebos, and the combined and sequential groups were in the second month of active pills. In Fig. 7 although it is less clear in the placebo group, all groups show a luteal trough on "he wanted" during cycle 1. During the third cycle, the placebo group shows the same pattern as in the first cycle The two groups on active pills, however, show a dramatic rise in "he wanted." We have omitted cycle 2 only to keep the graphs from becoming too confusing. The second cycle for the placebo group does not differ from cycles 1 and 3. The second cycle for each of the active pill groups lies between the first and third cycles, suggesting that the full effect of the pill is not evident until the women have been on active pills for more than one cycle. It is in retrospect unfortunate that we did not keep the women under treatment for a longer period of time so that we could see if the discrepancy between pill and natural cycles continued to increase with longer treatment.

From the data in Figs. 6 and 7, it is not possible to reject the third hypothesis. The clarity of the change in male desire patterns remains even when we examine individual cycles for individual groups.

4. According to the fourth hypothesis, cyclic androgen production is responsible for the observed sex cycles. Altered androgen levels, specifically testosterone, a hormone which has been associated with sex drive, will change under pill administration and cause altered sex patterns. It has been noted in females that testosterone production follows a cyclical pattern, with evident peaks of output during the ovulatory and luteal phases of the normal menstrual cycle (Ismail *et al.*, 1968; Lobotsky *et al.*, 1964). Another study found that the cyclical changes were eliminated in women on contraceptive pills (Apostolakis *et al.*, 1966). If the production of testosterone were affecting the "feeling state" of the women, we would expect these patterns to be similar. Neither is the case. Testosterone production during the normal menstrual cycle is high during the luteal phase, while in pill cycles it is not. Sex frequency, on the other hand, is low during the luteal phase of natural cycles and high during the luteal period of pill cycles. Without measuring androgens daily, we cannot definitely exclude the androgen hypothesis. But the contradiction between our patterns of observed sexual behavior and patterns of androgen production in previous studies reduces the probability of androgen implication in the patterns observed.

There remains to be explored the possibility that the "he wanted" data do not accurately reflect the male's desire but are simply an imputation to him by the woman on the basis of her own feeling or an after-the-fact conclusion following intercourse. The data argue against this interpretation in two ways. First, nothing in her reports of her general feelings supports this interpretation (Fig. 4). Second, if we examine the intercourse data by individual cycles by groups, as we did for the "he wanted" data in Fig. 7, the differences between pill experience and no-pill experience are not as large, although they do follow the same general pattern.

Our data do not positively exclude other interpretations, but they are completely consistent with the idea that the differences in the patterning of sexual frequency between women who are on active pills and women who are not on active pills are brought about by the male's responses to differences in nonbehavioral cues emitted by the woman. This is the same conclusion that Michael reached in studying the effect of contraceptive pills on the sexual behavior of the rhesus monkey (Michael and Plant, 1969).

The nature of the effect we have observed in humans, however, is quite different from that reported in monkeys by Michael. He found that after their sex partners had been on pills for *several* months, the sexual performance of the males was progressively interfered with. He did not mention an effect on cyclicity. We cannot say that we would not have obtained the same effect as he observed had we used dosages as high as his (about five times as great by body weight as ours), for as long as he did. During the period of our observation, there was no indication that the pills affected sexual behavior in any way except to alter its distribution during the menstrual cycle.

CONCLUSIONS

The depression of sexual frequency for natural cycles during the luteal phase and the lack of depression for pill cycles are probably a function of the presence of endogenous progesterone during natural cycles and its absence during pill cycles. Our data are consistent with (but not direct enough to establish) the following explanation of this function: The presence of endogenous progesterone during the natural cycles affects the male so that he does not desire coitus as frequently during the luteal phase. The absence of endogenous progesterone during pill cycles removes whatever restraint progesterone had on the male. Since there are no data indicating that female feelings and overall activity level are changed, we believe a nonbehavioral mechanism should be sought in humans to account for the change in male desire. This interpretation is consistent with Michael's observation in rhesus monkeys that males were not sexually attracted to and not sexually effective with females treated with progesterone (Michael *et al.*, 1967*b*).

REFERENCES

Apostolakis, M., Becker, H., and Voight, K. D. (1966). The effect of lynestrenol administration on testosterone, estrogen, pregnanediol and total gonadotropin excretion during the menstrual cycle. *Steroids* 7: 146-156.

Ismail, A. A. A., Harkness, R. A. H., and Loraine J. A. (1968). Some observations on the urinary excretion of testosterone during the normal menstrual cycle. *Acta Endocrinol. (Kbh.)* 58: 685-695.

Lobotsky, J. H. L., Wyrs, E. J., Segre, J., and Lloyd, C. W. (1964). Plasma testosterone in the normal woman. *J. Clin. Endocrinol. Metab.* 24: 1261-1265.

Michael, R. P., and Plant, T. M. (1969). Contraceptive steroids and sexual activity. *Nature* 222: 579-581.

Michael, R. P., Herbert, J., and Welegalla, J. (1967a). Ovarian hormones and the sexual behavior of the male rhesus monkey (*Macaca mulatta*) under laboratory conditions. *J. Endocrinol.* 39: 81-98.

Michael, R. P., Saayman, G., and Zumpe D. (1967b). Inhibition of sexual receptivity by progesterone in rhesus monkeys. *J. Endocrinol.* 39: 309.

Michael, R. P., Keverne, E. B., and Bonsall, R. W. (1971). Pheromones: Isolation of male sex attractants from a female primate. *Science* 172: 964-966.

Thorneycroft, I. H., and Stone, S. C. (1972). Radioimmunoassay of serum progesterone in women receiving oral contraceptive steroids. *Contraception* 5: 129-146.

Udry, J. R., and Morris, N. (1968). Distribution of coitus in the menstrual cycle. *Nature* 220: 593-596.

Udry, J. R., and Morris, N. (1970). The effect of contraceptive pills on the distribution of sexual activity in the menstrual cycle. *Nature* 227: 502-503.

23

JAMES A. KENNY

Sexuality of Pregnant and Breastfeeding Women

The effect of pregnancy and lactation on the sexual behavior of women was studied, using a retrospective questionnaire answered by a nonrandom sample of 33 women. Sexual functioning was operationally defined by four categories: desire, frequency, enjoyment, and orgasm. Five time periods were studied: the three trimesters of pregnancy, the period of breastfeeding and the period after weaning. Most of the mothers reported that their sexual behavior was "about the same" during pregnancy as before except for the third trimester, where desire, frequency, and enjoyment decreased. Eighty-two percent of the mothers felt that sex relations should continue throughout all of the pregnancy. Sexual functioning during breastfeeding was reported to be "about the same" as before pregnancy by 75% of the women. Desire returned for most women by 4 weeks after childbirth, earlier than many of them felt it safe to resume sex relations. Women who had been married longer, with more children and more breastfeeding time, reported an earlier return of sexual interest and felt it safe to resume sex relations earlier. Most women reported their sexual interest after weaning was "about the same." No one reported a decrease in sexual interest after weaning. All of the women reported breastfeeding to be enjoyable. Younger marrieds were apt to rate breastfeeding even higher than older marrieds. Also, younger marrieds felt freer about breastfeeding in public. Sexual relations continue when procreatively unfruitful and even when difficult in humans. This underscores the importance of the bonding value of sex.

INTRODUCTION

What effect do pregnancy, childbirth, and breastfeeding have on the sexual behavior of women? A nonrandom sample of 33 women was asked to complete a confidential questionnaire bearing on this question. Although the questionnaire focuses primarily on sexual intercourse one could legitimately ask whether pregnancy, childbirth, and breastfeeding (and the menstrual cycle) are a part of women's sexuality in their own right. Positive and negative factors in pregnancy and breastfeeding are explored briefly in this larger extragenital sense.

Newton (1955) argues for a broader approach to the study of female sexuality: "Sexual intercourse is, of course, just as important a phase of women's reproductive role as menstruation, pregnancy, childbirth, and lactation. However, it has often been singled out as if it were the only important part of women's sexuality and role." The Kinsey study (Kinsey, *et al.,* 1953) makes no specific mention of the effect of pregnancy and breastfeeding on women's sexual functioning. This omission is all the more glaring in a section under "Marital Coitus." Mention is made of age, education, sex techniques, etc., but there is no reference to pregnancy or breastfeeding. It would seem that even if a woman did not spend 9 or more months of her life pregnant, the fear of or hope for conception would be a factor of some significance in her sexual relations. Newton feels that the reason for this omission is that "the Kinsey study concentrates on only those portions of women's sexual behavior that are similar to what men experience." This narrowness has been considerably redressed since Kinsey's study. However, there is still a need for continued studies of female sexuality that are not limited by a male model.

REVIEW OF THE LITERATURE

Ford and Beach (1951) set human female sexuality in the context of mammalian sexuality. They point out that pregnancy is accompanied by major modifications in the hormonal balance of females, i.e., high estrogen levels. However, the closer one gets to the human female the less influence an increased estrogen level has on sexual behavior. They find a "clear-cut relationship between reproductive fertility and sexual responsiveness in females of lower mammalian species. . . . The correlation . . . is less well-defined in subhuman primates and completely obliterated in the human female. This suggests an evolutionary change involving progressive relaxation of hormonal control of feminine eroticism."

Ford and Beach offer data from 60 societies on the occurrence of sexual intercourse during pregnancy (Table I). The authors note that the sex taboo during pregnancy is usually rationalized as an attempt to prevent the fetus from injury. Further, all but two of the 21 societies that prohibit sex during all or most of the pregnancy are polygynous. This means that the husband has other legitimate sexual outlets.

The best study of sex during pregnancy to date has been done by Masters and Johnson (1966). They used two study groups: first, a group of six women whose sexual functioning was directly observed and measured in their research laboratory and, second, a group of 111 women who gave a regular verbal report as their pregnancies progressed. The six pregnant women who were directly observed ranged in age from 21 to 36. In general, their sexual responses were physiologically the same as those of nonpregnant women. Masters and Johnson did note some increased breast tenderness, a heightened arousal during the

Table I. Occurrence of Sexual Intercourse During Pregnancy (Ford and Beach, 1951)

Month of pregnancy	Societies permitting sex relations	
	%	No.
2nd	70	42
3rd–5th	63	38
6th–7th	50	30
8th	40	24
9th	25	15

second trimester, and the fact that the resolution phase (after orgasm) took longer and was less complete than in nonpregnant women.

In their study using the verbal report of 111 pregnant women, Masters and Johnson divided the material into the three trimesters. In the first trimester, most women having their first baby reported a decrease in sexual interest and responsiveness. However, of the 68 women who had delivered at least once previously, four reported an increase in sexual function, 57 reported "no change" from before they were pregnant, and seven reported a decrease. In the second trimester, the "sexual partners generally reflected a marked increase in eroticism and effectiveness of performance regardless of the parity or ages of the women interrogated." Eighty-two out of 101 women reported this increase. In the third trimester, many women reported some loss of interest. Masters and Johnson feel that this may have been due to the fact that 77 of the 101 had been warned by their physicians to avoid intercourse for at least part of the time. Thus, based on their research, one could propose the following "norms" for sexual desire and functioning during pregnancy: the same degree of sexual functioning in the first trimester, an increase in the second, and a decrease in the third.

With regard to postpartum sex, Ford and Beach report that "the majority of lower mamalian females do not normally become receptive until their young are weaned." Further, "during the first several post-partum months, the physiology of the female body is different from what it was before and during pregnancy. This is especially true if the mother nurses her infant." Finally, the authors point out that the physiology involved in breastfeeding and that involved in mating are in some ways antithetical. "Nervous stimuli evoked by suckling appear to prevent the anterior pituitary gland from secreting gonadotrophic hormones, and as a result the ovaries do not produce the sex hormones necessary to mating behavior." Ford and Beach present cross-cultural data from 66 societies with a postpartum sex taboo (Table II).

Masters and Johnson (1966) studied the sexuality of women after delivery. They report a range of delay of return of sexual desire after childbirth of from 2 or 3 weeks to over 3 months. They also report that the 24 mothers in their study

Table II. Postpartum Sex Taboo Length in 66 Societies
(Ford and Beach, 1951)

Length of taboo	Societies permitting sex relations	
	No.	Cumulative %
Short delay of 1-2 weeks	6	9
2 weeks to 1 month	15	32
1 month to 6 weeks	8	44
2-4 months	10	59
8-10 months	2	62
Until dentition, walking, etc.	5	70
Throughout lactation (2-3 years)	20	100

who were breastfeeding indicated a prompter return of sexuality and a return to higher levels of functioning than the others. In fact, three women reported experiencing orgasm during breastfeeding. Sexual arousal was the occasion of "deep guilt feelings" in 12 of the mothers. Masters and Johnson conclude with the comment that medical reasons for refraining from sexual intercourse after childbirth usually end after the third postpartum week.

METHODOLOGY

A questionnaire was developed with the assistance of Gebhard (1971) to query the recollections of women about their sexual behavior during pregnancy and breastfeeding. The questionnaire was given to 45 women known to the author. Confidentiality of the respondent was assured by providing stamped and addressed envelopes in which to return the questionnaires. Thirty-three women returned completed questionnaires. Of these 32 had breastfed their last child. One was pregnant (she answered for a previous pregnancy), and eight were actively breastfeeding.

Although there were too few subjects for extensive controlled analysis, four control variables were selected. Dichotomies were formed so that at least ten subjects fell into each group. "Length of time married" was divided into 1 to 5 years and 6 to 18 years. "Number of children" was divided into women who had only one child and those who had more than one. "Physical state during pregnancy" was split by combining "better" with "same" and "worse" with "variable." The rationale for this combination was that the "worse/variable" group felt physically worse for at least part of their pregnancy. "Total time spent breastfeeding" was divided into women who had breastfed for 1 year or less and those who had breastfed for more than 1 year. Where the differences in percent appear significant (usually 25% or more), they are commented on in the text under the appropriate topic.

A general description of the research population is as follows: number of

Table III. Sexual Relations During First Trimester

	Desire		Frequency		Enjoyment		Orgasm	
	No.	%	No.	%	No.	%	No.	%
More	7	21	8	24	4	12	2	6
Same	15	45	14	42	21	64	27	82
Less	10	30	11	33	8	24	3	9
Other	1	3	0		0		1	3
	33		33		33		33	

subjects: 33 (32 for breastfeeding section); mean age: 29.0 years (age range 22 to 43 years); mean length of time married: 7.0 years (range 1½ to 18 years); mean number of children: 2.4 (range one to ten children); mean age of youngest child: 1.9 years (range 2 months to 7 years); mean length of time breastfeeding last child: 8 months (range 2 weeks to 27 months); mean total time spent breastfeeding: 15 months (range 2 weeks to 91 months) (all children included).

RESULTS

Sexual Relations During Pregnancy

Desire, frequency, enjoyment, and orgasm are treated as separate variables in sexual functioning. In every case a plurality of women reported that their sexual functioning was the same during the first trimester as before they became pregnant (Table III). In the categories of "enjoyment" and "orgasm," the numbers reporting "about the same" increased to a majority. One third or less of the women reported a decrease in any of the categories of sexual functioning in the first trimester.

Physical State

Forty percent of the women who felt physically well during pregnancy, and only 11% of those who felt worse reported an increase in frequency of intercourse in the first trimester. A large majority of women felt "about the same" in each of the four categories in the second trimester (Table IV). Further, those

Table IV. Sexual Relations During Second Trimester

	Desire		Frequency		Enjoyment		Orgasm	
	No.	%	No.	%	No.	%	No.	%
More	8	24	8	24	6	18	4	12
Same	24	73	21	64	24	73	24	73
Less	0		4	12	3	9	4	12
Other	1	3	0		0		1	3
	33		33		33		33	

who reported "more" outnumbered those who reported "less" in each category except orgasm (a tie). This is the reverse of what happened in the first trimester, where "less" outnumbered "more" in each category. Apparently, the second trimester does not present obstacles to adequate sexual functioning. Only about one-tenth of the women reported a decrease in sexual functioning.

A plurality of women reported a decrease in desire frequency, and enjoyment during the third trimester (Table V), but a majority (52%) reported that "orgasms" were about the same as when not pregnant. A large number of women commented that the problems related to intercourse began only in the last 6 weeks. The first half of the last trimester was more like the second trimester. These comments suggest an appropriate revision in the questionnaire.

Length of Time Married

Forty percent (40%) of the young marrieds and only 11% of the old marrieds experienced a decrease in orgasms in the last trimester. A similar difference (nearly 25%) was noted in desire, frequency, and enjoyment. Apparently, the older marrieds (6 to 18 years) were not as apt to let the last trimester interfere with their sexual functioning as the younger married women. This probably reflects their greater sexual experience. It does not reflect more pregnancies for the older marrieds, since differences between the one-child mothers and the multiple mothers are not at all evident in the data.

Total Time Spent Breastfeeding

None of the more experienced breastfeeders and 42% of the less experienced ones reported a decrease in orgasms in the last trimester. Thirty-nine percent (39%) of the more experienced breastfeeders and 68% of the less experienced breastfeeders reported a decrease in sex frequency. The more experienced breastfeeders were more apt to report that frequency and orgasms were "about the same." One hypothesis to explain this might be that women who breastfeed more are or become more physical and sensual than other mothers.

Table V. Sexual Relations During Third Trimester

	Desire		Frequency		Enjoyment		Orgasm	
	No.	%	No.	%	No.	%	No.	%
More	8	24	5	15	4	12	3	9
Same	11	33	10	30	13	39	17	52
Less	14	42	18	55	16	48	8	24
Other	0		0		0		5	15
	33		33		33		33	

Continuation of Intercourse in Pregnancy

To the question "Should sexual intercourse continue throughout pregnancy?" 27 women (82%) said yes and six (18%) said no; i.e., a large majority felt that sexual intercourse should continue. The women felt that sex should stop designated a time in the last 2 months. All but one of the longer breastfeeders felt that sex should continue throughout pregnancy.

When asked about petting as an alternative to sexual intercourse the great majority favored petting to mutual climax (Table VI). One woman reported that she enjoys bringing her husband to climax by petting but feels guilty about letting him do the same to her. All four of the women who proposed that the wife should bring the husband to climax by petting were young marrieds (1 to 5 years) and less experienced breastfeeders (0 to 12 months).

Postpartum Sexual Intercourse

Most of the women (52%) felt that it was safe to resume sexual intercourse after childbirth when the vaginal discharge stopped, even if this was before the "6-week checkup" (Table VII). This corresponds with the advice of Masters and Johnson that sex relations can usually be safely resumed 3 to 4 weeks after delivery. Many women reported that desire returned before they felt that it was safe to have sex. Forty-two percent were interested at a time when only 12% felt

Table VI

"If through choice or for medical reasons sexual intercourse cannot be had at some stage of pregnancy, do you feel   that . . ."

No.	%	
2	6	Both husband and wife should abstain from any sexual activity.
4	12	The wife should bring the husband to climax by petting.
0		The husband should bring the wife to climax by petting.
27	82	Both husband and wife should reach climax by petting.
33		

Table VII. Sexual Abstention After Childbirth

Safe to resume		Interest resumes		
No.	%	No.	%	
4	12	14	42	Earlier than 4 weeks
17	52	9	27	Discharge stops (about 4 weeks)
12	36	4	12	Medical OK (about 6 weeks)
0		6	18	After 6 weeks
33		33		

that it was safe. At the other end, none of the women felt that sex relations were unsafe after 6 weeks, although 18% still reported a lack of interest.

Length of Time Married

Eighty-four percent of the older marrieds and only 40% of the younger marrieds felt that it was safe to resume sex relations after the discharge had stopped. This undoubtedly reflects the greater experience of the older marrieds, indicating that, for them, the cessation of discharge rather than the medical checkup was the signal for sex to resume. It may also reflect the more rapid return of desire in the older marrieds, since 78% of those married 6 to 18 years and 60% of the 1 to 5 year group mentioned that interest had returned by the time the discharge had stopped.

The same pattern held with number of children and total time spent breastfeeding. Those women with more children (difference of 22%, 72% to 50%) and those who had breastfed longer (difference of 37%, 85% to 48%) felt it was safe to resume sex earlier (after the discharge had stopped). More of those who breastfed longer expressed interest in resuming sex relations even before the discharge had stopped (54% to 32%).

Postpartum Sex

Only 18% of the women in this group felt that their sexual interests declined as a result of childbirth (Table VIII). Childbirth itself was not seen as a major deterrent to postpartum sexual enjoyment. Write-in comments included the note that sexual experience was more likely than childbirth to cause a greater interest in sex and, further, that problems in the marriage were more likely than a fear of childbirth to cause a decrease in sexual interest.

Number of Children

Forty-three percent of the multiple mothers and only 8% of those with one child reported that childbirth increased their sexual desire. The same trend is seen in "total time spent breastfeeding," where 46% of the longer breastfeeders and only 16% of those who breastfed 1 year or less felt childbirth had heightened their sexual interest.

Table VIII. Effect of Childbirth on Sexual Desire

No.	%	
10	30	Made you more interested
17	52	Made little or no difference
6	18	Made you less interested

Advantages and Disadvantages of Pregnancy and Breastfeeding

The primary advantages of being pregnant reported by this group are clearly psychological ("feel creative," "fulfillment") (Table IX). The primary disadvantages of pregnancy as reported are physical ones (Table X).

All 32 of the mothers found breastfeeding "enjoyable," and 72% of them went so far as to say it was "exceptionally meaningful" (Table XI). None of the breastfeeders felt the experience was neutral or disagreeable Apparently, there is little ambivalence; no one in this group seemed to breastfeed out of a sense of duty.

Eighty-seven percent of the younger marrieds and 59% of the older marrieds found breastfeeding "exceptionally meaningful." This tendency is reversed,

Table IX. Advantages of Being Pregnant

No.	%	Rank	
10	30	1	Felt creative ("wonderful joy of having a living being within you," etc.)
9	27	2	Feeling of fulfillment (felt important, special, feminine, etc.)
9	27	2	No fear of getting pregnant (can relax with sex; no need to think of contraceptives; etc.)
6	18	4	Physical well-being (feel better physically; face blemishes disappear, no blemishes; large bust; etc.)
5	15	5	Anticipation (something to look forward to; preparing and planning for a baby; etc.)
5	15	5	Enjoy the extra attention
2	6	7	Feel closer to husband and family
2	6	7	None ("no other way to have a baby")
48			

Table X. Disadvantages of Being Pregnant

No.	%	Rank	
20	61	1	Physical discomfort (sick to stomach; tired and lack energy; heartburn; can't breathe; frequent urination, etc.)
6	18	2	Awkwardness (too big; clumsy; full of arms and legs, etc.)
4	12	3	Activities restricted (diet; sleep; can't play tennis; etc.)
3	9	4	Psychological upset (become emotional; low frustration tolerance; etc.)
3	9	4	None
2	6	6	Clothes won't fit
2	6	6	Too many babies
1	3	8	Unfit world ("have I a right to bring a child into this dismal world?")
41			

Table XI. Attitudes Toward Breastfeeding

No.	%	
23	72	An exceptionally meaningful experience
9	28	Enjoyable
0		Neutral—just a necessary part of infant care
0		A bothersome chore for the infant's sake
0		Definitely disagreeable
32		

Table XII. Breastfeeding in Social Groups

No.	%	"Would you feel comfortable or at ease breastfeeding . . ."
32	100	With your husband present?
31	97	With female friends and relatives present?
20	63	With female and male friends and relatives present?
13	41	With practically anybody present?⁻

however, when number of children is considered. Sixty-four percent of the one-child mothers and 76% of the multiple mothers saw their breastfeeding experiences as "exceptionally meaningful." This same trend is noted in total time spent breastfeeding. Those who breastfed longer (77%) were more apt to see breastfeeding as "exceptionally meaningful" than those who breastfed for 1 year or less (68%). In other words, positive feelings about breastfeeding increased with time spent breastfeeding and number of children, but decreased with length of time married.

Eighty-three percent of those who felt worse and 57% of those who felt the same or better during their pregnancy saw breastfeeding as "exceptionally meaningful." This could be a case of those who paid a higher price valuing the "merchandise" more.

With respect to feeling comfortable about breastfeeding in social groups, the biggest drop (97% to 63%) occurred when males other than the husband were present (Table XII). Still, a majority of mothers (63%) claimed that they felt at ease breastfeeding among known persons of either sex. Three women wrote in that their being at ease depended more on the attitude of the people present toward breastfeeding. One woman reported feeling at ease breastfeeding in the presence of friends but not of relatives. Forty-one percent reported feeling at ease breastfeeding in almost any group.

Eighty-percent of the younger marrieds and only 47% of the older marrieds reported feeling at ease breastfeeding in the presence of known persons of both sexes. This same trend is present, but less obvious when number of children is considered. Seventy-three percent of the one-child mothers and 57% of the multiple mothers reported feeling at ease in a known but mixed group. This trend does not hold with time spent breastfeeding, where the percentages are about even.

Three-fourths of the mothers reported that breastfeeding had little effect on their sexual lives (Table XIII). The control variables did not seem to be significant in causing any major fluctuations. However, these questions on breastfeeding occasioned more write-in comments than any other part of the questionnaire.

Several mothers commented that they experienced less desire during the first few months and the same or more desire later on. Since almost everyone observes a sex abstention of from 3 to 6 weeks after delivery, the questions on breastfeeding might have been split into "first 2 months after childbirth" and "2 months and longer after childbirth." This would separate the physical recovery after childbirth from the specific influence of lactation on sexual behavior.

One mother wrote in some detail about the relationship between breastfeeding and sex, summing up many of the other comments: "You have to distinguish between the first couple of months after childbirth and the later breastfeeding period. To me, sex is best of all during the later breastfeeding period because (1) I feel physically better than at any other time (2) no fear of pregnancy and no contraceptives needed because for me breastfeeding is a 100% effective contraceptive for at least one year after the birth of a baby, and (3) there is something about nursing a little baby that gives you an 'all's right with the world' kind of feeling. I feel so happy and loving toward my whole family, husband, and other children as well as the baby. Sex just seems to be a nice natural expression of this good feeling." Obviously, it is difficult here to isolate the specific effects of lactation on sexual behavior from other postpartum

None of the mothers reported less sexual interest after breastfeeding (Table XIV). Most said their interest remained "about the same." The only noteworthy

Table XIII. Sexual Relations During Breastfeeding

	Desire		Frequency		Orgasm	
No.	%	No.	%	No.	%	
More	2	6	2	6	3	9
Same	24	75	25	78	24	75
Less	4	13	4	13	3	9
Other	2	6	1	3	2	6
	32		32		32	

Table XIV. Interest in Sexual Relations After Weaning

No.	%	
5	16	More interested than when you were breastfeeding
18	56	About the same
0		Less interested
9	28	Other (haven't weaned yet)

Table XV. Advantages of Breastfeeding

No.	%	Rank	
22	69	1	Closeness to baby (symbiosis; relationship with baby; forces you to spend time with baby; etc.)
16	50	2	Convenient and practical (no worries over spoiled milk, formula, or sterile bottles; great for trips; saves time; easy; etc.)
11	34	3	Emotional fulfillment (knowledge that baby depends on you for survival; satisfaction in supplying food and love; feel important; sense of accomplishment; wonderful experience; holding a soft warm baby; etc.)
9	28	4	Physical advantages for baby (advantages of human milk over cow's milk; fewer respiratory ailments and allergies; no colic; natural immunities; etc.)
6	19	5	Psychological advantages for baby (baby is contented; knows he's loved; sense of security; etc.)
4	13	6	Physical advantages for mother (figure comes back sooner; draws uterus back more quickly; keeps mom super-thin; breasts are pretty containers; etc.)
2	6	7	Saves money
1	3	8	Physical pleasure for mother (oral stimulation of the engorged breast is very erotic)
1	3	8	Baby's excretions less unpleasant (stools and vomit not so smelly)
72			

Table XVI. Disadvantages of Breastfeeding

No.	%	Rank	
12	38	1	Can tie mother down (tend not to leave infant with babysitter; can't work an eight-hour day; feel uneasy breastfeeding in a group; etc. Note: At least four of the women gave this as a "tongue in cheek" disadvantage, implying that it was not so bad to be tied down by the baby)
7	22	2	None
5	16	3	Physical unpleasantness for mother (breasts are sometimes uncomfortably full; milk leaks; etc.)
5	16	3	Physical appearance (can't wear certain clothes; can cause a weight increase, etc.)
5	16	3	Father can't participate or help (dad feels left out; father can't help out)
3	9	6	Nuisance (night feedings; less sex; baby won't take bottle)
2	6	7	Birth control a problem (rhythm and pill can't be used; too much female hormone in the milk)
2	6	7	Hard for mother to stop breastfeeding
1	3	9	Problem for baby (baby gains less weight)
42			

difference among the control variables occurred under "total time spent breast-feeding." Thirty-one percent of the longer breastfeeders and 5% of those who breastfed less reported that they were more interested in sex after weaning.

Ranking high among advantages of breastfeeding are psychological factors ("closeness to baby," "fulfillment") and practical ones ("convenient," "easy") (Table XV). It should be noted that 22% of the women reported that breastfeeding had no disadvantages (Table XVI).

DISCUSSION

The sexual functioning of pregnant women as reported in this study is generally the same as for nonpregnant women. This is in spite of the fact that the pregnant women in this study are an unusual group: all but one went on to breastfeed their infants. Meyer (1969) reports that only 18% of women in the United States leave the hospital breastfeeding. This similarity of prepregnancy and pregnancy sexuality flies in the face of hormonal changes but is consistent with Ford and Beach's finding that there is less hormonal control of female eroticism as one moves up the evolutionary scale from lower to higher mammalian species. However, there remains some considerable interdiction of female sexuality during pregnancy in many human cultures. Of 60 societies studied, 30% prohibit sex relations from the second month of pregnancy and 50% from the sixth month on. In other words, despite the relaxation of hormonal control, there is still some cultural reluctance to permit sexual functioning to continue freely during pregnancy.

Masters and Johnson report that sexual functioning is the same as before pregnancy during the first trimester. There is an increase during the second trimester and a decrease in the third trimester. The present study defines sexual functioning in four categories: desire, frequency, enjoyment, and orgasm. Most of the women in the present study reported that all four categories of sexual behavior were "about the same" during the first two trimesters as before pregnancy. Then in the third trimester, desire, frequency, and enjoyment decreased, but orgasms remained "about the same." An obvious explanation for the relatively higher number of orgasms is the corresponding decrease in sexual frequency. Another possible explanation would be the increased congestion in the genital area which may crave release. The present data do not support the finding of Masters and Johnson that there is an increase in sexual functioning over prepregnant levels in the second trimester. Otherwise the results are comparable. This support for a general continuation of normal sexual functioning during pregnancy should be evidence that the impact of morning sickness in the first trimester and awkwardness in the last need not and does not significantly impair sexual behavior.

Ford and Beach report a postpartum sex taboo which lasts from 2 to 4 months for half of the societies reported on, and longer for the rest. Masters and

Johnson report a range of from 2 weeks to 3 months in the return of sexual desire among women in the United States. Almost half of the women in the present study reported a resumption of sexual interest earlier than 4 weeks after parturition. Yet only 12% of these same women felt that it was safe to resume sex relations that soon. Masters and Johnson report that there was a prompter return of sexual desire and a return to higher levels of sexual functioning among breastfeeding women than among women not breastfeeding. Thus the earlier return of sexual desire in the present study group may reflect the fact that these women are breastfeeders. When other variables are considered, a picture emerges of the women who have been married longer, with more children, and more breastfeeding time feeling that it was safe to resume sex relations earlier (after the discharge had stopped) and reporting an earlier return of sexual interest (even before the discharge had stopped). Thus age and experience seem positively correlated with sexual functioning.

However, this "age and experience" factor does not affect breastfeeding as positively as it affects sexual relations. Those who had breastfed longer were more apt to rate breastfeeding as "exceptionally meaningful." But this stimulation is reversed when "length of time married" is considered: 87% of the younger marrieds and only 59% of the older marrieds found breastfeeding an "exceptionally meaningful experience." Further, it is the younger marrieds and the one-child mothers who felt more at ease breastfeeding in a known group of mixed sex. Here again, it is the younger mothers who have the freer attitude It is possible that the older mothers are less idealistic and more honest. However, since this was a retrospective study, the more tenable explanation is that this represents a generation change, with the younger mothers possessing freer attitudes toward breastfeeding in public.

All the women in this group reported that they enjoyed breastfeeding The major reasons given were psychological ("closeness to baby," "emotional fulfillment") and practical ("convenient," "easy"). If breastfeeding is as enjoyable and fulfilling as these women say it is, then one might wonder why so few women (18% choose this option, even temporarily. Further, the reasons why women are reluctant to breastfeed in public could profitably be explored.

Finally, the questionnaire itself needs some revision. This present research should be taken as a pilot study. In future studies of this nature, the social class of the mother should be determined. Also, the third trimester of pregnancy ought to be split in half since it is generally the last 6 weeks that seem to affect sexual functioning. Further, the breastfeeding period might be split into the period before sexual relations are resumed, the period of transition, and thereafter. An even better approach might be to have a questionnaire filled out month-by-month during pregnancy and lactation, rather than employ a retrospective procedure. As for sampling technique, a stratified random sample should be obtained which permits adequate consideration of lower-class women.

The pregnancy group should be a separate group from the breastfeeding group, since breastfeeding in our culture is probably atypical. In our country, breastfeeding mothers tend to cluster in certain social classes, and they form a minority among mothers of any class in our society. Finally, breastfeeding itself needs more careful definition. A minimum duration of 6 months of breastfeeding for such a study would be advisable.

REFERENCES

Brecher, R., and Brecher, E. (1966). *An Analysis of Human Sexual Response*, Signet, New York.

Ford, C., and Beach, F. (1951). *Patterns of Sexual Behavior*, Perennial (Harper & Row), New York.

Gebhard, P. (Director, Indiana University Institute for Sex Research) (1971). Personal conversation.

Kinsey, A., Pomeroy, W., Martin, C., and Gebhard, P. (1953). *Sexual Behavior in the Human Female*, Pocket Books, New York.

Masters, W., and Johnson, V. (1966). *Human Sexual Response*, Little Brown, Boston.

Meyer, H. (1969). Breastfeeding in the United States: Report of a 1966 national survey with comparable 1946 and 1956 data. *Child and Family* 8: 230-239.

Newton, N. (1955). *Maternal Emotions*, Psychosomatic Medicine Monograph No. 13, Hoeber, New York.

Newton, N. (1971). Trebly sensuous woman. *Psychol. Today* 5(2): 68-71 and 98-99.

24

JACK H. HEDBLOM[1]

Dimensions of Lesbian Sexual Experience

Sixty-five female homosexuals, ranging in age from 18 to 55, completed a research questionnaire exploring their sexual relationships. Twenty-eight percent of the sample had become aware of their homosexual orientation between ages 6 and 10. First homosexual fantasies occurred between the ages of 11 and 15 for another 42%. More than two-thirds engaged in their first homosexual contact before the age of 20. These initial homosexual contacts were not exploitative. Rather, the respondents had been willing, cooperative partners. At the time of initial experience, there were as many who were seducers as there were those who were seduced. Forty percent achieved orgasm at the time of their first homosexual experience. Physical experience with another female preceded their entry into the homosexual community by several years. Nearly nine out of ten dated males during their homosexual careers, and more than half the respondents had had sexual experience with a male. A large number of female sexual partners was not the pattern of the respondents; four out of five had had physical intimacies with fewer than eight women.

INTRODUCTION

The findings reported are part of a larger study done in Philadelphia between 1964 and 1970. In its entirety, the study explored the social and attitudinal dimensions of the lesbian community. Combining participant observation and traditional survey techniques, it was intended to be exploratory in nature, generating only nominal data. It examined the process of becoming homosexual with special regard to age at first fantasy about women, age at first physical experience, and finally the age and process involved in identification with the homosexual community. Heterosexual physical experiences were explored with regard to the acts themselves, derived satisfactions, and the circumstances surrounding them. The administration of the questionnaire proved difficult during the pretest period. The male sex of the interviewer caused many potential interviewees to refuse cooperation. For this reason, the data were collected by a field interviewer who was herself homosexual.

[1] Assistant Professor of Sociology, Wichita State University, Wichita, Kansas.

Questions regarding sexual practices appeared in two places in the questionnaire. Some questions with regard to fantasies, initial experiences, subsequent experiences, and frequency of sexual acts appeared in the principal body of the questionnaire. The majority of questions dealing with sexual activities occurred in a section that was optional. Sixty-four of 65 respondents completed this section.

The sample was comprised of 65 lesbians ranging in age from 18 to 55 (see Tables I through IV for summaries of the data obtained). Thirty percent were strangers met in homosexual bars or through friends. Twenty percent were friends of the field investigator. The remaining 50% of the sample completing the questionnaire were slight acquaintances or acquaintances of close friends. Thirty-one of the sample were presently sharing a homosexual marriage arrangement, while 34 were not. Occupations and educational achievements were distributed from unskilled to professional and from elementary school to graduate university training.

The data were grouped for comparative purposes into age groups with an interval of 5 years and into homosexually married and unmarried.

Table I. Total Sample Characteristics

A. Age		Married	Unmarried	Total
6	41-45	3	2	5
5	36-40	4	3	7
4	31-35	4	3	7
3	26-30	9	18	27
2	21-25	11	7	18
1	16-20	0	1	1

46 of 65 total or 70% of sample are 30 years old or less
20 or 31 married or 68% of married sample are 30 years old or less
26 of 34 unmarried or 76% of unmarried sample are 30 years old or less

B. Years of schooling				
Graduate work		3	3	6
College	Graduate	3	3	6
	3 years	1	4	5
	2 years	3	2	5
	1 year	3	4	7
High school	Graduate	15	15	30
	3 years	2	2	4
	2 years		1	1
	1 year	1		1
Grade	8			
	7			
	6			
	5			

Table I. Continued

C. Occupation

Professional	4	5	9
Technical	5	6	11
Skilled	6	8	14
Semiskilled	5	12	17
Unskilled	5	2	7
Blue collar	5		5
No answer	1	1	2

D. Religious affiliation

Protestant	9	12	21
Catholic	16	16	32
Jew	1	2	3
Other	5	3	8
(1 no answer)			

E. Race (self-defined)

White	31	33	64
Negro		1	1
Mongol			
Other			

F. Marital status (heterosexual)

Single	24	33	57
Married	1		1
Separated	3		3
Divorced	3	1	4

G. Children

Male	2
Female	4
None	61

Table II. Religious Preference by Age Group[a]

Group	Total	Protestant	Catholic	Jew	Other
1. 16-20	1				1
2. 21-25	18	6	9	1	2
3. 26-30	27	9	14	1	3
4. 31-35	7	3	3		1
5. 36-40	7	1	3	1	1
6. 41+	5	2	3		
Totals[b]		21	32	3	8

[a] Race distribution was one Negro (she is in 26-30 age category) and 64 white.

[b] One no answer.

Table III. Marital Status by Age Group

Group	Total	Single	Married	Separated	Divorced
1. 16-20	1	1			
2. 21-25	18	16		1	1
3. 26-30	27	24	1	1	1
4. 31-35	7	6			1
5. 36-40	7	6		1	
6. 41+	6	4			1
Totals		57	1	3	4

Table IV. Parental Occupations and Education[a]

A. Parental occupations		Father	Mother	Total
		10	6	16
Professional		7	3	10
Technical		20	3	23
Skilled		9	40	49
Semiskilled		4	1	5
Unskilled			2	2
Blue collar				
		50	55	105
B. Parental years of school				
Graduate work		2	2	4
College	Graduate	10	3	13
	3 years			
	2 years	2	6	8
	1 year		1	1
High school	Graduate	22	21	43
	3 years		2	2
	2 years	4	1	5
	1 year	2	7	9
Grade	8	2	5	7
	7	3	5	8
	6	4	3	7
	5	2	1	3
Totals		53	57	110

[a] Figures do not total 65 for mother or father because not all respondents answered the question.

Respondents manifested a greatly varied educational experience. This background ranged from 1 year of high school to graduate school. The largest percentage of the sample were high school graduates who had not attended college. Forty-six percent of the sample, however, had attended college or were in the process of attending college. The pressure on the homosexual female to obtain a college education or vocational training is greater than it is on the average female in our society. The lesbian cannot look to a well-educated male to support her during her life, nor can she become a housewife and rely on her femininity to provide a living for her. The need for training and education is as great for her, therefore, as it is for the breadwinner male. Occupationally, this is reinforced in that 48% of the sample could be classified as skilled or semiskilled workers, with 32% fitting into the professional category. The female homosexual community clearly reflects the pressures toward occupational achievement.

DEFINITION–THE LESBIAN

For the purposes of this study, we defined the lesbian as a female who focuses her sexual attentions, fantasies, and activities upon members of her own sex. Persons who are so defined must identify themselves as homosexual and, as Goffman (1963) stated,

> participate in a special community of understanding wherein members of one's own sex are defined as the most desirable sex objects and sociability is energetically organized around the pursuit and entertainment of these objects.

Homosexuality is a stigmatized social adjustment. This stigmatization has resulted in the creation of a subculture and a status system based on what the individual is rather than what she might become. Commitment to a unique community of homosexuals not only provides an accepting milieu for the homosexual to interact in but also represents a kind of problem-solving behavior.

In evaluating any data relevant to homosexuality, the impact of participation in a deviant subculture must be considered. The simple fact of being homosexual creates innumerable difficulties in playing basic social roles. Being homosexual affects associations, entertainment patterns, and occupational roles, as well as delimiting the possibility of certain types of social mobility. Being a homosexual, male or female, eventually affects all family relationships, including those with parents and siblings. The social and sexual career of the lesbian is focused primarily upon her sex identification and places her in a special relationship to the larger society and to the conventional patterns of moving through life cycles that characterize that society (*cf.* Gagnon and Simon, 1969). The homosexual commitment, therefore, provides the hub around which the rest of the lesbian's life is arranged.

COMING OUT

In evaluating the coming-out process, defined as the emergent identification with homosexuality and growing self-awareness as a homosexual, we must consider that women are women first and homosexuals second. It is important to note that lesbians are exposed to the subtle influences and experiences as are the heterosexual females, many of which occur before actual sex experience.

Women constitute a more homogeneous group than males by virtue of their more rigid and organized socialization process. Within this frame of reference, we cannot view the female homosexual to be more concerned than the male homosexual with the establishment of the home and more likely to relate the act of sex to the psychological state of love. We would expect her to be more passive in her search for a mate-partner even in the established marketplace of the homosexual community. We would expect, therefore, the social career and the emergent sexual commitment of the female homosexual to parallel those of the female heterosexual. The findings of this study tend to reinforce this hypothesis to the extent that lesbian interaction with nonhomosexual males typically finds the lesbian playing an almost stereotypically passive role, sexually complementary to the straight male. Women are trained to be less aggressive and assertive in their roles and to cultivate sentimentality. We socialize our females to be mothers.

(This study also explored attitudes of female homosexuals toward male homosexuals. The findings tentatively supported the contention that lesbians have more in common with female heterosexuals than they do with male homosexuals. In fact, lesbians appear to view the male homosexual as being more promiscuous, more flighty, having more extremes in behavior that would tend to identify him as a deviant. He was interpreted as having more "one-night stands," as tending less toward the generation of a stable relationship. The data support the contention that female homosexuals tend to view male homosexuals pejoratively.)

The coming-out process involves many adjustment problems. The lesbian must contend with her differences from the straight community. The knowledge of her commitment affects friendships and dating patterns associated with girls emerging into the competitive sexual marketplace. She must also contend with the prospect of rejection on the basis of her condition.

Given expectations of family and peers, the lesbian may well repress or deny initial feelings of interest in women, resulting in a pretense of heterosexual patterns. Should such pretenses continue, the result may be pregnancy or marriage. The remaining choice is that of leading two lives, a surface life ostensibly nonhomosexual and a secret life involved with others who share similar status and adjustment problems. The fact that this problem is created by the nonhomosexual world is of little importance.

SEXUAL AWARENESS

Given the developmental pattern of the heterosexual female, it was felt that awareness of homosexuality would affect either grammar school or high school experiences. When asked if self-recognition of homosexuality affected elementary school experience, only 19% of the sample indicated that it had (Table V). Sixty-seven percent of the sample indicated that their high school experience was not affected by their awareness of their own homosexual commitment (Table VI). Given peer support for heterosexual dating patterns, as well as the possibility of the respondent feeling that what was happening to her with regard to her own sexual feelings was a passing phase and that all would be normal soon, these findings were not surprising. Regardless of her growing awareness of her own homosexuality, the lesbian continues her heterosexual dating patterns for some considerable period of time. She has little or no support from the homosexual community for her homosexuality unless she is immediately and deeply involved with it. She perceives pressures toward what is culturally defined as a more ordinary life style from peers and from her family, who generally tend to define this period in her life as the "fun period." As she matures, there is a decreasing emphasis on dating activities from peers and family accompanied by an emphasis on her emergent role as an adult female. With maturity and eventual emancipation from the home comes greater opportunity to explore other forms of life style and sexual adjustment. It is ordinarily at this point that serious involvement with the homosexual community begins.

The lesbian's involvement and eventual identification with the homosexual community closely parallel the heterosexual female's emancipation from high school peers and family and her emergence into the adult world.

Most female homosexuals maintain a front or posture of heterosexuality. Eighty-four percent of our sample indicated that they were comfortable with nonhomosexuals. Their comfort in interacting with the straight community suggests the effectiveness of this heterosexual front; it makes possible a considerable exchange between homosexual and heterosexual communities. The posture of heterosexuality allows the lesbian to act as a single girl in the nonhomosexual community. Since she was socialized in the straight community, such behavior is natural to her regardless of her sexual commitment. That she comfortably

Table V. Did Being a Homosexual Affect Your Elementary School Experience?

	Married	Unmarried	Total
Yes	3	9	12
No	27	25	52
No answer	1	0	1

Table VI. Did Being a Homosexual Affect Your High School Experience?

	Married	Unmarried	Total
Yes	9	13	22
No	22	21	43
No answer	0	0	0

interacts with the heterosexual community indicates that she has adjusted to her role in the homosexual community and is comfortable with it.

In order to examine the process of identification with homosexuality from initial awareness of sexual identity to permanent involvement with the homosexual community, we should examine the ages at which various stages occur.

Respondents indicated that typically first homosexual fantasies occurred between the ages of 11 and 15 (42%). Twenty-eight percent indicated that they were aware of their own homosexual inclinations between the ages of 6 and 10. Nineteen of the sample or 30% indicated awareness as occurring after 15. Sixteen of this group indicated awareness as occurring between the ages of 16 and 20. When asked when their first homosexual contact occurred, 79% of the sample indicated that it occurred before the age of 20. Twenty-one percent stated that they experienced it before the age of 15. Only eight of the sample indicated that the contact occurred before the age of 10.

The data suggest, therefore, that the female homosexual is aware of her homosexuality well before the age of 20. This awareness precedes by some considerable period of time her initial physical contact. Her initial homosexual contacts were not exploitative or characterized by the respondent's seduction into a homosexual posture. Instead, they were willing, cooperative exploration of homosexual tendencies. Table VII indicates clearly that the sample contains as many seducers as seduced on first contact.

Fourteen percent of respondents indicated that this first physical contact had occurred before the age of 10. Seventy-nine percent of the respondents had a physical experience before the age of 20 and before entry into the homosexual community. Only 20% of respondents reported that their first physical experience had occurred after the age of 20 (typically before 25). These respondents indicated that they chose other homosexuals as their principal social group between the ages of 20 and 30, with only 45% of the sample making this choice before 25 years of age and another 35% between the ages of 26 and 30. Only four of the sample made this decision after 30. Physical experience thus precedes entry into the homosexual community by a considerable period of time. Membership in the homosexual community is, therefore, the result of feelings and events not necessarily sexual in nature resulting in awareness of self as homosexual and acceptance of the self as homosexual. By increasing involvement in the homosexual community, the female homosexual minimizes the stigma of her

Table VII. Were You at First Contact (1) Seduced or (2) Seducer?

	Married	Unmarried	Total
Seduced	14	16	30
Seducer	16	17	33
No answer	1	1	2

identity as something different from the normal population and finds support for her emotional as well as social career.

DATING PATTERNS

Although the frequency of dating patterns is similar to that of heterosexual dating patterns, the nature of the homosexual date differs from the heterosexual counterpart. Due to the covert nature of homosexuality, dating involves attendance at house parties, group outings, and other collective activities which conceal their basically homosexual nature. Sixty percent of the sample indicated that they relied on the network of friends and associates in the homosexual community for dates or other forms of interaction.

Despite clear-cut boundaries between heterosexual and homosexual worlds, interchanges between them occur. Eighty-nine percent of respondents reported that they had dated men during their homosexual careers. Thirty-seven of the 65 respondents also indicated that they had had sexual experience with men. Apparently, dating heterosexual men has sexual connotations. Respondents indicated that they dated straight men more often then they did gay men; in fact, 85% of the respondents indicated that they did not date gay men exclusively. Respondents typically dated once a week, with homosexually married couples dating less frequently than homosexually unmarried persons. Seventy-nine percent of respondents after being instructed to disregard their present involvement indicated that they dated at least once a week or four or more times per month.

SEX ACTIVITY

It is a popular myth in the heterosexual world that homosexuality occurs as the result of early corruption of children by persons already practiced in the "perversion." The data indicated that the initial homosexual contact was the result of mutual exploration occurring between partners or was initiated by the respondent herself. Of the 65 respondents, 51 or 79% indicated that they had thought about women sexually prior to their first physical contact. Only 13 (21%) indicated that they had not. According to the data, 95% of the sample had their first sexual fantasy about women before the age of 20 and 46 or 70% before the age of 15. Significantly, 16% of the sample indicated that the fantasy occurred before the age of 10. Ninety-three percent of the sample had such fantasies before the age of 20.

The majority of the sample had had their first physical homosexual experience before the age of 20, with 22 or 34% before the age of 15 and 29 or 45% between the ages of 16 and 20. Seventy-nine percent of respondents indicated that the first homosexual contact in the physical sense occurred before the age of 20. Twenty-one percent experienced such a physical experience before the age of 15. Only eight respondents indicated this as occurring before the age of 10. For an additional 20%, physical expression of their commitment occurred between 21 and 25 years of age.

When respondents were asked to describe what roles they played in their initial physical lesbian experience, approximately 50% (30 of 63 answering this question) stated that they played the role of the seducer. Respondents also indicated that they had already focused on women as their principal sex goal. Those remaining described their role as being seduced or somewhat passive. Typically then, fantasy occurs before physical contact. Thus physical contact is apparently accompanied by a willingness to explore the possibility of a relationship with another woman.

Further exploring the nature of the first sexual contact, respondents were asked whether the contact involved simply manual stimulation or involved the more complete act of oral-genital contact (cunnilingus). It was not expected that cunnilingus would occur on first contact. Of the sample of 65, 17 or 27% indicated that oral sex had been a part of their first contact, while 73% indicated that it had not.

An attempt was made to ascertain the point at which respondents achieved orgasm. We defined this as sexual satisfaction. The question provided three possible answers ranging from first contact to subsequent sexual contact. Of the sample, three individuals did not answer the question, and 26 or 40% indicated that they had achieved orgasm on first contact. Three or 5% indicated that they had done so on second contact and 33 or 51% on subsequent contacts.

These data suggest a readiness on the part of the respondents to engage in homosexual activities as well as fantasies about such activities. Although approximately 60% of respondents indicated achieving orgasm on subsequent contacts, 40% of respondents indicated orgasm on first contact. The immediacy of sexual gratification might be explained by the similarity of homosexual acts, i.e., physical manipulation and masturbation activities common to childhood. It is also possible that since the other female is not capable of penetrating as would a male sex partner be, this provides a relaxed frame of mind within which orgasm is more likely to occur.

Respondents were asked to indicate, when they were not involved with an individual in a marriage arrangement, what percentage of their dates resulted in sexual relations. Sixty-seven percent of the married group indicated that 20% of their dates resulted in sexual contact, while 55% of the unmarried group indicated that approximately 20% of their dates resulted in sexual contact. In the married group, 22% indicated that between 50 and 60% of their dates resulted in sexual contact. When asked whether or not sexual involvement required an emotional bond between consenting adults, over 90% of respondents indicated that it did. Ninety-eight percent of the sample stated that they preferred a stable relationship to "playing the field."

When exploring the frequency of sexual intercourse between girls involved in a stable relationship, predictably we found that the married group tended to have sex more frequently than did the unmarried group. Nineteen of the unmarried group or 58% indicated that sexual intercourse occurred five or fewer times per month. Of the total sample, homosexuality married and unmarried, 76% (48) engaged in sexual intercourse 15 or fewer times per month. There is apparently a greater amount of sexual activity occurring between respondents than is reported for heterosexual couples. It was the experience of the observation period that there was a great amount of emphasis on sex and sex-related activities in the homosexual world. This may be because the homosexual tends to relate her entire life style around her sexual preference, and this sense of difference and resultant perception of stigma create a gulf between her and the heterosexual community.

Despite persistent myths equating homosexuality with promiscuity, 82% of the sample indicated having physical intimacies with seven or fewer women in their entire career. Fifty-eight percent indicated intimacies occurring with four or fewer women.

Given the impermanence of the homosexual marriage, which has none of the legal or social supports of the heterosexual marriage, the lesbian cannot be defined as promiscuous.

HETEROSEXUAL EXPERIENCE

The optional section on heterosexual sex activities had six parts. The respondent was asked initially whether she had had sexual relations with a man. If she had not had relations with a man, the remainder of the questionnaire would be blank. Of the total sample, 37 indicated that they had had sexual relations with a man and 27 indicated that they had not. Twenty-two of this 37 came from the married group and 15 came from the unmarried group. A greater percentage of persons sharing a marriage relationship had had sexual relations with a man. The largest number who had sex with a man were between 21 and 25. The next largest number were between the ages of 26 and 30.

Respondents were asked if their sexual contact with the male involved penis in vagina penetration. Of the 37 who indicated that they had had sexual relations with a man, 33 indicated that penetration had occurred. Relations occurring between heterosexually oriented males and homosexual females are therefore not comprised of acts that would be expected to occur between consenting females.

When asked whether oral-genital contact had occurred, 20 (57%) indicated that it had not. Clearly, the heterosexual relationships of the lesbian are not directed, therefore, by what she is accustomed to sexually experiencing with other women and such are not mock versions of her homosexual relationships. Respondents described the role played in heterosexual encounters as an essentially passive or submissive one. This is, after all, the attitude culturally defined as appropriate for the female and one that she is socialized to perform. Of the 17 (26%) indicating oral-genital contact, eight stated that it had been mutual, three stated that only they had been involved (fellatio), and six indicated that only the male had been involved (cunnilingus).

Respondents were asked if in these heterosexual relationships orgasm had occurred. The data were evenly distributed, with 17 indicating "yes" and 18 indicating "no." Although some respondents were able to enjoy satisfying sexual relations with a man, the data indicated that they did not long continue having relationships with men after identification with the homosexual community. At least in some instances, therefore, the choice of sex partner was not based on the female's inability to have satisfying sexual relations with men but was a preference based on psychosexual identity. The choice of partner was, therefore, not entirely related to whether or not sexual gratification could be obtained with men in some cases.

Some respondents indicated that heterosexual intercourse had occurred 7–8 and in one case 16 years prior to the date of completing the questionnaire. The fact that ten of the 37 indicated that they had had sexual contact with a man, within the 12-month period preceding their completion of the questionnaire, is significant, since it is indicative of a greater involvement with the straight community than is typically assumed for the homosexual female. Comparing the responses of the married with the unmarried group, the data indicate that the existence of the homosexual marriage and the nature of the couple involvement in such an arrangement tended to limit the sexual access of the woman so involved to males. In this sense, the marriage appeared to limit the degree of interchange and the nature of interchange occurring between the homosexual and straight community. The married group who indicated having had sexual relations with a man largely stated that the experience occurred 4 or more years in the past. Only four of the group of 22 stated that this had occurred within the last 2 years, and only one of this group indicated that it had occurred within the last year. In the unmarried group (N=15) indicating that they had had sex with a man, 12 asserted the event had occurred within the past 2 years. Five indicated further that the event had occurred within the past 6 months. Thus the data indicated that in the unmarried group there was a greater probability of recently having had sexual relations with a man than in the homosexually married group. The differences in the responses of the two groups may relate to the greater social mobility of the unattached lesbian, who would have more opportunities to meet men and to be socially involved with them.

The data also indicate that oral sex with a male partner was not related to the achievement of orgasm for either the married or unmarried groups, or any particular age cohort. Sixteen of the 37 indicating that they had had sex with a man indicated that they had achieved orgasm; although the differences between the married and unmarried groups were minimal, the younger unmarried female homosexual tended to be more likely to achieve orgasm than an older, married woman. This difference might reflect the fact that the younger lesbian belongs to a generation that has different sexual values than older generations. These differences may be interpreted only as indicating possible directions. They cannot be representative of real differences due to sampling procedures and due to our relatively small sample size.

REFERENCES

Gagnon, J., and Simon, W. (eds.) (1969). *Sexual Deviance. The Lesbian, a Preliminary Overview*, Harper & Row, New York.
Goffman, E. (1963). *Stigma: Notes on the Management of Spoiled Identity*, Prentice-Hall, Englewood Cliffs, N.J.

PART V

SEX ROLES

SEX ROLES

The studies included in this section indicate sex role differences with the male seen as more capable, healthier, and concerned with maintaining a more powerful position vis-a-vis the female. If a woman succeeds it's attributed to greater effort rather than ability. One study notes that males respond maladaptively to female role change which can only serve to emphasize two distinct roles, the appropriateness of each depending on one's sex. Another study involving social learning theory indicates that situational factors can influence children to play with a so-called sex-inappropriate toy. Thus, the roles of both sexes need not be static and invariant.

25

DAVID TRESEMER AND JOSEPH PLECK‡

Sex-Role Boundaries and Resistance to Sex-Role Change†

SEX-ROLE stereotypes can be conceptualized as sets of widespread, stable, and consensual images in our culture (see the recent work on this in Broverman *et al.*, 1972). By virtue of being human, men and women are seen as identical on many traits, but the styles and activities that are characteristically attributed to one group but not to the other are at the core of the personality and are extremely important for the person in social relationships. The dichotomization of gender is perhaps the easiest and most powerful differentiation to which people cling. In this culture, there is a tendency to associate one pole on a large number of abstract bipolar dimensions (warm–cold, earth–heaven, etc.) with one sex, the other pole with the other sex. Indeed, the widespread use of the concept "the *opposite* sex" indicates the way in which these two reference groups are considered to be unalterably opposed. Depending on one's sex label, there are different norms for behavior, demanding conformity to two distinct coherent social roles, delineated by sex-role stereotypes. Along with the basic ascribed roles of age and race, sex label predicts a great deal of a person's behavior and also others' behavior toward the person.

---

†This paper is a slightly revised version of a paper presented at the Radcliffe Institute Conference, "Women: Resource for a Changing World," Cambridge, Mass., 18 April 1972.
‡The order of authorship was determined by the flip of a coin. Tresemer was primarily responsible for the introduction and first section; Pleck was primarily responsible for the second section.

Thus, sex-role stereotypes influence our perceptions of others as well as our (and their) actual behavior.

The functional value for the individual of sex-role stereotypes can be integrated with a number of traditional theories of personality development (see especially the conflicting theoretical positions in Maccoby, 1966), though most emphasize the very early learning of sex-role differences. Whichever way is most crucial for the development of sex-role-appropriate behavior in childhood, there is a great deal of cognitive energy expended in adolescence and adulthood to maintaining unambiguous boundaries for sex roles. Erik Erikson suggests there is a necessary opposition of these two comparative reference groups in order for normal growth to take place:

A clear elaboration of sexual types is always essential for the polarization of the sexes in sexual life and in their respective identity formation (1965, p. 236).

To reformulate this point in the language being developed here, cultural definition of sex roles, in the form of role-expectations or stereotypes, is required for an integrated sense of self with "inner continuity and sameness" (to use Erikson's phrase).

Consequently, sex roles have clear boundaries. And, by definition in a universe composed of two groups with sharp boundaries, to venture outside one's own boundary is to venture into the domain of the other. This implies conformity to sex roles has two more important functions—(1) reception of gratifying affection and acceptance for the "right" behavior, and (2) avoidance of punishment for overstepping the ascribed limits of one's sex role.

Analyses of the results of sex-typing of fields of graduate study (Davis, 1968) and professional occupations (Rossi, 1965; Epstein, 1970) illustrate the effects of these segregating influences but do not trace them back to attitudes or motives concerning perceived sex-role appropriateness or congruency. Of the three functions of conformity to sex-role stereotypes mentioned above, we have found that the last—avoiding the negative consequences of deviance—is far more obvious among our adolescent and adult subjects, in thematic imagery and behavior. A passage from Margaret Mead's *Male and Female* is instructive in this context:

Where an occupation or an art is defined as feminine, the males who are attracted to it are either already in some way injured or may be injured if they try to practise it. . . . When an occupation is defined as masculine, women who first enter it will be similarly handicapped (1949, p. 377).

In other words, given the negative consequences for transcending role boundaries which Mead talks about, individuals strive to avoid sex-role-incongruent behavior and thus to act in a way congruent with their appropriate sex role. We have to this point developed a model for the structure of the social definitions of sex roles, as well as an idea of the motivation for behavior congruent with that role. To establish stability and consistency in a personal sense of identity, to receive the expected praise for proper behavior, and to avoid censure from without, people tend to strive to conform to and tend to fear to deviate from the opinions and behaviors dictated by these prescribed roles. Perhaps, because the threat of "injury" appears much more specific and clear-cut than the possible advantages of praise for conformity or confirmation of an individual's sense of self, inhibition of negatively sanctioned behavior seems more common than concerns about acting in just the "right" way.

An interesting illustration of the perceptions of sex-role-congruent behavior and the awareness of negative consequences for violation of sex-role boundaries comes from a small study of the entire junior class of an Eastern suburban high school. As part of a survey sponsored by the Guidance Department, we asked 109 males and 84 females to rate a series of occupations on a set of nine-point evaluative scales. Each occupation was crossed by sex of incumbent so that we asked for evaluations of male medical doctor, female medical doctor, male home economist, female home economist and so on for chemist, interior decorator, market research worker, and registered nurse. We had chosen the occupations randomly from three groups of professions—those with low percentage of women in that profession across the nation, high percentage of women, and equal numbers of women and men. (Data were obtained from the Dept. of Labor's *Occupational Outlook Handbook*, 1969.) Each subject was asked to rate six randomly chosen combinations of sex and occupation, avoiding explicit comparisons between male and female incumbents for any occupation. For this discussion, we will use all this data, ignoring possible order effects, and we will look at the results on only one of the evaluative scales—masculine/feminine. Each of the points in Figure 1 represents the responses of half of the subjects, with equal numbers of males and females. By taking the means within each percentage group, we can plot a rough curve of percentages of females in an occupation by the evaluation as relatively masculine or feminine. Though a stronger support for congruency between sex role and sex-role-appropriate behavior would have been indicated in steeper slopes, Figure 1 shows that high school juniors, with minimal knowledge of what these occupations actually entail, see them as sexualizing their incumbents, making them more or less appropriately masculine or feminine. This involves a process of generalizing from the statistical properties of a whole profession to the personality

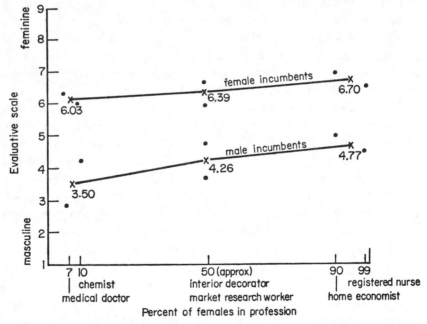

FIGURE 1   Ratings of male and female incumbents of different occupations representing three ranges of percentages of females in that occupation on a masculine/feminine evaluation scale. Each of the points represents one-half of the subjects (N=193), and the crosses the means within percentage category. (Data from a study carried out by Dane Archer, Buffy Aries, David Ruth and David Tresemer.)

characteristics of an individual in that occupation. One's actual sex is never forfeited (i.e. male nurses are not more feminine than female doctors), but it is clear what kind of occupation one should take up to be most in line with one's reference group. The more women in an occupation, the more a male worker in that occupation is conceived to be violating the boundaries of his sex role.

We might mention here that some of these expectations have been shown to have real negative consequences for male nurses, to take a well studied example (Segal, 1962; Etzkowitz, 1971)—they have low self-esteem as men and do shoddy work as nurses.

The above points about the properties and dynamics of sex roles can be supplemented by more formal social psychological theory, namely Leon Festinger's theory of social comparison processes (1954; see also Pettigrew, 1967): A basic desire to structure one's environment in order to define and preserve a stable and positive self-image leads to comparison with similar others and conformity with their opinions and behaviors; members of the positive referent group are influenced to conform while similarities to members of any negative referent group are rejected. Though the concepts of social role, social stereotypes, and even sex label as a referent affecting behavior are not explicitly stated in this theory, they clearly follow. Mischel (1970), for one, has suggested that sex-role-congruent behavior involves the maintenance of cognitive consistency and avoidance of cognitive dissonance.

In our analysis, which is derived from this theory, sex label is a powerful referent for evaluating similarity on important dimensions of behavior. Stereotypes are understood in terms of this theory as standards for evaluating conformity or deviance from the appropriate sex group. Thus, sex-role stereotypes are a potent cognitive factor in the regulation of the individual's own motivational system. They affect not only the individual's monitoring and surveillance of his/her own behavior, but of others' behavior too. In order to maintain the internal consistency and sameness of the referent group to which one strives to conform (and the internal consistency and differentness of the referent group(s) from which one strives to be different), one acts to reduce the deviance of members of these relevant groups, either with common techniques of social control—hostile jokes, threats, withdrawal of emotional or financial support, etc.—or by rejection or ostracism through re-labelling—"he's a queer," "she's a dyke." Thus, the social definitions of sex roles are maintained.

While rather simple, these propositions bear stressing: traditional theories of personality do not give much weight to culture-wide external norms, images, and stereotypes as determinants of behavior. Perhaps the social psychological view of social comparison, based on the idea that a person strives to create and maintain a definition of self consistent with the norms and values of a coherent world, makes a truer assessment.

We integrate these concepts as follows: widespread images of appropriate sex roles, associated with the general reference groups of men and women, give normative direction to the formation of sex-role identity; the process of enforcement of these norms takes place via social comparison with the immediate group of similar others (or peer group).

We would like to trace out in the remainder of this paper the impact of sex-role stereotypes (1) on the inhibition of sex-role-incongruent behavior in oneself and in one's own sex group (internal dynamics and own reference group), and (2) on men's response to the changes in women's role in society ("negative" or "opposite" reference group). While the first has traditionally been approached as a psychological problem, we intend to complement it with a more sociological point of view; while the second has normally been thought of as a social problem—how men as a group relate to women as a group—we intend to complement it with an understanding of the dynamics of the male personality.

I. FEAR OF SUCCESS AS THE INHIBITION OF SEX-ROLE-INCONGRUENT BEHAVIOR

Matina Horner's (1968) study of the motivation in women to avoid success is probably well known to this audience. Briefly, she found an important relation between anxious ideation concerning success and actual decrements in performance when confronted with a situation demanding competition with another. The "motive to avoid success" was assessed by scoring imagery in stories written to the thematic apperceptive cue, "At the end of first term finals, Anne finds herself at the top of her med school class" (see Atkinson, 1958, for a presentation of this tradition for assessing motives). Female subjects wrote about Anne at the top of the class and male subjects about John. Three kinds of themes were found for fear of success: (a) internal fears and negative effects—Anne feels guilty, unhappy, unfeminine, etc.; (b) social rejection as a result of success—"everyone hates and envies her," Anne has no boy friends, her classmates physically harm her; and (c) bizarre or exaggerated hostile responses, or denial of the cue altogether—Anne is at the top of her class but her boy friend is *higher*, Anne is a code name for a group of medical students who take turns taking exams for her. The stories of sixty-five percent of the females in the sample showed this fear of success imagery, a rate which incidentally has been found repeatedly since then (see Horner, 1972). Only ten percent of the males in the sample responded this way to John at the top of his med school class. Behavioral measures of performance on simple achievement tasks showed marked differences between those high and low in measured fear of success in the different conditions of her experiment, thus validating the inferences taken from these thematic productions. The group of females scoring high on the measure of fear of success performed much less well working in competing pairs than they did working alone, while females scoring low on this measure performed much better in the competitive situation, as did the males. In response to the expected negative consequences of success, women actually restricted their own performance capability (assessed in a "relaxed" noncompetitive setting).

Going back to our model, we might reinterpret these results as a reaction to violation of sex-role boundaries. This more general idea also anticipates a fear of success in men, though perhaps in different areas. Indeed, if the notions offered by Ruth Hartley (1959) and Myron Brenton (1966) about the greater narrowness and restrictiveness of the male sex role are true, we might possibly find much larger areas and greater intensity of inhibition for males. We must first suspend the common value judgment that male success is the only success or indeed the only form of competence, a position which we feel obscures the entrapment of males and the fulfillment of females in their respective roles in society. Each sex has successfully developed certain faculties and underdeveloped others, based on conformity to appropriate sex roles. Just as both men and women have different areas of success, they both have fears of success in areas perceived as inappropriate to their sex role. Indeed, to meet their needs, the two sexes often rely on various interdependent relationships. This leads not only to the wife's vicarious experience of her husband's achievement competence but also to the husband's vicarious experience of his wife's affiliative of social-emotional competence. (Some of the difficulties of this interdependence will be presented in the next section.)

Let us look at the original female story-writing cue in Horner's research in terms of sex-role-appropriate success. In the Anne/med school cue, Anne is successful in more than one way. She is "out of place" in two senses, both of which might elicit stronger success-avoidant imagery. First, Anne is excelling above all her peers, regardless of their sex (i.e. top of the class), a style of dominance associated with men rather than women, and, second, Anne is doing competently at a task that has been defined in this culture as the behavioral territory or domain of the male (i.e. med school). Though Horner was careful to label this a "motive to avoid success in intellectual competition and/or leadership ability," the literature which cites the results of this and related studies seems to ignore these two factors with the simpler explanation that Anne is afraid of being *competent*. Taking these factors into account in terms of sex-role-appropriateness, we would not expect to find high levels of fear of success imagery to the cue, "At the end of first term finals, Anne finds she is *doing well* in her *nursing school* class."

We can systematically divide the differences in behavior between males and females into two factors based on those developed above: (a) different classes of appropriate *tasks*, all of which require achievement motivation to handle effectively, and (b) different *styles* of relating to one's surroundings, often thought of as character traits. This parallels the state (or content) versus process dichotomy in psychology. The notion of success involves both of these, not only the goal to be attained but the means for attaining it.

In terms of *tasks*, males do not often engage in child-care, house cleaning, cooking, and a host of other tasks reserved in this culture for the homemaker, the wife. Stylistically, the male is commonly seen as more aggressive and power-seeking, less dependent and nurturant, less able to give or receive help or love, less able to deal with his own emotions or with others' emotional needs. This differentiation parallels the "competence" versus "warmth" clusters of traits for men and women found by Broverman *et al.* (1972) and the classic "instrumental" versus "expressive" factors theorized by Parsons and Bales (1955), though appropriate content has been separated from appropriate style.

Manipulations of *style* can make inappropriate tasks appear appropriately handled. When males engage in tasks defined as feminine, they publicly complain or fumble, joke it off, or profession-alize the job by performing with exaggerated masculine demeanor. In other words, by appropriately managing style, males can some-times masculinize a task labeled as feminine. Though Horner's definition (above) seems to emphasize success as a state, it is clear that style is a crucial element in the appropriateness of competence for the male and female sex roles. Perhaps this analysis suggests why fear of success imagery is found in stories written by women to the cue, "Mary has found out that she has been made head cheerleader for her school's cheerleading squad"—though it is a sex-role-appropriate task, it is a masculinized style.

Taking these considerations into account, our model of tendencies to avoid sex-role-incongruency would predict high levels of success-avoidant imagery to cues such as "John is getting very good at changing diapers for his newborn child" (inappropriate task) or "John is a warm and affectionate person" (inappropriate style). These high levels of anxiety in response to these stimuli would be reactions to success at tasks and at ways of dealing with people and things traditionally associated with the female sex role. Cues such as these need testing to support the notions presented here.

Up to this point, we have been talking about particular aspects of situations which arouse motivation to avoid sex-role-incongruence, applied to people in general. But people vary in how sensitive they are to these situations. There is not a uniformly strong tendency to conform to the role demands of one's appropriate sex group. We hypothesize that the key factors in explaining these individual differences are (a) variation in the perception or awareness of sex-role stereotypes as they are defined and continually reinforced in our culture, and (b) conscious attempts to modulate one's own concepts about sex role and sex-role-congruent behavior. Possibly to the extent that a person perceives or believes in stereotypical differences between the sexes is he/she motivated to conform to sex-role-congruent attitudes and behaviors while rejecting sex-role-incongruent attitudes and behaviors. The measure used to assess this was devised by Tresemer, using a format suggested by Brigham (1970) and twelve items randomly chosen from the list of stereotypic traits presented in Broverman *et al.* (1972). Subjects are asked to indicate what percent on a five-point scale from 0 to 100 of males they think have a particular trait; then they are asked for perceptions of percentages for females. Differences in the traditionally defined direction are added (and differences in the opposite direction subtracted) to give the score of perceived differences between the sexes. The measure has been found to have a high range of scores. A preliminary analysis of the relation of this measure to fear of success imagery in a small sample of females from a state teachers' college yielded surprisingly strong results (cf. Figure 2). Fear of success was scored for half the subjects on the Anne/med school cue; for the other half on the following roughly equivalent cue: "Diane has just received word that she is one of the three students in the state to get a perfect score on the LSAT (Law

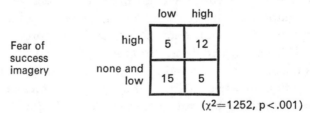

Perceived differences between sexes

		low	high
Fear of success imagery	high	5	12
	none and low	15	5

$(\chi^2=1252, p<.001)$

FIGURE 2 Number of subjects scored for fear of success imagery in thematic apperceptive stories and on perceived differences between the sexes (N=37). (Fear of success imagery scored by Robert Watson and Prof. M. S. Horner at Harvard University in a pilot study supervised by Prof. Horner.)

School Admission Test)." It appears that the more one perceives differences between the sexes in terms of conventional stereotypical traits, then the more one engages in success-avoidant ideation concerning sex-role-incongruent tasks, and (using the extension from Horner's thesis, 1968) the more one actually avoids success in those tasks.†

Though in general throughout our culture, images of sex roles and the stereotypes associated with them have great salience for behavior, our closing point for this section is that we must remember that they affect people very differently, perhaps for different reasons. Perhaps exaggerated differences between the sexes have been learned early in life and have a primary importance of their own later on—in so far as these convictions affect the expectancy and the value of success in a particular activity, we expect alterations in motivation to do well in that task or to inhibit performance depending on the sex-role congruence or incongruence of that activity. Or perhaps attitudes about differences between the sexes might be a secondary process or epiphenomenon of more basic personality traits—perhaps exaggerated differences between the sexes belies a too great reliance on external standards for comparison, evidence of a conflicted ego or weak sense of personal ability.

II. MALE RESPONSE TO THE CHANGING ROLE OF WOMEN

Observers such as Rossi (1970, p. 539) and Erikson (1965, p. 237) have forebodingly anticipated a "male backlash" to contemporary change in women's role in society. Whether backlash or not, change in the ambitions and goals of women today does present problems of personal accommodation and adjustment to many men. In analyzing these problems of adjustment, we find it useful to distinguish two areas of female role change to which men are responding. Our

---

†These particular findings should be viewed with some caution since subsequent analysis of a number of samples has shown that this relation does not always hold true.

analysis draws on Parsons and Bales' (1955) formulation of traditional sex role differentiation, in which instrumental/task functions are assigned to males, and expressive/social-emotional functions to females. First, men are responding to women becoming more instrumental and task-oriented, challenging traditional male instrumental dominance. Second, men are responding to women becoming less expressive and social-emotional for men, specifically, women becoming less willing to exclusively serve male emotional needs at the expense of other goals and ambitions. This change in women frustrates traditional male emotional dependence on women.

Descriptions of male socialization (Mead, 1949, chap. 15; Hartley, 1959) have emphasized that male expectations of instrumental superiority over women derive ultimately from pressures on the male child to achieve and to conform to sex role norms. In these accounts, denigration of female instrumental ability and exclusion of females from competition serve as outlets for the inner tensions produced by this society's pressure on the male child to perform. Adult female achievement can be seen in this light as disrupting the often uneasy fashion in which achievement strivings are integrated into male personality.

There has been relatively less written about men's dependence on women for the satisfaction of their emotional needs and for the facilitation of their own emotional expression. Because of traditional male emotional constriction, many men feel that without women they are unable to experience themselves emotionally. A scene from the recent film *Carnal Knowledge* provides a striking illustration. In this scene Art Garfunkel tells his roommate, played by Jack Nicholson, that their mutual girl friend "expresses thoughts for me that I never even knew I had." In the next scene, Nicholson jealously and violently demands of her, "you tell him his thoughts, you have to tell me my thoughts!" Both statements reflect male expressive dependency on women, men's need for women to help them express what they are feeling, differing only in the extent of its gratification.

That many women live vicariously through their husbands' achievement has often been pointed out; that their husbands are simultaneously living through their wives' emotionality has not. This complementarity, in both the instrumental and expressive areas, reflects a traditional interdependence of male and female roles which is increasingly being called into question by contemporary change in women. Analyzing this traditional complementarity from the point of view of men, we may speak of men having a "psychological investment" in the traditional sex role performance of women, specifically, in women's being expressive but not instrumental. These traditional female behavioral styles gratify male needs. The depth of male psychological investment in the traditional sex role status of women, not so evident in the past when women accepted traditional roles, is increasingly revealed by the intensity of many men's reactions to female role change.

In our analysis, male psychological investment in instrumental superiority over women and investment in expressive dependency on women are relatively independent. That is, for some men, increased female achievement, with its threat to male instrumental superiority, is the major threat posed by female role change. For others, the major threat is the decrease in women's willingness to serve male emotional needs, with its frustration of male expressive dependency. For still others, both aspects of female role change are threatening, and become merged or fused together. For yet others, neither is threatening. The relative independence of these two factors occurs because male psychological investments in the two areas derive from different domains in male personality and from different developmental experiences, which may or may not co-exist or co-occur.

In our pilot work, we have examined male reactions to female role change in the instrumental/task area. (A parallel analysis of the impact of change in the expressive area is currently underway.) One hundred and seventeen male subjects wrote brief imaginative stories to the Anne/medical school cue described earlier.† This cue would clearly be expected to elicit material relating to male investment in instrumental superiority over women. In examining the stories, we assume that their form and content reflect general features of the subjects' cognitive and defensive styles.

---

†These stories were collected in two separate samples by Robert Watson of Harvard University and Dr. Peter Wish of Framingham State College, who kindly made them available for this reanalysis.

In trying to understand men's stories in response to this cue, we theorized that there are two major maladaptive ways for men to deal with female achievement, or two major *defensive styles* to female achievement. We called these styles *stereotyping* and *hostile resistance*. Many men did not employ either style in their stories, and dealt with the female achievement cue adaptively and positively. We feel, though, that stereotyping and hostile resistance are relatively widespread, and grounded in the traditional male sex role. We see many men responding to the current increase in women's achievement by exaggerating and elaborating these defensive styles—much as individuals generally respond to novelty and crisis by directing additional energy to previously adaptive defenses. For clarity of presentation, we will describe stereotypers and hostile resisters as two distinct groups (although these two styles are not necessarily mutually exclusive). Some of the attributes of each group have been speculatively inferred from our data, and thus should be regarded as tentative. Table 1 summarizes some central differences between the two styles.

Stereotypers approach experience through rigid and pervasive cognitive categories. Since female achievement does not fit easily into their system, they inattend to it, have a high threshold for perceiving it, and easily forget it once they have noticed it. Since achievement is discrepant with their image of women, based on traditional stereotypes, they view it as highly exceptional, explicable only on the basis of unusual life experience. In short, an instance of female achievement is the exception that proves their rule. They feel that most women want not equality, but traditional complementarity, with the compensatory satisfactions of their traditional role. When stereotypers allow themselves to be aware of many women's desires for achievement and equality, they see women as internally conflicted by these desires. They focus on these conflicts in a superficially sympathetic but actually hyperalert way. They view these conflicts not as evidence that the socialization of women needs to be changed, but rather as evidence that sex role change should "go slow," accommodating rather than fundamentally challenging traditional female achievement conflicts.

Developmentally, we infer that this defensive style derives from a

TABLE 1

	Defensive style	
	Stereotyping	Hostile resistance
Core attitude	Women are instrumentally weak and dependent	Women are formidable, but will be overcome by men
Elaboration of core attitude	Idealization, chivalry, *noblesse oblige*	Woman-baiting
Attitude to female achievement	Superficially sympathetic; hyperalert to achievement conflicts	Overtly hostile, unempathic to women's conflicts
Perceptual threshold for female achievement	High, inattending	Low, hyperalert
Perceived block to female achievement	Internal conflicts in women	External resistance by men
Perceived demand from women	Traditional complementarity	Superiority
Ego strength and self-esteem	High, reflecting successful internalization of cultural norms	Low
Characteristic SES	High	Low

resolution of the dynamic problems of male childhood through a motivated perception that women are instrumentally weak and dependent, a perception reinforced by many elements in the socialization of the male child's female peers. This perception forms part of the basis of later cultural and romantic idealization of women, and feelings of chivalry and *noblesse oblige* toward women. In general, stereotyping is associated with high self-esteem and high ego strength, as these terms are generally understood, reflecting the successful and unconflicted internalization of dominant cultural values and norms, with reliance on relatively high level defenses. It is probably associated with higher rather than lower socioeconomic status. Although stereotypers do not take female achievement too seriously, they do not react to it with hostility, aggression, or inner disturbance and turmoil.

Hostile resisters see women as wanting not equality, but superiority. They fear that women wish to make men dependent on them. In contrast to stereotypers, they have a relatively low perceptual threshold for evidence of female achievement and power. In an apparently unerring and hyperalert way they get entangled in relationships with powerful women. For hostile resisters, achievement and power are not the goals of a few exceptions to the general pattern of female dependence, as stereotypers see it, but rather the secret (or not so secret) wishes of every woman. Hostile resisters show markedly little interest and involvement with traditionally feminine, passive women, apparently needing strong women against whom to struggle and resist. They react to achieving women with conscious and overt hostility as well as turmoil. In contrast to stereotypers, who are hyperalert to women's inner conflicts, resisters block out any empathic awareness of women's inner concerns.

Developmentally, we infer that hostile resistance derives from a resolution of the dynamic problems of male childhood based on organizing self-esteem around the ability to resist, flaunt, and defy what is perceived as the formidable power of women. This dynamic resolution is modeled and reinforced by many themes in male primary school culture, especially its sanctioned rebellion against female teachers and its terrorization of female peers. This dynamic resolution also forms a major part of later "woman-baiting." Hostile resistance is probably associated with lower rather than higher socioeconomic status, and low ego strength and self-esteem generally.

Now to apply this theoretical typology to our stories. Features of these stories interpreted as reflecting stereotyping included (1) perceptual distortions of the cue which minimize or overlook the female achievement, such as describing Anne as a nurse, or introducing a boy friend who got higher grades; (2) highly unusual life circumstances to justify the achievement, such as having a parent who died of a rare illness whose cure Anne will discover; (3) internal psychological conflict in the hero, especially around sex role concerns, most often resolved by Anne reducing her achievement.

Story elements consistent with hostile resistance included (1) the intrusion of power themes in the motives and consequences of Anne's achievement, and in others' responses to it, e.g. "now Anne wants everyone to bow down to her"; (2) fall in male self-esteem around performance, e.g. "the men in the class are mad because a woman is number 1"; (3) presence of primitive violence and aggression, especially directed against Anne; (4) deliberately "spoiling" the cue through highly idiosyncratic and bizarre interpretations (as contrasted with the stereotyper's well-meaning misinterpretations), e.g. "The med school is an *avant-garde* medical school where the goal of its graduates is not so much to save lives, but to make healthy and mildly sick people die with maximum finesse. Anne is thus a proficient and subtle murderess." (5) Loss of organization and coherence in the story, reflecting the arousal of anxiety.

When this method and our analysis are more refined, it will be possible to give some reliable estimate of the prevalence of these two defensive styles in men. We are currently extending our research by studying male response to change in women in the social-emotional/expressive area, using similar methods. We anticipate that there will be two parallel defensive styles relating to female expressive change, one which stereotypes and idealizes women's ability to gratify men emotionally, and another which is organized around fears of loss of emotional gratification.

In conclusion, although we have focused here on maladaptive male responses to female role change, we believe that men have the inner resources to adapt to the changing status of women in a humanly creative way, and to find in the realignment of the sexes new freedom and new liberation for themselves. The intention of this analysis is not to point an accusing finger at the manifold forms of male chauvinism. Rather, its real intention is to give both men and women insight into the different kinds of emotional resistances, based on sex role stereotypes, men experience in confronting contemporary change in women. Hopefully, both can learn to transcend and outgrow these resistances, so each can reap the human benefits which loosening and change in traditional sex-role definitions offers.

References and Notes

Atkinson, J. W. (Ed.), *Motives in fantasy, action, and society* (Princeton, N.J.: Van Nostrand, 1958).

Brenton, M., *The American male* (Greenwich, Conn.: Fawcett, 1966).

Brigham, J., "Ethnic stereotypes," *Psychol. Bull.*, (1971), **76,** 15–38.

Broverman, I. *et al.*, "Sex-role stereotypes: a current appraisal," *J. Social Issues*, 1972, **28,** 59–78.

Davis, J. A., *Great aspirations* (Chicago: Aldine, 1968).

Dept. of Labor, *Occupational outlook handbook* (Washington, D.C.: Government Printing Office, 1969).

Epstein, C., *Woman's place* (Berkeley: Univ. of California Press, 1970).

Erikson, E. H., Concluding remarks. In J. A. Mattfeld and C. G. Van Aken (Eds.), *Women and the scientific professions* (Cambridge, Mass.: M.I.T. Press, 1965).

Etzkowitz, H., "The male sister: sexual separation of labor in society," *J. Marriage and the Family*, 1971, **33,** 431–433.

Feifer, J., *Carnal Knowledge* (New York: New American Library, 1971).

Festinger, L., "A theory of social comparison processes," *Human Relations*, 1954, **7,** 117–140.

Hartley, R. E., "Sex-role pressures and the socialization of the male child," *Psychol. Rep.*, 1959, **5,** 457–468.

Horner, M. S., "Sex differences in achievement motivation and performance in competitive and noncompetitive situations." Unpublished doctoral dissertation, Univ. of Michigan, 1968.

Horner, M. S., "Toward an understanding of achievement related conflicts in women," *J. Social Issues*, 1972, **28,** 157–175.

Maccoby, E. (Ed.), *The development of sex differences* (Stanford, Calif.: Stanford Univ. Press, 1966).

Mead, M., *Male and female* (New York: William Morrow, 1949).

Mischel, W., "Sex-typing and socialization." In P. H. Mussen (Ed.), *Carmichael's manual of child psychology*, 3rd ed. (New York: Wiley, 1970), 3–72.

Parsons, T. and Bales, R. F., *Family, socialization, and interaction process* (Glencoe, Ill.: Free Press, 1955).

Pettigrew, T., "Social evaluation theory," *Nebraska Symposium on Motivation*, 1967, 241–311.

Rossi, A. S., "Barriers to the career choice of engineering, medicine, or science among American women." In J. A. Mattfeld and C. G. Van Aken (Eds.), *Women and the scientific professions* (Cambridge, Mass.: M.I.T. Press, 1965), 51–127.

Rossi, A. S., "Women—the terms of liberation," *Dissent* (Nov.–Dec. 1971), 531–541.

Segal, B., "Male nurses: a case study in contradiction and prestige loss," *Social Forces*, 1962, **41,** 31–38.

Watson, R., "Male and female responses to the succeeding female cue." Unpublished manuscript (Harvard University, 1971).

Wish, P. A., "The motive to achieve success and the motive to avoid failure: psychological determinants of choosing a college major." Unpublished doctoral dissertation, Boston College, 1970.

26

THOMAS M. WOLF[2]

Effects of Live Modeled Sexual Inappropriate Play Behavior in a Naturalistic Setting[1]

In a naturalistic setting, boys and girls were exposed to a same- or opposite-sex live peer model who played with a sex-inappropriate toy for the children. Thirty boys and 30 girls were randomly assigned to one of three conditions. A 2 × 3 factorial design, with sex of subject (male or female) and sex of model (male, female, or no-model control) was used. Generally play behavior with the sex-inappropriate toy was promoted following exposure to a same-sex model relative to an opposite-sex model or no-model control group. The findings were interpreted within a social learning theory.

There are a variety of theoretical interpretations of the acquisition of sex-typed behaviors (e.g., Mussen, 1969). Cognitive-developmental theorists (e.g., Kohlberg, 1966) maintain that a child labels himself as a "boy" or "girl" and this self-categorization then becomes the major organizer of his sex-typed behaviors. Once these self-categorizations become stabilized at approximately 5 or 6 years of age, they tend to be fixed, generalized, and irreversible. Psychoanalytic and trait theorists (see Mischel, 1970) assume that individuals early in life have certain response dispositions or traits which also tend to be fixed, generalized, and irreversible. On the other hand, social learning theorists (e.g., Mischel, 1970) maintain that a child's acquisition and performance of sex-typed behaviors is not governed by his sex identity but rather by his social learning history. No assumptions are made about the generality or consistency of sex-typed behaviors across stimulus situations, but the extent to which similar responses are displayed in a variety of situations is a function of the degree of learned stimulus generalization for that response pattern and the specific contingencies in the situation (Mischel, 1966). Few studies have been conducted relating to the effects of models on the modifiability of sex-typed behaviors in naturalistic settings, although this issue has important theoretical implications relating to the reversibility and generality of sex-typed behaviors.

Previous findings from laboratory studies indicate that boys display earlier and more clearly defined sex-appropriate behavior than girls (e.g., Mussen, 1969). Many girls between the ages of 3 and 10 show a strong preference for masculine games, activities, and objects; whereas, it is unusual to find many boys who prefer feminine activities (Brown, 1957; Hartup & Zook, 1960; Kagan, 1964). Furthermore, many girls state a desire to be a boy or a daddy relative to few boys who state a desire to be a girl or a mommy (Brown, 1957).

The perceived similarity between the model and observer has been shown to influence the amount of observational learning in laboratory studies (e.g., Kagan, 1958; Rosekrans, 1967). Children have been shown to attend more closely to same-sex models (Maccoby & Wilson, 1957; Maccoby, Wilson, & Burton, 1958), and observational learning is promoted by exposure to same-sex models (Hetherington & Frankie, 1967;

[1] The author would like to express his appreciation to William Johnstone and Bonnie Barrett for serving as experimenters. Thanks to Bill Toner, Director of the summer YMCA, for his cooperation. Portions of this article were presented at the Eastern Psychological Association, Boston, April 1972.

[2] Requests for reprints should be sent to the author, Department of Psychology, State University of New York, College at Cortland, Cortland, New York 13045.

Maccoby & Wilson, 1957; Maccoby, Wilson, & Burton, 1958). Also, Mischel (1970) has indicated that in some areas, such as toy and activity preferences, children's sex-typed behaviors may be influenced to a greater extent by peers than by parents (Mussen & Rutherford, 1963). Kobasigawa (1968) found that young boys displayed more sex-inappropriate play behavior following exposure to a same-sex model relative to an opposite-sex model or no-model control group, while this modeling effect was not found for girls.

In contrast to the above laboratory studies, few studies have been conducted in naturalistic settings. The present study used a naturalistic setting to determine the effects on children of modeled sex-inappropriate play behavior. Children were exposed to a live peer model (male or female) who played with a toy that was sexually inappropriate for the children. It was hypothesized that (a) children would imitate a same-sex model to a greater extent than an opposite-sex model and (b) girls would display sex-inappropriate behavior to a greater extent than boys.

Method

The subjects were 30 boys (mean age = 8 years 8 months, *SD* = 14 months) and 30 girls (mean age = 9 years 4 months, *SD* = 20 months) enrolled in a summer YMCA camp. The subjects were all white except for one black child and came from predominantly middle-class families. Male and female undergraduate students served as experimenters and male and female 8-year-old children served as live peer models. A 2 × 3 factorial design, with sex of subject (male or female) and sex of model (male, female, or no-model control) was used.

The subjects were secured individually from different camp activities by the same-sex experimenter in order to attend another activity. The male or female model who appeared to be a camper standing next to a group of other children was picked up on the way to the experimental situation. They were brought to a section of an open field set off from the camp and next to a wooded area. The children were told they could play with some toys resting on a blanket on the ground and that the model would play first. The subject then sat down on the ground next to the experimenter and observed the model play with the toy that was sexually inappropriate for the subjects for approximately 3 minutes. The play behavior was standardized and essentially the same for all subjects. On the basis of a preliminary toy preference

study, a truck with a tire on it and an oven with a kettle on it were selected as the male- and female-appropriate toys, respectively.[3]

Following exposure to the model, the experimenter indicated that it was time to take the model back to camp but that the child could play while they were gone. An observer hidden in a jeep, pulled into the woods, recorded the subject's play behavior for 5 minutes through a specially constructed window. From these records, latency to first response and total time spent playing with the sex-inappropriate toys were calculated. The subject was then asked a standard set of questions. One question dealt with whether he liked or disliked the model. The following items on a sheet of paper were read to each subject by the experimenter: like a lot (1), like a little (2), dislike a little (3), and dislike a lot (4). Then the subjects were told not to tell other campers about the toy playing situation because it should be a surprise for them.

Results

The means for each group are presented in Table 1. Analyses of variance indicated that no main effects were found for subjects or models on either the latency or duration measure. There was a significant Sex of Subject × Sex of Model interaction for the latency (*F* = 3.48, *df* = 2/54, *p* < .05) and duration (*F* = 6.70, *df* = 2/54, *p* < .01) measures. Boys played with the sex-inappropriate toy longer following exposure to a same-sex model relative to an opposite-sex model (*t* = 2.67, *p* < .01), and girls played with the sex-inappropriate toy more quickly (*t* = 2.00, *p* < .05) and tended to play longer (*t* = 1.77, *p* < .08) following exposure to a same-sex model relative to an opposite-sex model.

Females exposed to a female model played with the sex-inappropriate toy significantly

---

[3] In a preliminary toy preference study, 10 white boys and 10 white girls (mean age = 7.6 years, with a range from 6 to 9 years) from predominantly middle-class families were left alone in an empty classroom with an oven with kettle, doll carriage with doll, truck with tire, and wheelbarrow with shovel while their play behavior was recorded for 5 minutes through a one-way mirror. The clearest sex difference as measured by total time spent playing with the toys was found for the oven and truck. Boys played with the truck for a significantly longer period of time than did girls (*t* = 3.52, *p* < .01), while girls played with the oven for a significantly longer period of time than did boys (*t* = 4.65, *p* < .01). A rank ordering of the toys following the play period was found to be consistent with the above results.

TABLE 1

GROUP MEANS FOR LATENCY AND DURATION
MEASURES

Model	Boys		Girls	
	Latency	Duration	Latency	Duration
Male	40.80	144.60	156.00	55.60
None	47.50	77.70	135.80	36.80
Female	112.90	40.70	52.90	122.30

longer than female subjects who saw no model ($t = 2.63$, $p < .01$), and there was a tendency for males exposed to a male model to play with the sex-inappropriate toy longer than male subjects who saw no model ($t = 1.73$, $p < .08$). The groups in which subjects were exposed to opposite-sex models did not differ from their respective control groups.

A 2 × 2 analysis of variance computed for the rated attractiveness of the models indicated that no main effects were found. However, there was a significant Sex of Subject × Sex of Model interaction ($F = 6.86$, $df = 1/36$, $p < .05$). This interaction indicated that boys rated a same-sex model as more attractive than an opposite-sex model ($t = 3.00$, $p < .003$), while no difference was found for girls.

Discussion

The general finding that children's play behavior with the sex-inappropriate toy was promoted following exposure to a same-sex model relative to an opposite-sex model or no-model control group lends support to a social learning interpretation of sex typing (Mischel, 1970). Observational learning is promoted in children following exposure to same-sex models, with no adverse consequences to either the subject or model. This finding indicates the importance of situational variables in the performance of sex-typed behaviors. The results are not consistent with cognitive-developmental, psychoanalytic, or trait theories of sex typing which maintain that once sex differences become stabilized at an early age they tend to be fixed, generalized, and irre-

versible. If this were the case, boys and girls in the present study would have been more resistant to the modeled sex-inappropriate play behavior because of their desire to play with toys that are congruent with their own sex identity.

Mischel (1970) has indicated that children are probably more frequently rewarded for watching and imitating same-sex models, especially when the models display sex-typed behaviors. Perhaps in the present study there was greater perceived similarity (e.g., Kagan, 1958) as well as greater attending behavior (e.g., Maccoby & Wilson, 1957) to a same-sex model and observational learning was promoted as a result (e.g., Hetherington & Frankie, 1967). Boys did rate same-sex models as more attractive than opposite-sex models, while no differences were found for girls. Maybe this finding is due to more rigid sex typing for boys than for girls in our society (Lynn, 1959). It would be desirable to take objective measures of perceived similarity and attending behavior in future studies.

Contrary to prediction, girls did not display more sex-inappropriate play behavior than did boys. Several factors may have contributed to this unexpected finding. Since the children were given no instructions by the experimenter about the appropriateness of the toys, they may have tended to match the behavior of the same-sex model. All subjects observed the model play with the sex-inappropriate toy in the presence of the experimenter without any adverse consequences administered to either the subject or the model. This nonreaction by the experimenter may have conveyed to the subjects the permissibility of playing with the sex-inappropriate toy. Because boys are more rigidly sex typed and are typically more accustomed to receiving or observing other boys receiving negative consequences for displaying sex-inappropriate behavior than are girls (Lynn, 1959), the nonreaction by the experimenter may have been particularly effective in disinhibiting boys' play behavior with the sex-inappropriate toy. In addition, it is conceivable that children are more inclined to display sex-inappropriate behavior in a naturalistic setting in which they are probably less suspicious about possible external surveillance than would be the case in a laboratory setting. It has also been shown that boys are more likely to play with sex-inappropriate toys than are girls when an adult authority figure is absent than when the adult is present (Hartup, Moore, & Sager, 1963).

The present study was a controlled experiment conducted in a naturalistic setting familiar to the children. Many investigators have pointed out the need for conducting research on imitation in naturalistic settings (e.g., Mischel, 1966). Willems (1965) has argued that if a scientist is concerned with how findings, laws, and theories generalize to real-life behavior, then an ecological orientation is required to discover the conditions for application. It would be meaningful, for example, to test for the generality of sex-typed behaviors in one setting to a variety of other settings which could vary on the basis of physical and cognitive similarity. It would also be desirable to test for the generality of the findings with a wider variety of sex-typed toys than were used in the present study.

REFERENCES

BROWN, D. Masculinity-femininity development in children. *Journal of Consulting Psychology,* 1957, **21,** 197–202.

HARTUP, W., MOORE, S., & SAGER, G. Avoidance of inappropriate sex-typing by young children. *Journal of Consulting Psychology,* 1963, **27,** 467–473.

HARTUP, W., & ZOOK, E. Sex-role preference in three- and four-year-old children. *Journal of Consulting Psychology,* 1960, **24,** 420–426.

HETHERINGTON, E., & FRANKIE, G. Effects of parental dominance, warmth, and conflict on imitation in children. *Journal of Personality and Social Psychology,* 1967, **6,** 119–125.

KAGAN, J. The concept of identification. *Psychological Review,* 1958, **65,** 296–305.

KAGAN, J. Acquisition and significance of sex-typing and sex role identity. In M. Hoffman & L. Hoffman (Eds.), *Review of child development research.* Vol. 1. New York: Russel Sage, 1964.

KOBASIGAWA, A. Inhibitory and disinhibitory effects of models on sex-inappropriate behavior in children. *Psychologia,* 1968, **11,** 86–96.

KOHLBERG, L. A cognitive-developmental analysis of children's sex-role concepts and attitudes. In E. Maccoby (Ed.), *The development of sex differences.* Stanford: Stanford University Press, 1966.

LYNN, D. A note on sex differences in the development of masculine and feminine identification. *Psychological Review,* 1959, **66,** 126–135.

MACCOBY, E., & WILSON, E. Identification and observational learning from films. *Journal of Abnormal and Social Psychology,* 1957, **55,** 76–87.

MACCOBY, E., WILSON, W., & BURTON, R. Differential movie-viewing of male and female viewers. *Journal of Personality,* 1958, **26,** 259–267.

MISCHEL, W. A social-learning view of sex differences in behavior. In E. Maccoby (Ed.), *The development of sex differences.* Stanford: Stanford University Press, 1966.

MISCHEL, W. Sex-typing and socialization. In P. Mussen (Ed.), *Carmichael's manual of child psychology.* Vol. 2. New York: Wiley, 1970.

MUSSEN, P. Early sex-role development. In D. Goslin (Ed.), *Handbook of socialization theory and research.* Chicago: Rand McNally, 1969.

MUSSEN, P., & RUTHERFORD, E. Parent-child relations and parental personality in relation to young children's sex-role preferences. *Child Development,* 1963, **34,** 589–607.

ROSEKRANS, M. Imitation in children as a function of perceived similarity to a social model and vicarious reinforcement. *Journal of Personality and Social Psychology,* 1967, **7,** 307–315.

WILLEMS, E. An ecological orientation in psychology. *Merrill-Palmer Quarterly of Behavior and Development,* 1965, **11,** 317–333.

(Received December 27, 1972)

27

VIRGINIA ELLEN SCHEIN[1]

The Relationship Between Sex Role Stereotypes and Requisite Management Characteristics

Three hundred male middle managers rated either women in general, men in general, or successful middle managers on 92 descriptive terms. The results confirmed the hypothesis that successful middle managers are perceived to possess characteristics, attitudes, and temperaments more commonly ascribed to men in general than to women in general. There was a significant resemblance between the mean ratings of men and managers, whereas there was no resemblance between women and managers. Examination of mean rating differences among women, men, and managers on each of the items disclosed some requisite management characteristics which were not synonymous with the masculine sex role stereotype. Implications of the demonstrated relationship for organizational behaviors are discussed.

Although women make up 38% of the work force (Koontz, 1971), the proportion of women who occupy managerial and executive positions is markedly small. One extensive survey of industrial organizations (Women in the Work Force, 1970) revealed that 87% of the companies surveyed had 5% or fewer women in middle management and above.

According to Orth and Jacobs (1971), one reason for the limited number of women managers and executives is that " . . . traditional male attitudes toward women at the professional and managerial levels continue to block change [p. 140]." Bowman, Worthy, and Greyser (1965) found that of 1,000 male executives surveyed, 41% expressed mildly unfavorable to strongly unfavorable attitudes toward women in management. This negative reaction to women in management suggests that sex role stereotypes may be inhibiting women from advancing in the managerial work force.

The existence of sex role stereotypes has been documented by numerous researchers (Anastasi & Foley, 1949; Maccoby, 1966; Wylie, 1961). For example, Rosenkrantz, Vogel, Bee, Broverman, and Broverman (1968) found that among male and female college students, men were perceived as more aggressive and independent than women, whereas women were seen as more tactful, gentle, and quiet than men. In addition, these researchers found that the self-concepts of men and women were very similar to their respective stereotypes.

One way in which sex role stereotypes may impede the progress of women is through the creation of occupational sex typing. According to Merton, " . . . occupations can be described as 'sex-typed' when a large majority of those in them are of one sex and when there is an associated normative expectation that this is how it should be [Epstein, 1970, p. 152]." Judging from the high ratio of men to women in managerial positions and the informal belief that this is how it should be, the managerial job can be classified as a masculine occupation. If so, then the managerial position would seem to require personal attributes often thought to be more characteristic of men than women. Basil (cited by Brenner, 1970), using a nationwide sample of present managers, found that the four personal characteristics rated as most important for an upper management position were seen as more likely to be possessed by men than women. Thus, in general, sex role stereotypes may effectuate the perception of women as being less qualified than men for high-level management positions.

Also, sex role stereotypes may deter women from striving to succeed in managerial positions. In a theory of work behavior, Korman (1970) maintains that " . . . individuals will

[1] I would like to thank John C. Sherman for his assistance with the statistical analyses.

Requests for reprints should be sent to Virginia Ellen Schein who is now with Personnel Research, Metropolitan Life Insurance Company, 1 Madison Avenue, New York, New York 10010.

engage in and find satisfying those behavioral roles which will maximize their sense of cognitive balance or consistency [p. 32]." If a woman's self-image incorporates aspects of the stereotypical feminine role, she may be less inclined to acquire the job characteristics or engage in the job behaviors associated with the masculine managerial position since such characteristics and behaviors are inconsistent with her self-image.

Despite the apparent influence of stereotypical attitudes on the selection, placement and promotion of women, there is a dearth of studies that analyze the operation of sex role stereotypes within organizations. Although stereotypical masculine characteristics have been found to be more socially desirable (Rosenkrantz et al., 1968) and more similar to the characteristics of the healthy adult (Broverman, Broverman, Clarkson, Rosenkrantz, & Vogel, 1970) than stereotypical feminine characteristics, Schein (1971) found a paucity of studies dealing with psychological barriers, such as sex role stereotyping, that prevent women from achieving in the work force.

Since there have been no empirical studies except for Basil's demonstrating the existence of a relationship between sex role stereotypes and the perceived requisite personal characteristics for the middle management position, the purpose of the present study was to examine this association. Specifically, it was hypothesized that successful middle managers are perceived to possess those characteristics, attitudes and temperaments more commonly ascribed to men in general than to women in general. Bowman et al. found that male acceptance of women managers increases with the age of the respondent. Therefore, it was also hypothesized that the association between sex role stereotypes and requisite management characteristics would be less strong among older managers than among younger ones.

METHOD

Sample

The sample was composed of 300 middle line male managers of various departments within nine insurance companies located throughout the United States. Their ages ranged from 24 to 64, with a median of 43 years, their years of experience as managers, from 1 to 40 years with the median being 10 years.

Measurement Instrument

In order to define both the sex role stereotypes and the characteristics of successful middle managers, three forms of a Descriptive Index were developed. All three forms contained the same descriptive terms and instructions, except that one form asked for a description of women in general (Women), one for a description of men in general (Men) and one for a description of successful middle managers (Managers).

In developing the Descriptive Index, 131 items that differentially described males and females were garnered from studies by Basil (In Brenner, 1970), Bennett and Cohen (1959), Brim (1958), and Rosenkrantz et al. (1968). Using these items, a preliminary form of the Descriptive Index was administered to 24 male and female college students. Half of the subjects were given the Women form and half the Men form. In order to maximize the differences in the descriptions of Women and Men, an analysis of all the means and standard deviations was performed and an item was eliminated if (a) its mean descriptive rating was the same for both Women and Men, (b) it was judged by the experimenter and a staff assistant independently to be similar in meaning to one or more other items but it had a smaller mean difference between descriptions of Women and Men, or (c) its variability on both forms was significantly greater than the overall mean variability.

The final form of the Descriptive Index contained 92 adjectives and descriptive terms. The instructions on the three forms of the Index were as follows:

On the following pages you will find a series of descriptive terms commonly used to characterize people in general. Some of these terms are positive in connotation, others are negative, and some are neither very positive nor very negative.

We would like you to use this list to tell us what you think (women in general, men in general, or successful middle managers) are like. In making your judgments, it may be helpful to imagine that you are about to meet a person for the first time and the only thing you know in advance is that the person is (an adult female, an adult male, or a successful middle manager). Please rate each word or phrase in terms of how characteristic it is of (women in general, men in general, or successful middle managers).

The ratings of the descriptive terms were made according to a 5-point scale, ranging from 1 (not characteristic) to 5 (characteristic) with a neutral rating of 3 (neither characteristic nor uncharacteristic).

Procedure

Within each company, a representative with research experience randomly distributed an equal number of the three forms of the Index to male managers with a salary range of approximately $12,000 to $30,000 and a minimum of one year of experience at the managerial level.

Each manager received only *one* form of the Index. The cover letter to the participants stated that the researcher was " . . . engaged in the establishment of a Descriptive Index to be used for management development" and informed the participants that "since various forms of the questionnaire are being distributed within your company, high quality research results can only be obtained if you do not discuss your questionnaire or responses to it with anyone in your company." The questionnaires were returned in individually sealed envelopes.

Of the total number of Descriptive Indexes distributed, 76.62% or 354 out of 462 were returned. The return rates for the various forms of the Index were as follows: Women, 76.62%; Men, 77.27%; and Managers, 75.97%. The usable number of questionnaires was reduced to 300 (88 Women, 107 Men, and 105 Managers). Questionnaires were eliminated if (a) demographic data, such as age and sex, were not indicated or (b) the questionnaires were completed by females. Of the latter, 17 out of 26 were Women forms, which accounts for the lower number of usable Women questionnaires.

RESULTS

The degree of resemblance between the descriptions of Men and Managers and between Women and Managers was determined by computing intraclass correlation coefficients (r') from two randomized groups analyses of variance (see Hays, 1963, p. 424). The classes (or groups) were the 92 descriptive items. In the first analysis, the scores *within* each class were the mean item ratings of Men and Managers, while in the second analysis, they were the mean item ratings of Women and Managers. According to Hays, the larger the value of r', the more similar do observations in the same class tend to be relative to observations in different classes. Thus, the smaller the within item variability, rela-

TABLE 1

ANALYSES OF VARIANCE OF MEAN ITEM RATINGS
AND INTRACLASS COEFFICIENTS

Source	df	MS	F	r'
Men and managers				
Between items	91	1.27	4.23*	.62
Within items	92	.30		
Women and managers				
Between items	91	.89	1.13	.06
Within items	92	.79		

*$p < .01$.

TABLE 2

INTRACLASS COEFFICIENTS WITHIN
THREE AGE LEVELS

Age level	Intraclass coefficients	
	Men and managers	Women and managers
24–39 ($n = 113$)	.60**	.01
40–48 ($n = 95$)	.64**	.00
49 and above ($n = 92$)	.60**	.16*

* $p < .05$.
** $p < .01$.

tive to the between item variability, the greater the similarity between the mean item ratings of either Men and Managers or Women and Managers.

According to Table 1, which presents the results of the analyses of variance and the intraclass correlation coefficients, there was a large and significant resemblance between the ratings of Men and Managers ($r' = .62$) whereas there was a near zero, nonsignificant resemblance between the ratings of Women and Managers ($r' = .06$), thereby confirming the hypothesis that Managers are perceived to possess characteristics more commonly ascribed to Men than to Women.

To determine if age moderates the relationship, the total sample was divided into three age levels, with an approximately equal number of subjects distributed within each age level and within each Women, Men, and Manager group. Intraclass correlations between the mean ratings of Men and Managers and between Women and Managers were computed within each of the three age levels. According to the results, as shown in Table 2, the main hypothesis is less strongly supported among subjects 49 years and above than among younger subjects. Within all three age levels, there was a significant resemblance between the mean ratings of Men and Managers. Among subjects 24 to 39 years and those 40 to 48 years, there was no resemblance between Women and Managers; however, among subjects 49 years and above there was a small but significant resemblance between the ratings of Women and those of Managers.

In addition to intraclass correlation coefficients, Pearson product moment correlation coefficients were computed in order to determine the linear relationships between the mean ratings among the three groups. According to the results, there was a significant correlation ($r = .81$, $p < .01$) between the mean ratings of Men and Managers, but the correlation between the mean ratings of Women and Managers was not significant ($r = .10$). Within all three age levels the r between Men and Managers was significant at the .01 level ($r_1 = .77$; $r_2 = .80$; $r_3 = .79$). Within the two younger groups the correlation between Women and Managers was not significant ($r_1 = .04$; $r_2 = .05$); however, there was a significant correlation between the mean ratings of Women and Managers among subjects 49 years and above ($r_3 = .23$, $p < .05$).

Although the determination of the degree of resemblance between the mean ratings of Men and Managers and the degree of resemblance between the mean ratings of Women and Managers was considered to be the primary test of the hypothesis, an exploratory examination of the specific descriptive items on which Women or Men were perceived as similar to or different from Managers was also carried out so as to obtain a better understanding of the relationship. For each of the 92 items a 3×3 factorial analysis of variance, incorporating the three groups (Women, Men, and Managers) and the three age levels, was performed. According to the results, there was a significant group effect for 86 of the 92 items. An alpha level of .0005 was used as the criterion of significance; therefore, the probability of obtaining one or

more spuriously significant F ratios was .045. There were no significant age effects, nor were there any significant age $\times$ group interactions.

For each of the 86 items displaying a significant group effect, Duncan's multiple range test for unequal n's (see Kramer, 1956) was used to determine the significance of the difference (alpha = .01) between the mean ratings of Men and Managers, Women and Managers, and Men and Women. The results revealed that on 60 of these 86 items, ratings of Managers were more similar to Men than to ratings of Women; for 8 of the 86 items the ratings of Managers were more similar to those of Women than to Men; and for the remaining 18 items with significant group F ratios there was no relationship between sex role stereotypes and perceptions of managerial characteristics—both the mean ratings of Women and Men were significantly different from those of Managers, but there were no significant differences between the mean ratings of Women and Men.[2]

Items representative of the first outcome category, in which Managers were more similar to Men than to Women, were as follows: Emotionally Stable; Aggressive; Leadership Ability; Self-Reliant; (not) Uncertain; Vigorous; Desires Responsibility; (not) Frivolous; Objective; Well Informed and Direct. These items were judged to be representative of the total group of 60 items by three advanced psychology students unfamiliar with the aims of the study. Table 3 presents the items in the latter two outcome categories, in which the predicted direction of mean differences did not occur.[3]

TABLE 3

ITEMS DISPLAYING LACK OF SIMILARITY
BETWEEN MANAGERS AND MEN

Category	Item	
Managers more similar to women than to men	Understanding Helpful Sophisticated Aware of feelings of others	Intuitive Neat (Not) Vulgar Humanitarian Values
Sex role stereotypes not related to management characteristics	Competent Tactful Creative Courteous (Not) Exhibitionist (Not) Devious (Not) Deceitful (Not) Strong Need for Social Acceptance (Not) Desire to Avoid Controversy (Not) Dawdler and Procrastinator (Not) Desire for Friendship	Intelligent Persistent Curious (Not) Quarrelsome (Not) Hasty (Not) Bitter (Not) Selfish

[2] Since the 92 items are undoubtedly intercorrelated, the number of significant item differences within each of the three outcome categories should not be viewed as a test of the hypothesis. The *N* within each of the Women, Men, and Manager groups approximated the number of items, thereby precluding a factor analysis within groups, and a factor analysis combining the responses to the three different forms of the Descriptive Index would be misleading due to the possibility of differing factor structures within the three stimulus groups (see Nunnally, 1967).

[3] A complete list of the items and Women, Men, and Manager mean ratings within the three outcome categories is available upon request from the author (see address in Footnote 1).

DISCUSSION

The results confirm the hypothesis that successful middle managers are perceived to possess those characteristics, attitudes and temperaments more commonly ascribed to men in general than to women in general. This association between sex role stereotypes and perceptions of requisite management characteristics seems to account, in part, for the limited number of women in management positions, thereby underscoring the need for research on the effect of these stereotypical attitudes on actual behavior, such as organizational decision making and individual job performance.

The results suggest that, all else being equal, the perceived similarity between the characteristics of successful middle managers and men in general increases the likelihood of a male rather than a female being selected for or promoted to a managerial position. In a study of hiring practices in colleges and universities, Fidell (1970), using hypothetical descriptions of young PhDs which were identical except for sex, found that the modal level of job offer was lower for women (assistant professor) than for men (associate professor). The present findings imply that similar types of discriminatory selection decisions occur in industrial settings.

To the extent that a woman's self-image incorporates the female sex role stereotype, this relationship would also seem to influence a woman's job behavior. For example, in a laboratory task study pairing high and low dominance subjects, Megargee (1969) found that where the same sex subjects or high dominance males and low dominance females were paired, the high dominance subject, regardless of sex, assumed the leadership role; however, where high dominance females were paired with low dominance males, the high dominance females did not assume the leadership role. In this particular pairing, evidently, assumption of the leadership role was inconsistent with the females' feminine self-image and, therefore, they preferred to maintain their cognitive consistency by not being leaders. Given the high degree of resemblance between the perceived requisite management characteristics and characteristics of men in general, women may suppress the exhibition of many managerial job attributes in order to maintain their feminine self-image. Certainly, additional research is needed to determine if this relationship between sex role stereotypes and management characteristics exists among female middle managers.

Although approximately the same degree of resemblance between the characteristics of successful middle managers and those of men in general was found within all three age levels, only subjects within the 49 and above age group perceived a resemblance between the characteristics of Managers and those of Women. This finding suggests a slight reduction of the differential stereotypical perceptions of men and women among older managers. Examination of the degree of resemblance between the characteristics of Men and Women within the three age levels supported this notion. There was no significant resemblance between Women and Men within the two younger age levels ($r'_1 = -.14$; $r'_2 = .07$), whereas there was a significant resemblance between Women and Men among the oldest group of managers ($r'_3 = .30$, $p < .05$).

Certain concomitants of age, such as experience, may somewhat reduce the perceptual 'male-typing' of the managerial job. For example, experienced managers (the r between age and managerial experience was .76) probably have had more exposure to women as managers, thereby modifying some of their stereotypical perceptions of women. Perhaps more influential to their perceptions may be the changing roles of the wives and female social peers of these older managers. According to Kreps (1971), the proportion of women in the work force increases from age 16 until early 20s, then declines sharply but rises to a second peak of participation that is reached at about age 50. Older male managers may have more interaction with women for whom the role of labor force participant is more salient than that of mother–homemaker. This age effect interpretation implies that as more women become active participants in the labor force, the increased experience with working women will reduce to some extent the relationship between sex role stereotypes and requisite management characteristics among all age groups. Consequently, this psychological barrier to women in management will be lowered, thereby affording a greater opportunity for women to enter into and advance in managerial positions.

The results disclosing certain managerial characteristics that were not synonymous with the masculine sex role stereotype indicate areas in which women presently may be more readily acceptable in and accepting of managerial positions. Examination of the items in Table 3 suggests that "employee-centered" or "consideration" behaviors, such as Understanding, Helpful, and Intuitive, are requisite managerial characteristics that are more commonly ascribed to women in general than to men in general. In certain situations, exhibition of these stereotypical feminine behaviors may be advantageous. For example, in an experimental study, Bond and Vinacke (1961) used a task that required coalition formation for success. Males tended to use exploitative strategies, while females tended to use accommodative techniques. For this particular task, females outperformed the males. Perhaps focusing more attention on the feminine characteristics that are related to managerial success will foster a climate of greater receptivity to women managers.

Turning again to Table 3, some of the perceived requisite characteristics that were not related to sex role stereotypes, such as Intelligent, Competent, and Creative, can be classified as ability or expertise factors. That expertise is perceived to be as characteristic of women as of men supports Brenner's suggestion that women can be placed in managerial positions in which expertise is an important component of authority and explains Bowman et al's. finding that male managers perceive more opportunity for women managers in staff than in line positions. Most of the remaining items in this outcome category appear to be socially undesirable personality traits, such as Quarrelsome, Bitter, Devious, and Deceitful. These traits were less characteristic of successful managers than of either men or women, but no difference in the possession of these traits was perceived between men and women. Here, too, accentuation of the finding that certain attributes required of successful managers may be found more or less as easily among women as men may enhance the status of women in management.

REFERENCES

ANASTASI, A., & FOLEY, J. P., JR. *Differential Psychology.* New York: Macmillan, 1949.

BENNETT, E. M., & COHEN, L. R. Men and women: Personality patterns and contrasts. *Genetic Psychology Monographs,* 1959, 59, 101–155.

BOND, J. R., & VINACKE, W. E. Coalitions in mixed-sex triads. *Sociometry,* 1961, 24, 61–75.

BOWMAN, G. W., WORTHY, N. B., & GREYSER, S. A. Are women executives people? *Harvard Business Review,* 1965, 43, 14–16+.

BRENNER, M. H. Management development activities for women. Paper presented at the meeting of the American Psychological Association, Miami, September 1970.

BRIM, O. G. Family structure and sex-role learning by children: A further analysis of Helen Koch's data. *Sociometry,* 1958, 21, 1–16.

BROVERMAN, I. K., BROVERMAN, D. M., CLARKSON, F. E., ROSENKRANTZ, P. S., & VOGEL, S. R. Sex-role stereotypes and clinical judgments of mental health. *Journal of Consulting and Clinical Psychology,* 1970, 34, 1–7.

EPSTEIN, C. F. *Woman's place.* Berkeley: University of California Press, 1970.

FIDELL, L. S. Empirical verification of sex discrimination in hiring practices in psychology. *American Psychologist,* 1970, 25, 1094–1098.

HAYS, W. L. *Statistics for psychologists.* New York: Holt, Rinehart & Winston, 1963.

KOONTZ, E. D. The progress of the woman worker: An unfinished story. *Issues in Industrial Society,* 1971, 2, 29–31.

KORMAN, A. K. Toward a hypothesis of work behavior. *Journal of Applied Psychology,* 1970, 54, 31–41.

KRAMER, C. Y. Extension of multiple range tests to group means with unequal numbers of replications. *Biometrics,* 1956, 12, 307–310.

KREPS, J. *Sex in the marketplace: American women at work.* Baltimore: Johns Hopkins Press, 1971.

MACCOBY, E. E. (Ed.) *The development of sex differences.* Stanford: Stanford University Press, 1966.

MEGARGEE, E. I. Influence of sex roles on the manifestation of leadership. *Journal of Applied Psychology,* 1969, 53, 377–382.

NUNNALLY, J. C. *Psychometric theory.* New York: McGraw-Hill, 1967.

ORTH, C. D., & JACOBS, F. Women in management: Pattern for change. *Harvard Business Review,* 1971, 49, 139–147.

ROSENKRANTZ, P., VOGEL, S., BEE, H., BROVERMAN, I., & BROVERMAN, D. M. Sex-role stereotypes and self-concepts in college students. *Journal of Consulting and Clinical Psychology,* 1968, 32, 287–295.

SCHEIN, V. E. The woman industrial psychologist: Illusion or reality? *American Psychologist,* 1971, 26, 708–712.

Women in the work force. *Management Review,* 1970, 59, 20–23.

WYLIE, R. *The self concept.* Lincoln: University of Nebraska Press, 1961.

(Received September 20, 1971)

28

WALTER R. GOVE

Adult Sex Roles and Mental Illness[1]

Mental illness has been the focus of innumerable studies, many of which have looked at the relationship between sociological variables and psychiatric disorders. It has, by now, been established that there is an inverse relationship between social class and mental illness (e.g., Hollingshead and Redlich 1958; Dohrenwend and Dohrenwend 1969; Rushing 1969), although the cause of this relationship is still debated. However, the relationships between mental illness and most other sociological variables remain unclear.

This paper will explore the relationship between adult sex roles and mental illness. Previous attempts to clarify this relationship have produced inconsistent and contradictory results (see, e.g., Dohrenwend and Dohrenwend 1965, 1969; Manis 1968). We believe that a major reason that these results occur in studies dealing with persons in psychiatric treatment is that mental illness has frequently been treated as a residual category in which diverse and unrelated disorders have been grouped (Scheff 1966). In this paper, mental illness will be treated as a fairly specific phenomenon —a disorder which involves personal discomfort (as indicated by distress, anxiety, etc) and/or mental disorganization (as indicated by confusion, thought blockage, motor retardation, and, in the more extreme cases, by hallucinations and delusions) that is not caused by an organic or toxic condition. Two major diagnostic categories which fit our definition are the neurotic disorders and the functional psychoses. The chief characteristic of the neurotic disorders is anxiety in the absence of psychotic disorganization. The functional psychoses (schizophrenia, involutional psychotic reaction, manic depressive reaction, psychotic depressive reaction, and paranoid reaction) are psychotic disorders with no (known) organic cause (American Psychiatric Association 1968).

The two other major diagnostic psychiatric categories, the personality

[1] A condensed version of this paper was presented at the September 1971 meeting of the American Sociological Association. We would like to thank S. Frank Miyamoto for encouraging the pursuit of some suggestive relationships discovered in work done under his very helpful supervision (see Gove 1967), and Antonina Gove, William Rushing, James Thompson, Bruce Dohrenwend, and Mayer Zald for their comments on an earlier draft of this paper. The research for this paper was supported by the Vanderbilt University Research Council.

disorders and the acute and chronic brain disorders, do not conform to our conception of mental illness. Persons with a personality disorder do not experience personal discomfort, being neither anxious nor distressed, nor are they suffering from any form of psychotic disorganization. They are viewed as mentally ill because they do not conform to social norms and are typically forced into treatment because their behavior is disruptive to others. These persons are characterized by aggressive, impulsive, goal-directed behavior which is either antisocial or asocial in nature (American Psychiatric Association 1968; Rowe 1970; Klein and Davis 1969). Not only are the symptoms associated with the personality disorders different from those associated with mental illness (as we are defining it), but the forms of therapy effective in the treatment of mental illness are typically not effective in the treatment of the personality disorders. In fact, it is only recently that the personality disorders have come to be considered within the domain of psychiatry (e.g., Robbins 1966, p. 15). The brain disorders (the acute and chronic brain syndromes) are caused by a physical condition, either brain damage or toxins, and are not a functional disorder. Since personality and brain disorders do not conform to our conception of mental illness, in this paper neither of these disorders will be treated as mental illness.[2]

Almost all psychiatric patients are classified under the diagnostic categories already discussed. Three of the remaining categories, "mental deficiency," "without mental disorder," and "undiagnosed," are largely self-explanatory, infrequently used, and are not relevant to the present paper. The remaining two categories may be of interest. The transient situational (personality) disorder is an acute symptom response to an overwhelming situation where there is no underlying personality disturbance.[3] When the situational stress diminishes, so do the symptoms. This diagnostic

[2] We would emphasize that in our view there are a number of advantages to limiting the category mental illness to the neuroses and the functional psychoses. Most important, we believe that with mental illness delineated in this manner, it is possible to develop a general theory of mental illness. Some work has already been done along these lines (Gove 1968, 1970a). For instance, it has been shown how acute distress may lead to the development of psychotic disorganization in the mentally ill. We recognize that not all readers will agree with our definition of mental illness. Regarding this, we would note that one of the most critical problems in the development of a viable theory is the delimitation of the phenomenon to be explained. As we know from the history of science, attempts at such delimitation are controversial, even when they lead to a synthesis previously lacking (Kuhn 1970). If, using our conception of mental illness, we are able to discover patterns of mental illness that appear to be theoretically meaningful (as we think we do in the latter part of the paper), it is up to the critics of our definition to support their criticism by a systematic marshaling of contrary evidence.

[3] Up until 1968, when the *Diagnostic and Statistical Manual on Mental Disorders* was revised (see American Psychiatric Association 1968), the transient situational disorders were referred to as the transient situational personality disorders.

category is applied mainly to children and adolescents, but it is also occasionally used with adults. Perhaps a person so diagnosed should be included in our conception of mental illness, but it is not absolutely clear. The other category is comprised of the psychophysiologic disorders which are characterized by somatic symptoms that appear to be the consequence of emotional tension although the person is frequently unaware of emotional stress.

We will now turn to a discussion of the characteristics of adult sex roles which we believe are related to mental illness. Implicit in our analysis is the assumption that stress may lead to mental illness. We would like to emphasize that our discussion will be limited to the modern industrial nations of the West, particularly the United States. After looking at the relationship between adult sex roles and mental illness (as indicated by neurosis and the functional psychoses), we will briefly look at other disorders where there is almost undeniably a high degree of distress or anxiety, namely, the transient situational disorders, the psychophysiologic disorders, and suicide.

SEX ROLES

In Western society, as elsewhere, sex acts as a master status, channeling one into particular roles and determining the quality of one's interaction with others (Hughes 1945; Angrist 1969). There are several reasons to assume that, because of the roles they typically occupy, women are more likely than men to have emotional problems. First, most women are restricted to a single major societal role—housewife, whereas most men occupy two such roles, household head and worker. Thus, a man has two major sources of gratification, his family and his work, while a woman has only one, her family. If a male finds one of his roles unsatisfactory, he can frequently focus his interest and concern on the other role. In contrast, if a woman finds her family role unsatisfactory, she typically has no major alternative source of gratification (Bernard 1971, pp. 157–63; also see Lopata 1971, p. 171; Langner and Michael 1963).

Second, it seems reasonable to assume that a large number of women find their major instrumental activities—raising children and keeping house—frustrating. Being a housewife does not require a great deal of skill, for virtually all women, whether educated or not, seem to be capable of being at least moderately competent housewives. Furthermore, it is a position of low prestige.[4] Because the occupancy of such a low-status,

---

[4] Most authors routinely assume that the role of housewife has little prestige (e.g., Harrison 1964; Rossi 1964; Friedan 1963; Parsons 1942; Bardwick 1971; Bernard 1971); however, we have been unable to locate any systematic evaluation of this assumption.

technically undemanding position is not consonant with the educational and intellectual attainment of a large number of women in our society, we might expect such women to be unhappy with the role.

Third, the role of housewife is relatively unstructured and invisible. It is possible for the housewife to put things off, to let things slide, in sum, to perform poorly. The lack of structure and visibility allows her to brood over her troubles, and her distress may thus feed upon itself. In contrast, the job holder must consistently and satisfactorily meet demands that constantly force him to be involved with his environment. Having to meet these structured demands should draw his attention from his troubles and help prevent him from becoming obsessed with his worries.[5]

Fourth, even when a married woman works, she is typically in a less satisfactory position than the married male. There has been a persistent decline in the relative status of women since 1940 as measured by occupation, income, and even education (Knudsen 1969). Women are discriminated against in the job market, and they frequently hold positions that are not commensurate with their educational backgrounds (Harrison 1964; Knudsen 1969; Epstein 1970; Kreps 1971). Furthermore, working wives are typically viewed by themselves and by others as primarily supplementing the family income, which makes their career involvement fairly tenuous (Harrison 1964, p. 79; Epstein 1970, pp. 3–4; Hartley 1959–60). Perhaps more important, working wives appear to be under a greater strain than their husbands. In addition to their job, they apparently typically perform most of the household chores, which means that they work considerably more hours per day than their husbands.[6]

Fifth, several observers have noted that the expectations confronting women are unclear and diffuse (Goode 1960; Parsons 1942; Angrist 1969; Rose 1951; Epstein 1970); many have argued that this lack of specificity creates problems for women[7] (see esp. Rose 1951; Parsons 1942; and Cottrell 1942). Rose (1951), Angrist (1969), Epstein (1970), and Bardwick (1971) note that the feminine role is characterized by the adjusting to and preparing for contingencies. Rose (1951), for example, found that women tend to perceive their career in terms of what men will do, whereas men perceive their career in terms of their own needs. At

---

[5] Although this analysis is somewhat speculative, evidence consistent with it is provided by Langner and Michael (1963, pp. 301–57), Phillips and Segal (1969), Gove (1967), and especially Bradburn and Caplovitz (1965, pp. 95–127).

[6] The evidence indicates this is the case in Europe (Haavio-Manila 1967; Prudenski and Kolpakov 1962; Dahlström and Liljeström 1971), and it appears to be the case in the United States (Hartley 1959–60).

[7] Some investigators (e.g., Mead 1949; Komarovsky 1946; Friedan 1963; Steinmann and Fox 1966; Bardwick 1971) have suggested that the expectations confronting women are not merely diffuse but are in fact contradictory and that women are placed in a serious double bind.

best, it is likely that many women find the uncertainty and lack of control over their future frustrating.

Many authors (Komarovsky 1950; McKee and Sherriffs 1959; Friedan 1963; Mead 1949; Gavron 1966; Rossi 1964; Hartley 1970) have viewed the difficulties confronting women as being a result of recent changes in the woman's role in industrial societies. According to this argument, women previously had a more meaningful role. Families were large, and during most of their adult life women were responsible for the care of children. Without the conveniences of modern industrial society, housework required more time and skill and was highly valued. Since the family's economic support was frequently provided by a family enterprise, the wife played a role in supporting the family. With the development of industrialization and the small nuclear family, the woman's child-rearing years were shortened, her domestic skills were largely replaced by modern conveniences, and she was no longer part of a family enterprise supporting the family. During this time, both sexes were receiving more education; for the male, education produced occupational advancement and diversity; for the female, education was accompanied by a role shrinking in importance. These changes in women's roles were accompanied by changes in the legal and ideological structure, which held that the same standards should apply to men and women. However, instead of being treated as equals, women remained in their old institutionalized positions. If this analysis is correct, much of the presumed stress on women is a relatively recent phenomenon.

To summarize, there are ample grounds for assuming that women find their position in society to be more frustrating and less rewarding than do men and that this may be a relatively recent development. Let us, then, at this point postulate that, because of the difficulties associated with the feminine role in modern Western societies, more women than men become mentally ill. Our analysis of roles has focused primarily, but not exclusively, on the roles of married men and women, and it is within this group that we might expect to find the greatest difference in the rates of mental illness of men and women. Unfortunately, most existing data are presented by sex and not by sex and marital status.

Before we turn to an analysis of the data on mental illness, we might note two types of evidence that appear to support our framework. First, there is considerable evidence that women have a more negative image of themselves than men have of themselves (McKee and Sherriffs 1957, 1959; Sheriffs and McKee 1957; Gurin, Veroff, and Feld 1960, p. 70; Rosenkrantz, Vogel, Bee, Broverman, and Broverman 1968). Second, the available evidence on depression uniformly indicates that women are more likely to become depressed than men (e.g., Silverman 1968).

RATES OF MENTAL ILLNESS FOR ADULT MALES AND FEMALES

To evaluate rates of mental illness for males and females we will look at community surveys, first admissions to mental hospitals, psychiatric admissions to general hospitals, psychiatric care in outpatient clinics, private outpatient psychiatric care, and the prevalence of mental illness in the practices of general physicians. The National Institute of Mental Health (NIMH) provides data for the United States on first admissions to mental hospitals, psychiatric admissions to general hospitals, and psychiatric care in outpatient clinics. Because these data are much more comprehensive than any provided by individual investigators, our discussion of such treatment will be limited to these data. For community surveys and private outpatient care, we will, of course, have to depend upon the outcomes of individual studies (and our ability to locate them).

Community surveys.—In keeping with our concern with sex roles in modern industrial societies, we will discuss only community studies conducted after World War II.[8] We were able to locate 21 community studies done within the time period which dealt with the relationship between sex and mental illness. Three of these studies investigated a population which we felt was probably not relevant for our purposes,[9] and a fourth study provided only very limited information,[10] leaving 17 relevant and usable

[8] There are a number of reasons for taking the period around World War II as a cutoff point. We are concerned with adults, and much of their frame of reference will have been determined by the type of world they grew up in. Women received the vote in 1920, and persons born at this time were only 25 years old at the end of World War II. Furthermore, the major impact of industrialization did not really start until around World War I. Thus, persons much older than 25 at the end of World War II were raised in a situation where the roles and expectations were quite different than they are now. Perhaps one of the best indicators of the change in the woman's role is the proportion of married women who hold jobs, and it wasn't until World War II that a significant proportion of married women held jobs.

[9] The studies were those of Eaton and Weil (1955) who investigated mental illness in the Hutterites, Bellin and Hardt (1958) who investigated mental illness in the aged, and Helgason (1964) who investigated mental illness in all persons born in Iceland between 1895 and 1897. All of these studies, incidentally, found women to have higher rates of mental illness than men.

[10] The reports of the Midtown study (Srole, Langner, Michael, Opler, and Rennie 1962; Langner and Michael 1963) present no statistical breakdown by sex. Of the community studies of mental illness that do not break mental illness down into diagnostic categories, this is the only one whose authors include the personality disorders within their operational definition of mental illness. Thus, their conception of mental illness does not correspond to ours. Using their measure of mental illness, they report they found no significant sex differences at four age levels. Women, however, did report more psychoneurotic and psychophysiological symptoms than men (Langner and Michael 1963, p. 77). As most persons with a personality disorder are men, it would appear (although we cannot be sure) that there were more men with a personality disorder and more women with a psychoneurotic disorder and that they tended to balance each other out.

studies. These studies range from prevalence at a particular point of time (cf. Essen-Möller 1956), to incidence over a specified proportion of time (cf. Hagnell 1966), to an attempt to identify an incident of mental illness at any time in the respondent's lifetime up to the time of the study (Leighton, Leighton, Hardin, Macklin, and MacMillan 1963). Most of the studies focus primarily, although not exclusively, on prevalence at the time of the study. In all the studies that do not provide a diagnostic breakdown, the measures of mental illness relate very well to our conception of mental illness. The results of these studies are presented in table 1. In each case more women than men were found to be mentally ill.

First admissions to psychiatric hospitals.—There are three types of psychiatric hospitals in the United States—public mental hospitals (state and county), private mental hospitals, and VA psychiatric hospitals. The NIMH reports yearly on first admissions to public and private mental hospitals. According to their definition, first admissions include only persons with no prior inpatient psychiatric experience. Their definition thus not only excludes persons who have previously been in a mental hospital but also those who have received inpatient psychiatric treatment in a general hospital (NIMH 1967a, p 16). Using these reports (NIMH 1967a, 1967b), we have calculated the rates of admissions to public and private mental hospitals in the United States by diagnosis for persons 18 and over.[11] These rates are based on the estimates for 1967 of the number of persons in the civilian[12] resident population who are 18 and over and have been age adjusted (standardized).[13] The only relevant information available on the VA psychiatric hospitals is the total number of psychiatric admissions (first admissions and readmissions) with no diagnostic break-down (Administrator of Veterans' Affairs 1967, p. 207). We have there-fore had to estimate the number of first admissions to the VA hospitals. Because VA patients are predominantly male, and we have predicted that more women than men would be mentally ill, we have made estimates which we are virtually certain are too large to avoid favorably biasing our results.[14]

---

[11] The reports on the hospitals are not entirely complete, with 9.1% of public hospitals and 11.1% of private hospitals not reporting. In computing the rates we have corrected for these hospitals by assuming that their rates were equal to the overall hospital average.

[12] By taking the civilian population we are slightly inflating the male rate which from our point of view unfavorably biases the results. It should be noted that the military population has received a psychiatric screening which leaves a dispropor-tionate number of mentally ill persons in the civilian population.

[13] The age-specific rates were calculated using the U.S. Bureau of the Census (1970) estimates of the 1967 population. These rates were then standardized on the 1966 population (U.S., Bureau of the Census 1966).

[14] The specific procedures used in making these estimates as well as our rationale

TABLE 1

PERCENTAGE OF MEN AND WOMEN FOUND TO BE MENTALLY ILL IN
COMMUNITY SURVEYS

Source	Male	Female	Sample Size
	A. Rates Based Solely on Responses to Structured Interview		
Martin, Brotherston, and Chave (1957, p. 200) ..	25	Over 40	750
Phillips and Segal (1969, p. 61)	21.2	35.5	278
Phillips (1966)	21	34	600
Bradburn and Caplovitz (1965, p. 30)	31	54	2,006
Tauss (1967, p. 122)	18.4	38.0	707
Taylor and Chave (1964, p. 50)	22	43	422
Gurin et al. (1960, p. 189)*	22	40	2,460
Haberman (1969):			
Washington Heights	18.2	25.3	1,865
New York City	14.9	33.3	706
Hare and Shaw (1965, p. 25):			
New Adam	15.6	22.9	1,015
Old Bute	13.1	26.3	924
Public Health Service (1970, p. 27)†	14.9	34.2	6,672
Bradburn (1969, p. 119)‡	20.3	38.9	2,379
Melle and Haese (1969, p. 239)	...	§	5,498
	B. Rates Based on Clinical Evaluation (Psychosis and Neurosis)		
Pasamanick et al. (1959, p. 188)	4.2	7.1	809
Primrose (1962, pp. 18–24)‖	4.7	14.7	1,701
Essen-Möller (1956, pp. 148–49)	1.7	3.7	2,550
Hagnell (1966, pp. 99–103)‖,#	6.0	15.6	2,550
	C. Rates Based on Several Sources** (Psychosis and Neurosis)		
Leighton et al. (1963, pp. 265–67)	45	66	1,010

* Gurin et al. (1960) present their data along four symptom factors—psychological anxiety, physical health, immobilization, and physical anxiety. The figures presented refer to a score of 5 or more on the psychological anxiety factor. Women also scored higher than men on the other three factors.
† Rate indicates persons with three or more symptoms.
‡ Rates of persons high on symptoms of anxiety.
§ 2.5 times male rate.
‖ Study involved the complete survey of an entire community and excludes psychosis due to organic disorder.
Rates for neurosis calculated by authors from data on pp. 99–102. (Child neurosis was not considered when calculating the rates.)
** Rates combine psychosis and neurosis and are based on interviews, observations of interviewer, hospital and other institutional records, impressions of physicians in contact with respondent, and impressions of community informants.

The data on first admissions to mental hospitals are presented in table 2. Because we have overestimated VA admissions, the true rate falls somewhere between the combined rate for public and private hospitals and

---

for them are available from the authors upon request. We would simply note here that data presented by Pollack, Radick, Brown, Wurster, and Gorwitz (1964, p. 511) for Louisiana and Maryland indicate that our estimates for VA admissions are between two and four times too large.

TABLE 2

First Admissions to Mental Hospitals in the United States
(Persons per 100,000)

	State and County	Private	Combined	Ratio F/M	VA Hospitals Over-estimate	All Hospitals	Ratio F/M
Functional psychosis:							
Male	293	89	382		61	443	
				1.27			1.10
Female	322	162	484		2	486	
Neurosis:							
Male	107	99	206		22	238	
				1.68			1.46
Female	165	182	347		1	348	
Total:							
Male	400	188	588		83	671	
				1.41			1.24
Female	487	344	831		3	834	

the rate presented for all hospitals. Even looking at the all-hospital rate, which inflates the rate for males, it is obvious that there are more mentally ill women admitted to mental hospitals.

Psychiatric care in general hospitals.—About as many persons receive inpatient psychiatric treatment in general hospitals as are cared for in mental hospitals. Such treatment is generally quite brief with most of the persons returning to the community, although a few go on to become patients in mental hospitals. The NIMH reports yearly on the number and characteristics of the psychiatric discharges from general hospitals with inpatient psychiatric services. This report does not cover general hospitals under federal control. Using the NIMH (1967d) report, we have calculated the discharge rates for 1967 by diagnosis for persons 18 and over in the United States.[15] As before, these rates are based on estimates of the civilian population 18 and over (U.S., Bureau of the Census 1970) and have been age standardized. Because of the rapid patient turnover in general hospitals, the psychiatric admission rates (first admissions and readmissions combined) and discharge rates should be virtually equivalent. For the VA general hospitals we have the total

[15] The reports on the general hospitals with psychiatric inpatient services are not complete, with 31.4% of the hospitals not reporting. In computing the rates we have corrected for these hospitals by assuming that their discharge rates were equivalent to the average of the other hospitals.

number of psychiatric admissions but lack additional information (Administrator of Veterans' Affairs 1967, p. 207). In calculating these rates, we, therefore, have had to make estimates for two parameters.[16] From the Public Health Service (1967) we have discharge data on all public health general hospitals by sex and diagnosis. In the same manner as before we have used these data to calculate age-standardized rates. More mentally ill women are treated in general hospitals, with the discrepancy between men and women being even greater than in the mental hospitals (table 3).

TABLE 3

PSYCHIATRIC CARE IN GENERAL HOSPITALS IN THE UNITED STATES
(PERSONS PER 100,000)

	Nonfederal Hospitals*	VA General Hospitals†	Public Health Hospitals*	All General Hospitals	Ratio F/M
Functional psychosis:					
Male	816	109	6	931	1.44
Female	1,334	3	0	1,337	
Neurosis:					
Male	959	128	₌11	1,098	1.89
Female	2,068	4	4	2,076	
Total:					
Male	1,775	237	17	2,029	1.68
Female	3,402	7	4	3,413	

* Rates based on discharges.
† Rates based on admissions.

Psychiatric out-patient care (excluding private practice).—The NIMH (1967e) also conducts a yearly survey of outpatient psychiatric facilities. In their yearly report, they present information on terminations by age, sex, and diagnosis. We have, as before, used this information to compute age-standardized rates based on the civilian population for persons 18 and over for 1967.[17]

[16] To estimate the proportion of men and women who were discharged we used the proportion of men and women who were psychiatric residents in the VA hospitals in 1967 (NIMH 1967c). To estimate the diagnostic distribution of admissions to the VA hospitals we used the diagnostic distribution of men and women discharged from the nonfederal general hospitals.

[17] The reports on the outpatient clinics not associated with the VA are not complete, with 27.2% of such clinics not reporting. In computing the rates we have corrected for these clinics by assuming that the termination of the nonreporting clinics were

The rates for men and women are quite similar to those which dealt with psychiatric hospitalization, with more mentally ill women than men treated in these clinics (table 4). It should be noted that the NIMH report does not include facilities where a mental health professional other than a psychiatrist directs the mental health program and assumes responsibility for the patients. However, a study by Zolik and Marches (1968) indicates that the proportions of men and women who are treated as mentally ill in such facilities are very similar to the proportions presented here.

TABLE 4

Care in Psychiatric Clinics in the United States (Persons per 100,000) Rates Based on Terminations

	All Outpatient Clinics (Except VA)	VA Outpatient Clinics	All Clinics	Ratio F/M
Functional psychosis:				
Male	573	114	687	
Female	832	2	834	1.21
Neurosis:				
Male	433	122	555	
Female	956	3	959	1.73
Total:				
Male	1,006	236	1,242	
Female	1,788	5	1,793	1.44

Private outpatient psychiatric care.—To discover the relative proportions of mentally ill men and women in private outpatient psychiatric care we again must turn to studies conducted by various investigators. Unfortunately, we have only been able to locate a few studies which indicate the sex distribution of the practices of psychiatrists. As indicated in table 5, these studies all found that more women than men are seen by psychiatrists. The magnitude of this relationship may be somewhat obscured by the fact that all of these studies include disturbances such as the personality disorders.

Most persons who receive treatment for mental illness are treated by physicians in the community who lack special psychiatric training. These

equivalent to the average of the reporting clinics. The rates for the VA clinics are based on estimates made by the NIMH for *all* VA clinic terminations.

TABLE 5

Contact with a Psychiatrist—All Types of Mental Disorders

Source	Men (%)	Women (%)	Patients (N)
Private office practice:			
Gordon and Gordon (1958, p. 544):			
Bergen County	41	59	(746)
Ulster County	34	66	(264)
Cattaraugus County	37	63	(239)
Bahn, Gardner, Alltop, Knatterud, and Solomon (1966, p. 2046)	...	*	(270)
Referred to psychiatrist:			
Watts, Caute, and Kuenssberg (1964, p. 1355) Referrals	39	61	(4,452)†
Innes and Sharp (1962, p. 449) Referred from general population in given year	0.5	0.6	(2,003)
Outpatients:‡			
Hagnell (1966, p. 46)	2.9	7.6	(2,550)

* Rates higher for females.
† Based on a study of 261 general practices.
‡ Persons from the general population who saw a psychiatrist as outpatients over a 10-year period.

physicians also play a major role in channeling persons into more specialized psychiatric care (see Susser 1968; p. 246). Most of the mentally ill persons treated by general physicians are suffering from a psychoneurotic disorder. In table 6 we have presented some of the findings regarding the proportion of men and women that are treated for mental illness by general practitioners.[18] All of the studies that have looked at this relationship have found that more women receive such treatment. The finding by Shepherd, Cooper, Brown, and Kalton (1964, p. 1361) that psychiatric disorders ranked third among presenting conditions for women and seventh among men suggests that this relationship cannot be explained by assuming that women simply go to physicians more frequently than men.

In summary, *all* of the information on persons in psychiatric treatment indicates that more women are mentally ill. This information exactly parallels the data from the community studies and is thus consistent with our formulation that the adult woman in modern industrial society is more likely to experience mental illness.

Other relevant psychiatric disorders.—Earlier, while discussing the relationship between the various diagnostic categories and mental illness (as

[18] Table 6 does not present all the relevant studies, being limited to those that are relatively recent and readily available. For a discussion of the earlier and less easily located studies, see Ryle (1960) and Watts (1962).

TABLE 6

TREATMENT OF MEN AND WOMEN FOR MENTAL ILLNESS BY GENERAL PRACTITIONERS

Source	Men (%)	Women (%)	Patients (N)	Practices Studied (N)
	A. Percentage in Specified Population Being Treated			
Hare and Staw (1965, p. 26):				
New Adam	3.0	7.5	(990)	...
Old Bute	3.4	7.4	(875)	...
Taylor and Chave (1964, p. 118)	5.5	9.4	(2,826)	...
	B. Percentage of Mentally Ill Patients in Practice			
Fry (1960, p. 86)	7.1	16.3	(5,471)	(1)
Ryle (1960, p. 324)	1.4	7.1	(2,400)	(1)
Logan and Cushion (1958, pp. 69–70)	3.0	6.4	(114,294)	(106)
Kessel (1960, p. 18)	11.1	15.8	(670)	(1)
Martin et al. (1957, p. 199)	3.5	7.5	...	...
Shepherd et al. (1964, p. 1361)	5.9	12.6	(14,697)	(40)
Cooper (1966, p. 9)	17.4	27.2	(7,454)	...
Cooper, Brown, and Kalton (1962)	6.9	15.6	(743)	...
	C. Sex Distribution of Patients Receiving Treatment for Mental Illness			
Watts et al. (1964, p. 1355)	32.0	68.0	(6,123)	...
Mazer (1967)	31.8	68.2	(154)	...

we have identified it), we noted that there were two relatively infrequently used categories—the transient situational personality disorders, and the psychophysiologic disorders—which appear to reflect a high degree of anxiety or distress.

As noted, the transient situational personality disorders are characterized by an acute symptom response to an overwhelming situation which is followed by the disappearance of the symptoms when the stress is withdrawn. Using the same sources and techniques as before, we calculated the rates in the United States for the transient disorders for persons 18 and over by (1) first admissions to mental hospitals, (2) psychiatric treatment in general hospitals, and (3) terminations from outpatient clinics. There are many more women treated for transient disorders in general hospitals and outpatient clinics (table 7). Only a very few persons with transient disorders are admitted to mental hospitals, and here the rates for males and females are roughly equal. These data, taken together, indicate that considerably more women experience a transient situational personality disorder.

The psychophysiologic disorders are characterized by a somatic disorder that appears to result from emotional tension. Some authors have

TABLE 7

PSYCHIATRIC TREATMENT OF THE TRANSIENT SITUATIONAL DISORDERS IN
THE UNITED STATES (PERSONS PER 100,000)

Type of Hospital	Male	Female
First Admissions to Mental Hospitals		
State and county	26	23
Private	5	6
VA (high estimate)	5	0
Total	36	29
Psychiatric Care in General Hospitals		
Nonfederal*	65	120
VA†	9	0
Public health*	...	...
Total	74	120
Care in Psychiatric Outpatient Clinics‡		
All except VA	166	271
VA	0	0
Total	166	271

* Rates based on discharges.
† Rates based on admissions.
‡ Rates based on terminations.

speculated (e.g., Hagnell 1966, p. 155) that men tend to react to stress by developing a psychophysiologic disorder, while women may in comparable situations become mentally ill, and that this may explain the higher rate of psychiatric morbidity in women. In the same manner as before, we have calculated the rates in the United States for the psychophysiologic disorders for persons 18 and over by (1) first admission to mental hospitals, (2) psychiatric treatment in general hospitals, and (3) terminations from outpatient clinics (table 8). A few of the community surveys and three of the studies of the practices of general physicians present the proportion of men and women with a psychophysiologic disorder. The data on psychiatric treatment,[19] the practices of general physicians, and the results of the community surveys all indicate that more women than men have a psychophysiologic disorder (table 8). The data on the transient and the psychophysiologic disorders thus supplement the earlier finding that women are more likely than men to be mentally ill.

[19] It is only in the general hospital that many persons receive psychiatric treatment for psychophysiologic disorders, and it is only here that there is a difference between male and female rates.

TABLE 8

PSYCHOPHYSIOLOGIC AND PSYCHOSOMATIC DISORDERS
A. PSYCHIATRIC TREATMENT OF PSYCHOPHYSIOLOGIC DISORDERS IN THE UNITED STATES
(PERSONS PER 100,000)

Type of Hospital	Male	Female
	First Admissions to Mental Hospitals	
State and county	2	2
Private	2	2
VA (high estimate)	0	0
Total	4	4
	Psychiatric Care in General Hospitals	
Nonfederal*	70	137
VA general†	9	0
Public Health	2	0
Total	81	137
	Care in Psychiatric Outpatient Clinics‡	
All except VA	20	27
VA	6	0
Total	26	27

B. COMMUNITY SURVEYS

Source	Male (%)	Female (%)	Sample Size
Pasamanick, Roberts, Lemkau, and Kreuger (1959, p. 188)	18.9	52.4	809
Essen-Möller (1956, pp. 148–49)§	18.2	30.7	2,550
Llewellyn-Thomas (1960, p. 201)	31.0	59.0	274
Leighton et al. (1963, p. 264)	65.0	71.0	1,010

C. STUDIES OF PRACTICES OF GENERAL PHYSICIANS

Source	Male (%)	Female (%)	Sample Size	Practices Studied (N)
Shepherd et al. (1964, p. 1361)‖	2.5	3.5	14,697	(46)
Mazur (1967)#	41.6	58.4	89**	(5)
Watts (1962, p. 40)††	...	‡‡	114,294	(106)

* Rates based on discharges.
† Rates based on all admissions.
‡ Rates based on terminations.
§ Persons age 15 and over.
‖ Proportion of persons over age 15 with psychosomatic disorders.
\# Sex distribution of patients with psychophysiologic disorders.
** Patients with disorder.
†† Sex distribution of patients with psychosomatic disorders.
‡‡ 3 women to 2 men.

Suicide.—Although not a form of mental illness, suicide reflects a high degree of distress. More men than women commit suicide (Farberow and Schneidman 1965; Stengel 1969; Maris 1969), which might be taken as suggesting that more men are distressed. However, "the number of suicidal attempts is six to ten times that of the suicides, at least in urban communities" (Stengel 1969, p. 89), and women are much more likely to attempt suicide (Stengel 1969; Farberow and Schneidman 1965). Thus, if we look at suicide attempts (including those that were successful), we would conclude that women are more distressed than men. In short, a simple comparison of the suicidal behavior of men and women gives ambiguous results and makes any generalization rather tenuous. However, as shown elsewhere (Gove 1972a), a more detailed analysis does seem to support our role framework. To cite simply one example, in England and Wales (Stengel 1969, p. 26) and in the United States (Maris 1969, p. 7) the rates of suicide among women have greatly increased in recent years whereas they have not among men, which, of course, is consistent with the discussed changes in the woman's role in Western society.

All the data on mental illness (as we have defined it) indicate that more women than men are mentally ill. It is especially important to note that this finding is not dependent on who is doing the selection. For example, if we look at admissions to mental hospitals, where the societal response would appear to be of prime importance, women have higher rates; if we look at treatment by general physicians, where self-selection would appear to be of prime importance, women have higher rates; and if we look at community surveys, where the attempt is to eliminate selective processes, women have higher rates.

Before we evaluate other explanations for the sex difference in the rate of mental illness, we will briefly discuss some data that suggest that this difference results from the characteristics of male and female roles in modern society.

EVIDENCE FOR THE ROLE EXPLANATION

If the reader reviews our argument regarding why women are more likely to be mentally ill then men, he will note that we focused primarily on the roles of married women and men, which we indicated were quite different. In contrast, the roles of unmarried men and women appear to be more similar. Thus, our role analysis suggests that the major difference in rates of mental illness between men and women is found among married men and women.

Elsewhere, Gove (1972b) has reviewed the studies in the modern industrial nations conducted after World War II that present the relationship between marital status and mental disorder. Unfortunately, these studies use quite varying definitions of mental disorder. However, all these studies indicate that married women are more likely to have a mental disorder than married men. The results were quite different for unmarried persons. When never-married men were compared with never-married women, divorced men with divorced women, and widowed men with widowed women, it was found that within each of these statuses some studies indicated that men had higher rates and others that women had higher rates. Furthermore, if there was a pattern within these categories, it was that men were more likely than women to be mentally ill, for within each of the unmarried statuses more studies found men to have the higher rates of mental illness.

Because woman's position in our society has undergone major changes in the relatively recent past, we might expect some changes over time in the ratio of men to women that were mentally ill. There is, in fact, some evidence that there was a change in this ratio some time around World War II. It appears, for example, that prior to World War II more men than women with psychotic disorders were admitted to mental hospitals (Landis and Page 1938, p. 40; Goldhamer and Marshall 1953, p. 65; U.S., Bureau of the Census 1930, 1941). Furthermore, the community studies cited by Dohrenwend and Dohrenwend, which they feel indicate that there is no sex difference in rates of mental illness, also suggest a shift toward relatively higher rates of mental illness in women. Of the studies they cite, which were conducted in Western Europe or North America following World War II, 12 showed higher rates for women, while none showed higher rates for men. However, of the pre–World War II studies conducted in these areas, three show higher rates for women and eight show higher rates for men (Dohrenwend and Dohrenwend 1969, p. 15).

Further evidence that the disproportionately large number of mentally ill women is a product of the social system is provided by the community study by Leighton et al. (1963, pp. 322–53). As in other community surveys, they found that in general more women than men were mentally ill. More important, they discovered two types of communities that had con-trasting results, namely a set of three communities that were undergoing a severe economic depression, and an Acadian French village which was extremely well integrated. As one might expect, the depressed communities had a higher than average rate of mental illness. What is interesting is that in these communities men had somewhat higher rates of mental illness than women. This makes sense considering that an extremely poor employment situation probably has more impact on men. The integrated French Acadian community had very low rates of mental illness, with women being noticeably lower than men. This community was an extremely close-knit, traditional, family-oriented village, culturally isolated from the larger society. It is likely that in this community the woman's role corresponded rather closely to that of a preindustrial Western society.

ALTERNATIVE PERSPECTIVES

The societal reaction perspective.—During the past decade the societal reaction perspective has been one of the most pervasive and influential sociological approaches to deviance (e.g., Becker 1963; Erikson 1964; Scheff 1966; Schur 1969). Scheff (1966), in particular, has used this approach to explain stabilized mental illness. According to this perspective, a person comes to occupy the role of the mentally ill primarily because of the actions of others. It is Scheff's (1966) formulation that: (1) virtually everyone at some time commits acts that correspond to the public stereotype of mental illness; (2) if these acts should become public knowledge, the individual may, depending upon various contingencies, be referred to the appropriate officials; and (3) the person will then be routinely processed as mentally ill and placed in a mental institution. In short, a person becomes mentally ill primarily because others perceive him as mentally ill and act accordingly.

There is fairly strong evidence that if both men and women perform acts indicative of mental illness, men are much more likely to be perceived and reacted to as mentally ill. For example, Phillips (1964), using hypothetical case descriptions of mental illness, consistently found that men were rejected more strongly than women even though the behavior in each case was the same. The discrepancy between the sexes was the greatest in the case of the simple schizophrenic characterized primarily by the nonperformance of instrumental roles. Fairly similar findings have been presented by Larson (1970) and Fletcher (1969). Furthermore, the evidence from these case descriptions appears to reflect real processes. For example, psychotic males are hospitalized at an earlier age than psychotic women (e.g., Gove 1972c), and an important finding by Raskin and Golob (1966) indicates that the males' earlier hospitalization is not due to an earlier manifestation of symptoms but to a quicker response by society to their psychotic symptoms.

If the rates of manifest distress and disorganization were equal for males and females, the fact that such symptoms are more inconsistent with the masculine role would lead people to perceive and respond to males as mentally ill more frequently than to females. Thus, the societal reaction perspective leads (at least in its pure form) to the prediction that more males than females would be treated as mentally ill.[20] As we have seen,

[20] This prediction is obvious in the area of psychiatric hospitalization, where societal reaction typically plays a major role in effecting entrance into treatment. Societal

this prediction is incorrect, for women appear, on all indicators, to have higher rates of mental illness. Furthermore, we do not feel that the societal reaction perspective could be used to explain the patterned variations discussed in the previous section. We therefore conclude that the societal reaction perspective does not provide a satisfactory explanation for the data presented in this paper. 'This finding complements other evidence (Gove 1970b), which indicates that the societal reaction perspective does not provide a valid general theory of mental illness.

Women are expressive.—Phillips and Segal (1969) recently noted that community studies of mental illness which are based on self-reported symptoms find that women have a higher rate of psychiatric disturbance than men. They believe, however, that this is due not to "real sex differences in frequency of disturbance but rather to man's greater reluctance to admit certain unpleasurable feelings and sensation," since men believe such behavior is not masculine (Phillips and Segal 1969, p. 69). In other words, it is "more culturally appropriate and acceptable for women to be more expressive about their difficulties" (Phillips and Segal 1969, p. 59). However, they apparently do not feel that the simple willingness to express symptoms would lead persons to seek professional help, for they note that when other relevant variables are controlled the expression of such symptoms is not related to seeking medical help, and they feel that "respondents themselves probably do not often interpret these psychiatric symptoms as indicators of illness—physical or psychological—that could profit from professional attention" (Phillips and Segal 1969, p. 65).

The Phillips-Segal explanation is based on the different cultural roles of men and women. Because space does not permit us to systematically evaluate all the possible elaborations of this type of explanation, we will simply point to some areas which suggest that this approach will not serve as a general explanation of the differences in the rates of mental illness of men and women. First, unmarried men have as high, if not higher, rates of mental illness as unmarried women. Second, the fact that the rates for men appear to have been higher prior to World War II would appear to contradict the "women are expressive" explanation. Third, we do not see how the expressive explanation can account for women having higher rates of admissions to mental hospitals, for typically hospitalization is initiated by someone else. Fourth, all the community studies based on a *clinical* evaluation, which (presumably) are not affected by the expressiveness of women, found women to have higher rates of mental illness.

---

reaction theorists generally have not dealt with the issue of voluntary self-referrals. However, we (perhaps debatably) reason that males would be more likely than females to perceive the manifestation of psychiatric symptoms as indicating they were mentally ill, for such symptoms are more out of tune with the masculine than the feminine stereotype.

Although we feel the expressiveness explanation does not account for the main thrust of the data presented in this paper, we do tentatively accept the hypothesis that women are more expressive than men, and we would like some solid data on how this trait interacts (if at all) with the various ways of identifying mental illness.

SUMMARY

We have argued that the woman's role in modern industrial societies has a number of characteristics that may promote mental illness and have explored the possibility that in such societies women have higher rates of mental illness than men. In our analysis we have utilized a fairly precise definition of mental illness, limiting it to functional disorders characterized by anxiety (neurosis) and/or mental disorganization (psychosis). The information on first admissions to mental hospitals, psychiatric treatment in general hospitals, psychiatric outpatient clinics, private outpatient psychiatric care, the practices of general physicians, and community surveys all indicate that more women than men are mentally ill. A survey of the information on two other diagnostic categories which may reflect mental illness (as we have defined it)—the transient situation disorders and the psychophysiologic disorders—also revealed that women are more likely to have these disorders. Patterned variations in the rates of mental illness among men and women have been described suggesting that the ordering of these rates is a reflection of the position of men and women in society. However, we would like to emphasize that we need to know much more about how the woman's role produces high rates of mental illness, and without more research we can only speculate, as we have done, on what the important factors might be.

REFERENCES

Administrator of Veterans' Affairs. 1967. *Annual Report 1967.* Washington, D.C.: Government Printing Office.
American Psychiatric Association. 1968. *Diagnostic and Statistical Manual on Mental Disorders.* Washington, D.C.: American Psychiatric Association.
Angrist, Shirley. 1969. "The Study of Sex Roles." *Journal of Social Issues* 25 (January): 215–32.
Bahn, Anita, Elmer Gardner, Lacoe Alltop, Genell Knatterud, and Murray Solomon. 1966. "Admission and Prevalence Rates for Psychiatric Facilities in Four Register Areas." *American Journal of Public Health* 56 (December): 2033–51.
Bardwick, Judith. 1971. *The Psychology of Women: A Study of Bio-Cultural Conflicts.* New York: Harper & Row.
Becker, Howard. 1963. *Outsiders: Studies in the Sociology of Deviance.* New York: Free Press.
Bellin, Seymour, and Robert Hardt. 1958. "Marital Status and Mental Disorders among the Aged." *American Sociological Review* 23 (April): 155–62.
Bernard, Jessie. 1971. *Women and the Public Interest.* Chicago: Aldine-Atherton.

Bradburn, Norman. 1969. *The Structure of Psychological Well-being.* Chicago: Aldine.

Bradburn, Norman, and David Caplovitz. 1965. *Reports on Happiness.* Chicago: Aldine.

Cooper, Brian. 1966. "Psychiatric Disorder in Hospital and General Practice." *Social Psychiatry* 1(1): 7–10.

Cooper, B., A. C. Brown, and G. G. W. Kalton. 1962. "A Pilot Study of Psychiatric Morbidity in General Practice." *Journal of the College of General Practitioners* 5 (November): 590–602.

Cottrell, Leonard. 1942. "The Adjustment of the Individual to His Age and Sex Roles." *American Sociological Review* 7 (October): 617–20.

Dahlström, Edmund, and Rita Liljeström. 1971. "The Family and Married Women at Work." In *The Changing Roles of Men and Women,* edited by Edmund Dahlström. Boston: Beacon.

Dohrenwend, Bruce, and Barbara S. Dohrenwend. 1965. "The Problem of Validity in Field Studies of Psychological Disorder." *Journal of Abnormal Psychology* 70(4): 52–69.

———. 1969. *Social Status and Psychological Disorder.* New York: Wiley.

Eaton, Joseph, and Robert Weil. 1955. *Culture and Mental Disorders.* Glencoe, Ill.: Free Press.

Epstein, Cynthia. 1970. *Woman's Place.* Berkeley: University of California Press.

Erikson, Kai. 1964. "Notes on the Sociology of Deviance." In *The Other Side,* edited by Howard Becker. New York: Free Press.

Essen-Möller, Erik. 1956. "Individual Traits and Morbidity in a Swedish Rural Population." *Acta Psychiatrica et Neurologica Scandinavica,* Supplementum 100: 1–160.

Farberow, Norman, and Edwin Schneidman. 1965. *The Cry for Help.* New York: McGraw-Hill.

Fletcher, Richard. 1969. "Measuring Community Mental Health Attitudes by Means of Hypothetical Case Descriptions." *Social Psychiatry* 4(4): 152–56.

Friedan, Betty. 1963. *The Feminine Mystique.* New York: Norton.

Fry, John. 1960. "What Happens to Our Neurotic Patients?" *Practitioner* 185 (July): 85–89.

Gavron, Hannah. 1966. *The Captive Wife: Conflicts of Housebound Mothers.* London: Routledge & Kegan Paul.

Goldhamer, Herbert, and Andrew Marshall. 1953. *Psychosis and Civilization: Two Studies in the Frequency of Mental Disease.* Glencoe, Ill.: Free Press.

Goode, William. 1960. "Norm Commitment and Conformity to Role Status Obligations." *American Journal of Sociology* 66 (November): 246–58.

Gordon, Richard, and Katherine Gordon. 1958. "Psychiatric Problems of a Rapidly Growing Suburb." *A.M.A. Archives of Neurology and Psychiatry* 79 (May): 543–48.

Gove, Walter. 1967. "Types of Psychiatric Patients." Master's thesis, University of Washington, Seattle.

———. 1968. "A Theory of Mental Illness: An Analysis of the Relationship between Symptoms, Personal Attributes and Social Situations." Ph.D. dissertation, University of Washington, Seattle.

———. 1970a. "Sleep Deprivation: A Cause of Psychotic Disorganization." *American Journal of Sociology* 75 (March): 782–99.

———. 1970b. "Societal Reaction as an Explanation of Mental Illness: An Evaluation." *American Sociological Review* 35 (October): 873–84.

———. 1972a. "Sex Roles, Marital Status and Suicide." *Journal of Health and Social Behavior* 13 (June): 204–13.

———. 1972b. "The Relationship between Sex Roles, Mental Illness and Marital Status." *Social Forces,* vol. 51 (September).

———. 1972c. "The Interaction of Sex Roles and Mental Illness as a Factor Determining Time of Entrance into Treatment and the Development of Chronicity." Unpublished manuscript.

Gurin, Gerald, Joseph Veroff, and Sheila Feld. 1960. *Americans View Their Mental Health*. New York: Basic.

Haavio-Mannila, Elina. 1967. "Sex Differentiation in Role Expectations and Performance." *Journal of Marriage and the Family* 29 (August): 368–78.

Haberman, Paul. 1969. "Cross-Survey Analysis of Psychiatric Symptomology: A Corroborative Report on Subgroup Differences." Paper read at annual meeting of the American Sociological Association, San Francisco.

Hagnell, Olle. 1966. *A Prospective Study of the Incidence of Mental Disorder*. Sweden: Berlingska Boktryckeriet.

Hare, E. H., and G. K. Shaw. 1965. *Mental Health on a New Housing Estate*. London: Oxford University Press.

Harrison, Evelyn. 1964. "The Working Women: Barriers in Employment." *Public Administration Review* 24 (June): 78–85.

Hartley, Ruth. 1959–60. "Some Implications of Current Changes in Sex Role Patterns." *Merrill-Palmer Quarterly of Behavior and Development* 6 (April): 153–64b.

———. 1970. "American Core Culture: Changes and Continuities." In *Sex Roles in a Changing Society*, edited by Georgene Seward and Robert C. Williamson. New York: Random House.

Helgason, Thomas. 1964. "Epidemiology of Mental Disorders in Iceland." *Acta Psychiatrica Scandinavica*, Supplementum 173:1–258.

Hollingshead, August, and Fredrick Redlich. 1958. *Social Class and Mental Illness*. New York: Wiley.

Hughes, Everett. 1945. "Dilemmas and Contradictions of Status." *American Journal of Sociology* 50 (March): 353–59.

Innes, George, and Geoffrey Sharp. 1962. "A Study of Psychiatric Patients in North-East Scotland." *Journal of Mental Science* 108 (July): 447–56.

Kessel, W. I. N. 1960. "Psychiatric Morbidity in a London General Practice." *British Journal of Preventive Social Medicine* 14 (January): 16–22.

Klein, Donald, and John Davis. 1969. *Diagnosis and Drug Treatment of Psychiatric Disorders*. Baltimore: Williams & Wilkins.

Knudsen, Dean. 1969. "The Declining Status of Women: Popular Myths and the Failure of Functionalist Thought." *Social Forces* 48 (December): 183–93.

Komarovsky, Mirra. 1946. "Cultural Contradiction and Sex Roles." *American Journal of Sociology* 52 (November): 184–89.

———. 1950. "Functional Analysis of Sex Roles." *American Sociological Review* 15 (August): 508–16.

Kreps, Juanita. 1971. *Sex in the Market Place: American Women at Work*. Baltimore: Johns Hopkins Press.

Kuhn, Thomas. 1970. *The Structure of Scientific Revolutions*. Chicago: University of Chicago Press.

Landis, Carney, and James Page. 1938. *Modern Society and Mental Disease*. New York: Farrar & Rinehart.

Langner, Thomas, and Stanley Michael. 1963. *Life Stress and Mental Health*. New York: Free Press.

Larson, Richard. 1970. "The Influence of Sex Roles and Symptoms on Clergymen's Perceptions of Mental Illness." *Pacific Sociological Review* 13 (Winter): 53–61.

Leighton, Dorothea, Alexander Leighton, John Hardin, David Macklin, and Allister MacMillan. 1963. *The Character of Danger*. New York: Basic.

Llewellyn-Thomas, Edward. 1960. "The Prevalence of Psychiatric Symptoms within an Island Community." *Canadian Medical Association Journal* 83 (July): 197–204.

Logan, W. P. D., and A. A. Cushion. 1958. *Morbidity Statistics from General Practice*. Vol. 1. Studies on Medical Population Subjects no. 14. London: Her Majesty's Stationery Office.

Lopata, Helena. 1971. *Occupation Housewife*. New York: Oxford University Press.

McKee, John, and Alex Sheriffs. 1957. "The Differential Evaluation of Males and Females." *Journal of Personality* 25 (March): 356–71.

————. 1959. "Men's and Women's Beliefs, Ideals and Self-Concepts." *American Journal of Sociology* 64 (January): 356–63.

Manis, Jerome. 1968. "The Sociology of Knowledge and Community Mental Health Research." *Social Problems* 15 (Spring): 488–501.

Maris, Ronald. 1969. *Social Forces in Urban Suicide.* Homewood, Ill.: Dorsey.

Martin, F. M., J. H. F. Brotherston, and S. P. W. Chave. 1957. "Incidence of Neurosis in a New Housing Estate." *British Journal of Preventive Social Medicine* 11 (October): 196–202.

Mazer, Milton. 1967. "Psychiatric Disorders in General Practice: The Experience of an Island Community." *American Journal of Psychiatry* 124 (November): 609–15.

Mead, Margaret. 1949. *Male and Female.* New York: Morrow.

Meile, Richard, and Philip Haese. 1969. "Social Status, Status Incongruence and Symptoms of Stress." *Journal of Health and Social Behavior* 10 (September): 237–44.

National Institute of Mental Health. 1967a. *Patients in State and County Mental Hospitals 1967.* Washington, D.C.: Government Printing Office.

————. 1967b. *Patient Characteristics Private Mental Hospitals 1967.* Washington, D.C.: Government Printing Office.

————. 1967c. *Veterans with Mental Disorders 1963–1967.* Washington, D.C.: Government Printing Office.

————. 1967d. *General Hospital Inpatient Psychiatric Service 1967.* Washington, D.C.: Government Printing Office.

————. 1967e. *Outpatient Psychiatric Services 1967.* Washington, D.C.: Government Printing Office.

Parsons, Talcott. 1942. "Age and Sex in the Social Structure of the United States." *American Sociological Review* 7 (October): 604–16.

Pasamanick, Benjamin, Dean Roberts, Paul Lemkau, and Dean Krueger. 1959. "A Survey of Mental Disease in an Urban Population: Prevalence by Race and Income." In *Epidemiology of Mental Disorder,* edited by Benjamin Pasamanick. Washington, D.C.: American Association for the Advancement of Science.

Phillips, Derek. 1964. "Rejection of the Mentally Ill: The Influence of Behavior and Sex." *American Sociological Review* 29 (October): 679–87.

————. 1966. "The 'True Prevalence' of Mental Illness in a New England State Community." *Mental Health Journal* 2 (Spring): 35–40.

Phillips, Derek, and Bernard Segal. 1969. "Sexual Status and Psychiatric Symptoms." *American Sociological Review* 34 (February): 58–72.

Pollack, Earl, Richard Redick, Vivian Brown, Cecil Wurster, and Kurt Gorwitz. 1964. "Socioeconomic and Family Characteristics of Patients Admitted to Psychiatric Services." *American Journal of Public Health* 54 (March): 506–18.

Primrose, E. J. R. 1962. *Psychological Illness.* Springfield, Ill.: Charles C Thomas.

Prudenski, G., and B. Kolpakov. 1962. "Questions concerning the Calculations of Non-working Time in Budget Statistics." *Problems of Economics* 6 (April): 12–31.

Public Health Service. 1967. *Division of Direct Health Service Annual Statistical Summary Fiscal Year 1967. Part II. Diagnostic and Demographic Data.* Washington, D.C.: Government Printing Office.

————. 1970. *Selected Symptoms of Psychological Distress.* Public Health Service Publication no. 1000, ser. 11, no. 37. Washington, D.C.: Government Printing Office.

Raskin, Allen, and Risa Golob. 1966. "Occurence of Sex and Social Class Differences in Premorbid Competence, Symptom and Outcome Measures in Acute Schizophrenia." *Psychological Reports* 18 (February): 11–22.

Robbins, Lewis. 1966. "A Historical Review of the Classification of Behavior Disorders and Once Current Perspective." In *The Classification of Behavior Disorders,* edited by Leonard Eron. Chicago: Aldine.

Rose, Arnold. 1951. "The Adequacy of Women's Expectations for Adult Roles." *Social Forces* 30 (October): 69–77.

Rosenkrantz, Paul, Susan Vogel, Helen Bee, Inge Broverman, and Donald Broverman.

1968. "Sex Role Stereotypes and Self-Conceptions in College Students." *Journal of Consulting Psychology* 32 (3): 287–95.

Rossi, Alice. 1964. "Equality between Sexes: An Immodest Proposal." *Daedalus* 93 (Spring): 607–52.

Rowe, Clarence. 1970. *An Outline of Psychiatry.* Dubuque, Iowa: Brown.

Rushing, William. 1969. "Two Patterns in the Relationship between Social Class and Mental Hospitalization." *American Sociological Review* 34 (August): 533–41.

Ryle, A. 1960. "The Neuroses in a General Practice." *Journal of the College of General Practitioners* 3 (August): 313–28.

Scheff, Thomas. 1966. *Being Mentally Ill: A Sociological Theory.* Chicago: Aldine.

Schur, Edwin. 1969. "Reactions to Deviance: A Critical Assessment." *American Journal of Sociology* 75 (November): 309–22.

Shepherd, Michael, Brian Cooper, A. C. Brown, and G. W. Kalton. 1964. "Minor Mental Illness in London: Some Aspects of a General Practice Survey." *British Medical Journal* 2 (November): 1359–63.

Sherriffs, Alex, and John McKee. 1957. "Qualitative Aspects of Beliefs about Men and Women." *Journal of Personality* 25 (June): 450–64.

Silverman, Charlotte. 1968. *The Epidemiology of Depression.* Baltimore: Johns Hopkins Press.

Srole, Leo, Thomas Langner, Stanley Michael, Marvin Opler, and Thomas Rennie. 1962. *Mental Health in the Metropolis.* New York: McGraw-Hill.

Steinmann, Anne, and David Fox. 1966. "Male-Female Perceptions of the Female Role in the United States." *Journal of Psychology* 64 (November): 265–79.

Stengel, Erwin. 1969. *Suicide and Attempted Suicide.* Baltimore: Penguin.

Susser, Mervyn. 1968. *Community Psychiatry: Epidemiologic and Social Themes.* New York: Random House.

Tauss, W. 1967. "A Note on the Prevalence of Mental Disturbance." *Australian Journal of Psychology* 19 (August): 121–23.

Taylor, Lord, and Sidney Chave. 1964. *Mental Health and Environment.* London: Longman's Green.

U.S., Bureau of the Census. 1930. *Mental Patients in State Hospitals 1926 and 1927.* Washington, D.C.: Government Printing Office.

———. 1941. *Patients in Mental Institutions 1938.* Washington, D.C.: Government Printing Office.

———. 1966. "Estimates of the Population of the United States by Age, Color, Sex: July 1, 1966." Current Population Reports Series P-25, no. 352. Washington, D.C.: Government Printing Office.

———. 1970. "Estimates of the Population of the United States by Age, Race, and Sex: July 1, 1967 to July 1, 1969." Current Population Reports Series P-25, no. 441. Washington, D.C.: Government Printing Office.

Watts, C. A. H. 1962. "Psychiatric Disorders." In *Morbidity Statistics from General Practice.* Vol. 3. Studies on Medical Population Subjects no. 14. London: Her Majesty's Stationery Office.

Watts, C. A. H., E. C. Caute, and E. U. Kuenssberg. 1964. "Survey of Mental Illness in General Practice." *British Medical Journal* 2 (November): 1351–59

Zolik, Edwin, and Joseph Marches. 1968. "Mental Health Morbidity in a Suburban Community." *Journal of Clinical Psychology* 24 (January): 103–108.

29

JANET TAYNOR AND KEY DEAUX[2]

When Women Are More Deserving Than Men: Equity, Attribution and Perceived Sex Differences[1]

Male and female subjects read descriptions of either a male or a female stimulus person performing well in an emergency situation that had been previously shown to be more masculine than feminine. The subjects then allocated rewards and evaluated performance, effort, and ability of the stimulus person. On the basis of equity theory it was assumed that being a woman in a masculine situation would be perceived as a nonvoluntary constraint, and thus it was predicted that the female would be rated as more deserving of reward than the male for an equivalent performance. It was further predicted from both an equity theory and an attribution theory standpoint that performance would be correspondingly inflated to balance the increased deservingness of reward and that effort, an unstable internal attribute, would be used in preference to ability, a stable internal attribute, in explaining the performance. Both predictions were confirmed, and the results were discussed in relation to recent sex difference research.

Recent claims of discrimination against women suggest the need to study systematically when, if, and how women are discriminated against. It seems likely that the problem involves not only overt discrimination but also more subtle processes in evaluation of abilities, performance, and other attributes of men and women. Recent research in the area of perceived sex differences, while not wholly consistent, has nevertheless suggested that the abilities and performance of men and women may be differentially perceived. Men have been rated superior to women on a task involving ratings of professional journal articles (Goldberg, 1968). Men have been judged to be superior to women in the context of an art contest, but the difference has disappeared when an authoritative opinion (a judge's decision) has been passed announcing a winner of the contest (Pheterson, Kiesler, & Goldberg, 1971). Men have been judged superior to women in the context of applying for a study abroad program when the merits of each were high, but women were judged superior to men when the merits of each were low (Deaux & Taynor, 1973).

In part, the absence of any clear-cut trend in these cited findings may reflect a rather haphazard choice process in selecting situations for evaluation. While a choice based on the relevance of the situation to an actual applied setting is in some respects commendable, it seems more profitable at this point to select situations which can also clearly relate to existent social psychological theory with the hope of integrating the study of perceived sex differences with more established bodies of theory.

In an effort to study the problem of perceived sex differences within a theoretical context, the equity model appears to be a likely candidate for the task. The equity model (Adams, 1965) states that members of a dyad allocate rewards to self and other in proportion to the contributions of self and other. Person A is motivated to attempt to make his own outcomes and inputs proportional to Person B's outcomes and inputs. As conceptualized by Adams, outcomes are rewards that A perceives that he and B are receiving in a specific situation. An example of this would be salary and status received in a job situation.

[1] This study represents work completed in partial fulfillment of the master's degree by the first author under the direction of the second author. The authors thank Richard Stotts for his assistance in conducting the experiment and Donn Byrne and Richard Heslin for their helpful comments throughout the research. Portions of this study were presented at the May 1972 meeting of the Midwestern Psychological Association, Cleveland.

[2] Requests for reprints should be sent to Kay Deaux, Department of Psychological Sciences, Purdue University, West Lafayette, Indiana 47907.

Inputs are such things as level of performance, effort, age, sex, and a host of other personal attributes that are relevant to the particular exchange.

When a person is not an actual member of the exchange relationship but is put in the situation of being able to allocate rewards to the members of the exchange, he allocates rewards along the lines predicted by the equity model. Leventhal and Michaels (1971) asked subjects to rate the deservingness of reward of athletes who had different inputs. Inputs were divided into four components: performance, effort, training, and body height. Height was classified as a constraint over which the individual had no control (called nonvoluntary constraint). Effort was classified as a constraint over which the individual did have voluntary control (called voluntary constraint). The results of this study showed that the subjects rated individuals who were operating under nonvoluntary constraints to be more deserving of reward than individuals not operating under nonvoluntary constraints.

Thus, the equity model predicts that an individual working under a nonvoluntary constraint is perceived as more deserving of reward than someone not working under such a constraint. Extending this model to the area of perceived sex differences, if being a woman can be assumed to be a constraint in some situations, then it follows that a woman would be rated as more deserving of reward than a man for a comparable performance in that situation.

If it is true that the woman would be assigned greater rewards in some situations, then equity theory would require that one or more of the input variables would have to be inflated in order to balance the increased outcome, that is, deservingness of reward. While equity theory does not provide a specific indication of which variables would be so inflated, Weiner and Kukla (1970) have provided evidence that there is a linear relationship between performance and assigned rewards. As the most direct link, therefore, we would predict that greater deservingness of reward would be accompanied by an increased evaluation of performance. Other factors, specifically ability and effort, can be considered as internal loci of cause for a given perfor-

mance, and in line with attribution theory, at least one of these factors should also be increased to explain the increased performance. There are at least two reasons to predict that in the present situation subjects would inflate the effort variable rather than the ability variable. First, Weiner and Kukla's data suggest that effort is a more salient determinant of reward than is ability. Second, in terms of the present situation in which a woman is performing well in a situation in which her capability is assumed to be lower, the more temporary attribute of effort would appear to be more susceptible to change than the stable attribute of ability.

In summary, it was hypothesized that when a man and a woman perform the same act in a masculine situation, (*a*) a woman is perceived as more deserving of reward than an equally performing man; (*b*) a woman is perceived as performing better than the comparable man; and (*c*) a woman is perceived as expending more effort than the comparable man.

In addition, two other variables were considered in terms of their possible influence on evaluative judgments. While equity theory has in general used a paradigm in which a comparison person is present, Pritchard (1969) has suggested that internal comparison others are always present and hence need not be presented by the experimenter. To determine the effect of the presence or absence of a comparison other, the male or female actor was described as being alone or in the company of an opposite-sex other.

Further, it was considered desirable to consider individual difference variables which might differentiate subjects with varying dispositions toward women acting in unanticipated ways. Based on the work of Adorno, Frenkel-Brunswik, Levinson, and Sanford (1950), the F scale was selected, as high scorers on this scale have been found to have more respect for authority and rules and to be less tolerant for those who do not follow prescribed rules of behavior.

METHOD

Summary of Design

A $2 \times 2 \times 2$ analysis of variance factorial design was used in which sex of subject, sex of stimulus, and presence or absence of a nonacting opposite-sex other were used as independent variables. Male and female subjects were presented a description of a stimulus man or stimulus woman performing well (in a desirable and appropriate manner) in a civic emergency situation in either a condition of the stimulus person's being alone while taking appropriate action or being with a nonacting member of the opposite sex while taking appropriate action. A completely between-subjects design was used.

Subjects

Sixty-one male and 60 female introductory psychology students participated in this experiment as partial fulfillment of course requirements. The subjects were run in groups of approximately 30, with subjects randomized across conditions within groups. One male and one female experimenter were present during the entire experiment.

Procedure

The subjects were told that they were participating in a study designed to investigate why people do or do not respond in an emergency situation. They were told that they would be asked to evaluate the performance of individuals in a civic emergency situation. The subjects were then given the following written description of the stimulus person:

Bob Carter is 35 years old. He is the father of two children and resides with his children and wife in a large suburban development outside of one of the country's larger cities. Bob is thought of as a typical person and fairly representative of the community in which he lives. In interviewing Bob and some of his friends, we discovered that he and his friends generally agreed about the type of person he is. Bob and his friends generally agreed that Bob could be described by the following list of adjectives: likeable, mild-mannered, alert, masculine, and capable.

For the female stimulus condition the name Linda was used with appropriate substitution of pronouns. The adjective feminine was given in place of the adjective masculine.

The subjects were then asked to rate the stimulus person on a series of 7-point bipolar adjective scales, including adjectives that relate to male–female dimensions, such as dominant–submissive, strong–weak, and masculine–feminine.

After the subjects had completed this rating, they read a description of the critical situation in which the condition of the nonacting opposite-sex other was manipulated (the stimulus person being alone or together with a nonacting opposite-sex other). In the alone–male condition, the subjects saw the following description of the situation:

This is the situation in which Bob was involved. Bob was on his way to meet an old friend for lunch. He parked his car in a high-rise parking lot and boarded the elevator to get to the street level. The elevator descended two floors when a man entered. As soon as the elevator started again, this man pushed the "stop" button, pulled out a gun, and demanded Bob's money. When the elevator reached the street level, the gunman fled into the street, after threatening Bob's life if he left the elevator before the gunman was safely into the street.

Later that afternoon the gunman was apprehended. It was learned that this was one of a series of similar incidents, in one of which two of the victims of the crime had been killed.

The alternative together conditions were identical to the alone conditions except that a member of the opposite sex was also present in the elevator and was also a victim of the holdup man. No further description was provided of either the characteristics or behavior of the nonacting other.

The subjects in the alone condition then were asked to predict how the stimulus person would behave. In the together condition the subjects predicted the behavior of both the stimulus person and the nonacting opposite-sex other. These predictions were made on three dimensions: performance (What is the likelihood that _____ would take constructive measures to apprehend the gunman?), effort (How hard would _____ try to take constructive measures in this situation?), and ability (Would _____ have the ability to do anything constructive in this situation?). Each dimension was rated on an 11-point scale, on which 0 indicated a lack of the characteristic and 10 indicated an abundance of the characteristic. Verbal labels were used to divide the scales into five equal categories (e.g., not try at all; not try; neither try nor not try; try; try very hard).

Following this prediction, the subjects read a description of how the stimulus person actually behaved in the emergency situation. Pretesting had established that this behavior (described below) was considered to be more masculine than feminine and highly desirable in nature. The subjects in both the alone and together conditions read the following description (with appropriate sex of stimulus person):

It might be of interest to find out whether Bob did react in this civic emergency in an expected or unexpected manner.

From the police report it was learned that Bob handled himself very well. After the gunman had left, having threatened him with his life if he left the elevator before the gunman could blend into the pedestrians on the street, Bob had thought to close the elevator door and go up one floor where he would be safe from the gunman while he called the police. Upon leaving the elevator to call the police, Bob looked down over the railing of the parking lot, watched the gunman long enough to tell which way he was going, and was able to tell the police in which direction the gunman had gone. This quick action, which alerted a passing patrol car, enabled the police to catch up with the gunman before he had gone several blocks. Bob also had remembered very much about the gunman, including his looks, his dress, and his mannerisms.

The police told Bob that his quick thinking and cool-headedness had enabled them to catch the gunman and had probably saved the life of a future victim.

After reading this account of the stimulus person's behavior in the described emergency situation, the subjects were then asked to rate the stimulus person on an 11-point scale measuring deservingness of reward (How deserving of reward is _____ ?). The subjects also rated the stimulus person on the dimensions of performance, ability, and effort. These scales were constructed in the same way as the earlier scales except for the appropriate changes in verb tense. In addition, ratings were obtained on confidence (How confident are you of your ratings of _____'s actual performance?), likelihood of similar future performance (How would _____ perform in another similar incident?), and deviation of performance from expectancy (Did _____'s performance differ from what you expected?), each on a similar 11-point scale. In the together condition both the stimulus person and the nonacting other were evaluated. The subjects then reevaluated the stimulus person on the original adjective rating scale and completed a 22-item modification of the F scale (Mitchell & Byrne, 1973).

Following this procedure, the experimenters discussed with the subjects the nature of the experiment and the hypotheses being tested and answered any questions which arose.

RESULTS

Effectiveness of the Manipulations

An overall main effect was seen for the masculine–feminine, dominant–submissive, and strong–weak dimensions on the original adjective rating scale, which the subjects completed prior to reading the situational description. The man was seen as more masculine ($p < .01$), more dominant ($p < .01$), and stronger than the woman ($p < .01$), indicating that the male and female stimulus persons were clearly distinguished.

Despite the fact that pretesting had shown the situation to be clearly a male-associated task, initial predictions of performance, ability, and effort did not differ significantly between the male and female stimulus persons. Significant differences were found on each of these measures, however, when the nonacting male was compared to the nonacting female. The nonacting male was predicted to perform better ($p < .0001$), to have more ability (p

$< .0001$), and to exert greater effort ($p < .0001$) than the parallel nonacting female. Furthermore, in each case in which both a male and a female were described as being present in the situation, the mean predicted values for the male were higher than for the female, regardless of which one was the more extensively described stimulus person.

Evaluation of the Stimulus Person

Because of somewhat uneven distribution in cells when subjects are classified by scores on the F scale, the initial analyses were performed using a three-way unweighted-means analysis of variance without regard to F scale scores.

The major prediction was that the female stimulus person would be seen as more deserving of reward than the male. As indicated in Tables 1 and 2, females were rated as significantly more deserving of reward than males ($p = .012$). A significant Sex of Subject × Condition (Alone versus Together) interaction resulted from the fact that women made higher ratings than men in the together condition, independent of sex of stimulus person, while men assigned higher ratings in the alone condition.

Similarly, considering the subjects' evaluations of the stimulus person's performance, the female stimulus person was again rated more highly than the male ($p = .015$).[3] A significant Sex of Stimulus × Condition interaction ($p = .043$) was found, and a simple effects analysis (Winer, 1971) indicated that while females were seen as performing significantly better than males in the alone condition, there was no difference between them in the together condition.

Analysis of variance of the effort measure showed the predicted difference between male

---

[3] Consideration was given to the possibility of computing change scores that would compare predicted performance, ability, and effort to the ratings obtained after subjects had read the description of the actual behavior. However, information obtained from subjects during debriefing indicated that many subjects made their predicted ratings on the basis of possible physical encounter with the gunman, whereas the actual behavior described involved behavior of a more cognitive nature. Thus, change scores computed from these two rather different conceptions did not appear to be a valid choice.

TABLE 1

MEAN RATINGS OF STIMULUS PERSON ON DESERVING-
NESS OF REWARD, PERFORMANCE,
EFFORT, AND ABILITY

Subjects	Deserv-ingness	Perform-ance	Effort	Ability
Males				
Male alone (15)	7.60	7.60	7.80	7.53
Male together (19)	7.00	7.95	7.47	7.63
Female alone (16)	8.19	8.88	8.38	8.25
Female together (11)	7.54	7.91	7.36	6.73
Females				
Male alone (14)	6.36	7.71	7.36	7.78
Male together (13)	7.85	8.54	8.00	7.54
Female alone (14)	8.14	9.14	8.86	8.36
Female together (19)	7.89	8.84	8.68	8.16

Note. Numbers in parentheses indicate cell frequencies.

and female stimulus persons, again favoring the female. Females were rated as trying significantly harder ($p = .014$). None of the interactions were significant. Analysis showed no differences in ability ratings with the means for male and female stimulus persons nearly identical on this measure.

Questions dealing with the deviation of performance from expectancy, the likelihood of a similar performance in the future, and confidence in overall ratings showed no differences among conditions.

Evaluation of the Nonacting Other

In the together conditions, the stimulus person was accompanied by a person of the opposite sex who took no action in the situation. Parallel ratings were obtained of these nonacting others, and a 2 × 2 analysis of variance (Sex of Subject × Sex of Nonacting Other) was performed on each of these response measures.

No differences were found between male and female nonacting persons on measures of deservingness of reward, likelihood of similar performance, performance, effort, or confidence in overall ratings. Two interesting differences did appear in these analyses, however. Despite the fact that neither person was depicted with any detail, the subjects rated the male as having significantly more ability than the female ($F = 8.72$, $df = 1/58$, $p = .005$). In a similar vein, responses to the question dealing with deviation of the performance from expectancy showed that the subjects found the female's lack of action to be significantly more similar to their expectations than was the male's ($F = 18.08$, $p = .0002$). There were no main effects of sex of subject or a Sex of Subject × Sex of Stimulus interaction on either of these measures.

High versus Low Authoritarians

The total distribution of scores on the F scale was split in half ($Mdn = 66.3$, $M = 65.9$), and a four-way unweighted-means analysis of variance was then performed on all of the response measures, with cell ns varying from 5 to 14. Analysis of variance indicated that high-authoritarian subjects rated both the male and female stimulus persons higher on measures of predicted performance ($F = 7.34$, $df = 1/105$, $p = .008$), predicted effort ($F = 4.50$, $p = .03$), and predicted ability ($F = 4.55$, $p = .03$). Relatively few interactions between authoritarianism and the other variables were sigificant. The exception to this statement was the Sex of

TABLE 2

SUMMARY OF ANALYSES OF VARIANCE OF RATINGS OF DESERVINGNESS OF REWARD, PERFORMANCE,
EFFORT, AND ABILITY

Source	Deservingness		Performance		Effort		Ability	
	MS	F	MS	F	MS	F	MS	F
Sex of subject (A)	.016	<1	6.666	2.50	6.526	3.14	5.283	2.46
Sex of stimulus (B)	16.152	6.40**	16.170	6.06**	12.874	6.20**	1.846	<1
Alone–together (C)	.000	<1	.017	<1	1.381	<1	6.422	2.99
A × B	.902	<1	.450	<1	5.422	2.61	3.486	1.62
A × C	11.309	4.48*	2.392	<1	5.994	2.89	1.755	<1
B × C	5.807	2.30	10.906	4.09*	4.132	1.99	4.539	2.11
A × B × C	5.271	2.09	.065	<1	.031	<1	5.110	2.38
Error	2.524		2.668		2.075		2.147	

Note. For all main effects and interactions, $df = 1/113$.
* $p < .05$.
** $p < .025$.

Stimulus × Condition × Authoritarianism interaction, which was significant for deservingness of reward ($F = 4.11$, $p = .04$), effort ($F = 6.84$, $p = .01$), and ability ($F = 21.998$, $p = .0001$). In each of these instances, the pattern of differences showed high authoritarians to rate the male stimulus person more favorably in the alone condition as opposed to the together condition; low authoritarians, in contrast, consistently rated the male more favorably in the together condition than in the alone condition while rating females more favorably in the alone condition.

DISCUSSION

The results of this experiment demonstrate the applicability of the equity model to the study of perceived sex differences. The prediction from equity theory that a female, presumably acting under nonvoluntary constraints by virtue of being a female, would be perceived as being more deserving of reward in a masculine situation than an equally performing male was confirmed. The inflated measure of performance for the female stimulus person is consistent with the equity assumption that input and outcome must be balanced. The fact that the inflated performance of females was more pronounced in the alone condition than in the together condition may suggest that when the female stimulus person is alone in the elevator with the gunman, her helplessness is made more salient. Thus her femininity is more evident, increasing the magnitude of the constraint she is under and precipitating a higher rating of performance to compensate for the perceived constraint. Alternatively, the female in the company of a male may be seen as under less constraint; further, her taking action when a male is present may be subject to negative evaluation by virtue of the fact that the male becomes less masculine in appearance.

Of specific relevance for the equity model is the fact that the deservingness of reward was evident in both the alone and together conditions. This finding suggests that a comparison other does not have to be present physically in all situations for the equity model to hold, confirming the suggestion by Pritchard (1969) that a comparison other is internalized within an individual and is always available for comparison. These data provide support for this supposition and appear to extend the equity model.

Suggestive, if not conclusive, evidence is provided for the relevance of attributional hypotheses to the study of perceived sex differences. Although equity theory considers ability, effort, and performance as parallel types of input variables, an attributional analysis would look at ability and effort as two possible causal factors to be used in explaining a given performance. In the present situation it was predicted and found that effort, a less stable attribute, is preferred over ability in explaining the female's better performance and greater deservingness in a situation in which the female would normally not be expected to do as well. If we consider the data for the nonacting other, it can be seen that ability as a stable attribute is again less susceptible to change. The subjects predicted, in advance of the description of outcome, that the nonacting male would perform better, would have more ability, and would exert more effort than the nonacting female. With evidence that the nonacting person was indeed nonacting, ratings of both performance and effort were altered to conform with the reality, but males were still seen as having greater ability than females. These results are consistent with the recent findings of Kepka and Brickman (1971), who showed that the discrepancy between performance and ability is explained by invoking motivational factors.

Authoritarianism, which was included in the study to test its viability as a potential mediating variable in the evaluation of male and female performance, offered relatively little assistance. The consistent tendency for high authoritarians to find the female's performance more creditable in the together condition than in the alone condition, while low authoritarians rated the female higher in the alone condition than in the together condition, is of some interest and may relate to more structured role definitions on the part of high authoritarians. High authoritarians may view the female's behavior in the together condition as more acceptable by assuming that the male, though unstated, was in fact supporting or guiding the female in her actions, and thus the female's behavior was not terribly deviant; in the alone condition, in contrast, the action clearly originated with the female, a situation which low authoritarians found more acceptable than did high authoritarians.

We might consider how prevalent the tendency to overrate the female performer in a more typically masculine situation is, particularly in view of studies by Goldberg (1968), Pheterson et al. (1971), and Deaux and Taynor (1973), all of which suggested that the male is more typically upgraded in comparison to the female. The present situation has at least two characteristics that are not found in the previously cited experiments: First, the situation was transitory in nature and does not imply a history of such action; and second, details of the performance, including the outcome of that performance, were explicit, thus minimizing additional assumptions on the part of the subjects. With reference to the first point, each of the previous experiments supplied evidence that would suggest a history of some accomplishment in the form of professional journal writing, artistic endeavors, or evidence of high school and college accomplishments. In such situations subjects may be evaluating not only the evidence directly presented but assumptions of long-term continuity which through actual frequency of encounter may favor the male. More specifically, there are more successful male artists, journal writers, and the like. In contrast, the present situation asked the subjects only to evaluate a single incident that did not require implicit assumptions of continuity. As to the second point, the subjects in the present experiment had more precise information about the behavior to be evaluated than the subjects did in other cited experiments. They were clearly told that the stimulus person had performed successfully and that the police had commended him or her for actions taken, whereas the subjects in other experiments were asked to judge the quality of a painting or of a professional journal article, tasks for which they presumably had little expertise. Thus, given uncer-

tain performance and implied continuity of that performance, a bias in favor of males may result; given more specific details of performance and no implied history of that performance, the female can be seen as more deserving of reward for an unexpectedly good performance. Consistent with this interpretation, Pheterson et al. (1971) did not find a male bias in the situation in which they gave clear evaluation of the performance, that is, a judge's decision of award for the painting.

As a parallel to the present results, equity theory should also predict that in a situation in which females are assumed to be of superior ability, an unexpectedly good performance by a male would also be overrewarded. The problem in this regard is defining a situation that meets these criteria, and to date no satisfactory situation has been found. A further question arising from this study is the effect of the presence of the opposite-sex other as opposed, for example, to a same-sex other. We suspect that these two situations would not produce equivalent evaluations of the stimulus person.

While additional research is needed to determine the limits and potentials of the equity interpretation, it is nonetheless clear that specific predictions can be made regarding the evaluation of male and female behavior that, in addition to being socially relevant, are also based on existent social psychological theory.

REFERENCES

ADAMS, J. S. Inequity in social exchange. In L. Berkowitz (Ed.), *Advances in experimental social psychology.* Vol. 2. New York: Academic Press, 1965.

ADORNO, T. W., FRENKEL-BRUNSWIK, E., LEVINSON, D. J., & SANFORD, R. N. *The authoritarian personality.* New York: Harpers, 1950.

DEAUX, K., & TAYNOR, J. Evaluation of male and female ability: Bias works two ways. *Psychological Reports,* 1973, 32, 261–262.

GOLDBERG, P. A. Are women prejudiced against women? *Transaction,* 1968, 5, 28–30.

KEPKA, E. J., & BRICKMAN, P. Consistency versus discrepancy as clues in the attribution of intelligence and motivation. *Journal of Personality and Social Psychology,* 1971, 20, 223–229.

LEVENTHAL, G. S., & MICHAELS, J. W. Locus of cause and equity motivation as determinants of reward allocation. *Journal of Personality and Social Psychology,* 1971, 17, 229–235.

MITCHELL, H. E., & BYRNE, D. The defendant's dilemma: Effects of jurors' attitudes and authoritarianism on judicial decisions. *Journal of Personality and Social Psychology,* 1973, 25, 123–129.

PHETERSON, G. I., KIESLER, S. B., & GOLDBERG, P. A. Evaluation of the performance of women as a function of their sex, achievement, and personal history. *Journal of Personality and Social Psychology,* 1971, 19, 114–118.

PRITCHARD, R. D. Equity theory: A review and critique. *Organizational Behavior and Human Performance,* 1969, 4, 176–211.

WEINER, B., & KUKLA, A. An attributional analysis of achievement motivation. *Journal of Personality and Social Psychology,* 1970, 15, 1–20.

WINER, B. J. *Statistical principles in experimental design.* (2nd ed.) New York: McGraw-Hill, 1971.

(Received May 19, 1972)

30

RHODA K. UNGER, BETH J. RAYMOND
AND STEPHEN M. LEVINE

Are Women a "Minority" Group?
Sometimes!

Beginning with Helen Hacker's (1951) well-known article, there have been a number of attempts to extend the definition of minority group to women. Obviously, such a definition cannot be defended statistically since women make up more than fifty percent of the population. Therefore, attempts have centered about the role characteristics of members of minority groups—in particular, the fact of discrimination and the awareness of such discrimination. Women, because of their high social visibility and ascribed social and intellectual inferiority, have sometimes been compared to blacks in our society by Women's Lib "activists."

Despite these characterizations of women as a minority group, little empirical data have been gathered on behavior toward women vis-à-vis other minority groups. It is particularly

AUTHORS' NOTE: *The authors would like to thank Elaine Brigante and Barry Kovin for assistance in the collection of the data. This article is the complete version of a paper presented in abbreviated form at the annual convention of the American Psychological Association, Honolulu, Hawaii, September 1972.*

important that such data be obtained for the various groups in identical social situations and without the knowledge of the individuals under study. It is also necessary that the situations chosen can be demonstrated to produce discriminatory behavior toward members of already clearly defined socially deviant groups—e.g., blacks or hippies. The recent experimental literature on cooperation appears to offer such situations.

A number of studies have attempted to determine the relationship of membership in a socially deviant group to cooperation. In a variety of nondemand situations requiring help, blacks receive significantly less assistance than do whites (Bryan and Test, 1967; Piliavin et al., 1969; Gaertner and Bickman, 1971). Deviant dress also produces significantly less cooperation than conventional attire when the individuals from whom cooperation is requested are members of the general population (Raymond and Unger, 1972; Keasey and Tomlinson-Keasey, 1971; Darley and Cooper, 1972; Samuel, 1972).

It is difficult to predict the relationship of sex and cooperation in nondemand studies. On one hand, there is much data to indicate that perception of dependency greatly increases cooperative behavior (Berkowitz, 1970; Schopler and Bateson, 1965). Under laboratory conditions, females who asked for help received more help than females who did not request such aid and more help than dependent males (Gruder and Cook, 1971). There was no relationship due to the sex of the potential helper. On the other hand, there are data which indicate that in some situations requiring cooperation—e.g., petition-signing (Keasey and Tomlinson-Keasey, 1971) and being in a stalled car (Deaux, 1971), females received less cooperation than males. Behavior toward females in these situations was comparable to that received by deviantly dressed or low-status individuals under similar conditions. Such data would seem to provide empirical evidence that women are, at least sometimes, members of a minority group.

The present study attempts to clarify the nature of the situations which do or do not lead to discriminatory behavior toward women. An attempt was made to compare women, under identical stimulus conditions, with a group known to receive discriminatory treatment—e.g., hippies. Sex and social deviance were factorially combined in two experimental conditions requiring cooperation. In the first condition, subjects were requested to grant a small favor—i.e., permit the experimenter to go before them on a checkout line. In the second, the experimenter's car apparently stalled at an intersection (Doob and Gross, 1968), and cooperation was measured in terms of the length of the interval before the subject reacted by honking his or her horn.

It is hypothesized that individuals dressed in deviant attire, regardless of sex, would receive less cooperation in both experimental situations. Sex, however, should produce a differential effect in the two experimental situations. When a favor is requested, female dependency becomes salient, and females should receive more cooperation than males. When no help is required other than resistance of frustration, females, like other minority groups, should receive less cooperation than males. No interaction between sex and social deviancy is expected in either situation.

EXPERIMENT I

METHOD

Experimenters. The Es were one male and one female undergraduate psychology majors at Hofstra, aged 21 and 20, respectively, both white. Each E served in both the conventional and deviant role.

Conventional attire for the male E consisted of a business suit, white shirt and tie, and neatly combed hair. For the female E, it consisted of a suit and neat grooming. Deviant appearance for the male E included brightly colored paisley pants, ribbed body shirt, sandals, an army jacket, and a peace medallion around his neck. He was unshaven and wore a wig of long and uncombed hair. Deviant appearance for the female E included brightly colored tie-dye pants, a flowered shirt, fringed vest, sandals, round metal rim glasses, and a peace medallion about her neck. Her hair was long and relatively ungroomed.

Subjects. Ss were approached on checkout lines in a number of supermarkets and department stores. Ss were chosen without regard to race, sex, or age. Only 1 S on a line was studied at any one time. A total of 371 individuals were approached: 214 males and 157 females.

Location. The study was conducted in four stores in Nassau County, Long Island, New York. The stores that were chosen served shoppers of both middle and lower-middle socio-economic levels.

Procedure. The different experimental conditions were counterbalanced so that each store was sampled once under each condition. The same departments in each store were visited under each condition. Data collection took place on two days with one intervening day.

The E approached S, who was the third or fourth person standing on a fairly long checkout line and who had more than one item to purchase. E carried one item, purportedly to be purchased, and asked politely, "Excuse me, I'm in a terrible hurry and I was wondering if I could get ahead of you." If the S cooperated, E left the line before reaching the register, remarking that he or she was in too much of a hurry to wait or that he or she had forgotten something. Once E was away from S, the S's sex and estimated age (below 30, 30-45, above 45) were recorded, as well as whether or not he or she had cooperated.

RESULTS

A 2 x 2 x 2 x 3 chi square (sex of S x age of S x sex of E x attire of E) was used to analyze the data (Winer, 1962). Age was included as a blocking variable. Although there appear to be some interesting results involving age, a discussion of them is beyond the scope of the paper. The main effects of E's sex, χ^2 (1) = 11.24, p < .01; attire, χ^2 (1) = 10.27, p < .01; and S's sex, χ^2 (1) = 4.49, p < .05 were significant. The female E received more cooperation than the male E (81.9% versus 66.7%);

conventionally dressed Es received more cooperation than deviantly dressed Es (81% versus 66.5%); and male Ss cooperated more than female Ss (78.5% versus 68.8%).

The interaction of E's sex x S's sex, χ^2 (1) = 9.77, p < .01, indicated that female Ss cooperated equally with male and female Es (70% and 68% cooperation, respectively), however, male Ss cooperated more with female Es than male Es (92% and 64% cooperation, respectively).

Finally, the interaction of E's sex x attire x S's sex, χ^2 (1) = 6.47, p < .05 indicated that, although deviant attire always resulted in less cooperation than conventional attire, the male Ss tolerated deviant dress in the female E much more than the male E, while the reverse was true of female Ss—they were much less tolerant of deviant dress in the female E than in the male E (see Table 1).

EXPERIMENT II

METHOD

Experimenters. The Es were the same as in Experiment I. However, in this experiment conditions resembling those of the Doob and Gross (1968) study were introduced. In the conventional conditions, Ss drove a middle-status automobile with no insignia of any kind on it. In the deviant conditions, Ss drove a similar type of automobile festooned with stickers, peace signs, and pasted-on flowers.

Subjects. Subjects consisted of 408 drivers divided equally into each of the 24 experimental conditions: sex and condition of deviancy of E, sex and age of S who happened to pull up behind one of the experimental cars.

TABLE 1
PERCENTAGE OF Ss COOPERATING AS A FUNCTION OF Es SEX, Es ATTIRE AND Ss SEX

Subjects	Male Experimenters		Female Experimenters	
	Deviant	Conventional	Deviant	Conventional
Male	53	75	88	95
Female	64	73	58	80

Location. The study was conducted on a number of major thoroughfares in central Nassau County, Long Island, New York. The streets were selected according to the following criteria: (1) there were many drivers, (2) they served neighborhoods of both middle and lower-middle socioeconomic level, (3) there were drivers of both sexes.

Procedure. The procedure used was similar to that employed by Doob and Gross (1968). E drove his or her car until a red light was reached. When the light changed, E did not start immediately, but appeared to be busy changing the radio station or gazing from side to side. These behaviors were engaged in until either the driver in the car behind honked his horn or fifteen seconds had elapsed. An observer hidden in the back seat of the car recorded the latency of the first honk as well as the sex and estimated age of the subject.

RESULTS

A 2 x 2 x 2 x 3 analysis of variance (sex of E x condition of deviancy x sex of S x age of S) was used in order to analyze the data. As in Experiment I, age was included as a blocking variable and is not discussed in the paper.

Since almost every driver honked before fifteen seconds had elapsed, data could not be analyzed in terms of the percentage of drivers honking for the various experimental conditions. Therefore, the latency before the first honk was calculated and used as the dependent measure.

All the main effects were highly significant. Female Es were honked at faster than Male Es, 7.4 versus 9.2 seconds, $F (1,384)$ = 83.36, $p < .01$. The conventional Es were afforded more time before being requested to move on via the horn honk than the deviant Es, 9.1 versus 7.6 seconds, $F (1,384)$ = 64.86, $p < .01$. Female Ss were more patient than male Ss, 9.2 versus 7.5 seconds, $F (1,384)$ = 70.71, $p < .01$.

As in Experiment I, sex of S and sex of E interacted significantly, $F (1,384)$ = 17.85, $p < .01$, although the direction of the effect was different. Although both male and female Ss honked faster at the female E than at the male E, the difference was greater for the male Ss. Male Ss increased their response speed from 8.9 to 6.1 seconds when the E was female rather than male while the female Ss changed their speed of honking from 9.6 to 8.7 seconds.

The interaction, sex of S x condition of deviancy was also significant, F (1,384) = 10.02, p < .01. Male Ss honked faster at deviant versus conventional drivers, 7.0 versus 7.9 seconds, however, female Ss differentiated between the drivers even more. They honked after 8.1 seconds when the driver was deviant as compared to 10.3 seconds when the driver was conventional.

The interaction of sex of E x condition of deviance, F (1,384) = 9.23, p < .01, indicated that although deviance in general resulted in faster honking, the difference was greater when the E was male. For the male E, deviant attire changed honking from 10.3 to 8.2 seconds while for the female E, honking changed from 7.9 to 7.0 seconds.

Finally, the interaction of sex of E x condition of deviancy x sex of S, F (1,384) = 7.73, p < .01 (see Table 2) indicated that, when the experimenters changed from the conventional to the deviant condition, both male and female Ss decreased their latency of response. Only in the combination of the female E and male S is this decrease absent. Since this condition receives extremely rapid honking, it is possible that we are limited by reaction time, and there is no room for further decline.

DISCUSSION

The study demonstrated that whether or not a "minority group" effect is produced with sex as a variable depends upon the nature of the experimental task. When "femaleness" and "social deviance" were factorially combined and the same experimental manipulations utilized, social deviants were uni-

TABLE 2
MEAN LATENCY OF FIRST HORN HONK IN SECONDS AS A FUNCTION OF Es SEX, Es CONDITION OF DEVIANCY, AND Ss SEX

Subject	Male Experimenters		Female Experimenters	
	Deviant	Conventional	Deviant	Conventional
Male	7.77	9.95	6.31	5.90
Female	8.54	10.65	7.41	9.83

formly discriminated against while females were favored in one case and treated negatively in the other.

The results of the present experiment are similar to those already reported in the literature for the two variables considered separately. Deaux (1971), in a similar horn-honking study, also found that female drivers were treated less patiently than were male drivers in the same situation. She attributed her results to the presumed lower status of the female driver. Both Deaux (1971) and Doob and Gross (1968) have shown that low-status cars are honked at much more rapidly than high-status cars.

A number of other studies utilizing a variety of tasks requiring cooperation have demonstrated that those dressed in a deviant manner receive less cooperation than those conventionally attired (Raymond and Unger, 1972; Keasey and Tomlinson-Keasey, 1971; Darley and Cooper, 1972; Samuel, 1972). In the present experiment, it is not surprising that deviant individuals receive less cooperation under all conditions than do conventional individuals. The question that must be answered is: If women are a "minority" group, why is there a reversal of the relationship that sex has to other people's cooperation when we change the nature of the task?

While a number of studies have shown no relationship of sex to cooperation, those that do indicate that females are more likely to be helped than males (Berkowitz et al., 1964; Gruder and Cook, 1971). The latter authors state that the sex difference in helping behavior is due to the sex of the recipient and apparently depends upon the perception of dependency of the individual from whom help is requested. By extension, one could assume that females are perceived as being more dependent than males, particularly when they request aid. The results of Experiment I are consistent with those of a field replication of Gruder and Cook's (1971) study—females requested help and received more cooperation than dependent males.

The authors feel that a more extensive differentiation between the situations in Experiment I and in Experiment II is required in order to understand these results. It is believed that perception of dependency is a limited aspect of a more general phenomenon related to the power relationship between the cooperator and the cooperatee.

In the first experiment, the female's behavior fit the stereotype of the "poor damsel in distress." In this situation, the female, especially if conventionally dressed, has indicated that she has no power, but that rather all power is in the hands of the other individual. In the second experiment, however, the female possesses some degree of social power by virtue of her ability to frustrate another individual. Although the car may have stalled, it is not obvious she is in a dependency relationship with the driver behind her. In fact, she has placed herself in at least a position of equality with that driver.

The differential effect of social deviance and sex on the two tasks provides interesting information about this hypothesized power relationship. Social deviance uniformly produces discrimination in both situations. Moreover, it reduces cooperation toward women in all experimental conditions. It is possible that choice of deviant clothing and personal style reflects a challenge to social power which lacks any real power to back it up. Studies have shown that the probability of an aggressive response occurring following frustration is related to the status attributed to the frustrator (Cohen, 1955; Hokanson and Burgess, 1962). Doob and Gross (1968) attribute their results to the ability of the frustrating individual to exercise sanctions. The higher the status, the more power; the more power, the more cooperation elicited. Conversely, females and deviants may receive less cooperation because they have lower status and power.

Males may be perceived as being more legitimate sources of power and authority than females. Both men and women are more ready to sign a petition when it is presented by a male than by a female (Keasey and Tomlinson-Keasey, 1971). Women who engage in behavior similar to that of men are not apt to acquire similar social status from it. Pheterson et al. (1971) have shown that women's work will be evaluated less well than men's even by other women in situations where social influence is ambiguous. Only when the female work is given supposed social sanction (winning of a contest) is it evaluated as being equal to that of men.

Another major factor which may affect these results is interpersonal attraction toward members of the opposite sex. This factor seems to operate most clearly in the face-to-face situation of Experiment I. As has been shown in a number of previous field experiments, women, in general, cooperate less than men (Raymond and Unger, 1972; Gaertner and Bickman, 1971; Wispe and Freshley, 1971). However, in the present experiment there is also a sex of subject x sex of experimenter interaction. Males cooperate with females more than with other males, while females do not differentially respond to the sex of the individual requesting the favor. These results may be due to the social expectation that males, but not females, are permitted to show attraction to the opposite sex.

The effects of interpersonal attraction apparently interact with the effects of deviant attire. While deviance decreases cooperation for all individuals under all conditions, individuals are least tolerant of deviant individuals of their own sex. Women are least cooperative with female deviants, and men are least cooperative with male deviants. This effect for women holds up even under the non-face-to-face conditions of Experiment II.

It is hypothesized that females will be treated as members of a minority group when they aspire to equal power or status with men. They will receive decreased cooperation from both men and women under these circumstances. Membership in other minority groups (e.g., social deviants) will further decrease cooperation even in tasks in which they are favored as dependent individuals. Females apparently react against disturbance of the social order more than males. Thus, they, as well as males, may oppose the gaining of power by females.

Of course, there are a number of other factors operating in these experiments. The age of the subject and the similarity between the subject and experimenter are apparently of importance. It is also an open question as to why so many more effects were obtained than in most experiments. It is possible the answer lies in the nature of the field experiment. Subjects were not aware of what was required of them and in these naturalistic settings freer rein was given to the working out of power relationships than would otherwise be the case in the laboratory situation.

REFERENCES

BERKOWITZ, L. (1970) "The self, selfishness and altruism," in J. Macaulay and L. Berkowitz (eds.) Altruism and Helping Behavior. New York: Academic.

——— S. KLANDERMAN, and R. HARRIS (1964) Effects of experimenter awareness and sex of subject and experimenter on reactions to dependency relationship." Sociometry 27: 327-337.

BRYAN, J. H. and M. J. TEST (1967) "Models and helping: naturalistic studies in aiding behavior." J. of Personality and Social Psychology 6: 400-407.

COHEN, A. R. (1955) "Social norms, arbitrariness of frustration and status of the agent in the frustration-aggression hypothesis." J. of Abnormal and Social Psychology 51: 222-226.

DARLEY, J. M. and J. COOPER (1972) "The 'Clean for Gene' phenomenon: the effects of students' appearance on political campaigning." J. of Applied Social Psychology 2: 24-33.

DEAUX, K. K. (1971) "Honking at the intersection: a replication and extension." J. of Social Psychology 84: 159-160.

DOOB, A. N. and A. E. GROSS (1968) "Status of frustrator as an inhibitor of horn-honking responses." J. of Social Psychology 76: 213-218.

GAERTNER, S. and L. BICKMAN (1971) "Effects of race on the elicitation of helping behavior." J. of Personality and Social Psychology 20: 218-222.

GRUDER, C. L. and I. D. COOK (1971) "Sex, dependency and helping." J. of Personality and Social Psychology 19: 290-294.

HACKER, H. M. (1951) "Women as a minority group." Social Forces 30: 60-69.

HOKANSON, J. E. and M. BURGESS (1962) "The effects of status, type of frustration and aggression on vascular processes." J. of Abnormal and Social Psychology 65: 252-257.

KEASEY, C. B. and C. I. TOMLINSON-KEASEY (1971) "Social influence in a high-ego-involvement situation: a field study of petition signing." Presented at Eastern Psychology Association Convention, New York.

PHETERSON, G. J., S. B. KIESLER, and P. A. GOLDBERG (1971) "Evaluation of the performance of women as a function of their sex, achievement and personal history." J. of Personality and Social Psychology 19: 114-118.

PILIAVIN, J. M., J. RODIN, and J. A. PILIAVIN (1969) "Good samaritanism: an underground phenomenon." J. of Personality and Social Psychology 13: 389-300.

RAYMOND, B. J. and R. K. UNGER (1972) " 'The apparel oft proclaims the man': cooperation with deviant and conventional youths." J. of Social Psychology 87: 75-82.

SAMUEL, W. (1972) "Response to Bill of Rights paraphrases as influenced by the hip or straight attire of the opinion solicitor." J. of Applied Social Psychology 2: 47-62.

SCHOPLER, J. and N. BATESON (1965) "The power of dependence." J. of Personality and Social Psychology 2: 247-254.

WINER, B. (1962) Statistical Principles in Experimental Design. New York: McGraw-Hill.

WISPE, L. G. and H. B. FRESHLEY (1971) "Race, sex and sympathetic helping behavior: the broken bag caper." J. of Personality and Social Psychology 17: 59-65.

PART VI

CROSS-CULTURAL STUDIES

CROSS-CULTURAL STUDIES

Cross-cultural studies are of particular importance in this reference volume because they are not always readily available to readers in the United States. The International Year of the Woman, sponsored by the United Nations, has made us particularly aware of the need to know more about the role and status of women around the world. Comparative studies of women in many parts of the world, as well as those that focus specifically on France, Israel and England are included here.

31

BIRGITTA LINNER

Status of Women-Population-Development

The three concepts of my title may be regarded as substructures within that larger structure which we call a society. These substructures are interconnected with each other (and with other substructures). If you affect one, you affect the others.

Every society strives for development. Also, most countries have some kind of a population policy. The status of women is no less important. Much lip service is paid to it, but all too often it is not taken seriously. Nevertheless, the status of women is not only affected by changes in development, population policy, etc. (everybody would agree there); it affects development and other areas of society. It is one of the keys to development, and it has to be used if we wish to open the door to a better future.

I am concentrating here on the situation of the developing countries.

The downward spiral

In 1972, the UNICEF and WHO joint Committee on Health Policy in
Geneva pointed out that women of child-bearing age and children
compose approx. 70% of the population in some developing countries,
and that "it is clear that they constitute a vulnerable group which
demands priority attention in family health care". I am thinking
of Kenya which I visited recently. As in all Africa, the trend toward
urbanisation is very strong. (Academician V.G. Solodovnikov has
given the figure of 5% of the population per year for the developing
Africa (1). Young women who leave their village hardly know how
they get pregnant, and still less how to avoid it. The result is
a staggering number of unwanted pregnancies. Consequently, the rate
of abortions is very high; many of them are fatal or medically
harmful. For the rest, there is a growing number of mothers unable
to provide for their children. Everybody will agree that this is
a serious problem. Women - young women in particular - find themselves in a downward spiral.

Colombia offers another instance of the negative spiral. Lack of
education and too many children are two forces jointly pulling
downwards. A recent report states as follows:

"Fertility is inversely related to the level of education reached:
the pregnancy rate in women with no schooling is 58% higher than
that of women with some secondary education; the pregnancy rates
of women whose husbands are farmers or laborers is higher than that
of wives of professionals, administrators and skilled workers; and
women in the rural areas or of the poorer socio-economic level have
a higher fertility rate than those in the urban areas or of the
higher socio-economic groups. The implication of these findings is
that improving the quantity and quality of educational opportunity
in the rural areas and among the lower income groups in the cities
could help control population growth". (2)

According to the same report, the absolute number of illiterates
in Colombia shows an increase, and illiteracy remains almost three
times higher in the rural areas (41%) than in the urban areas (15%)
We are confronted here with a vicious circle (illiterate women tend
to have more children who, in their turn, will be illiterate and
have more children, etc.), which has to be broken. The conclusion
drawn by the report is "that a major effort is needed to improve
primary education with special emphasis on rural education, and
secondly to locate first-cycle comprehensive secondary schools to
serve the rural and rural-urban areas."

Colombia illustrates a general tendency here: the number of illiterates in the world is increasing today, especially among women.

Status of Women and Family Planning

It is often said that women want to have many children. The number
of abortions contradicts this theory. So does a recent survey of
attitudes to family size in Kenya:

"Thus in one survey convering a number of groups which together account for 70% of Kenya's African population, it was found that 38% of rural women saw nothing good at all' in having many children. Not unexpectedly, the chief explanation was above all the heavy burden of expenditures for school fees, food and clothing, which no less than 75% of the women found onerous." (3)

There has been much talk about "quality of life" at this conference. Let me point out that "quality of life" implies the possibility of planning one's children. That possibility - or freedom - is denied the majority of the world's women. They do not have access to education about the functions of human reproduction, nor to the methods of reproduction control offered by modern science. Many countries - both developed and developing - do not include fertility control in their health services or social welfare programs. This in spite of the United Nations Human Rights Declaration as amended in 1968: "Couples have a basic human right to decide freely and responsibly on the number and spacing of their children and a right to adequate education and information in this respect...." If women are not given access to information regarding human reproduction and to family planning services, the human right to space children is illusory as far as they are concerned.

(It has been estimated that the establishing of a maternity health program, including family planning services, which were to cover the whole world, would cost about ten billion Swedish crowns (roughly one billion pounds). The yearly operating costs would be about 3.5 billion Sw crowns. Compare the military budgets! Obviously, the problem is not basically of a financial nature.)

Three roads to an improvement

The first two have been mentioned above: 1) family planning and health services, 2) education. The third one is: 3) employment for women.

Traditionally, child-bearing is the main role of women. If the pattern is to be broken, she must be offered other alternatives. Dr. Aziz Bindary [x]), chairman of the Supreme Council for Family Planning of Egypt, recently pointed out that getting the women out into the labor market is probably the most important factor in curbing the population growth.

Declarations and action

The United Nations have spoken up on several occasions against the discrimination of women and for equal rights and equal status of women, for example in a declaration of 1967:

"Discrimination against women, denying or limiting as it does their equality of rights with men, is fundamentally unjust and constitutes an offence against human dignity."

In the strategy of the second decade of development of the United Nations it is emphasized that "women s integration in the total process of development must be encouraged". [xx])

I could easily go on quoting declarations of this kind for a long
while, and you would all nod your heads in agreement. "How very
true, how very good!" And so what? It is a sad fact that speaking
of human dignity, particularly where women are concerned, has little
effect. The status of women is left to feminists and humanitarians.
This is why I am not speaking in either capacity here. Rather, I am
speaking in terms of development and too fast population growth. If
we wish to promote development and to curb over-population, we have
to realize that the status of women is a key factor in that social
change, the urgency of which is recognized by all.

Notes

x) At the Pugwash-conference at Aulanko, Finland, September 1973.

In recent years the Pugwash Movement has taken up the population
problems as one of their issues. Thus, at the 21st Pugwash Conference at Sinaia, Romania, 1971, the following statement was adopted:

"Although the rate of population growth differs widely between
countries, the rapid increase in world population is an alarming
threat to the future of mankind. In many less-developed countries,
the annual increase in population is virtually as large as the
annual increase in production. Also the increase in population
in the highly developed countries is serious. In many techno-
logically developed countries, the depletion of natural resources
and pollution will cause eventually serious consequences if the
countries delay too long to take steps to limit the increase
in population...."(4)

xx) The United Nations has designated 1974 as World Population Year,
and a World Population Conference will be arranged in Bucharest,
August 19-30, 1974. The UN Conference will be the first world
conference for policy-makers on population problems.(5)

It should also be mentioned that the United Nations has designated the following year, 1974, as the International Women's Year.

It is remarkable to note that staff and delegates within the UN
organisations itself are almost totally male. "The UN population"
does not reflect the world's population. The situation seems
particularly absurd when considering questions like the ones
discussed here. For a description, see "The Situation of Women
in the United Nations, UNITAR 1973" by Prof. Alexander Szalai,
University of Economic Sciences in Budapest. (6)

Footnotes

1) Solodovnikov, V.G. 1973. Problems of the Developing Nations.
The Africa Institute of the Academy of Sciences of the USSR,
Moscow

2) Economic Growth of Colombia. Problems & Prospects. World Bank
Country Economic Report. The John Hopkins University Press,
Baltimore and London, 1972

3) Employment, Incomes and Equality. A Strategy for Increasing
Productive Employment in Kenya. International Labor Office,
ILO, Geneva, 1972

4) Problems of World Security, Environment and Development.
Proceedings of the Twenty-First Pugwash Conference on Science
and World Affairs, Sinaia, Romania, August 26-31, 1971

5) World Population Year 1974. Purposes, Principles, Programmes.
United Nations Fund for Population Activities, New York. USA

* * *

32

UNITED NATIONS ECONOMIC AND SOCIAL COUNCIL/COMMISSION ON THE STATUS OF WOMEN

Study on The Interrelationship of The Status of Women and Family Planning
(Report of the Special Rapporteur Addendum)

1. The meaning of "family planning"

1. The concept of "family planning" is difficult to define precisely, especially so because the phrase apparently means very different things to different people, depending on their social or political perspective. This problem became especially apparent in seminar discussions on the relationship between the status of women and family planning and in Government responses to the question "How would you define 'family planning' as applicable in your country?".

2. For some the term "family planning" refers to specific techniques of contraception, whereas for others it refers to very broad programmes for improving the physical and social well-being of all families. Similarly, some view "family planning" benignly as any purely voluntary service aimed primarily at assisting individuals in having the number of children they want when they want them. Others associate it with particular national programmes to encourage or discourage large families, and still others view it as a deliberate and sometimes suspect policy of wide-scale fertility limitation.[1] Unfortunately, this lack of consensus on the meaning of "family planning" severely hinders open discussion of the issue, especially where "family planning" programmes are equated well attempts at population control.

---

[1] The word "fertility" in this report refers to the actual number and spacing of births, whereas "fecundity" refers to the biological capacity for reproduction.

2.   Family planning as a human right

3.   For the purpose of this report, "family planning" is interpreted as
meaning the right of all persons to determine freely and responsibly the
number and spacing of their children, including the right not to have
children. This interpretation follows the principles set forth in the
Declaration on Population, issued on Human Rights Day, 10 December 1966
"... that the opportunity to decide the number and spacing of children
is a basic human right"; in resolution XVIII of the International
Conference on Human Rights held at Tehran in 1968 "... that couples have
a basic human right to decide freely and responsibly on the number and
spacing of their children and a right to adequate education and information
in this respect"; and in the Declaration on Social Progress and Development
(General Assembly resolution 2542 (XXIV), adopted on 11 December 1969, that
"parents have the exclusive right to determine freely and responsibly the
number and spacing of their children", and the State has an obligation to
provide families with "the knowledge and means necessary to enable them to
exercise this right". It is also consistent with the Programme of Concerted
International Action for the Advancement of Women (General Assembly
resolution 2716 (XXV), adopted unanimously on 15 December 1970), which
recommends certain objectives to be achieved during the Second United
Nations Development Decade, among them the following:

> "Making available to all persons who so desire the necessary
> information and advice to enable them to decide freely and
> responsibly on the number and spacing of their children and to
> prepare them for responsible parenthood, including information on
> the ways in which women can benefit from family planning. Such
> information and advice should be based on valid and proven
> scientific expertise with due regard to the risks that may be
> involved".

4.   Family planning programmes are those organized activities, whether publicly or privately administered, aimed specifically at assisting individuals in exercising their right to plan effectively the number and spacing of their children (if any). They include programmes of education and communication in matters of fertility regulation as well as the direct provision of birth control advice, services and supplies (including contraceptives, abortion, sterilization) and treatment for sterility or subfecundity in both clinical and non-clinical settings. Related programmes in medical care, nutrition, social welfare and other fields, although they may have a significant impact on fertility, are in this report discussed as essential adjuncts to direct family planning activities rather than as part of the core programmes themselves.[2]

5.   The right to decide freely and responsibly on the number and spacing of children cannot be considered apart from other human rights. It takes on its full meaning only in the context of a wide array of human rights on which it depends, among them the right to adequate health care, to education, to employment, and to a decent standard of living. More specifically, free and responsible planning depends not only on universal education in human reproduction, sexuality, birth control and family living and on free access of all persons to birth planning information, services and supplies, but also on the provision of universally accessible high-quality medical care for the protection of mothers and children and on national social and economic policies assuring individuals and families freedom from hardship and want, regardless of their marital status or the number of their children.

---

[2] For a similar distinction, see Report of the Interregional Meeting of Experts on the Social Welfare Aspects of Family Planning, United Nations Headquarters, 22-30 March 1971 (United Nations publication, Sales No. E.71.IV.11).

6. The objective of family planning is clearly the _enrichment_ of human life, not its restriction.[3] Family planning is an essential element of the right of women as individuals to self-determination. It recognizes their deep concern with the protection and sanctity of their bodies; their right to personal autonomy, joy and happiness; their interest in developing the full range of their talents and abilities; and their equal rights and responsibilities with men not only within the family but also in the economic, cultural, social and political life of their communities and of their nations, including their right to equal participation in decision-making at all levels. In this context, family planning contributes both to the fulfilment of personal aspirations and to the achievement of broad national social goals.

3. <u>The relation between family planning and fertility</u>

7. When family planning refers to the right of individuals to decide freely and responsibly on the number and spacing of their children, it is clear that family planning is not synonymous with fertility reduction. In fact, the practice of family planning is compatible with high fertility on both an individual and national level. Contraceptive information and services may be supplied and utilized for the planning of reproduction, but these are tools that individuals may use to any end. If the motivation for large numbers of children is high, if couples want to begin childbearing early and space their children close together, and do so, then they are in fact practising "family planning". On the other hand, low levels of fertility may be the unwanted or unintended consequences of subfecundity, sterility or other cultural practices, rather than of deliberate attempts to limit births.

----

[3] Declaration on Population by World Leaders, 10 December 1966: "We believe the objective of family planning is the enrichment of human life, not its restriction, that family planning, by assuring greater opportunity to each person, frees man to attain his individual dignity and reach his full potential."

8. The degree of knowledge and use of contraception may be usefully viewed as
a variable intervening between the social structure and fertility, as one
practice, among many, either directly or indirectly influencing reproduction.[4]
In addition, we must distinguish between the ability to space and limit births
and the actual decision to do so. The latter decision rests solely on the
individual or the couple, whereas the former condition depends in greater measure
on the distribution of information, education and services in the society at large.

9. Where pro-natalist forces in a society are strong and anti-natalist forces
are weak - that is, where social and economic conditions encourage early and
frequent childbearing - then the provision of family planning services may have
very little impact on fertility. Clinics in some countries report more interest
in treatment for subfecundity and sterility than in contraception.[5] In other
countries, family planning clinics have been utilized most heavily by high-parity
women, who might otherwise have resorted to other methods of birth control,
including abstinence or illegal abortion, and utilized least by women in their
early years of childbearing. Thus, birth rates drop little if at all in societies
where the motivation for children remains high, even in the face of large-scale
national family planning programmes.

10. In the context of changing social and economic conditions that raise the
cost of children and/or reduce their benefits, however, couples tend to find
ways to lower their fertility, whether or not an official family planning
programme is in existence. The most notable case of rapidly declining birth
rates at a time of great social and economic upheaval is that of Western Europe in
the nineteenth and early twentieth centuries, when delayed marriage, celibacy and
coitus interruptus (among other practices) substituted for more "modern" methods
of birth control.

---

[4] Kingsley Davis and Judith Blake, "Social structure and fertility: an
analytic framework", Economic Development and Cultural Change, vol. 4, No. 3
(April 1965), pp. 211-235.

[5] In the Medical Advice Centre in Tema, Ghana, half of the patients
attending in 1966-1968 came for subfertility treatment and slightly under half
came for contraception (Christian Council of Ghana, Committee on Christian
Marriage and Family Life, Annual Report, 1968, p. 5). At the beginning of the
family planning programme in Sandyoung, Egypt, those coming for
infertility cases far outnumbered those coming for birth control (Aziza Hussein,
"Recent developments in the United Arab Republic").

11. Thus the ability to determine the number and spacing of children is most likely to lead to delayed childbearing and lower fertility when social and economic conditions strongly motivate individuals to do so. Expanding the range of opportunities for women so that they share equally with men in the social, economic, political and cultural activities of their communities and nations may well be a major force towards this end. In this light, the right of women as individuals to control their reproductive behaviour takes on broader meaning and importance.

4. Limitations on the individual's right to determine family size

12. If we affirm the right of individuals to decide freely and responsibly on the number and spacing of their children, we must address the issues of what "freely" and "responsibly" mean in this context and what limits may legitimately be set on the individual's right to determine family size.

13. A reasonable decision must rest, in so far as possible, on full awareness of the actual and potential consequences of the decision for the individual, for his or her sexual partner, for the child, for the family and for the community at large. This awareness depends in turn both on adequate education in family living and in the costs and benefits of population growth, to the community and nation, and on the individual's personal sensitivity regarding the needs of those who will be most closely affected by the decision. Among the latter, the needs and rights of the child are paramount. It should not be forgotten that these include the child's right to develop physically, mentally, morally, spiritually and socially in a healthy and normal manner in conditions of freedom and dignity, and the child's right to protection against all forms of neglect, cruelty and exploitation.[6] Thus, the responsible decision takes into account, among other factors, the right of every child to be a wanted child and the needs of the community as a whole.

---

[6] See Declaration of the Rights of the Child (General Assembly resolution 1386 (XIV)). The Declaration on the Elimination of Discrimination against Women (General Assembly resolution 2263 (XXII)) specifies, in article 6, that in situations involving the rights and duties of parents, the interests of the children shall be paramount.

14.   A free decision must rest, in so far as possible, on the availability of a wide range of socially accepted and financially feasible alternatives with regard to the number and spacing of children (which in turn depend on larger social and economic conditions), and on the availability of family planning services assisting individuals in carrying out their decisions. Although the freedom of individuals to determine the number and spacing of their children according to their own goals, values and beliefs is considered to be a fundamental right, to be protected from outside interference, it is important to realize that family planning decisions are made in concrete social and economic situations. They are thus by their very nature influenced and constrained by "outside" factors such as living standards, housing conditions, social welfare policies, cultural traditions, and so on.[7] Within this broad framework, however, we may reaffirm the right of individuals to choose freely among a number of alternatives, including the option of not having children at all.

5.   The role of Governments

15.   General Assembly resolution 2211 (XXI) of 17 December 1966 on population growth and economic development recognized the sovereignty of nations in formulating and promoting their own population policies, with due regard to the principle that the size of the family should be the free choice for each individual family. What happens when these two principles conflict? Whose will should predominate?

16.   If the right of the individual to full knowledge of and access to means of safe control over reproduction is a fundamental human rights, then it is clear that this right, like other human rights, cannot be abridged by any State. Thus nations do not have a sovereign right to force women to bear

---

7/ Report of the Expert Group Meeting on Family Planning and Social Policy in Europe (SOA/ESDP/1971/2), p. 41.

children against their will, either by denying them information or education
in family planning matters, or by restricting their access to safe and
effective means of birth control (whether deliberately or as a consequence of
governmental non-intervention in this "private" area). Nor do nations have
a sovereign right to force women to restrict their childbearing, either through
forced abortion or sterilization or through severe social, economic or legal
sanctions.[8/] These statements are consistent with article 4 of the
United Nations Declaration on Social Progress and Development, which states
that parents have the exclusive right to determine freely and responsibly the
number and spacing of their children.[9/]

17. What methods may Governments legitimately use in formulating and promoting
particular demographic policies, especially those relating to reproductive
behaviour?

18. Participants in a United Nations Seminar on Family Planning and Social
Policy in Europe criticized heavily those policies that try to achieve their
ends by denying people access to family planning services, declaring that it
is especially intolerable for the State deliberately to use its power to
limit the effectiveness with which people are able to plan the number and
spacing of their children.[10/]Another group of experts on population policy,
while appreciating the dilemma posed by the discrepancy between individual
and national needs, declared that close attention should be paid to any
potentially undesirable social ramifications of policies proposing incentives
or disincentives for childbearing. Moreover, some policies suggested in the
literature, such as outright legal restrictions on the number of children in
a family, should be regarded as a clear violation of basic human rights.

8/ Particularly when measures intended to prevent births are aimed at
destroying, in whole or in part, a national, ethnic, racial or religious group.
The Convention on the Prevention and Punishment of the Crime of Genocide, which
entered into force on 12 January 1952, states that persons conspiring to or
committing genocide shall be punished, whether they are constitutionally
responsible rulers, public officials or private individuals.

9/ General Assembly resolution 2542 (XXIV).

10/ Provided that the means employed to control births do not encroach
on the rights of others, as does infanticide, for example. Report of the
Expert Group Meeting on Family Planning and Social Policy in Europe (SOA/ESDP/1971/2),
pp. 8 and 37.

19. Governments may, however, consider ways to influence the social and economic milieu in which reproductive decisions are made in order to bring personal goals more in line with national needs. Educating the population on the relation between population growth and national development, providing social security for the aged, the ill and the unemployed, expanding opportunities for women to work outside the home, improving standards of living by equalizing the distribution of material resources, and similar policies, need not conflict with the principle that family planning is the exclusive right of individuals. Ideally, "it is to be expected that a wise government would help people to exercise that right in a way that did justice to their own and others' interests, present and future".[11/] Under these conditions, individuals may continue to act freely on their own goals and values if they find government policies inconsistent with them.

6. Other limitations

20. If Governments do not have the sovereign right to deny individuals the right to determine freely the number and spacing of their children, neither do particular groups who may have an interest, for various reasons in restricting the access of their members or of other groups or persons to information, education, or services permitting them to govern their own reproductive behaviour. It is important to reaffirm the right of individuals to act in this intimate area according to their own values and beliefs, but it is equally important to protest against the imposition of the values and beliefs of one group on another, especially when those values and beliefs conflict and when the one attempts to deny the basic human rights of the other.

11/ Ibid.

21. Conflicts of interest within the family, between husband and wife, or
between unmarried sexual partners pose even more of a dilemma for the protection
of basic rights. The issue of whose will should predominate when a consensus
cannot be reached is highly sensitive, both emotionally and politically.
However, keeping in mind the principle that one individual does not have the
right to exploit another person's body or labour against his or her will;
that pregnancy and childbirth may severely endanger a woman's health, or even
her life; and that in the eyes of the family, the society and the mother herself,
the greatest responsibility for nurturing, protecting and caring for young
children usually rests with the woman; then it follows that where parties
disagree, the woman should ultimately bear the final right and responsibility
for determining the number and spacing of the children she bears.

7. Family planning and population control

22. Family planning is very different from population control. However,
when family planning programmes are sponsored as one component of a deliberate
policy to reduce birth rates in particular nations or among particular subgroups
within nations; when the rationale of family planning is phrased in terms of
population control rather than in terms of expanding individual rights to self-
determination; and when family planning services are promoted apart from and
without including reforms in general health care, social justice and the
redistribution of wealth; then family planning programmes are on occasion
naturally met with suspicion by those very nations or groups for whom they were
intended. Unfortunately the confusion of family planning with population control
may lead to the false rejection of the former for political reasons, so that
persons who genuinely desire family planning information and services under
the appropriate conditions are, under these conditions, forced to reject them.

23. The focus of this report is therefore on family planning as a fundamental
human right rather than as a means to fertility reduction. Family planning in
the absence of other programmes for social and economic progress - including
programmes for the advancement of women to full equality with men in every
sphere of life - is a hollow accomplishment, and one not likely to lead to
significantly lower birth rates in countries of high fertility. But where
a combination of progressive forces does lead to lower birth rates, the fertility
reduction may best be seen as a beneficial side effect of social and economic
progress, and not as the sole purpose of family planning.

II.   THE IMPORTANCE OF FAMILY PLANNING FOR WOMEN AS INDIVIDUALS
AND ITS IMPACT ON THEIR ROLES IN SOCIETY

A.   Focusing on the individual woman

24.   Discussions of the need for family planning programmes and/or other
population policies most frequently appear to emphasize the importance of
the relationships between population growth, the age structure of populations,
and the requirements of social and economic development on a national and
international scale.   For those concerned with problems of "over-population",
the Malthusian fears of food shortages and, more recently, of scarcities in
essential natural resources are also cited as rationales for policies designed
to reduce rates of population growth.   For those who view "under-population" as
a threat in their countries, the widespread dissemination of family planning
information and services is sometimes rejected on the grounds that it is not
compatible with national needs.   Whatever the particular demographic situation,
however, these discussions tend to place family planning primarily in the
perspective of national and international population goals and priorities.

25.   Less attention has been paid to the human rights aspects of family planning,
that is, to the necessity of providing family planning information, education
and services for the direct purpose of guaranteeing to all persons the right to
determine freely and responsibly the number and spacing of their children,
regardless of the population factor in the countries concerned.   And even less
attention has been paid to the necessity of providing family planning services
as a means, among others, of enabling women to free themselves as individuals
and to exercise fully their rights to social, economic and political equality
with men.   Where women are considered at all in the formulation of population
policies, they tend frequently to be viewed as either passive recipients of
family planning services or, if their motivation to alter their childbearing
patterns in the desired directions (whether up or down) is low, as obstacles to
the achievement of national social and economic goals.   The inherent justice of
a policy that would help in raising the status of women and in promoting equality
between men and women, in and of itself, is rarely mentioned as a goal.

26. In the first chapter the concept of family planning as a fundamental human rights was briefly discussed. In this chapter we will outline the extent to which the exercise of the right to decide whether and when to have children, or the inability to exercise this right, may help or hinder women as individuals in exercising their various social, economic and political rights. These rights are set forth in the Declaration on the Elimination of Discrimination Against Women, among other instruments.[12]/

27. One problem in analysing the impact of family planning is to isolate the specific influence of the number and spacing of births from the multitude of other factors that facilitate or impede the exercise of women's rights. Economic, social, cultural and political forces unique to every country shape the structure of opportunities for health care, education, employment and political participation, as well as the institution of the family. Moreover, the nature and consequences of these forces are constantly changing. The question is whether it is possible to describe those conditions under which certain patterns of reproductive behaviour can make a difference to the individual woman's ability to exercise her rights, apart from the effect of these other forces.

28. A second problem concerns the separation of cause from effect in the relationship between reproductive behaviour and women's social roles. In a sense the organization of this report into chapters distinguishing between the impact of family planning and fertility on women's status, and the impact of women's status of family planning and fertility, creates an artificial conceptual distinction that may not exist in fact. The best example of this dilemma appears in the association between female employment and fertility. The question always arises as to which "causes" which: are women who have fewer children (for a variety of reasons) more likely to seek employment because they are freer to do so, or are employed women more likely to keep their family size deliberately small

---

12/ For the text of the Declaration on the Elimination of Discrimination Against Women and other relevant instruments. see Human Rights: A Compilation of International Instruments of the United Nations (United Nations publication, Sales No. E.73.XIV.2).

so that they may continue to work? Obviously both factors play a part, but it is difficult for the researcher to decide which factor may be more important in any given situation, especially on the basis of statistical information alone.

29. Finally, in assessing the impact on the individual woman of the ability to regulate fertility, one must distinguish between her knowledge of. contraception and its actual consequences as manifested in altered fertility patterns. Obviously a woman may practise "family planning" effectively, begin childbearing early and bear many children while having "just as many children as she wants, when she wants them". Nevertheless, the knowledge itself of how to regulate births, regardless of its direct effect on fertility, gives women the power to plan their lives in ways undreamed of by those who have never questioned the inevitability of their childbearing, or who have resorted in desperation to cumbersome, ineffective and often. dangerous methods to stop unwanted births. As the Netherlands response points out, "family planning will greatly enhance people's awareness of the possibility of shaping their own destinies".

30. When the power to space and limit pregnancies is translated into an actual decision to do so, the impact on women's status may be measured more accurately. Disaggregated into its components of the ability to delay the first birth, to space births several years apart, to stop childbearing earlier in the life cycle and to limit the total number of births,[13]/ each aspect of birth planning may be examined separately for its effect on the woman's health and on the exercise of her economic, social and political rights in the society and in the family.

---

[13]/ Including forgoing childbearing altogether.

B.   Recent evidence on reproductive patterns and
     contraceptive knowledge and practice

31.   Table 1 (E/CN.6/575/Add.3) shows the average number of children born alive
per thousand women of specified ages for about 70 countries for which information
is available for 1960 or later.[14]   At first glance it is apparent that the
highest fertility rates on a regional basis are found in Oceania, where women in
five countries averaged 6,259 live births per thousand women aged 45-49, or over
six children per woman by the end of her reproductive years.   Women in the
African countries listed bore fewer children -- an average of 4,977 per thousand
women aged 45-49 -- with women in Asia bearing 4,882, in the Americas 4,215, and
in Europe 2,988. Averages for the individual countries listed range from
approximately two children per woman in England and Wales to over six in Kenya, Southern
Rhodesia, Jordan, Thailand, Bahrain, Tonga and Fiji, and almost eight in
Western Samoa.

32.   These figures represent the accumulated number of live births to women
passing through their prime reproductive years in the decades of the 1930s and
1940s.   Changing fertility patterns in more recent years are revealed in the
number of children born per thousand women in the younger age brackets, many
of whom may not reach the larger family sizes of the older generation.[15]

33.   The childbearing patterns of these younger women in their late teens and
early twenties may be even more relevant to the question of the impact of
childbearing on women's roles than is the total number of children born to women,
for reasons suggested in the following discussions of female education and
employment.   Because the figures in table 1 refer to both married and unmarried
women, it is difficult to tell whether a low figure means that married women were
having fewer children, or whether only a small proportion of women in that age

---

[14]   Problems associated with the evaluation and accuracy of these statistics
are discussed in notes to the tables in the United Nations Demographic Yearbooks
listed as sources.

[15]   On the other hand, some may surpass them.   Women aged 35-39 in Hong Kong
in 1966, for example, are shown as already having borne more children than those
aged 40-44 or 45-49, although figures for women in the older age groups may be
artificially depressed by memory loss regarding the total number of live births. A
similar situation is shown in several Latin American and Caribbean countries.

group were married, or living in reproductive unions. But on a cumulative
basis the figures do suggest the extent to which a particular age group of women
as a whole might be bound to the care of children. In Puerto Rico, for example,
about 1,000 children had already been born alive per 1,000 women aged 15-19, or
one per woman, suggesting an early and quite universal commitment to child care
among teenage girls. But in Czechoslovakia, Guadeloupe, Khmer Republic,
Martinique, Réunion, Romania and Tonga, fewer than 100 children had been born
for every thousand women in this age group, leaving them relatively free to
pursue other activities.

34. The point will be consistently stressed in this report that reproductive
patterns are the end result of many economic, social, cultural and biological
factors, of which the practice or non-practice of deliberate contraception is
only one. Thus it is a mistake to assume that the high birth rates shown in
some countries in table 1 are inevitably the consequence of lack of contraceptive
knowledge or practice, or that low birth rates indicate widespread, conscious
birth control. Moreover, lack of contraceptive knowledge cannot adequately
explain the absence of contraceptive practice, because it only begs the question
of why people are so little motivated to learn of a method in the first place.
Nevertheless, evidence on contraceptive knowledge and practice does provide us
with an approximate idea of the extent to which couples believe they can regulate
the timing and number of their births, and thus, gives a hint of the size of the
population in various countries covered in discussions of the importance of
family planning for women as individuals and its impact on their roles in society.

35. World-wide surveys on knowledge, attitudes and the practice of contraception
("KAP" studies) among married couples of reproductive age have shown that as few
as 15 per cent of women in some rural areas of developing countries claim to
know of any method of birth control,[16]/ although in general the figures in

---

16/ Rural Ghana, 1965/66, in John C. Caldwell, "Anti-natal practice in
Tropical Africa", International Union for the Scientific Study of Population,
International Population Conference, London 1969, vol. II (Liège, Belgium, 1971),
pp. 1228; Rural Algeria, 1967/68, in Association algérienne pour la recherche
démographique, économique et sociale; La Régulation des naissances, opinions et
attitudes des couples algériens: résultat préliminaire d'une enquête nationale,
(Algeria, summer 1968); Rural Mysore, India, early 1960s in Parker Mauldin,
"Fertility studies: knowledge, attitudes and practice", Studies in Family Planning,
No. 7 (New York, The Population Council, June 1965), p. 7.

Asian, African and Latin American studies tend to run closer to 30 to 50 per cent, and are higher in urban areas, among men, and among the better educated.[17]   Among some highly educated populations in developing countries and in most industrialized countries, from 90 to 100 per cent of women likely to know of a method.

36. These figures are always difficult to interpret for they depend on how the question is worded (the difference between "knowing of" and "knowing how to use" a method, for example), whether specific methods are named as examples, whether the question refers to preventing pregnancies or preventing births (which would permit abortion as a possible response), and whether a woman is willing to admit she knows of a method, among other factors.[18]   However, even allowing for the probable overestimation of contraceptive ignorance in many studies (and a similar overestimation of "willingness to learn"), it seems clear that many women -- and especially poor women, uneducated women, and women in many rural areas -- are totally unaware of any safe, effective method for controlling their own fertility.

37. The percentages of couples who say they have actually practised some method tend to fall even lower. Again it is difficult to untangle the meaning of these figures, for they depend so much on the interview situation and on whether methods such as abstinence or abortion are specifically included as alternatives. Nevertheless, figures as low as 1 per cent have been reported in some studies made during the 1960s,[19] with a more typical range of 5-20 per cent for Africa, 20-40 per cent for Asia, 40-60 per cent for Latin America and from 75-90 per cent for industrialized countries.[20]   These approximate figures might well be kept in mind in the discussions that follow.

---

[17] Summary tables supplied by the Population Council, New York.

[18] For a discussion of the problems of interpreting KAP surveys, see Philip M. Hauser, "Family planning and population programs", Demography, vol. 4, No. 1, 1967, pp. 397-414; John C. Caldwell, op.cit.; and Lawrence W. Green, "East Pakistan: Knowledge and use of contraceptives", Studies in Family Planning, 39 (March 1969), pp. 9-14, among others.

[19] Urban Kenya, 1966, Thomas E.Dow,Jr., "Attitudes toward family size and family planning in Nairobi", Demography, vol. 4, No. 2, 1967, pp. 780-797; Rural Morocco, 1966, in tables supplied by the Population Council.

[20] Summary tables supplied by the Population Council, New York.

C. The impact of family planning on maternal and child health

1. The right to health

38. United Nations instruments recognize the right of everyone to the enjoyment
of the highest standards of physical and mental health.[21] Among other measures,
they propose that steps be taken to reduce the rate of stillbirth and infant
mortality in all countries and to assure the healthy development of the child.
It is clear that these rights are closely related to the right to family planning
information and services, and, more broadly, to the right to decide freely and
responsibly on the number and spacing of children. A decision to have a child
is not free if it poses a grave risk to the life or health of the woman or the
child in question. Nor is it free if it is made in ignorance of ways to space
or limit births.

39. The positive effects of family planning on maternal and child health appear
to be universally recognized by Governments. All who responded to the guidelines
reported that in their opinion, family planning was beneficial to the
health and well-being of mothers, children and families. Thus it is not surprising
that family planning programmes are often supported for health reasons alone.

40. Health services personnel have also come to realize that action to achieve
optimal reproductive patterns is as fundamental an aspect of health care as,
for example, nutritional care, environmental sanitation and communicable disease
control.[22] Growing recognition of the relationships between the occurence,
timing and spacing of pregnancies, and physical and mental health has led in many
cases to the redefinition of family planning as a vital preventive and positive
health measure.

21/ For example, article 12, International Covenant on Economic, Social
and Cultural Rights (General Assembly resolution 2200 A (XXI)).

22/ World Health Organization, Technical Report Series, No. 476, "Family
planning in health services, report of a WHO Expert Committee" (Geneva, 1971),
p. 13.

41. It is important to bear in mind, however, that factors such as illiteracy, poverty, malnutrition, poor medical services or inadequate child care may have a far greater adverse effect on maternal and child health than does the age of the mother, or the number or spacing of her previous pregnancies. Under good conditions a woman may bear six or eight children in relative safety, space them close together and be assured that they will all survive their childhood. Under poor conditions, childbirth can pose grave risks to maternal or infant health even where pregnancies are spaced and limited. Family planning is not a substitute for necessary improvements in the distribution of health-related resources such as food, medical care, adequate housing and health education and information.

2. The association between reproductive patterns and maternal and child health

42. An association between large or closely spaced families and poor maternal or child health does not prove that the former causes the latter, for both conditions may result independently from low levels of living.[23] Maternal and infant survival rates and health levels vary greatly across countries and across major population subgroups, depending on economic, social and cultural conditions. Nevertheless, within countries and within groups of differing socio-economic levels, similar patterns appear. The evidence appears unambiguous that, other things being equal, maternal and infant morbidity and mortality are lower when births are postponed to the late teens or early twenties, when childbearing ceases by the mid-thirties, when births are spaced from two to three years apart, and when the total number of births does not exceed four or five.[24]

23/ Report of the Expert Group Meeting on Family Planning and Social Policy in Europe (SOA/ESDP/1971/2), p. 39.

24/ World Health Organization,"Health aspects of family planning", Technical Report Series, No. 442 (Geneva 1970); International Planned Parenthood Federation, "The relationship between family size and maternal and child health"; Abdel R. Omran, The Health Theme in Family Planning, Monograph 16 (Chapel Hill, N.C., Carolina Population Center, 1971); The International Federation of Gynaecology and Obstetrics, Proceedings of the International Seminar on Maternal Mortality, Family Planning and Biology of Reproduction, Bombay, March 1969 (Bombay, the Federation of Obstetric and Gynaecological Societies in India); World Health Organization, "Health, family planning and the status of women", paper prepared for the Seminar on the Status of Women and Family Planning, Istanbul, 11-24 July 1972.

43. There are a number of dangers to maternal health arising out of pregnancies following closely on one another, high parity (many births) and pregnancies occurring to women over the age of 35. The dangers are compounded when two or three of the above conditions occur together,[25/] and when they are associated with overcrowding, poverty, poor nutrition, poor hygiene, illiteracy, or lack of access to medical advice and services.

44. Maternal death is often caused by ante-partum or post-partum haemorrhage or shock, especially among poor, older and multiparous women.[26/] The chief source of maternal deaths in Africa is said to be anaemia, caused by a deficiency of animal protein in the diet, the infestation of the intestinal tract with parasites, and the very rapid and debilitating succession of births.[27/] Rapid childbearing and high parity has been found to be associated with obstetric disease and gynaecological complications as well as aggravating the incidence of a large number of other diseases such as cancer, cardio-vascular disease, epilepsy, severe anaemia, and diabetes, among others. [28/]

45. Evidence also points to greater risks of fetal and infant deaths or illness with high parity, advanced maternal age and short birth intervals. Correlations have been found between these reproductive patterns and spontaneous abortion (miscarriage), stillbirths, premature births, low birth weights, infant deaths, birth deformities and infant and child malnutrition and disease.[29/] Again, risks of death or illness are aggravated by conditions of poverty, ignorance and poor medical care.

25/ Risks are higher, however, among older women who are bearing their first child than among those of slightly higher parity in the same age groups.

26/ International Planned Parenthood Federation, "The relationship between family size and maternal and child health".

27/ Ibid.

28/ Ibid.

29/ See foot-note 24/.

46. Several countries in their responses declared that declining birth rates in their countries had been accompanied by declining maternal and infant mortality rates,[30] although the relationship was not necessarily a causal one. Reductions in birth rates among older women were singled out as especially important in a few countries.[31]

47. Others specifically mentioned a reduction in illegal abortion as a beneficial consequence of family planning.[32] Morbidity and mortality rates resulting from illegal abortion are of course difficult to obtain, but the World Health Organization estimates that mortality rates may reach or exceed one per hundred illegal abortions in some large communities where abortions are primarily self-induced or performed by unskilled personnel.[33] Many women are hospitalized with complications following abortion attempts.[34] On the other hand, where abortions - legal or illegal - are performed by skilled medical practitioners, mortality and morbidity rates are much lower. Under ideal medical conditions with good health services, mortality from legal abortions may fall considerably below that from childbirth.[35]

30/ Indonesia, working paper (WP/2) for the Seminar on the Status of Women anf Family Planning, Istanbul, 11-24 July 1972; response of Japan; response of the United Kingdom.

31/ Response of Fiji; response of Thailand; Finland working paper (WP/3) for the Seminar on the Status of Women and Family Planning, Istanbul, 11-24 July 1972.

32/ United States of America and Yugoslavia, working papers for the Seminar on the Status of Women and Family Planning, Istanbul, 11-24 July 1972; Belgium, Cameroon and Italy responses

33/ "Spontaneous and induced abortion: report of a WHO scientific group", World Health Organization, Technical Report Series, No. 461 (Geneva, 1970), pp. 38-40.

34/ For example, 15 per cent of all admissions to the Farah Maternity Hospital in Iran are post-abortion cases, numbering 6,000 in 1969-1970. See Population and Family Planning in Iran (ST/SOA/SER.R/13).

35/ Ibid.

3. Health conditions affecting reproduction

48. The interrelationship of maternal and child health with reproduction is
complex. Not only do the number and timing of pregnancies (among other important
factors) affect the woman's and child's chances for survival and good health, but
general health conditions affect in turn the number and timing of pregnancies.

49. Perhaps the clearest example of this latter association is the common
situation in which high infant mortality motivates couples to begin childbearing
early and to produce as many children as possible in rapid succession in the
hopes that at least, some will survive to adulthood. Yet frequent pregnancies
create an additional drain on maternal health and shorten the duration of breastfeeding of infants. As a consequence, pregnancies are less likely to be carried
to term successfully and infants are less likely to survive their early years, a
pattern which in turn perpetuates the desire for additional children.

50. Poor health conditions tend to depress fecundity and increase infant mortality.
But rapid declines in infant and childhood mortality rates, which are occurring in
many developing countries as a consequence of improvements in nutrition and the
control of infectious diseases, produce in many cases unexpectedly large families.[36]
These may not only pose further limitations on the improvement of family health,
but also depress the whole socio-economic status of the family, and especially of
women who bear the primary responsibility for child care.[37] The problem is
especially critical where there is little awareness that effective birth control
is possible, or where women depend on unreliable methods or hazardous abortions
rather than face the consequences of further unwanted pregnancies. It is clear,
then, that improvements in health care and in material standards of living must
be provided in conjunction with family planning information and services. Neither
is sufficient without the other.

---

[36] "Health, family planning and the status of women", paper prepared by the
World Health Organization for the Seminar on the Status of Women and Family Planning,
Istanbul, 11-24 July 1972, p. 1.

[37] Ibid.

4.   Family planning programmes as an element of maternal and child health care

51. The integration of family planning services with maternal and child health
care delivery systems is obviously advantageous in a number of respects, especially
in countries with well-developed health resources.[38/] Family planning programmes
can benefit greatly from the established organizational structure, procedures,
skilled personnel, and opportunities for family planning counselling that existing
medical services provide. In cultural settings where women are reluctant to seek
out family planning information or services, or are reluctant to be seen entering
special family planning clinics, the integration of functions may be particularly
beneficial. Moreover, delivering family planning services (including treatment
for subfecundity or sterility) in the context of general maternal and child health
care may create a greater sense of trust among Governments and among subgroups in
the population who might otherwise suspect the goals of family planning programmes
as being aimed primarily at population control, rather than at improvement in the
lives of individuals.

52. Several countries pointed out in their responses that many of the advantages
of medically oriented family planning programmes derive from the opportunity to
provide other forms of health care along with family planning advice and services.
Included among these are general health education, prenatal and post-natal counselling,
subfecundity and sterility treatment, and veneral disease and cervical cancer
detection, among others.

53. On the other hand, some observers have criticized the tendency to overemphasize medical or health aspects of family planning. The problem of relying heavily
on health care delivery systems for family planning is especially acute in
countries with limited and already strained resources. Some countries have one
doctor for as few as four or five hundred people, for example, but in others the
ratio of doctors to population may be only one per fifty thousand.[39/] Within

---

38/   For a more detailed discussion, see World Health Organization, "Family
planning in health services: Report of a WHO Expert Committee", WHO Technical
Report Series, No. 476 (Geneva, 1971), pp. 31-40.

39/   Statistical Yearbook, 1971 (United Nations publication, Sales
No. 72.XVII.1), pp. 712-715.

many countries, medical care tends to be concentrated in major metropolitan centres, frequently leaving rural dwellers entirely without services. Moreover, family planning programmes serving women who are hospitalized for childbirth, miss women who want to postpone their first birth, and those who are not hospitalized for childbirth, as well as those who may not wish to bear children at all. Although in some industrialized countries virtually all women give birth in health institutions,[40] in others hospitalization is very rare. Most rural dwellers, especially those who are poor and uneducated, live far from medical centres and cannot afford the time or money to make regular visits to clinics for family planning or pregnancy-related medical care.

54. Where health care delivery systems are inadequate, there is clearly an urgent need for them to be greatly expanded to ensure that everyone is able to exercise his or her right to the highest standards of physical health. Information, education and services relating to fertility regulation are an essential element of these programmes. However, other channels of education, information and family planning services should also be utilized so that all persons are simultaneously able to exercise their right to decide when, and whether, to have children.

5. Mental health aspects of planned childbearing

55. Less attention has been paid to the mental health aspects of family planning than to its implications for physical health, partly because the effects of timing and limiting births are even more difficult to isolate from the effects of other factors in this area. Nevertheless, Governments which responded to the guidelines were in general agreement that the ability to bear children by choice is beneficial to the full development of the woman, the child and the family.

40/ Poland, for example, reported that 99 per cent of births in that country are attended by medical or paramedical personnel in health institutions (response of Poland).

56. A number of studies have suggested that the "mental health"" of women and children, as measured by various indicators of social and psychological well-being, is highest when births are planned and wanted.[41/] From the point of view of the child, the quality and quantity of parental care may diminish as additional children are born. Psychological needs of children are closely linked with love and affection, but it may be impossible for a parent to give full attention to each of a large number of children spaced close together.[42/] Unwanted children may (and often do) suffer even more from lack of love and affection which may amount to extreme neglect.[43/] The problem is aggravated when the society does not provide high-quality infant and child care services, including health care and when there are no facilities to relieve mothers of the heavy burdens of domestic labour. The situation is further aggravated when mothers must assume the major responsibility for the day-to-day care and nurturing of their children, and the obligations of the fathers in this respect are not recognized.

57. Several country participants in United Nations Seminars on the Status of Women and Family Planning pointed to the beneficial effects of family planning on the woman's psychological and social well-being. For example, the Ghanian participant at the Seminar on the Status of Women and Family Planning, Istanbul, reported that the woman who has spaced her family "can enjoy a better and healthier marital life with her partner without the fear of an unwanted pregnancy"; as well as enjoying greater emotional stability and fuller life for herself and her family.[44/] The Kenyan participant reported that the parents are able to decide the

---

41/ See foot-note 24/.

42/ ST/TAO/HR/46, pp. 10-11.

43/ For example, several studies show that mortality is higher among infants born out of wedlock than within marriage. See The Relationship between Family Size and Maternal and Child Health, International Planned Parenthood Federation (1970), p. 9.

44/ Working paper prepared by Ghana for the Seminar on the Status of Women and Family Planning, Istanbul, 11-24 July 1972.

size of their families, mothers may plan better their participation in employment, social activities and family affairs. Their improved chances of enjoying good mental and physical health provide an incentive to become fully involved in nation building.[45]

58. However, the New Zealand Government in its response expressed a more cautious opinion in warning of the possible consequences of reduced family size, when alternatives roles for women outside the family are limited:

> "There is no doubt that the health of mothers and children is improved by the spacing and, in many cases, the limitation of family. There are, however, many other factors which might well operate against this improvement in health and these are becoming evident in this country. Mothers with fewer children and more time on their hands become dissatisfied and restless, or seek satisfaction in work outside the home. These situations are providing their own problems and are affecting the physical and mental health of the mother, child and family as a whole. There is no doubt that smaller and satisfactorily spaced families increase the possibility of health for the family, but this will only be maintained if women find satisfaction in other ways, and the well-being of the children they have is safeguarded".

59. It is questionable, however, to assume that an increase in the number of children necessarily decreases the psychological stress of mothers who lacking in possibilities of other creative outlets and fuller life of participation in the community, are intellectually frustrated.

60. The crux of the argument on the benefits of family planning for the individual woman may be exactly this: that it depends on the extent to which the cultural and structural conditions of each society make alternative roles available to women beyond their traditional obligations in marriage and motherhood. This is equally true of societies where woman's status may be regarded as "high" in accordance with the number of children she bears, where depriving her of that position without an alternative role which is equally highly regarded may in effect lower her prestige in the eyes of the community. Some of these roles and their relationship to family planning are discussed in the following sections.

---

[45] Working paper prepared by Kenya for the Seminar on the Status of Women and Family Planning, Istanbul, 11-24 July 1972.

D. The impact of family planning on women's roles in society

1. The right to an education

61. According to the Universal Declaration of Human Rights, everyone has the
right to an education. In the Declaration on the Elimination of Discrimination
against Women, among other documents, girls and women, married or unmarried, are
to be assured equal rights with men in education at all levels, including study
in educational institutions of all types, the same choice of curricula, and
equal access to scholarships and other financial support.[46]

62. Equal education has proved to be an elusive goal, however. As table 2
shows (E/CN.6/575/Add. 3), in many countries a much smaller proportion of women
than men, aged 15 and over is literate. In countries for which information is
available in Africa and Asia, for example, adult women are on the average only
slightly over half as likely as men to be able to read and write.[47] The degree
of sex inequality is especially severe where over-all literacy rates are low, with a
female rates falling to one quarter of male rates and below in a few countries
where only a tiny minority of adult women is literate.

63. The ratio of female to male literacy rates improves in every country when
only those between the ages of 15 and 19 are considered, suggesting that sex
inequality is slowly being reduced in this area as general levels of literacy
rise. However there are still some countries in which teenage girls are less
than half as likely as boys to be able to read and write. And in many countries
where literacy courses are offered for adults, women make up only a small fraction
of those enrolled.[48]

46/ ' Universal Declaration on Human Rights, article 26; Declaration on
the Elimination of Discrimination against Women, article 9; UNESCO Convention
and Recommendation against Discrimination in Education, 1960.

47/ See also United Nations Educational, Scientific and Cultural
Organization, Equality of Access to Literacy (ED/MD/14).

48/ Ibid.

64. Females are also frequently under-represented in school enrolments, with their under-representation becoming more extreme at the higher levels of education. The influence of this absolute and relative lack of schooling may be felt throughout the lives of women in severely limiting their potential for any but unskilled, poorly paid employment. School attendance rates of girls aged 5 to 14, shown in table 3, range from an average of 79 per cent of boys' rates in Africa and Asia to 100 per cent in the Americas. At ages 15 to 19, girls' rates average from 47 per cent of boys' rates in Africa to 92 per cent in Europe. But young adult women aged 20 to 24 are only 15 per cent as likely to be enrolled in school as are men in Africa, 44 per cent in Asia, 57 per cent in Europe and 63 per cent in the Americas. In many areas the relative under-representation of females appears to be compounded by an over-all scarcity of educational resources that place them at an even greater competitive disadvantage, although it is interesting to note that in Latin America girls appear to be less disadvantaged in schooling as compared to boys than they are on the average in Africa or Asia, even at similar levels of male enrolment.

65. Even when school enrolment rates are approximately equal for males and females, certain fields of study are often strongly sex-typed as appropriate for females only, or males only. For example, in Swedish Vocational Schools in 1969, 95 per cent of nursing students and 86 per cent of students in domestic work were women, but only 12 per cent of those in technical education and 8 per cent in industry and crafts were women.[49] In the Swedish universities, women predominated in the humanities, while men totally dominated the technological side.[50] Women in Hungary constituted 82 per cent of the students in technical schools of economics in 1968-1969, but only 17 per cent of those in industrial technical schools.[51] The nature and degree of sex-typing of

---

49/ Response of Sweden.

50/ Ibid.

51/ Response of Hungary. Other similar examples are mentioned in the response of Jordan and in the working paper prepared by New Zealand for the Seminar on the Status of Women and Family Planning, Istanbul, 11-24 July 1972.

fields varies greatly across countries. A number of Governments pointed out in their responses that women are increasingly entering fields of training that were formerly closed to them.[52]

66. What effect does the ability to determine the number and spacing of children have on the exercise of the woman's right to an education and to equal treatment in schools at all levels?

67. Delaying the onset of childbearing, either through delaying marriage itself,[53] or by postponing the first birth within marriage, is the most relevant aspect of fertility regulation in this regard. Postponing the first birth should have the greatest impact on a woman's opportunities for vocational training or for secondary, college or university education in those countries or among socio-economic groups in which (a) she had a high probability of pursuing an education beyond the normal first years of childbearing to begin with, and (b) the birth of a child would effectively limit her chances of staying in school.

68. On the first point, where few girls receive higher education, delaying the first birth is likely to make little if any difference as to their educational opportunities (although it may well have a significant effect on other aspects of their lives).[54] Table 3 shows that in the African countries for which information was available, on the average only about 19 per cent of girls between the ages of 15 and 19 were enrolled in school during the 1960s. Comparable figures for Asia were 28 per cent, the Americas, 29 per cent, and Europe, 32 per cent. (The range for individual countries listed spread from 3 per cent in Pakistan and 5 per cent in Sierra Leone to 63 per cent in Japan and 67 per cent in the United States of America.)

---

[52] Egypt, Fiji, Jordan, Thailand.

[53] "Marriage" is used here to refer to any more or less permanent sexual union.

[54] Iran, Jamaica and Singapore reported that lack of family planning knowledge can impede women's educational opportunities, however.

69. It is doubtful whether the lack of the knowledge or means to plan and space children per se is as much responsible for the initially lower school enrolment rates of females and their higher dropout rate, as the economic, social and cultural ressures that define sex roles and contribute to a preference for early marriage over continued schooling for girls.[55/] Scarce resources for over-all educational investment are also constraining factors. That is, both the absence of family planning and the low levels of female education may derive from similar underlying social, economic and cultural factors, rather than one "causing" the other. But where higher education for women on a large scale is economically feasible and socially valued, then the ability to delay or forgo marriage and/or the first birth becomes increasingly salient in enabling the individual woman to exercise her rights in this area.[56/]

70. The second point concerns the likelihood of women discontinuing their schooling when they marry or have children. Many women who might otherwise remain in school drop out on marraige or when they have children of their own volition, because they are forced to, or because it is expected of them. In the United States, for example, of a national sample of young men and women who began college in the late 1960s, 75 per cent of females who married and had children dropped out before completing college, as compared to 52 per cent of married males with children, 22 per cent of single women and 27 per cent of single men.[57/] If couples had known how to prevent an early pregnancy or had

---

55/ Jordan, for example, reported that, in the past, prevailing social customs which kept women as prisoners in their homes and favoured early marriage, and frequent childbearing prevented women from receiving an education, along with male opposition to female schooling and generally low levels of education and literacy. Participants in the Istanbul Seminar advocated for change in the traditional attitudes which presented women as domestic stereotypes and family planning directed at both men and women, in order to encourage women to complete their schooling. Participants emphasized the fact that a rising age at marriage would also foster the accomplishment of a higher level of education for women and permit practical training for employment.

56/ Responses of Finland, Sweden and the United States of America stated that effective birth control was an almost indispensable prerequisite for the attainment of equality with men in a society where educational requirements are rising and young men and women become sexually active at a relatively early age.

57/ Unpublished data from A. J. Jaffe and Walter Adams, Bureau of Applied Social Research, New York.

been sufficiently motivated to do so,[58] the tendency for females to drop out
of school because of family obligations might have been significantly reduced.
On the other hand, if financial support is available to enable young adults to
stay in school and if the society places high priority on the provision of
child-care services for infants and young children, then an early birth is less
likely to impede a woman's educational opportunities.

71. Spacing pregnancies, keeping family size small and ending childbearing
earlier in the life cycle should have less of an impact on formal schooling
than delaying the first birth. It may be important, however, in freeing women
for continuing education such as adult literacy courses.[59]   A UNESCO study of
sex inequality in literacy found that heavy domestic obligations prevented the
participation of many women in literacy programmes.[60]   Other obstacles to their
initial or continued participation included: time-consuming agricultural and
non-agricultural employment; geographical isolation and negative attitudes to
female literacy in the community and on the part of husbands, such attitudes
ranging from indifference to hostility.[61]

72. Under some conditions, family planning - especially the postponement of
motherhood - can clearly make a difference in enabling women to exercise their
right to an equal education. It may have an even greater impact on the second
generation where a smaller family size reduces the pressure on daughters to
drop out of school to look after their younger siblings. And in the long run,

---

58/ It was estimated in the United States that, between 1964 and 1966, over
two fifths of all births to married women between the ages of 15 and 19 were
premaritally conceived (United States of America, Bureau of the Census;
Fertility Indicators, 1970, Series P-23, No. 36).

59/ In many cases the problem of trying to motivate women to complete their
education and vocational training after childbirth could be avoided if women
learned how to practise family planning while still in school (working paper
prepared by Iran for the Seminar on the Status of Women and Family Planning,
Istanbul, 11-24 July 1972).

60/ UNESCO, op. cit., p. 20.

61/ Ibid., pp. 20-28.

one would expect that, as women spend shorter and shorter periods of their lives in childbearing, their claim to equality in education will become all the more persistent. But the adoption of family planning in and of itself, in the absence of other necessary cultural and structural changes expanding the opportunities for women outside the home, may not be sufficiently powerful to effect a real transformation in this area. Only in interaction with other progressive forces is family planning likely to expand women's educational opportunities significantly, and where this is the case, it is likely to be an essential component.

2. Rights pertaining to employment

73. International instruments declare that everyone has the right to work, to free choice of employment, to just and favourable conditions of work, to protection against unemployment, to fair remuneration and to equal pay for equal work, among other economic rights.[62] Women, married or unmarried, are to have equal rights with men in this regard. In addition, in order to eliminate other forms of discrimination against women in employment, measures are to be taken to prevent their dismissal in the event of marriage or maternity, to provide paid maternity leave with the guarantee of returning to former employment, and to provide child-care facilities and other necessary social services.[63]

74. It is interesting to note at the outset that although rates of male labour force participation vary little from country to country or through the normal working years of the life cycle, rates of female employment differ widely across nations and within major subgroups of the population. They often follow well-defined patterns by age, and generally vary quite dramatically according to women's marital status and the number and ages of their children. It should be noted that "employment" generally refers to work from which an income is derived, however, thus excluding from the labour force statistics, most women who work at unpaid domestic or agricultural labour, that is, the vast majority of women in a great number of countries.

---

[62] Articles 23 and 24, Universal Declaration of Human Rights; articles 7 and 10, International Covenant on Economic, Social and Cultural Rights.

[63] Article 10, Declaration on the Elimination of Discrimination against Women; ILO Convention on Equal Remuneration (1951); ILO Discrimination Convention (1958); ILO Employment Policy Convention (1964) and ILO Convention on Maternity Protection (1921).

75.   Table 4 (E/CN.6/575/Add.3) shows that among countries for which
information was available on female employment during the decade of the
1960s, the proportions of females of all ages (including children) who
were classified as "economically active"[64] ranged from lows of 5 per cent
or less in a number of North African and Middle Eastern countries, to
over 40 per cent in some sub-Saharan African nations, Thailand and several
Eastern European countries, including the Union of Soviet Socialist Republics.
Considering only the prime childbearing years of 20 to 24, which removes the
effect of differing population age distributions on the total employment rates,
female economic activity ranged from a low of 5 per cent or less in Algeria
and the Libyan Arab Republic, through an average of 25 per cent in the
African region, 35 to 40 per cent in Asia, the Americas and Oceania, 58 per cent
in Europe, to a high of 87 per cent in Thailand. Because male rates range
only between about 75 and 95 per cent among this age group, the ratio of female
to male employment tends to decline as female rates themselves decline, with
the greatest inequalities appearing in those countries where female employment
rates are lowest.

76.   Women's labour force participation also fluctuates according to their
age, marital status, duration of marriage, number of children and the age of
the youngest child. These fluctuations tend to follow well-defined patterns

---

64/ Much of the apparent variation in rates across countries may be due
to differing definitions of "economically active" populations (see foot-note
to table 4, E/CN.6/575/Add.3). Inconsistencies are especially likely to arise
in the treatment of agricultural workers. Specific figures are to be interpreted
with caution.

within groups and within countries even when the absolute levels of
employment differ markedly across groups or countries.[65/] Employment
rates of currently married women vary internationally more than those
of widowed or divorced women, with single women having the highest and least
variable rates of economic activity.

77. A number of countries declared in their responses that family planning
facilitates women's participation in the labour force.[66/] For example, delaying
marriage and/or the first birth may enable women to complete their education
and vocational training so that they are qualified for more highly skilled
jobs, and also to establish themselves in a profession.[67/] Controlling the
timing of births permits women to combine employment and childbearing in the
least disruptive way, permitting at the same time a greater degree of work
commitment and improved chances of advancement on the job.[68/] Keeping the
family size small (or forgoing children altogether) frees women to work who
might otherwise be overwhelmed by domestic responsibilities, while reducing

---

65/ See, for example, Nicole Nubrulle, "Communication sur l'emploi féminin
en Europe", Council of Europe, European Population Conference, Strasbourg, 1966,
section C 48; Tomas Frejka "Demographic aspects of women's employment",
International Union for the Scientific Study of Population, International
Population Conference, London, 1962, vol. III, pp. 1559-1571; Jerzy Berent "Some
demographic aspects of female employment in Eastern Europe", ibid., pp. 1572-1588;
Juan Carlos Elizaga, "Demographic aspects of women's labour force in Latin
America and Chile", ibid., pp. 1589-1600; Stuart Garfinkle, "Work in the lives
of women", ibid., pp. 1601-1613; Eva Garzouzi, "The demographic aspects of
women's employment in the United Arab Republic", ibid., pp. 1620-1623;
Françoise Guelad-Leridon, "Quelques aspects démographiques et sociaux de l'emploi
féminin dans les pays d'Europe occidentale", ibid., pp. 1626-1635.

66/ For example, Cameroon, Finland, France, India, Italy, Singapore,
and the United States of America; St. Joan's International Alliance (Belgium).

67/ Response of the United States of America.

68/ Response of Finland.

the number of work interruptions caused by pregnancy, childbirth and infant and child care.[69/] Participants in the Seminar on the Status of Women and Family Planning at Istanbul pointed out that increasing family size was in many instances associated with decreased chances of employment, and that women with large families, who were in most need of supplementing the family income through employment, tended to be poorly represented in any but the unskilled and lower-paid jobs.[70/] This was partly due to their heavy domestic commitments and partly to their lack of education and training. Finally, women who stayed home to raise their children may be encouraged to re-enter the labour force if they have their last child relatively early in the life cycle.[71/] Viewed in this light, the exercise of the right to determine the number and spacing of children can have a direct impact on the woman's exercise of her economic rights.

69/ Responses of Finland, France, Sweden; response of St. Joan's International Alliance (Belgium); working paper prepared by the United States of America for the Seminar on the Status of Women and Family Planning, Istanbul, 11-24 July 1972. The effect of the number of children on participation in the labour force may drop off after the third or fourth child, however; beyond that number, further increase in family size may not significantly reduce the rates of mothers' employment. See Elizaga, op. cit., p. 1596; and Berent, op. cit. In Sweden the biggest decline in female employment came with the birth of the second child; additional births were relatively less constraining (response of Sweden).

70/ ST/TAO/HR/46, para. 50.

71/ The right of the youngest child was given special significance in responses from Finland, France and Sweden. Stuart Garfinkle found in the United States that the major proportion of most women's work life occurs after she has raised her family and re-entered the labour force. A woman marrying at 20 years of age with one child had in 1960 a work life expectancy essentially of the same length (25 years) as a 35-year-old working woman who has completed her family (Garfinkle, op. cit., p. 1603).

78. Individual women may be better able to take advantage of existing economic opportunities by practising family planning. But it is apparent that the obligations of childbearing and childrearing are often used to justify discrimination against women as a group, in the economic sphere, often regardless of the individual woman's reproductive behaviour or expectations.[72/] The fact or even the assumption of the primacy of women's familial roles may also serve to legitimate the concentration of the female labour force in lower-level, more poorly paid positions, women's lower pay, even when they work at the same tasks men do, their frequently greater vulnerability to layoffs in time of unemployment and their numerical dominance in certain "feminine" occupations.[73/]

[72/] Cameroon, for example, responded that employers would probably be more willing to hire women if there were fewer work interruptions from pregnancy and childbirth.

[73/] The tenacity of sex inequalities in economic life are revealed in responses from several countries that have made deliberate efforts to remove them. In Finland, for example, although equal rights are guaranteed by law, in practice women are more often employed in jobs which do not offer any opportunities for advancement, even when they have the same training as men. Thus, although equal pay is guaranteed by law for equal work, women average only 60 to 80 per cent of men's earnings (response of Finland). A similar situation is reported in Sweden, where 76 per cent of salaried government employees in the lower end of the pay scale in 1968 were women, but only 2 per cent of those at the top (response of Sweden). For a review of international instruments, national legislation and major obstacles to the achievement of equal pay for men and women, see the report prepared by the ILO for the Commission on the Status of Women, "Equal pay for work of equal value" (E/CN.6/519).

79.   The Declaration on the Elimination of Discrimination Against Women calls
for the provision of paid maternity leaves, child-care facilities and other
supporting services in order to eliminate forms of economic discrimination
against women that are based on their childbearing functions. Where labour
is in short supply and the demand for female workers is high, Governments may
be stimulated to provide such services in order to take advantage of an
under-utilized labour pool.[72/] But when these benefits are required of
employers for their female workers during periods when male workers are plentiful,
the tendency may be for employers to hire only men. Thus, the fear is sometimes
expressed that these types of protective guarantees for women can be used not
to "protect" women, but to discriminate further against them.[73/]

80.   The consistent assumption throughout, of course, is that childcare is
primarily the women's responsibility, and that such services need only to be
provided for women workers. If men assumed an equal responsibility for caring for
their young children, however, and if Governments and employers recognized
this equal responsibility and their own responsiblity as well, parental leaves
and childcare facilities would be provided for both men and women workers. Under
these conditions, the basis for additional discrimination against women on account
of "their" reproductive behaviour could then be largely removed.[74/]

[72/] For example, Japan responded that labour shortages in that country
were partially responsible for the creation of various facilities such as
nurseries and dormitories, to free women for employment.

[73/] See, for example, ESA/SDHA/AC.1/26 and ESA/SDHA/AC.2/21.

[74/] Paternity leaves have been proposed in Finland but their general
adoption appears "distant" (response of Finland).

81. It should be emphasized that the "supply" of female labour as influenced
by the number, spacing and ages of children is only one factor, among many,
determining the nature and extent of female labour force participation, however.
For example, some participants in the Seminar on the Status of Women and Family
Planning at Istanbul felt that family planning would help in relieving
many of the difficulties that women face in the economic sphere by
reducing their domestic obligations. Others, however, stressed the
responsibility of Governments to create more favourable conditions for all
working women, and especially for those women with children who must work for
financial reasons.[75/] The adequacy of child care services, the extent
to which husbands are willing to share in childrearing and household chores,[76/]
and the availability of other domestic assistance or labour-saving devices
are important factors helping or hindering women in the exercise of their economic
rights.[77/] The degree of prejudice against the idea of wives or mothers taking
gainful employment, and the actual extent of discrimination against them, are
also crucial.[78/]

[75/] ST/TAO/HR/46, para. 50.

[76/] A Czechoslovakian report states that "A major factor which causes
difficulty to employed women is still the unequal division of responsibility
as regards the home; the weight of domestic responsibilities and care of
children continues to rest mainly - and in some cases completely - on women".
Employed women in one survey averaged four hours on household chores on workdays
and six hours on free days. H. Vinterová, "Report for the United Nations
Commission on the Status of Women: Information from a survey of views of
women on employment, the family and the home in the Czechoslovak Socialist
Republic" (January 1972), pp. 8 and 13.

[77/] Responses of Japan, Sweden and the United States of America; working
papers prepared by New Zealand, Poland and Yugoslavia for the Seminar on the Status
of Women and Family Planning, Istanbul, 11-24 July 1972.

[78/] India reported for example that "the reluctance to employ women in
industry is... a more important factor than fertility" in accounting for low
levels of female employment in that sector (response of India).

82. Finally, the structure of the labour market itself shapes the opportunities
for women's employment, whether or not women are relatively "free" to work.
Several countries mentioned that female employment increased considerably when
there was a high demand for it, as in wartime, post-war reconstruction, under
centrally planned economic systems and during periods of rapid economic
expansion.[79/] The growth of particular occupations or sectors of the economy
employing predominantly women also creates a demand, especially where part-time
work is offered.[80/] But high levels of male unemployment and under-employment
exacerbate the competition for all kinds of jobs and place women at an additional
disadvantage.[81/]

83. As fertility increasingly becomes a matter of choice, women will not only
be more free to take advantage of existing economic opportunities but may well
exert pressure on the public and private sectors to provide more jobs and
greater equality of opportunity than many are now able or willing to provide. On
the other hand, the extent to which fertility is likely to be significantly
reduced depends in turn partially on the availability of employment for women.
The nature of this interdependence is discussed more thoroughly in chapter III.

[79/] Responses of Czechoslovakia and Japan; working paper prepared by the
Republic of Viet-Nam for the Regional Seminar on the Status of Women and Family
Planning for Countries within the Economic Commission for Asia and the Far East
Region, Jogjakarta, Indonesia, 20-30 June 1973.

[80/] Response of Sweden.

[81/] Responses of Czechoslovakia, France and Jordan. In response to the
common argument that increases in female employment will produce corresponding
decreases in male employment, the ILO reports that

"On the contrary, increased earnings opportunities for women have not only
made it possible for them to live and to support their children (in many
developing countries women have very heavy responsibilities in this regard),
but have also often stimulated consumer demands for food, goods and services
which, in turn, have generated additional opportunities for employment and
self-employment" (Statement of the representative of the International Labour
Organisation at the Regional Seminar on the Status of Women and Family
Planning for Countries within the Economic Commission for Asia and the Far
East Region, Jogjakarta, Indonesia, 20-30 June 1973).

3. Rights pertaining to marriage and the family

84. Perhaps no issue in the area of women's rights has been as sensitive or
as controversial as the principle of equal rights of men and women "as to
marriage, during marriage and at its dissolution", even though this a
is a principle clearly stated in article 16 of the Universal Declaration of
Human Rights. In many countries, the principle of equality within the family
has not yet been recognized in civil law and, upon marriage, women may be
deprived of many civil rights, such as the independent ownership of property,
or the right to work without their husband's consent. But even in countries
where legislation favours equal rights, traditional cultural patterns of male
dominance in private life are slow to change. Could the widespread practice
of family planning significantly alter the status of women as compared to men
in private life, and especially at the time of marriage, during marriage and
at its dissolution?

85. With reference to the timing of marriage, the United Nations has declared
that child marriage and the betrothal of young girls before puberty shall be
prohibited. Women shall have the same right as men to free choice of a spouse,
and to enter into marriage only with their free and full consent. The inheritance of widows is banned. Minimum standards for age at marriage are to be
set in every country at not less than 15 years, with all marriages being
officially registered.[82]

82/ Universal Declaration of Human Rights, article 16; International
Covenant on Economic, Social and Cultural Rights, article 10; Declaration on
the Elimination of Discrimination Against Women, article 6; Convention and
Recommendation on Consent to Marriage, Minimum Age for Marriage and Registration
of Marriages (1962 and 1965); Supplementary Convention on the Abolition of Slavery,
the Slave Trade and Institutions and Practices Similar to Slavery (1956), article 1.

86. In examining the effect of family planning on the exercise on an equal
basis with men of a woman's right to decide whether, when and whom to marry,
one must take into consideration the cultural mores of each society. The
essential contribution of birth control is the separation of sexual behaviour
from reproduction. In societies where premarital heterosexual relations are
common, the ability to delay the first birth could serve to raise the average
age at first marriage and to place women in a more favourable position as
regards the choice of a spouse. This is especially true where a high proportion
of early first marriages appear to be "caused" by an unplanned pregnancy. Some
participants at the Seminar on the Status of Women and Family Planning
at Istanbul expressed reservations concerning proposals that contraceptive
information and supplies be made available to young girls as a protective
measure, especially in cultures where a strong emphasis was placed
on the requirement of virginity for brides.[83] But others pointed out that
young girls were often unaware of their reproductive functions and suffered as
a result of their ignorance. It was noted that in some countries, births to
unwed teenage girls were very frequent and that such pregnancies usually meant
the loss of education, job training and future social standing.[84] At the same
time, early marriages hastily contracted to "legitimate" the birth of a child
tended to be less stable than those contracted under less compelling conditions,
frequently causing much unhappiness to the mother, father and child alike.

87. Effective birth planning can also lower the average age at first marriage
by making it possible for couples to marry relatively early, while postponing
their childbearing to a time when their education is completed and their
employment prospects more secure. In either case, the separation of sexual
activity from reproduction allows a greater degree of control over the choice of
a spouse and the decision of whether or not to marry than could otherwise be
achieved.

---

[83] ST/TAO/HR/46, para. 55.

[84] Ibid.; response of Austria.

88. The preceding discussion assumes that women do have a choice in deciding
whether, when and whom to marry. But in many traditional societies these crucial
decisions remain predominantly or solely in the hands of elders who may have
a vested interest in arranging marriages that solidify ties between particular
families while maintaining complex systems of social stratification. Under
these conditions a girl may well be married shortly after reaching puberty, in
which case any knowledge she may have about birth control will make little
difference as to the exercise of her rights on entering the marriage. Moreover,
in some societies where high fertility is valued and a woman's fecundity must be
proven before she is acceptable as a bride, there would be little motivation for
birth planning at this stage in the life cycle. Indeed, the absence of a
pregnancy might ruin a woman's chances for a successfully arranged match.

89. As for the marriage itself, United Nations instruments declare that men and
women are to share equal rights and responsibilities, including equal rights and
duties in matters relating to their children.[85/] Some respondents viewed family
planning in its broadest sense as a positive force in marriage that, as well as
freeing women to play a larger role in the society at large, could contribute to
the ideal of a true partnership of the spouses based on the principle of
equality, love and mutual responsibility for the creation, care and nurturing
of children.[86/] One consequence would be a decline in the patriarchal concept of
the family in which the man automatically assumes the role of head and provider
while the woman is expected to subjugate herself without question to his authority.[87/]
It was recognized, however, that where patriarchal attitudes are still strong,

---

85/ Declaration on the Elimination of Discrimination Against Women,
article 6; General Assembly resolution 2200 A (XXI); International Covenant on
Civil and Political Rights, article 23.

86/ Responses of Austria and Yugoslavia; ST/TAO/HR/46, para. 46.

87/ Responses of Austria and Yugoslavia.

there is frequently a great deal of resistance on the part of husbands to their wives learning about or using female methods of birth control.[88] Such attitudes are often associated with double standards of sexual behaviour that allow men considerable permissiveness both before and during marriage while requiring strict fidelity from women.[89] Male resistance is apparently often founded in the belief that wives will no longer remain sexually faithful or generally submissive to their husbands if they acquire the knowledge of how to prevent pregnancies. The implicit assumption in these fears is that birth planning can indeed be a powerful means to greater independence for the woman in the family, especially if it increases her opportunities to exercise other rights as well.

90. Once again, however, in cultural situations in which a woman's status is defined almost entirely by the number of children she bears, or by the number of her sons, her power and authority in the family and in the community might be considerably reduced if she were to bear no children, or only one or two. The experience of family planning clinics in several African countries, for example, has been that women are often more interested in learning about ways to increase their fertility than to decrease it.[90] In the context of such beliefs it would be detrimental to the woman's status to practise contraception as long as no alternative roles were possible under existing economic and social conditions.

---

[88] One in four Puerto Rican women who did not use contraceptives cited their husband's objections as the reason, in one survey. See Ofelia Mendoza, "What are the factors in Latin American culture that might stimulate or discourage fertility control?", Proceedings of the Seventh Conference of the International Planned Parenthood Federation, Singapore, February 1963 (Amsterdam, Excerpta Medica Foundation), p. 70.

[89] Working paper prepared by Turkey for the Seminar on the Status of Women and Family Planning, Istanbul, 11-24 July 1972.

[90] Hassan M. Hussein, "Evaluation of progress in fertility control in the United Arab Republic", World Population Conference, 1965, vol. II (United Nations publication, Sales No. 66.XIII.6) p. 143; Christian Council of Ghana (response of Ghana).

91. The same argument applies to women's rights at the time of marital dissolution. The United Nations has not addressed the question of whether couples have a basic right to terminate an unhappy marriage. Its instruments do declare that whatever the degree of restrictiveness a State imposes regarding divorce, the grounds for dissolving a marriage, and the rights and obligations following its dissolution, should be the same for men and women. Yet where women have few social or economic options outside of marriage, and especially where the husband has the unilateral power to divorce his wife at will and take another, the fear of repudiation may motivate women to have many children as a form of social insurance.[91]

92. In industrialized societies with liberal divorce laws and greater options for women beyond the home, remaining childless or having only one or two children may well place women in a more advantageous position than those with larger families, by lifting the compulsion to remain in an unhappy marriage. Some studies show that women who are gainfully employed have a higher probability of divorcing than do housewives,[92] and that divorce tends to be more frequent among couples with no children or with small families even when the tendency for these marriages to be of shorter duration is taken into account.

93. In cases of marital dissolution through the death of the husband or through separation, desertion or annulment, as in divorce, the influence of family planning and family size on the individual woman's exercise of her equal rights and responsibilities relating to support, property and children depend on many factors. Under some cultural conditions and in some legal systems, women with few children may have an advantage over those with many, whereas in other systems the opposite may be true. But there seems to be little doubt that knowledge of family planning methods can permit a degree of self-determination at the time of marriage, during marriage and at its dissolution that is essential to the maximization of the happiness of the individual and the family.

---

[91] Economic and Social Council resolution 1068 F (XXXIX); working paper prepared by Indonesia for the Seminar on the Status of Women and Family Planning, Istanbul, 11-24 July 1972, p. 21; ST/TAO/HR/46, para. 85.

[92] For example, H. Han Sluwka, "Divorce in Austria", International Union for the Scientific Study of Population, International Population Conference, London, 1969, vol. III, p. 1837.

4.   Participation in public life

94. The United Nations has declared the right of women to participate in
public life and political decision-making on equal terms with men. In particular;
women are to be assured of the right to vote in all elections, to be eligible for
all publicly elected bodies, to hold public office and to exercise all public
functions.[93]

95. In so far as family planning contributes to freeing women from heavy domestic
responsibilities, it can facilitate their active participation in community,
national and international affairs.[94] And in so far as the act of planning the
spacing and number of births accustoms women to the possibility of acquiring greater
control over their own lives, it may encourage them to play a more active role in
public decision-making as well. However, even in some countries where birth planning
is widely practised and where average family size is very small, women continue
to face obstacles in reaching higher levels of policy formulation through elective
or appointive office.[95] Attitudes and prejudices about women's capacities are
slower to change than the actual social and economic conditions of their position
in society.[96] But where smaller families and the sharing of responsibilities
for childrearing by husbands and by the community do release women for a greater
degree of direct participation in public decision-making than they have formerly
achieved, they may well become a very strong force for social change in many
countries. And if these forces are channelled also into the struggle for
women's rights, the impact will be felt in changing legislation and practices
in all areas of education, employment and the family.[97]

---

[93] Universal Declaration of Human Rights, article 21; Convention on the
Political Rights of Women (1952); International Covenant on Civil and Political
Rights, article 3; Declaration on the Elimination of Discrimination against Women,
article 4.

[94] Responses of Fiji, Finland, Jamaica, Japan, Jordan, the Netherlands and
the United States of America.

[95] Response of Finland.

[96] Response of India.

[97] The response of the United States of America cites the example of
the newly formed Women's National Political Caucus which is dedicated to
increasing the political power and the rights of women and all under-represented
groups. A number of their guidelines involve issues with an immediate and
direct impact on women, as in the areas of contraception and abortion.

III. THE STATUS OF WOMEN AS A FACTOR
      INFLUENCING FERTILITY

A. The status of women as a demographic variable

96. Although demographers and policy-makers have long been interested in the
effect on birth rates of such processes as urbanization, industrialization,
modernization and economic growth -- and of such economic characteristics (usually
attributed to the male) as occupation, education and income -- little interest
has been expressed to date in the effect on fertility of the status and roles of
women. Yet each of these variables, if they are to influence a woman's reproductive behaviour, must act by shaping the opportunity structure in which decision-
making occurs. This is the case whether such decisions are directly or indirectly
related to reproduction, or whether they are made deliberately or implicitly.
The woman's experiences, aspirations and range of options must play a central role.

97. In this chapter the effect on family planning and family size of the status
of women in the family and in society is examined. Although the evidence suggests
that the status of women, or the degree of equality between men and women, is
one of the most crucial variables affecting reproductive behaviour, one must be
cautious about making generalizations, based on statistical associations, rather
than on demonstrated causal relationships. Evidence of the latter type is
particularly difficult to obtain. For example, although female employment may
be strongly associated with smaller family size, when a cross-section of employed
and non-employed women is compared at one point in time, an increase over time
in the national rate of female employment may not necessarily result in lower
birth rates, if other factors (such as strong social pressures towards large
families) simultaneously work in the opposite direction. It is true that, in
the absence of extensive female employment, the birth rate might have been even
higher, but the immediate causal effect of such employment in reducing fertility
may frequently be lost to the viewer.

98. Nevertheless, the strong association revealed in the following sections
between the exercise of women's rights and the timing and spacing of children
suggests that such factors as women's employment, education and their position
in the family may well have a direct impact. This appears to be the case even
when the enormous diversities of culture and social structure across and within
countries are taken into account, and even at different stages of economic development.

B. The effect of the educational level of women

1. Association of schooling with other factors

99. The educational level of women appears to be one of the most important
factors influencing family size and birth rates. Such widely disparate countries
as Egypt, Finland, Guatemala, India, Jamaica, the Philippines, Singapore, the
Syrian Arab Republic, Turkey,[98]/ and Yugoslavia declared in their responses to the
United Nations guidelines that, in their countries, the average number of children
was smaller among women with higher education. Moreover, where comparisons can be
made, studies show that the educational level of the wife is more strongly
correlated with a couple's fertility than the educational level of the husband,[99]/
suggesting that investments in female education may have a greater impact on
fertility than the same investment in schooling for men.

100. The relationship is not a simple one, however, nor is it inverse in all cases.
The number of years of schooling a woman has received is, after all, only one
factor among many influencing her reproductive behaviour. Other biological,
economic, social and cultural variables affecting fecundity, family size preferences
and access to birth control may render it more or less functional.

101. Also, it may be, as some writers have suggested, that the number of years of
formal schooling is simply the most visible and quantifiable element in a cluster
of interdependent forces affecting fertility, and that it is not higher education
per se but its association with factors such as openness to new ideas, higher
socio-economic status and standards of living, exposure to an urban environment,
and a greater range of options and interests outside the home that is responsible
for the apparent influence of one on the other. This poses methodological
problems in examining the relationship between the two.

98/ Working paper prepared by Turkey for the Seminar on the Status of Women
and Family Planning, Istanbul, 11-24 July 1972.

99/ Ibid.; E. D. Driver, Differential Fertility in Central India (Princeton,
New Jersey, Princeton University Press, 1963); United Nations and the Government
of India, Mysore Population Study, Population Studies No. 34 (United Nations
publication, Sales No. 61.XIII.3); Halvor Gille, "Summary Review of fertility
differentials in developed countries", IUSSP, International Population Conference,
London, 1969, vol. III, pp. 2018-2019.

2. Marriage patterns, contraceptive practice and desired family size

102. The question is, how, and under what conditions, does the amount and type of a woman's formal education make a difference? It is usually hypothesized that higher education for women can work indirectly to reduce fertility in at least three ways, through (a) delaying marriage and increasing the probability of non-marriage, thus reducing or eliminating the time span of exposure to the possibility of conception;[100/] (b) reducing desired family size, by creating aspirations for a higher level of living for the couple and their children and by stimulating women's interest and involvement in activities outside the home, especially employment; and (c) exposing women to knowledge, attitudes and practices favourable to birth control, including a higher level of communication between husband and wife, enabling them to bring their actual reproduction in line with their desired family size.

103. First, educated women marry later and often postpone childbearing until they attain the required qualifications or degrees,[101/] although there appears to be a tendency in some industrialized countries for women to marry earlier even while they are still attending an educational institution.[102/] Highly educated women may also have less opportunity (or inclination) to marry because of the smaller chances of meeting men with similar education or position,[103/] because of their own greater opportunities for social and financial independence which reduces the need to marry, and because of reluctance on the part of many

---

100/ Assuming either a low degree of sexual contact outside of marriage and/or a high degree of birth control.

101/ Background paper prepared by Dubrovka Stampar for the Seminar on the Status of Women and Family Planning, Istanbul, 11-24 July 1972, p. 14. Educational differentials in age at first marriage were reported by Austria, Belgium (response of St. Joan's International Alliance), Cameroon, Czechoslovakia, Fiji, Finland, Guatemala, Jordan, the Netherlands, New Zealand, the Philippines, Poland, Singapore, Sweden, and the United States of America; none reported that such differentials did not exist. The Republic of Korea included a document showing that in 1967, 61.4 per cent of a sample of illiterate women had married before 17 years of age, compared to 24.3 per cent of those with primary school education, 4.9 per cent of those with high school and 4.3 per cent of those with college. Only 1.8 per cent of illiterate women married at 24 years or later, compared to 5.0 per cent with primary school, 20.5 per cent with high school and 56.5 per cent with college. See The Findings of the National Survey on Family Planning, 1967 (Republic of Korea, Ministry of Health and Social Affairs, December 1968) p. 174.

102/ Response of Finland, among others.

103/ Stampar, op. cit.

males to marry a highly educated woman. In the Regional Seminar on the Status
of Women and Family Planning for Countries of the Western Hemisphere, Santo Domingo,
9-22 May 1973, for example, participants pointed out that the fear of not finding
a husband frequently caused women to drop out of school by age 16 or 18
(encouraged by their parents) in order not to become "overeducated" for the
marriage market. Those who remained in school did marry later, and higher
proportions were removed from the "procreative stream" by not marrying at all
(and not bearing children out of wedlock).[104]/

104. The difference in average age at first marriage between less and more
educated women in some cases appears to account for most if not all educational
differentials in completed family size,[105]/ especially where those who marry
later make up for their delayed childbearing by reproducing more abundantly after
marriage. In these latter instances, late marriage and the postponement of the
first birth do not necessarily result in a lower completed family size, for
educational differentials, while strong in the early adult years, may diminish
or disappear by the time childbearing is completed.[106]/

105. Secondly, higher education may also reduce desired family size by raising
the woman's aspirations for her own level of living and that of her children
(especially in regard to their education); improving her employment opportunities
and participation in social, public and political activities; reducing her
dependence on large numbers of children for social and economic support in old
age; and creating favourable conditions for the preservation of the child's life
and health.[107]/ This last point received much attention at the Regional Seminar

---

104/ ESA/SDHA/AC.1/26, para. 25.

105/ For example, J.C. Caldwell "Some factors affecting fertility in Ghana",
IUSSP, International Population Conference, London 1969, vol. I (Liège, 1971),
pp. 751-758.

106/ Patrick Chadike "The possibility of fertility change in modern Africa;
a West African case", IUSSP, International Population Conference, London 1969,
vol. I, p. 809; C.V. Kiser "Social, economic and religious factors in the
differential fertility of countries of low fertility", World Population Conference,
1965, vol. II, pp. 219-222; P.O. Olusanya "Modernization and the level of fertility
in Nigeria", IUSSP, International Population Conference, London 1969, vol. I, p. 819.

107/ Stampar, op. cit.

on the Status of Women and Family Planning for Countries within the Economic Commission for Asia and the Far East Region, Jogjakarta, where high levels of infant and child morbidity and mortality were cited as key reasons for high birth rates among the poor and less educated.[108] On the other hand, good general education provides for a better infant survival rate to compensate for lower fertility, thus reducing the desire for large families in order to ensure that at least some children will live to adulthood.[109]

106. Thirdly, higher education with its social and economic correlates is more likely to expose women to a wide range of general information and to greater possibilities for decision-making and choice in many areas. Among these is exposure to attitudes favourable to birth planning, knowledge of the means to do so, and access to the more modern and effective contraceptive methods. Many Governments responding to this item confirmed the association,[110] which continues to be one of the basic findings of the many Knowledge and Practice Studies undertaken in both industrialized and developing countries.[111] Thus, whether there are educational differentials in desired family size or not, better educated women are more likely to be able to avoid unwanted births and to space their births effectively than are illiterate women or those with only a few years of schooling.

---

[108] ESA/SDHA/AC.2/21, para. 25.

[109] "Introductory statement on the subject of the status of women as a factor influencing fertility", background paper prepared by S. Anandalakshmy for the Regional Seminar on the Status of Women and Family Planning for Countries within the Economic Commission for Asia and the Far East Region, Jogjakarta, 20-30 June 1973.

[110] Belgium, (St. Joan's International Alliance), Finland, Guatemala, India, Japan, Jordan, Philippines, Poland, Sweden, United States of America and Yugoslavia. None reported contradictory findings.

[111] See references in IUSSP, International Population Conference, London, 1969; World Population Conference, 1965, vol. II, (United Nations publication, Sales No. 66.XIII.6); Proceedings of the Eighth International Conference of the International Planned Parenthood Federation, Santiago, 1967; and Knowledge and Practice Studies, such as Studies in Family Planning (New York, The Population Council), among others.

3. The impact of education in industrialized and developing countries

107. In developing countries for which information is available, the education
of women appears, at the individual level, to have a very strong impact on
fertility. The greatest reduction in family size appears among women with
secondary or higher education, but where access to this level of schooling is
confined to a small élite (see E/CN.6/575/Add. 3, table 3), then its effect on
over-all birth rates is slight.[112]

108. The majority of women of reproductive age in a number of developing
countries, especially in rural areas, is illiterate (E/CN.6/575/Add. 3, Table 2).
Illiteracy, with its usual correlates of material poverty and restricted
opportunity, presents a severe obstacle to the motivation for, or acceptance of,
family planning.[113] However, even the transition from illiteracy to literacy
resulting from low levels of schooling is shown to have some influence in
reducing family size.[114] The rare exceptions, in which illiterate rural women

---

[112] For example, in a national sample survey of 3,200 currently married
Turkish women under 45 years of age conducted by the Hacettepe Institute of
Population Studies in 1968, university graduates averaged 1.4 live-born children
as compared to 2.0 for high school graduates (12 years), 2.1 for elementary
school graduates (eight years), 2.8 for women with at least five years of primary
school, 3.2 for women with fewer than five years, and 4.2 for illiterates. However,
university graduates were only 0.5 per cent of the sample while two thirds were
illiterate. Serim Temur "Socio-economic determinants of differential fertility
in Turkey", The Second European Population Conference, Strasbourg, 1971.

[113] The Governments of Cameroon, Egypt, Fiji, India, Jamaica, Jordan
and Singapore mentioned that illiteracy blocked information and access to
family planning in their countries.

[114] As in foot-note [112] above.

have lower birth rates than women with some primary schooling, appear to be caused by poorer health and subfecundity among the least educated group.[115/]   Other exceptions appear when cultural pressures toward large families in rural areas are so strong as to obliterate the effect of a few years of schooling entirely.[116/]

109. In most industrialized countries the inverse relationship between education and average family size appears to have diminished over the past several decades but not disappeared, except in some cases where women above a certain income level with the most schooling have larger families on the average than women with somewhat less education.[117/]   The effect of a woman's education also depends in part on the level of her schooling relative to that of her husband and her parents.[118/]   This reduction of the traditionally strong educational differentials in many countries is apparently a response to increasingly homogeneous behaviour in all three aspects of the education fertility correlation, that is, in average age at first marriage, in desired family size, and in the knowledge and practice of birth control as it becomes diffused through the entire population.

115/ V. Erlich, Family in Transition (Zagreb, Naprijed, 1954), p. 39; National Centre for Social and Criminological Research, Cairo, Status of Women in Relation to Fertility and Family Planning in Egypt (1973), p. 82.

116/ For example, J. M. Stycos and R. N. Weller found that in the rural areas of Turkey neither female employment nor schooling was related to fertility, while in urban areas, fertility was differentiated quite clearly by schooling; see "Female working roles and fertility", Demography, vol. 4, No. 1 (1967). Finding similar situations in Latin America, Stycos suggested that a certain amount of urbanization may be necessary to "activate the effect of education on fertility", J. M. Stycos, Human Fertility in Latin America (Ithaca. Cornell University Press, 1968), p. 269.

117/ Austria responded that the number of children born decreases with higher levels of education among lower-income groups but increases with education among higher-income groups. Se also Halvor Gille, "Summary review of fertility differentials in developed countries", International Population Conference, London, 1969, vol. III, (Liège, IUSSP, 1971), pp. 2011-2025; Council of Europe, Second European Population Conference, Strasbourg, 1971, CDE (1971), T. III, pp. 131-139.

118/ N. V. Muhsam, op. cit., p. 1871; David M. Heer, "Educational advance and fertility change", IUSSP, International Population Conference, London, 1969, vol. III, p. 1905; Constantina Safilios-Rothschild, op. cit., p. 605.

4.   The need for relevant education

110. It is clear that not only the number of years of schooling, but the type or quality of the schooling makes a difference. Women trained in fields traditionally thought to be "female" are shown in some studies to have higher fertility than women in less "feminine" fields with equal or fewer years of schooling.[119] Participants in the Regional Seminar on the Status of Women and Family Planning for Countries of the Western Hemisphere, Santo Domingo, pointed out that traditional education for girls in Latin America was often viewed primarily as preparation for marriage rather than for a job or career, with the result that little vocational or professional training was offered and the schooling had little effect in changing women's roles or aspirations, which might reduce their desired family size.[120] A similar issue was raised in the Regional Seminar on the Status of Women and Family Planning for Countries within the Economic Commission for Asia and the Far East Region, Jogjakarta. Not only were girls more likely to drop out of school than boys, but the formal education that both received was often inherited from colonial systems in which the curricula were inappropriate for the development needs of the country.[121]

111. This leads to the point that even a high level of education may not contribute to a lower desired or actual family size if a women does not find adequate outlets for her skills in a career or other rewarding non-familial activities. The interaction of education with employment may explain the U-shaped relationship reported earlier for some industrialized countries in which highly educated, affluent women have larger families and are less likely to work than those with more moderate levels of education.[122] Similarly, female employment

---

119/ Constantina Safilios-Rothschild, "Sociopsychological factors affecting fertility in urban Greece: a preliminary report", Journal of Marriage and the Family, vol. 31, No. 3 (August 1969), pp. 597-598.

120/ ESA/SDHA/AC.1/26, para. 28.

121/ ESA/SDHA/AC.2/21, para. 27.

122/ It is more usual for a direct relationship to exist between education and employment however. For example, in Chile in 1960, 11.4 per cent of women without education participated in the labour force, 19.3 per cent of those with six years of schooling, 34.5 per cent of secondary school graduates, and 71.4 per cent of college graduates. Juan Carlos Elizaga "Demographic aspects of women's labour force in Latin America and Chile", IUSSP, International Population Conference, London, 1969, vol. III, p. 1594.

itself may not influence fertility significantly unless a woman's education
has prepared her for something more than subsistence agricultural labour,
unpaid work in a family enterprise, or other low-status, low-paying jobs.

C. The effect of women's employment

1. Role incompatibility: the forced choice

112. To what extent might the full exercise of women's rights to equality with
men in employment influence the number and spacing of their children? If a
consistent causal effect were to be found, the implications for development
strategies would be clear: ensuring women's right to equal work and equal pay
should result in lower birth rates while simultaneously facilitating economic
and social development. However, the relationship depends not on the simple
fact of employment alone but on the sector of the economy in which the woman is
employed, her education, skills, occupation, income, work commitment, duration
or continuity of employment, whether it is full or part-time, the availability
of child care, and other factors. Moreover, as was the case for education, it
is not always possible to distinguish cause from effect when female employment
and fertility are considered. In any given situation, is it the case that
women who work outside the home are deliberately keeping their family size
small, or is it the case that women who have smaller families or no children,
for a variety of reasons, are more free to take outside employment?

113. Female employment may contribute to a later age at marriage and a higher
probability of non-marriage, especially where such employment offers women
significant social satisfaction and provides a sense of financial independence
which would reduce the need to marry for economic support. In this sense,
employment may perhaps be viewed as a partial functional alternative to marriage.
But the greatest impact of such employment would appear at the professional
levels, where there is an obvious interaction with the effect of higher education
on the timing and probability of marriage. At less skilled occupational levels
one would expect the association between female employment and marriage patterns
to diminish or disappear.[123]/

---

[123]/ The response of the Philippines declared that the nature of the work
experience is critical: relatively late marriage in that country occurred only for
women "whose employment took them outside the context of family and family
enterprise into the non-familial, non-traditional world of wages and salaries".

114. Most research has focused on the concept of role incompatibility within marriage in attempting to explain variations in the strength of the association between female employment and fertility. Employment should reduce fertility most effectively when birth planning is widely practised and when the roles of worker and mother are most incompatible, that is, when (a) the place of work is away from the home, which may pose practical problems relating to child care; (b) women believe that they should devote full time to their children, which creates a psychological dilemma in choosing between employment and children; or (c) the woman's employment provides her with significant social, psychological or economic rewards which she may be unwilling to forgo in order to have another child. Thus in societies or among subgroups in which birth control is not widely practised and/or women are financially compelled to work outside the home in any case, then we should not expect to find a strong association between employment and fertility. Indeed, both mother and worker roles may be equally assumed of women. The same argument holds for those situations in which the two roles can be easily combined, for example when the demands of the job are relatively flexible and when domestic help is readily available.

115. It may be that the greatest degree of perceived role conflict exists among employed women of relatively high socio-economic status who neither need to work outside the home nor are expected to do so. The motives for seeking work must influence the degree of role conflict experienced. A study of working women in India revealed that women who worked primarily because they were interested in their work or because it gave them a sense of economic independence did not view their employment as interfering with child care responsibilities.[124/] Indeed

---

124/ K. P. Singh, "Career and family: women's two roles", *Indian Journal of Social Work*, vol. 33, No. 3 (1972), pp. 277-281, as cited in "Introductory statement on the status of women as a factor influencing fertility", background paper prepared by S. Anandalakshmy, for the Regional Seminar on the Status of Women and Family Planning for Countries within the Economic Commission for Asia and the Far East Region, Jogjakarta, 20-30 June 1973.

"the sense of fulfilment or gratification that came from their jobs may have made the women more able psychologically to deal with the situation of their regular absence from the home" [125]/ But women who worked primarily because of economic necessity saw their work as an unwanted obstacle to spending more time with their children.

116. If employment is not economically essential and if the rewards for working are not sufficiently attractive women may more readily sacrifice their jobs in order to bear and raise children than forgo childbearing for the sake of remaining employed.[126]/ That is, the choice the woman makes may depend in large part on the perceived amount of social approval for the economic role as compared to the domestic role. It has been suggested that if women's employment outside the home is to affect fertility significantly, it must be socially valued and rewarded at least as highly as childbearing.[127]/ This is where an official public ideology can have important consequences in tipping the balance one way or another.

117. Participants in the Seminars on the Status of Women and Family Planning in Santo Domingo and Jogjakarta noted that women have always worked. The point is, they have usually not been paid for it. Thus one must be careful in discussing the effect of female employment on fertility to specify that such employment generally refers to the gainful employment of women outside the home. Many censuses underestimate the extent of female employment because vast numbers of women working in agriculture, handicrafts, trade or family enterprises are not counted as gainfully employed, in spite of the productive value of their labour.[128]/

125/ S. Anandalakshmy, op. cit., p. 6.

126/ "The status of women, fertility and family planning", paper prepared by the International Planned Parenthood Federation for the Seminar on the Status of Women and Family Planning, Jogjakarta, 20-30 June 1973.

127/ Ibid.

128/ ESA/SDHA/AC.1/26, para. 30; ESA/SDHA/AC.2/21, para. 33.

2. Differential effects in industrialized and developing countries

118. It is in the industrialized countries that the relationship between female employment and fertility seems most clear when currently employed and non-employed women are compared. Women who are employed full-time tend to have smaller families (or to remain childless) more often than those who are employed part-time or not at all.[129/] Those who have worked for a major part of their married lives have smaller families than those who have worked for only short periods or sporadically.[130/] Women in white-collar and professional occupations - occupations which require higher education and provide greater social and economic rewards - have smaller families than do women in blue-collar and service occupations.[131/] Women with a high degree of work commitment (for example, women who would continue to work even if their husbands made all the money they needed) are more likely to practise modern and effective birth control methods and to bear fewer children than those who work for economic necessity.[132/] In rural areas of many industrialized countries, however, where traditional agricultural labour is not so incompatible with raising a family, the relationship between female employment and fertility often disappears.[133/]

129/ Halvor Gille, op. cit., pp. 2011-2025; United Nations European Social Development Programme, Family Planning and Social Policy in Europe (SOA/ESDP/1971/2), p. 14. Census statistics from Yugoslavia showed that women aged 25-30 in 1961 who were defined as "economically active" were from two to four times as likely to be childless as "inactive" women. (Zagorka Aničić, "Certain indicators of recent fertility trends of Yugoslav population", IUSSP, International Population Conference, London, 1969, vol. I, p. 498).

130/ Gille, op. cit.; Stanley Kupinsky, "Non-familial activity and socio-economic differentials in fertility", Demography, vol. 8 (August 1971), p. 358.

131/ Aničić, op. cit., p. 499.

132/ Constantina Safilios-Rothschild, op. cit., p. 599; Family Planning and Social Policy in Europe (SOA/ESDP/1971/2).

133/ For example, in Poland, Czechoslovakia and France, see Tomas Frejka, "Demographic aspects of women's employment", IUSSP, International Population Conference, London, 1969, vol. III, p. 1567.

119. Most industrialized countries responding to this section of the
United Nations survey agreed that female employment results in a smaller
family size (Finland, France, Japan, the United States of America, for example).
However, Austria and the Netherlands noted that birth rates were dropping
in their countries without a corresponding increase in female labour force
participation, and others have noted that major declines in Western European birth
rates in the late nineteenth and early twentieth centuries often preceded major
expansions in women's employment. These apparent contradictions suggest that
on a national level changes in female employment rates and fertility many
may not appear to be causally related over time because of the simultaneous
influence of other, sometimes contradictory, forces; but at any one point in
time, employed women may nevertheless have fewer children and space them
differently than those who are not employed.

120. In developing countries the employment/fertility relationship is less
clear, although a distinction must be made between urban and rural areas and
between the "modern" and "traditional" sectors of the society.

121. In rural areas, paid employment (where it exists) usually has little
impact on fertility, partly because birth control is not widely practised where
the value of large numbers of children remains strong, and partly because the
employment is likely to be of an agricultural, marketing or cottage industry
type in which a woman may either keep her young children with her while she
works or leave them with other family members.[134/] Much employment may not be
paid but produces some income, either directly or indirectly. Not only may it
offer little motivation to reduce fertility but it may actually increase the
advantages of a large family if all members, including children, are put to some
productive use.

134/ Background paper A prepared by Dubrovka Stampar, for the Seminar on
the Status of Women and Family Planning, Istanbul, 11-24 July 1972; H. Yuan Tien,
"Employment and education of women in China: implications for fertility change",
IUSSP, International Population Conference, London, 1969, vol. III, pp. 1981-1982.

122. Thus, in countries where most female employment is agricultural, it is not surprising that birth rates sometimes (but not always) remain high. Table 5 (E/CN.6/575/Add.3) shows that on the average, about half of the female population defined as "economically active" in 16 African countries for which information was available worked in agriculture, ranging from only 6 per cent in Zambia to over 90 per cent in Botswana, Gabon, Liberia and the Niger. (Definitions of "economic activity" differ widely from country to country, however.)

123. In 22 Asian countries, half of the economically active women were also engaged in agriculture, with a similarly wide range of under 5 per cent in Hong Kong, Kuwait and Macau to over 90 per cent in Nepal and the Syrian Arab Republic. Employed women are far less likely to be found in agriculture in the Americas, with a range of 2 per cent in Chile, Puerto Rico and the United States of America to 32 per cent in Ecuador and Peru and an average for 28 countries in the region of 12 per cent. Agricultural labour is more frequent in the Union of Soviet Socialist Republics and Eastern Europe, and less frequent in northern and Western Europe.

124. In the cities and towns of developing countries, woman's paid employment is more likely to be incompatible with raising a family if it takes her out of the home and if she has difficulty in finding ways to care for her children.[125/] She is also more likely to learn about birth control and have access to family planning services in cities than in the countryside, although much depends on the sector of the economy in which she works.. Some studies have shown that women in the professions and in white-collar occupations are more favourably disposed towards the use of contraceptives and have fewer live births than do skilled manual workers, who in turn have smaller families than do women in sales and trade.[126/]

125/ Sidney Goldstein, "The influence of labour force participation and education on fertility in Thailand", Population Studies, vol. 26, No. 3 (November 1972), pp. 419-436.

126/ Patrick Chadike, "The possibility of fertility change in modern Africa: a West African case", IUSSP, International Population Conference, London, 1969, vol. I, p. 809.

125. Consistent with these findings, Guatemala, India, Jordan, the Philippines, and the Syrian Arab Republic reported that the negative relationship between female employment and fertility appeared strongest in urban areas, among non-agricultural workers and in conjunction with higher education. In the countryside, where the majority of women lived, employment frequently had no effect in delaying marriage or reducing family size.

3.   The issue of protective legislation

126. The question arose at the Seminars on the Status of Women and Family Planning as to whether protective legislation and other measures such as paid maternity leaves and child care services for employed women were pronatalist or antinatalist in their effect. Surprisingly little factual information is available on this topic. Some participants from Latin American and Asian countries argued that employers in their countries often used these requirements, where they existed, as additional excuses for not hiring women, especially when men were actively competing for the same jobs.[127/] If such legislation did prevent some women from working, they might be less motivated to keep their family size small and the result would be pronatalist. Similarly, if women had the right to an unlimited number of paid maternity leaves, if they were guaranteed the same or equivalent jobs on their return and if nurseries were available, they might also be less inclined to delay or prevent additional births.

127. On the other hand, the experience of some Scandinavian and Eastern European countries with liberal maternity benefits suggests that paid leaves and crèches are entirely compatible with low birth rates.[128/] Indeed, such benefits appear to

---

127/ ESA/SDHA/AC.1/26, para. 32; ESA/SDHA/AC.2/21, paras. 34 and 35.

128/ For example, government responses stated that Finland grants to female government employees two months' maternity leave with full pay plus six months' unpaid leave with guaranteed return. Poland provides 16 weeks at full pay with an option of three years' unpaid leave (working paper prepared by Poland for the Seminar on the Status of Women and Family Planning, Istanbul, 11-24 July 1972) Czechoslovakia, Hungary, Romania and Sweden also reported very liberal maternity leave policies.

facilitate the entry of women into the labour force and their continuation
in it, especially where the demand for labour and the need or desire to work
is high. At the same time, women are exposed to non-familial interests,
activities and rewards over long periods of time which may reduce their desire
for additional children and have an antinatalist effect. Thus the impact of
this type of legislation appears to depend on other social, economic and
cultural conditions in the society and particularly on the demand for female
labour. In any case, international standards in this field are clear. Paid
maternity leave, nursing breaks and adequate child care facilities should be
provided.

4.   Future trends in female participation in the labour force

128. What might the effect of female employment be in the future? Australia,
Canada, Japan, New Zealand and the United States of America and many Eastern
and Western European countries have experienced large increases in female
participation in the labour force over the past two decades, most notably among
married women and women with young children. The International Labour Office predicts
that the female labour force will continue to grow more rapidly than the male labour
force at least to 1985 in the industrialized regions of the world, with the
exception of Eastern Europe and the Union of Soviet Socialist Republics where
women are already employed at near peak capacity (and where some social policies
are directed towards encouraging more women to stay home to raise children).[129]
Given that female employment in these countries is largely non-agricultural
(E/CN.6/575/Add. 3, table 5) and of a type that appears to influence the timing
and number of births, one might expect that birth rates could remain low or decline.

---

[129]   International Labour Organisation, 1965-1985 Labour Force Projections,
Part V (Geneva, 1971), tables 4 and 5.

129. Generally speaking, however, the opportunities for labour force participation of women in non-agricultural sectors of the economies of many developing countries have been extremely limited. As a number of writers have pointed out, the process of economic development is not a unilinear one, leading inevitably to the greater integration of women in non-agricultural production.[130] The experience of many African countries and of India, for example, shows that rural-urban migrations accompanying development frequently deprive women of their formerly productive role in agriculture, handicrafts or village marketing, without offering a substitute role in the modern sector of the towns, where unemployment is usually high.[131] Under these marginal conditions one would not expect urban birth rates to decline rapidly. Moreover, when the development effort is heavily capital-intensive rather than labour-intensive, women may find it particularly difficult to compete with men for scarce, mechanized, "male-type" jobs. On the other hand, opening up new fields of work in economic development may relax barriers to women's employment in countries where cultural factors previously limited women's participation in agriculture.[132]

130. The ILO predicts declines in rates of female labour force participation during the prime childbearing years in all major regions of Asia (excluding Japan) and in Africa, with the exception of North Africa where women's employment is already minimal. No major change is predicted for Latin America or the Caribbean.[133] Again these projections are significant for their potential impact on fertility as well as for standards of living and for the status of women. They suggest that in the absence of major efforts at social engineering (such as those undertaken in China), many developing countries will not be able to absorb the growing supply of female labour.

131/ See, for example, Demographic Aspects of Manpower, Report 1: Sex and Age Patterns in Economic Activities (ST/SOA/SER.A/33), 1962; Andrew Collver and Eleanor Langlois, "The female labour force in metropolitan areas: an international comparison", Economic Development and Cultural Change, vol. 10 (July 1962), pp. 363-385; Ester Boserup, Women's Role in Economic Development (New York, St. Martin's Press, 1970).

131/ Ester Boserup, op. cit., pp. 174-195, 208-209; K. M. Kapadia and S. D. Pillai, Industrialization and Rural Society (India, Popular, 1972).

132/ Pakistan, country paper for the Regional Seminar on the Status of Women and Family Planning for Countries within the ECAFE Region, Jogjakarta, 20-30 June 1973.

133/ International Labour Organisation, op. cit.

131. Some critics have suggested that alternative forms of development be
pursued, which take advantage of local conditions by emphasizing full employment
through labour-intensive development, over rapid economic growth based on capital-
intensive models.[134/] Such a strategy, by mobilizing women fully into economic
production, might well lead to more rapid economic growth in the long run and
to lower birth rates. In areas where cultural disapproval of women's employment
currently runs high, new fields of employment might be created specifically
to attract women into the labour force without their having to compete directly
with men. For example, in Egypt, small-scale rural industries in such fields
as garment making, textiles and food processing are being proposed in an attempt
to raise the status of women in the villages, while providing an attractive
alternative to childbearing.[135/]

[134/] An extensive bibliography on this topic is contained in
William C. Thiesenhusen, Employment and Latin American Development; in Peter Dorner
(ed.) Land Reform in Latin America: Issues and Cases, (Madison, Wisconsin,
University of Wisconsin, Land Economics Monograph No. 3, 1971). See also
Gamani Corea, "A third style for Asia", Ceres, Food and Agriculture Organization
of the United Nations, vol. 5, No. 5 (September-October 1972), pp. 9-17.

[135/] Aziz Bindary, "New approaches to rural population problems", paper
prepared for United Nations/FAO/UNFPA Seminar on Population Problems as Related
to Food and Rural Development in the Near East, Cairo, December 1972. For
additional proposals, see "Integration of women in development: report of the
Secretary-General" (E/CN.5/481), 14 December 1972.

D. The effect of family laws and practices

1. Legal rights and obligations

132. The United Nations has declared that men and women are entitled to equal rights at the time of marriage, during marriage and at its dissolution.[136/] Few Governments have fully incorporated the principle of equality into their family legislation, however. In some, the law upholds an explicit double standard in which women on marriage become virtually the private property of their husbands. In some countries civil codes relating to marriage and the family are not binding on major segments of the population who are subject to customary or religious law.[137/] In others, legal systems inherited from colonial pasts, have little relevance to prevailing practices or needs.[138/] Even where family legislation is relatively egalitarian, many women may not be aware of their rights or may be afraid to fight for them at the risk of alienating a man on whom they depend for social and economic survival.[139/]

133. In this section a brief attempt is made to explore some of the possible implications for fertility of the position of women at the time of marriage, during marriage and at its dissolution. Because little research has been done in these areas that would permit separation of the effects of family structure or behaviour from other related factors, answers to most questions must remain subject to clarification or revision in the light of new evidence as it appears.

136/ Article 6, Declaration on the Elimination of Discrimination against Women.

137/ For example, in Indonesia, the Adat or customary law applies to "Indigenous Indonesians", the "Marriage Ordinance for Indonesian Christians" applies to Indigenous Indonesian Christians residing in certain territories; the customary law of their respective religions applies to Arabs and other foreigners of Asian origin (except Chinese); and the Civil Code (inherited from Dutch colonialism) applies only to Europeans and Chinese. Indonesian Planned Parenthood Association, Legal Aspects of Family Planning in Indonesia (September 1971), p. 12.

138/ See ESA/SDHA/AC.1/26, paras. 19-21.

139/ Ibid., para. 24.

2.   International variations in age at marriage

134. The average age at first marriage for women ranges across countries
from about 16 years to 24 or 25. Where legal minimums have been set they
range from 12 to 20.[140] In general, the pattern in Western industrialized
societies has been one of delayed marriage (mid-twenties) and relatively high
proportions of women remaining single throughout their childbearing years
(from 10 to 20 percent), while in developing countries early (mid to late teens)
and universal marriage (all but one or two percent) for girls has been more the
rule.[141] However, there are important exceptions to this generalization. In
the past two decades, in particular, the marriage patterns of many developing
and industrial countries appear to be converging toward an intermediate position
in which women marry on the average in their early twenties and perhaps 6 to 10
percent never marry.[142]

135. Social and economic pressures to marry girls off while they are very young
remain strong in many regions, however (for example, in some Moslem countries,
parts of India and in some tribal African societies). Early, arranged marriages
are frequently a common feature in predominantly agricultural societies where
the family is a direct unit of economic production and marriage and childbearing
are economic necessities.[143] Alliance between families, created and maintained
through inter-marriage, form the basis of social, political and economic cooperation in the community. If the bride is very young she is more likely to comply
with her parents' wishes with respect to the choice of a spouse and the timing
of the marriage. Virginity is easy to assure if the girl is married at puberty.

---

[140] Measures, Policies and Programmes Affecting Fertility, with Particular
Reference to National Family Planning Programmes (United Nations publication,
Sales No. E.72.XIII.2), p. 49.

[141] John Hajnal, "European marriage patterns in perspective", in D. V. Glass
and D.E.C. Eversley (eds.), Population in History, (Chicago, Aldine, 1965), pp. 101-
143.

[142] India and the Philippines among others reported rising ages at marriage;
Austria, Finland, New Zealand and the United States of America reported declining
ages. See also Ruth B. Dixon, "Explaining cross-cultural variations in age at
marriage and proportions never marrying", Population Studies No. 25, July 1971,
pp. 215-233; S.N. Agarwala, "Pattern of marriage in Some ECAFE countries", IUSSP,
International Population Conference, London 1969, vol. III, pp. 2106-2125.

[143] Aziza Hussein, "Recent developments in the United Arab Republic",
paper presented at the Symposium on Birth Control and the Changing Status of
Women, New York, 18-19 October 1966.

In many cultures an unmarried daughter past a certain age may be considered an embarassment or disgrace to the family, and spinsterhood is virtually unheard of.

136. One generally finds that in countries where girls marry very early, the age gap between males and females on entering marriage may average as high as eight to 10 years.[144/]   Thus the girl's already subordinate position at the time of her marriage is compounded by the additional advantages her husband has accrued with his age and "experience". Where women marry later the difference in ages is usually much smaller. In most countries the average age at first marriage for women is higher, and the age gap between brides and grooms smaller; among educated and employed women and among those living in cities or towns.[145/]

137. Table 6 (E/CN.6/575/Add.3) gives some idea of the range of patterns across countries in the timing of marriages among women. Over 70 per cent of females between the ages of 15 and 20 were already married in Chad, India, Mali, Nepal, the Niger, Pakistan and the United Republic of Tanzania, whereas fewer than 5 per cent were married at this age in a number of European countries and in French Guiana, Guadeloupe, Hong Kong, Japan, the Republic of Korea, Macau, Martinique and the Ryukyu Islands. On the average about 40 per cent of those 15 to 19 were married in the countries listed for the African region, 30 per cent in Asia, 15 per cent in the Americas and in Oceania, 9 per cent in the Union of Soviet Socialist Republics, and 7 per cent in Europe. The question is, how much impact do these variations have on birth rates? And would the abolition of child marriage, along with the exercise of the right to free choice of a spouse and to marry only with free and full consent, make a difference?

144/ Dixon, op. cit.

145/ For example, the Philippines (response); Turkey (working paper for the Seminar on the Status of Women and Family Planning, Istanbul, 11-24 July 1972); India (Ishrat Z. Husain, "Mean age at marriage and differential fertility", IUSSP, International Population Conference, London, 1969, vol. I, p. 466); Ghana (D. I. Pool, "The rural-urban fertility differential in Ghana", IUSSP, op. cit., p. 837); ECAFE countries (Agarwala, op. cit.).

3. <u>Influence of marriage age on family size</u>

138. We would expect variations in nuptiality to determine fertility levels
and differentials most strongly in societies in which (a) birth control is
not widely practised within marriage and (b) few children are born outside of
marriage. The decline of birth rates in Western Europe in the late nineteenth and
early twentieth centuries, for example, has been attributed in good part to patterns
of late marriage, with high proportions of women -- perhaps one tenth to one
quarter -- never marrying.[146] Contraception <u>within</u> marriage was not adopted
on a wide scale until somewhat later, and in most European countries the social
sanctions against out-of-wedlock births tended to be rather severe. On the
other hand, the early and universal marriage of girls in many developing countries
and the infrequent practice of marital contraception creates a potential for high
levels of relatively uncontrolled fertility. It has been suggested that delayed
marriage and non-marriage could have a great impact on fertility in a region such
as tropical Africa, for example, where marital fertility is high, if changing
patterns of nuptiality were not offset by increases in out-of-wedlock births.[147]

139. For countries in which birth planning within marriage is widely practised
the timing of marriage itself (or even the proportions who marry) is less
influential in determining fertility levels and differentials. Declining ages
at marriage may be offset by greater control over the timing and number of births,
thus obscuring major differences in family size between women who married early
or late. The differences that do appear are more likely to be due to other
factors associated with early versus late marriage, such as education, occupation
and income.

146/ Hajnah, op.cit.

147/ A. Romaniuk, "Fertility trends in Africa", IUSSP, op. cit., p. 746.

140. When de facto marriages are frequent, as in many countries in Latin America and the Caribbean where they may constitute well over half of all unions, formal marriage patterns are also less likely to have a significant effect on fertility. The relatively low percentages of married women aged 15 to 19 shown in table 6. (E/CN.6/575/Add. 3) for the Americas conceal the fact that in many areas of the region birth rates are rather high among this age group. Discussions at the Regional Seminar on the Status of Women and Family Planning, Santo Domingo, revealed that frequently only middle- and upper-income couples could afford to marry legally because of the high expectations for dowries, housing, employment and general standards of living considered appropriate to married life. Some among this group did not marry or have children at all.[148] But rural dwellers and the urban poor were likely to enter common-law unions or more casual visiting unions in which virtually every woman became a mother, and did so early.

141. Would legislation raising the legal minimum age for marriage to 16 or 18 years make a significant difference to birth rates in countries with currently high fertility? Most evidence suggests that it would not. In Latin America and the Caribbean, for example, such legislation would have no relevance to the large numbers of women who do not marry legally and yet begin childbearing early. And women who do marry legally in such settings are likely to do so at a later age than that set by law: the legal minimum in Mexico is 14, for example, but in 1967 the average age of brides was 23.[149] Fiji reported that proposals to raise the minimum to 16 in that country would have little effect because the majority of marriages occurred two to three years later in any event.[150] Thailand reported a legal minimum age for marriage of 15 but a median age for brides of about 21.[151]

---

[148] ESA/SDHA/AC.1/26, para. 18.

[149] Response of Mexico.

[150] Response of Fiji.

[151] Response of Thailand.

142. What of those countries where girls are married very young? It is extremely difficult to change these patterns by legislative fiat alone. Raising the legal minimum in India and in some Moslem countries to 15 or 16 appears not to have entirely eliminated child betrothal or the marriage of girls at puberty, for cultural pressures to do so remain strong in many areas.[152] Furthermore, the law can be avoided by failing to register the marriage or by registering it several years later.

143. Even if the law were effective in actually raising the age at marriage to 16 or 18 in these early marrying societies, the impact on over-all birth rates is likely to be slight. Various cultural practices, combined with the phenomenon of low adolescent fecundity, frequently delay the first birth to an average of 17 or 18 years even in marriages that were initiated at 12 or 14. A later age at marriage may only shorten the interval between marriage and the first birth.[153] Indian studies suggest that brides would have to be at least 19 or 20 years old on the average, to begin to have a significant demographic impact in that country.[154]

144. Later marriage among women could have an indirect effect on reproduction if it increased the likelihood of their staying in school, completing an education and finding skilled, paid employment. Each of these factors in turn, along with the greater maturity and independence of the woman herself, should create a more positive attitude towards the practice of family planning. Legislation postponing the marriage of girls to the same age that is considered legally permissible for boys would simultaneously work towards greater equalization of rights on entering marriage. Currently, most countries legislate inequality by setting a higher minimum age for marriage of boys than girls, although recent legal changes in some countries are moving towards greater equality in this regard.

---

[152] ST/TAO/HR/46, para. 73; working paper prepared by India for the Seminar on the Status of Women and Family Planning, Istanbul, 11-24 July 1972; working paper prepared by Indonesia (p. 9) and working paper prepared by Iran (p. 2) for the Regional Seminar on the Status of Women and Family Planning for Countries within the ECAFE Region, Jogjakarta, 20-30 June 1973.

[153] V. C. Chidambaram and A. V. Zodegkar, "Increasing female age at marriage in India and its impact on the first birth interval: an empirical analysis", IUSSP, International Population Conference, London, 1969, vol. I, pp. 437-447.

[154] S. N. Agarwala, "Social and cultural factors affecting fertility in India", Proceedings, Seventh Conference of IPPF, Singapore, 1963, p. 102; N. C. Das, "A note on the effect of the postponement of marriage on fertility", World Population Conference, 1965, vol. II (United Nations publication, Sales No. 66.XIII.6).

145. The difficulties of trying to create conditions favourable to a later age of marriage for females in the face of cultural obstacles were stressed by participants in the Regional Seminar on the Status of Women and Family Planning, Jogjakarta, who agreed that laws postponing marriage would not be effective without other concurrent measures of obvious benefit to the families and girls involved, such as educational and employment opportunities.[155/] However, in order to overcome the resistance of parents who are afraid that their daughters may become unmarriageable once they pass the age of 16 or 18, massive educational campaigns may also be necessary to stress the advantages of a later age at marriage. China, for example, appears to have had great success in promoting the ideology of delaying marriage to the mid-twenties for women and the late twenties for men although 18 and 20 are the ages stipulated by law.[156/] In that country the advantages to both the individual and the nation are stressed: young people, by postponing family burdens, can preserve their health, gain additional maturity, and devote their energies to social reconstruction through education, work and political activity.[157/] Of course, structural and cultural alternatives to early marriage and childbearing for women have simultaneously been created, without which efforts at persuasion would probably have little effect. Marriage in the mid-twenties for women is symbolic of a radical improvement in their status over the arranged matches and child brides of only a few decades ago.

155/ ESA/SDHA/AC.2/21, para. 18.

156/ "Delayed marriage and planned birth", compiled by the Planned Birth Leadership Group of the Kwangtung Provincial Revolutionary Committee. Translated into English by Loren Fessler, the American Universities Field Staff, *Fieldstaff Reporter*, East Asia Series, vol. XX, No. 1, p. 2.

157/ Ibid., p. 3.

4.   Other practices at the time of marriage

146. With regard to the question of the right to marry only with free and full consent and the right to free choice of a spouse, the loss of parental control over the arrangement of their children's marriages, in so far as such control is frequently associated with early and universal marriage within an extended family system, should also serve to delay marriage on the average and to increase the probability of non-marriage for some women, either voluntarily or involuntarily.[158] Courtship takes time and an independently contracted marriage requires a degree of maturity not expected of a young girl whose primary obligation is to obey the wishes of her husband and her elders.   The free choice of a spouse -- even with a considerable amount of parental guidance -- also implies a degree of equality between husband and wife at the time of their marriage that may be essential to effective communication about family planning.

147. Along with child betrothal and the parentally arranged match, the practice of exchanging large dowries or dowers at the time of the marriage has also been challenged on the grounds that it reduces the contract to a financial transaction between families.   Patterns of exchange vary widely across cultures as to the amount and type of material goods that are to be transferred, the expected donor, the recipient, and the use to which the goods are put.   But whether the bride's family receives a bride-price from the groom's family at the time of marriage as reimbursement for the loss or her services or is expected to provide a dowry to the groom, the need for parents to retain strict social controls over their marriageable daughters in these circumstances, is likely to remain strong.   As for its impact on the status of women and fertility,

---

158/ A high degree of parental control is also compatible with late marriage in some societies, however. See Judith Blake, "Parental control, delayed marriage and population policy", World Population Conference, 1965, vol. II (United Nations publication, Sales No. 66.XIII.6), pp. 132-136.

attempts in India to abolish the dowry derived partially from the extreme
financial hardships that low-income parents faced when they had to provide
unrealistically large dowries to find husbands for their daughters. As a
consequence the birth of girls was often dreaded and they were sometimes abandoned
or sold by desperate parents.[159] The birth of girls would presumably be more
welcome in societies where bride-prices are expected. Both systems may influence
birth rates by encouraging early marriage and shaping sex preferences among
offspring, although the nature of these relationships is not yet clear.

5.   Cultural beliefs regarding the role of women in the family

148. Once women are married, how does their position in the family affect
reproductive decisions? Do the degree of male dominance within the household, the
nature of the everyday division of labour and the legal rights and obligations of
the couple vis-à-vis one another and their children have a significant impact on
fertility?

149. Participants in the Seminars on the Status of Women and Family Planning
mentioned a number of beliefs and customs in their countries which they felt
encouraged high fertility, especially in rural areas and among the urban poor.
Government responses contained additional information. In traditional extended
families, for example, elders frequently exerted great influence on young brides
to begin childbearing right away and to have as many children as possible.
Mothers-in-law could sometimes increase their power and authority within the
family with every child that was born into the household.

159/ Over 90 per cent of abandoned babies in Delhi are girls; "Introductory
statement on the subject of the status of women as a factor influencing fertility",
background paper prepared by S. Anandalakshmy for the Regional Seminar on the
Status of Women and Family Planning for Countries within the ECAFE Region,
Jogjakarta, 20-30 June 1973.

150. Male dominance with its consequent male privilege and prerogative was
mentioned many times as a source of female oppression and an obstacle to the
acceptance of family planning. Participants at the Regional Seminar on the
Status of Women and Family Planning for Countries of the Western Hemisphere,
Santo Domingo, talked of <u>machismo</u> -- the need to prove masculinity through
sexual promiscuity and the frequent fathering of children -- and the corresponding belief that a woman must prove her "womanliness" through early and frequent
childbearing. Childlessness was a source of shame. Double standards of sexual
behaviour whereby premarital and extramarital sexual relations were tolerated
or even expected of men, but strictly forbidden to women compounded the low
status of women and encouraged reproductive irresponsibility on the part of men.
Many men were said to view their wives, mistresses and children as personal
possessions to be used and displayed like material goods. Women in many cultures
lived first under the guardianships of their fathers, then their husbands and
finally their sons, sometimes in the strictest isolation, without even the right
to leave their homes.

151. The level of communication between husbands and wives on matters of sex,
family size and family planning was said in the Seminars to be frequently very
low. Sex as a topic of conversation was often taboo. Whereas the double
standard valued premarital virginity, absolute marital fidelity, sexual ignorance
and extreme modesty in the "good" wife or sister or daughter, women in lower-
income groups were often exploited sexually and left with children to raise on
their own. Many men resisted having their wives learn about birth control for
fear that they would become sexually unfaithful as a result.

152. Beliefs in the basic inferiority of women were said to be pervasive in
many countries. Thus even in societies in which women had achieved considerable

advances in education and employment, old notions about "woman's place" were slow to die.[160/] The virtuous wife and mother was one who devoted herself to the care of her husband, children and home, continuously sacrificing her own interests to the welfare of her family. Employed women were often expected to continue unassisted in this role in addition to their work outside the home.

153. Preferences for children of a particular sex were also said to encourage additional births, although the statistical evidence on the impact of sex preferences on birth rates is somewhat ambiguous. The general tendency in most cultures was for boys to be valued over girls, although in some matrilineal descent systems or where bride prices were paid, girls were sometimes more highly valued. Extreme evidence regarding the preference for male offspring was cited at the Regional Seminar on the Status of Women and Family Planning for Countries within the Economic Commission for Asia and the Far East Region, Jogjakarta. In several countries in the region the death rates for female infants and children were significantly higher than those for males.[161/] Females were sometimes permitted to eat only when all the males in the household had finished. Where nutrition was already poor, this cultural practice frequently meant the difference between survival and death for the female child. A United Nations team in one country reported that "the mission saw villages where all the boys were in school and no girls. In hospitals it noticed that the proportion of boys receiving health care was larger than that of girls.[162/]

160/ The working paper prepared by Finland for the Seminar on the Status of Women and Family Planning, Istanbul, 11-24 July 1972, for example, cited a study in which the traditional female image of the sacrificing, hard-working wife and mother who was a good cook and housekeeper prevailed among all age, educational and class groupings. "The persistence of this traditional image in the face of otherwise rapidly changing society is quite remarkable." (p. 13).

161/ ESA/SDHA/AC.2/21, para. 45; working paper prepared by ECAFE for the Regional Seminar on the Status of Women and Family Planning for Countries within the ECAFE Region, Jogjakarta, 20-30 June 1973, pp. 13 and 14.

162/ Population and Family Planning in Iran (ST/SOA/SER.R/13), p. 104.

6. Equality and fertility

154. The low status of women within the family appears to have major repercussions on their knowledge of family planning methods, their access to the means to regulate their pregnancies and even on the desire to do so. But the status of women within the home depends in great part on the structural conditions shaping their opportunities for control over resources outside the home. Evidence from many surveys suggests that in practice, the greater are the resources that a woman brings into her marriage relative to those of her husband (especially in regard to her education and outside paid employment or essential agricultural production), the more equal her voice is likely to be in the major decisions of the family.[163/] Studies of married couples in predominantly urban areas in both industrialized and

---

163/ National Centre for Social and Criminological Research, Cairo, Status of Women in Relation to Fertility and Family Planning in Egypt (1973), p. 165; Council for Social Development, New Delhi, "Status of women and family planning in India", draft report, part I, p. 61; Johannes Noordhoek and Yrsa Smith, "Family and work" (in Danish), Acta Sociologica, 14, (1971) No. 1-2, pp. 43-51; Constantina Safilios-Rothschild, "A comparison of power structure and marital satisfaction in urban Greek and French families", Journal of Marriage and the Family, 29 (1967), pp. 345-352; A. Beluhan, "Survey of knowledge and practice of family planning and problems connected with motherhood in two factories in Zagreb", Zena, 29 (1971), p. 77; R. H. Weller, "The employment of wives, role incompatibility and fertility: a study among lower and middle class residents of San Juan, Puerto Rico", Milbank Memorial Fund Quarterly, 46 (1968), p. 507. A considerable amount of "cultural lag" between the gaining of relative equality outside the home and a breakdown of the traditional pattern of decision-making and division of labour in the home has been reported for a number of countries, however, including Denmark (Noordhoek and Smith, op. cit.); Czechoslovakia (response); Finland and Jamaica (working paper for the Seminar on the Status of Women and Family Planning, Istanbul, 11-24 July 1972); and India (Promilla Kapur, "The changing role and status of women", The Indian Family in the Change and Challenge at the Seventies (New Delhi, Sterling Publisher, 1972), p. 53.

developing countries also indicate that the more equal or "non-traditional" is the division of labour (including decision-making) in the home, the more likely it is that couples will (a) communicate with one another about sex, family size desires and birth planning; (b) report a high degree of sexual satisfaction; (c) express a desire for small families and (d) practise effective contraception.[164]

155. The crux of the argument in the assocation between activities outside the home, relationships within marriage and fertility appears to be the issue of alternative roles. When non-familial activities for women are highly valued and rewarded, wives' participation in them would seem to bring a greater degree of equality into the marriage. Greater equality in turn tends to create an interpersonal relationship more favourable to birth planning and to a smaller family size. But where non-familial alternatives are not available for women, that is, where the division of labour follows highly traditional, segregated lines and the individual woman has little autonomy, then frequent childbearing is usually rewarded and encouraged. A woman's prestige in the eyes of her husband, her relatives and the community at large may depend largely on the number of children she bears.

---

[164] National Centre for Social and Criminological Research, Cairo, op. cit.; India (response); India, Iran, the Philippines and Singapore (working paper prepared by ECAFE for the Regional Seminar on the Status of Women and Family Planning for Countries within the ECAFE Region, Jogjakarta, 20-30 June 1973, pp. 10 and 11); Attiya Inayatullah, "Impact of culture on fertility in Pakistan", Proceedings, Seventh Conference of the International Planned Parenthood Federation, Singapore, 1963, p. 113; Robert E. Mitchel, "Husband-wife relations and family planning practices in urban Hong Kong", Journal of Marriage and the Family, 31 February 1972, pp. 130-146; J. C. Caldwell, "The control of family size in tropical Africa", Demography (October 1968), pp. 612-614; E. Garcia and A. Ramirez, Informe Final del Estudio Sobre Valores y Actitudes de los Jefes de Familia Respecto al Mejoramiento de los Niveles de Vida en la República Dominicana (Santo Domingo, Research Centre of the National University Pedro Henriquez Urena, 1971); Reuben Hill, J. M. Stycos and Kurt Back, The Family and Population Control: A Puerto Rican Experiment in Social Change, (Chapel Hill, University of North Carolina Press, 1959); R. H. Weller, loc. cit.; B. C. Rosen and A. B. Simmons, "Industrialization, family and fertility, a structural psychological analysis of the Brazilian case", Demography, 8 (1971), pp. 42-47; Constantina Safilios-Rothschild, "Family and fertility in urban Greece", IUSSP, International Population Conference, London, 1969, vol. III, pp. 1852-1860; Lee Rainwater, Family Design: Marital Sexuality, Family Size and Contraception (in the United States) (Chicago, Aldine, 1965).

7.   Variations in family structure

156. The nature of the association between the personal relationship between
husband and wife and their reproductive behaviour is also likely to depend on
the type of marital union (whether monogamous or polygamous, legal or consensual)
and on the structure and composition of the household and the larger kin group
of which they are a part (whether nuclear or extended, matrilocal or patrilocal
etc.). These factors in turn are usually associated with socio-economic status.
For example, we noted that in the Latin American and Caribbean region, legal
marriage (and non-marriage) was more characteristic of higher socio-economic
groups while consensual unions were found more often among those with low income.
In some societies where women's role outside the home is restricted, polygamy
may be found only among the wealthiest men, whereas in many other societies where
women play an active role in economic production, even the poorest man may be
able to "afford" several wives.[165]

157. Evidence regarding the effect of these differences in family structure
on fertility is as yet inconclusive. Much remains to be done in specifying
the conditions under which the type of marital union and the household living
arrangements influence the spacing and number of births. It is usually assumed,
for example, that women living in extended households, where the pressures from
elders for early and frequent childbearing are likely to be great, and where
child care and household help are easily available, will have more children than
women living in more isolated nuclear households. Yet in some studies this does

---

[165] See Esther Boserup on "The economics of polygamy" in Women's Role in
Economic Development, (New York, St. Martin's Press, 1970), pp. 37-52. A similar
situation was reported for informally polygamous males with several self-supporting
common-law wives, by participants in the Regional Seminar on the Status of Women
and Family Planning for Countries of the Western Hemisphere, Santo Domingo, 9-22
May 1973.

not prove to be the case.[166/] Investigations of such a relationship are complicated by the fact that, among other things, couples may experience several different living arrangements throughout their lifetimes, and a wide variety of household compositions can be found in most countries. Moreover, whereas the household itself may be nuclear in type, the couple will frequently continue to maintain very close ties with and receive assistance from the larger family unit.

158. It is also frequently assumed that women in polygamous unions have more children than those in monogamous unions. This is due to the belief that wives sharing the same husband may compete with one another to have many children as a sign of the husband's special favour, as a claim to inheritance, or that the polygamous male may be more likely to resist the idea of contraception, and so on. However, some studies show that individual women in monogamous unions bear more children than those in polygamous unions, where long taboos on sexual intercourse during lactation can more easily be observed.[167/] In polygamous societies as a whole, birth rates may nevertheless be higher if women marry earlier, more universally, and remarry quickly, giving maximum exposure in the population to the possibility of conception.

166/ ESA/SDHA/AC.2/21, para. 26; response of the Philippines, p. 10; James A. Palmore, "Population change, conjugal status and the family", Population Aspects of Social Development, Asian Population Series No. 11 (1972) (United Nations publication), p. 58; Moni Nag, "Family type and fertility", World Population Conference, 1965, vol. II (United Nations publication, Sales No. 66.XIII.6); P. C. Bebarta, "Family structure and fertility", Proceedings of the 51st and 52nd Sessions of the Indian Science Congress, part III (Calcutta, 1964).

167/ ESA/SDHA/AC.2/21, para. 19; response of India, p. 7. This observation is nevertheless consistent with the finding that women in monogamous unions may be more likely to practise contraception; see Gyorgy T. Acsadi, Adenola A. Igun and Gwendolyn Z. Johnson, Surveys of Fertility and Family Planning in Nigeria, Institute of Population and Manpower Studies, University of Ife (1972), pp. 103, 117 and 128. See also A. Romaniuk, "Fertility trends in Africa", IUSSP, op. cit., vol. I, pp. 746 and 747, and Measures, Policies and Programmes Affecting Fertility ..., pp. 51 and 52.

159. With regard to the legality of the marital union, women in consensual or "visiting" unions may have their first sexual experiences and begin childbearing earlier than legally married women in the same society. Some studies show, however, that births in such unions, on the average, are spaced at wider intervals and result in an equal or lower completed family size than among married women.[168/] One Caribbean study shows that women in visiting unions are more likely to be childless than those in common law unions, who in turn are more likely to be childless than women in formal marriages.[169/]

8.   Legal rights and obligations during marriage

160. The nature of the specifically legal rights and obligations of married couples towards one another and towards their children may also have a bearing on reproductive decisions, although it must be kept in mind that customary practice is likely to play a much larger role. Because there is little systematic data in this area, we can as yet only speculate on the answers to most questions. For example, how does the denial of certain civil rights, such as a woman's right to own, inherit or bequeath property, affect her desired family size? Where only male children inherit property, does fertility increase until a desired number of sons are born? Is a woman who bears no children or who bears only one or two, or only daughters, disadvantaged under some legal systems more than others?

168/   ESA/SDHA/AC.1/26, para. 18; G.W. Roberts, "Fertility in some Caribbean countries", IUSSP, op.cit., vol. I, p. 702; Judith Blake, Family Structure in Jamaica: The Social Context of Reproduction, (New York, Free Press, 1961). For an analysis of the relationship between agricultural systems, the status of women and types of marital unions, see John Stuart Macdonald, "Family-household structure and agricultural organization in the southern Caribbean", IUSSP, op.cit., vol. III, pp. 2234-2240.

169/   Roberts, loc.cit., p. 702.

161. There is little doubt that the denial to married women of independent
rights over property reduces their status within the family. Where a woman cannot
work without her husband's written permission, for example, and where she has no
inheritance rights, "... she is completely dependent on the man for all her needs
and has also to submit to his wishes. The woman under these conditions has
little voice in taking decisions in important problems such as the number of
children she should have or when she should have them".[170/] The denial to women
of the right to inherit property, or the restriction of their allowable share
to half of the male portion as specified in some systems may also contribute
to a preference for sons, and thus increase the over-all birth rate.[171/]

162. Perhaps of more importance in determining desired family size is the nature
of parental rights and duties regarding their children, and the reciprocal rights
and duties of children regarding their parents. On the latter question, the
expectation that adult children will support and care for their parents in sickness
and old age is frequently mentioned as an incentive for large families, especially
sons. The expectation becomes a virtual necessity in countries that have no
social security systems for disability, unemployment and old age. It is the poor
in these countries who are most likely to feel the greatest need for large
families as a means of survival. It is also the poor who are most likely
to depend on even young children to provide additional family income, for the
smallest contribution from child labour may make a significant difference to the
family as a whole.[172/] In rural areas children can be an essential source of
agricultural and domestic production, while in towns and cities they may produce
handicrafts, engage in petty trade or find other sources of gainful work.

170/ Response of India, p. 7.

171/ Working paper prepared by Indonesia for the Regional Seminar on the
Status of Women and Family Planning for Countries within the ECAFE Region,
Jogjakarta, 20-30 June 1973, p. 10.

172/ For a brief discussion of the effect of child labour laws and
compulsory school attendance on fertility, see Measures, Policies and Programmes
Affecting Fertility ..., pp. 36 and 37.

163. On the other hand, where children become primarily consumers of material resources rather than producers and, where parents are expected to support their children financially at least until their early adult years (including, perhaps, an expensive education) then the costs of a large family are likely to override its benefits.173/ This phenomenon appears most frequently in the middle socio-economic groups and as an accompaniment to urbanization, industrialization and "modernization".

164. What effect does the division of parental rights and responsibilities have on family size decisions? Speculation on the differences between husbands and wives in their desire for additional children sometimes focuses on the assumption that because women tend to carry the major responsibility for the day-to-day care of children, whereas men are removed from its immediate burdens, women would be more motivated than men to keep the family size small.174/ But alternative hypotheses suggest that men, being more closely associated with the financial responsibilities of children and more exposed to "modern" ideas outside the home should be more intensely motivated to limit family size. Clearly the nature of the perceived costs and benefits of having an additional child must differ for each spouse depending on their concrete experiences and on the cultural and structural conditions of the society that determine the division of labour between them. It may also rest with the nature of parental rights and responsibilities at the time of marital dissolution, whether through death, divorce or desertion.

173/ For a discussion of the possible effects on fertility of child allowances and tax benefits, see Measures, Policies and Programmes Affecting Fertility..., pp. 17-29.

174/ One review of Knowledge and Practice Studies conducted in the 1960s showed that in 11 out of 12 cases in which it was possible to compare male and female responses, a larger proportion of women than men reported wanting no more children. The 11 were: Bangladesh (Dacca, 1963 and 1964), Ghana (1963), India (Delhi, 1958-1961), Indonesia (Jakarta, 1968), Kenya (Nairobi, 1966), Morocco (urban 1966, rural 1967, small towns 1967), Pakistan (Lahore, 1960) and Thailand (1968). The exception was Algeria (urban 1967-1968). See Dorothy Nortman, "Population and family planning: a factbook", Reports on Population/Family Planning, No. 2 (Fourth edition) (New York, The Population Council, September 1972), pp. 68-71.

9. The impact of marital dissolution

165. The impact on fertility of marital dissolution depends to a large extent on its timing, frequency and on patterns of remarriage, that is, on the length of reproductive time a woman "loses" between sexual unions. When death rates are high and life expectancies short, many couples will not survive their potential childbearing years together. An Indian study showed that seven or eight years of the reproductive period could be lost on an average by the death of either the husband or wife, or both.[175/] Widowed women at age 45 in one area averaged 5.5 children, compared to 6.6 children among all women aged 45 who had ever been married.[176/] If the remarriage of widows is forbidden, as it was in Hindu tradition (at least among the upper castes), fertility is inevitably depressed. If widows remarry easily, however, or are "inherited" by one of their husband's brothers, as in some societies, then fertility may not be reduced at all.

166. Similarly, the impact of divorce, annulment or separation depends on the probabilities of the woman's remarriage or her entry into another type of sexual union. The lower fertility of women in consensual unions as compared to legal marriages in some parts of the Caribbean, for example, has been attributed to the intermittent loss of childbearing potential when women in the former category are "between unions" and not engaging in sexual activity.[177/]

167. Apart from the actual fact of divorce itself, what impact might the perceived ease or difficulty of obtaining a divorce have on family-building behaviour? It has been suggested that the husband's arbitrary right to divorce his wife at will in some countries frightens women into having many children in order to bind their husbands more securely to them. And where childlessness or

---

175/ S.N. Agarwala, "Social and cultural factors affecting fertility in India", Proceedings, Seventh Conference of the International Planned Parenthood Federation, Singapore, 1963, p. 102.

176/ Ibid., p. 103.

177/ Roberts, loc. cit.

the absence of sons is a justifiable grounds for divorce, the woman with the most children is likely to feel the safest in her marriage -- a marriage she depends on for her social and economic survival. In this context, one in which women have few options outside of marriage, the threat of divorce could have a pronatalist effect.

168. On the other hand, ease of divorce in societies where women do have alternative means of social and economic support may have an antinatalist effect in ending marriages that might otherwise produce more children.[178/] Once again, however, much depends on the remarriage of the woman. Some commentators suggest that couples entering new unions even with "completed" families from former marriages are likely to have additional children in order to solidify the new relationship.[179/] Whether this additional childbearing compensates for the time spent between marital unions is not known, however.

169. Other aspects of the rights and obligations of spouses at the time of marital dissolution need to be more carefully examined with respect to their influence on the status of women and on fertility. What rights does a woman have to inheritance at her husband's death or to support for herself and her children after a divorce? Do children remain with their mother or return to their father's family? What legal rights do women have in consensual or common-law unions? Does the financial obligation on the part of the male to support his children born out of wedlock reduce the number of such births? What legal control does a man retain over a wife and children whom he has deserted, and how does this affect a woman's future sexual and reproductive decisions? Do couples actually take the possibility of death, divorce or desertion into account when they have children, and if so, how?

[178/] Working paper prepared by the United States of America for the Seminar on the Status of Women and Family Planning, Istanbul, 11-24 July 1972, p. 19.

[179/] For example, ESA/SDHA/AC.1/26, para. 17. It was also noted that legal prohibitions of divorce could not prevent couples from breaking up and forming new unions, except that the new unions were not legally recognized or protected.

170. Many questions remain unanswered in the whole area of the relationship between family laws, family practices, the position of women and fertility. But in general the evidence suggests that the expansion of opportunities for women outside the home is reflected, albeit slowly, in greater autonomy and equality as to marriage, during marriage and at its dissolution. Greater autonomy and equality in turn favour closer communication between sexual partners, effective birth planning practices and greater freedom of choice as regards family size.

171. At the same time, the development process itself entails "a shift from major dependence on relatively self-contained local institutions (such as family and village) to dependence on larger social, economic and political units".[180/] As the family becomes more specialized in its function, high fertility is likely to become irrelevant or burdensome, in which case the pressure on women to adhere strictly to domestic roles is reduced.

E. Participation in public life and decision-making

172. The belief where it prevails that woman's proper sphere is in the closed intimacy of home and family is inevitably matched with the corresponding belief that man's role is to deal with the larger matters of the outside world. It is interesting to note that even where women have made major gains in acquiring access to knowledge, training and economic independence, their share in decision-making in both the family and in public life - that is, their share of political power — appears to lag behind their share in other resources.

180/ Ronald Freedman, in <u>World Population Conference, 1965</u>, vol. I, (United Nations publication, Sales No. 66.XIII.5), pp. 39-40.

173. The United Nations has declared the right of women to participate in public life and political decision-making on equal terms with men, specifically the right to vote in all elections, to be eligible for all publicly elected bodies, to hold public office and to exercise all public functions.[181] Women have won the right to vote in all but a handful of countries, but in most nations -- even those that guarantee equality in the law -- women are poorly represented at the upper levels of decision-making in government offices or elective bodies. Their greatest successes have occurred in countries where Governments actively promote an ideology of equality between the sexes in public and private life, thus breaking down some of the traditional resistance to placing women in leadership positions. But in hardly any country can it be said that women play an equal role with men in political life. The tendency is usually to point to the one or two women in conspicuously high positions as examples of women's participation while ignoring the weight of evidence on the extreme underrepresentation of women as a group.

174. What does this say about the status of women, and what does it mean for their reproductive behaviour?

175. Participation in public life can of course have the same direct influence on fertility as other forms of employment. Women with reduced domestic responsibilities are more free to involve themselves in community or national activities, while women whose political involvement takes them out of the home and into a world of wider interests and rewards may desire and have smaller families.

---

[181]/ Article 21, Universal Declaration of Human Rights (1948); Convention on the Political Rights of Women (1952); article 3, International Covenant on Civil and Political Rights (1966); article 4, Declaration on the Elimination of Discrimination Against Women (1967).

176. But beyond this relatively direct association between public life and reproduction among those who are themselves active participants, an expanded engagement of women in public affairs may have a far broader -- though less direct and more difficult to measure -- impact on fertility patterns by providing a community or a nation with highly visible models of women who are active and competent leaders and decision-makers. Such women can be a powerful force towards changing attitudes regarding female roles and responsibilities. And at the individual level, even the simple act of voting itself may encourage women to have greater confidence in their own capacity or independent thought and action, a confidence that could carry over into the more private activities of sex and childbearing.

177. Of course the participation of women in political areas specifically devoted to improving the status of women, promoting equality between the sexes or expanding birth planning information and services can have a tremendous impact on the questions we have been discussing. Women's groups throughout the world are developing political skills and applying pressure in many areas to expand the rights of women in public and private life and to challenge prevailing sex stereotypes and eliminate discriminatory practices. As they become increasingly successful, women will find new freedom to develop their own potential as full multidimensional human beings in the context of a radically transformed society.

178. In the field of development planning and population policies, where women have been severely underrepresented in the past, many are also beginning to take note of the overwhelmingly masculine character of research institutes and decision-making bodies. Women are demanding to play a larger role in determining and evaluating demographic policies that affect their lives so intimately. In the long run, the direction of development planning and population research, along with priorities for action, may shift considerably as the relationships between social and economic structures, equal rights and demographic behaviour are more fully understood, and as women insist on playing an equal role with men in deciding their own future.

IV. IMPLICATIONS FOR THE STATUS OF WOMEN OF
     CURRENT POPULATION TRENDS

179. The central question of this chapter is the extent to which current and
projected population trends in different regions of the world in turn affect
the status of women. Is it possible to isolate particular aspects of population
processes in order to identify their influence on women's status now and in the
future? More specifically, how is the position of women in education, employment,
public and private life shaped under different conditions of population growth,
structure and distribution? What demographic conditions appear to facilitate
equality between the sexes and what conditions appear to hinder it?

A. Population growth and the age structure

180. In discussing the impact of population trends on the status of women it
is not so much the absolute size of populations that must be taken into account,
but their rate of growth and the ratio of persons of dependent age to those of
prime adult working ages. In 1972 the world's population was growing at the
rate of 2 per cent per year, enough to double its numbers -- or add another
3.8 billion people -- in 35 years.182/ Regional growth rates ranged from less
than 1 per cent in Europe and the Union of Soviet Socialist Republics (doubling
times of from 75 to 100 years) to 2.3 per cent in Asia (30 years), 2.6 per cent in
Africa (27 years) and 2.8 per cent in Latin America (25 years). Within these
regions the conditions of individual nations varied considerably. And within
nations, rates of birth, marriage, death, migration and other demographic
processes also differed across major population subgroups, by region and for
rural and urban areas.

182/ The source of all statistics in this chapter unless otherwise noted
is the 1972 World Population Data Sheet - Population Reference Bureau, Inc.
(Washington, D.C.).

1.   Countries with high growth rates

181. Dramatic declines in death rates in many developing countries since the 1940s, combined in many cases with continuously high birth rates, have produced unprecedented rates of natural increase over wide regions. The death rate in Latin America, for example, had dropped by 1972 to approximately 10 per thousand, a level identical with that of industrialized countries in North America, Europe and the Union of Soviet Socialist Republics.[183/] Yet its birth rate was a high 38 per thousand, leaving a growth rate of 2.8 per cent per year. The population of Asia, with a similarly high birth rate of 37 and a death rate of 14, increased at 2.3 per cent per year. In Africa, the very high birth rate of 47 per thousand was somewhat counteracted by a death rate of 21, producing a 2.6 per cent growth rate. Presumably as health conditions improve in the African region and fertility remains high (or increases under the influence of better health), the population there will grow at even greater speed. It is expected that in the relatively brief period between 1972 and 1985, Africa will add 166 million to its population, Asia, 726 million and Latin America, 135 million.

182. A number of countries are growing at a rate of over 3.2 per cent, which would double their populations in approximately 20 years. Among these are Algeria, Colombia, the Dominican Republic, Ecuador, Iraq, Jordan, Mexico, Morocco, Pakistan, Paraguay, the Philippines, the Syrian Arab Republic, Thailand and Venezuela.

183/ The low death rate is partially a function of the young age distribution in Latin America, in which children and young adults who have lower death rates than older people make up the bulk of the population. Average life expectancies tend to be considerably lower in Latin America and other developing regions than in the industrialized countries.

183. Such increases in population clearly place a tremendous burden on a country's material resources and services. Even if land, food, housing, schools, jobs, health services and other resources are not now in short supply, they must be doubled within two decades in order to keep pace with the demands of growing numbers, while merely maintaining existing levels of living. Participants at all the Seminars on the Status of Women and Family Planning expressed the fear that under extreme competition for source resources, women, who are already disadvantaged, would suffer even greater disabilities.[184] In the absence of a deliberate policy to the contrary, the promotion of equality between men and women might be sacrificed to even stronger preferential treatment for males in education, training and employment. Thus women would be left with few options but to continue in their traditional roles in a patriarchal society, perhaps under even worse material and social conditions that before. In turn, of course, this situation would most likely encourage and foster the maintenance of high birth rates, perpetuating the vicious cycle of growth and scarcity of resources.

184. The decline in mortality which precipitated these high growth rates would appear on the surface to benefit women greatly, especially in reducing the risks of infant and maternal death. However, it has frequently been pointed out that the drop in death rates in many developing countries often represents not a fundamental improvement in the level of living of the masses but imported medical technology such as immunization, which has reduced the toll of major contagious diseases. A higher survival ratio among infants, if it occurs at a time of food shortages, could mean that female children are even more likely to be deprived of adequate nourishment where cultural practices give males priority for scarce resources within the family. And even broader improvements in health care, sanitation and nutrition, while making conception easier and childbearing safer, could be disadvantageous if it means an "unwanted" increase

---

[184] ST/TAO/HR/46, paras. 102-133; ESA/SDHA/AC.1/26, para. 45; ESA/SDHA/AC.2/21, paras. 54-55; responses of Egypt, India, Indonesia and Nigeria; working paper prepared by ECAFE for the Regional Seminar on the Status of Women and Family Planning for Countries within the ECAFE Region, Jogjakarta, 20-30 June 1973, pp. 12-15.

in fecundity among women who are already burdened with family responsibilities
and who lack the knowledge and means to prevent further pregnancies. This again
points to the need for an integrated approach in development planning and
population policies.

185. Whatever the level of mortality, high birth rates produce a broad-based
age pyramid which may further depress the level of living as well as the capacity
of women to participate fully in economic and political life. In Africa, Asia and
Latin America between 40 and 45 per cent of the population of the regions as a whole
are children under 15 years of age. Only 50 to 55 per cent are working age adults
between 15 and 64. In contrast, 25 per cent of Europe's population are under 15
and about 65 per cent are in the working ages. Although the tendency for children
to start working younger and perhaps for old people to retire later in the
developing countries may partially offset the lower proportion in the prime
working ages, the rates of underemployment and unemployment tend to be higher.[185/]
"On balance, the ratio of dependents to producers is substantially higher in the
less developed countries."[186/] The dependency burden on the generally meagre
incomes of productive workers and on the heavy domestic labours of women is
clearly enormous.

2.   The transition to lower fertility

186. The broad-based age pyramid engendered by high birth rates carries within
it the potential for continuing high or increasing rates of population growth,
even when the number of children per couple begins to decline.

> "This occurs because a rapid transition from high to low birth and death
> rates is in general accompanied by a temporary inflation in the proportion of
> women in the reproductive ages. This proportion will eventually stabilize
> at a lower level, but in the meantime the birth rate /and thus the growth
> rate/ will be correspondingly inflated relative to its final stable level".[187/]

Considerable increases in population are therefore inevitable in the near future
in high-fertility countries, whether or not birth rates decline.

185/ "Introductory statement on the subject of the implications for the
status of women of current trends in population growth", working paper prepared by
Anuree Wanglee for the Seminar on the Status of Women and Family Planning, Istanbul,
11-24 July 1972, pp. 1 and 2.

186/ Ibid., p. 2.

187/ Ibid.

187. Nevertheless, both short-run and long-run advantages accrue from the transition to low fertility that, while benefiting both men and women, should be more keenly felt by women. For example, fewer births would have an immediate impact on the domestic burdens of women, particularly with reference to the age groups of children under 5, freeing women to participate more fully in life outside the home. As the younger cohort reaches school age, the pressures of sheer increasing numbers on the educational system should be relieved somewhat, with the possibility that the chances of girls to attend school would improve, not only absolutely but relative to boys. A similar process would be expected as the young men and women reach the age of entry into the labour force. However, as we noted in chapter II, even at similar over-all levels of school enrolment and employment the differentials between men and women vary greatly across countries. The underlying social and cultural causes of these differentials must also be overcome, if relief from demographic pressure is to be translated into real advantages for women.

3. Countries with low growth rates

188. Low rates of population growth resulting from controlled levels of mortality and fertility may not only reflect a higher status of women but also facilitate additional improvements in their potential for equality with men. In Europe, the Union of Soviet Socialist Republics and North America, birth rates in 1972 averaged about 16 or 17 per thousand and death rates about 8 to 10, creating an annual rate of natural increase of 1 per cent or less. Some countries grew at a rate of half of 1 per cent or less. It would, for example, take from 139 to 700 years or more for populations to double at current growth rates in Austria, Belgium, Czechoslovakia, Denmark, Finland, the Democratic Republic of Germany, the Federal Republic of Germany, Hungary, Luxembourg, Sweden and the United Kingdom.

189. Under such conditions the pressures on resources are clearly quite minimal when increases in numbers alone are considered. Indeed, in the face of rapid

economic expansion and low birth rates, some countries are anticipating labour shortages.[188/] For this and other reasons, policies in the Eastern European countries in particular are directed towards improving women's working conditions and maternity benefits, so that both employment and childbearing may be developed to the optimal extent.

190. Although the demographic pressures on resources of industrialized high-income countries may be reduced through low population growth rates, pressures deriving from high and rising standards of living may be severe. These very improvements in standards of living are potentially of great benefit to women, however, if they lead to reduced domestic chores, improved and expanded facilities for day care, more adequate housing, health care and social services, and maximal opportunities for education, employment and political participation. The question is, do these benefits automatically accrue under "advantageous" demographic conditions?

4.   Population growth in the context of social, economic and
     political conditions

191. It is difficult, if not impossible, to isolate the effect of demographic trends such as population growth from related factors influencing the status of women, especially so because the highest growth rates tend to occur in the poorest regions of the world, while the lowest growth rates are found in the wealthier regions. But participants in a Seminar on the Status of Women and Family Planning for Countries of the Western Hemisphere concluded that population growth was mediated by the social, economic and political processes of each country.[189/]

188/ Responses of Finland, Japan and Sweden.

189/ Report of the Regional Seminar on the Status of Women and Family Planning for Countries of the Western Hemisphere, Santo Domingo, 9-22 May 1973 (ESA/SDHA/AC.1/26), paras. 43-44.

As such it affected the position of women only indirectly. Of more consequence
were the historical conditions producing the current rates of fertility and
mortality, without which the position of women could not be understood. Similarly,
future developments were said to depend primarily on the social, economic and
political decisions made by each country.[190/] Demographic pressures such as rapid
population growth and heavy rural-urban migration were likely to exacerbate
problems of inequality and marginality of major population subgroups, for example,
but there was no proof that these problems would be dealt with effectively if the
population grew at a slower pace. Countries with similar birth, death and growth
rates might show very different patterns of male and female school enrolment,
male and female employment rates, distribution of income across social classes,
and so on. Much depended on the priorities set by Governments. If Governments
regarded economic growth primarily as a means of achieving social progress,
including the full social, economic and political participation of every member
on an equal co-operative basis, then the status of women would improve regardless
of demographic conditions. Their improved status in turn should result in the
voluntary adoption of family planning and a family size based on freedom of
choice. But where Governments attached priority to economic growth with little
regard for the distribution of income or the promotion of equality between groups
(including men and women), then the competition for scarce resources was likely to
strengthen the traditional division of labour based on sex, thereby increasing
women's social isolation and decreasing their control over material resources.[191/]

190/ Response of Finland; working paper prepared by Yugoslavia for the
Seminar on the Status of Women and Family Planning, Istanbul, 11-24 July 1972.

191/ ESA/SDHA/AC.1/26, paras. 43 and 44.

B. Geographical distribution of population

192. Patterns of human settlement, along with processes of internal and
international migration, have been very little studied with respect to their
implications for the status of women. Because there is so little systematic
evidence in this area, only a few questions will be touched on here. How are
women's lives affected by urbanization, for example? Does the move from rural
village to town or city expand or contract women's rights, and in what ways?
How are the timing and probability of marriage influenced, or the spacing and
number of children? These questions are of special relevance in view of the rapid
rates of urbanization in many countries, over the past two decades. An estimated
one quarter of the world's population lived in cities of 100,000 or more in 1970.
Africa remains the least urbanized region with 11 per cent, followed by Asia at
16 per cent, Latin America and the Union of Soviet Socialist Republics at
31 per cent, and Europe at 38 per cent. In the Oceania region, 49 per cent of
the population lived in major cities, and in North America, 57 per cent.

193. Urban populations in every region have been growing faster than the
population as a whole.[192/] The same pattern is predicted for the next several
decades. For countries within the geographical scope of the Economic Commission
for Asia and the Far East, for example, rural populations are expected to increase
by 33 per cent in the last three decades of the twentieth century, but urban
populations are expected to treble.[193/] Thus, not only will population density
on already crowded arable rural lands double, but urban problems of housing,
congestion, services and unemployment will be severely aggravated.

192/ Kingsley Davis, World Urbanization 1950-1970, vol. I (Berkeley,
California, Institute of International Studies, University of California, 1969),
pp. 141-160.

193/ "Introductory statement on the subject of the implications for the
status of women of current trends in population growth", background paper prepared
by Sultan Hashmi for the Regional Seminar on the Status of Women and Family
Planning for Countries within the ECAFE Region, Jogjakarta, 20-30 June 1973,
p. 8.

194. In the African and Asian regions, the exodus from rural areas has consisted primarily of adult males of prime working ages. What does this do to the status of women remaining in the villages? It is possible that under some conditions they may improve their position by taking over many activities formerly performed by men and acquiring a major decision-making role in the family and in the community. On the other hand, it may mean only a double burden for the women left behind who are forced to struggle with agricultural as well as household chores. They may remain under the authority of their absent husbands, or of elder family members. In addition, as participants in the Regional Seminar on the Status of Women and Family Planning for Countries within the ECAFE Region, Jogjakarta, pointed out, each time the men returned to their villages for a visit there were additional births, and so women's domestic burdens often remained unabated.

195. As a consequence of the migration patterns, men tend to outnumber women in urban areas of Asia and Africa. In Iran in 1971, for example, there were 108 males in the towns and cities for every 100 females.[194/] During the same period the ratio of males per 100 females was 116 in India, 117 in the United Republic of Tanzania, 120 in Uganda and 138 in Kenya.[195/] What impact does this numerical dominance have on the position of women in the cities, particularly on their access to scarce resources of education and employment? Are prostitution, polygamy and consensual unions encouraged? Do women marry earlier and more universally than they might if the ratio between the sexes was more balanced?

[194/] Calculated from Demographic Yearbook, 1971 (United Nations publication, Sales No. E/F.72.XIII.1), table 5.

[195/] Ibid.

196. In Europe and the Americas, women usually constitute a majority in the stream of migrants to towns and cities. As a consequence, the ratio of urban males to females was 91 in Chile in 1970, 95 in Brazil, 96 in Mexico, 93 in the United States of America and 94 in England and Wales.[196/] Again, how does this numerical imbalance affect women's rights and their reproductive behaviour?

197. Under some conditions the move from village to town may represent real freedom for women from the constraints and traditions of village life. It may also offer a range of opportunities for schooling, vocational training, gainful employment, child-care services, health care, family planning services and other amenities that were simply not available in rural areas.

198. However, the move to town may also result in a lower level of living if the woman's formerly productive role in agriculture or other goods-producing activities is lost without substitution by wage labour. A formerly supportive environment in which child care and other forms of mutual assistance were readily available might give way to an isolated existence for women, in which the division of labour between husband and wife is more rigid than the one left behind.

199. Participants in the Regional Seminar on the Status of Women and Family Planning for Countries of the Western Hemisphere, Santo Domingo, noted that the heavy migration of uneducated, unskilled rural peasants to many cities in the Latin American region caused special problems for women.[197/] Many migrants "... were young, single women who entered the lower levels of service occupations in the cities, were exploited economically and sexually, and often ended in prostitution. Others were married women confined with their children almost as prisoners in miserable shanty towns while their husbands looked for work".[198/] Where population pressures in both rural and urban areas aggravated problems of unemployment and alienation, males often acted out their frustrations in exaggerated aggressive behaviour, sexual promiscuity and irresponsible procreation.[199/]

[196/] Ibid.

[197/] See also ESA/SDHA/AC.2/21, para. 59, and Esther Boserup, Woman's Role in Economic Development (New York, St. Martin's Press, 1970), chap. 10.

[198/] ESA/SDHA/AC.2/21, para. 46.

[199/] Ibid.

200. Participants also pointed out that the "brain drain" of the more educated, ambitious and skilled persons from rural to urban areas and from developing countries to industrialized regions adversely affected those who were left behind by depriving them of talented leadership and more "modern" ideas. For example, parents migrating to cities sometimes left their children in the villages for relatives to care for, meaning that traditional beliefs regarding the "proper" role of women were more likely to be perpetuated.[200] And in the country as a whole, the loss of highly educated men and women could reduce the pressure on Governments to develop innovative programmes for the promotion of full employment, a more just distribution of wealth and the equal rights of men and women.

201. Although it is generally assumed on the basis of historical evidence from the non-industrialized countries that voluntary migration occurs in the direction of better opportunities and living conditions, thereby serving as a valuable mechanism of adjustment of population to resources, there is a growing body of evidence suggesting that rural-urban migration in many developing countries may reduce rural population pressures only slightly, if at all; may lower agricultural productivity; and may create demands for urban employment and services far beyond the capacity of the cities to absorb them. In this context it is especially important to analyse the changing position of women in both rural and urban areas as it is affected by the process of migration, among other factors. In turn, the changing position of women under these conditions will have basic implications for future trends in family planning and family size.

---

[200] ESA/SDHA/AC.1/26, para. 47.

33

Salon, Foyer, Bureau: Women and the Professions in France[1]

During the great revolution of 1789—rhetorically dedicated to abstract equality—the women of France rioted, demonstrated, and struggled in the cause. However, apart from references to *citoyennes*—the female version of the new, universal social rank, *citoyen*—women received no substantive benefits from the redistribution of rights after the destruction of the monarchy and aristocracy (see Duhet 1971).[2] Such a pattern has long characterized the situation of women in France—not least those women who seek to enter the most skilled and prestigious occupational positions, the professions. France has long been characterized by abstract commitments to equality—but also by strong familistic traditions stressing women's subordinate and domestic role. Since 1900, higher education has been available to women in proportions that compare favorably with other European societies; yet today they are minimally represented at the highest professional levels. At the same time, French women have wider access to professional careers than do their counterparts in many other Western societies.

Thus, French women are very far indeed from that "equality" proclaimed in the Republic's motto, but simplistic images of "repression" or "discrimination" are insufficient for an adequate sociological understanding of the professional aspirations, frustrations, and achievements of women in France. The situation of professional women in France reveals some of the complex interactions among economy, polity, and culture defining "women's place," illuminating by comparison and contrast the more familiar situation in English-speaking societies.

THE CLASS AND OCCUPATIONAL SETTING

Some distinctive characteristics of French social and occupational structure must be understood as a prologue to analysis. Professional occupations in

[1] I wish to acknowledge the help of Elinor Barber and Allan Silver in the preparation of this paper.

[2] The Constitution of 1791 treated women as *passif* rather than *actif* citizens; the legislative committee of the Convention in 1793 excluded women—together with minors, the mad, and the criminal—from political rights; shortly after, they were prohibited from attending any political assembly (Duhet 1971, pp. 165–66). The Revolution's unprecedented provision for divorce, however, formally conferred equal rights on both spouses.

France cannot be taken as the direct equivalents of American ones. They include, of course, the classic "liberal professions"—law, medicine, the professoriat; but in France, *professeurs* are found not only in universities but at the educational level just below, the *lycées*. High government administrators—*cadres supérieurs*—are more highly professionalized in France, both in occupational style and educational requirements (roughly equivalent to American graduate studies short of the doctoral dissertation). For this reason, as well as the traditional dignity and prestige of the higher public administration in France, government administration is appropriately regarded as a profession.

Other occupations, too, are more readily accorded professional status in France. This is true of some in which women are numerous, such as teachers below the *lycée* level (*instituteurs*), and middle-level administrators; such strata comprise the *cadres moyens*. Both *cadres supérieurs* and *cadres moyens* are classifications used by the French census, but they are also terms of daily speech used to describe social distinctions in French society.

These distinctions suggest how inapplicable to France is the American notion of a broad middle class which—however heterogeneous in occupational, educational, and ethnic terms—nonetheless shares core social values which widely serve as models for other strata. The term *bourgeoisie*, often translated misleadingly as "middle class," refers to about 26% of the French population (in 1962), a group sharply distinguished both from manual workers (*ouvriers*) and white-collar personnel (*employés*). Within the *bourgeoisie* must be distinguished the 4% or 5% of the population forming the *grande bourgeoisie*—*cadre supérieurs*, the liberal professions, and the most wealthy property owners, employers, investors, and businessmen. The *grande bourgeoisie* differs significantly not only in wealth and status but also in values and style of life from the *petite bourgeoisie* (10% of the population) and the *bourgeoisie moyenne* (12%) (who include the *cadres moyens*, i.e., *instituteurs*, nurses, administrators, and smaller businessmen and property owners). As we shall see, distinctions between the values of the *grande bourgeoisie* and other strata are important in understanding the position and opportunities of professional women.[3]

PROFESSIONAL WOMEN IN THE OCCUPATIONAL STRUCTURE

Compared with other Western nations, the proportion of women employed in nonagricultural occupations in France ranks among the highest—36%

[3] The status and life styles of professions and the *bourgeoisie* in France are also affected by the continuing presence of very large proportions of rural and manual workers. Of the labor force, 15% (a proportion applying to both sexes) are in the agricultural sector—three times that of Britain, and almost twice that of the United States. Fully 39% of the total labor force are manual workers, *ouvriers*; of working women, 22%

(Organisation Internationale du Travail 1967).[4] However, the extent of women's participation in the labor force is an ambiguous indicator of equality between the sexes; a high rate may denote women's large-scale relegation to low-paying, unskilled, and dead-end positions, whose major social function is to supplement low family incomes or to support families without male heads of households. The nature of women's participation in professional occupations partakes of analogous ambiguities. In the non-agricultural labor force, the proportion of each sex who are professionals (the liberal professions, *cadres supérieurs, cadres moyens*) is essentially identical—17% for women, 17.8% for men. But distinguishing within professional occupations, only 18% of professional women are in the higher-status positions (liberal professions, *cadres supérieurs*) compared with 42% of the men. The absolute number of French professional women is about half that of men—in 1968 there were 1,002,940 such women, compared with 2,003,960 men.

Although French women enjoy considerable access to the professions, they tend to cluster in the middle ranks. Yet this state of affairs is in some ways not so unsatisfactory as the comparable one in the United States. The relatively high status of middle-level professionals in France, and some distinctive characteristics of professional occupations like teaching and public administration—in which women are heavily concentrated—work to modify somewhat what would otherwise be a position of very marked inferiority in professional life.

The most important case in point is that of *lycée professeurs*, of whom 55% were women in the school year 1968–69. In all, 46,307 were *lycée professeurs*, constituting one-quarter of all women in the *cadre supérieur* and liberal professions. *Lycées*, although the stage before university studies, are hardly the same as American high schools. Academically, their last two years are comparable with the first two in superior American colleges. The selection of teachers is rigorous, and requirements are intellectually strenuous. Candidates receive specialized educations in the Ecoles Normales Supérieures, at academic levels higher than that provided in university faculties attended by students of the same age. Both *lycée* and university *professeurs* usually pass a difficult competitive examination, the *agrégation*, requiring several years of preparation and testing general culture as well as specialized knowledge. Teaching staffs in *lycées* are organized in a hierarchy of ranks, and high rank is achieved both by seniority and by indications of professional achievement. These schools are understood to be vehicles of high culture, and successful completion of such a school

---

are *ouvrières*. (All descriptive statistics not otherwise attributed have been drawn from 5% samples of census data; these figures are drawn from the 1968 census.)

[4] Other "leaders" in this respect are Finland (42% in 1960), Denmark (38% in 1967), and the United States (36% in 1967).

provides an automatic entitlement to university admission. Thus, *lycée* teaching is clearly assimilated to university education rather than lower education; it represents an arduous and prestigious achievement. *Lycée professeurs* are widely regarded as representatives of science and culture in a society where official values accord high status to these domains. That half of these *professeurs* are women meets an abstract criterion of equality without devaluating the profession by "overfeminizing" it, in a society in which women are not admitted on equal terms to the highest occupational ranks. In both qualitative and quantitative senses, then, *lycée* teaching represents a most significant professional area available to women, one essentially lacking in American society.[5]

Similar considerations apply to *instituteurs*. In 1962, 72% of these were women (Ministère de l'Education National 1968–69)—certainly a high proportion but lower than the comparable figure for primary school teachers in the United States, which is more than 90% (Institut National de la Statistique et des Etudes Economiques [INSEE]). As representatives of culture in a society which officially holds its culture to be a national treasure, their prestige benefits; also, their professional preparation is clearly superior to that of their American counterparts.[6] Thus, at all levels of state-supported teaching below the university, but particularly in *lycées*, teaching careers open to women are significantly more professionalized than their American counterparts.

There remain the universities. As is well known, the distinction between academic ranks is far sharper than in the United States, with the professoriat constituting by far a smaller fraction of the total teaching staff, and exercising distinctive kinds of authority.[7] In these ranks, women are indeed few—less than 2% in the faculties of law and medicine, 4.5% in the *facultés des lettres* (teaching literature, philosophy, and social science), and 6% in the science faculties. However, below the professorial rank—at instructional levels which in rights and relative compensation rank below associate and assistant professors in the American system—the proportion of women jumps to 25% (reaching 35% in the *facultés des lettres*)

[5] Conditions of employment and compensation have been equal for men and women in *lycée* teaching since 1927. It is important to add, however, that positions of higher administrative authority within *lycées* are dominated by men. *Lycées* are sexually segregated, both as to students and teaching staff—a circumstance that has offered women "built-in" *entrée* to this important profession.

[6] Equality of working conditions among *instituteurs* of both sexes was achieved in 1882. We may note that women staffing the *écoles maternelles*—caring for children between the ages of three and six years—must have achieved essentially the same educational qualifications as *instituteurs* and have often begun advanced studies (Berger 1952).

[7] The rank of university professor usually requires the completion of the *thèse d'Etat*—a degree more strenuous than the American Ph.D that normally requires 10 years for completion.

(Dumas 1965). In the United States in 1961, 9% of university full professors were women, and 16% of the associate professors (Fogarty et al. 1971). Once again, a characteristic pattern emerges—a tiny participation of women at the very highest professional levels but a very considerable presence at the middle levels, one comparing favorably indeed with other Western societies.

Given the significance of academic intellectuals in defining and interpreting the nature of social problems, it is curious that this discrepancy between women's participation at high and low levels of instructional authority within the university has not produced in France an ideological focus upon the special problems of academic women, as it has in the United States. Data are lacking to show how long this sort of discrepancy has characterized French university faculties, but, in any case, the general problems of French universities—overcrowding, concentration of authority in the professorial "mandarinate," restricted opportunities for nonprofessorial staff, and others—have overshadowed concern with the problems of women. None of the major competing interpretations of the universities' difficulties—financial, administrative, Marxist, *gauchiste*, or other—stresses discrimination against women, as compared with such issues as class inequality, generational conflict, disputes about intellectual authority, or insufficient resources.

Apart from teaching, public administration is the other large-scale set of professional opportunities sponsored by the state. Its significance is very great, given the long tradition in France of centralized state administration, the high qualifications required for it, and the prestige surrounding it. Women were first admitted into the civil service at the end of the last century, but it was the First World War which significantly widened their opportunities in the state sector and led to a formal equality of treatment and conditions in most respects. Only after the Second World War, however, were the highest administrative positions made accessible to women, who were admitted to the Ecole Nationale d'Administration, the intellectually rigorous and key point of entry into these posts. As of 1962, 11.2% of the highest administrative positions—finance inspectors, members of the Conseil d'Etat, and others—were women. In the United States as of 1961, the proportion of women in the highest grades of the civil service was 4.4% (Fogarty et al. 1971). Nonetheless, whole ministries—Justice, Foreign Affairs, Finance—have very few women in higher positions, and admission to some administrative careers remains formally closed.[8] Women

---

[8] Women are excluded from the Ecole des Mines, Ecole du Génie Rural, and the Ecole des Eaux et Forets. On the other hand, although data are lacking, their presence at responsible levels in the Ministries of Education, of Labor, and of Health appears to be significant.

are still formally barred from the office of *préfet*—the extremely important representatives of central government in the *départements* into which France is administratively divided. Indeed, the very law which established equal rights for women in the public service provided also for exceptions due to the "physical unfitness" of women and "psychological difficulties which the presence of women might provoke" (Michèl and Texier 1964).[9] Nonetheless, public administration clearly represents an important professional opportunity for women. Among women in positions of high administrative responsibility, three-quarters are in the public service (*Avenir* 1965). Furthermore, the rate at which the number of women administrators among the *cadres supérieurs* is increasing is the highest of any profession; and this rate is double that of the increase among males (OCDE 1970).[10] As of 1962, 21,000 women were at administrative ranks corresponding to the *cadres supérieurs* compared with 172,740 men. The major significance of public administration as a profession for women lies in the *cadres moyens*, where in 1962 there were 79,060 women (and 168,700 men).

We have already observed that the high qualifications and prestige of public administration in France lend it both the aura and the substance of a professional career.[11] But this rather high participation of women professionals in public administration occurs in the context of their low participation in the liberal professions. Law and medicine remain heavily masculine (15% of French physicians are women); and engineering even more so (3% of the latter are women).[12] The achievement of professional women in France is thus very much weighted on the side of public employment, especially in teaching and government administration, at the expense of accomplishment in entrepreneurial and private professions.

Given the "statist" tradition of France—in which, historically, public administration and education have played central roles as stabilizing and conservatizing forces—this means that professional women are largely engaged in the least dynamic and change-oriented aspects of French life. As we shall see below, when analyzing aspects of French culture, this is but one way in which French professional women are particularly affected by the most conservative tendencies in French society. At this point, it is sufficient to point out that in the context of France, professional achievements by women do not necessarily contribute to accelerated social change.

---

[9] "L'inaptitude physique," "les difficultés psychologiques que pourraient soulever une présence féminine" (Michel and Texier 1964).

[10] The rate is even higher in the private sector, where the absolute number of women is smaller.

[11] The substantive benefits are described by Vimont (1965, pp. 23–55).

[12] One percent of architects are women.

ACCESS TO HIGHER EDUCATION IN PROFESSIONAL CAREER LINES

Higher education being an indispensable prerequisite for entry to professional occupations, it is necessary to consider women's access to universities. In these terms, France emerges as among the most egalitarian of European nations: in 1963, 43% of university students were women, compared with 32% in Britain, 35% in Denmark, 24% in Germany, and 22% in Norway (OCDE 1970).[13] And the significant proportion of women among French university students has not been a recent development: from 2.5% in 1900, it grew to 12.5% in 1920, 26% in 1930, and fully 34% at the start of the Second World War. The postwar period saw a slowing of the growth of female representation as the total university population began to expand considerably; from 38% in 1959 it moved to 43% in 1963, where it has roughly remained (UNESCO 1968).

France has thus made higher education available to women on a larger scale, and over a longer period, than has been the case in many other, if not all, Western European countries. However, access of women to higher education in France is largely a function of class inequality. The *grande bourgeoisie* in 1962 represented 4% of the population but 29% of the university students; the *cadres moyens* amounted to 7.8% of the population but 18% of the students (OCDE 1965). Among women university students, the proportion of *bourgeois* origin is higher than among men. Thus, higher education in France consolidates the class position of the *bourgeoisie* more often among women than among men (Bourdieu and Passeron 1964). The daughters of the *bourgeoisie* are more likely to go to universities than the sons of nonmanual occupational strata, let alone of *ouvriers*. Women in France are by no means denied access to professions because they are blocked off from university education. There is a marked discrepancy between their educational opportunities and the extent of their professional achievement. This situation, now developing on a large scale in the United States and some other nations for the first time, has existed in France for decades. Yet women in France have displayed less overt discontent on this account or indeed on any other account that involves woman's place. Tellingly, Simone de Beauvoir's subtle and powerful *De deuxième sexe,* published in 1949, was the first notable occasion on which the problem of women's role was comprehensively raised; by no means restricted to France, it analyzes those aspects of French society which women of Beauvoir's stamp find particularly irksome. In France today, this book can still be regarded as ahead of its time— its impact having been limited to some intellectual and ideological circles—while, in translation, it has been widely read in the English-speaking societies, where

[13] Comparisons with the United States are more difficult, given the far greater heterogeneity of post–high school educational institutions in America than in Western Europe.

the problem was raised decades earlier in both intellectual and agitational terms. To understand why feminist formulations and movements have been so slow to develop in France, we may begin with a discussion of some cultural factors particularly distinctive to French society.

CULTURAL DEFINITIONS OF WOMEN

If it is true that everywhere images of women's nature play a large role in defining and reinforcing "appropriate" roles for them, in no Western society is this more palpably obvious than in France. Surely no other Western culture has developed more elaborated and intricate ideas about women and more closely interwoven them with the "high culture" and the style of life of whole social classes. The two centuries that produced the classical culture of France, the 17th and 18th, also produced a series of women eminent as both sponsors and creators of high culture. Beside such names as la duchesse de Rambouillet, la marquise de Sevigné, Madame de Lafayette, Madame de Maintenon, Mademoiselle de Lespinasse, and Madame de Staël, corresponding figures in Anglo-American culture (Jane Austen and Emily Dickinson, for example) are comparatively pale and late. Women helped shape the core values and the very language that are crucial to the substance of French culture. Such women, of course, were few and highly privileged, flourishing in the setting of an aristocratic social order. The rise of commercial society in the 19th century demoted women from the highest reaches of cultural creativity and participation as key sponsors of culture. Balzac and Flaubert, among others, described the emergence of a new type of woman—a highly elaborated aesthetic object, the property of men, and seeking expression as wife or mistress. "The destiny of woman and her sole glory," writes Balzac in his *Physiologie du mariage,* "is to excite the hearts of men. Woman is a property acquired by contract; she is disposable property, . . . in short, woman properly speaking is only an annex of man" (cited by Beauvoir 1949). Older themes portraying woman as an idealized erotic object, finding fulfillment and power over men in love, certainly persisted; but more significant by far was the new dominance of the domestic ideal, associated above all with the most prosperous *bourgeoisie.* The focus of emotional life became the *foyer*—an idea for which "home" is a weaker equivalent; as an arena for women, the *foyer* was far more restricted and passive than the aristocratic milieu.[14]

It would be anachronistic to regard this development solely as a decrease of *bourgeois* women's power. On the contrary, their enhanced role within

[14] A succinct contrast of *bourgeois* and aristocratic notions of women and family life is found in Barber (1955, pp. 78–81). For more extended statements, see the essays by Xavier Lannes and Jean Maitron on the 18th and first half of the 19th centuries, respectively, in Prigent (1954). A large historical view is offered by Ariès (1962, esp. pt. 3).

the family—the expectation of being loved, some responsibility for the rearing and education of children—represented a significant improvement. Until about the middle of the 18th century, *bourgeois* and aristocratic women had little or nothing to do in these terms. On the whole, they neither reared children nor administered households; these tasks were discharged by servants, nurses, and tutors under the ultimate direction of husbands. Ironically, in view of later developments, among the first conquests and achievements of higher-status women in France was the role of *maîtresse de maison* (see Sullerot 1968). (The very phrase, the counterpart of *maître de maison,* differs from the English "housewife" [*ménagère*]; it implies an important and distinct role in the administration of the home as a social and moral entity.) We shall see that the impact of this "achievement" is still meaningful among *bourgeois* women in contemporary France. To appreciate this, we must understand the historical and cultural aspects of prevalent ideology about the family and women's place in it as they evolved in France.

After the Bourbon Restoration of 1815, conservative ideologists elaborated a social philosophy which defined the domestic, nuclear family as a major element of social stability. This represented a shift in the alleged basis of social stability from earlier emphases upon the extended aristocratic lineage, public ties of dependence and obligation based upon locality, the "corporations" of artisans and merchants, the parish, and other groupings—all of them larger than the domestic family and, of course, excluding women from significant power. The influential conservative Bonald, for example, worked out such a theory, comparing domestic authority with fundamental social and political authority, and assigning to women a subordinate but vital place in the newly significant domestic scheme.[15]

Such values, however, were very far from the exclusive property of the Catholic reaction. Rousseau, seminal both for Romanticism and the Enlightenment, called for domesticated, loving motherhood, even to the point of having mothers nurse their own children—a suggestion ridiculed in the aristocratic *salons* as an expression of "les vanités de la mamelle."[16] The

[15] "L'homme est à la femme ce que la femme est à l'enfant; ou le pouvoir [sovereign authority] est au ministre, ce que le ministre est au sujet" (cited by Beauvoir 1949, p. 186). As we have observed it was a *gain* for women to be regarded as "ministers" in Bonald's sense. (This did not prevent Bonald from describing the adultery of men as a cause only of personal unhappiness to wives, while that of wives represented the destruction of the family—a widespread French perspective.) On the distinctive contribution of the domestic family to social order in Bonald's thought, see his "Du divorce consideré au XIXe siècle relativement à l'état domestique et à l'état public de la société" (in Bonald 1864, esp. chaps. 2, 3, 4). At more popular levels, comparable images of the family and women's role were promulgated during the Restoration with unprecedented scope and intensity. See Deniel (1965).

[16] Awkwardly translated, at best, as "the conceit of breasts" (Sullerot 1968, p. 80).

apostle of rational progress, Comte, saw women as inferior by reason of their "biological childishness" (*infantilisme biologique*). He rather vaguely sentimentalized them as morally superior to men, but saw men as stronger "not only in body, but also in intellect [*esprit*] and character. . . . We must above all act and think, struggling against the difficulties of our real destiny; thus, men must command, despite their lesser morality" (Comte 1848, p. 204). Comte, like Rousseau and Bonald, saw woman's chief role and contribution as lying in the *foyer,* in the education of children and the refinement of emotional impulses. Like Rousseau's, his definition of women's role was not seen as reactionary and retrograde but was linked to a vision of progress. "In order to assure [woman's] emotional destiny," Comte wrote, man must make woman's life "more and more domestic," and "above all detach her from all outside work. . . . *The man must feed the woman*: this is the natural law of our species" (Comte 1848, pp. 242–43). To grasp how such a vision could possibly be understood as expressing a kind of liberating progress, the briefest excursion into Comtean thinking is necessary. For him, the domestication of women was a phase of progress in emotional life—part of the grand Comtean vision—in which society would pass from family arrangements, like those of aristocracy, linking it to the past; move on to the new type of voluntary, conjugal, and domestic arrangement linking it to the present and the living; and finally arrive at "paternal" impulses expressing a "universal sociability" linking humanity to the future (Comte 1848, p. 91). Such perspectives may seem obscure, muddled, or quaint; but only by grasping them do we understand how the domesticizing of higher-status women in France was understood as a form of progress rather than a regressive and reactionary development.

Perhaps the most indigenously French founder of the European Left, Proudhon, was a fervent mysogynist. Woman was fit only to choose between being "mistress or housewife" (*courtisane ou ménagère*).[17] Her inferiority was intrinsic, not conditioned; in the family—as much the cell of social stability, in Proudhon's thought, as in the reactionary Bonald's—her task was to educate children in moral duty, but "under paternal sanction," since she was only a "living reflection, her mission [being] to embody, simplify and transmit to young minds the father's thought."

Even Emile Durkheim, later in the century, explained some sex differences in suicide rates as a function of women's less complex and sensitive

---

Rousseau's family doctrine is found chiefly in his didactic novels, *Emile* and *La nouvelle Héloise* and included, it must be noted, a parallel domestication of men.

17 Proudhon did not regard the woman question lightly. In his *De la justice dans la Révolution et dans l'Eglise* (1858) he devoted 300 pages to "Amour et mariage"; just before his death, he wrote another 270 pages replying to female critics, under the title *La pornocratie; ou les femmes dans les temps modernes* (see Maitron 1954).

emotional character, requiring lessened dependence upon social control.[18]

Neither a radical thinker like Fourier nor, more important, writers in the mainstream of French Marxism or socialism subscribed to these perspectives. Attacking the *bourgeois* family, they included women's subjection among the evils of capitalist society. But French Marxism has always interpreted the subjection of women in a context of class conflict. The powerful emphasis on class themes in French social protest has operated to discourage specifically "feminist" diagnoses of women's situation such as those characteristic of England and America. As we have seen, such advantages as higher-status women do enjoy in France—in state employment and access to higher education—are indeed strongly linked to the political and social status quo. The problems of lower-status women have characteristically been assimilated to a class- rather than a women-centered definition of the situation.

We see that important representatives of widely diverse and opposed French thought—Catholic conservatives, Romantic individualists, scientific progressivists, antibourgeois polemicists—have all agreed, in different tones and in different perspectives, on the value or necessity of women's domestic and subordinate mission. There was no French counterpart to the role played by a John Stuart Mill in the struggle for women's rights in the 19th century. The dominant conservative impulses found wide echo, and still do. "She is to charm, console, understand. Her role is that of a helpful, available assistant, but without initiative. She exists essentially in relation to others; her place in the scheme of things is not in the outside world of action, but in the privacy of the home, where she arranges and prepares the times of relaxation" (Chombart de Lauwe 1963, p. 120). Thus does a sociologist, summing up contemporary research findings, describe the modal image of women in France.

To assess this image only as passive and self-effacing is to underestimate its strength and appeal. It also provides a positive role for woman, interpreting her familial functions as crucial rather than ornamental, dignified rather than subordinate. Thus, the woman becomes the agent of high culture within the domestic circle—not only in substantive terms that provide a function for women's education—but also as teacher and exemplar of *la politesse* to children—a concept of far greater social scope and cultural resonance than its American analogues, 'politeness" or "good manners." This value complex is strongest in the *bourgeoisie*. Thus, we will

[18] "Her sensibility is rudimentary rather than highly developed. As she lives outside of community existence more than man, she is less penetrated by it; society is less necessary to her because she is less impregnated by sociability. With a few devotional practises and some animals to care for, the old unmarried women's life is full. . . . Man, on the contrary, is hard beset in this respect. . . . Because he is a more complex social being, he can maintain his equilibrium only by finding more points of support outside himself" (Durkheim 1951, pp. 215–16).

see below, familistic definitions of woman's role are strongest precisely in that stratum which, in Anglo-American societies, is among the least familistic.

Such values were, until very recently, strongly reflected in French laws. The Napoleonic Code, drawing often on Roman models, found both precedent and conceptual imagery for reaffirming the domestic hegemony of the *pater,* and conceiving of women only in a domestic context. Until 1938, women could not work, attend universities, or participate in decisions about childrens' education, without their husbands' permission; husbands were administrators of their wives' property and wealth; women were defined, with the criminal, the insane, and children, as legally "unfit." The Napoleonic Code defined the obedience of wives to husbands as a legal obligation. After 1938, only a successful request for a special form of marriage contract could prevent husbands from being invested with total ownership of family property, including that owned by women before marriage; in recent years, about three-quarters of French women have been married without making such requests. Husbands are still legally defined as the *chef de la communauté* and *chef de famille*—both much more extensive notions than "head of the family." In France, it has been secular law, not religious ritual, that proclaimed the wife's duty to "obey the man." As *chef de la communauté* he was entitled to make major financial, educational, and other decisions without consulting the wife. Until 1965, when some reforms were introduced, wives needed the formal consent of husbands to work outside the home or to buy on credit; even those reforms left many of the husbands' privileges untouched.[19]

Thus, married women in France have long suffered from legal disabilities. Yet French values assign far higher social esteem to the married than the unmarried woman; the single state is regarded as deeply anomalous for women, and nowhere except in deviant subcultures is it identified with notions of freedom and self-determination. These values are not peculiar to France, of course, but are especially deep there. A forceful indicator of their strength is found in a recently enacted law providing that all women

[19] A good summary of these aspects of French law is given in Michael and Texier (1964, pp. 71–106). They led, in the words of these authorities, to a situation in which "a sane wife is never the [legal] equal of a mad husband" (p. 73). The concept of the *foyer* and of women's place in it is clearly expressed in an aspect of French marriage law which provided that adultery by husbands was punishable only by light sanctions, unless the offense was actually committed in his home, in which case it was cause for divorce. Adultery by wives anywhere was cause for divorce and sometimes imprisonment. The backwardness of French law on women is hardly restricted to family life. Women did not receive the right to vote until 1945, when their participation in the Resistance was frequently cited as justification for enfranchising them. They thus received, after the Second World War, what American and British women received after the First World War without having had to become heroines or martyrs to do so.

over the age of 25 are entitled to be addressed as *Madame,* even if unmarried; and that an unmarried woman above that age who is persistently
addressed as *Mademoiselle* may bring legal action for slander.[20] Thus,
single women in France have traditionally been subject to social depriva-
tions, and married women, to legal ones. Expressive of these attitudes were
debates that occurred in the French Assembly after World War I, on the
subject of enfranchising women: it was argued, in opposition, that the vote
should be given to unmarried but not to married women, on the grounds
that married women could not be "political individuals" with wills other
than those of their husbands. This reverses the view, conventional in
England and America, that the married are in general more "mature" or
"responsible" than the unmarried.[21]

To call these perspectives "traditional" would suggest an unbroken
continuity that, as we have seen, distorts history. In fact, they are linked
above all to a class which only developed in the 19th century, the
bourgeoisie; and this historical association is strongly manifested in contemporary data on the distribution of family values and behavior in French
society. Repeatedly, the *bourgeoisie* emerges as *more* "traditional" in these
areas than the *classe moyenne* or the working class. Thus, *the very class
whose cultural, economic, and social advantages are such as to render many
of its women qualified candidates for professional careers is that least
disposed to approve and provide for women's work outside the home.*

The data are striking indeed—perhaps especially to American readers
who are likely to think of higher social status and education as implying
greater approval for the equality of women. In France, the percentage of
women who play significant roles in decisions about the family budget is
15% among the *bourgeoisie,* 53% for the *classe moyenne,* and 78% in the
working class. The lower the social class, the more likely men are to help
in domestic tasks. The higher the class, the more women's working outside
the home is perceived as incompatible with the obligations of family life
(Chombart de Lauwe 1963, p. 158).

In professional strata, the strength of the *femme au foyer* image remains
very strong. Among professional women with at least one child, two-thirds
think it wise to remain at home while children are small (Andrieux 1962,
pp. 351 ff.). It is not unduly speculative to imagine the psychic cost to
those professional women who, accepting this ideology, continue careers
through this stage of the life cycle. The great majority of these women

[20] These provisions contrast sharply with the emergence of "Ms." as a form of address
that ignores marital status, in the United States, or the general use of "Miss" as a
way to gain the attention of receptionists, sales personnel, and waitresses.

[21] In Britain the vote was, in fact, extended during the 1920s to women in two stages,
beginning with those above the age of 28, with no attention paid to marital status.
Thus, in Britain it was considered anomalous for *younger* women, and in France, for
married women, to vote.

regard their family roles as requiring a full-time commitment. Not only familistic but "women-of-cultivated-leisure" imagery is very strong: 59% of professional women express the desire to cease work in order to pursue cultural interests after children have left the home (Andrieux 1962, pp. 351 ff.). Thus, professional commitments among French women are accompanied both by familistic commitments and the attractions of a consummatory attitude to culture as a substitute for a professional career.

That this "traditionalism" is apparently especially strong among the *bourgeoisie* means that there is a greater tendency for women professionals to come from the *classe moyenne,* who are more disposed to utilize higher education as a means of social mobility and comparatively less inhibited by such values (Chombart de Lauwe 1963, pp. 197–205). Thus, the greatest opportunities for professional advances have been made available to those women whose class and family styles are least likely to encourage serious professional commitments. Indeed, among the few women who have achieved the highest positions in the professional civil service, the proportion of unmarried ones is extremely high—50% (Vimont 1965, pp. 23–52). In France, the claims of family and profession are incompatible for women to a degree extraordinary in a modern society. Each is treated as sovereign, making the kind of claims upon life and being that do not easily tolerate the coexistence of the other.

CONCLUSIONS

Characterized by strong commitments to abstract equality and universalism, France has long evolved a richly wrought set of conservatively defined roles and values governing the social existence of women. These values have continuing and compelling influence.[22] Their fulfillment is conceived as rewarding, not merely as restrictive and constraining, by many French women. The role of the women in the *foyer,* especially in the more advantaged classes likely to furnish higher proportions of professionals, is charged with satisfying content, psychologically and culturally. Even among those who choose professional life, the competing tug of the *femme au foyer* remains strong.

But French women have also achieved considerable professional success and have long enjoyed access—within the limits of overarching class inequalities—to free higher education. As we have seen, many of their successes are within the context of state-sponsored activity. Indeed, there is a sense in which the state has created the professional women in France.

---

[22] The continuing social conservatism of French women can be shown by their disproportionate electoral support for the parties of order and hierarchy in postwar France, regardless of age or social class. The number of women in elective office at all levels has, in fact, declined considerably since a high point after the Liberation (see Duhamel 1971).

Thus, the extent and nature of women's professional activities reflects the characteristic French cleavage between the society's modal social values, on the one hand, and those of the French state, on the other—a difference that has led some to describe France as an "administered" rather than a "governed" society. In these respects, the professional successes of French women run against the grain of the culture, in much the same way as the universalism of the French government has often ignored or overridden the localism, Catholicism, and individualism of the French people.

This sort of state-sponsored success for women's professional aspirations involves considerable costs. It fails, of course, to eliminate the tensions and limits imposed by the continuing cultural conservatism of French society with respect to women's place and role. Indeed, given the great gap in France between those values suffusing government and public administration and those of the society, the professional aspirations of many women can be seen as diverted into insulated and conservative sectors of French life.

We saw earlier that French women made a large advance into the professional labor market after the First World War, but that there were signs of a decline or stagnation in the situation after the Second World War. Rapid defeat and occupation meant that France did not experience prolonged mobilization of the domestic economy, unlike other Western nations during 1939–45. The French economy since 1945 has grown at a rate that has not compelled a major "talent hunt" among women for scarce aptitudes required in newly emerging specialties. Men have only slowly, if at all, "abandoned" the less dynamic professional careers to women, as might happen to a greater extent in a more rapidly growing economy (we have seen a few signs of this in the sex patterns of professional employment in government and the private sector).

Despite the holding of an "Estates-General" of Women at Versailles in the fall of 1970—an event which surprised many by the vigor and clarity of the complaints and demands that the delegates and leaders manifested—there is little sign of the emergence of a modern women's movement in search of expanded opportunities. Forces of the Left—above all, the Communist party—are slow to deal with the question of women's rights, least of all those of women professionals. Themes of protest center on the rigidities of administration in government and institutions; the insufficiency of resources for education, housing, and transport; inflation and the slow rate of economic growth; and the maldistribution of wealth and income in a society that has not become significantly less socially hierarchical in the postwar period. The few groups—among them, weak and scattered *gauchistes*—who raise the issue of women's role as such, often in accents borrowed from contemporary American polemic, are barely heard and widely ignored.

In such a setting, the prospects for an expansion of professional opportunities for women are not encouraging. Whether one defines the situation as depressing or moderately promising is a matter of personal style and social ideology. But, in any event, it seems unlikely that the weight of French tradition in the matter of women will be rapidly lightened in the decades to come. The limited and deeply ambiguous "success" of French professional women is likely to endure for some time.

REFERENCES

Andrieux, Cécile. 1962. "Ideologies traditionelle et moderne dans les attitudes sòciales feminines." Thèse de troisième cycle, Université de Paris.
Ariès, Phillipe. 1962. *Centuries of Childhood*. London: Cape.
Avenir. "Les carrières feminines" (April–May 1965).
Barber, Elinor. 1955. *The French Bourgeoisie in the Eighteenth Century*. Princeton, N.J.: Princeton University Press.
Beauvoir, Simone de. 1949. *Le deuxième sexe*. Paris: Gallimard.
Berger, Ida. 1952. *Les maternelles*. Paris: Centre d'Etudes Sociologiques.
Bonald, Louis de. 1864. "Du divorce considéré au XIXᵉ siècle relativement à l'état domestique et à l'état public de société." In *Oeuvres complètes*. Vol. 2. Paris: Migne.
Bourdieu, Pierre, and J. C. Passeron. 1964. *Les héritiers*. Paris: Editions de Minuit.
Chombart de Lauwe, Paul-Henry. 1963. *La femme dans la société: Son image dans différents milieux*. Paris: Centre Nationale de la Recherche Scientifique.
Comte, Auguste. 1848. *Discours sur l'ensemble du positivisme*. Paris: Mathias.
Deniel, Raymond. 1965. *Une image de la famille et de la société sous la Restauration (1815–1830)*. Paris: Editions Ouvrières.
Duhamel, Alain. 1971. "Les femmes et la politique." *Monde* (March 10).
Duhet, Paul-Marie. 1971. *Les femmes et la Révolution*. Paris: Juillard.
Dumas, Francine. 1965. "La femme dans la vie sociale." In *Femmes du XXᵉ siècle*. Paris: Presses Universitaires de France.
Durkheim, Emile. (1897) 1951. *Suicide*. Trans. John Spaulding and George Simpson. Glencoe, Ill.: Free Press.
Fogarty, Michael, et al. 1971. *Sex, Career and Family*. Beverly Hills, Calif.: Sage.
Institut National de la Statistique et des Etudes Economiques (INSEE). 1970. *Annuaire statistique de la France*. Paris.
Maitron, Jean. 1954. "Les penseurs sociaux et la famille dans la première moitié du XXᵉ siècle." In *Renouveau des idées sur la famille*, edited by Robert Prigent. Paris: Presses Universitaires de France.
Michèl, Andrée, and Geneviève Texier. 1964. *La condition de la française aujourd'hui*. Paris: Gauthier.
Ministère de l'Education Nationale. 1968–69. *Le personnel de l'enseignement public. Statistique des enseignants*. No. 3 (1). Paris.
Organisation de la Coopération et du Dévelopment Economique. 1965. *Origines sociales des professeurs et instituteurs*. Paris: Direction des Affaires Scientifiques.
————. 1968. *Enseignement primaire et secondaire*. Paris: Direction des Affaires Scientifiques.
————. 1970. *L'emploi des femmes*. Paris: Seminaire Syndicale Regional.
Organisation Internationale du Travail. 1967. *Annuaire statistique du travail*. Paris.
Prigent, Robert, ed. 1954. *Renouveau des idées sur la famille*. Paris: Presses Universitaires de France.
Sullerot, Evelyne. 1968. *Histoire et sociologie du travail feminin*. Paris: Presses Universitaires de France.
UNESCO. 1968. *World Survey of Education*. Paris: UNESCO.
Vimont, Claude. 1965. "Un enquête sur les femmes fonctionnaires." *Population* (January-February), pp. 22–55.

NANCY DATAN

34

Your Daughters Shall Prophesy: Ancient and Contemporary Perspectives on The Women of Israel [1]

Israel, where feminists coexist uncomfortably with traditionalism and orthodoxy, contains a broad spectrum of dramatically contrasting life-styles; and these contrasts, I believe, can provide some unique insights into the changing meanings of female and male which are evolving out of today's movements for women's rights. My contribution to the issue of women's liberation is a set of paradoxes which I encountered as an American woman and a social scientist who immigrated to Israel, and there participated in a cross-cultural study of 1200 women of five Israeli sub-cultures, ranging from modern European Jewish immigrants to traditional Arab Muslim villagers. [2]

Before I contrast ancient and contemporary role expectations for the women in Israel and the peculiar consequences my colleagues and I have discovered, I would like to highlight some of the contrasts between the worlds of American and Israeli women. In the United States, Shirley Chisholm's declaration of candidacy elicited the question, "Is this country ready for a woman president?" That question was not asked in Israel when Golda Meir stepped into the office of Prime Minister - yet when one says "husband and wife" in Hebrew, one says "ba'al v'ishah" - owner and woman; and among the standard congratulatory telegram forms, one may say to the parents of a new-born baby girl, "A firstborn

[1]In: Michael Curtis and Mordecai Chertoff (eds.). Israel: Social Structure and Change. New Brunswick, NJ: Transaction Books (1973).

[2]The study was directed by Aaron Antonovsky of the Israel Institute of Applied Social Research; Benjamin Maoz of the Beilinson Medical Center was project codirector. The study was supported by a grant from the U.S. National Institute of Mental Health (P.L. 480 Agreement No. 06-276-2).

daughter is a sign of many sons." In brief, then, in Israel one sees that a woman of ability can rise to the head of government - side by side with indications that, among certain sectors of the population, women are emphatically the second sex.

Recently there has been some criticism within Israel of the self-righteous smugness of Israeli women who have, by and large, disdained the American women's movement. Shulamit Aloni (1971) claims that their disdain is increasingly unjustified. It is true that in Israel a framework of progressive legislation is already present; and Mrs. Aloni notes almost in passing that in the professions and in the universities success is as open to women as to men, both because there is no discrimination by sex and because the recent history of the state includes the tradition of the dynamic, pioneering woman. Before I move to her criticisms, I want to point out that these are exactly the goals toward which the American Women's Liberation Movement is striving, and of course Israel is sometimes described as a feminist's utopia.

Shulamit Aloni, however, argues that the achievements of the early pioneers are steadily being eroded by a number of factors: the hardships of the early days, when the scarcity of manpower forced women into the fields and onto the frontiers, have given way to comparative affluence. Affluence has in turn permitted women to withdraw from the labour market, and simultaneously led to a trend in advertising oriented toward the woman as consumer in a life-style of leisure. Mrs. Aloni concludes that the women of Israel need to be responsive to the world-wide women's rebellion while it is still true that no rebellion is needed in Israel, and while there is still time to achieve equality of status merely by exercising rights already written into the laws of the land.

While I support this position in most respects, I find the collapse of the Israeli feminist revolution - which is paralleled by a decline in American

feminism from 1920 until quite recently - intriguing rather than dismaying.
It suggests that equality of opportunity will not lead at once to the disappearance of sex-role differentiation, and it raises the possibility that there may be
something of value in traditional sex roles.

I want to note briefly some of the ancient Judaic traditions which affect
women, and the transformations which took place a century ago in Europe. Then
I want to describe some reasonable expectations and some peculiar findings which
came out of research on Israeli women of modern and traditional cultures which
was carried out by Aaron Antonovsky, Benjamin Maoz, and myself. Next, I shall
describe some of the facets of contemporary Israeli life which illustrate not a
single, liberated female role model, but rather a complex, conflicting, and
contradictory set of role models in Israel today. Finally, I want to offer the
germ of a theory about male and female roles and some personal speculation about
the implications of this theory for the observations I have made about Israeli
culture.

Israel is the land which gave Western civilization its traditions of male
dominance and female subordination. The traditional sex roles are expressed in
Genesis as Adam and Eve are expelled from the Garden of Eden: Eve is told, "In
sorrow thou shalt bring forth thy children; the desire shall be to thy husband
and he shall rule over thee," and Adam is told, "In the sweat of thy face shalt
thou eat bread." With the passing of time, men's sweat is mitigated by modern
industrial technology, and modern medicine mitigates women's woe in childbirth;
most recent of all has been the challenge to the husband's rule.

There are a number of facets of Orthodox Judaism which are, according to
most anthropological criteria (Bart, 1967), constraints on women, and indicative
of male dominance and female subordination: these include the traditional
bride-price, menstrual separation, ritual periods of uncleanness following

childbirth - and the fact that the period of uncleanness is twice as long for the birth of a daughter as for a son.

Judaic ritual was very little altered until the period of enlightenment in Europe. A movement to reform Jewish religious practices grew up in Central Europe in the nineteenth century: women no longer sat to worship in the screened, secluded gallery, but sat together with men; the elaborate network of sexual and menstrual taboos was simplified and reduced, with more room for individual variation in ritual observance. These changes signified a rejection of the traditional subordinate status of women set out in Biblical codes (Learsi, 1966).

Simultaneously with the movement for religious reform in Judaism, in nineteenth century Europe the economic changes which accompanied increasing urbanization led to a strong movement for equality of women's rights, and in turn women began to achieve prominence in a number of areas. Although there was a high proportion of Jewish women in the movement for emancipation, no specific large-scale Jewish women's movement existed until the twentieth century with the reappearance of anti-semitism (Sacher, 1958; Roth, 1961).

Israel's primary role models, of course, were the women of Russia who immigrated in the Second Aliyah, between 1905 and 1914, bringing with them a pioneering ideology, secular and egalitarian, which was perfectly suited to the circumstances of the land: dry, or swampy, or rocky: available for redemption only through the marshalling of all available human resources. Radical changes in sex roles occurred in the pioneering period, well-known to everyone who has taken an interest in the kibbutz: childrearing was collective, freeing women to share the duties of heavy labour and military defense. Men did not, however, take the primary responsibility for childrearing by becoming child caretakers, so we might say in a sense that the kibbutzim, at least at first, masculinized everyone in the service of egalitarianism.

The pioneering farmwomen were joined by the subsequent wave on immigration from Central Europe in the 1930's; this second stream brought an alternate model of the emancipated woman, professional rather than farmer. A number of forces converged at this point in the history of Israel to support and further the emancipation of women from their traditional roles; and at the time of the founding of the State, a number of fundamental laws were passed guaranteeing equal rights irrespective of sex.

It should be pointed out, however, that coexisting with these poineering women who are so familiar to us were groups of women who were quite traditional in various ways. There were devout, orthodox Jews of Central Europe, who were as highly educated as their secular, pioneering counterparts, but continued to observe religious ritual. There were Jews from Near Eastern countries, where no comparable movement for religious reform had occurred, and where the movement for the emancipation of women which had occurred in Europe a hundred years ago was only beginning in the Near East at the start of this century. Finally, there were traditional Arab Muslim villagers, whose life style has been compared by Raphael Patai (1959) to that of the Biblical Hebrews.

Aaron Antonovsky, Benjamin Maoz, and I carried out a study of 1200 Israeli women from five ethnic groups which represent varying degrees of modernization. We studied modern, urban Europeans; transitional Turks, Persians, and North Africans; and traditional Arab villagers. Our study did not include kibbutz women or significant numbers of devout but highly educated Europeans, or modern, urban Muslim or Christian Arabs, so many fascinating questions about various subtle facets of modernity and the revolution in women's roles in Israel were not tested in our research.

We were interested in a rather straightforward issue: what is the effect of the degree of modernity on a woman's success in adapting to the changes in middle age? We had some tentative hypotheses as we began our work. My male colleagues felt that the traditional woman would adapt more successfully: she had borne a large family; she could expect to rise to the status of matriarch, with authority over her sons' wives and greater personal freedom than before. Conversely and certainly not by chance, I was convinced that the modern woman would adapt more successfully: she had alternate roles and was not dependent on motherhood for self-esteem, so the departure of children from the home would pose no crisis. Support could be found for either viewpoint in the conflicting literature on the psychology of women.

It should be stressed that we all expected that the degree of modernity would bear a linear relationship to the measure of adaptation; we differed in the direction of our predictions. Some of our findings have been reported in detail elsewhere (Datan et al., 1970; Maoz et al., 1970; Datan, 1971, Datan, 1972; Antonovsky et al., 1971); for the purposes of the present paper, I simply want to describe the fate of our predictions. On such measures as social role satisfaction, psychological well-being, and response to menopause, we obtained a fairly clear answer to the question of the effect of the degree of modernity on the success of adaptation to middle age. It turned out that each theory was half right: the most successful adaptation was seen at the two poles of the traditionalism-modernity continuum - among the Arabs and the Europeans.

With the wisdom of hindsight, we all wondered why we could not have foreseen this pattern as the most likely. Clearly the Europeans and the Arabs, despite the dislocations of World War II and the Israeli wars of Independence, Sinai, and 1967, were living in relatively stable environments in terms of cultural

continuity. It may be surmised that the transitional women were subject to a
particular stress in that cultural cues learned in childhood and young adulthood no longer serve them. The immigrant European entered a society where the
dominant cultural values were those of enlightened European Jewry; the Arab
woman, like the immigrant Near Eastern Jew, also witnessed the penetration of
new life styles, but change came more gradually into the villages. The
transitional women, born in countries where the transformation from folkways to
modernization was taking place fairly rapidly, were then transplanted to a
country where modernization was complete and their relatively traditional
life styles were outmoded; their greater negativism may have been due to the
stress of meeting the demands of a modern environment with outmoded responses.

As we move from traditional through transitional to modern groups in this
study, we see the emergence of the woman from a position of subordination and
subservience to a more egalitarian status. In general, the process of modernization has been associated with raised psychological well-being (Lerner, 1958).
Many factors are involved in this pattern: socioeconomic status rises with
modernization; furthermore, even most of the traditional villagers have some
exposure to the mass media, and therefore some awareness that the world is
moving on while they are not, that material comforts are available but not to
them - and that their children may move forward to achieve these comforts and in
rejecting traditional folkways perhaps reject their parents as well. Yet in our
study, the transition toward modernity, and with it emancipation and liberation,
did not by itself bring about improved psychological well-being: on the
contrary, as I have remarked elsewhere (1972), the process of liberation appears
costly and painful.

At one level of interpretation, I have suggested that modern and traditional
women are alike in that each is adapted to her environment, with the appropriate

skills for manipulation. Magic and ritual evolved as tools for control, the
primitive forerunners of a professional education: both groups of women, then,
are educated for achievement, each in her own way. This is certainly an adequate
explanation of our data, and indeed, we do not have sufficient exploratory,
descriptive data to permit any more elaborated explanations.

However, I have been intrigued by the similarity in successful adaptation
seen at the two extremes of the traditionalism-modernity continuum in our study,
and my exposure to the American Women's Liberation Movement over the past year
and a half in the United States has sensitized me still further to the puzzles of
bisexuality. Accordingly, I have some speculations to offer about some aspects
of maleness and femaleness which I have observed under the special conditions of
dramatic contrast which obtain in Israel.

In addition to the legally prescribed favouritism shown to males, Israel
is guilty of many practices which discriminate between men and women. The
language itself discriminates: Hebrew is a highly inflected language and one
cannot make a simple declaration such as "I work" without simultaneously declaring
one's sex through the form of the verb. Just as in English, the generalized
singular pronoun is "he" - but worse than that, there is no common plural gender
in Hebrew corresponding to the English "they" or "them", so that if there is a
gathering in Israel of nuclear physicists, comprising two hundred women and one
man, the press will use the masculine plural to describe the crowd.

I would like to suggest, however, that discrimination between men and women
is not inevitably discrimination against women. Only where sex is inextricably
bound to status does it seem necessary to strive for the elimination of sex-based
differentiation. I have previously noted that the kibbutzim, even at their most
revolutionary, always assigned women to the children's houses, and I have heard

American feminists criticize this practice as discriminatory. What is not obvious to an American audience is that the role of caretaker is very much prized, and so women seek to achieve it, rather than seeking to be liberated from it. On a similar note, a Communist Chinese woman declared, "The education of children is directly related to the liberation of women," and I agree, but she went on to say, "Women used to worry about how to run a family and serve her husband, but now our great ambition is to make revolution." I don't think that is the liberating message in the excellent system of pre-school education in China or in Israel. Rather, a nation which cares so intensely about the education of its children is raising the status of its women in a far more essential way than merely by "liberating" them from child care: it is affirming their irreplacable importance as childbearers by sharing in the process of child rearing. And before we assume that all societies are deeply concerned for their children, we might recall that the schools of Chicago were scheduled to close for twelve days in December 1971 because no public funds could be found to meet the educational budget.

One of the paradoxes of the feminist revolution on the Israeli kibbutzim was that women aspired to the role of caretaker in the children's house. This is in no way inconsistent with the emphasis Judaism has always placed on the education of its children, but it is inconsistent with the apparent aim of the kibbutzim to achieve complete egalitarianism in sex roles. It suggests, in fact, that when the traditional role of housekeeper-mother does not entail secondary status, it exerts a powerful attraction even to pioneers and revolutionaries, and this in turn helps to explain the endurance of traditions which appear to discriminate against women without any obvious compensation.

Arguments against sex discrimination have by now become public currency. I
don't dare argue in a public forum _for_ sex discrimination of any sort, because
the issue has become so polarized that I would find myself in the company of a
number of ideological bedfellows whose views I do not share in any way. However,
I have begun to feel that the continual, rather tense interplay between tradition
and liberation in Israel serves a number of functions. First, tradition defines
the status of women with absolute clarity. This has two consequences: for the
traditional woman, a viable set of guidelines is provided for a role which,
although it is secondary in status, is vital to family functioning.

The best illustration of the breadth of ritual expectations is in the verses
"Eshet hayil," a woman of valour, whose price is above rubies. The woman of
these verses is very different from the current stereotype of the traditional
woman, for she not only sees to the household but conducts a thriving business in
linen with the Canaanites - in short, she is exercising a broad range of talents
in a variety of roles both domestic and economic. To repeat: she is not
"confined" to the household; more likely, her energies and abilities are
stretched as far as they will go, within _and_ outside the home. This has been
true of traditional women generally, and it is only when industrialization and
urbanization remove most of the traditional woman's economic and domestic
functions that we begin to see the stereotype emerge: a woman confined, whose
energies are going to waste. However, Orthodox Judaism continues to provide
vital roles for women with regard to religious ritual, and my observation -
although I would like to see the question systematically tested by research-
is that Orthodox Judaism provides sustenance for women as well as men.

However, feminists, myself included, are bound to remark that certain
meanings in the very beautiful verses of "eshet hayil" emerge more clearly if

it is altered slightly and we recite, "A man of valour, who can find? for his price is above rubies." There is no question at all in my mind that no man would want his price discussed - no matter how high it is fixed - for it immediately raises the question, as it should, who is doing the buying and selling?

This leads me to the second consequence of the clear traditional prescriptions on the status of women. While the traditional woman is obviously given a definite set of guidelines, paradoxically, I believe, the woman who is seeking a new self-definition is also aided by the clarity of tradition. By contrast to American women, who currently oppose not only legal inequities but also a set of diffuse, invisible constraints in the unspoken American role models, and are forced to extremes of protest in order to make these contraints visible at all, those who oppose the status of women in Judaism deal with specific instances where women and men do not have equality. I have begun to feel that the visibility of these constraints serves to liberate women from diffuse feelings of inferiority by defining the issues they wish to challenge.

I have said that the interplay between tradition and liberation in Israel serves to define the status of women in two ways: first, the traditional role of wife, mother, and homemaker is a clear one, and even to an outsider like myself much of the religious ritual assigned to women can be seen as the source of great potential satisfaction. Second, the clarity of definition also delineates areas of controversy on the status of women, and I have suggested that this may indirectly lead to a measure of psychological liberation for the feminist.

Now I want to come to my final point. I was not able to formulate a fully-elaborated theory of human sexuality in time for this conference, and so I was forced to decide whether I should remain within the relatively conservative confines of the inferences growing out of my research and my observations, or

if I might share some speculations which constitute the germ of a theory. I have
made two observations about Israeli life which bear on feminist concerns.
First, the Israeli revolution for equality of sex rights has lost much of its
original impetus, and on the kibbutzim as well as elsewhere there has been a
return, to some extent, to the traditional feminine role. Second, our research
suggested that both traditional and modern women were better off than women in
the middle, transitional between traditionalism and modernity. It seems apparent
that these observations grow out of a common base, which is the viability of the
traditional female role.

I have come to believe that feminists and revolutionaries have something to
learn from tradition. I suspect that the history of feminism in Israel
teaches us that a movement intended to erase sex-role differences is bound to
fail, simply because in its strong opposition to sex-linked status inequities
the movement ignores the appeal of tradition. I am not, then, predicting total
failure for the feminist revolution: instead, I would assert that the future
of female roles will forever involve tension between sex-typed roles and
egalitarianism. The pull toward sex typing is rooted in male and female
polarities, biological imperatives which urge us into a sexual dialectic,
a part of which is to affirm our sexual differences.[3]

I want to suggest, further, that signs of sex discrimination in Israel such
as those that I have earlier described may have a latent function in addition to
their manifest function of preserving tradition. These sexual labels of language

---

[3]These remarks grew out of David Gutmann's defense of male chauvinist pigs:
he observed that they were the last remnants of humanity who still enjoyed
the natural antagonism between men and women.

work, and ritual - sexual stigmata, if you wish - also serve as sexual self-affirmation. For the feminist in Israel, then, tradition serves not only to state issues to which she is opposed, but also to define her as female - sparing her, it may be,   the need to take on a sex-typed role to maintain this definition.

I take as axiomatic that the assertion of femaleness and maleness is natural to us, and that the expression of one's sexuality is intrinsically good. But sex differences have been linked to status differences throughout human history and so feminist movement of the past and present have generally had to strive to eliminate both. This has been true of the feminism of the pioneering generation in Israel and will be true also, I expect, of any Women's Liberation Movement in Israel today. But the unique good fortune of the women of Israel is the remarkable cultural pluralism in contemporary Israeli society, offering a spectrum of role models from the secular pioneer to the traditionalist. This cultural pluralism includes contradiction is inherent in attempts to resolve sexual identity with equality, and this resolution may forever take the form of ongoing conflict between some form of sex-typing and some form of egalitarianism - and pluralism may be the most successful outcome.

HELEN MAYER HACKER

The Socio-Economic Context of Sex and Power: A Study of Women, Work and Family Roles in Four Israeli Institutional Frameworks

Introductory Statement

This research proposal is instigated by the concern felt by the
leadership of the Moshav Ovdim Shitufi (cooperative small holders'
settlement) in Israel in regard to the occupational dissatisfaction
of their female members. This is a type of social organization which
represents a compromise between a kibbutz and a regular Moshav.
Productive work is carried out on a communal basis, as in the kibbutz,
but each family lives in its own house, as in the moshav, and draws
up its own budget. The collective income is distributed to families
on the basis of the number of persons in the household. Men and women
alike are expected to work an eight hour day, but married women are
given "credit" towards their required hours for the performance of
household tasks. The number of hours so credited varies according
to the number of children in the family. The principle of "self
labor" prescribes the employment of any household help, so that, in

the absence of husbandly assistance, the full burden of maintaining
the home falls upon the wife-mother. Although women's services in
the home were given social and financial recognition, the automatic
assignment of married women to domestic duties led to their virtual
exclusion from the more specialized and skilled tasks of either an
agricultural or industrial nature.

Establishment of the Moshavim Shitufim began in the late 1930's,
thus allowing time for a group of "unemployed matriarchs" to appear.
These women have become discontent with their limited lives, much
like their American counterparts, and have expressed the wish to
undertake various business enterprises, such as a motel for tourists.
This outlet for their creative energies, however, is blocked on the
objective side by the prohibition of hired labor, and, motivationally,
by the fact that such activity will not add to the family income
which is based solely on "need."

For younger, better educated and more professionally trained women
the problem is even more acute. Full time commitment to a "career"
would entail their carrying a double burden without extra reward. It
might be supposed that other, "less ambitious" women might be assigned the task of doing the housework of those of their sisters who
preferred to work outside the home, but, apart from the demeaning
aspect of such labor in a private rather than a collective setting,
they would not be permitted to reap any benefit in addition to that
gained from taking care of their own homes.[1]

The presenting social problem, then, from the point of view of the
Moshav Shitufi as a community is the loss of potential female productive power, while on the part of individual women, it is a loss

---

1. This situation makes quite explicit the fact, partially obscured
in non-socialist societies, that, to the extent that husbands do not
share in household chores or men not make up half the personnel in
collectivized services, some married women can achieve economic
equality with men only at the expense of other women.)

of material and psychic rewards. This problem of female "underemployment" becomes especially pressing and poignant for an encapsulated,
egalitarian society because not only does the presumed disaffection
of half its members undermine its raison d'être and set in motion a
whole chain of dysfunctional consequences in its social life, but
even more threatening is the likelihood that a substantial portion
of the younger generation will leave the Moshav unless the work interests of the young women can be accommodated.

The proposed research project, however, has a twofold objective.
The first, and applied, aim is to provide the basic data that would
help the leadership to solve--or at least to clarify--the policy
problems posed by the present occupational arrangements. It is
possible that the leadership define the problem differently from the
majority of the members. Basic fact-finding in the first phase of
the research will be directed to measuring the extent and dimensions
of work-related dissatisfactions among both men and women, and the
personal and social characteristics with which these are associated.
(The procedures to be used in the preliminary stages of the investigation and the kinds of data they may be expected to yield are described below under the heading of SOURCES AND METHODS TO BE USED)

The second, more theoretical aim consists of taking advantage of
the natural field experiment which the several settlement patterns in
Israel afford in order to test the relationship among certain controlled and key variables, which in the last analysis may condition
women's work opportunities in any society. Here the hope is to make
some contribution to the basic question of whether, in the present
state of the industrial arts, including our knowledge of psycho-bio-

logy and the workings of society, any institutional framework can be
engineered which provides equally for the expressive and economic
desires of both men and women--or whether there are inherent limitations on such equality, arising either from the social consequences
of biological differences between men and women and/or the functional
prerequisites of any type of social organization.

As to the key variables, many theorists have postulated a vital
linkage among men's primacy in the occupational structure, women's
whole or partial immersion in the home, and the political-legal
structure of the society. A very crude and simplistic expression of
this notion is that male control over economic resources has enabled
men as a group to bend the polity to their interests and as individuals to exercise hegemony in their own homes. Technological, along
with ideological, change, however, has threatened male dominance by
enabling women to obtain independent sources of livelihood and thus
to contribute more resources to the marriage. In the wake of this
development, a whole spate of studies have been made--(see RELATION
TO WORK BEING DONE BY OTHERS in the same general area for a sampling
of them)--which explore the relationship between the wife's employment and her marital power.

Investigations, however, of the relationship between women's
political power in the general society and their marital power, despite an impressive pseudo-historical literature on matriarchy, have
not been conducted along empirical lines. It is this relationship
which I would like to test in the almost ideal laboratory conditions
afforded by Israel. That is, I propose to examine the relationship
between male-female conflict at the micro - i.e. familial and the

macro or institutional levels. Is there indeed any correlation between reward-seeking attainment in marriage, including the satisfaction
of occupational wishes, with the economic and political balance of
power between men and women in the larger society?

Although marriage and family institutions have traditionally been
viewed in functional interdependence with political and economic
institutions, they have not been given equal weight. Thus, such
economic and technological determinists as Engels, Veblen, Ogburn
grant priority to economic institutions in forming family structures,
while some sociologists, most notably William Goode and Marion Levy,
Jr., stress the importance of family organization and values as an
independent variable in industrialization.

This difference in emphasis upon the direction of causality has
practical implications for the policies recommended to alleviate the
situation of women in the modern world. Radical feminists, defined
by Shulamith Firestone[1] as those who hold the sexual class system
to provide the basis for the "exploitative" economic class system,
assert that genuine feminine equality must wait upon the dissolution
of the nuclear family which inevitably casts men into the role of
chief provider and "patriarch." In other words, the nuclear family
must cease to be the unit of income production, consumption, or even
child rearing. On the other side are those feminists and sociologists[2] who consider the demand for the abolition of the family as
not getting to the crux of the question of sex equality, and who
place greater stress on women's access to the productive resources
of society which alone will afford them the power base to bargain and
and conflict for equality. In this view the nuclear family may be

---

1. Shulamith Firestone, The Dialectic of Sex, New York, Bantam
Books, 1970, p. 37.
2. See Juliet Mitchell, "Women: The Longest Revolution," NEW LEFT
REVIEW, December, 1966; and John Scanzoni, SEXUAL BARGAINING: POWER
POLITICS IN THE AMERICAN MARRIAGE, Prentice-Hall, 1972, p. 183.

retained, if women are able to achieve an equal sharing of economic
and expressive roles--i.e. role-interchangeability between husband
and wife--within marriage.[3] It permits a dynamic interaction between the struggle of women as a conflict interest group and the
power which individual women can exert in the marital relationship.

These two outlooks find expression in the avenues which have been
taken, if not to make women full economic competitors with men, at
least to free them for gainful employment outside the home. "Marxist"
societies have chosen not to tamper with the male role, but to
collectivize women's domestic and child-rearing responsibilities--
at least in principle, if not in practice. Democratic, welfare-
oriented nations, on the other hand, have concentrated more on measures to help husbands and wives share in both the internal and external
maintenance of the home. Neither type of society has achieved great
success in its objective, whether by reason of military exigency
emphasis upon capital accumulation, ideological hangovers from the
past, a spontaneous or induced rebirth of familism or varying combinations of these factors.

Basic to the question of restructuring men's and women's occupational
and familial roles is the consideration of dominant value orientation.
While two income or two job families have been found compatible with
our economic value system, there has been considerable questioning
of the possibility of two career families. The intermittent and/or
part-time character of women's employment, among other factors, has
condemned them to second rate careers. But as long as the majority
of women accept the primary responsibility for the care of the home
and of children, they will not be able to compete on an equal basis

---

3.   The reluctance of American women to revolutionize marriage is
expounded in Margaret N. Poloma and T. Neal Garland, "The Married
Professional Woman: A Study in the Tolerance of Domestication,"
JOURNAL OF MARRIAGE AND THE FAMILY, 33, August, 1971, 531-540.

with men. Further, so long as this remains the dominant pattern, those husbands who do share these responsibilities with their wives will be placed at a competitive disadvantage with other men who are free to devote all their time and energy to their work, often with wifely assistance either in concrete form or merely providing what Jessie Barnard has termed the "stroking function" of women.

Even retaining the primacy of an achievement orientation, however, there is the possibility that if women continue to press their demands for equal treatment in industry that the cultural expectation of the husband as the principal breadwinner will change, and that individual couple choices as to whether the wife or the husband will be the stay-at-home or secondary career partner may split 50-50. In this event the family will still be one primary career, but the "careerist" will be as likely to be the wife as the husband.

As stated previously, there are only two other, and rather dubious, conditions which would permit a two-career family. The first is that private services in the form of domestic help could be utilized to free the wife for full career commitment. We have already seen that this solution is forbidden to female members of the kibbutz and the moshav shitufi on ideological grounds. Such a development is also imminent in the United States to the extent that we are trying to implement equality of opportunity for every person regardless of sex, race, nationality, religion, or "disadvantaged" background. As this equality becomes more and more of a reality, fewer women will be available as servants--unless, of course, their scarcity enables them to bargain for wages and other perquisites which will render domestic work as attractive as other alternatives. The second condition, as discussed above, would be an acceleration of the transfer of family functions to other agencies--a process which has already begun to be reversed in the kibbutz. Whether this trend back to familism in the kibbutz represents a "natural" response or merely the re-emergence of a European cultural concept of the good wife and mother, long repressed, but not forgotten, is a moot question. In any event, clarification of this matter in Israel will have important implications for social policy in the United States.

There is yet a third possibility, one which involves the redefinition of careers along "feminine" or humanist lines. In such a shift of values recognition and material reward may be downplayed in favor of the "quality of life." Should this re-orientation come to pass, reduced work schedules and shared marital roles may be desired by the majority, with only a few of the most gifted or most ambitious insisting on complete dedication to their work. Very likely, such individuals may abjure marriage and parenthood althogether--a sacrifice which most such men have not had to make in the past.

All the foregoing possibilities have been realized to some extent in Israel. It is hoped that a systematic examination of the four kinds of social organization along a continuum from complete collectivism to private enterprise which currently co-exist in Israel will help to identify those variables which are crucial to the questions raised in this study. Israel provides unique opportunities as a social laboratory not only for its conjunction of varying degrees of mixed farming, manufacturing, and other enterprises in differing normative environments, but also for its high percentage of immigrants representing a variety of cultural backgrounds. The following chart presents a rough schemata of the differences and similarities in the four institutional frameworks under consideration.

	KIBBUTZ	MOSHAV SHITUFI	REGULAR MOSHAV	PRIVATE SECTOR
Product				
Ownership of means of production	Communal	Communal	Individual*	Private
Responsibility for production decisions, including allocation of work tasks	Communal	Communal	Individual	Individual
Purchasing and selling unit	Joint	Joint	Joint	Individual
Characteristics of "productive" workers	Member, disproportionately male	Member; predominantly male	Member** and/or hired labor	Disproportionately male
Consumption				
Criteria for allocation of income	Need (quantitatively defined)	Need	Earnings of family	Earnings of family
Unit which makes budget decisions	Communal	Individual	Individual	Individual
Housing				
Dining facilities	Communal	Individual	Individual	Individual
Extent of housekeeping	Simple, communal	More elaborate Individual	More elaborate Individual	More elab. or variable Individual
Division of household tasks between spouses	Joint (theoretically)	Mainly wife	Mainly wife	Probably wife
Family "provider"	Both spouses	Both	Mainly husband	Mainly husband
Family "spender"	Neither spouse	Mainly wife	Mainly wife	Mainly wife
Childrearing				
Principal socializing agents	"Nurses" Peers, teachers	Mainly wife	Mainly wife	Mainly wife
Parental role differentiation	None	Traditional	Traditional	Traditional

* Heavy machinery may be owned cooperatively
** Wives may raise chickens, vegetables, etc.

Notes:
1. A more elaborate taxonomy would indicate variations within each framework.
2. This table provides no information on the relationship between husband and wife along the dimensions of power, prestige, communication, affective emotional ties, or relative participation in larger kinship or friendship groups because these have not as yet been adequately determined.

(1)THE QUESTIONS WHICH YOUR RESEARCH IS DIRECTED TOWARD ANSWERING
     AND THEIR SIGNIFICANCE

As previously stated, the principal focus of the present research is
to explore the possible range of relationships among certain dimensions
of marital interaction, wives' attitudes and behaviors in regard to
work, and the participation in and power of women in the decision-
making activities of the community, and to find out whether these
relationships vary in the four institutional frameworks under study:
the kibbutz, the Moshav Shitufi, the regular Moshav, and the private
sector as represented by an urban sample of married students and/or
personnel at the University of the Negev--in other words, an investigation of the interplay between the micro or familial and macro or
institutional levels.

In pursuit of this objective, some of the specific questions which
suggest themselves include: (Please note that a comparison among the
four frameworks is implied for each question.)

1. How do men and women define the roles of the two sexes, especially
with regard to work behaviors and attributes? What are their desired
self-images?

2. What, if any, are the differences in male and female attitudes
towards work?

3. What are the pressures which motivate women either to aspire
to a "male model" of work or to be satisfied with a different or lesser
commitment? Which women are vulnerable to which pressures? i.e. as
described in terms of age, education, number and ages of children,
husband's attitude toward wife's work, husband's help in home, with
children, and in wife's "vocation," husband's prestige and/or earnings
by virtue of his work or other activity.

4. In regard to the factors listed in question 3, what is the

direction of causality--or which are facilitatiiong and which are motivating factors? For example, does a wife seek education, limit the number of children, insist on husband's help, etc. because she has certain work aspirations or does she enter into a given work situation only if these enabling factors are present.

5. What kinds of satisfactions do wives seek, and how do they rank them in importance? To what extent are deficiencies in some areas compensated for by gratifications in others? How do these change over the life cycle, either in actuality or in anticipation? Do women formulate life plans? To what extent and in what ways do couples view their families as a "set of intercontingent careers?"

6. What kinds of satisfactions are sought in work? What is the relative importance of psychological and economic rewards? How do these differ for men and women? (If they do.)

7. Is there any relationship between the husband's commitment to work and that of his wife? Similarly, for community activities?

8. Does the wife's involvement in decision-making or other community activity vary according to the nature and extent of her work outside the home?

9. In what ways, if any, is the wife's attitude toward work affected by such aspects of marital interaction as relative dominance, power in decision-making, extent of communication between husband and wife, and overall "happiness" in marriage? Similarly, the husband's?

10. Is the perception of such expressive benefits of marriage as companionship, empathy, physical love and affection similar for both spouses? Are such perceptions influenced by the work of either spouse?

11. Do the attitudes of husband and wife towards the wife's work differ from or resemble that of the following kinds of persons:

a. their work associates
b. their ten best friends, whether male or female, or those with whom they have the most frequent contact
c. their siblings or other relatives of their own generation
d. their parents or other relatives of the ascendant generation
e. their adolescent or adult children (if they have any.)

12. What is the relationship between women's past work experience and their present vocational plans or aspirations? Does dissatisfaction with her job evoke a wish for a different assignment or to be exempt from "productive" tasks?

13. (Where applicable) How do work-assigning committees view women's roles and what criteria do they apply in making assignments--for both sexes?

In a sense the significance of these questions has already been indicated in the INTRODUCTORY STATEMENT. It is hoped that the data gathered in the attempt to answer them will clarify both the obstacles and the inducements to the full utilization of the productive capacities of women--on both the individual and the group level. More specifically, this research should:

a. specify work motivations for women, as well as men, since it brings into sharp relief the separation of economic from psychological rewards.

b. discover whether sex differences in regard to work are accentuated or attenuated in varying social contexts.

c. contribute a provisional answer to the perennial question of what is biological and what is cultural in the role differentiation of men and women.

d. identify those problems of women which emerge from specific types of social structures, thus providing leads for their alleviation

(2)RELATION TO WORK BEING DONE BY OTHERS IN THE SAME GENERAL AREA

To my knowledge no work is currently being done either on the
Moshav Shitufi nor on the hypothetical linkage of women's general
status in society to their marital power. Nor, for that matter, do
books abound on the regular Moshav. A recent work by Maxwell I. Klayman
entitled THE MOSHAV IN ISRAEL: A CASE STUDY OF INSTITUTIONAL BUILDING FOR
FOR AGRICULTUAL DEVELOPMENT published by Praeger in 1970 does not give
special attention to women's occupations. While studies based on individual families seem also to be lacking for Israel, there is of
course a substantial literature on the Kibbutz. Of special relevance
to the present problem are Yonina Talmon's paper "Sex-Role Differentiation
in an Equalitorian Society" in Thomas E. Lasswell and Burma's SOCIETY
AND SOCIAL LIFE and her chapter in M. F. Nimkoff's COMPARATIVE FAMILY
SYSTEMS called "The Family in a Revolutionary Movement--The Case of the
Kibbutz in Israel."

The relationship between the wife's employment status and her power
vis à vis her husband, however, has been examined in a variety of
cultural settings. While most studies are concerned with the effect
of the wife's employment on her influence on various family decisions,
including the number of children, many also deal with the prior question
of the husband's control over his wife's work behavior. The following
list is only partial:

United States

> Blood, Robert O., Jr. and Donald M. Wolfe. HUSBANDS AND WIVES.
> Glencoe, Ill., Free Press, 1960.

> Conters, Richard et al., "Conjugal power structure: a re-exam-
> ination," AMERICAN SOCIOLOGICAL REVIEW 36 (April) 1971, 264-278.

> Heer, David M., "Dominance and the working wife," in F. Ivan
> Nye and Lois W. Hoffman, eds. THE EMPLOYED MOTHER, Chicago:
> Rand-McNally, 1963.

United States (continued)

Komarovsky, Mirra. BLUE-COLLAR MARRIAGE. New York: Random House. 1964

Papanek, Miriam L., "Authority and sex roles in the family," JOURNAL OF MARRIAGE AND THE FAMILY 29 (May) 1969, 359-363.

(My own dissertation (1961) revealed that husband's attitude, in contradiction to Mildred Weil's[1] findings, did not seem to have great predictive value for the wife's decision to work, but rather changed in accommodation to it. My as yet unpublished research in Italy and in India, while not specifically directed to this area, did show spousal agreement in regard to the wife's working outside the home.)

Germany

Lamouse, Annette, "Family roles of women: a German example," JOURNAL OF MARRIAGE AND THE FAMILY 31 (February) 1969:145-152.

Lupri, Eugen, "Contemporary authority patterns in the West German family: a study in cross-national validation," JOURNAL OF MARRIAGE AND THE FAMILY 31 (February): 1969, 134-144.

Greece

Safilios-Rothschild, Constantina, "A comparison of power structure and marital satisfaction in urban Greek and French families," JOURNAL OF MARRIAGE AND THE FAMILY 29 (May) 1967: 290-302.

(Of interest to the Mosnav Shitufi situation is her finding that the advent of babies does not keep the Greek wife at home, be- because female relatives serve as babysitters, perhaps paralleling the old Negro grandmother in the United States.)

France

Michel, Andrée, "Comparative data concerning the interaction in French and American families," INTERNATIONAL JOURNAL OF COMPARATIVE SOCIOLOGY 11 (June) 1967: 157-165.

Denmark

Kandel, Denise and Gerald S. Lesser. "Marital decision-making in American and Danish urban families: a research note," JOURNAL OF MARRIAGE AND THE FAMILY 34 (February) 1972: 134-138.

---

1. Mildred W. Weil, "An Analysis of the Factors Influencing Married Women's Actual or Planned Work Participation," AMERICAN SOCIOLOGICAL REVIEW, 26, (February, 1961) 91-96.

Yugoslavia

Buric, Olivera and Andjelka Zecevic, "Family, authority, marital satisfaction, and the social network in Yugoslavia," JOURNAL OF MARRIAGE AND THE FAMILY 29 (May) 1967: 325-336.

Japan

Blood, Robert O., Jr. and Yuzura John Takeshita, "Development of cross-cultural equivalence of measures of marital interaction for the U.S.A. and Japan." TRANSACTIONS OF THE 5th WORLD CONGRESS OF SOCIOLOGY, 1964, Louvain, International Sociological Association, 333-44.

Puerto Rico

Weller, Robert H., "The employment of wives, dominance, and fertility," JOURNAL OF MARRIAGE AND THE FAMILY 31 (August) 1968: 437-442.

Ghana

Oppong, Christine, "Conjugal power and resources: an urban African example." JOURNAL OF MARRIAGE AND THE FAMILY 32 (November): 676-680.

For preliterate societies, Morris Zelditch is outstanding for his analysis of the data contained in the Human Relations Area Files.

(Zelditch, Morris, Jr., "Role differentiation in the nuclear family: a comparative study," in Talcott Parsons and Robert F. Bales, eds. FAMILY, SOCIALIZATION, AND INTERACTION PROCESS. Glencoe, Ill., Free Press, 1955, 307-351.)

Two other works which concentrate on the roles and power of women are:

Paulme, Denise, ed.WOMEN OF TROPICAL AFRICA. Berkeley: University of California Press, 1963.

Kaberry, Phyllis M. WOMEN OF THE GRASSFIELDS. London: Her Majesty's Stationery Office, 1953.

One cannot hope even to tap all the empirical studies and impressionistic analyses of the general status of women in societies, historically and cross-culturally. The present study should qualify, refine, and hopefully augment the body of general propositions relating to the three variables under consideration.

(3)SOURCES AND METHODS TO BE USED

I. Resources

Dr. Dorit P. Pandan-Eisenstark, Deputy Head, Department of Behavioral Science, University of the Negev, will act as co-director of this study. Dr. Chana Rapaport, Director of the Henrietta Szold Institute for Research in Behavioral Science has expressed his willingness to give counsel, and to make office space available to me at the Institute. I have also several other professional contacts in Israel at the University of Haifa, the Hebrew University, and Bar-Ilan University who will serve as consultants.

II. Planned phases of Study

A. My first month in Israel will be spent in generalized fact-finding: library research, interviews with consultants and informants, including the leaders of the Moshavim Shitufim, and visiting many of the 26 settlements presently in existence. I will also consult with social scientists who have special knowledge of the kibbutz and the regular moshav.

Then I will spend several weeks as a participant-observer in the moshav shitufi selected for this investigation, perhaps substituting for bona fide members on various work assignments.

B. On the basis of these experiences, with the cooperation of Dr. Pandan-Eisenstark, I will construct a relatively brief questionnaire which will be administered to every adult in the moshav, probably between 150 and 250 persons. This census will inquire into work history, work plans, division of household tasks, leisure time activities, community participation, attitudes towards cooperative child care, involvement in kin networks, sociometric ratings of other households, place on scales measuring various attitudes, including acceptance of

socialist ideology, motivations for work, sex roles, and whatever else
may emerge as relevant during my stay in the moshav. The consus will
also include background data on the composition of the household,
country of origin, length of time in Israel and in the moshav, extent
of religious observances.

C. On the basis of the census results certain households will be
selected for intensive interviewing. The aim of this sampling would
be to obtain as complete a representation as possible of the various
combinations of background factors and attitudinal constellations.
Only married couples would be included, and husbands and wives would
be interviewed separately. (A similar procedure is projected for the
other three institutional frameworks.) The size of the sample selected
for in-depth interviewing will depend upon the availability of funds,
and the possibility of conducting interviews in English and/or obtaining
the services of volunteer interviewers or interpreters.

It is hoped that a minimum of 80 couples or 160 persons will be interviewed, stratified as follows:

> Moshav Shitufi   30
> Kibbutz   20
> Regular Moshav   15
> University of the
>   Negev personnel   15
>
>   80

Tentatively, the interviewing schedule would probe the following
areas:

(1) basic ideas and values concerning the differences and similarities, both actual and ideal, in the work and family roles of men and
women.

(2) basic value orientations along the lines suggested by Parsons'
pattern variables, Lynds' "The Middletown Spirit," or Riesman's
typology.

(3) power differentials between husband and wife, perhaps utilizing
Strodtbeck's "revealed differences" technique or role-played scenes
at the end of the interview.

(4) perception of the marital relationship, including extent of
communication, empathy, moral support, affection, etc. Areas of greatest
satisfaction and dissatisfaction.

(5) child-rearing attitudes and practices, including changes, if
any, from the way they were socialized which parents are implementing
or would like to implement for their children. Number of children
desired.
Aspirations for children.

(6) frequency and content of interaction with relatives, friends.

(7) exposure to media, travel, other "outside influences; army
service

(8) participation in community affairs, committee work, official
positions, "avocations."

(9) conceptions of "masculine" and "feminine" tasks, and attitudes
towards undertaking them.

(10) extent of religious feelings and observances

(11) overall assessment of work, family, and community life in their
own setting, as well as in the other three.

(12) extent to which husband and wife discuss certain topics with
each other: children, work, plans for future, problems, common interests

(13) attitudes towards their own and spouse's work assignment;
relative satisfaction and dissatisfaction; anticipations of change or
lack of change. Extent to which husband and wife "help" each other.

(14) perception of their "standing" in the community, and whether
similar or divergent for husband and wife.

(4)PRESENT STATE OF THE PROJECT. i.e. WHETHER IT IS IN PROCESS, PROGRESS
DATE, AND EXPECTATION AS TO COMPLETION.

The project is still in the planning stage. Such a study, however,
has been requested by the leadership of the Moshavim Shitufim, which
is much concerned with the problem posed by the underemployment of their
women members and the latter's discontent. It is expected that the
federation of these Moshavim will fund a more extensive, quantitative
study, especially if the findings of the exploratory study provide
promising leads for further research, possibly of the action variety.
At the present time Dr. Dorit P. Pandan-Eisenstark, who, with me, will
be co-investigator on this project, is carrying on

She is coming to the United States in August, 1973, when we will
confer both on this project and on a research seminar on women which
we will be conducting jointly at the University of the Negev during
the spring of 1974. Some of the seminar students may also aid in the
interviewing and preliminary analysis of the data.

While it is hoped that this exploratory study will be completed by
the time I leave Israel in the late summer of 1974, my minimum expectation
is that data collection and analysis will have been accomplished at
least for the Moshav Shitufi.

(5)GOALS TO BE ACCOMPLISHED DURING FELLOWSHIP PERIOD AS WELL AS THE
ULTIMATE GOAL OF THE PROJECT.

As stated under (4) my goal for the fellowship period is the preparation of a preliminary report based on the findings from the Moshav
Shitufi portion of the study. Depending upon the availability of
funds and/or volunteer interviewers, interviews from the other three
samples--kibbutz, regular moshav, and the University of the Negev--will
also be done. Codes constructed for the analysis of the data from

the Moshav Shitufi should also apply in large measure to these samples,
so that little change need be made in the program for the computer.
If the results of machine tabulation are not forthcoming by the time
I leave Israel to resume my teaching duties at Adelphi in the fall
of 1974, Dr. Pandan-Eisenstark can send me copies of the print-out
sheets so that we can collaborate on the analysis of the data via
correspondence. If necessary, I will return to Israel during the
summer of 1975.

It may well be that this exploratory study will lead to certain inno-
vations in policy and suggest a follow-up study to assess the success
of such change. This additional study may be considered the ultimate
goal of the project. My participation would depend on my appraisal
of its theoretical importance and practical applicability to problems
in the United States.

(6)YOUR EXPECTATION AND PLANS CONCERNING PUBLICATION

The study should eventuate in the publication of a monograph or short
book in both English and Hebrew. Mr. Richard C. Rowson, Director of
Praeger Special Studies has expressed an interest in it. Other
possibilities include Schocken Books and Prentice-Hall. An article
based on the report will be submitted either to the AMERICAN
SOCIOLOGICAL REVIEW, JOURNAL OF MARRIAGE AND THE FAMILY, INTERNATIONAL
JOURNAL OF COMPARATIVE SOCIOLOGY, or some other sociological, social
psychological, or anthropological journal.

Likely avenues for publication in Hebrew or republication in English
would include the Israel Universities Press, Magnes Press at the Hebrew
University, Sifriat Ha-Poalim, Am-Oved Press in Tel Aviv, and the Social
Research Centre in Givat Haviva. An article might appear in the SOCIAL
RESEARCH REVIEW published at the University of Haifa or in any one of

the several social science journals in Israel.

(7)THE PLACE OR PLACES WHERE WORK WILL BE CARRIED ON

Field work will be conducted in Israel, probably in the Galilee area. As stated under (3): sources and methods to be used--respondents will be selected from one or two of the Moshavim Shitufim, kibbutzim, regular Moshavim, and the student body and staff of the University of the Negev in Beer-Sheva. Analysis of the data and writing of the report may be completed in Israel, but it is possible that these phases will be carried over to the United States, where some assistance will be forthcoming from Adelphi University.

REFERENCES

Aloni, Shulamit. Israeli Women Need Women's Lib! Israel Magazine,
     Vol. III, No. 4, 58-68.

Antonovsky, Aaron; Maoz, Benjamin; Datan (Dowty), Nancy; and
     Wijsenbeek, Henricus. Twenty-Five Years Later: A Limited Study of the
     Sequelle of the Concentration Camp Experiences. Social Psychiatry,
     Vol. 6, No. 4, 1971, 186-193.

Bart, Pauline. Depression in Middle-Aged Women: Some Socio-Cultural Factors.
     Ph.D. diss., University of California at Los Angeles, 1967.

Datan (Dowty), Nancy. Women's Attitudes towards the Climacterium in Five
     Israeli Sub-Cultures. Ph.D. diss., University of Chicago, 1971.

Datan (Dowty), Nancy. To Be A Woman In Israel. School Review, Vol. 80,
     No. 2, (February, 1972), 319-332.

Datan (Dowty), Nancy; Maoz, Benjamin; Antonovsky, Aaron; and
     Wijsenbeek, Henricus. Climacterium in Three Cultural Contexts.
     Tropical and Geographical Medicine, 22 (1970), 77-86.

Learsi, Rufus. Israel: A History of the Jewish People. Cleveland and
     New York: The World Publishing Company, 1966.

Lerner, Daniel. The Passing of Traditional Society: Modernizing the
     Middle East. Glencoe, Illinois: The Free Press, 1958.

Maoz, Benjamin; Datan (Dowty), Nancy; Antonovsky, Aaron; and
     Wijsenbeek, Henricus. Female Attitudes to Menopause. Social
     Psychiatry, 5 (1970), No. 1, 35-40.

Patai, Raphael. Sex and Family in the Bible and the Middle East. Garden
     City, New York: Doubleday and Company, Inc., 1959.

Sacher, Howard Morley. The Course of Modern Jewish History. New York:
     Dell Publishing Co., 1958.

THE ECONOMIST

The Life and Death of Ms. Solomon Grundy

At least 700 babies were born in Britain on the first day of this year —or should have been if Britain's mums held to the statistical rules. Unless these new year babies were a very unrepresentative lot, the girls among them were certainly in a minority. That is unlikely to stop them breaking into more and more male preserves by the time they grow up. Law reform and women's lib will see to that. But the notion that women and men are coming to lead identical lives is nonsense. As some differences are eroded, by education or the greater determination of married women to work outside the home, others are thrown more sharply into relief, mostly because women live longer. More women will continue to live alone, to be poor and to fill up certain kinds of hospitals simply because more of them are old.

The chart opposite shows which differences between the lives led by men and women are now slim, and which are still vast. Some differences have even increased, as a woman's expectation of life (partly because of the rapid decline in maternal deaths even since the second world war) has improved more than a man's. Some differences between men and women—like the poor proportion of girls taking science subjects at school—seem obstinately ineradicable. Others— like the proportion of women in the workforce—have changed greatly in the past 20 years.

Still different

Still other differences—like boys being more accident-prone than girls—seem just to be facts of life. The chart shows how men and women compare over a range of indicators running from birth to senility. The majority of male babies has been reduced somewhat even by the time children leave school. Baby boys are more likely to die in their first year than baby girls. As they get older, the high accident rate among boys means that a greater proportion of them find themselves in hospital with injuries. This imbalance is greatest with school-age children. The proportion of boys aged 5–14 finding themselves in hospital because of accidents was, in 1972, nearly twice as large as the proportion of girls. Oddly, the difference between the sexes is as marked as for the age-group 15–44, when the predominance of men in dangerous jobs would seem to explain their higher accident rate. But men, as well as boys, are accident-prone in the home. Among the same 15–44 age-group, more men than women die from accidents in the home. Only when very old do women seem to stand a much higher chance of dying from home accidents: fractured femurs are much more common among old women than old men.

At school, nearly the same proportion of girls as boys stay on beyond leaving-age. But the proportion going on to university is still very much lower, and the imbalance between boys and girls has been decreasing only slowly over the past 20 years. But more girls than boys now go into some kind of post-school education. In colleges of education, the proportion of girls entering to train as teachers is more than three times as high as the proportion of boys. Polytechnics are a male preserve. Some 2.3% of all boy school-leavers went to them, in England and Wales in 1973, compared with 1.3% of girls. But in the rest of the further education sector, boys are heavily outnumbered by girls. More boys than girls go straight into employment on leaving school. But the proportion of girls going into apprenticeships or other employment involving training is minute, compared with boys.

Easy options

Some of these differences are all too easily explained by patterns of education in school. Just under half of all GCE A-level entries by boys in England and Wales in 1972 were in science subjects, as compared with only 24% of girls' entries. This distinction has changed little over the past decade—except that the proportion of science entries made by both sexes has fallen. Girls still, proportionately, take fewer A-levels than boys. Their success rate is rather higher, which suggests that they (or their teachers) are less ready to take a chance. However, there is also some evidence that arts exams are simply easier to pass than maths and science.

An equal proportion of boys and girls smoke heavily. Only among the older age-groups do women smoke less heavily than men, possibly a relic of earlier generations' attitudes. The proportion of 15–19-year-olds who smoke is still below the proportions, for both sexes, of those in their 20s, but depressingly high. In Britain in 1972, nearly 40% of these older teenagers smoked.

Twice married

Women still marry much younger than men. In 1972, the average age of marriage for men in Britain was just under 25, while for women it was just under 23. It looks as if the steady decline in the age at which both men and women marry (which in 1901 was 27 for men and 25½ for women) has at last tailed off. Men re-marry older than women, too: in 1972, the average age of re-marriage was, for men, 45 and,

for women, just under 41. But the chances of remarrying seem to be much lower for women than for men. This distinction appears, oddly, to be greatest for the younger age-group. In 1971, three-quarters of the divorced or widowed men aged 25–29 re-married, as compared with under half the women in the same age-group.

The proportion of women economically active (which means in a job, looking for one or off sick) has been rising extremely fast. The increase has been among married women. Only 22% of them were found to be economically active when the 1951 census was taken in Britain; by the 1971 census, that figure had risen to 42%. Among single women, the proportion economically active had actually fallen (partly, of course, because an increasing proportion of them were old) from 55% to 44%. The proportion of men economically active had fallen from 88% to 81%.

Nearly a third of all women who work (and a very much higher proportion of married working women only) do so only part-time. Some 70% of these part-timers, in 1973, worked less than 24 hours a week. Even among those who do work full-time, the number of hours worked was at the same date, on average, eight less than those worked by men. Equally, the wages earned by full-time women are well below those earned by men. The proportion of full-time working women taking home more than £50 a week in 1973 was only a tenth of the proportion of full-time men. However, since 1970 wage rates have risen faster for women than for men.

The General Household Survey for 1971 found that women were more likely to be satisfied with their jobs than men. They were sacked or made redundant far less frequently, too. But they left more frequently for personal or domestic reasons. Proportionately, a tiny number of women could be classed as administrators or managers; but they are beginning to erode the imbalance in some of the professions. Because of their concentration in clerical, semi-skilled and service jobs, a social class breakdown shows disproportionately more women than men in classes III and IV and disproportionately fewer in class II. As for class I, very few women make that on their own account.

The proportion of women owning assets is equally small, but increasing fast as more and more couples put their homes (usually their only asset) in joint names. As most wealth statistics are based on death duties, that will take time to filter into them.

Better citizens

Proportionately fewer women belong to clubs and societies—at least, to ones that take them outside the home. That is not so true for teenagers. For example, while the number of Scouts has been declining, the number of Girl Guides has been increasing, and is now far higher. But leisure surveys show television to be equally addictive to both sexes.

The peak ages for criminality, for both sexes, are the late teens: the crime rates are highest for 17–21-year-old boys and girls. But for girls the peak is less marked. Under 19% of all offences by females are committed by this group, as compared with over 26% of all offences committed by men. Very many fewer women than men are found guilty of indictable crime, but it is interesting that the distinction—while still large—is not so great between the numbers of men and women cautioned by the police. Do women get off more lightly than men?

The proportion of women convicted of indictable crime who are sent to prison is vastly lower than the proportion of convicted men. This is partly because a very much smaller proportion of these convicted women have been found guilty of violent crime (in 1973 in England and Wales, 5% compared with 11% of convicted men) or of burglary (4% as compared with 18%), but also because sending a woman to prison usually means sending at least one child into the care of the local authorities. That is a powerful argument from which women probably benefit.

The most marked distinction is between the number of men and women found guilty of minor motoring offences. This need not all be credited to careful women drivers: the number of miles driven by men is vastly much greater than those driven by women.

And better health

Male drug addicts greatly outnumber female; and the imbalance is nearly as great among those treated by hospitals for venereal disease. The proportion of men treated in hospital for heart disease and the like is considerably greater than the proportion of women; but the predominance of women among the arthritic is much greater, partly, of course, because a greater proportion are old.

Over 65, a pretty equal proportion of men and women complain of some long-standing illness. This is surprising, since the average age of women in this group is higher than the average age of men. This age difference partly explains the relative poverty of old women, but this is also explained by the fact that more men more often have extra income beyond their pension.

Once women have reached the age of 75, they outnumber men by 5 to 2. They have been in a majority among all age-groups beyond the middle-age turning point of 40, but this has got greater and greater with age. Worse still, the age-difference between the average married couple means that women outlive their husbands by about two years more than the six years' difference in life expectancy. So, among those over 75, the number of women living alone is vastly greater than the number of men. What is more, the proportion of very old women living alone, usually a dismal and dangerous state, is more than twice as high. And that is a distinction that all the women's liberation in the world cannot erode—except by abolishing marriage or persuading men to marry women much older than themselves.

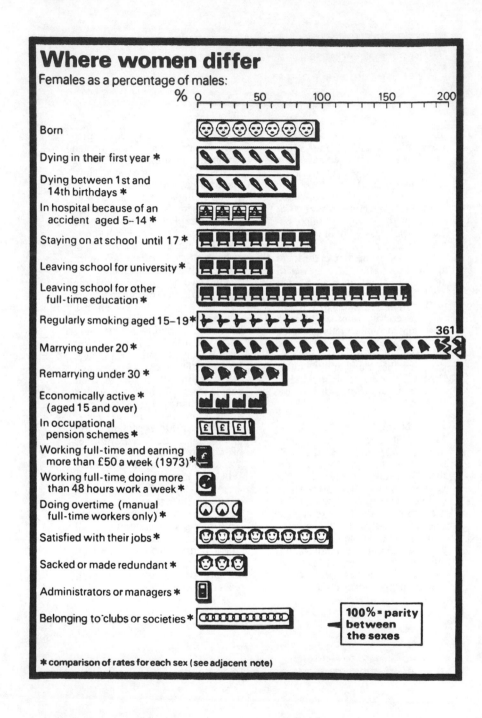

Where women differ

Females as a percentage of males:

% 0   50   100   150   200

Born

Dying in their first year *

Dying between 1st and
  14th birthdays *

In hospital because of an
  accident aged 5–14 *

Staying on at school until 17 *

Leaving school for university *

Leaving school for other
  full-time education *

Regularly smoking aged 15–19 *

Marrying under 20 *   361

Remarrying under 30 *

Economically active *
  (aged 15 and over)

In occupational
  pension schemes *

Working full-time and earning
  more than £50 a week (1973) *

Working full-time, doing more
  than 48 hours work a week *

Doing overtime (manual
  full-time workers only) *

Satisfied with their jobs *

Sacked or made redundant *

Administrators or managers *

Belonging to clubs or societies *

100% = parity
between
the sexes

* comparison of rates for each sex (see adjacent note)

Where women differ

Females as a percentage of males:

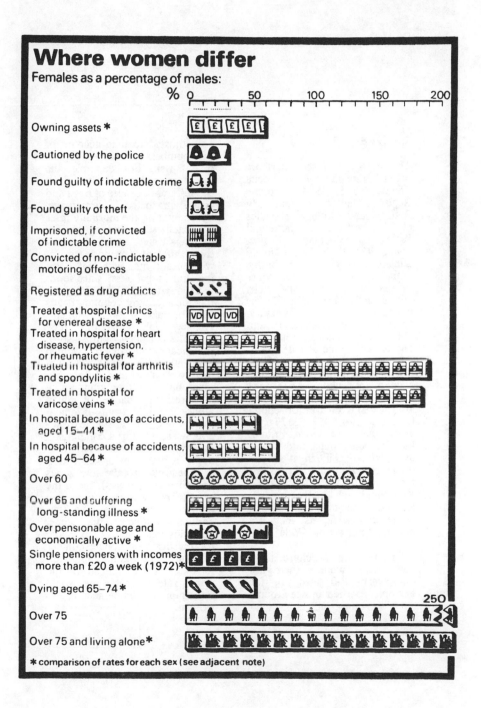

% 0 — 50 — 100 — 150 — 200

Owning assets *

Cautioned by the police

Found guilty of indictable crime

Found guilty of theft

Imprisoned, if convicted of indictable crime

Convicted of non-indictable motoring offences

Registered as drug addicts

Treated at hospital clinics for venereal disease *

Treated in hospital for heart disease, hypertension, or rheumatic fever *

Treated in hospital for arthritis and spondylitis *

Treated in hospital for varicose veins *

In hospital because of accidents, aged 15–44 *

In hospital because of accidents, aged 45–64 *

Over 60

Over 65 and suffering long-standing illness *

Over pensionable age and economically active *

Single pensioners with incomes more than £20 a week (1972)*

Dying aged 65–74 *

Over 75   250

Over 75 and living alone *

* comparison of rates for each sex (see adjacent note)

Sources

The statistics in the chart are taken principally from Social Trends No 5 (1974); also the Registrar-General's Quarterly Returns and Criminal Statistics (1973), both for England and Wales, and Population Projections, 1973–2013, for the United Kingdom. Figures for births, crime, earnings, overtime, hours worked, drugs, VD and clubs and societies are for 1973; for illness, accidents, mortality, smoking, marriage, wealth and old people's incomes for 1972; and for economic activity, occupation and occupational pensions, job satisfaction, redundancies, children at school, remarriage and old people living alone they are for 1971. Figures for school-leavers are for 1972–73. Figures are usually for Great Britain; but for age-groups, old people living alone, children at school, drugs and occupational pensions they are for the whole United Kingdom, while for school-leavers, long-standing illness, crime and accidents they are only for England and Wales.

The bars on the charts show how many women there are for every 100 men in, for example, particular age-groups; but for other indicators they are adjusted to take account of the numbers of women eligible or at risk. For example, the infant mortality indicators show the different chances of boys and girls dying before a certain age, by comparing the mortality rates for each sex. The figures for earnings and overtime show the different proportions of women and men with high earning and long hours; since fewer women work, an absolute comparison made by counting heads would make working women's chances look worse than they are. The bar showing the disproportionate number of women living alone similarly shows, not merely that women outnumber men, but that they stand twice as great a chance of living alone. The only group of indicators for which a simple head-count, rather than a comparison of proportions, is used is— apart from the obvious exception of age-group totals—the series on crime (and drugs). Since the excess of women over men comes in the age-groups that commit relatively little crime, adjusting the figures to allow for the disproportionate number of women in the adult population to make a comparison of the crime rate for each sex would be unfairly complimentary to women.